D1309615

新 GRE

写作思路剖析与题库精讲

张雷冬 ➡ 编著

群言出版社
Qunyan Press

图书在版编目(CIP)数据

GRE写作思路剖析与题库精讲 / 张雷冬编著 . — 北京 : 群言出版社，2012（2014.9重印）
ISBN 978-7-80256-332-2

Ⅰ．①G… Ⅱ．①张… Ⅲ．①GRE—写作—自学参考资料 Ⅳ．①H315

中国版本图书馆CIP数据核字（2012）第092764号

责任编辑　　陈丹丹
封面设计　　大愚设计+黄　蕊
出版发行　　群言出版社(Qunyan Press)

地　　址　北京市东城区东厂胡同北巷1号（100006）
网　　站　www.qypublish.com
电子信箱　bj62605588@163.com　qunyancbs@126.com
总编办　　010-62605588　65265404　65138815
发行部　　010-62605019　62263345　65220236
经　　销　全国新华书店
读者服务　010-62418641　65265404　65263345
法律顾问　北京市君泰律师事务所

印　　刷　北京鑫海达印刷有限公司
版　　次　2012年6月第1版　2014年9月第3次印刷
开　　本　880×1230　1/16
印　　张　26
字　　数　596千字
书　　号　ISBN 978-7-80256-332-2
定　　价　48.00元

本书献给豆豆、麒麒以及支持和鼓励我的家人

前　言

　　GRE考试在2002年以分析性写作代替了原有的逻辑分析之后，在2011年8月又经历了一次比较大的变革。此次改革后作文考试的基本结构还是由Analysis of an Issue和Analysis of an Argument两部分构成，主要变化体现在：

1. 两部分的题库规模都进行了缩减：Issue从以前的244道题目删减为149道题目；Argument从以前的242道题目删减为174道题目；

2. Issue写作时间从以前的45分钟缩短为30分钟；

3. 每道题目都增加了具体的写作要求。比如Issue要求考生讨论在多大程度上支持或反对题目观点，并要求分析实施观点的后果、导致观点成立与否的条件、可能的相反观点等等；而Argument要求考生讨论题目推理有哪些假设、需要提供哪些额外证据可以评价推理、需要回答哪些问题可以评价结论等等。

　　改革后作文部分的基本思路和写作方式没有本质变化，但由于附加了上述具体的写作要求，而且从ETS官方网站公布的GRE作文部分的考试说明和要求也可以看出，当前的作文对于考生文章的整体逻辑性和结构严谨性要求更高。比如，Argument不能像以前一样，随意找出题目中几个有疑问的句子加以驳斥，而要注意所有论证点之间的逻辑联系；Issue也不是仅仅堆砌大量支持或反对题目观点的例子就足以构造文章，而要针对写作要求调整论证内容的侧重点。

　　很多考生在准备Issue时难以找到分析切入思路、论证内容欠缺逻辑性和必要联系；或者对于题目的推理结构认识不到位而导致正文论证层次散乱、寻找论证点没有把握。作为一本GRE作文分析的工具书，本书针对这些问题提供了GRE作文所有题目的思路和结构方面比较全面详尽的分析，供考生查阅参考。本书的核心内容是针对Issue和Argument每道题目详尽地展开思路和论证，而GRE作文的句式、素材、例证等已有很多参考书提供了大量材料，故本书在这方面不再专门拨出篇幅叙述。

　　全书共分七章，具体内容安排如下：

第一章　Issue写作思路简介
　　众所周知，Issue写作思路较为灵活，很难套用某一种固定的分析写作模式。本书基于笔者数年教学经验总结出一种行之有效的对Issue题目进行分析、思考、构建文章的思维方法。这一方法特别适用于考生对于题目的背景知识、学科领域不太熟悉的情况；并可在考场上思维受阻、想不出论证内容的情况下作为行之有效的应急处理手段。

第二章　Issue题目分析思路参考
　　结合第一章介绍的搜集素材、拓宽思路、构架文章的方法，本章给出了每道题目比较全面的分析框架。要注意这些分析内容只是针对这道题目的一种可能分析思路，以帮助考生理解第一章介绍的分析方法，考生应该结合自己的专业以及比较熟悉或擅长的领域构建自己的论证思路体系。每道题目都列出了比较详尽的正面、负面、发散的论证内容，这些论证点并不要求在一篇Issue文章中全部体现，考生应该对一道题目先进行全面思考，再总结提炼自己的观点立场。

第三章　Issue参考范文
　　这里提供了题库中比较有代表性的5道题目的参考范文。如前所述，本书目的并不在于给考生提供大量的素材句式语料库，这些范文的用意主要是使考生更加深刻地体会前面介绍的分析方法。

第四章　Argument写作思路简介

Argument写作思路和文章结构相对比较简单。这里着重介绍了题目推理过程中频繁出现和写作时经常深入论证的常见逻辑问题以及针对新GRE Argument作文写作要求的应对方案。

第五章　Argument题目结构和论证要点详细分析

这是本书比重最大也最有特色的部分。这里首先分析了每道题本身的逻辑成分，即题目中哪些语句是作者的论据、哪些是假设、哪些是结论；其次，提供了每道题目的推理结构脉络，即作者是如何从论据出发一步一步推出假设和结论的，分析了论据、假设、结论之间的逻辑关系；最后，给出了每道题目针对其写作要求比较详尽的可能论证点。同样，这些论证点也不要求在一篇Argument文章中全部体现，其目的在于帮助考生全面完整地把握对题目推理的分析过程；写作时，只需挑选若干在逻辑上比较重要、自己比较擅长论证的环节深入展开即可。

第六章　Argument主要逻辑问题论证模板

本章针对Argument经常分析论证的逻辑问题提供了展开写作的语言结构参考。这些语言结构主要用于让考生体会这类逻辑问题的展开思路和层次，考生应结合自己的思维特点和论证习惯，构建属于自己的分析结构。

第七章　Argument参考范文

同样，本章选编了题库中比较有代表性的5道题目的参考范文，覆盖了Assumption、Question、Evidence、Alternative Explanation 4种写作类型，帮助考生体会文章论证结构的构建和对写作要求的具体应对。

本书具有以下特点：

一、全面

针对每道Issue题目的论证层面、每道Argument题目几乎所有可能的论证点给出了全面详尽的分析。

二、简明

语言简练，要点清晰。每道题的思路结构一目了然，帮助考生节约备考时间。

三、实用

书中没有复杂的句式、高深的例证，思路和方法都很容易掌握。因此，本书对于备考时间短，语言、思维基础又不是特别扎实的考生具有很高的实用价值。

为给考生提供翔实准确的参考，本书编写自当力求准确无误，校对、订正不厌其烦。但限于时间、精力、学识，各方面纰漏在所难免，因此也恳请读者不吝指出，从而使本书能够不断得以完善和改进。

本书在编写过程中受到了多方支持：

首先，要感谢大愚文化传播有限公司的编辑们，他们在写作方式和内容编排方面提供了很多极具价值的建议。

此外，还要感谢众多GRE考生的支持和鼓励，正是你们的期望和鼓舞使我在繁忙的教学之余有毅力将本书完成并不断完善。希望这本书对你们的考试准备能有所助益，也预祝你们在未来的考试和学习、工作中获得成功。

最后，要感谢在我写作无暇顾及其他的时候默默支持我事业、照顾我的家人，谢谢你们。

张雷冬

目 录

Issue 题库题号与页码对应表

题库题号	页码	题库题号	页码	题库题号	页码	题库题号	页码
1	45	39	86	77	26	115	31
2	25	40	88	78	42	116	71
3	81	41	21	79	79	117	26
4	68	42	74	80	22	118	74
5	25	43	46	81	24	119	104
6	68	44	33	82	61	120	37
7	55	45	75	83	20	121	38
8	95	46	56	84	34	122	33
9	98	47	89	85	40	123	76
10	11	48	65	86	30	124	63
11	27	49	73	87	51	125	12
12	15	50	29	88	23	126	54
13	55	51	22	89	92	127	39
14	69	52	17	90	89	128	77
15	83	53	91	91	47	129	86
16	28	54	61	92	66	130	93
17	98	55	67	93	92	131	19
18	72	56	50	94	40	132	48
19	18	57	100	95	24	133	102
20	84	58	42	96	70	134	103
21	50	59	43	97	62	135	84
22	32	60	29	98	87	136	88
23	48	61	51	99	27	137	82
24	16	62	43	100	63	138	75
25	16	63	14	101	47	139	31
26	46	64	49	102	57	140	59
27	100	65	77	103	52	141	94
28	35	66	78	104	44	142	90
29	17	67	15	105	53	143	60
30	20	68	99	106	53	144	94
31	13	69	44	107	45	145	39
32	85	70	57	108	80	146	79
33	64	71	22	109	65	147	41
34	72	72	19	110	80	148	13
35	82	73	59	111	96	149	97
36	18	74	101	112	58		
37	20	75	34	113	36		
38	41	76	73	114	31		

Argument 题库题号与页码对应表

题库题号	页码	题库题号	页码	题库题号	页码	题库题号	页码
1	126	45	208	89	276	133	154
2	127	46	210	90	141	134	287
3	128	47	211	91	277	135	289
4	130	48	214	92	278	136	288
5	131	49	209	93	157	137	290
6	134	50	215	94	186	138	166
7	134	51	151	95	196	139	233
8	138	52	188	96	197	140	291
9	139	53	216	97	280	141	234
10	142	54	219	98	135	142	292
11	145	55	222	99	137	143	235
12	146	56	223	100	171	144	217
13	147	57	224	101	278	145	228
14	148	58	185	102	172	146	228
15	150	59	226	103	279	147	257
16	155	60	227	104	179	148	257
17	156	61	232	105	180	149	258
18	160	62	237	106	181	150	229
19	162	63	240	107	245	151	218
20	161	64	242	108	246	152	293
21	143	65	243	109	158	153	294
22	163	66	244	110	159	154	230
23	144	67	247	111	212	155	231
24	167	68	248	112	213	156	259
25	170	69	249	113	281	157	295
26	168	70	250	114	265	158	296
27	175	71	252	115	251	159	132
28	169	72	253	116	266	160	296
29	176	73	254	117	267	161	285
30	177	74	255	118	149	162	236
31	178	75	260	119	164	163	192
32	178	76	261	120	165	164	174
33	183	77	262	121	238	165	220
34	184	78	264	122	239	166	193
35	187	79	268	123	203	167	182
36	191	80	269	124	239	168	299
37	194	81	270	125	204	169	263
38	195	82	225	126	282	170	300
39	198	83	271	127	284	171	129
40	201	84	271	128	189	172	298
41	202	85	272	129	190	173	133
42	205	86	274	130	152	174	199
43	206	87	273	131	153		
44	207	88	140	132	286		

第一章　Issue写作思路简介

Issue写作要求考生结合写作要求讨论对题目观点的认同程度。

在备考Issue写作时可以按照以下几个步骤进行：

一、把所有题目按照题材、核心思想、论证结构分类；

二、针对每个领域、每类主题的题目发挥发散性思维，搜集写作论证素材；

三、结合每道题目的特点和写作要求构建文章结构。

一　题目分类

不论考生打算花多少时间准备Issue写作，都要把题目进行分类。这样做一方面节约时间——有些相近甚至几乎相同的题目可以互相参考共用素材；另一方面很多题目之间存在一定的内在联系——题目本身就能提供很多思路和素材方面的参考。

Issue题目涉及的题材领域非常广泛，因而观察和分类的角度也多种多样。这里介绍本书涉及的三种分类方式供考生参考：

❶ 按照题目讨论的题材领域分类

在第二章中每道题目最前面的底纹框（如**自然**）标示了该题目的题材领域，共分自然、教育、科技、社会、政治、认知6类；这一分类方式主要用于考生针对不同领域的现象或话题搜集例证。

❷ 按照题目的核心思想分类

按照题目的核心思想分类即按照题目讨论主题之间的逻辑关系分类，也就是第二章的A~H类，共8类。

A类：眼前问题与长远问题的关系；

B类：个体与整体（领导/名人与社会）的关系；

C类：科技与人性（机器与人）的关系；

D类：理性与感性的作用；

E类：学科之间的交叉影响；

F类：统一与分歧（竞争与合作）的关系；

G类：理想与现实的关系；

H类：传统与创新的关系。

同一类的题目因为核心思想相近，故很多例证或某些论证段落可以通用或互相参考借鉴。

❸ 按照正文段落之间的逻辑结构分类

根据题目观点的表达方式，可以把正文之间的逻辑关系分为4类：对比型（comparison）、问题解决型（solution）、推理型（reasoning）、观点型（claim）。第二章每道题目之后的方括号（比如[claim→ solution]）标示了每道题的参考逻辑结构。关于逻辑结构的详细分类和相应思路可以参考本章下面的内容。

用上述第二种题目分类方法整理好的题目，因为核心主题相近，故可以针对每类主题建立一个素材库，这个素材库中的材料在论证这类主题的很多题目时都可以使用。在搜集素材时可以先把同一个主题题库的题目通读一遍，有时题目本身就能给同一题库的其他题目提供很多现成的思路和参考。然后针对这一主题进行一些思维发散和联想的工作，看看能想到哪些和该主题相关的概念、观点、理论、事件、人物，这一过程也通常被称为Brain Storming，即"头脑风暴"。平时考生要勤于思考和留心积累，把看到的能用于Issue文章论证的事件和观点及时进行整理，同时还要有针对性地搜寻一些素材。在搜集素材和思考论证思路时可以参考以下5个层面，为便于记忆，这5个层面可以简写为"DCDRE"：

1. ［D］**DEFINITION of the critical term and concept**：人们通常如何定义和理解题目中涉及的关键概念。把这一点想清楚一方面可以明确论证对象，避免考生产生误解；另一方面有些题目仅从核心概念的定义出发就可以构建文章。

比如Issue作文题库第85题：Some people believe that in order to thrive, a society must put its own overall success before the well-being of its individual citizens. Others believe that the well-being of a society can only be measured by the general welfare of all its people.

对于前一类观点的论证出发点之一就在于对overall success（总体成功）的理解。所谓"总体成功"是指在政治上取得霸权？经济上形成垄断？还是社会基本福利和人权的完善提高？在正文段落中就可以从这几种不同的理解出发，分别分析对于成功的不同定义对原题观点会产生如何的影响。

2. ［C］**CATEGORIES of the critical term and concept**：题目中关键概念的分类。很多题目经常讨论一些笼统抽象的概念，比如culture、information等，对于这类题目不应泛泛地讨论，而应该先把这些抽象概念分类，再分门别类讨论针对不同的概念种类题目的观点能否成立。

3. ［D］**DOMAINS that would be affected by the claim**：题目观点可能会影响到的领域。比如作者提出的行为或观点是否在政治上产生影响？或在文化上有所体现？还是会影响到社会、科技、艺术等领域？

这里，请注意Domain和Category的区别。Category指的是一个概念自身能分成多少类；而Domain指的是某概念、某行为在哪些其他领域会产生影响。比如"文化"这个概念，从Category的角度来考虑就可以分成"当代文化"、"传统文化"；"主流文化"、"非主流文化"；"本土文化"、"外来文化"等类别；而从Domain的角度来考虑就可以思考文化这个概念会对哪些领域产生影响，比如文化会影响到社会生活、外交、经济等层面。

Domain这一层面还包含2个分支：C & P

- ［C］CONDITION: Under what CONDITION is the claim valid? 题目的观点、看法在什么情况下成立？或题目观点的成立需要具备哪些前提？一般不会存在百分之百无条件绝对成立或不成立的论述，因此可以分情况讨论：题目观点在什么条件下合理，什么条件下不合理。
- ［P］PERIOD: At what historical PERIOD is the claim valid? 题目的观点、看法在不同的历史时期有哪些不同的影响和体现？即在过去成立与否，在今天有无合理性，在将来又会如何。

前3个层面"DCD"主要用于结合自己的知识体系特点来构架文章整体层次。有些题目,假如考生对历史比较了解,可以从[P]Period角度展开,几个正文段落分别讨论题目观点在不同历史时期的正误;如果对自己的知识面比较有把握,可以从[C]Category或者[D]Domain来展开,几个正文段落分别讨论题目观点对于不同的概念类别或在不同的领域有哪些不同影响;如果对于逻辑论证比较擅长,可以从[C]Condition的角度来展开,讨论在不同的情况下,题目观点有哪些合理或不合理的地方。因此,有些题目仅仅依靠这3个层面就足以构建整篇文章。有些题目讨论的内容决定了在展开时只能或必须从这3个层面展开。

比如Issue作文题库第41题:The greatness of individuals can be decided only by those who live after them, not by their contemporaries.

本题在构建正文时必须从Domain的角度分别分析不同领域的个人成就能否由同时代的人来评价。因为对于不同领域的名人(比如政治、军事、科技、艺术等)情况都是不一样的,如果笼统论断他们能或不能由同时代的人评价将会使文章流于空泛。

又如Issue作文题库第9题:In any field of endeavor, it is impossible to make a significant contribution without first being strongly influenced by past achievements within that field.

本题也必须从Domain的角度分别讨论不同领域的重大进步是否必须借鉴该领域的以往成果。

4. **[R] REASONS that would probably lead people to come to such claim**:人们得出题目观点的理由可能是什么。比如是出于政治目的?还是历史原因?或是利益驱使?抑或是不得已而为之?

在分析理由的时候可以从3个角度思考:
- [I] IMPORTANCE 重要性:采纳题目观点有哪些重要意义?
- [B] BENEFITS 利益性:题目观点对于各个方面会产生哪些好处?或题目讨论的主体之间出于哪些利益考虑和利益关系而采取题目中的做法或形成题目中所描述的态势。
- [N] NECESSITY 必须性:出于哪些不得已之处不得不采取题目所说的行为。

5. **[E] EFFECTS that would possibly be brought about by the claim**:接纳题目的看法或实施题目所描述的行为可能会产生什么后果。

R和E这两个层面主要是在论证某一点的时候深入挖掘论证层次时使用的。找到作者提出某种观点的理由、动机以及后果、影响之后,再去评价、确立对题目观点的立场就有依据了。R和E这两点和前三点DCD会有一定程度的重叠,也就是在考虑前因和后果的时候可能会考虑某一观点对于不同概念种类的前因后果,在不同领域的前因后果,不同时期的前因后果,不同条件下的前因后果,等等。

有了以上层面作为基本构架之后,还需要有针对性地搜集各个领域和主题的具体例证,即一些有代表性的事件、人物、概念、理论。搜集例证时有几条原则需要注意:

- Issue使用的例子没有任何限制,并不是只有伟人、大事才可以用作例证。任何和话题相关的、能够说明自己观点的人或事都可以用于Issue例证。
- 搜寻例子要扬长避短,尽可能从自己熟悉、喜欢、擅长的领域或自己的专业领域搜寻。这样找到的例子自己最熟悉,论证时会更加得心应手,也不容易雷同。
- 要按照需求寻找例子,而不要大海捞针。Issue所需要的例证都是具有某些突出特点的人物和事件,因而要结合自己的背景知识积累,有针对性地去搜寻,而不能把某些长篇著作全部读完再从中摘取能够用得上的例子。
- 有些存在分歧、没有最终统一看法的例子,或是解释起来会比较费时费力的例子,尽管可能非常精彩,也具有独特性,但在写作时还是应尽量避免使用。一方面容易产生争议;另一方面,30分钟的写作时间也不允许对例子作深入分析和解释。

三 构建文章结构

❶ 对题目话题展开分析的思路

Issue写作从题目的理解角度、文章结构到例证素材都非常灵活。理论上说，让100个人去答一道Issue题目，在他们都不偷懒并进行独立思考的前提下，应该得到100种不同的分析方式。下面介绍其中一种从题目观点本身的语言表达特点出发构造正文论证结构的思路。这是一种比较强调文章整体逻辑性，而且几乎所有考生——不论其专业和背景知识——都能够掌握的分析方式。通过这种思路来构架正文有几点优势：

- 能够保证正文围绕题目讨论的Central Issue展开而不会跑题。
- 能够保证正文段落之间的逻辑关系严谨。Issue文章是表达自己的观点，但不是散文。写作时一定要注意正文段落论证内容之间的逻辑性。以这里介绍的方式展开正文，其整体逻辑关系一般可以构造得比较严谨。

但还要再次强调，这里介绍的展开思路只是一道题思路的诸多展开方式中的一种，其最主要的功能是当考生在考场上看到题目，发现其讨论的领域自己不十分了解，例证搜集积累得不充分，以及找不到明确的展开思路时作为辅助分析的工具来使用。它并不一定是这篇文章最佳的或唯一的展开结构，更不是所谓的标准答案。

根据题目观点的语言表达特征，正文段落之间的逻辑关系可以定义为4类：对比型（comparison）、问题解决型（solution）、推理型（reasoning）、观点型（claim）。

1）对比型（comparison）

对比型即题目中对比了A和B两种概念或行为。对比型题目在题库中有两种表现形式：显性对比和隐性对比。

所谓显性对比，是在题目中直接把两方观点进行比较。

比如Issue作文题库第7题：Some people believe that government funding of the arts is necessary to ensure that the arts can flourish and be available to all people. Others believe that government funding of the arts threatens the integrity of the arts.

所谓隐性对比，即在题目中并没有列出两方观点，而是暗含了对A、B两个概念或行为的比较。这类题目语言表达经常为：It is more important to do A than to do B, A rather than B，等等。

比如Issue作文题库第19题：Governments should focus on solving the immediate problems of today rather than on trying to solve the anticipated problems of the future.

在对对比型题目展开论证时，首先应该想一想针对这道题所在的题库进行发散性思维所得到的"DCDRE" 5个层面有没有可以应用于这道题的素材。比如，本题能不能从各个领域分别展开讨论，能不能从不同时期分别分析，能不能分不同情况加以考虑等等。这5个层面不仅在对比型题目论证时可以使用，在其他几种题目类型中也可以使用。这些层面都是构造论证文章的一些基本元素。

其次，任何一道对比型题目都可以应用的通用展开思路，就是分别分析对比双方的正负优劣，作出综合判断。即第一种观点或行为A有哪些优势和劣势；分析的另外一种观点或行为B又有哪些优势和劣势。然后作出自己的综合判断。

另外，对于有些对比型题目还可以考虑一下A、B两者有没有对比的可能性和必要性，或能否找到途径使A、B双方得以调和，即找到一种折中途径：既能吸取A的优势，又能保证B的优势。

2）问题解决型（solution）

这类题目是出题人提出了一个问题或一个目标，同时提供了一个解决问题、实现目标的方案。这类题目的典型语言表达为：

To do sth., one must do sth.

或The way to do sth. is...

以及以through、by引导的方式状语。

比如Issue作文题库第2题：To understand the most important characteristics of a society, one must study its major cities.

问题解决型题目的正面论证内容有2个层面可以展开：

- 出题人提出题目中解决方案的可能理由。这个理由可以参考本章提到的分析Reason的3个角度：Importance / Benefits / Necessity。即采纳题目解决方案有哪些重要意义、对各方面有哪些利益影响以及出于哪些不得已之处只能采用题目方案解决问题。
- 题目解决方案的合理性。即采用题目方案确实能在一定程度上解决题目提出的问题。

问题解决型题目的负面论证有3个层面可以展开：

- 题目解决方案的局限性或问题。即在某些情况下，题目方案无法解决题目提出的问题；或题目方案自身就存在某些漏洞或缺陷。
- 题目方案的可行性。即题目方案尽管理论上可以解决问题，但在现实中存在某些障碍导致该方案无法操作。

  以上两条负面论证并非适用于所有问题解决型题目，而下面的这一条是对任何一道问题解决型题目都适用的"通用"的负面论证：

- 要达到作者提出的目标或解决题目提出的问题，还可能存在哪些其他解决方案。

这3点负面论述之间的逻辑关系非常紧密：首先，题目方案可能无法完美解决问题；其次，即使理论上能解决，现实中可能也难以操作；再次，既然题目方案无法解决问题或不可行，我们应该通过其他手段实现题目目标或解决题目问题。

3）推理型（reasoning）

这类题目的结构有些类似Argument：出题人从一些论据出发推出自己的观点。推理型题目也分为显性推理和隐性推理：

显性推理即题目自身已经把讨论内容分为Reason和Claim两部分。比如Issue作文题库第131题：

Claim: Researchers should not limit their investigations to only those areas in which they expect to discover something that has an immediate, practical application.

Reason: It is impossible to predict the outcome of a line of research with any certainty.

隐性推理即题目并没有把讨论内容直接分成Reason和Claim两部分，但从逻辑上来说是从一些论据、出发点推出一个观点。这类题目在语言表达上通常会出现because、therefore、thus等词汇。

比如Issue作文题库第64题：The human mind will always be superior to machines because machines are only tools of human minds.

这类题目在展开论证时，正面内容可以从3个层面进行思考：

- 题目的理由（论据）确实有一定合理性。
- 题目的推理过程有一定合理性：即从题目的论据确实可以推出题目的观点，其推理过程有一定必然性和充分性。但在实际论述时真正能够应用这一点的题目非常少。
- 题目的观点有一定的合理性。

同样，负面论证内容也可以从3个层面进行思考：

- 题目的理由在某些情况下不合理，存在问题或缺陷。
- 题目的推理过程存在问题：即使上述理由成立，仅有这些理由也不足以推出题目观点。
- 题目的观点本身有问题，或如果接受、采纳题目观点，将可能造成一些不利影响。

另外，推理型题目还有2个发散层面可以进行思考。所谓发散，即这些层面和题目论证是相关的，但难以严格界定属于正面还是负面素材：

- 题目的推理过程是否存在一些前提、假设、必须要满足的条件；如果有，可以用一个乃至几个段落来讨论这些前提或条件是否能够满足。
- 当题目观点是出题人提出的一种行为时，可以讨论该行为的可行性。

4）观点型（claim）

这类题目本身没有任何思维过程，而是直接提出了出题人的一个观点或判断。这类题目在表达上通常是判断句形式，比如：

It is necessary to do sth. / It is important to do sth.；

或经常以出现should为标志，如Government should...

比如Issue作文题库第63题：There is little justification for society to make extraordinary efforts—especially at a great cost in money and jobs—to save endangered animal or plant species.

这类题目在展开论证时，正面论述可以分2个层面：

- 出题人之所以提出题目观点的主观理由，即题人可能出于什么目的或动机而提出题目观点。这个理由通常可以参考Reason的Benefits和Necessity2个分支加以思考。即出题人可能出于哪些利益驱使，或出于哪些迫不得已的原因而得出题目中的看法。
- 题目观点的客观合理性：这一点通常会从Reason的Importance分支以及Effect来考虑。即接纳题目观点有哪些重要意义，或对各方面会产生哪些正面的、积极的影响。

观点型题目的负面论证最基本的出发点就是讨论题目观点本身的不合理性，即观点本身存在哪些问题，或如果接受题目观点将会引发哪些不良后果。另外，在进行负面分析时观点型题目可以根据具体情况向其他几种论证结构转化。

这里简单说明一下以上4种逻辑结构之间的内在联系：

这4种论证结构并不是孤立存在的，它们之间存在一些逻辑上的互通性。有些题目同时具有几种不同论证结构的特点，这类题目可以应用不同结构的思路来进行分析。有些时候，某些题目论证到一定层面时可以进行论证结构的转化。

在这4种结构中，对比型最为基本，几乎任何一道题目最终都可以转化成对比型进行论证。问题解决型可以看成是对比型的一种特殊形式，可以理解为题目解决方案和其他方案之间的对比。推理型和观点型题目在分析时只要能找到出题人观点的对立面，或题目提出的行为以外的其他可能行为，就可以理解成题目观点和对该问题其他观点之间的对比。

观点型题目在条件成熟的情况下，论证负面内容时可以向其他3种论证结构转化。观点型题目在展开分析的时候，可以先思考一下出题人提出题目观点有可能出于哪些理由？有可能为了达到什么目的？与题目行为相对应的其他行为可能有哪些？

如果能找到出题人提出题目观点的理由，就可以把题目转化成推理型（Reason → Claim）的结构进行分析，讨论由该理由是否足以推出题目观点，或该推理过程是否存在某些前提或要满足某些条件。如果能找到出题人提出题目观点或行为的目的，那么就可以把题目转化成问题解决型加以分析，讨论要达到上述目的还有没有其他解决手段和途径。如果能找出出题人提出的行为的对立面或相对应的其他行为，就可以转化成对比型加以分析，讨论题目提出的行为和其他行为的正负优劣。

比如Issue作文题库第148题：Nations should pass laws to preserve any remaining wilderness areas in their natural state.

从题目表达来说本题应该属于观点型。在分析的时候首先可以想一想，出题人为什么要提出把原始环境保留在自然状态？因为人类活动和干预或多或少会对原始环境产生破坏和干扰。这样在分析负面的时候就可以转化成推理型进行思考：人类活动会对自然产生干扰这条理由是否足以让我们推出应该把原始环境保持在自然状态的结论？这个推理过程的成立有哪些前提和条件需要满足？

其次，也可以想一想，出题人要把原始环境保留在自然状态的目的是什么？通常来说是为了环保，为了让这些原始环境更好地服务于社会发展。这样在分析负面的时候就可以转化为问题解决型进行思考：要达到这一目的，除了像作者说的把原始环境保持在自然状态以外，还有没有其他方式和途径？

还可以想一想，对于原始环境的处理方法，与出题人提出的保持在自然状态不加干预相对应的其他行为是什么？比如可以进行一定的人为干预，进行适度的开发甚至获得一些经济效益等。这样在分析负面的时候就可以转化为对比型进行思考：对于原始环境的处理方式，保持其自然状态和进行适当的人为干预各有哪些利弊。

从以上4种基本论证结构出发能够发散思考出很多层面的素材，在进行写作的时候并不需要把这些素材全部加以深入分析，而是应在准备题目的时候先针对一道题进行正负各方面的全面思考，然后再构架自己的立场和文章结构，而不要先确定自己想写的立场，再去构架论证：一方面这不是思考论证的正常思路；另一方面这样处理不容易保证正文的逻辑。

❷ 正文段落的总体结构

确定了一道题目的基本立场后，就可以对上述正负素材进行筛选，并按照一定的正文段落结构展开论述。一般来说，根据Issue的考试时间和论证深度，一篇文章写2~4个正文段落比较合适。这些正文段落之间的总体关系可以分为3类：

1）直线型

即所有正文段落都向同一个逻辑方向层层递进，全部正文段落都讨论正或者负其中一方面的素材。考生经常提出这样的疑问：Issue题目往往带有一定学术深度和思想性，要是写成完全支持或完全反对不显得自己思维过于简单么？这一点不必担心，不用为了表达思维全面性非要写另外一面。有些题假如写完全支持或反对就可以写得很有道理，或题目观点本身就过于极端或没有太多道理，那么，正文处理成直线型完全没问题。

2）有保留的支持或反对

对于题目观点基本支持，但有一些保留意见需要讨论；或反之，对题目观点基本不赞成，但也有一些合理性值得肯定。假如正文写3段，如果是有保留的支持，可以用正、正、负的结构，即用前2段对这道题目的正面素材加以分析论述，第3段转折，用1个段落讨论一下题目观点的负面内容；如果是有保留的反对，则可以用正、负、负的结构，即先用1个段落讨论题目的正面意义，整体作为让步，转折后用2段平行或递进讨论题目的2个负面层面；或者用负、负、正的结构，即先用2段讨论对题目的负面看法，最后一段转折肯定一下题目观点的合理性。

3）平衡结构

即题目看法有利有弊，有合理性的一面，但也存在一些不合理性，两方面比重基本相当。这种结构正文一般可以用2段或4段构造：2段是1正1负；4段则2正2负。

❸ 展开正文时感觉没得写怎么办?

有了正文的基本结构之后,接下来就是每个正文段落展开的问题了。要提高正文段落的质量还需从语言和思维两方面入手。一方面,要大量阅读各种范文、Verbal部分的阅读长文章和外文期刊的评论型文章提升语感,逐渐提高自己用规范学术英语进行论证的能力;另一方面,要大量积累素材、例证,并在平时对各类问题、各种现象勤于思考,锻炼自己批判性思维的能力。

在展开正文分析时,由于上了考场时间紧迫心理紧张,如果感到某些正文段落实在没得可写、无法深入分析,那么以下几种增加正文段落论证内容的方法和思路可供大家参考:

1)分析理由

把题目中提出的现象、行为产生的理由进行深入分析,可以结合前述分析Reason的3个分支:Importance、Benefits和Necessity。对某些现象、观点和行为深入剖析其成因,一方面可以加深论证层次,另一方面能够使自己的分析论证过程更有逻辑性和说服力。

2)分析例子

把说明自己论点所用具体例子的定义、特点、事件过程,以及该例子和论点之间的具体逻辑联系进行适度深入的解释说明。有些考生写作时仅仅把自己用作例证的人或事摆出来,但假如这个人物或事件并不是尽人皆知的,那么就可能令人难以理解。另外,考生也可以说明这个例子是如何与这段要说明的论点之间一步一步建立论证联系的,如果有必要也应该说明其中的推理论证过程。

3)加反证

即把本段段首句的论点正话反说一下,用双重否定句重新诠释段首句。比如(Issue作文题库第19题)某正文段段首句为:政府应集中精力解决当前问题才能保证社会稳定。如果感觉没有可以论证的内容了,那么可以对段首句进行反证:如果政府没有及时解决当前问题,就会造成一定的不良社会影响。这样就可以得到很多展开论证的思路。

4)推极端

主要是在分析某些题目的负面内容时,如果找不到针对某些观点和行为的负面分析素材,可以把该行为或观点推向极端进行尝试。一般来说,任何行为或观点都有一个限度,过分之后一般都会产生问题。还以Issue作文题库第19题为例:要思考政府解决当前问题会有什么负面影响,可以把这种行为推向极端——政府按照一定原则适度解决急迫问题是必需的,但如果政府过分重视解决当前需求的重要性,就会产生一定的社会危害。

❹ 对写作要求的呼应

Issue对考生提出了6种可能的写作要求:

1) Write a response in which you discuss the extent to which you agree or disagree with the statement and explain your reasoning for the position you take. In developing and supporting your position, you should consider ways in which the statement might or might not hold true and explain how these considerations shape your position.

写文章分析你在多大程度上赞同或反对题目的观点并解释理由。在展开论证自己的观点时,应考虑观点何时成立、何时不成立,并解释这些方面对于你观点的形成有何影响。

2) Write a response in which you discuss the extent to which you agree or disagree with the recommendation and explain your reasoning for the position you take. In developing and supporting your position, describe specific circumstances in which adopting the recommendation would or would

not be advantageous and explain how these examples shape your position.

写文章分析你在多大程度上赞同或反对题目的建议并解释理由。在展开论证自己的观点时，需描述采纳上文建议可能会有利或不利的特定情形，并解释这些例子对于你观点的形成有何影响。

3）Write a response in which you discuss your views on the policy above and explain your reasoning for the position you take. In developing and supporting your position, you should consider the possible consequences of implementing the policy and explain how these consequences shape your position.

写文章分析你对上文政策的看法并解释理由。在展开论证自己的观点时，应考虑实施该政策可能产生的后果，并解释这些后果对于你观点的形成有何影响。

4）Write a response in which you discuss the extent to which you agree or disagree with the claim AND the reason on which that claim is based.

写文章分析你在多大程度上赞同或反对题目的观点以及基于的理由。

5）Write a response in which you discuss which view more closely aligns with your own position and explain your reasoning for the position you take. In developing and supporting your position, you should address both of the views presented above.

写文章分析哪一方观点更加贴合你的看法并解释理由。在展开论证自己的观点时，应对双方观点都给予回应。

6）Write a response in which you discuss the extent to which you agree or disagree with the claim. In developing and supporting your position, be sure to address the most compelling reasons or examples that could be used to challenge your position.

写文章分析你在多大程度上赞同或反对题目观点。在展开论证自己的观点时，需对可能用于挑战你观点的最有说服力的理由和例子给予回应。

在这6种写作要求中，前3种可以说没有太大差别。它们只是针对不同性质的题目观点提出的不同表达。如果题目观点是出题人的一个判断，则可能用第一种写作要求；如果题目观点是一种建议或提案，则可能用第二种写作要求；如果题目本身是一种国家政策，则可能用第三种写作要求。对于后半句"考虑何时成立何时不成立、有利或不利的特定情形"云云，对文章的总体展开思路没有根本性影响，只要在论证层面的选择、论证素材的侧重上加以体现即可。在论证素材选择方面第一种写作要求最为宽泛，几乎与题目观点相关的所有内容都可以阐述；第二种写作要求则应侧重于论述要保证题目建议有效而应满足的前提，即前述思考题目思路中的Condition层面；第三种写作要求则应侧重于论述题目行为可能产生的后果，即前述思考题目思路中的Effect层面。

第四和第五种写作要求是专门针对题库中的显性推理型和显性对比型题目提出的特别要求。

显性推理型题目如Issue作文题库第131题：Claim: Researchers should not limit their investigations to only those areas in which they expect to discover something that has an immediate, practical application.

Reason: It is impossible to predict the outcome of a line of research with any certainty.

显性对比型题目如Issue作文题库第7题：Some people believe that government funding of the arts is necessary to ensure that the arts can flourish and be available to all people. Others believe that government funding of the arts threatens the integrity of the arts.

对于第四种写作要求展开论证时，参考前述对于推理型题目的展开思路进行分析即可；对于第五种写作要求，既可以按照前述对于对比型题目的展开思路进行分析，也可以把双方观点看成两道不同的题目，根据其语言表达特点归入相应的论证结构进行分析，最后再进行整体归纳判断。

第六种写作要求稍微有些特殊，它要求考生在论证时考虑和自己观点相反的另一种看法并对其给予回应。因此考生在思考和论证时需要多想一步，思考一下和自己立场不同的人可能出于什么考虑会提出相反观点。这类题在思考相反观点时，有时可以参考同一题库近似题干的对比型题目。

比如Issue作文题库第94题：

The effectiveness of a country's leaders is best measured by examining the well-being of that country's citizens.

Write a response in which you discuss the extent to which you agree or disagree with the claim. In developing and supporting your position, be sure to address the most compelling reasons and/or examples that could be used to challenge your position.

这道题属于第六种写作要求。

在考虑评判领导人业绩还有其他哪些不同看法时可以参考Issue作文题库的第85题：

Some people believe that in order to thrive, a society must put its own overall success before the well-being of its individual citizens. Others believe that the well-being of a society can only be measured by the general welfare of all its people.

Write a response in which you discuss which view more closely aligns with your own position and explain your reasoning for the position you take. In developing and supporting your position, you should address both of the views presented.

这道题属于第五种写作要求，它就给Issue作文题库第94题的论证思路提供了一些参考：有些人会认为领导人的能力应该用国家的总体成功和地位来衡量。因而在论证Issue作文题库第94题时，就可以把题干转化成类似Issue作文题库第85题的对比型结构寻找论证素材和思路，再结合写作要求把这些论证素材加以整理即可。

综上所述，在准备Issue写作时最关键的环节就是展开思路、寻找素材和组织语言，训练自己的思考和论证能力。在展开思路方面，本章提供了一种可供参考的、比较实用的、而且对题目进行快速分析非常有效的分析方法；在本书第二章也提供了根据这种方法对每道Issue题目进行分析得到的结果。但这些思路和框架只是一种启发和参考，考生一定要结合自己的思维特点和知识体系构建一套有特点且行之有效的题目分析方法。考生在平时也应该注重思考能力的训练，多从不同层面考虑一下某些事件和别人的一些观点，分析它们的前因后果、成立的前提以及适用的领域等等。在写作素材方面，需要考生结合本章所介绍的搜寻例证的原则，挖掘积累一些有一定通用性（即能用于论证很多题目），又有一定独特性（即没有被大多数考生注意到或被前人用得很滥）的例证。在语言方面，考生需要大量阅读各种范文、GRE Verbal部分的阅读文章、外文期刊中的社论等论证文章来提高语感。

Issue题目涉及层面非常广泛，写作思路又非常灵活，因此很难用一种固定套路或思维来解答所有题目。考生一定要进行大量阅读积累，勤于思考，勤于下笔练习，对所有主要领域和主要论证结构的题目都有比较深入的了解和成熟的应对方法，才能在做到考场上游刃有余。

本章列出了Issue题目的参考分析思路。

题目顺序已重新编排。首先，主题相同或相近的题目编排在了一起，便于考生查阅参考；其次，所有149道Issue题目又按照其核心思想分为8大类：

A类：眼前问题与长远问题
B类：个体与整体（领导/名人与社会）
C类：科技与人性（机器与人）
D类：理性与感性
E类：学科之间的交叉影响
F类：统一与分歧（竞争与合作）
G类：理想与现实
H类：传统与创新

同一类别的题目核心思想相近，论证结构、内容、素材可以互为参考。

每道题目之前的文字底纹框，比如**自然**，标示了这道题目的学科领域，考生在搜集例证时应从不同领域出发分别挖掘。每道题目之前的数字底纹框，比如**10**，标示了这道题目在Issue作文题库中的序号。每道题目之后的方括号，比如[claim → solution]标示了这道题的参考分析结构。

接下来的思路参考，则是从给出的分析结构出发而构建的正面、负面、发散的论证内容。但要注意：

- 如前所述，每道题目在每位写文章的作者心中应该有不尽相同的理解和展开思路。因此这里所列的只是针对这道题目的一种可能论证结构，而绝非标准答案。其主要用意在于为考生在面对题目感觉无从入手分析的时候提供一种思路启发。
- 每道题目列出的是正负各方面相对比较全面的论证点，写文章时不需要把这些点全部涵盖和展现出来，一般只要选择2~4个比较值得展开、有道理可说的论证点支持自己的立场即可。
- 这部分的主要目的是给考生提供思路参考，因而语言力求简练易懂。有些用英文表达过于繁琐或有理解难度的句子就直接用中文表达。

此外，为节省篇幅，每道题的写作要求在此都简化表达。

A Urgent and Long Run 眼前问题与长远问题

1. **自然** Nations should pass laws to preserve any remaining wilderness areas in their natural
10 state, even if these areas could be developed for economic gain. [claim→solution]

国家应该立法将所有现存原生态地区保持在自然状态，即使对这些地方的开发能够产生自然经济效益。

Discuss your views on the policy and consider the possible consequences of implementing the policy.

【作者提出该观点的目的是什么？】

- 更好的环保，使原始环境能更好地服务于现代社会的总体需求。

【该观点有合理性吗？】

- ［从主观合理性来说］It's one of the primary tasks of government. A nation ought to actively seek effective measures to protect such areas which are worth preserving.

- ［从必须性来说］Human interference will more or less disturb natural environment. Blind and large scale development will pose irreversible effects on environment, as confirmed by numerous examples.

  One without distant care must have near sorrow.

【实施题目所述的政策可能带来哪些正面效果？】

- Effective protection of those areas will benefit future generation.

【与之相对的观点有道理吗？】

- ［从重要性来说］Economic development might be a more critical task for some societies.

- ［从被保护地区的条件来说］可以从wilderness areas的分类来展开。对于有保护价值的原始环境，采纳题目所说的政策固然不错，但不应一刀切，并非所有原生态环境都值得完全保留。

  Some wilderness areas have little value to preserve. Careful investigation and differentiation on their value are necessary before we take steps.

【要达到作者的目的，有没有其他方案？】

- Environmental protection and economic gain are not necessarily mutually exclusive.

  我们可以找到一些折中方案，既能有效环保，又能产生一定经济收益。

- Other solutions

  ［example］eco-tourism

  Attracting tourists to these areas through environmentally sensitive projects could help raising fund for environmental protection, and could make the society give more attention to the protection of these areas.

---

2. 自然/社会 Some people claim that a nation's government should preserve its wilderness
125 areas in their natural state. Others argue that these areas should be developed for potential economic gain. [comparison/solution]

有些人认为政府应该保存原始区域的自然状态。另一些人提出应该开发这些地区以产生经济效益。

Discuss which view more closely aligns with your own position and address both of the views presented.

【第一种观点有道理吗？】

- It's one of the primary tasks of government. A nation ought to actively seek effective measures to protect such areas which are worth preserving.

- ［从后果来说］Effective protection of those areas will benefit future generation.

- ［从必须性来说］Human interference will more or less disturb natural environment.

【第一种观点存在问题吗？】

- Totally keeping these areas untouched may not be the best solution for the protection of these areas.

- Sometimes environmental protection and economic gain are not necessarily mutually exclusive.

【第二种观点有道理吗？】

- ［从重要性来说］Economic development might be a more critical task for some societies.

- [从被保护地区的条件来说] 不应一刀切，有些没有太多保留价值的原生态环境可以进行适当的开发和改造。

  Some wilderness areas have little value to preserve, careful investigation and differentiation on the value are necessary before we take steps.

【第二种观点存在问题吗？】

- Human interference will more or less disturb natural environment. Blind and large scale development will pose negative effects on environment, as confirmed by numerous examples.

【两种观点有没有调和的可能？】

要实现环保，可能还有其他解决途径，将环保和获得经济收益有效结合。

- Other solutions

  [example] eco-tourism

  Attracting tourists to these areas through environmentally sensitive projects could help raising fund for environmental protection, and make the society give more attention to the protection of these areas.

---

3. 自然 Nations should pass laws to preserve any remaining wilderness areas in their natural
148 state. [claim→solution]

国家应该立法保存原生态区域的自然状态。

Discuss the extent to which you agree or disagree with the claim and address the most compelling reasons and/or examples that could challenge your position.

思路参考

【作者提出该观点的目的是什么？】

- 更好的环保，使原始环境能更好地服务于现代社会的总体需求。

【该观点有合理性吗？】

- It's one of the primary tasks of government. A nation ought to actively seek effective measures to protect such areas which are worth preserving.
- [从后果来说] Effective protection of those areas will benefit future generation.
- [从必须性来说] Human interference will more or less disturb natural environment.

【可能存在哪些相反观点？】

- Some people may propose that these areas should be developed for potential economic gain.
- Economic development might be a more critical task for some societies.

  [回应] Environmental protection is of greater importance in the long run.

- Some wilderness areas have little value to preserve.

  [回应] Damage to regional environment will trigger chain-reaction, therefore affecting the whole global eco-system.

【发散】

- 要实现环保，可能还有其他解决途径。

  〈略，参考 10 , 125 〉

---

4. 自然 Society should make efforts to save endangered species only if the potential extinction of
31 those species is the result of human activities. [claim]

只有当某物种将来的灭绝由人类活动导致时，社会才应该努力拯救该濒危物种。

Discuss your views on the policy and consider the possible consequences of implementing the policy.

【作者提出该观点的理由可能是什么？】

- ［从合理性来说］The extinction of some species has nothing to do with human activities.
- ［从可行性来说］The protection of some species is beyond human capability.
- ［从人类社会客观现实来说］Some urgent problems of human society have higher priority than to save endangered species.

【上述理由存在问题吗？】

- Almost all extinctions of species today are caused by human activities, directly or indirectly.

【作者的推理过程合理吗？】

- Human society has the responsibility to save those species even if they will be naturally extinct.

【实施题目所述的政策可能带来哪些后果？】

- Some species possess great value to human race, some of which are not realized by human yet. The extinction of them will bring great loss to human society.
- ［example］

  Every species plays an important role in the eco-system; their extinctions will trigger chain-reaction, therefore affecting the bigger eco-system.

  Some species could provide materials for scientific research and medical, industrial use, or they could be an icon of a nation, or simply they are friends of human.

---

5. **自然** There is little justification for society to make extraordinary efforts—especially at a great
63 cost in money and jobs—to save endangered animal or plant species. ［claim］

社会没有理由付出额外努力——特别是大量金钱和人力——去拯救濒危植物物种。

Discuss the extent to which you agree or disagree with the statement, consider ways in which the statement might or might not hold true.

【作者提出该观点的理由是什么？】

- ［从合理性来说］The extinction of some species has nothing to do with human activities.
- ［从可行性来说］The protection of some species is beyond human capability.
- ［从人类社会客观现实来说］Some urgent problems of human society have higher priority than to save endangered species.

【这些理由充分吗？】

- The extinctions of some species are caused by human activities, directly or indirectly: human constructions and developments may ruin their living environment, destroy their habitat, result in vanishing of their foods, or humans have hunted them to cause their extinction.

【上述理由足以推出观点吗？】

- Human society has the responsibility to save those species even if they will be naturally extinct.

【题目所述的行为本身有道理吗？】

- Some species possess great value to human race, some of which are not realized by human yet. The extinction of them will bring great loss to human society.
- ［example］

  〈略，参考 31〉

14

6. **自然** Some people believe that society should try to save every plant and animal species, despite the expense to humans in effort, time, and financial well-being. Others believe that society need not make extraordinary efforts, especially at a great cost in money and jobs, to save endangered species. [comparison]

一些人认为社会应该拯救所有动植物物种，不论花费多少人力、时间和金钱。另一些人认为社会没有必要付出额外努力——特别是大量金钱和人力——去拯救濒危物种。

Discuss which view more closely aligns with your own position and address both of the views presented.

思路参考

【第一种观点有道理吗？】

- ［从合理性来说］The extinction of some species has nothing to do with human activities.
- ［从可行性来说］The protection of some species is beyond human capability.
- ［从人类社会客观现实来说］Some urgent problems of human society have higher priority than to save endangered species.

【第一种观点存在问题吗？】

- The claim that society should save every species at all cost is open to doubt:

    ［从可行性来说］The protection of some species is beyond human capability.

    ［从人类社会客观现实来说］Some urgent problems of human society have higher priority than to save endangered species.

【第二种观点有道理吗？】

- The extinction of some species has nothing to do with human activities.

    〈略，可参考第一种观点的阐述〉

【第二种观点存在问题吗？】

    〈略，可参考第一种观点的阐述〉

7. **教育** Governments should offer a free university education to any student who has been admitted to a university but who cannot afford the tuition. [solution]

政府应该对所有被大学录取但无法负担学费的学生提供免费大学教育。

Discuss your views on the policy and consider the possible consequences of implementing the policy.

思路参考

【提出上述政策的目的可能是什么？】

- 使公民享有平等受教育的权利，使社会充分发掘潜在的智力资源。

【采纳该政策可能带来哪些正面影响？】

- Some students with special talent could not afford the tuition; depriving them of the right of education will actually affect the future of a nation.
- ［从重要性来说：题目方案能否达到以上目的？］By doing so we could guarantee that every citizen can enjoy the right of being educated, and promote the equity of the society.

【采纳该政策可能带来哪些负面后果？】

- Such policy may render those students overly depend on financial aids, and will go against the cultivation of their personalities.

【要达到作者的目的，有没有其他方案？】

- Government could provide those students with certain kind of loan, which should be paid after their graduation.

---

8. **教育** Governments should offer college and university education free of charge to all students.

25 [claim]

政府应对所有学生提供免费的大学教育。

Discuss the extent to which you agree or disagree with the recommendation and describe specific circumstances in which adopting the recommendation would or would not be advantageous.

思路参考

【作者提出该观点可能出于哪些考虑？】

- To guarantee that every citizen could enjoy the equal right of being educated.
- Some students with special talent may not be able to afford the tuition; deprive them of the right of education will actually affect the future of a nation.

【何时应该采纳作者提出的方案？】

- 当社会公民无法完全享有平等受教育的权利时可以采取作者的方案，以避免社会各方面的不公平和差距进一步拉大。

【何时不必采纳作者的方案？】

- 当公民受教育的权利已经基本保障，高等教育已经成为人们自觉主动的选择和需求，而且大多数公民已经有能力负担高等教育支出时，不一定非要采取以上手段。

【作者提出的方案存在问题吗？】

- Such policy may render some students deem higher-education a deserved matter, and will go against the cultivation of their personalities.

【有没有其他替代方案？】

- 对于确实无法负担学费的学生，学校、社会可以提供有偿助学贷款；对于完全有能力支付学费的学生则不必一定如此。

---

9. **教育** The best way to teach is to praise positive actions and ignore negative ones. [solution/

24 comparison]

教学的最好方法就是夸奖正面行为，忽略负面行为。

Discuss the extent to which you agree or disagree with the statement and consider ways in which the statement might or might not hold true.

思路参考

【作者提出的方案有没有合理之处？】

- [从后果来说] Approval of positive actions helps forming good habits.
- 对正面行为的肯定对受教者是一种鼓励，引导他们懂得更多道理。
- Overemphasis or harsh punishments on negative actions could result in inadequate personalities.

【作者的方案存在问题吗？】

- Always praising positive actions may cause undesirable results, such as overconfidence, pride, etc.
- Totally ignoring negative actions is not helpful for the forming of appropriate value system.

  建议从Condition角度来展开：不同程度、不同类别的错误行为应区别对待。

- Minor negligence could be ignored, while serious delinquency must be warned or even punished.

【除了作者的方案，有没有其他教导方法？】

- 对于这一问题不应绝对化处理，而应分不同情况区别对待：

  In some cases, moderately praising positive actions is necessary; while some negative ones should also be corrected in time.

- Making the educator himself a role model or a good example might be a better way to teach.

【思路提示】

本题可以从Domain的角度展开，分别分析在家庭、学校、科研、工作各领域的教育过程中，题目所述的行为是否合理有效。

---

10. **教育** The best way to teach—whether as an educator, employer, or parent—is to praise [29] positive actions and ignore negative ones. [solution/comparison]

教学的最好方法——不论作为教育者、雇主还是家长——就是夸奖正面行为，忽略负面行为。

Discuss the extent to which you agree or disagree with the claim, address the most compelling reasons and/or examples that could be used to challenge your position.

思路参考

【作者提出的方案有没有合理之处？】

- [从后果来说] Approval of positive actions contributes to forming good habits.
- 对正面行为的肯定对受教者是一种鼓励，引导他们懂得更多道理。
- Overemphasis or harsh punishments on negative actions could result in inadequate personalities.

【可能存在哪些相反的看法？】

- Always praising positive actions may cause undesirable results, such as overconfidence, pride, etc.
- Totally ignoring negative actions is not helpful for the forming of appropriate value system.

【对于这些问题应该如何解决？】

- In some cases, moderately praising positive actions is necessary; while some negative ones should also be corrected in time.
- Making the educator himself a role model or a good example might be a better way to teach.

---

11. **教育** The best way to teach is to praise positive actions and ignore negative ones. [solution/ [52] comparison]

教学的最好方法就是夸奖正面行为，忽略负面行为。

Discuss the extent to which you agree or disagree with the recommendation, describe specific circumstances in which adopting the recommendation would or would not be advantageous.

思路参考

【作者提出的方案有没有合理之处？】

- 在各个领域，鼓励正面行为一般都有助于良好习惯的形成和人格的培养。
- 对正面行为的肯定对受教者是一种鼓励，引导他们懂得更多道理。
- 对于负面行为过分苛责会产生心理阴影。

【作者的方案存在问题吗？】

- 对正面行为的过分褒奖可能导致骄傲、自负等问题。
- 完全无视负面行为会导致行为准则的模糊，不利于正确价值观的形成。

【发散】

〈略，参考 **24**, **29** 〉

【思路提示】

〈略，参考 **24** 〉

---

12. 社会 Governments should focus on solving the immediate problems of today rather than on

19 trying to solve the anticipated problems of the future. [comparison]

政府应集中精力解决当前紧迫问题而不是试图解决未来预期问题。

Discuss the extent to which you agree or disagree with the recommendation and describe specific circumstances in which adopting the recommendation would or would not be advantageous.

思路参考

【解决当前问题有哪些重要意义？】

- ensuring the survival of a society
- keeping social stability

【解决当前问题有哪些负面影响？】

- Overemphasis of some existing problems could cause harmful effects.

【解决未来问题有哪些重要意义？】

- contributing to the development of a society in the long run
- helping future generations

【解决未来问题有哪些负面影响？】

- The consequences of some future researches are unclear and therefore governments should not hastily invest in solving such problems.

【两方面能否调和】

- 一般情况下，当前和长远问题都需要重视，权衡处理才能保证社会稳定发展。

【思路提示】

- 建议从Category或Domain角度展开，分别分析在不同领域当前和长远问题的重要性。

---

13. 科技 Governments should not fund any scientific research whose consequences are unclear.

36 [claim]

政府不应资助任何结果不明的科学研究。

Discuss the extent to which you agree or disagree with the recommendation and describe specific circumstances in which adopting the recommendation would or would not be advantageous.

思路参考

【作者提出该观点的理由是什么？】

- The result of some researches will pose harmful effects on society.

【作者的推理过程合理吗？】

- Not all researches whose consequences are unclear will bring about negative effects.

【作者的观点是否存在问题？】

- Hastily denying funding for all such researches may go against social improvement.

【有没有调和的可能性？】

- Careful investigation and demonstration should be carried out before we fund such projects.
- Indiscriminately denying funding or blind investment could be equally harmful.

---

14. 科技 Governments should not fund any scientific research whose consequences are unclear.

72 ［claim］

政府不应资助任何结果不明的科学研究。

Discuss your views on the policy, consider the possible consequences of implementing the policy.

思路参考

【作者提出该政策的理由是什么？】

- The result of some researches will pose harmful effects on society.

【该政策有可能产生什么后果？】

- ［正面］preventing potential negative effects
- ［负面］Not all the researches whose consequences are unclear will bring about negative effects. Consequently, hastily denying funding for all such researches may go against social improvement and prevent important and valuable discoveries to emerge.

【发散】

- Careful investigation and demonstration should be carried out before we fund such projects.
- Indiscriminately denying funding or blind investment could be equally harmful.

---

15. 科技 Claim: Researchers should not limit their investigations to only those areas in which they

131 expect to discover something that has an immediate, practical application.

Reason: It is impossible to predict the outcome of a line of research with any certainty.

［reasoning→comparison］

观点：研究人员不应该把他们的研究局限于那些可能会得到有直接现实应用价值的成果的领域。

理由：要确定预测某研究的成果是不可能的。

Discuss the extent to which you agree or disagree with the claim and the reason on which that claim is based.

思路参考

【题目陈述的理由合理吗？】

- 有些研究确实很难预测其结果和影响。
- 某些领域的重大发现和发明是在研究其他领域课题的时候偶然做出的。（可参考E类 56 ）

【题目观点有合理性吗？】

- Limiting investigations to those areas will obviously go against the development of a society in the long run.

【题目的理由有问题吗？】

- 并非所有研究结果都不可预测。

【题目的论证过程有问题吗？】

- 不赞成把研究局限于上述领域并非出于作者陈述的理由，而是社会长远发展的考虑。

16. 教育 Teachers' salaries should be based on their students' academic performance. ［claim→
30 solution］

教师工资应取决于其学生的学术表现。

Discuss the extent to which you agree or disagree with the claim and address the most compelling reasons and/or examples that could be used to challenge your position.

思路参考

【题目提出该观点的目的是什么？】

- 为了提高教学质量，更加公平有效地确定教师薪酬。

【题目观点有合理性吗？】

- ［从后果来说］It's an incentive for teachers to improve their teaching quality.
- ［回应］The proposal could be unfair for some teachers because the talents of their students might be greatly different.

【题目观点有不合理性吗？】

- ［从教学对象的实际情况来说］学生的天资有很大差别，用这种方式决定教师待遇可能有失公允。
- ［回应］决定教师待遇可以采取其他方法。

【其他确定教师薪酬的方案】

- The salaries could be based on the evaluation of students toward teachers' teaching quality.
- adopting a more comprehensive assessment system which will take all relevant factors into account

17. 教育 Teachers' salaries should be based on the academic performance of their students.
83 ［claim→solution］

教师薪酬应取决于其学生的学术表现。

Discuss the extent to which you agree or disagree with the recommendation and describe specific circumstances in which adopting the recommendation would or would not be advantageous.

思路参考

【题目提出该观点的目的是什么？】

- 为了提高教学质量，更加公平有效地确定教师薪酬。

【题目行为能达到该目的吗？】

- ［从后果来说］It's an incentive for teachers to improve their teaching quality.

【题目行为何时合理？】

- 如果不同教师的教学对象各方面条件差别不大，那么，采用这种方法就是合理的。

【题目行为何时不合理？】

- 如果不同教师教授的学生天资等各方面条件有很大差别，那么，用这种方式决定教师待遇可能有失公允。

【发散】

〈略，参考 30 〉

18. 教育 Society should identify those children who have special talents and provide training for
37 them at an early age to develop their talents. ［claim］

社会应挖掘有特殊天赋的儿童，并在早期训练他们以开发其天赋。

Discuss the extent to which you agree or disagree with the recommendation and describe specific circumstances in which adopting the recommendation would or would not be advantageous.

【题目所述提案的意义】

- 充分发挥这些儿童的天赋，使之服务于社会发展。

【题目所述提案能达到该目的吗？】

- ［从必须性来说］Some talents must be cultivated at an early stage to be fully developed.

【题目所述提案达到目的的前提是什么？】

- An effective evaluation-system must be established to accurately assess and determine children's talent.
  要发挥这些儿童的天赋，首先应建立一套积极有效的天赋评价机制。
- 所谓的天赋应该有益于社会发展。
- 对这些天赋的早期培养和步入社会后的工作、生活不应脱节。

【题目所述提案在什么情况下会有问题？】

- 儿时显露的天赋有时并不能一直持续到成年；相反，有些儿时普通的孩子长大后反而有突出贡献。
  Some great people did not show special talent when they were young or even were regarded as imbecilities.
- 如果处理不好对所谓天才儿童的发掘和对待方式，那么，对其他儿童以及天才儿童自身都会有不良影响。
- 如果没有正确的培养方式，将产生揠苗助长的后果。
- 对儿童天赋的培养如果不能和成年后的工作、生活有效衔接，使这些特殊天赋有效服务于社会，那么题目所述提案就没有任何意义。

---

19. **社会** The greatness of individuals can be decided only by those who live after them, not by their
41 contemporaries. [claim/comparison]
个人的伟大只能由后人而不是其同时代的人评判。

Discuss the extent to which you agree or disagree with the statement and consider ways in which the statement might or might not hold true.

【思路提示】

- 本题通常从Domain的角度来展开，即讨论不同社会领域的成就能否由同时代的人评判。

【题目观点的理由可能是什么？】

- The thoughts and ideas of some brilliant minds are so advanced that it would take several decades or even centuries for people to understand them.
- 同时代的人有时出于社会、政治乃至利益原因，不能或不愿对有些成就作出公正评价。

【题目说法合理吗？】

- ［商业领域］Business success and achievements can usually be recognized immediately.
- ［自然科学］It depends. The significance of some research was recognized almost immediately, while the greatness of some research was realized and confirmed by people after decades or centuries.
- ［艺术］It also depends. The themes of some great art works are so plain that almost everyone could understand them, while the greatness of some artists and their works regain their honor and appreciation after hundreds of years.（可参考E类 **55** ）
- ［政治］For political leaders, fair, objective and accurate evaluation of their greatness was often carried out only by later generations.
- On the one hand, it took decades for the impacts of their political decisions, policies to emerge.
- On the other, some contemporaries do not dare to make fair assessment for political purpose or for the concern of their personal safety.

20. 社会 Young people should be encouraged to pursue long-term, realistic goals rather than seek
[51] immediate fame and recognition. [comparison]

应该鼓励年轻人追求长远现实的目标而不是迅速成名。

Discuss the extent to which you agree or disagree with the recommendation and describe specific circumstances in which adopting the recommendation would or would not be advantageous.

思路参考

【作者提出该观点的目的可能是什么？】

● 使年轻人树立正确的价值观和目标，发挥自身的天分，使之能更好地服务于社会发展的总体目标。

【追求长远目标有意义吗？】

● helpful for young people to achieve true greatness
● helpful for young people to overcome greater difficulties
● important for the well-being of the whole society

【追求长远目标在可行性方面有问题吗？】

● [前提未必能保证] 能树立长远目标固然不错，但要树立正确目标需要恰当的引导和环境的熏陶；对于年轻人来说，由于缺乏所需的经验和阅历，有时会接受错误的价值观，追求不正确的目标。
● [从年轻人的客观特点看] 年轻人仍然处于人生的探索阶段，更乐于尝试、体验和冒险，让他们固守所谓长远目标可能有一定难度。

【追求快速成名有意义吗？】

● Undoubtedly, immediate fame and recognition could bring young people material abundance and great fulfillment.

【追求快速成名有问题吗？】

● But, greater emptiness will follow when the fame and recognition fade. This could even lead people to misdeeds, as evidenced by numerous examples of famous people.
● Seeking immediate fame and recognition will be no good for the overall well-being of a society.

21. 社会 Young people should be encouraged to pursue long-term, realistic goals rather than seek
[71] immediate fame and recognition. [comparison]

应该鼓励年轻人追求长远现实的目标而不是迅速成名。

Discuss the extent to which you agree or disagree with the statement, consider ways in which the statement might or might not hold true.

思路参考

〈略，参考 [51]〉

22. 社会 Nations should suspend government funding for the arts when significant numbers of their
[80] citizens are hungry or unemployed. [claim→solution]

当大量国民处于饥饿和失业状态的时候，国家应暂缓对于艺术的资助。

Discuss the extent to which you agree or disagree with the recommendation and describe specific circumstances in which adopting the recommendation would or would not be advantageous.

【题目描述背景的暗含含义是什么？】

- The circumstance described by the speaker（significant numbers of citizens are hungry or unemployed）may indicate negligence of government in properly allocating its money and making correct decisions.
- Understandably, government funding should be used for more urgent purposes under such circumstance.

【题目所述观点有合理性吗？】

- [从政府职责来看]政府有义务合理分配、使用其财政收入，保证社会稳定发展和公民的基本生存权。如果大批公民的生存无法得到保证，那么，对于艺术这种精神需求的投入应该延缓。皮之不存，毛将焉附？

【题目所述的观点有问题吗？】

- 艺术的存在和发展有其必要性，没有艺术，人类的社会文化发展将没有任何意义。
- Suspending government funding for art until hunger and unemployment are eliminated may suggest that the funding will never be put in place.

【有没有其他解决方案？】

- Art patronage is not a necessary function of government.
- Art could be funded by wealthy individuals, private foundations, and social institutions.

---

23. 社会 Claim: Nations should suspend government funding for the arts when significant numbers of their citizens are hungry or unemployed.

88

Reason: It is inappropriate—and, perhaps, even cruel—to use public resources to fund the arts when people's basic needs are not being met. [reasoning→solution]

观点：当大量国民处于饥饿和失业状态的时候，国家应暂缓对于艺术的资助。

理由：当人民基本需求无法得到满足的时候，用公共资源资助艺术是不妥当的甚至可能是残酷的。

Discuss the extent to which you agree or disagree with the claim and the reason on which that claim is based.

【题目的理由有道理吗？】

- 如果大批公民的生存无法得到保证，那么，对于艺术这种精神需求的投入应该延缓。皮之不存，毛将焉附？

【题目观点有道理吗？】

- [从政府职责来看]政府有义务合理分配、使用其财政收入，保证社会稳定发展和公民的基本生存权。

【题目推理的前提有问题吗？】

- The circumstance described by the speaker（significant numbers of citizens are hungry or unemployed）may indicate negligence of government in properly allocating its money and making correct decisions.
- Understandably, government funding should be used for more urgent purposes under such circumstance.

【题目的理由有问题吗？】

- 艺术的存在和发展有其必要性，没有艺术，人类社会文化发展的意义将大大降低。
- [从行为后果来说]Suspending government funding for art until hunger and unemployment are eliminated may suggest that the funding will never be put in place.

【有没有其他解决方案？】

- ［从题目观点的前提来说］Art patronage is not a necessary function of government.
- Art could be funded by wealthy individuals, private foundations, and social institutions.

---

24. 教育 All parents should be required to volunteer time to their children's schools. ［claim → 81 solution］

应该要求所有家长在孩子的学校参加志愿工作。

Discuss the extent to which you agree or disagree with the recommendation and describe specific circumstances in which adopting the recommendation would or would not be advantageous.

思路参考

【提出上述观点的目的是什么？】

- 为了让孩子得到更适合其发展的教育。

【采纳上述建议的意义何在？】

- ［从必须性来说］Parents know what kind of educational activities are most suitable for their children.
- ［从利益性来说］Parents are most motivated to take proper measures to ensure their children receiving the best education.

【题目所述建议能达到上述目的吗？】

- Parents' interests on their children's activities might be the best encouragement for the children's education.
- Parents' supervision on school activities could ensure proper educational choices.

【题目所述建议在什么情况下会有问题？】

- ［从建议成立的前提来说］Though their intentions might be justified, parents are not necessarily equipped to know what is best for the education of their children.
- ［从建议产生的后果来说］The proposed actions may interfere with normal school activities.
- ［从建议的可行性来说］强行要求所有家长参与学校活动可能存在困难。

【有没有其他解决方案？】

- 学校应该根据家长的具体情况恰当安排他们辅助教学的活动，硬性统一要求未必产生良好效果。

---

25. 教育 All parents should be required to volunteer time to their children's schools. ［claim → 95 solution］

应该要求所有家长到他们孩子的学校参加志愿工作。

Discuss the extent to which you agree or disagree with the claim and address the most compelling reasons and/or examples that could be used to challenge your position.

思路参考

【提出上述观点的目的是什么？】

- 为了让孩子得到更适合其发展的教育。

【采纳上述建议的意义何在？】

- ［从必须性来说］Parents know what kind of educational activities are most suitable for their children.
- ［从利益性来说］Parents are most motivated to take proper measures to ensure their children receiving the best education.

【题目建议能达到上述目的吗？】

- Parents' interests on their children's activities might be the best encouragement for the children's education.
- Parents' supervision on school activities could ensure proper educational choices.

【可能存在哪些相反观点？】

- ［从建议成立的前提来说］Though their intentions might be justified, parents are not necessarily equipped to know what is best for the education of their children.
- ［从建议产生的后果来说］The proposed actions may interfere with normal school activities.
- ［从建议的可行性来说］强行要求所有家长参与学校活动可能存在困难。
- ［回应］应根据家长的具体情况给他们安排适当的学校活动，并对家长参与的程度制定合理有效的原则，避免对正常教学秩序造成干扰。

B Individual and Group (Leaders/Celebrities and Society)
个体与整体(领导/名人与社会)

1. 社会 To understand the most important characteristics of a society, one must study its major
   ② cities. ［solution］
   要了解一个社会的最重要特征，必须研究其主要城市。
   Discuss the extent to which you agree or disagree with the statement and consider ways in which the statement might or might not hold true.

思路参考

【题目提出的方法有意义吗？】

- It is primarily in major cities that a nation's mainstream culture, politics, and business activities take place, therefore, the features of major cities could reflect the characteristics of many aspects of a society.

【题目提出的方法有问题吗？】

- The condition of major cities could only represent some superficial aspects of a society.
- Under the influence of globalization, modern cities have become more and more uniform, and the features of major cities might be little indication of a society's tradition, custom, and history.

【要了解社会特点，有没有其他途径？】

- To fully understand the characteristics of a society, one must study other aspects, such as its rural areas, citizens（their hobbies, living habits, traditions, diet, etc.）

2. 社会 Claim: Governments must ensure that their major cities receive the financial support they
   ⑤ need in order to thrive.
   Reason: It is primarily in cities that a nation's cultural traditions are preserved and generated.
   ［reasoning］
   观点：政府必须确保其主要城市获得繁荣所需的财政支持。
   理由：一个国家的文化传统主要是在城市得以保存和创造。
   Discuss the extent to which you agree or disagree with the claim and the reason on which that claim is based.

思路参考

【题目的理由有道理吗？】

- Admittedly, some aspects of a nation's cultural traditions are preserved and generated in cities.

【题目的观点有道理吗？】

- It is one of the primary tasks of government to ensure the development of its cities.
- [从必要性来说] Government funding is necessary for the survival of cities.

【题目的理由有问题吗？】

- Many aspects of a nation's cultural traditions, such as handcrafts, folk art, custom and traditional festivals, are generated and preserved intact in small towns and rural regions.

【题目的推理过程有问题吗？】

- The mere fact that a city generated or preserved cultural traditions does not sufficiently illustrate that government should give priority to that city when considering the allocation of the budget.

【有没有其他解决方案？】

- The development of cities could also be subsidized by wealthy individuals, private foundations, and social institutions.

---

3. 社会 It is primarily in cities that a nation's cultural traditions are generated and preserved.
117 [claim→solution]
一个国家的文化传统主要在城市产生和保留。
Discuss the extent to which you agree or disagree with the statement and consider ways in which the statement might or might not hold true.

思路参考

【思路提示】

- 本题最好结合Category来展开，分别分析讨论不同种类的文化传统主要在哪里产生。

【题目的观点有合理性吗？】

- Admittedly, some aspects of a nation's cultural traditions are preserved and generated in cities.

【题目的观点有问题吗？】

- Many aspects of a nation's cultural traditions, such as handcrafts, folk art, custom and traditional festivals, are generated and preserved intact in small towns and rural regions.

【题目提出的问题有其他方面的可能性吗？】

- Some cultural traditions could be preserved through other media.

---

4. 社会 The most effective way to understand contemporary culture is to analyze the trends of its
77 youth. [solution]
了解当代文化的最有效途径就是分析年轻人的潮流。
Discuss the extent to which you agree or disagree with the statement and consider ways in which the statement might or might not hold true.

思路参考

【思路提示】

- 本题最好从Category的角度展开，分别讨论要研究不同种类的当代文化，分析年轻人是否是最佳方案。

【题目提出的方法有意义吗？】

- Youth are the group of people who most eagerly present themselves; analysis of the trends of youth is essential for understanding many aspects of contemporary culture.

【题目提出的方法有问题吗？】

- The trends of youth could only reflect some fashionable, or even avant-garde aspects of culture, and may not accurately represent the mainstream of culture.

【要了解当代文化，有没有其他途径？】

- Adults and seniors dominate many fields of social activities; analysis of the trends of those people might be a more crucial approach to understand the mainstream of culture.
- To thoroughly study contemporary culture, one should also analyze other aspects of a society, such as cities and rural areas, citizens (their hobbies, living habits, traditions, diet, etc.)

---

5. 社会 People's behavior is largely determined by forces not of their own making. ［claim→
   11 solution］
   人们的行为很大程度上是由自己无法控制的力量决定的。
   Discuss the extent to which you agree or disagree with the statement and consider ways in which the statement might or might not hold true.

思路参考

【题目的说法在什么情况下有合理性？】

- Absolute freedom does not exist at all. Any choice or behavior is more or less influenced by immediate environment.
- ［个人先天条件一般都无法由自己控制］One's inherent condition, such as physical condition, family condition, nationality, etc., could not be determined by an individual; behavior related to those aspects is largely determined by external forces.

【题目的说法在什么情况下不一定正确？】

- ［后天的很多因素可以通过自身努力加以完善和提高］One's knowledge, culture, thoughts, wisdom could be acquired through his interaction with society.

【发散：有没有其他决定个人行为的因素？】

- One should consciously look for his strong points and advantages, and cultivate the ability of seizing the opportunities he faces.

---

6. 社会 People's behavior is largely determined by forces not of their own making. ［claim→
   99 solution］
   人们的行为很大程度上是由不受自己控制的力量决定的。
   Discuss the extent to which you agree or disagree with the claim and address the most compelling reasons and/or examples that could be used to challenge your position.

思路参考

【题目的说法有道理吗？】

- Absolute freedom does not exist at all. Any choice or behavior is more or less influenced by immediate environment.
- ［Compelling reason: In everyday lives, we all have almost infinite number of choices. The only reason why people feel they have no choice is that they do not dare to undertake the cost of making correct choices.］
- ［回应］作为理性个体，一个人在社会中生存，趋利避害几乎可以说是本能反应。因而没有采取在道德良知上完全正确的行为也不可过多指责。

- ［个人先天条件一般都无法由自己控制］One's inherent condition, such as physical condition, family condition, nationality, etc., could not be determined by an individual; behavior related to those aspects is largely determined by external forces.

【题目的说法在什么情况下不一定正确？】

- ［后天的很多因素可以通过自身努力加以完善提高］One's knowledge, culture, thoughts, wisdom could be acquired through his interaction with society.

- ［Compelling reason: However, one's inherent condition largely determines his later development.］

- ［回应］无论如何，最终控制个人思想和行为的还是人本身，因而个人必须对自身各方面的完善提高负责任。

---

7. **政治/社会** Some people believe that in order to be effective, political leaders must yield to public **16** opinion and abandon principle for the sake of compromise. Others believe that the most essential quality of an effective leader is the ability to remain consistently committed to particular principles and objectives. ［comparison→solution］

有些人认为作为有力的政治领导人必须屈从于大众观点并为妥协而放弃原则。另外一些人认为有力的领导人最重要的品质就是一贯忠于某种特定原则和目标的能力。

Discuss which view more closely aligns with your own position and address both of the views presented.

思路参考

【第一种观点有道理吗？】

- ［观点成立的前提］The public opinion does not conflict with the primary goal of social development and progress.

- ［从领导人的职责来说］The ultimate goal of political leaders is to serve the people, and to enhance the general welfare of the society. They ought to compromise when their political principles conflict with public interest.

【第一种观点有问题吗？ / 对第一种观点的回应】

- People are more likely to think of their personal interests. Indiscriminately compromising to their opinion may jeopardize the general welfare of the society.

- Sometimes adhering to correct principles is more important than satisfying the public. It is necessary for leaders to weigh the advantages and disadvantages thoroughly before they take steps.

【第二种观点有道理吗？】

- ［观点成立的前提］The so-called principles are really worth being adhered to.

- ［观点存在的客观意义］Adherence to correct principle is important and necessary for social development and progress.

【第二种观点有问题吗？】

- Commitment to incorrect principles and totally ignoring the public may bring disastrous result to a nation.

【两种观点有调和的可能吗？】

- ［合理制度的约束更为重要］With proper system setting, we can prevent disaster of a nation due to the leaders' fault.

8. 政治 Politicians should pursue common ground and reasonable consensus rather than elusive
60 ideals. [claim/comparison]

政治人物应该追求共同利益和合理的共识而不是难以捉摸的理想。

Discuss the extent to which you agree or disagree with the recommendation and describe specific circumstances in which adopting the recommendation would or would not be advantageous.

思路参考

【追求共识有合理性吗？】

- ［从政治活动的最终目的来说］The ultimate goal of politics is to serve the people, and to enhance the general welfare of the society. Politicians ought to search for common ground and reasonable consensus, and to compromise when their political principles conflict with public interest.

【追求共同利益有问题吗？】

- People are more likely to think of their personal interests. Indiscriminately compromising to their opinion may jeopardize the general welfare of the society.
- Sometimes adhering to correct ideals is more important than searching for consensus. It is necessary for politicians to weigh the advantages and disadvantages thoroughly before they take steps.

【追求理想有合理性吗？】

- ［观点成立的前提］The so-called ideals are really worth being adhered to.
- ［观点存在的客观意义］Adherence to correct ideals is important and necessary for social development and progress.

【追求理想有问题吗？】

- Commitment to incorrect ideals and totally ignoring the public may bring disastrous result to a nation.

【两种行为有调和的可能吗？】

- Reasonable consensus and political ideal need not be mutually exclusive.

---

9. 政治 Government officials should rely on their own judgment rather than unquestioningly carry
50 out the will of the people they serve. [comparison]

政府官员应依靠自己的判断而不是盲目地服从民众的意愿。

Discuss the extent to which you agree or disagree with the recommendation and describe specific circumstances in which adopting the recommendation would or would not be advantageous.

思路参考

【政府官员何时应该坚持自己的判断？】

- ［坚持判断的前提］The officials are proficient enough to make correct judgment.

  Their judgment does not conflict with general welfare of a society.
- ［从该行为的必要性来说］The settlement of some accidents requires instant response based on experience and judgment of officials.
- People are more likely to think of their personal interests. Indiscriminately carrying out their will may jeopardize the general welfare of the society.

【政府官员坚持自己的判断会有问题吗？】

- ［在有些情况下］The judgment of some officials might be biased or unjust, due to their political interest.
- ［从该行为可能的后果来说］The recommendation would lead to undue freedom of officials to carry out

their own will, and disaster of the nation would follow.

【政府官员是否应该服从民众意愿？】

- ［从官员的职责来说］The ultimate goal of officials is to serve the people, and to enhance the general welfare of the society. They should carry out the will of people if only their will does not conflict with the primary goal of social development and progress.

【两种行为有调和的可能吗？】

- ［合理制度的约束更为重要］Overly relying either on the judgment of officials or on the will of people would bring about harmful effect. Proper system setting is necessary to prevent both tendencies.

---

10. **政治** Some people believe that government officials must carry out the will of the people they
86 serve. Others believe that officials should base their decisions on their own judgment.
   ［comparison→solution］
   一些人认为政府官员必须遵从人民意愿。另一些人认为官员应基于自己的判断作出决策。
   Discuss which view more closely aligns with your own position and address both of the views presented.

思路参考

【第一种观点有道理吗？】

- ［观点成立的前提］The will of people does not conflict with the primary goal of social development and progress.
- ［从官员的职责来说］The ultimate goal of officials is to serve the people, and to enhance the general welfare of the society. They should carry out the will of people whenever the will does not conflict with the primary goal of social development and progress.

【第一种观点有问题吗？】

- ［从公众的客观情况来看］People are more likely to think of their personal interests. Indiscriminately carrying out their will may jeopardize the general welfare of the society.
- Sometimes adhering to correct judgment is more important than satisfying the public. It is necessary for officials to weigh the advantages and disadvantages thoroughly before they take steps.

【第二种观点有道理吗？】

- ［坚持判断的前提］The officials are proficient enough to make correct judgment.
- Their judgment does not conflict with general welfare of a society.
- ［从该行为的必要性来说］The settlement of some accidents requires instant response based on experience and judgment of officials.

【第二种观点有问题吗？】

- ［在有些情况下］The judgment of some officials might be biased or unjust, due to their political interest.
- ［从该行为可能的后果来说］The recommendation would lead to undue freedom of officials to carry out their own will, and disaster of the nation would follow.

【两种行为有调和的可能吗？】

- ［合理制度的约束更为重要］Overly relying either on the judgment of officials or on the will of people would bring about harmful effect. Proper system setting is necessary to prevent both tendencies.

11. 政治 Government officials should rely on their own judgment rather than unquestioningly carry
`115` out the will of the people whom they serve. [comparison]

政府官员应依靠自己的判断而不是盲目服从民众的意愿。

Discuss the extent to which you agree or disagree with the statement and consider ways in which the statement might or might not hold true.

思路参考

〈略，参考 `50` 〉

12. 政治 Any leader who is quickly and easily influenced by shifts in popular opinion will accomplish
`114` little. [claim]

迅速且轻易受公众意见变化影响的领导不会有什么作为。

Discuss the extent to which you agree or disagree with the statement and consider ways in which the statement might or might not hold true.

思路参考

【该观点存在的理由是什么？】

- ［观点存在的必要性］Adherence to correct principle is important and necessary for achieving the primary goal, and is also an useful virtue of an effective leader.
- ［从公众的客观特点来说］The general public are more likely to think of their personal interests, and are less informed than the leaders. Indiscriminately compromising to their opinion may jeopardize the general welfare of the group.

【该观点有问题吗？】

- ［从行为产生的后果来说］Stubborn commitment to certain objective may result in arbitrary decisions, or even autarchy.

【思路提示】

- 本题和前面几题的不同之处在于：主题词leader前面没有任何限定，因而可以从Domain的角度来展开，分别讨论政治、宗教、经济、文化、科技等各领域的领导是否适用上述判断。

13. 政治 Claim: Major policy decisions should always be left to politicians and other government
`139` experts.

Reason: Politicians and other government experts are more informed and thus have better judgment and perspective than do members of the general public. [reasoning→solution/comparison]

观点：主要政治决策都应该留给政治家和其他政府专家。

理由：政治家和其他政府专家消息更加灵通，从而比一般公众具有更好的判断力和视角。

Discuss the extent to which you agree or disagree with the claim and the reason on which that claim is based.

思路参考

【题目的理由有道理吗？】

- ［从客观现实来说］Generally speaking, politicians and experts are more informed and experienced and therefore have advantages in making judgment.

【题目的观点有道理吗？】

- ［观点成立的前提］The politicians and experts have enough expertise and experience and are fully informed to make correct decisions.
- The political purpose of those politicians does not conflict with general welfare of the society.
- ［从必要性来说］The settlement of some accidents requires instant response based on experience and judgment of politicians and experts.
- ［从民众的客观特点来讲也有必要性］Citizens are more likely to think of their personal interests; indiscriminately compromising to their opinion may jeopardize the general welfare of the society.

【题目的理由有问题吗？】

- Without an effective system of selecting, appointing, and assessing officials and experts, we cannot ensure that politicians are more experienced than the public to make correct decisions.

【题目的推理过程有问题吗？】

- ［即使政治家和专家更有能力］There is no guarantee that political decisions they made will always be in the interest of general public, due to certain political purpose of the politicians.
- Similarly, how can we prevent corruption, faulty decision without effective supervision from the public?

【题目的观点有问题吗？】

- ［从政治活动的终极目标来说］The ultimate goal of officials is to serve the people, and to enhance the general welfare of the society. They should carry out the will of people whenever the will does not conflict with the primary goal of social development and progress.
- ［从观点可能产生的后果来说］Undue freedom of politicians to carry out their own will may bring about disaster of the nation.
- ［从民众参与决策的必要性来说］Encouraging people to participate in the process of public policy making is necessary for ensuring the general welfare, and could help the government to develop correct and scientific decisions.

【有没有其他可能采取的措施？】

- ［合理的制度更为重要］Overly relying either on the judgment of officials or on the will of people would bring about harmful effect. Proper system setting is necessary to prevent both tendencies.

【思路提示】

- 本题最好结合Condition来展开，分别讨论在不同的情形下，处理事务应该依赖专家还是听取大众的意见。

---

14. 社会 Claim: The best way to understand the character of a society is to examine the character of the men and women that the society chooses as its heroes or its role models.

Reason: Heroes and role models reveal a society's highest ideals. ［reasoning+solution］

观点：了解一个社会特点的最好方法就是研究被该社会选为英雄或者榜样的人的特点。

理由：英雄和榜样揭示了社会的最高理想。

Discuss the extent to which you agree or disagree with the claim and the reason on which that claim is based.

思路参考

【题目的理由有道理吗？】

- Many heroes do embody some virtues and ideals admired or approved by the society who chooses them as heroes.

【题目的理由有问题吗？】
- Some people were chosen as heroes just because they have some virtues or characters that were very rare in their society. In this case, examination of their character will be of no use for understanding the character of their society.

【题目的推理过程有问题吗？】
- 即使被选为英雄的人确实反映了社会的最高理想，但这些理想就能够代表全部的社会特点吗？

【研究社会特点有没有其他解决方法？】
- To fully understand the characteristics of a society, one must study other aspects, such as its cities, ordinary people (their hobbies, living habits, traditions, diet, etc.).

【思路提示】
- 本题可以结合Domain来展开，分别讨论军事、政治、科技、体育、娱乐、经济各领域的英雄能否反映社会理想，进而反映社会特点。同时也可以参考 **2** 、 **77** 的一些素材。

---

15. 社会 The best way to understand the character of a society is to examine the character of the **122** men and women that the society chooses as its heroes or its role models. [solution]

了解一个社会特点的最好方法就是研究被该社会选为英雄或者榜样的人的特点。

Discuss the extent to which you agree or disagree with the claim and address the most compelling reasons and/or examples that could be used to challenge your position.

思路参考

【题目提出的了解社会特点的方法有道理吗？】
- Many heroes do embody some virtues and ideals admired or approved by the society who chooses them as heroes.
- [回应][应根据不同情况判断] Some people were chosen as heroes just because they have some virtues or characters that were very rare in their society; in this case, examination of their character will be of no use for understanding the character of their society.
- [回应][了解社会还有其他途径] To fully understand the characteristics of a society, one must study other aspects, such as its cities, ordinary people (their hobbies, living habits, traditions, diet, etc.).

【思路提示】
- 本题建议结合Domain来展开，分别讨论军事、政治、科技、体育、娱乐、经济各领域的英雄能否反映社会特点，以及各个领域的英雄在反映社会特点方面会存在什么问题。

---

16. 社会 Claim: It is no longer possible for a society to regard any living man or woman as a hero.
44 Reason: The reputation of anyone who is subjected to media scrutiny will eventually be diminished. [reasoning]

观点：一个社会不再可能把任何在世的个人当成英雄。

理由：任何暴露在媒体审查之下的人的名声最终都将消亡。

Discuss the extent to which you agree or disagree with the claim and the reason on which that claim is based.

思路参考

【题目的理由有道理吗？】
- [从媒体的客观条件来说] The modern media are so powerful that they can raise someone up to a hero

while devastating someone's reputation forever.

- ［从媒体运行的利益关系来说］The media are usually run by profit-seeking groups; they may find out that the misfortunes and misdeeds of people, especially those of heroic figures, often bring them more profits than the virtues and accomplishments of those people do.
- ［从社会客观条件来说］The general public usually expect that their heroes are guilty of some sort of character flaw or misdeed, and are willing to hear about scandals.

【题目的推理过程有合理性吗？】

- A flawed public figure can hardly be deemed as a hero.

【题目的理由有问题吗？】

- ［不能一刀切，对于有些英雄来说］The reputations of some people who possess true virtues have not been damaged, if not enhanced, by media scrutiny.

【题目的推理过程有问题吗？】

- ［即使媒体有摧毁个人声誉的力量，也未必说明所有在世的人都不可能被看作英雄］Not all heroes have dazzling reputation; some ordinary people could also be considered as heroes, and they are more resistant to media scrutiny.

【思路提示】

- 本题可以从Domain的角度考虑，分别讨论政治、经济、社会、娱乐、科技各领域被人们视为英雄的人物对媒体审查的抵抗力如何，以及他们之所以被称为英雄和他们的声誉之间的关系是否紧密。

---

17. 社会 In this age of intensive media coverage, it is no longer possible for a society to regard any
75 living man or woman as a hero.［claim/reasoning］
在媒体高度覆盖的今天，社会不可能再把任何在世的人视为英雄。
Discuss the extent to which you agree or disagree with the statement and consider ways in which the statement might or might not hold true.

思路参考

〈略，参考 **44** 〉

---

18. 社会 It is no longer possible for a society to regard any living man or woman as a hero.
84 ［claim→reasoning］
社会不可能再把任何在世的人视为英雄。
Discuss the extent to which you agree or disagree with the claim and address the most compelling reasons and/or examples that could be used to challenge your position.

思路参考

【作者提出上述观点的理由可能是？】

- ［从媒体的客观条件来说］The modern media with intensive coverage are so powerful that they can easily raise someone up to a hero while devastating someone's reputation forever. Therefore the fame of some superficial heroes who are subjected to media scrutiny might be quickly diminished.
- ［从媒体运营的利益关系来说］The media are usually run by profit-seeking groups; they may find out that the misfortunes and misdeeds of people, especially those of heroic figures, often bring them more profits than the virtues and accomplishments of those people do.
- ［从社会客观条件来说］The general public usually expect that their heroes are guilty of some sort of

character flaw or misdeed, and are willing to hear about scandals.

- [回应][不能一刀切，对于有些英雄来说] The reputations of some people who possess true virtues have not been damaged, if not enhanced, by media scrutiny.

【从上述理由能推出作者观点吗？】

- A flawed public figure can hardly be deemed as a hero.
- [回应][即使媒体有摧毁个人声誉的力量，也未必说明所有在世的人都不可能被视为英雄] Not all heroes have dazzling reputation; some ordinary people could also be considered as heroes, and they are more resistant to media scrutiny.

【思路提示】

- 本题可以从Domain的角度分别举例说明政治、经济、社会、娱乐、科技各领域是否有可能将在世的人视为英雄。

---

19. 社会 The surest indicator of a great nation is represented not by the achievements of its rulers, 28 artists, or scientists, but by the general welfare of its people. [comparison/solution]

一个伟大国家的最可靠指标不是由其统治者、艺术家或科学家的成就来体现，而是由其人民的总体利益来体现。

Discuss the extent to which you agree or disagree with the statement and you should consider ways in which the statement might or might not hold true.

思路参考

【题目中提及的统治者、艺术或科学家的成就对于衡量国家的伟大有意义吗？】

- 这些人的突出贡献也是衡量一个国家的指标之一，他们的成就有助于提升一个国家的总体实力和形象。
- [从个人贡献的重要性来说]不可否认，科学、艺术、政治等很多领域杰出人物的贡献对于国家的生存发展是必不可少的。
- General welfare is the end product of individual achievements. The contributions of those people will enhance the general welfare of the nation.

【强调统治者、艺术家或科学家的成就存在问题吗？】

- [从后果来说]过分强调名人的作用会导致危险的社会倾向，会导致社会过分沉醉于某些圈子和群体的成就，从而忽视普通民众的真实需求。
- A nation overemphasizing the contribution of its famous people while ignoring the demand of its citizens will eventually achieve nothing.
- [从统治者、艺术家或科学家成就的客观影响来说]
  他们的成就未必总是能促进社会总体利益的提升。
  比如：科技的发展会影响人们的生活质量、私密性、效率、社会安全各方面（可参考C类：科技对社会影响的负面素材）。
  政治人物的追求和利益假如不能和人民利益相协调也会阻碍社会进步（可参考 61 、 86 等关于政治人物应基于什么标准作决策的素材）。
- [从充分性来说]仅有统治者、艺术家或科学家的成就不足以保证国家的发展和强大。

【人民总体利益对于衡量国家的伟大有什么意义？】

- [从国家社会发展的最终目标来说] The ultimate goal of social progress is to enhance the general welfare of citizens. A nation which cannot ensure the general welfare of its people is far from a great nation.
- [从现实世界客观状况来说] Some countries with high social welfare could also be considered as great nations although they might have no prominent achievement in the fields mentioned above.

【强调人民总体利益有问题吗？】
- 可参考本题第一个论证层面：统治者、艺术家或科学家成就的意义中关于重要性的论述。

【两方面能否调和？】
- 显然，一个既有统治者、艺术家或科学家的突出贡献，又能保证人民利益和社会发展的国家无疑可称为真正伟大的国家。

【思路提示】
- 本题举例时可以参考Domain，分别讨论政治、艺术、科学领域的成就对于社会利益和国家的伟大有没有作用，而不要一概而论。另外，展开时也可以结合Period，讨论不同历史时期衡量伟大国家的标准是什么。一个强盛帝国的评价标准和衡量一个民主国家的成功标准会有很大差别。

---

20. 社会 Claim: The surest indicator of a great nation is not the achievements of its rulers, artists, or
113 scientists.

Reason: The surest indicator of a great nation is actually the welfare of all its people. [reasoning/comparison/solution]

观点：一个伟大国家的最可靠指标不是其统治者、艺术家或科学家的成就。

理由：一个伟大国家的最可靠指标实际上是其所有人民的利益。

Discuss the extent to which you agree or disagree with the claim and the reason on which that claim is based.

思路参考

【题目的理由有道理吗？】
- [从国家社会发展的最终目标来说] The ultimate goal of social progress is to enhance the general welfare of citizens. A nation which cannot ensure the general welfare of its people is far from a great nation.
- [从现实世界客观状况来说] Some countries with high social welfare could be considered as great nations although they might have no prominent achievement in the fields mentioned above.

【题目的观点有道理吗？】
- [从后果来说] 过分强调名人的作用会导致危险的社会倾向，会导致社会过分沉醉于某些圈子和群体的成就，从而忽视普通民众的真实需求。

  A nation overemphasizing the contribution of its famous people while ignoring the demand of its citizens will eventually achieve nothing.
- [从名人成就的客观影响来说]

  名人的成就未必能促进社会总体利益的提升。

  比如：科技的发展会影响人们的生活质量、私密性、效率、社会安全各方面（可参考C类：科技对社会影响的负面素材）。

  政治人物的追求和利益假如不能和人民利益相协调也会阻碍社会进步（可参考 16 、 86 等题目关于政治人物应基于什么标准作决策的素材）。
- [从充分性来说] 仅有名人的成就不足以保证国家的发展和强大。

【题目推理的前提有问题吗？】
- 出题人的假设：名人成就和人民利益没有关联，是相互排斥的。

  但实际上，科学、艺术、政治等很多领域的杰出人物的贡献往往有助于提升人民的总体利益。

  General welfare is the end product of individual achievements. The contributions of those people will enhance the general welfare of the nation.

【题目的观点有问题吗？】
- 这些领域名人的突出贡献也是衡量一个国家的指标之一，他们的成就有助于提升一个国家的总体实力和形象。

【发散/总结】
- 显然，一个既有名人突出贡献，又能保证人民福利和社会发展的国家无疑可称为真正伟大的国家。

【思路提示】
〈略，参考 **28** 〉

---

21. 社会 Claim: The surest indicator of a great nation must be the achievements of its rulers, **120** artists, or scientists.

Reason: Great achievements by a nation's rulers, artists, or scientists will ensure a good life for the majority of that nation's people. [reasoning→comparison/solution]

观点：一个伟大国家最可靠的指标一定是其统治者、艺术家或科学家的成就。

理由：一个国家的统治者、艺术家或科学家的伟大成就将保证该国大多数民众的美好生活。

Discuss the extent to which you agree or disagree with the claim and the reason on which that claim is based.

思路参考

【题目的理由有道理吗？】
- [从个人贡献的重要性来说] 不可否认，科学、艺术、政治等很多领域杰出人物的贡献对于国家的生存发展是必不可少的，也有助于提升社会总体利益。

  General welfare is the end product of individual achievements. The contributions of those people will enhance the general welfare of the nation.

【题目的观点有道理吗？】
- 这些领域名人的突出贡献确实是衡量一个国家的指标之一，他们的成就有助于提升一个国家的总体实力和形象。

【题目的理由存在问题吗？】
- [从名人成就的客观影响来说]

  名人的成就未必总是能促进社会总体利益的提升。

  比如：科技的发展会影响到人们的生活质量、私密性、效率、社会安全等各方面（可参考C类：科技对社会影响的负面素材）。

  政治人物的追求和利益假如不能和人民利益相协调也会阻碍社会进步（可参考 **16** 、**86** 题目关于政治人物应基于什么标准作决策的素材）。

【题目的推理过程存在问题吗？】
- [从充分性来说] 即使名人成就确实有利于保障人民生活，但仅有名人的成就不足以保证国家的发展和强大。

【题目的观点存在问题吗？】
- [从后果来说] 过分强调名人的作用会导致危险的社会倾向，会导致社会过分沉醉于某些圈子和群体的成就，从而忽视了普通民众的真实需求。

  A nation overemphasizing the contribution of its famous people while ignoring the demand of its citizens will eventually achieve nothing.

- [从国家社会发展的最终目标来说] The ultimate goal of social progress is to enhance the general welfare of its citizens. A nation which cannot ensure the general welfare of its people is far from a great nation.

- [从现实世界客观状况来说] 题目的表述过于武断。名人成就虽然是衡量国家伟大的指标之一，但并不是绝对的唯一标准。

Some countries with high social welfare could also be considered as great nations although they might have no prominent achievement in the fields mentioned above.

【思路提示】

- 本题举例时可以参考Domain，分别讨论政治、艺术、科学领域的成就对于保证人民生活有没有作用，而不要一概而论。另外，展开时也可以结合Period，讨论不同历史时期衡量伟大国家的标准是什么。一个强盛帝国的评价标准和衡量一个民主国家的成功标准会有很大差别。也可以分析在不同时期政治、艺术、科学各方面影响对于提升人们生活质量有没有帮助。

---

22. 社会 Some people claim that you can tell whether a nation is great by looking at the
121 achievements of its rulers, artists, or scientists. Others argue that the surest indicator of a great nation is, in fact, the general welfare of all its people. [comparison/solution]

一些人认为能够从一个国家的统治者、艺术家或科学家的成就看出这个国家是否伟大。另一些人认为一个伟大国家的最可靠依据实际上是其所有人民的总体利益。

Discuss which view more closely aligns with your own position and address both of the views presented.

思路参考

【第一种观点有道理吗？】

- 这些领域名人的突出贡献确实是衡量一个国家的指标之一，他们的成就有助于提升一个国家的总体实力和形象。
- [从个人贡献的重要性来说] 不可否认，科学、艺术、政治等很多领域杰出人物的贡献对于国家的生存发展是必不可少的，有助于提升社会总体利益。
  General welfare is the end product of individual achievements. The contributions of those people will enhance the general welfare of the nation.

【第一种观点有问题吗？】

- [从后果来说] 过分强调名人的作用会导致危险的社会倾向，导致社会过分沉醉于某些圈子和群体的成就，从而忽视了普通民众的真实需求。
  A nation overemphasizing the contribution of its famous people while ignoring the demand of its citizens will eventually achieve nothing.
- [从名人成就的客观影响来说] 名人的成就未必总是能促进社会总体利益的提升。
- [从充分性来说] 仅有名人的成就不足以保证国家的发展和强大。

【第二种观点有道理吗？】

- [从国家社会发展的最终目标来说] The ultimate goal of social progress is to enhance the general welfare of its citizens. A nation which cannot ensure the general welfare of its people is far from a great nation.
- [从现实世界客观状况来说] Some countries with high social welfare could also be considered as great nations although they might have no prominent achievement in the fields mentioned above.

【第二种观点存在问题吗？】

- 社会和人民的福利有时依赖于一些杰出人物的贡献。

【两方面能否调和？】

- 一个既有名人突出贡献，又能保证人民福利、社会发展的国家无疑可称为真正伟大的国家。

【思路提示】

〈略，参考 28 〉

23. **社会** The surest indicator of a great nation is not the achievements of its rulers, artists, or
127 scientists, but the general well-being of all its people. [comparison/solution]

一个伟大国家最可靠的指标不是其统治者、艺术家或科学家的成就，而是所有人民的总体利益。

Discuss the extent to which you agree or disagree with the claim and address the most compelling reasons and/or examples that could be used to challenge your position.

思路参考

【题目中提及的名人成就对于衡量国家的伟大有意义吗？】

- 这些领域名人的突出贡献也是衡量一个国家的指标之一，他们的成就有助于提升一个国家的总体实力和形象。
- ［从个人贡献的重要性来说］不可否认，科学、艺术、政治等很多领域杰出人物的贡献对于国家的生存发展是必不可少的。

  General welfare is the end product of individual achievements. The contributions of those people will enhance the general welfare of the nation.
- ［回应］［从后果来说］过分强调名人的作用会导致危险的社会倾向，导致社会过分沉醉于某些圈子和群体的成就，而忽视普通民众的真实需求。

  A nation overemphasizing the contribution of its famous people while ignoring the demand of its citizens will eventually achieve nothing.
- ［回应］［从名人成就的客观影响来说］名人的成就未必总能促进社会总体利益的提升。
- ［回应］［从充分性来说］仅有名人的成就不足以保证国家的发展和强大。

【人民的总体利益对于衡量国家的伟大有什么意义？】

- ［从国家社会发展的最终目标来说］The ultimate goal of social progress is to enhance the general welfare of its citizens. A nation which cannot ensure the general welfare of its people is far from a great nation.
- ［从现实世界客观状况来说］Some countries with high social welfare could also be considered as great nations although they might have no prominent achievement in the fields mentioned above.
- ［回应］社会和人民的福利有时依赖于一些杰出人物的贡献。

【思路提示】

〈略，参考 **28** 〉

24. **社会** The general welfare of a nation's people is a better indication of that nation's greatness
145 than are the achievements of its rulers, artists, or scientists. [comparison/solution]

相对于国家的统治者、艺术家或科学家的成就，民众的总体利益是一个国家伟大程度的更好指标。

Discuss the extent to which you agree or disagree with the claim and address the most compelling reasons and/or examples that could be used to challenge your position.

思路参考

〈略，参考 **127** 〉

25. 社会 Some people believe that in order to thrive, a society must put its own overall success
[85] before the well-being of its individual citizens. Others believe that the well-being of a society can
only be measured by the general welfare of all its people. [comparison/solution]

一些人认为社会要繁荣，必须把其总体成功置于个人利益之上。另一些人认为社会成就只能由
其所有人民的总体利益来衡量。

Discuss which view more closely aligns with your own position and address both of the views presented.

思路参考

【第一种观点有道理吗？】

- ［从社会成就的客观作用来说］Sometimes the overall success of a society could enhance the general
  welfare of the nation.
- ［从客观必须性来看］The government need to sacrifice individual citizen's interest for the greater profit of
  the society under certain circumstances.

【第一种观点有问题吗？】

- ［从观点产生的后果来说］Overemphasizing the importance of a society's overall success may damage the
  well-being and human right of individual members.

【第二种观点有道理吗？】

- ［从国家社会发展的最终目标来说］The ultimate goal of social progress is to enhance the general welfare
  of its citizens. A nation which cannot ensure the general welfare of its people is far from success.
- A society which secures its people's general welfare has already succeeded.

【两方面能否调和？】

- 只有当社会总体成就有利于提升人民福祉时才是有意义的。有时为了更大的群体利益可能需要暂时
  牺牲一部分人的个人利益，在这种情况下必须要对受损失的个体做出合理补偿，这可以通过完善的
  制度设计加以保障。

【思路提示】

- 本题展开时可以结合Domain，分别讨论政治、军事、科技、经济、基本福利、人权等各方面要获得成
  功是否需要牺牲个体。

26. 社会/政治 The effectiveness of a country's leaders is best measured by examining the well-
[94] being of that country's citizens. [solution]

国民的利益是衡量国家领导业绩的最佳标准。

*Discuss the extent to which you agree or disagree with the claim and address the most compelling
reasons and/or examples that could be used to challenge your position.*

思路参考

【题目的说法有道理吗？】

- ［从国家社会发展的最终目标来说］The ultimate goal of social progress is to enhance the general welfare
  of its citizens.
- The leader of a country which secures the well-being of its citizens is clearly an effective leader.

【题目的说法有问题吗？】

- 过分强调国民个体利益有时可能会影响更大范围的发展。

【思路提示】

- 衡量领导人成就有没有其他指标？可以从Domain的角度展开，讨论各领域(如文化、艺术、科技、经
  济)的成就能否成为衡量领导者业绩的指标。

27. 社会/政治 The effectiveness of a country's leaders is best measured by examining the well-being of that country's citizens. [solution]

147 国民的利益是衡量国家领导业绩的最佳标准。

Discuss the extent to which you agree or disagree with the statement and consider ways in which the statement might or might not hold true.

思路参考

【题目的说法有道理吗？】

- ［从国家社会发展的最终目标来说］The ultimate goal of social progress is to enhance the general welfare of its citizens.
- The leader of a country which secures the well-being of its citizens is clearly an effective leader.

【题目的说法在何种情况下会有问题？】

- 当小范围国民利益可能影响到更大群体的总体利益时，需要个体做一些让步和妥协。在这种情况下必须要对受损失的个体做出合理补偿，这可以通过完善的制度设计加以保障。

【思路提示】

- 衡量领导人成就有没有其他指标?社会各个领域(如文化、艺术、科技、经济)的成就也可以作为衡量领导者业绩的指标，可以从Domain的角度来展开。

28. 社会 It is primarily through our identification with social groups that we define ourselves.

38 [solution]

我们主要是通过社会群体的认同来定义自身的。

Discuss the extent to which you agree or disagree with the statement and consider ways in which the statement might or might not hold true.

思路参考

【题目的说法有道理吗？】

- ［从人类行为的特点来说］Human beings naturally tend to seek out different groups to which they feel they have a certain sense of belonging, and to identify themselves.
- ［从社会群体的客观作用来说］The characteristics of social groups could reflect many aspects of human lives.
- ［从某些个人的特定需求来说］There are individuals who demonstrate very clearly who they are by their identification with certain social groups.
- Other people's attitude and feedback serve as a mirror, which could reflect one's disposition and values.

【题目的说法有问题吗？】

- ［从社会群体本身特性来说］Each social group has an enormous number of components and each component has its own specific characteristics.

  以群体特征定义个体可能会抹杀个体差别和特征。
- ［从社会群体之间的关系来说］Since everyone could belong to more than one social groups, the image reflected by incompatible groups will sometimes distort.

【自我界定有其他途径吗？】

- ［从人的成长阶段来说］Usually young people are more willing to identify themselves through social groups, while adults tend to define themselves more by their marital status, parental status, and occupations.

- [从自我界定的内涵来说] Some aspects of self-definition, such as one's inner feelings and subjective experiences, can be most effectively acquired through introspective method.

---

29. **社会** People's attitudes are determined more by their immediate situation or surroundings than by society as a whole. [claim/solution]

相对于整个社会，人们的看法更多是由其身边环境决定的。

Discuss the extent to which you agree or disagree with the statement and consider ways in which the statement might or might not hold true.

思路参考

【题目的看法有道理吗？】

- 身边环境给予人们最直接的影响；近朱者赤，近墨者黑。
  People with whom one frequently interacts and the immediate surroundings in which one lives usually exert more influence on one's values and attitude.

【这个推理过程充分吗？】

- 尽管身边环境对人们的态度影响更直接，但任何小环境都是社会总体环境的构成部分，因而不可避免地会受大环境的影响和制约。

【对于这个问题有没有其他可能性？】

- 人们的内在性格特征可能是决定其看法更主要的因素。
  Internal characteristics govern immediate attitude.

【总结】

- In determining one's attitude, the immediate situation and the whole society may play equally important roles. But one's internal characteristic might be more decisive.

---

30. **教育** Learning is primarily a matter of personal discipline; students cannot be motivated by school or college alone. [reasoning/comparison/solution]

学习主要是个人行为；学生学习不能仅仅由学校推动。

Discuss the extent to which you agree or disagree with the statement and consider ways in which the statement might or might not hold true.

思路参考

【前半句观点有道理吗？】

- [从学习过程的本质和目标来说] Learning is a process through which an individual could improve himself intellectually; the process of learning is most effective when it is motivated by one's inner initiatives.

- [从自学的客观可能性来说] Modern technologies could provide most knowledge for one to be educated, making self-learning possible.

【前半句观点有问题吗？】

- 尽管学习是个人需求和行为，但学习——以及教育——的目的之一是使个人能更好地融入社会，因此学习和教育必然受到社会环境和需求的影响。

【后半句观点有道理吗？】

- [从个人内在动因的必要性来说] Without one's inner initiative, school education could be useless.

- ［从学校等教育机构的作用来说］College and universities are the places where most knowledge generated; one's learning process is highly related with those educational institutions even if the process is not being in those institutions.
- ［从学校在教育方面的优势来说］Education provided by schools and colleges might be more professional and effective.
- ［从学校教育相对于个人教育的特点来说］Students could acquire appropriate values, thoughts and characters through interaction with other students, which cannot be acquired through self-learning.

---

31. 科技 Scientists and other researchers should focus their research on areas that are likely to 59 benefit the greatest number of people. ［claim］

科学家及其他研究人员应该将研究聚焦在能为尽可能多的人造福的领域。

Discuss the extent to which you agree or disagree with the recommendation and describe specific circumstances in which adopting the recommendation would or would not be advantageous.

思路参考

【人们提出上述观点的主观动因是什么？】

- 社会资源、科研经费、研究力量是有限的，为了更好地利用这些科研资源，从优先级来说应该优先发展可能造福更多人的研究。

【题目观点成立的前提是什么？能否成立？】

- ［前提］The outcome of a line of research could be predicted with certainty.
- But, sometimes we come across the answer to some question while seeking the answer to another.

【前述动因足以推出题目观点吗？】

- 科学研究是互相关联的，任何领域的研究都是在填补人类认知的空白，从而从整体上促进人类的总体利益和发展。
- 有些当前看似无用的研究结果在将来可能产生巨大价值。

【发散】

- Some processes of research are sheer fulfillment of some scientists' whimsicalities or may pose potential threat to human societies. We should make careful differentiation on these kinds of research, and to resist them when necessary.

【思路提示】

- 本题可参考A类 131 和D类 56 的一些分析过程和例证。

---

32. 社会 Leaders are created by the demands that are placed on them. ［solution］

62 领导是由加在他们身上的需求造就的。

Discuss the extent to which you agree or disagree with the statement and you should consider ways in which the statement might or might not hold true.

思路参考

【题目观点有道理吗？】

- ［从客观条件的必要性来说］Special social and historical demands are fundamental conditions for the creation of a leader.

- 并非所有领导都由需求造就，有些领导的智慧通过一些平常事就能得到体现。

【要造就领导仅有需求就足够了吗？】

- For a leader to be successful, many other characteristics, such as wisdom, justice, courage, are necessary.

【思路提示】

- 本题可以结合Domain展开，分别讨论军事、政治、经济各方面的需求对于造就领导的重要性。

---

33. 政治 Some people believe it is often necessary, even desirable, for political leaders to withhold
69 information from the public. Others believe that the public has a right to be fully informed.
[comparison]

一些人认为政治领导者向公众隐瞒信息通常是必要的，甚至是符合人们意愿的。另一些人则认为公众有权利知道全部真相。

Discuss which view more closely aligns with your own position and explain your reasoning for the position you take and address both of the views presented.

思路参考

【第一种观点有道理吗？】

- ［从控制信息的意义方面来说］Withholding information could help to serve some strategic or political purposes.
- ［从行为的必要性来说］Disclosure of certain types of information would threaten national security.

【第一种观点有问题吗？】

- ［从行为可能产生的后果来说］Undue information-control would raise public distrust or even hostility against the government.
- 有可能导致不受约束和监督的权力，从而导致腐败，甚至独裁专制。

【第二种观点有道理吗？】

- ［从行为的必要性来说］To avoid unnecessary social disturbance and chaos, leaders should ensure the public informed.
- The settlement of some accidents requires instant information-publication.
- ［从行为的后果来说］A gesture of sincerity and forthrightness is a demonstration of a concern for the broader interests of the public and the democratic system.

【第二种观点有问题吗？】

- 有些情况下某些信息没有必要让公众全部掌握。该观点中fully informed的表达过于绝对。

---

34. 政治/社会 To be an effective leader, a public official must maintain the highest ethical and
104 moral standards. [claim/solution]

作为有效的领导者，公职人员必须具备最高道德标准。

Discuss the extent to which you agree or disagree with the claim and address the most compelling reasons and/or examples that could be used to challenge your position.

思路参考

【提出上述观点的目的是什么？】

- 探讨作为有效的领导者必须具备的条件和要求。

【题目提出的条件有道理吗？】

- ［从观点的必要性来说］As public figures, officials should maintain high ethical and moral standards to be effective role models for the public.

- ［从观点产生的效果来说］Honest, trustworthy public officials could promote the well-being of the society.

【回应1】【题目提出的条件有问题吗？】

- ［从行为产生的后果来说］过分地用道德标准要求公职人员可能会导致一些虚伪和作秀的行为，也会对其发挥领导才干形成掣肘。
- ［从伦理道德的界定分类来说］Personal morality might be unrelated to effective political leadership. Public morality is necessary for successful leadership.

【回应2】【题目提出的条件有可行性吗？】

- 人无完人，要求公职人员保持最高伦理道德标准不太现实。既然最高标准难以满足，以此作为要求也就没有意义，不如制定适当的标准来要求公职人员。

【回应3】【有没有其他衡量标准？】

- The effectiveness of public officials could be better measured by their ability to keep their institution operating smoothly and efficiently and to promote the general welfare of the society.

---

35. 政治/社会 To be an effective leader, a public official must maintain the highest ethical and

107 moral standards. ［claim/solution］

作为有效的领导者，公职人员必须具备最高道德标准。

Discuss the extent to which you agree or disagree with the statement and consider ways in which the statement might or might not hold true.

思路参考

〈略，参考 **104** 〉

C Technology and Humanity（Machine and Human） 科技与人性（机器与人）

1. 科技 As people rely more and more on technology to solve problems, the ability of humans to

1 think for themselves will surely deteriorate. ［reasoning］

随着人们越来越多地依赖科技解决问题，人类独立思考的能力肯定会衰退。

Discuss the extent to which you agree or disagree with the statement and consider ways in which the statement might or might not hold true.

思路参考

【题目的观点有合理性吗？】

- ［从思考能力的种类来说］因为有了现代科技的辅助，有些可以用科技手段替代的能力，比如记忆、计算能力等，由于没有以往那么高的要求，可能有一定程度的退化。
- ［从人类社会的宏观发展来说］Technology creates more problems than it solves, and may threaten or damage the quality of life. From this point of view, it seems unwise for humans to develop technologies.

【题目的理由有问题吗？】

- Technologies and machines are only tools of human minds. They extend humans' ability of thinking.

【题目的推理过程有问题吗？人们依赖科技就会造成思考能力的退化吗？】

- Modern technology could make human lives more efficient and relieve people from mundane works, enabling humans to have more time to think and introspect.

【发散】

- Technology can only change the material world, but not the condition of humanity.

---

2. 社会 The luxuries and conveniences of contemporary life prevent people from developing into 〔26〕 truly strong and independent individuals. [claim]

当代生活的奢侈和便利妨碍人们成为真正强大和独立的人。

Discuss the extent to which you agree or disagree with the statement and consider ways in which the statement might or might not hold true.

思路参考

【题目的观点有道理吗？】

- 由于有了现代科技的辅助，有些可以用科技手段替代的能力，比如记忆、计算能力，有一定程度的退化。
- 现代社会奢华舒适的生活在一定程度上导致人们的思考能力下降，生活上也越来越依赖一些科技手段。
- ［从"强大"和"独立"的定义来说］真正的强大和独立是个人内心和思想的强大；现代奢华和便利的生活使人们沉迷于物质享受和追求，从而无暇顾及内心修养的完善和提高。

【题目的观点有问题吗？】

- ［从"强大"和"独立"的定义来说］Some modern facilities, such as automobile and the Internet, provide humans with more mobility and reduce one's dependence on other people.

  Those conveniences make human lives more efficient, therefore ensure people to have more time thinking for themselves and to engage in more meaningful activities.

【思路提示】

- 本题可以从"奢侈"和"便利"的定义来展开；奢侈和便利对人类生活和个人发展的作用是有区别的，最好分别讨论。还可以结合Category或Domain来展开，讨论不同领域的奢华和便利对人类发展产生何种影响。此外，也可以从"强大"和"独立"的定义来展开，分别讨论奢华便利对物质、肉体、精神等方面的强大和独立的影响。

---

3. 社会 The increasingly rapid pace of life today causes more problems than it solves. [claim] 〔43〕 当前越来越快的生活节奏在解决了一些问题的同时，产生了更多的问题。

Discuss the extent to which you agree or disagree with the statement and consider ways in which the statement might or might not hold true.

思路参考

【产生题目观点的理由可能是什么？】

- 出于人类本性中的贪欲和骄傲，各方面效率的提高反而放大了人们的欲望，人性中的很多问题通过比以往更突出的方式展现出来。

【题目观点有合理性吗？】

- 本题观点的合理性可以从Domain的角度来展开，分别讨论在不同层面或不同领域由科技进步带来的问题，e.g.:

  ［从个人生活来说］The rapid pace of life, most often results from technological improvement, adversely affects quality of living and impairs personal privacy.

[从社会整体来说] The rapid development of society makes human live (and the society as a whole) unstable and unsafe, and causes many social problems such as unemployment.

【题目观点有问题吗?】

- 同样,该观点的问题也可以从Domain的角度来展开,讨论现代社会生活的效率给我们带来的便利,e.g.:
  The rapid pace of life also brings us greater efficiency, creating more social services and benefits, such as better living condition, education, health-care, and so on.

【发散】

- Social and technological improvement can change the material world, but could not solve problems related to human nature. On the contrary, it sometimes magnifies the sins (pride, greed, envy, etc.) and desires of human.

---

4. 科技 The primary goal of technological advancement should be to increase people's efficiency

91 so that they have more leisure time. [claim→reasoning]

科技进步的主要目标应该是提高效率从而使人们有更多的休闲时间。

Discuss the extent to which you agree or disagree with the statement and consider ways in which the statement might or might not hold true.

思路参考

【题目中关于发展科技的目的的论述有合理性吗?】

- [从人类发展科技的主观动机来说] One of the purposes of human to develop technology is to both increase efficiency and relieve people from repetitive works.
- [从科技发展产生的客观影响来说] Technological advancement does increase people's efficiency in many aspects.
  这一点可以结合Domain来举例,分析在不同领域科技对于人们效率的影响。

【题目中关于发展科技的目的的论述有问题吗?】

- [从人类发展科技的主要目的来说] The original mission of science and technology might be to help human better understand nature and make efficient use of the laws of nature.
- [从科技发展的作用来说] Technological advancement could also serve as a motivating force of social improvement.
- [科技发展的负面影响] Technological improvement does not always bring about comforting effects.

【科技发展能带来更多休闲时间吗?】

- Technological developments have actually contributed to a more rushed and frantic pace of human affairs, due to the human nature.

【发散】

- Technology can only change the material world, but not the condition of humanity.

---

5. 科技/教育 Although innovations such as video, computers, and the Internet seem to offer

101 schools improved methods for instructing students, these technologies all too often distract from real learning. [claim]

尽管像视频设备、电脑以及互联网这类新技术看起来为学校提供了先进的教学手段,但这些科技手段经常使学生的注意力从真正的学习上转移。

Discuss the extent to which you agree or disagree with the statement and consider ways in which the statement might or might not hold true.

【思路提示】

- 本题可以结合"real learning"的定义展开。学习的过程可能包括健全的人格心智、道德修养的培养，基本知识和思维方法的传授，基本技能的培训。题目中提及的科技手段对于不同领域的学习可能有不同的作用。

【题目的观点有道理吗？】

- ［对于人格道德方面的学习］The abuse of such innovations sometimes distracts students from learning or even endangers their psychological health.

- ［对于知识技能方面的学习］由于学生的心智还不十分成熟，自控能力较差，因此，这些高科技教育工具有时会使学生分散注意力，降低学习效率。

【题目的观点有问题吗？】

- ［从这些科技手段产生的效果来说］These advances provide effective assistance for learning, and could enhance and improve the educational process.

---

6. **科技** Some people believe that our ever-increasing use of technology significantly reduces our **132** opportunities for human interaction. Other people believe that technology provides us with new and better ways to communicate and connect with one another. ［comparison］

一些人认为对科技越来越多的应用显著减少了我们与他人之间交往的机会。另一些人相信科技给我们提供了与他人沟通联系更好、更新的方法。

Discuss which view more closely aligns with your own position and address both of the views presented.

【思路提示】

- 本题可以从"interaction, communication and connection"的定义出发讨论。交往包含了沟通和联系，因而前后两种观点并不矛盾。科技在沟通方面确实提供了更多途径提高了人们的效率，但在交往的其他方面，科技有可能造成负面影响。

【第一种观点有道理吗？】

- ［从科技产生的后果来说］Technology makes people rely more and more on instant and distant communication methods, therefore, the opportunities of face-to-face interaction between people diminish.

【第二种观点有道理吗？】

- ［从科技产生的后果来说］Modern technology does provide people with efficient and convenient ways of communicating and connecting.

---

7. **科技** Governments should place few, if any, restrictions on scientific research and development. **23** ［claim］

政府如要对科学研究和发展进行限制，也应该加以极少的限制。

Discuss the extent to which you agree or disagree with the recommendation and describe specific circumstances in which adopting the recommendation would or would not be advantageous.

【提出题目观点的理由可能是什么？】

- Too many restrictions on research may impede scientific progress.

【题目的观点在什么情况下有道理？】

- 对于不违反人类基本道德准则的科研，确实不必施加过多干预。

【题目的观点在什么情况下可能产生不利影响？】

- Some processes of research are sheer fulfillment of some scientists' whimsicalities or may pose potential threat to human societies.

- The consequences of some research are unclear, or controversial, or even will bring disastrous result to society.

- We should make careful differentiation on these kinds of research, and place strict restrictions on them when necessary.

【总结】

- To enhance the general welfare of the society, government should supervise the potential risk of research, and find a balance between the gains and risks of scientific research.

【思路提示】

- 本题可以从Condition或Category的角度展开，分别讨论不同类型的科研应如何对待。

---

8. 社会/科技 The human mind will always be superior to machines because machines are only
64 tools of human minds.〔reasoning/comparison〕

人脑永远胜于机器，因为机器只是人类思维的工具。

Discuss the extent to which you agree or disagree with the statement and consider ways in which the statement might or might not hold true.

思路参考

【题目的理由有道理吗？】

- Machines are tools of human minds. No machine could exist unless human invent it.

【题目的推理过程有道理吗？】

- Humans are superior in that, from ethical point of view, humans produce and dominate machines.

【题目的观点有道理吗？】

- 〔从思维能力的不同层面来说〕On the basis of creative thinking and emotional sensitivity, human minds are superior, for no machines could develop the ability to think on their own, or develop so-called "emotional intelligence" so far.

【题目的推理过程有问题吗？】

- Most tools are superior to humans in their special use—that's why humans devise them.

【题目的观点有问题吗？】

- 〔从思维能力的不同层面来说〕Machines can perform certain technical jobs with greater accuracy and speed than human minds ever could.

【思路提示】

- 本题可以围绕"superior"的定义展开；对"superior"不同层面的理解决定了对题目观点的不同判断。

1. **社会** Laws should be flexible enough to take account of various circumstances, times, and
21 places. [claim]

法律应足够灵活以考虑不同的环境、时间、地点。

Discuss the extent to which you agree or disagree with the statement and consider ways in which the statement might or might not hold true.

思路参考

【提出题目观点的理由可能是什么？】

- [从法律的最终目的来说] The ultimate goal of laws is to serve people and society; the particular demand and condition of individual members should be considered when applying laws.
- [从保持法律灵活度的必要性来说] To some extent, laws are reflections of a region's culture, tradition and values, which could be various in different parts of a nation. These variations should be considered when constituting laws.

【题目观点存在客观合理性吗？】

- [从题目行为产生的客观后果来说] Rigid laws can result in unfairness if applied inflexibly in all places at all times.

【上述理由足以推出题目观点吗？】

- The basic function of law is to bring stability and order to the society. Although particular individual cases should be taken into account, a knowable, fair and equally implemented law is necessary for a legal system to be effective.

【题目观点存在问题吗？】

- [从固定法律的必要性来说] Knowing the laws is the premise of compliance, and knowing the laws is impossible without relatively stationary and fixed laws.
- [从法律变通导致的后果来说] Flexible laws in an imperfect legal system may make it possible for some people or institutions to distort laws without restraint.

【总结】

- [从不同层面的法律来说] 原则性的基本法律应保持一定的连续性和稳定性，不能经常更改或变通；而有些细节性、法规性质的条款可以根据不同情况作不同考虑，以实现公正和人性化。
- [从地理区域来说] 从一个国家整体来看，各地区的法律可以根据不同的文化习惯有所差别；但对于某一个特定地区来说，法律应该有一致性，不应随意变更。

2. **认知** Many important discoveries or creations are accidental: it is usually while seeking the
56 answer to one question that we come across the answer to another. [reasoning]

很多重大发现或创造都是偶然的：我们通常在寻求一个问题的答案时会碰巧找到另外一个问题的答案。

Discuss the extent to which you agree or disagree with the statement and consider ways in which the statement might or might not hold true.

思路参考

【题目的理由有道理吗？】

- 不可否认，历史上很多重大发现确实是碰巧得到的。

- Many important discoveries and creations are based on laborious works, not accidental.

【题目的推理过程有问题吗？】

- We can hardly find any process of discovery which is purely accidental because human beings are constantly seeking to discover something.

【题目的观点有问题吗？】

- ［从题目观点可能产生的后果来说］有可能导致社会缺乏踏实严谨的科学态度，而希望凭运气偶然获得成果从而一举成名。

【思路提示】

- 本题涉及两个概念：发现和创造。实际上，很多重大发现确实是偶然的；但创造则不然，它通常是人们有目的探索研究的结果。本题可以从两个概念的区别出发展开论证。

---

3. 社会 People should undertake risky action only after they have carefully considered its
61 consequences. [claim]

人们应该只有在仔细考虑其后果后才采取冒险行为。

Discuss the extent to which you agree or disagree with the recommendation and describe specific circumstances in which adopting the recommendation would or would not be advantageous.

思路参考

【思路提示】

- 本题必须结合Domain, Condition或具体例子展开，讨论在不同领域、不同情况下何时应该快速反应、何时应该三思后行。

【提出题目观点的目的可能是什么？】

- To make thorough, appropriate decision.

【提出题目观点的理由可能是什么？】

- ［从后果来说］Being impetuous could be destructive.

【题目观点有道理吗？】

- ［从后果来说］Thorough and careful consideration before taking actions helps to make wise and conscious decisions.

【题目观点的前提能成立吗？】

- ［前提：充分考虑能保证决策合理］It is almost impossible for an individual to ponder over every possibility and factor, due to the limitations of an individual. Thus, a decision without any risk could not exist.

【题目观点有问题吗？】

- ［从快速反应的必要性来说］Some situations call for immediate responses.
  Spending too much time considering the consequences might result in harmful effects, or might make an individual to lose some opportunities.

---

4. 认知 Claim: Any piece of information referred to as a fact should be mistrusted, since it may well
87 be proven false in the future.

Reason: Much of the information that people assume is factual actually turns out to be inaccurate. [reasoning]

观点：任何被当作事实引用的信息应该被怀疑，因为它可能在未来被证明是错误的。

理由：人们认为是事实的很多信息最后都被发现是不准确的。

Discuss the extent to which you agree or disagree with the claim and the reason on which that claim is based.

【思路提示】

- 本题可以从"fact"的定义入手展开。上述论证的前提之一就是人们是否有区分事实和假设的能力。（人们亲眼所见的）事实应该相信，但假设（人们想当然的信息，或被主观情绪和动机歪曲了的事实）当然应该怀疑。

【题目的理由有道理吗？】

- 确实，历史上有很多曾经被认为是事实的信息后来被证明是不准确的或错误的。

【题目的观点有道理吗？】

- ［从客观合理性来说］Information is often being presented with the speaker's subjective judgment and processing, providing a distorted picture of the true reality.

- ［从社会发展的必须性来说］The development of many aspects of human society, especially natural science, is a history of challenges to so-called "facts" assumed by people.

- ［从质疑产生的后果来说］
  Questioning authorities is a motivating force of social improvements and innovations, and could avoid negative social tendency.

【题目的理由有问题吗？】

- 人们亲眼所见、而非脑中认定的事实不存在不准确的问题。

【题目的推理过程有问题吗？】

- 有些信息或观点尽管不准确，但也是前人经验、思想的积累，如果善加利用可以为后世提供参考和基础。仅仅因为有些信息不可靠就怀疑一切理由似乎不够充分。

【题目的观点有问题吗？】

- ［从题目行为产生的后果来说］The claim that any piece of information should be mistrusted goes to extremes. Undue skepticism might be counter-productive.

- ［从题目行为的前提来说］Careful differentiation between well-intentioned and vicious challenges should be made.
  Careful differentiation between assumptions, claims and facts should be made.

---

5. **认知** The best ideas arise from a passionate interest in commonplace things. [solution]

   103 最好的想法来源于对平凡事物的兴趣。

   Discuss the extent to which you agree or disagree with the statement and consider ways in which the statement might or might not hold true.

【题目的说法有合理性吗？】

- Most profound knowledge and discoveries come from observations and researches on mundane objects.

【题目所说的方式有问题吗？】

- Undue concentration on commonplace things may impede the intellectual progress.

【要获得好的想法有其他渠道吗？】

- Some ideas and creations come from people's inspiration and intuition.

- Sometimes people come across the answer to one question while seeking the answer to another.

【思路提示】

- 本题最好结合Domain来展开举例，讨论不同领域获得好想法的途径的例子，否则文章容易流于空泛。

6. **认知** Claim: Imagination is a more valuable asset than experience.

    105 Reason: People who lack experience are free to imagine what is possible without the constraints of established habits and attitudes. [reasoning/comparison]

    观点：想象力是比经验更有价值的财富。

    理由：缺乏经验的人可以不受已有习惯和态度的约束去自由想象。

    Discuss the extent to which you agree or disagree with the claim and the reason on which that claim is based.

思路参考

【题目的理由有道理吗？】

- ［从经验的负面影响来说］Limitations set by existing experience and habits will sometimes impede creative activities.

【题目的观点有道理吗？】

- ［从想象力的作用来说］Imagination could help us break previous rules and limitations.

【题目的理由有问题吗？】

- ［从经验的重要性来说］Imagination without the assistance of experience could fall into whimsicality or even fallacy.

【题目的推理过程有问题吗？】

- Although imagination is essential for the progress of many aspects of human society, the importance of experience should not be underestimated.

【题目的观点有问题吗？】

- ［从接受题目观点的后果来说］Overemphasis on the value of imagination would result in unpractical and unrealistic actions.

【总结】

- 一般来说，想象力和经验是同等重要的。想象力能保证创新和活力；经验保证我们不会出现重大失误。将两者有效结合是保证成功和取得进步的重要途径。

【思路提示】

- 本题最好结合Domain来展开，分别讨论不同领域（如科技、商业、政治、军事、艺术等）的想象力和经验在取得成就方面的作用。

7. **认知** In most professions and academic fields, imagination is more important than knowledge.

    106 [comparison]

    在大多数职业和学术领域中，想象力比知识更加重要。

    Discuss the extent to which you agree or disagree with the statement and consider ways in which the statement might or might not hold true.

思路参考

【想象力有重要性吗？】

- ［从想象力的作用来说］Imagination could help us break previous rules and limitations.

【题目的观点有问题吗？】

- ［从接受题目观点的后果来说］Overemphasis on the value of imagination would result in unpractical and unrealistic actions.

【知识有重要性吗？】

- Imagination without the assistance of knowledge could fall into whimsicality or even fallacy.

【过分依赖知识有问题吗？】

- ［从知识的负面影响来说］Limitations set by existing knowledge will sometimes impede creative activities.
- People who lack knowledge are free to imagine what is possible.

【总结】

- 一般来说，想象力和知识是同等重要的。想象力能保证创新和活力；知识保证我们不会出现重大失误。将两者有效结合是保证成功和取得进步的重要途径。

【思路提示】

- 本题应结合Domain来展开，分别讨论不同领域（如科技、商业、政治、军事、艺术等）的想象力和知识在重要性上的权重。

---

8. **认知** In most professions and academic fields, imagination is more important than knowledge.

126 ［comparison］

对于大多数职业和学术领域中，想象力比知识更加重要。

Discuss the extent to which you agree or disagree with the claim and address the most compelling reasons and/or examples that could be used to challenge your position.

思路参考

【想象力的重要性何在？】

- ［从想象力的作用来说］Imagination could help us break previous rules and limitations.

【可能有哪些相反观点？】

- Knowledge is also important in the process of research and decision-making.
- ［回应］［从知识的负面影响来说］Limitations set by existing knowledge will sometimes impede creative activities.
- People who lack knowledge are free to imagine what is possible.
- ［从接受题目观点的后果来说］Overemphasis on the value of imagination would result in unpractical and unrealistic actions.
- Imagination without the assistance of knowledge could fall into whimsicality or even fallacy.
- ［回应］Careful balance should be made between imagination and knowledge. Overly relying on either side will go against true progress.

【总结】

〈略，参考 106 〉

【思路提示】

〈略，参考 106 〉

E Interdisciplinary 学科之间的交叉影响

1. 政治/社会 Some people believe that government funding of the arts is necessary to ensure that
7 the arts can flourish and be available to all people. Others believe that government funding of
the arts threatens the integrity of the arts. [comparison]
有些人认为政府对艺术的资助对于保证艺术繁荣以及普及是必需的。另外一些人认为政府对艺术的资助威胁了艺术的完整性。

Discuss which view more closely aligns with your own position and address both of the views presented.

思路参考

【第一种观点有道理吗？】

- 对于艺术创作收入尚不能完全支持自己生活的年轻或不知名的艺术家来说，政府资助对于保证他们发挥艺术天分创作出有价值的艺术品可能是必需的。

【第一种观点有问题吗？】

[从行为的后果来说] 政府对艺术的资助和干预可能使艺术作品受到政治和意识形态的干扰，阻碍真正的艺术创作。也可能导致有些艺术家和艺术机构过分依赖政府资助，从而损害艺术探索自由精神的本质，并扼杀艺术创作的活力。

- Art patronage is not a necessary function of government.
- Art could be funded by wealthy individuals, private foundations, and social institutions.

【第二种观点有道理吗？】

- 〈略，参考"第一种观点有问题吗？"中"从行为的后果来说"的论述。〉

【第二种观点有问题吗？】

- [从提出该观点的前提来说] 如果政府在资助艺术的同时能够保证不对艺术创作进行其他方面，特别是政治和意识形态上的审查和干预，那么，政府资助对于艺术发展未尝不是一种值得尝试的途径。

2. 教育 Universities should require every student to take a variety of courses outside the student's
13 field of study. [claim→solution]
大学应该要求所有学生学习大量非本专业的课程。

Discuss the extent to which you agree or disagree with the claim and address the most compelling reasons and/or examples that could be used to challenge your position.

思路参考

【提出上述观点的目的可能是什么？】

- 为了让学生发掘自己的兴趣特长，得到真正全面的教育。

【题目的观点能达到上述目的吗？】

- Not every student exactly knows which academic field they are really interested in and can do well in the beginning of their college life. The proposed policy could provide an opportunity for students to find their interest.

- Many disciplines are related; knowledge from outside the field of study could help students to think and observe from various points of view.
  这一点可以参考E类 **143** 的论证内容和素材。

【有可能存在哪些相反看法？】
- ［从可行性来说］Not all universities and colleges are capable of providing various courses in various fields.

  Students may not have enough time and energy to deal with too many courses. Adopting the policy might impede the process of learning.
- ［从行为的后果来说］Obliging students to take a lot of courses may not be helpful for students to discover their true interest.
- ［从教育的前提和目标来说］The cultivation of the ability of critical thinking, logical reasoning and problem-solving might be more important than acquiring knowledge for college-education.

【要达到以上目的，有没有其他解决途径？】
- 这些非专业课程的学习应该和学生本人的兴趣和选择相结合，同时也要强调学生思考推理能力的培养，这样才能真正达到大学培养人才和发掘学生潜能的目的。

---

3. 教育 Universities should require every student to take a variety of courses outside the student's
46 field of study. ［claim→solution］

大学应该要求所有学生学习大量非本专业的课程。

Discuss the extent to which you agree or disagree with the recommendation and describe specific circumstances in which adopting the recommendation would or would not be advantageous.

思路参考

【提出上述观点的目的可能是什么？】
- 为了让学生发掘自己的兴趣特长，得到真正全面的教育。

【题目建议在什么情况下会有好处？】
- Not every student exactly knows which academic field they are really interested in and can do well in the beginning of their college life. The recommendation could provide an opportunity for students to find their interest.
- Many disciplines are related; knowledge from outside the field of study could help students to think and observe from various points of view.

  这一点可以参考E类 143 的论证内容和素材。

【题目建议在什么情况下可能有问题？】
- ［从可行性来说］Not all universities and colleges are capable of providing various courses in various fields.

  Students may not have enough time and energy to deal with too many courses. Adopting the recommendation might impede the process of learning.
- ［从行为的后果来说］Obliging students to take a lot of courses may not be helpful for students to discover their true interest.
- ［从教育的前提和目标来说］The cultivation of the ability of critical thinking, logical reasoning and problem-solving might be more important than acquiring knowledge for college-education.

【要达到以上目的，有没有其他解决途径？】
- 这些非专业课程的学习应该和学生本人的兴趣和选择相结合，同时也要强调学生思考推理能力的培养，这样才能真正达到大学培养人才和发掘学生潜能的目的。

4. **教育** Claim: Universities should require every student to take a variety of courses outside the
70 student's major field of study.

Reason: Acquiring knowledge of various academic disciplines is the best way to become truly
educated. [reasoning/solution]

观点：大学应该要求所有学生学习大量非本专业的课程。

理由：获取诸多学科的知识是受到真正教育的最好途径。

Discuss the extent to which you agree or disagree with the claim and the reason on which that claim is based.

思路参考

【题目的理由有道理吗？】

- Many disciplines are related; knowledge from outside the field of study could help students to think and observe from various points of view.

  这一点可以参考E类 **143** 的论证内容和素材。

【题目的观点有道理吗？】

- Not every student knows exactly which academic field they are really interested in and can do well in the beginning of their college life. The proposed policy could provide an opportunity for students to find their interest.

【题目的理由有问题吗？】

- ［从教育的前提和目标来说］The cultivation of the ability of critical thinking, logical reasoning and problem-solving might be more important than acquiring knowledge for college-education.

【题目的推理过程有问题吗？】

- 这些非专业课程的学习应该和学生本人的兴趣和选择相结合，同时也要强调学生思考推理能力的培养，这样才能真正达到使学生获得全面教育的目的。

【题目的观点有问题吗？】

- ［从行为的后果来说］Obliging students to take a lot of courses may not be helpful for students to discover their true interest.

- ［从可行性来说］Not all universities and colleges are capable of providing various courses in various fields.

  Students may not have enough time and energy to deal with too many courses. Adopting the policy might impede the process of learning.

5. **教育** Universities should require every student to take a variety of courses outside the student's
102 field of study. [claim→solution]

大学应该要求所有学生学习大量非本专业的课程。

Discuss your views on the policy and consider the possible consequences of implementing the policy.

思路参考

【提出上述观点的目的可能是什么？】

- 为了让学生发掘自己的兴趣特长，得到真正全面的教育。

【题目政策可能存在哪些好处？】

- Not every student exactly knows which academic field they are really interested in and can do well in the beginning of their college life. The policy could provide an opportunity for students to find their interest.

- Many disciplines are related; knowledge from outside the field of study could help students to think and observe from various points of view.

  这一点可以参考E类 **143** 的论证内容和素材。

【题目政策可能导致哪些有问题的后果？】

- ［从可行性来说］Not all universities and colleges are capable of providing various courses in various fields.
- ［从行为的后果来说］Obliging students to take a lot of courses may not be helpful for students to discover their true interest.

  Spending much time on those courses may take away time that could be used for deeper research on students' own field of study and might impede the process of learning.
- ［从教育的前提和目标来说］Overemphasis on the importance of acquiring knowledge outside the field of study may lead students to neglect the cultivation of the ability of critical thinking, logical reasoning and problem-solving, which might be more essential than acquiring knowledge for college-education.

【要达到上述目的，有没有其他解决途径？】

- 这些非专业课程的学习应该和学生本人的兴趣和选择相结合，同时也要强调学生思考推理能力的培养，这样才能真正达到大学培养人才和发掘学生潜能的目的。

---

6. 教育 Requiring university students to take a variety of courses outside their major fields of study **112** is the best way to ensure that students become truly educated. ［solution］

要求大学生学习多种非本专业课程是保证学生真正受教育的最好途径。

Discuss the extent to which you agree or disagree with the statement and consider ways in which the statement might or might not hold true.

思路参考

【题目行为能达到作者的目的吗？】

- Not every student exactly knows which academic field they are really interested in and can do well in the beginning of their college life. The policy could provide an opportunity for students to find their interest.
- Many disciplines are related; knowledge from outside the field of study could help students to think and observe from various points of view.

  这一点可以参考E类 **143** 的论证内容和素材。

【题目行为存在问题吗？】

- ［从行为的后果来说］Obliging students to take a lot of courses may not be helpful for students to discover their true interest.
- ［从教育的前提和目标来说］Overemphasis on the importance of acquiring knowledge outside the field of study may lead students to neglect the cultivation of the ability of critical thinking, logical reasoning and problem-solving, which might be more essential than acquiring knowledge for college-education.

【题目的方法有可行性吗？】

- Not all universities and colleges are capable of providing various courses in various fields.
- Students may not have enough time and energy to deal with too many courses. Adopting the recommendation might impede the process of learning.

【要达到作者的目的，有没有其他方法？】

- 这些非专业课程的学习应该和学生本人的兴趣和选择相结合，同时也要强调学生思考推理能力的培养，这样才能真正达到大学培养人才和发掘学生潜能的目的。

7. **教育** Some people believe that universities should require every student to take a variety of
140 courses outside the student's field of study. Others believe that universities should not force students to take any courses other than those that will help prepare them for jobs in their chosen fields. [comparison]

一些人认为大学应该要求所有学生参加大量非本专业的课程。另一些人认为除了能帮助学生在所学专业为就业作准备的课程以外，大学不应该强迫学生参加任何其他课程。

Discuss which view more closely aligns with your own position and address both of the views presented.

思路参考

【第一种观点有道理吗？】

- Not every student exactly knows which academic field they are really interested in and can do well in the beginning of their college life. The policy could provide an opportunity for students to find their interest.
- Many disciplines are related; knowledge from outside the field of study could help students to think and observe from various points of view.

  这一点可以参考E类 143 的论证内容和素材。

【第一种观点有问题吗？】

- ［从可行性来说］Not all universities and colleges are capable of providing various courses in various fields.

  Students may not have enough time and energy to deal with too many courses. Adopting the policy might impede the process of learning.

- ［从教育的前提和目标来说］Overemphasis on the importance of acquiring knowledge outside the field of study may lead students to neglect the cultivation of the ability of critical thinking, logical reasoning and problem-solving, which might be more essential than acquiring knowledge for college-education.

【第二种观点有道理吗？】

- ［从行为的后果来说］Obliging students to take a lot of courses may not be helpful for students to discover their true interest.

【第二种观点有问题吗？】

- 过于功利。
- 违背高等教育的真正目标：使学生在学术、思想、人格各方面都得到全面的教育和发展，发掘自己真正的优势和兴趣。
- ［从后果来说］导致学生知识面过窄，对于整个世界的运作和各学科的联系没有全面的认识，不利于学生建立完整的科学思维体系和世界观。

【两种观点有调和的可能性吗？】

- 这些非专业课程的学习应该和学生本人的兴趣和选择相结合，同时也要强调学生思考推理能力的培养，这样才能真正达到大学培养人才和发掘学生潜能的目的。

8. **教育** Colleges and universities should require all faculty to spend time working outside the
73 academic world in professions relevant to the courses they teach. [claim]

大学院校应要求所有教职员工花时间走出学校，从事与其教授课程相关的工作。

Discuss your views on the policy and consider the possible consequences of implementing the policy.

【提出题目政策的目的可能是什么？】

- 提高大学教师的教学和科研能力。

【提出题目政策的理由可能是什么？】

- ［从必要性来说］The knowledge and experience in certain field often lags behind current development and changes due to the rapid pace of society progress.

【题目政策能达到上述目的吗？】

- The quality of education and academic research could be improved when faculty complement academic duties with real-world experience.

【上述政策可能有哪些正面意义？】

- The proposed actions could bring fresh insights, contagious excitement and practical examples to class, thereby sparking students' interest.
- Keeping abreast with the changing demands of work can help the faculty to make more informed decisions.
- Experience in the field can help professors find out cutting-edge and controversial issues, which are essential for doing more valuable researches.

【上述政策可能有哪些问题？】

- ［从可行性来说］For some academic areas, especially those abstract sciences and humanities, there is no profession to speak of outside academia.
- ［从政策后果来说］Spending too much time working outside the academic world may influence faculty's quality of education and research.

【思路提示】

- 本题可结合Domain展开，分别讨论不同领域、不同学科中教育与实际工作相结合的必要性和可行性。

---

9. **认知** No field of study can advance significantly unless it incorporates knowledge and

143 experience from outside that field. ［claim→solution/comparison］

除非借鉴其他领域的知识和经验，否则任何领域都无法取得重大进步。

Discuss the extent to which you agree or disagree with the statement and consider ways in which the statement might or might not hold true.

【思路提示】

- 本题最好结合Domain展开，分别举例分析不同学科领域借鉴外部知识的重要性，否则文章会流于空泛。

【题目的说法有道理吗？】

- Many disciplines are related; knowledge from outside the field of research could help researchers and scientists to think and observe from various points of view.

    这里可以引用很多交叉学科的例子作为论证素材。

【题目的说法有问题吗？】

- ［从观点所述行为的必要性来说］Incorporating outsiders' knowledge and experience is neither necessary nor sufficient for a field of study to advance, i.e., some significant academic advances have nothing to do with experience from other subjects.
- ［从观点可能引发的后果来说］The claim may lead researchers to overly rely on the discoveries and achievements of other fields, and therefore impede true academic progress.

- ［从不同学科的特点来说］For some academic areas, such as abstract sciences, arts, humanities, little knowledge from outside could be or need to be incorporated.

【要取得学术进步有没有其他途径？】

- long-term academic accumulation, inspiration, emergence of genius, etc.

---

10. 教育 In order to become well-rounded individuals, all college students should be required to
54 take courses in which they read poetry, novels, mythology, and other types of imaginative literature. [solution]

为使他们成为全面发展的人，应该要求所有大学生都参加阅读诗歌、小说、神话以及其他想象文学的课程。

Discuss the extent to which you agree or disagree with the recommendation and describe specific circumstances in which adopting the recommendation would or would not be advantageous.

思路参考

【题目提出的方案有道理吗？】

- ［从其效果来说］Reading imaginative literature could enrich students' spiritual world and inspire their creativity and imagination.
- ［从其必要性来说］Pure scientific research without the aid of imaginative works and humanities will be meaningless for the progress of human society.

  关于这一点论述可以参考C类和D类一些题目的素材思路，比如 43 、 106 。

【题目提出的方案有问题吗？】

- ［从必要性来说］Not all students need to take such courses. For students who have already read a lot of such works, these courses could be set as elective.
- ［从后果来说］Mandatory attending of these courses may cause repulsion of students, and may not bring desired effect.

  Reading too many such materials may lead students to indulge in illusions and unrealistic imaginations.

  Spending much time taking those courses may take away time that could be used for deeper research on students' own field of study and might impede the process of learning.

【题目方案存在可行性方面的问题吗？】

- Not all universities and colleges are capable of providing high-quality courses in such fields.
- Students may not have enough time and energy to deal with those courses. Adopting the recommendation might impede the process of learning.

【有没有其他方案可以达到作者的目的？】

- Requiring students to take other courses outside their field of study, not necessarily courses on imaginative works, could also help students to think and observe from various points of view.
- The cultivation of the ability of critical thinking, logical reasoning and problem-solving is also essential for college-education.

  题目所述行为应该尊重和结合学生本人的意愿和兴趣，强制性的课程未必会带来良好的效果。

---

11. 教育 Colleges and universities should require their students to spend at least one semester
82 studying in a foreign country. [claim→solution]

大学院校应该要求学生至少用一个学期时间到其他国家学习。

Discuss the extent to which you agree or disagree with the recommendation and describe specific circumstances in which adopting the recommendation would or would not be advantageous.

【提出上述观点的目的可能是什么？】

- 为了让学生得到真正全面的教育。

【题目建议的提出有没有什么前提？】

- 学校应该精心选择目的国，保证该国社会文化、环境等各方面真正有利于学生兴趣和能力的培养。

【题目建议在什么情况下会有好处？】

- Studying abroad may give students inspiration and broaden their perspective.

- Every country has its character and advantage. Requiring students to study in foreign countries would be beneficial for the development of their own country.

【题目建议在什么情况下可能有问题？】

- ［从可行性来说］Not all universities and colleges are capable of providing the opportunity for students to study abroad.

  Some students may not be able to afford studying abroad.

- ［从行为的后果来说］The excitement of being abroad may distract young students from their true objectives of studying in a foreign country.

【要达到以上目的，有没有其他解决途径？】

- For some colleges and universities which cannot provide such opportunities, requiring students to take courses outside their field of study is also an effective method to ensure students becoming truly educated.

【思路提示】

- 本题可以结合Domain展开，分别举例分析不同专业学生到国外学习的必要性。对于纯理论类专业，去国外学习的必要性不是很突出；而对于人文社科或艺术工程类专业，到国外学习能够开阔眼界、拓宽思路。

---

12. **教育** Colleges and universities should require their students to spend at least one semester
97 studying in a foreign country. ［claim→solution］

大学院校应该要求学生至少用一个学期时间到其他国家学习。

Discuss the extent to which you agree or disagree with the claim and address the most compelling reasons and/or examples that could be used to challenge your position.

思路参考

【提出上述观点的目的可能是什么？】

为了让学生得到真正全面的教育。

【题目的建议有合理性吗？】

- ［从行为后果来说］Studying abroad may give students inspiration and broaden their perspective.

  Every country has its character and advantage. Requiring students to study in foreign countries would be beneficial for the development of their own country.

【可能有哪些相反观点？】

- ［从可行性来说］Not all universities and colleges are capable of providing the opportunity for students to study abroad.

  Some students may not be able to afford studying abroad.

  ［回应］For some colleges and universities which cannot provide such opportunities, requiring students to take courses outside their field of study is also an effective method to ensure students becoming truly educated.

- ［从行为的后果来说］The excitement of being abroad may distract young students from their true objectives of studying in a foreign country.

［回应］学校应该精心选择目的国，保证该国社会文化、环境等各方面真正有利于学生兴趣和能力的培养。同时学校应对在国外学习的过程给予必要的监督和指导，保证学生明确学习的目的。

【思路提示】

〈略，参考 **82** 〉

---

13. **教育** Colleges and universities should require their students to spend at least one semester **100** studying in a foreign country. ［claim→solution］

大学院校应该要求学生至少用一个学期时间到其他国家学习。

Discuss your views on the policy and consider the possible consequences of implementing the policy.

思路参考

【提出上述观点的目的可能是什么？】

- 为了让学生得到真正全面的教育。

【题目的方案能达到上述目的吗？】

- Studying abroad may give students inspiration and broaden their perspective.
- Every country has its character and advantage. Requiring students to study in foreign countries would be beneficial for the development of their own country.

【题目的方案在什么情况下可能有问题？】

- ［从可行性来说］There may be difficulties for some colleges and universities to implement such program. Some students may not be able to afford studying abroad.
- ［从行为的后果来说］The excitement of being abroad may distract young students from their true objectives of studying in a foreign country.

【对于上述问题有没有解决途径？】

- For colleges and universities which cannot provide such opportunities, requiring students to take courses outside their field of study could also be an effective method to ensure students becoming truly educated.
- 学校应该精心选择目的国，保证该国社会文化、环境等各方面真正有利于学生兴趣和能力的培养。同时学校应对在国外学习的过程给予必要的监督和指导，保证学生明确学习的目的。

【思路提示】

〈略，参考 **82** 〉

---

14. **教育** All college and university students would benefit from spending at least one semester **124** studying in a foreign country. ［claim→solution］

所有大学生都可以从在其他国家至少一个学期的学习中获益。

Discuss the extent to which you agree or disagree with the statement and consider ways in which the statement might or might not hold true.

思路参考

【思路提示】

- 本题最好结合Domain展开，分别举例分析到国外学习对于不同专业的好处。

- 为了让学生得到真正全面的教育。

【题目的观点有合理性吗？】

- Studying abroad may give students inspiration and broaden their perspective.
- Every country has its character and advantage. Requiring students to study in foreign countries would be beneficial for the development of their own country.

【题目的观点可能存在哪些问题？】

- ［从可行性来说］Not all universities and colleges are capable of providing the opportunity for students to study abroad.

  Some students may not be able to afford studying abroad.
- ［从行为的后果来说］The excitement of being abroad may distract young students from their true objectives of studying in a foreign country.

【对于上述问题有没有解决方法？】

- For colleges and universities which cannot provide such opportunities, requiring students to take courses outside their field of study could also be an effective method to ensure students becoming truly educated.
- 学校应该精心选择目的国，保证该国社会文化、环境等各方面真正有利于学生兴趣和能力的培养。同时学校应对在国外学习的过程给予必要的监督和指导，保证学生明确学习的目的。

---

15. 认知 As we acquire more knowledge, things do not become more comprehensible, but more

33 complex and mysterious. ［claim］

随着人们获得越来越多的知识，事情没有变得更好理解，而是更加复杂和神秘了。

Discuss the extent to which you agree or disagree with the statement and consider ways in which the statement might or might not hold true.

思路参考

【思路提示】

- 本题如果从纯理论的角度切入会比较难分析，建议从Definition（对知识的定义）、Category（知识的种类）和Domain（各个领域知识的影响）分别举例分析和组织文章。

【题目的观点有道理吗？】

从某种意义上说，人类面对的问题随着人类知识的增加确实越来越复杂了。因为：

- The more knowledge one acquires, the more awareness one possesses.
- The more intensive education one receives, the more will one's view of the world change.
- The more one knows, the more unknown area one will find.

  知识越多，人们意识到的问题、所发现的未知领域就越多，看问题的角度也会随之改变。因而人们会发现自己面对更多的问题。

【题目的观点有问题吗？】

- This complexity does not equal mystery.

  The world itself has not changed, but the way we view the world has become vastly different.

  Knowledge helps us get closer to the very essence of the real world, and helps humans get reassured.

  但是，这种复杂性不能等同于神秘。客观世界本身并没有变化，而是人们看待世界的视角改变了。知识可以帮助我们接近事实真相，也可以解决我们对世界的疑惑。
- The acquisition of knowledge and exploration of unknown field are basic instinct of human.

【发散】

- Science and most human knowledge can only change the material condition of our world, but many problems related to human nature, such as war, poverty, oppression, can hardly be solved with knowledge.

这一点可以参考C类关于"科技无法解决人类社会问题"的一些思路和素材。

---

16. 认知 Some people believe that scientific discoveries have given us a much better understanding
`109` of the world around us. Others believe that science has revealed to us that the world is infinitely
more complex than we ever realized. [comparison]

一些人认为科学发现使我们对周围的世界有了更好的认识。另一些人认为科学让我们认识到世界比我们所了解的复杂得多。

Discuss which view more closely aligns with your own position and address both of the views presented.

思路参考

【第一种观点有道理吗？】

- [从人类发展科技的主观动机来说] the original mission of human to develop science: to discover the laws of nature
- [从科技发展的客观效果来说] Scientific discoveries give us more comprehensive and deeper understanding of the world, and help us get closer to the very essence of the real world. Scientific knowledge also helps humans get reassured.
- The acquisition of knowledge and exploration of unknown field are basic instinct of human.

【第一种观点有问题吗？】

- Science can only change the material condition of our world, but aspects of human nature can be hardly explained by science.

【第二种观点有道理吗？】

从某种意义上说，人类面对的问题随着人类知识的增加确实越来越复杂了。因为：

- The more knowledge one acquires, the more awareness one possesses.
- The more intensive education one receives, the more will one's view of the world change.

【第二种观点有问题吗？】

- The world itself has not changed, but the way we view the world has become vastly different.

【发散】

两种观点其实并不矛盾：

- Scientific discoveries could help human to explain and solve many problems, but the more humans know, the more unknown field will humans discover.

【思路提示】

- 本题可以从Category(不同种类的科学发现)的角度展开，分别举例分析科学发现对人类认知的影响。

---

17. 教育 Educators should teach facts only after their students have studied the ideas, trends, and
`48` concepts that help explain those facts. [claim → reasoning/solution]

教育者应该只有在学生掌握了帮助解释某些事实的观点、趋势和概念之后再讲授这些事实。

Discuss the extent to which you agree or disagree with the recommendation and describe specific circumstances in which adopting the recommendation would or would not be advantageous.

思路参考

【提出上述观点的理由可能是什么？】

- [从行为的好处来说] Learning of related ideas, trends, and concepts is helpful for students to memorize the fact.

- ［从行为的必要性来说］Students will eventually learn little if they learn only a pile of facts.

【题目的观点有意义吗？】

- ［从行为的重要性来说］The cultivation of the ability of analyzing facts might be more essential than merely memorizing facts for education.

【上述理由存在问题吗？】

- ［从可行性和事实的类别来说］For some newly emerged phenomena and problems, one can hardly find any ideas or concepts to explain them.

【上述推理过程存在充分性吗？】

- 尽管学习相关知识对于记忆事实确实有一定意义，但并非只有在学习相关知识后才能记忆事实。有些领域事实的记忆不需要太多相关概念，有些领域事实的记忆反过来有助于相关知识的学习。

【上述推理的前提有问题吗？】

- ［从观点的性质来说］Ideas, trends, and concepts are only assumptions or individual opinions. Learning such unwarranted or even biased ideas may sometimes jeopardize real learning.

【题目的观点有问题吗？】

- ［从后果来说］The proposed actions may be harmful for cultivating students' inspiration, creativity, and the ability to think for themselves.

---

18. 教育 Educators should base their assessment of students' learning not on students' grasp of
92 facts but on the ability to explain the ideas, trends, and concepts that those facts illustrate.
［claim→solution］
教育者对于学生学习的评价不应基于学生对事实的掌握，而应基于他们解释这些事实所说明的思想、潮流和概念的能力。

Discuss the extent to which you agree or disagree with the recommendation and describe specific circumstances in which adopting the recommendation would or would not be advantageous.

思路参考

【提出上述观点的理由可能是什么？】

- ［从行为的好处来说］The ability to explain those ideas, trends, and concepts is helpful for students to memorize facts.
- ［从必要性来说］Students will eventually learn little if they only memorize a pile of facts.
- ［从后果来说］The proposed actions are helpful for cultivating students' creativity and the ability to think for themselves.

【题目的观点有道理吗？】

- ［从行为的重要性来说］The cultivation of the ability of analyzing facts might be more essential than merely memorizing facts for education.

【题目行为的可行性存在问题吗？】

- For some newly emerged phenomena or isolated facts, one can hardly find any ideas or concepts illustrated by them.

【有其他评价学生的方法吗？】

- 逻辑推理、分析的能力固然重要，对于有些基础知识的掌握对于教育也是必须的。有效的评价体系应该同时兼顾两方面的需求，不应过于偏重某一方。

19. **认知** In order for any work of art—for example, a film, a novel, a poem, or a song—to have **55** merit, it must be understandable to most people. [claim→solution]

任何艺术作品——例如电影、小说、诗歌或歌曲——要有价值，它必须能够被大多数人理解。

Discuss the extent to which you agree or disagree with the statement and consider ways in which the statement might or might not hold true.

思路参考

【思路提示】

- 本题的展开可以结合Category，分别讨论不同种类的艺术要具有价值是否必须被大众理解。也可以结合Period，讨论不同时期的艺术要具有价值是否必须被大众理解。

【题目的说法有道理吗？】

- ［从艺术本身的性质来说］Arts are expressions of thoughts and feelings. It is reasonable to request arts to be understandable to people.

- The theme, technique, and means of expression of some great art works are so simple that almost everyone could understand them.

  但是，这只能说明有些有价值的艺术作品具有容易理解的特性，并不能说明是因为其浅显而决定了其价值。

【题目的说法有问题吗？】

- Being understandable to most people is neither sufficient nor necessary for an art work to hold merit.

  ［从艺术作品的特性来说］Some art works are exclusive expressions of artists' inner feelings. Some great works contain ideas and thoughts that transcend the time. They often confront us with uncertainty and lack of reason.

- The fact that the majority of people could not understand them does not mean that those works are of no merit.

  艺术创作和艺术欣赏都是一个主观过程。审美和艺术欣赏的感受取决于欣赏者的经历、学识、审美经验、阶层、年龄等各方面。因此有些艺术作品不能被大众接受或欣赏是正常的，不能因为有些人无法理解就否定艺术作品的价值。

- ［从后果来说］Accepting the claim may lead artists to pander to public taste, thereby hindering real artistic creation.

  People may have misinterpretation of some great works which are seemingly easy to understand.

【题目说法的可行性存在问题吗？】

- For some types of arts, especially those pure art forms such as music（without lyrics and themes），as well as architecture, handcraft, there is nothing can be said to be understandable.

【有其他途径赋予艺术作品价值吗？】

- Art works that reveal otherwise hidden ideas and impulses could also have merit.
- Some art works hold merit through upsetting old ways of artistic creation.

---

1. 社会 Scandals are useful because they focus our attention on problems in ways that no speaker
4 or reformer ever could. [reasoning/solution]

丑闻是有用的，因为它以发言人和改革家都无法做到的方式把我们的注意力聚焦于问题上。

Discuss the extent to which you agree or disagree with the claim and address the most compelling reasons and/or examples that could be used to challenge your position.

思路参考

【题目的理由有道理吗？】

- Scandals reveal some problems that will otherwise be ignored by speakers and reformers, for they may not dare to or be willing to expose them.

- ［从丑闻的特点来说］The public are willing to hear about and talk about scandals, thus, scandals could call our attention to pervasive social or political problems that a society should address.

【题目的观点有道理吗？】

- ［从丑闻的作用来说］Scandals could help promoting social progress and solving social problems in that they offset the shortcomings of regular supervisory mechanism of a society.

【题目的推理过程存在问题吗？】

- 正因为丑闻往往是从负面角度吸引人们的注意力，因此对丑闻的揭发很容易演变成满足公众好奇心的过程。因此，要判断丑闻的价值就要看揭露它的目的是真正为了解决问题还是仅仅为了制造轰动效应和吸引眼球。

【题目的观点存在问题吗？】

- ［从后果来说］丑闻有时会使人们只关注一些有轰动效应的事件而忽视了更重要、更需解决的问题。对于丑闻的过度报道和关注不利于引导社会和公众正确的价值观，不利于社会的真正进步。

【发散】

- Unduly relying on scandals to discover problems may reveal the malfunction of the social system, especially its supervisory and legal ones.

---

2. 教育 A nation should require all of its students to study the same national curriculum until they
6 enter college. [claim→comparison/solution]

国家应该要求所有学生在上大学前学习同样的国家规定课程。

Discuss the extent to which you agree or disagree with the recommendation and describe specific circumstances in which adopting the recommendation would or would not be advantageous.

思路参考

【思路提示】

- 本题最好结合Condition和Category来展开，讨论不同条件的国家以及不同性质的课程是否存在统一安排的必要性。

【提出题目观点的目的是什么？】

- 使所有学生受到同等良好的教育，并为将来的高等教育做准备。

【题目的行为能达到上述目的吗？】

- ［从必要性来说］A common core curriculum which provides fundamental skills and knowledge is necessary for the preparation of the future higher education.
- ［从后果来说］A common core curriculum could ensure that students become reasonably informed, and that all students are taught core values upon which a democratic society depends to thrive.

【题目的观点在什么情况下可能有问题？】

- 在不能保证充分民主，甚至是独裁专制的国家：
  A mandatory national curriculum may facilitate the dissemination of propaganda and other dogma.
- 在多民族、多文化的国家：
  Requiring all students to study the same national curriculum may result in the intensification of racial or cultural conflict.
- ［从可行性来说］对于多民族、多文化、多语言、地域宽广的国家，很难要求每个地区都执行同样的课程设置。

【与题目行为相对的其他方案是什么？】

- 由地方院校，或者学生自行选择课程。

【这种做法在什么情况下合理？】

- Courses other than those providing basic skills and knowledge could be arranged by schools.
- ［从必要性来说］No country could guarantee all students the opportunity of higher education, therefore, some courses providing various technical skills are necessary for some students who cannot enter college.
- ［从效果来说］Allowing students to select the courses they would study, or planning courses according to the interests and suggestions of students is beneficial for motivating students to learn.
  这一论证点的展开可以参考G类 90 。

【总结】

- 国家安排和地方安排应有效结合，不能完全偏重于其中一方。
- 课程完全由国家安排可能会导致教学缺乏灵活性，忽视不同地区、不同文化的特点和需求，并可能阻碍社会进步。而地方获得过度安排课程的权力可能造成国家教育体系的混乱，不利于为高等教育提供基础。
- 因此，提供基本工具、基本常识的课程应该由国家统一安排，而有些职业技能培训、兴趣课程、特色课程完全可以由地方、学校乃至学生自行安排。

---

3. **教育** A nation should require all of its students to study the same national curriculum until they **14** enter college. ［claim→comparison］
   国家应该要求所有学生在上大学前学习同样的国家规定课程。
   Discuss your views on the policy and consider the possible consequences of implementing the policy.

思路参考

【思路提示】

- 本题最好结合Condition和Category来展开，讨论不同条件的国家以及不同性质的课程是否存在统一安排的必要性。

【上述政策的目的是什么？】

- 使所有学生受到同等良好的教育，并为将来的高等教育做准备。

【题目的政策可能有哪些正面效果？】

- A common core curriculum could provide fundamental skills and knowledge which are necessary for the future higher education.

- A common core curriculum could ensure that students become reasonably informed, and that all students are taught core values upon which a democratic society depends to thrive.

【题目政策可能有哪些负面效果?】

- 在不能保证充分民主,甚至是独裁专制的国家:

A mandatory national curriculum may facilitate the dissemination of propaganda and other dogma.

- 在多民族、多文化的国家:

Requiring all students to study the same national curriculum may result in the intensification of racial or cultural conflict.

【题目的政策可能存在哪些问题?】

- [从可行性来说]对于多民族、多文化、多语言、地域宽广的国家,很难要求每个地区都执行同样的课程设置。

【有没有其他安排课程的方式?】

- 由地方院校,或者学生自行选择课程。

【这种做法在什么情况下合理?】

〈略,参考 6 〉

【总结】

〈略,参考 6 〉

---

4. **教育** A nation should require all of its students to study the same national curriculum until they **96** enter college. [claim→comparison]

国家应要求所有学生在上大学前参加同样的国家规定课程。

Discuss the extent to which you agree or disagree with the claim and address the most compelling reasons and/or examples that could be used to challenge your position.

思路参考

【思路提示】

- 本题最好结合Condition和Category来展开,讨论不同条件的国家以及不同性质的课程是否存在统一安排的必要性。

【提出题目观点的目的是什么?】

- 使所有学生受到同等良好的教育,并为将来的高等教育做准备。

【题目的行为能达到上述目的吗?】

- [从必要性来说]A common core curriculum which provides fundamental skills and knowledge is necessary for the future higher education.

- [从后果来说]A common core curriculum could ensure that students become reasonably informed, and that all students are taught core values upon which a democratic society depends to thrive.

【可能有哪些与题目观点相反的看法?】

- 在不能保证充分民主,甚至是独裁专制的国家:

A mandatory national curriculum may facilitate the dissemination of propaganda and other dogma.

- 在多民族、多文化的国家:

Requiring all students to study the same national curriculum may result in the intensification of racial or cultural conflict.

- [回应]在这类国家,统一安排课程应慎之又慎,有些敏感、涉及文化或价值核心的课程可以由不同地区来安排。

- [从可行性来说] 对于多民族、多文化、多语言、地域宽广的国家，很难要求每个地区都执行同样的课程设置。
- [回应] 在这些地区，有些非核心课程可以由地方院校，或者学生自行安排。

   Courses other than those providing basic skills and knowledge could be arranged by schools.

【总结】

〈略，参考 **6** 〉

---

5. **教育** A nation should require all of its students to study the same national curriculum until they **116** enter college. [claim→comparison]

国家应该要求所有学生在上大学之前学习同样的国家规定课程。

Discuss the extent to which you agree or disagree with the statement and consider ways in which the statement might or might not hold true.

思路参考

【思路提示】

- 本题最好结合Condition和Category来展开，讨论不同条件的国家以及不同性质的课程是否存在统一安排的必要性。

【提出题目观点的目的是什么？】

- 使所有学生受到同等良好的教育，并为将来的高等教育做准备。

【题目的行为有合理性吗？】

- [从必要性来说] A common core curriculum which provides fundamental skills and knowledge is necessary for the future higher education.
- [从后果来说] A common core curriculum could ensure that students become reasonably informed, and that all students are taught core values upon which a democratic society depends to thrive.

【题目的观点可能存在哪些问题？】

- 在不能保证充分民主，甚至是独裁专制的国家：

   A mandatory national curriculum may facilitate the dissemination of propaganda and other dogma.

- 在多民族、多文化的国家：

   Requiring all students to study the same national curriculum may result in the intensification of racial or cultural conflict.

【题目观点的可行性存在问题吗？】

- 对于多民族、多文化、多语言、地域宽广的国家，很难要求每个地区都执行同样的课程设置。

【有没有其他安排课程的方式？】

- 由地方院校，或者学生自行安排课程。

【这种做法在什么情况下合理？】

- Courses other than those providing basic skills and knowledge could be arranged by schools.
- [从必要性来说] No country could guarantee all students the opportunity of higher education, therefore, some courses providing various technical skills are necessary for some students who cannot enter college.
- [从效果来说] Allowing students to select the courses they would study, or planning courses according to the interests and suggestions of students is beneficial for motivating students to learn.

   这一论证点的展开可以参考G类 **90** 。

【总结】

〈略，参考 **6** 〉

6. **社会** The well-being of a society is enhanced when many of its people question authority.

[18] [claim→solution]

当社会上很多人怀疑权威时，社会总体利益将得到提升。

Discuss the extent to which you agree or disagree with the statement and consider ways in which the statement might or might not hold true.

思路参考

【思路提示】

- 本题可结合Domain来展开，分别讨论政治、科技、艺术、社会等不同领域质疑权威的作用和意义。

【题目的观点有道理吗？】

- ［从后果来说］［对于政治方面的权威］The more the people are questioning authority, the more the society's people care about what the authority is doing. Questioning authority forces governments to be more democratic, efficient, responsible and honest.
- ［对于其他社会层面的权威］Questioning authorities promotes innovation, invention, and discovery.
- ［从必须性来说］The opinions, claims, and theories of authorities may become out of date, or have inherent drawbacks. Questioning existing authority is necessary for social progress.

【题目的观点有问题吗？】

- ［从后果来说］Mass resistance to authority can escalate to violent protest and rioting, and impede development and progress.
- ［对于社会层面的权威］Some positive challenges do not necessarily come from a large number of people; a few key individuals can pose profound impact.

【发散】

- It is necessary to make clear differentiation between positive and vicious challenge.

7. **认知** In any situation, progress requires discussion among people who have contrasting points

[34] of view. [claim/solution]

在任何情况下，取得进步都需要持相反观点的人们进行讨论。

Discuss the extent to which you agree or disagree with the statement and consider ways in which the statement might or might not hold true.

思路参考

【思路提示】

- 本题应该结合Domain来展开，分别举例讨论在不同领域（比如社会、政治、科技、艺术、生活等）与持相反观点的人讨论的意义。如果从纯理论角度分析肯定会流于空泛。此外，本题表述中的"any"一词过于绝对，并非所有领域的进步都需要与持相反观点的人讨论。

【提出题目观点的理由可能是什么？】

- The perspective of any individual inevitably has limitation.

【题目的观点存在合理性吗？】

- ［从行为导致的后果来说］People whose ideas contradict ours can make us think from different point of view, and can give us much more valuable enlightenment, thereby helping us find perfect solutions.

【题目的推理过程存在问题吗？】

- For some realms of human endeavor, such as arts and culture, their progress involves little discourse and debate with those who have contrasting viewpoints.

- Discussion with those people is not necessary for progress. In other words, some great achievements were the result of sheer talent or inspiration.

【题目的观点存在问题吗？】

- Undue and irrational disagreement may be counterproductive and cause distress, or even inhibit true progress.

---

8. 认知 Claim: We can usually learn much more from people whose views we share than from those whose views contradict our own.

   Reason: Disagreement can cause stress and inhibit learning. [reasoning/comparison]

   观点：相对于和我们观点相反的人，我们通常能从和我们观点相同的人那里学到更多东西。

   理由：争执产生压力并阻碍学习。

   Discuss the extent to which you agree or disagree with the claim and the reason on which that claim is based.

思路参考

【题目的理由有道理吗？】

- ［从后果来说］Undue and irrational disagreement may be counterproductive and cause distress.

【题目的观点有道理吗？】

- It is easier for people to understand each other when they find them sharing the same ground.

【题目的理由有问题吗？】

- Disagreement does not necessarily cause stress and inhibit learning. It depends on the motivations of disagreement, the individuals' age, mental maturity, etc.

【题目的观点有问题吗？】

- ［从必要性来说］The perspective of any individual inevitably has limitation.

- People whose ideas contradict ours can make us think from different point of view, and can give us much more valuable enlightenment, thereby helping us find perfect solutions.

---

9. 认知 We can usually learn much more from people whose views we share than from people whose views contradict our own. [comparison]

   相对于和我们观点相反的人，我们通常能从和我们观点相同的人那里学到更多东西。

   Discuss the extent to which you agree or disagree with the statement and consider ways in which the statement might or might not hold true.

思路参考

【和观点相同的人交流有哪些积极因素？】

- It is easier for people to understand each other when they find them sharing the same ground.

- Cooperating with people who have common ground of understanding promotes efficient progress.

【和观点相同的人交流有哪些问题？】

- Interacting only with people whose views we share tends to make us neglect flaws or drawbacks in our view or theory, and will limit our perspective.

【和观点相反的人交流有哪些积极因素？】

- People whose ideas contradict ours can make us think from different point of view, and can give us much more valuable enlightenment, thereby helping us find perfect solutions.

【和观点相反的人交流有哪些问题？】

- Undue and irrational disagreement may be counterproductive and cause distress.

【发散】

- Whether disagreement or agreement will promote learning depends on myriad factors such as the motivations of disagreement, the individuals' age, mental maturity, etc.

---

10. **认知** We can learn much more from people whose views we share than from people whose **118** views contradict our own. [comparison]

相对于和我们观点相反的人，我们能从和我们观点相同的人那里学到更多东西。

Discuss the extent to which you agree or disagree with the statement and consider ways in which the statement might or might not hold true.

思路参考

〈略，参考 **76**〉

---

11. **教育** Students should always question what they are taught instead of accepting it passively. **42** [claim/comparison]

学生应该质疑他们所学的内容，而不是被动地接受。

Discuss the extent to which you agree or disagree with the statement and consider ways in which the statement might or might not hold true.

思路参考

【提出题目观点的理由可能是什么？】

- Teachers and professors are human beings and are therefore not perfect. Flaws and mistakes will inevitably exist in the course of their teaching.

【题目的观点有合理性吗？】

- [从后果来说] Questioning teachers would make students be more active in their learning, through which the students could motivate themselves.
- A student can raise questions only after he or she has seriously considered the subject. This process could help students to learn what they are taught more effectively and deeply.
- The proposed action could hone the students' ability of critical thinking, which is fundamental in their further research and development.

【题目的观点有问题吗？】

- Questioning whatever they are taught might be counterproductive in a student's education, and might go against true development and progress.
- Undue skepticism might be detrimental to the cultivation of the students' healthy personalities, making them tend to regard everything as negative.

【要达到教育的目的有没有折中方案？】

- Students should assimilate what they are taught with discrimination. Questioning everything could be as harmful as passively accepting everything.

12. 教育 Competition for high grades seriously limits the quality of learning at all levels of education.

45 [claim]

对高分的竞争严重限制了各个教育阶段的学习质量。

Discuss the extent to which you agree or disagree with the statement and consider ways in which the statement might or might not hold true.

思路参考

【提出上述观点的理由可能是什么？】

- Exam scores could not reflect the actual effect of education.

【题目的观点有合理性吗？】

- ［从后果来说］Simply pursuing high grades may lead students to ignore the real goal of education (cultivation of critical thinking, logical reasoning, and flexible application of knowledge), and may prohibit developing their interests and potentials.

- Competition for high grades might be harmful for the cultivation of students' healthy personalities.

  ［for reference only］As there are natural sins such as pride, envy and greed in human nature, such competition may intensify those negative characters.

【题目观点有问题吗？】

- Moderate competition might be necessary for motivating students to work hard and improve performance.

【总结】

适当的竞争对于调动学生的积极性和进取心有一定好处，但是单纯为了高分而学习显然会偏离教育的本来目的。因此，一方面教育者应该积极探讨寻求更为全面、公正的衡量教育效果的标准，另一方面要对竞争加以一定的控制，避免单纯用分数来衡量学生，同时避免学生仅仅为了分数而学习。

另外，竞争的作用对于不同阶段的学习可能也是不同的。对于低年级的学生，自控能力和自主学习能力比较差，而且这个阶段的学习还不会涉及很多需要深入思考和分析的内容，这时鼓励他们争取高分对于调动其学习积极性有一定意义；而对于高年级和高等教育，主要目标是培养学生的科学精神、独立人格和思辨能力，这一阶段再强调高分就没有什么意义了。

13. 教育 Some people believe that competition for high grades motivates students to excel in the

138 classroom. Others believe that such competition seriously limits the quality of real learning.

［comparison］

一些人相信对高分的竞争可以激励学生在学校的优秀表现。另一些人认为这种竞争严重限制了真正的学习质量。

Discuss which view more closely aligns with your own position and address both of the views presented.

思路参考

【第一种观点有合理性吗？】

- Moderate competition might be necessary for motivating students to work hard and improve performance.

【第一种观点有问题吗？】

- Competition for high grades might be harmful for the cultivation of students' healthy personalities.

  ［for reference only］As there are natural sins such as pride, envy and greed in human nature, such competition may intensify those negative characters.

【第二种观点有合理性吗？】

- Exam scores could not reflect the actual effect of education.

- ［从后果来说］Simply pursuing high grades may lead students to ignore the real goal of education（cultivation of critical thinking, logical reasoning, and flexible application of knowledge）, and may prohibit developing their interests and potentials.

【总结】

〈略，参考 **45**〉

---

14. 社会 The best way for a society to prepare its young people for leadership in government, **123** industry, or other fields is by instilling in them a sense of cooperation, not competition.

［comparison］

社会把年轻人培养成政府、工商业或其他领域领导人的最佳方法就是给他们灌输合作而非竞争的思想。

Discuss the extent to which you agree or disagree with the claim and address the most compelling reasons and/or examples that could be used to challenge your position.

思路参考

【思路提示】

- 本题最好结合Domain展开，分别讨论不同领域竞争和合作的重要性：
  对于体育和竞技领域，竞争精神显然是必要的，除了一些团体项目需要合作外，总体来说"更快、更高、更强"的思想推动了人类体育事业的进步；对于商业、经济、科技等领域，竞争和合作同等重要——竞争能促使人们不断完善和提高已有的技术、产品和服务，而有效的合作可以保证各个领域的进步和发展；对于政治、军事等领域则要视情况具体分析。

- 或者，本题也可以从不同层面来展开分析：
  从较大的社会层面来说，我们需要充分的竞争，避免垄断现象的出现，以保证各个实体获得公平的发展机会，从而为社会提供更优质、成本更低的服务和产品；但是从某一个具体群体或单位层面来说，则更多地需要合作精神，这样才能保证其目标的实现。

【强调合作精神有合理性吗？】

- ［从必要性来说］Some developments and progress necessitate cooperation between people.

【强调合作精神有问题吗？】

- ［从后果来说］Overemphasis of cooperation may lead the members in a group to overly rely on others' work and achievements, and result in their inertia.

  Also, emphasizing cooperation will not be beneficial for some individual members to show their talents and creativities.

【强调竞争精神有合理性吗？】

- ［从必要性来说］A thriving society depends on a freely competitive environment.

  In today's hyper-competitive technology-driven society, a competitive spirit is critical.

- The sense of competition is essential for individuals to exhibit their talents and creativities.

【强调竞争精神有问题吗？】

- ［从后果来说］Undue competition may impede real progress, may result in psychological pressure or even unhealthy personalities, and may even raise resentment and hostility among team members.

【回应】【发散】

- ［回应］竞争对于取得进步和发展是必要的，但要适度，因而必须制定公平合理的竞争规则，避免恶意竞争。

- 另外，决定领导水平的不仅仅是合作意识或竞争意识，更重要的在于对领导者人格和领导、执行能力的培养。

15. 社会 Some people argue that successful leaders in government, industry, or other fields must `128` be highly competitive. Other people claim that in order to be successful, a leader must be willing and able to cooperate with others. [comparison→solution]

一些人认为政府、工商业或其他领域的成功领导者必须是充满竞争性的。另一些人指出要获得成功，领导者必须愿意而且能够与他人合作。

Discuss which view more closely aligns with your own position and address both of the views presented.

思路参考

【思路提示】

- 本题可以转化为Solution结构来进行论证，即讨论领导者要获得成功，除了竞争或合作意识以外还有没有其他必须满足的条件。此外，也可以参考 `123` 的思路提示。

【第一种观点有合理性吗？】

- ［从必要性来说］A thriving society depends on a freely competitive environment. Full competition ensures best product, best service, and best idea.
- The sense of competition is essential for individuals to exhibit their talents and creativities.

【第一种观点有问题吗？】

- ［从后果来说］Undue competition may impede real progress, may result in psychological pressure or even unhealthy personalities, and may even raise resentment and hostility among team members.

  ［for reference only］As there are natural sins such as pride, envy and greed in human nature, such competition may intensify those negative characters.

【第二种观点有合理性吗？】

- ［从必要性来说］Some developments and progress necessitate cooperation between people.

【第二种观点有问题吗？】

- ［从后果来说］Overemphasis of cooperation may lead the members in a group to overly rely on others' work and achievements, and result in their inertia.

  Also, emphasizing cooperation will not be beneficial for some individual members to show their talents and creativities.

【发散】

- 竞争对于取得进步和发展是必要的，但要适度，因而必须制定公平合理的竞争规则，避免恶性竞争。
- ［转化为Solution，讨论领导者成功的其他必要条件］

  demands placed upon leaders / knowledge and wisdom / vision / courage / broad-mindedness / personality / organization skills, etc.

  这一论证点可以参考B类 `62` 的一些素材。

16. 社会 Every individual in a society has a responsibility to obey just laws and to disobey and resist `65` unjust laws. [solution]

社会所有成员都有义务遵守公正的法律，抵制不公正的法律。

Discuss the extent to which you agree or disagree with the claim and address the most compelling reasons and/or examples that could be used to challenge your position.

思路参考

【思路提示】

- 本题可以结合Condition展开，分别讨论不同程度、不同情况下的不公正法律应该如何对待。

【对于公正的法律】

- Laws must be absolutely obeyed if only they are fair, for laws are basic guideline on the behavior of citizens.

【对于不公正的法律，题目提出的方案有合理性吗？】

- The very foundation of a legal system is the idea of justice.
- Unjust laws should be fought against under some extreme circumstances.

【题目中对于不公正法律的处理方式有哪些问题？】

- ［从行为的前提来说］How to define just and unjust? People may have different criterion in their judgment.
- ［从行为的后果来说］Disobedience of law may result in social disturbance and chaos.
- ［从可行性来说］Disobedience and resistance of law might be infeasible for citizens.

【回应】【上述两方面有没有调和的可能？】

- 对于不公正的法律，我们应该根据具体情况区别对待。有些极端的、违反人类社会基本准则、甚至是邪恶的法律，公民应该尽其所能对抗并改变它；而对于只是有些瑕疵，或由于立法者考虑不周而导致损害特定人群利益的法律，我们应该通过合理、合法且有利于社会发展的方式对其加以修正，比如通过完善的立法程序、通过媒体监督，或反映社情民意来敦促立法者修改一些不合情理的法律条款。

---

17. 社会 People who are the most deeply committed to an idea or policy are also the most critical of

66 it. ［claim］

最忠于某一信念或政策的人也是对它最挑剔的。

Discuss the extent to which you agree or disagree with the statement and consider ways in which the statement might or might not hold true.

思路参考

【思路提示】

- 本题可以从对"idea"定义的理解来展开。对于信仰层面的"idea"，投身于其中的人们很少对之提出批判；而对于科技、社会、文化等其他领域的一般性概念、想法，则要分情况考虑。

【提出题目看法的理由可能是什么？】

- When people are committed to certain idea or policy, they often anticipate that the idea or policy is perfect. It is understandable that those people will be critical of it.

【题目的观点有合理性吗？】

- ［对于一般的社会层面的想法和政策］People who are committed to an idea or policy are often critical of it in hope of improving it and making it flawless.
- Individuals most firmly committed to an idea or policy are usually most knowledgeable on the subject, therefore are in the best position to understand and find the flaws and problems with the idea or policy.

【题目推理的前提存在问题吗？】

- 如果人们主张某种理念或政策是出于某些特殊的政治、社会、经济目的，甚至是为了欺瞒或蒙骗另外一些民众，那他们就未必会对这些理念提出批判。
- 忠于某一信念或政策的民众假如缺乏独立思考的能力和批判精神，则往往会对某种信念盲从和愚忠，因而也未必会提出挑剔或批判的意见。

【题目的观点有问题吗？】

- ［对于信仰层面］Firm commitment to a belief often implies utmost confidence in it. How can one have firm confidence in an idea or policy when one finds flaws, drawbacks, and problems within it?

- Sometimes the harshest criticism comes from people who oppose the idea or policy.

18. 认知 Claim: The best test of an argument is its ability to convince someone with an opposing viewpoint.

79 Reason: Only by being forced to defend an idea against the doubts and contrasting views of others does one really discover the value of that idea. [reasoning/solution]

观点：对论证的最好检验就是其说服持相反观点的人的能力。

理由：只有被迫与对某观点持怀疑态度和相反意见的人辩护该观点时，才能真正发现该观点的价值。

Discuss the extent to which you agree or disagree with the claim and the reason on which that claim is based.

思路参考

【题目的理由有道理吗？】

- The process of defending an idea urges us to further think over the idea, make deeper understanding of it, which could help us discover its real value.
- Doubts and contrasting views of others help one find flaws and problems of an idea, thereby helping us to improve it.

【题目的观点有道理吗？】

- An argument or idea will be of no value if it was proved entirely unconvincing.

【题目的理由有问题吗？】

- The value of an idea could be discovered through other methods, such as further research and study, introspection, etc.

【以上述理由推出题目观点有什么前提吗？】

- 以说服反方的能力来检验论证这一方法的有效性取决于提出相反观点的人的出发点和动机。如果对方质疑的出发点是善意的，是为了辨明真理和促进双方的认识，那么，题目的方案是有效的；但如果对方是恶意的挑衅，那么以说服对方的能力来检验论证就毫无意义。

19. 认知 The best test of an argument is the argument's ability to convince someone with an 146 opposing viewpoint. [solution]

对论证的最好检验就是其说服持相反观点的人的能力。

Discuss the extent to which you agree or disagree with the statement and consider ways in which the statement might or might not hold true.

思路参考

【提出题目观点的理由可能是什么？】

- One may discover the value of an argument when defending it against the doubts and contrasting views of others.

【题目观点有道理吗？】

- The process of defending an argument urges us to further think over it, make deeper understanding of it, and discover possible flaws or problems in it.
- An argument will be of no value if it was proved entirely unconvincing.

【题目检验论证的方法有问题吗？】

- ［从方法成立的前提来说］这种检验方式的有效性取决于提出相反观点的人的出发点和动机。如果对方质疑的出发点是善意的，是为了辨明真理和促进双方的认识，那么，题目的方案是有效的；但如果对方是恶意的挑衅，那么以说服对方的能力来检验论证就毫无意义。

【检验论证还有其他方式吗？】

- An argument could also be tested through other methods, such as further research and study, introspection, etc.

---

20. 认知 Critical judgment of work in any given field has little value unless it comes from someone 108 who is an expert in that field. [claim]

对于任何领域成果的评判除非来自该领域的专家，否则就没有什么价值。

Discuss the extent to which you agree or disagree with the statement and consider ways in which the statement might or might not hold true.

思路参考

【思路提示】

- 本题最好结合Domain展开，分别讨论对于不同领域成果的评价是否只能参考专家的意见。

【提出题目观点的理由可能是什么？】

- Due to experts' experience and expertise, their opinions are usually more valuable.

【题目的观点有合理性吗？】

- For the realm of some pure sciences, such as physics and astronomy, the work of researchers can be judged only by their peers. Outsiders usually have neither equipment nor ability to evaluate works in these fields.

【从上述理由推出观点有什么前提吗？】

- 专家的理论、观点应该是准确可信的，能够反映客观事物的发展规律的。然而我们知道，专家也是人，其观点、理论难免有一些错漏缺陷；另外，专家观点也只是一些假说，即在一定时期、一定条件下才能解释一些现象。因而真理并不一定完全掌握在专家手中。

【题目的观点有问题吗？】

- 对于其他领域的成果，未必只能由本领域专家评价。

  As for some social sciences, such as anthropology, the work in that field necessitates expertise from other fields.

  In business or management, the effectiveness of a strategy or the quality of a product can be judged by the market, consumers, and employees.

  In the realm of politics, the effectiveness of a decision can surely be evaluated by the general public.

---

21. 认知 Critical judgment of work in any given field has little value unless it comes from someone 110 who is an expert in that field. [claim]

对于任何领域成果的评判除非来自该领域的专家，否则就没有什么价值。

Discuss the extent to which you agree or disagree with the claim and address the most compelling reasons and/or examples that could be used to challenge your position.

思路参考

【提出题目观点的理由可能是什么？】

- Due to experts' experience and expertise, their opinions are usually more valuable.

【题目的观点有合理性吗? 】

- For the realm of some pure sciences, such as physics and astronomy, the work of researchers can be judged only by their peers. Outsiders usually have neither equipment nor ability to evaluate works in these fields.

【可能存在哪些相反观点? 】

- 专家也是人, 其观点、理论难免有一些错漏缺陷; 另外, 专家观点也只是一些假说, 即在一定时期、一定条件下才能解释一些现象。因而真理并不一定完全掌握在专家手中。
- 对于其他领域的成果, 未必只能由本领域专家评价。

  As for some social sciences, such as anthropology, the work in that field necessitates expertise from other fields.

  In business or management, the effectiveness of a strategy or the quality of a product can be judged by the market, consumers, and employees.

  In the realm of politics, the effectiveness of a decision can surely be evaluated by the general public.

【回应】

- 对于题目讨论的话题必须分情况论述: 对于有些纯科学领域, 领域外人士没有足够的专业知识、工具和方法来评价该领域的成果; 而对于有些交叉学科和社会领域, 其成果完全可以由非专业人士评价, 甚至有些领域的成果必须借鉴其他学科的知识才能够作出准确的评价。

Ⓖ Idealism and Pragmatism 理想与现实

1. **教育** Educational institutions have a responsibility to dissuade students from pursuing fields of
   ③ study in which they are unlikely to succeed. [claim→solution]
   教育机构有责任劝阻学生, 不使他们在他们不太可能成功的专业发展。

   Discuss the extent to which you agree or disagree with the claim and address the most compelling reasons and/or examples that could be used to challenge your position.

思路参考

【提出题目观点的目的可能是什么? 】

- 为了让学生获得适合自己的教育, 发挥特长, 从而使学生能更好地适应社会发展并做出成就。

【提出题目观点的理由可能是什么? 】

- Educational institutions and educators are more experienced in teaching students how to achieve better result of education, therefore could raise more valuable suggestions on their development.

【题目观点存在合理性吗? 】

- 每个学生的天分不一样, 强行让学生在自己并不擅长的领域发展不但会导致其学习效率低下, 甚至可能会使学习过程本身变得很痛苦。
- Educational institutions should encourage students to explore their real interests and advantages in the early stage of education, which are a critical catalyst for students' learning and further research.

【可能存在哪些相反观点? 】

- 学生, 特别是年龄比较小的学生, 还处在心智的成长和发展阶段, 因而即便教育机构在教育理论和经验方面有一定优势, 也未必能准确判断一名学生的真正潜质和未来的发展方向。完全由教育机构决定学生的发展方向可能会导致有些学生的潜在天赋得不到充分发展。

【回应】【要达到上述目的有没有其他途径? 】

- In choosing the field of study, educators should take into account the students' interests and desire of their own.

2. 教育 Educational institutions should dissuade students from pursuing fields of study in which
[35] they are unlikely to succeed. [claim→solution]

教育机构应该劝阻学生，不使他们在他们不太可能获得成功的专业发展。

Discuss your views on the policy and consider the possible consequences of implementing the policy.

思路参考

【提出题目观点的目的可能是什么？】

● 为了让学生获得适合自己的教育，发挥特长，从而使学生能更好地适应社会发展并做出成就。

【提出题目观点的理由可能是什么？】

● Educational institutions and educators are more experienced in teaching students how to achieve better result of education, therefore could raise more valuable suggestions on their development.

【实施上述政策可能有哪些良好结果？】

● 每个学生的天分不一样，强行让学生在自己并不擅长的领域发展不但会导致其学习效率低下，甚至可能会使学习过程本身变得很痛苦。因而在教育的初始阶段就帮助学生了解自身的特点，有助于学生将来做出更大的成就。

Educational institutions should encourage students to explore their real interests and advantages in the early stage of education, which are a critical catalyst for students' learning and further research.

【从上述理由足以推出题目观点吗？】

● 学生，特别是年龄比较小的学生，还处在心智的成长和发展阶段，因而即便教育机构在教育理论和经验方面有一定优势，也未必能准确判断一名学生的真正潜质和未来的发展方向。完全由教育机构决定学生的发展方向可能会导致有些学生的潜在天赋得不到充分发展。

【要达到上述目的有没有其他途径？】

● In choosing the field of study, educators should take the students' interests and desire of their own into account.

3. 教育 Educational institutions have a responsibility to dissuade students from pursuing fields of
[137] study in which they are unlikely to succeed. [claim→solution]

教育机构有责任劝阻学生，不使他们在他们不太可能获得成功的专业发展。

Discuss the extent to which you agree or disagree with the statement and consider ways in which the statement might or might not hold true.

思路参考

【提出题目观点的目的可能是什么？】

● 为了让学生获得适合自己的教育，发挥特长，从而使学生能更好地适应社会发展并做出成就。

【提出题目观点的理由可能是什么？】

● Educational institutions and educators are more experienced in teaching students how to achieve better result of education, therefore could raise more valuable suggestions on their development.

【题目观点存在合理性吗？】

● 每个学生的天分不一样，强行让学生在自己并不擅长的领域发展不但会导致其学习效率低下，甚至可能会使学习过程本身变得很痛苦。

● Educational institutions should encourage students to explore their real interests and advantages in the early stage of education, which are a critical catalyst for students' learning and further research.

- 学生，特别是年龄比较小的学生，还处在心智的成长和发展阶段，因而即便教育机构在教育理论和经验方面有一定优势，也未必能准确判断一名学生的真正潜质和未来的发展方向。完全由教育机构决定学生的发展方向可能会导致有些学生的潜在天赋得不到充分发展。

【要达到上述目的有没有其他途径？】

- In choosing the field of study, educators should take the students' interests and desire of their own into account.

---

4. **教育** Educational institutions should actively encourage their students to choose fields of study **15** that will prepare them for lucrative careers. [claim→comparison]

教育机构应积极鼓励学生选择能为他们提供赚钱职业的专业。

Discuss the extent to which you agree or disagree with the claim and address the most compelling reasons and/or examples that could be used to challenge your position.

思路参考

【和题目提出的做法相对的其他做法是什么？】

- 鼓励学生树立正确的价值观和目标，发掘自己的真正兴趣和特长，使之能更好地服务于社会发展的总体目标。

【鼓励学生选择有"钱途"的专业有合理性吗？】

- 在当前的商业社会，一定的经济基础是年轻人生存发展的必要条件。
- Undoubtedly, a lucrative career could bring young people material abundance and great fulfillment.

【可能存在哪些相反观点？】

［鼓励学生选择有"钱途"的专业存在什么问题？］

- But, greater emptiness will follow when the thirst for wealth is fulfilled; this could even lead people to misdeeds.
- Basing only on the profitability of that field when choosing fields of study will be no good for the true development of the students as well as for the overall well-being of a society.

［教育的真正目的是什么？］

- The primary goal of education should be the cultivation of the ability of critical thinking and logical reasoning, healthy personalities, and correct values. Jobs, profits, fames, achievements will be automatically guaranteed for students with these qualities.

［鼓励学生发掘兴趣特长、追求长远目标有哪些意义？］

- helpful for young people to achieve true greatness
- helpful for young people to overcome greater difficulties
- important for the well-being of the whole society

【回应】【追求长远目标在可行性方面有问题吗？】

- ［前提未必能保证］能树立正确的目标固然不错，但要树立正确的目标需要对自己充分全面的认识和对各个学科领域的了解。而对于学生来说，因为缺乏一定的人生阅历和经验，可能难以发现自己真正的优势并找到正确方向。
- ［从年轻人的客观特点看］年轻学生仍然处于人生的起步积累阶段，如果每天忙于生计可能会使他们无暇发展自己真正的兴趣和特长。

【思路提示】

〈略，参考 **51**〉

5. 教育 Educational institutions should actively encourage their students to choose fields of study
[135] that will prepare them for lucrative careers. [claim→comparison]

教育机构应积极鼓励学生选择能为他们提供赚钱职业的专业。

Discuss your views on the policy and consider the possible consequences of implementing the policy.

思路参考

【和题目提出的做法相对的其他做法是什么？】
- 鼓励学生树立正确的价值观和目标，发掘自己真正的兴趣和特长，使之能更好地服务于社会发展的总体目标。

【鼓励学生选择有"钱途"的专业有合理性吗？】
- 在当前的商业社会，一定的经济基础是年轻人生存发展的必要条件。
- Undoubtedly, a lucrative career could bring young people material abundance and great fulfillment.

【鼓励学生选择有"钱途"的专业会产生哪些不良后果？】
- Greater emptiness will follow when the thirst for wealth is fulfilled; this could even lead people to misdeeds.
- Basing only on the profitability of that field when choosing fields of study will be no good for the true development of the students as well as for the overall well-being of a society.

【鼓励学生发掘兴趣特长、追求长远目标有哪些意义？】
- helpful for young people to achieve true greatness
- helpful for young people to overcome greater difficulties
- important for the well-being of the whole society

【发散】
- The primary goal of education should be the cultivation of the ability of critical thinking and logical reasoning, healthy personalities, and correct values. Jobs, profits, fames, achievements will be automatically guaranteed for students with these qualities.

【思路提示】
〈略，参考 [51] 〉

6. 教育 Some people believe that college students should consider only their own talents and
[20] interests when choosing a field of study. Others believe that college students should base their choice of a field of study on the availability of jobs in that field. [comparison]

有些人认为大学生选专业时应只考虑其天分和兴趣。另外一些人认为大学生应从就业前景出发选择专业。

Discuss which view more closely aligns with your own position and address both of the views presented.

思路参考

【第一种观点有道理吗？】
- Interest is the best teacher for students' education.
- Basing on their own talents and interests when choosing the field of study could help students to attain greater academic achievements, to overcome greater difficulties, and to improve the well-being of the whole society.

【第一种观点有问题吗？】
- [从观点的前提和可行性来说] 在就业形势严峻、就业机会不充分的社会，仅凭天分和兴趣来选择专业似乎不太可行。

- 由于缺乏必要的阅历和经验，有些年轻学生在挖掘兴趣和天分方面存在一些困难；另一些学生在对自己兴趣和天分的认知方面可能会存在一定偏差，而且人的兴趣会随着时间的推移有所变化。因此，依靠兴趣和天分决定专业的选择可能存在一定的盲目性。

【第二种观点有道理吗？】
- 在当前的商业社会，一定的经济基础是年轻人生存发展的必要条件。

  Basing only on talents and interests when choosing the field of study, totally ignoring the pragmatic concerns, would be unrealistic for students to survive.
- Undoubtedly, a better career could bring young people material abundance and great fulfillment.

【第二种观点有问题吗？】
- ［参考第一种观点的合理性］

  Basing students' choice of the field of study only on the availability of jobs would be no good for students to achieve true greatness, and for the society to promote its general welfare.

【发散】
- The primary goal of education should be the cultivation of the ability of critical thinking and logical reasoning, healthy personalities, and correct values. Jobs, profits, fames, achievements will be automatically guaranteed for students with these qualities.

---

7. **教育** College students should base their choice of a field of study on the availability of jobs in
32 that field. ［claim→solution/comparison］

大学生应该从就业前景出发选择专业。

Discuss the extent to which you agree or disagree with the claim and address the most compelling reasons and/or examples that could be used to challenge your position.

思路参考

【题目的观点有合理性吗？】
- 在当前的商业社会，一定的经济基础是年轻人生存发展的必要条件。

  Totally ignoring the pragmatic concerns in students' choice of the field of study would be unrealistic for students to survive.
- A better career could bring young people material abundance and great fulfillment.
- 在就业形势严峻、就业机会不充分的社会，以就业作为选择专业的重要因素完全无可厚非。

【可能存在哪些相反观点？】

［从后果来说］
- Basing students' choice of the field of study only on the availability of jobs would be no good for students to achieve true greatness, and for the society to promote its general welfare.

［确定专业还有其他方法：根据学生的兴趣和天分来确定］
- Interest is the best teacher for students' education.
- Basing on their own talents and interests when choosing the field of study could help students to attain greater academic achievements, to overcome greater difficulties, and to improve the well-being of the whole society.

［从教育的主要目标来说］
- The primary goal of education should be the cultivation of the ability of critical thinking and logical reasoning, healthy personalities, and correct values. Jobs, profits, fames, achievements will be automatically guaranteed for students with these qualities.

【回应】

[根据兴趣和天分确定专业可能存在哪些问题？]

- 由于缺乏必要的阅历和经验，有些年轻学生在挖掘兴趣和天分方面存在一些困难；另一些学生在对自己兴趣和天分的认知方面可能会存在一定偏差，而且人的兴趣会随着时间的推移有所变化。因此，依靠兴趣和天分决定专业的选择可能存在一定的盲目性。

[各方面问题有没有调和的可能性？]

- 在保证教育基本目标的前提下，选择专业应该综合考虑就业前景和学生的兴趣和天分，不能单纯地只从某一方面考虑。

---

8. **教育** College students should base their choice of a field of study on the availability of jobs in **129** that field. [claim→solution/comparison]

   大学生应该从就业前景出发选择专业。

   Discuss the extent to which you agree or disagree with the recommendation and describe specific circumstances in which adopting the recommendation would or would not be advantageous.

思路参考

【题目的观点有合理性吗？】

- 在当前的商业社会，一定的经济基础是年轻人生存发展的必要条件。

   Totally ignoring the pragmatic concerns in students' choice of the field of study would be unrealistic for students to survive.

- A better career could bring young people material abundance and great fulfillment.

【题目的观点在什么情况下有意义？】

- 在就业形势严峻、就业机会不充分的社会，以就业作为选择专业的重要因素完全无可厚非。

【题目观点在什么情况下会有不利影响？】

- [从后果来说] Basing students' choice of the field of study only on the availability of jobs would be no good for students to achieve true greatness, and for the society to promote its general welfare.

- [从教育的主要目标来说] The primary goal of education should be the cultivation of the ability of critical thinking and logical reasoning, healthy personalities, and correct values. Jobs, profits, fames, achievements will be automatically guaranteed for students with these qualities.

【发散】

- 在保证教育基本目标的前提下，选择专业应该综合考虑就业前景和学生的兴趣和天分，不能单纯地只从某一方面考虑。

- Interest is the best teacher for students' education.

- Basing on their own talents and interests when choosing the field of study could help students to attain greater academic achievements, to overcome greater difficulties, and to improve the well-being of the whole society.

---

9. **教育** College students should be encouraged to pursue subjects that interest them rather than **39** the courses that seem most likely to lead to jobs. [comparison]

   应该鼓励学生学习他们感兴趣的学科，而不是看起来最可能找到工作的课程。

   Discuss the extent to which you agree or disagree with the recommendation and describe specific circumstances in which adopting the recommendation would or would not be advantageous.

【鼓励学生学习感兴趣的学科的理由可能是什么？】

- Interest is the best teacher for students' education.

【根据兴趣选择学习方向在什么情况下有意义？】

- ［从后果来说］Basing on their own talents and interests when choosing the field of study could help students to attain greater academic achievements, to overcome greater difficulties, and to improve the well-being of the whole society.

- Basing students' choice of the subjects of study on the availability of jobs would be no good for students to achieve true greatness, and for the society to promote its general welfare.

【根据兴趣选择学习方向在什么情况下可能有问题？】

- ［从观点的前提和可行性来说］在就业形势严峻、就业机会不充分的社会，仅凭兴趣来选择发展方向似乎不太可行。

- 由于缺乏必要的阅历和经验，有些年轻学生在挖掘兴趣方面存在一些困难；另一些学生在对自己兴趣的认知方面可能会存在一定偏差，而且人的兴趣会随着时间的推移有所变化。在这种情况下，依靠兴趣决定专业的选择可能存在一定的盲目性。

- ［从考虑就业的必要性来说］在当前的商业社会，一定的经济基础是年轻人生存发展的必要条件。

  Basing only on talents and interests when choosing the field of study, totally ignoring the pragmatic concerns, would be unrealistic for students to survive.

  A better career could bring young people material abundance and great fulfillment.

【发散】

- The primary goal of education should be the cultivation of the ability of critical thinking and logical reasoning, healthy personalities, and correct values. Jobs, profits, fames, achievements will be automatically guaranteed for students with these qualities.

- 在保证教育基本目标的前提下，选择专业应该综合考虑就业前景和学生的兴趣和天分，不能单纯地只从某一方面考虑。

---

10. 教育 Educational institutions should actively encourage their students to choose fields of study
98 in which jobs are plentiful. ［claim→comparison］

教育机构应积极鼓励学生选择就业前景理想的专业。

Discuss your views on the policy and consider the possible consequences of implementing the policy.

【提出题目政策的理由可能是什么？】

- 在当前的商业社会，一定的经济基础是年轻人生存发展的必要条件。

  Totally ignoring the pragmatic concerns in students' choice of the field of study would be unrealistic for students to survive.

【题目政策有合理性吗？】

- 在就业形势严峻、就业机会不充分的社会，以就业作为选择专业的重要因素完全无可厚非。

【采纳题目政策会产生哪些正面效果？】

- A better career could bring young people material abundance and great fulfillment, providing material base for them to pursue subjects in which they are interested.

【采纳题目政策会产生哪些负面效果？】

- Basing students' choice of the field of study only on the availability of jobs would be no good for students to achieve true greatness, and for the society to promote its general welfare.

【发散】

- The primary goal of education should be the cultivation of the ability of critical thinking and logical reasoning, healthy personalities, and correct values. Jobs, profits, fames, achievements will be automatically guaranteed for students with these qualities.

- 在保证教育基本目标的前提下，选择专业应该综合考虑就业前景和学生的兴趣和天分，不能单纯地只从某一方面考虑。

---

11. 教育 Educational institutions should actively encourage their students to choose fields of study `136` in which jobs are plentiful. [claim→comparison]

教育机构应积极鼓励学生选择就业前景理想的专业。

Discuss the extent to which you agree or disagree with the claim and address the most compelling reasons and / or examples that could be used to challenge your position.

思路参考

〈略，参考 `32` 〉

---

12. 教 育 Claim: When planning courses, educators should take into account the interests and `40` suggestions of their students.

Reason: Students are more motivated to learn when they are interested in what they are studying. [reasoning→solution]

观点：在安排课程的时候，教育者应考虑学生的兴趣和建议。

理由：当学生对所学的东西感兴趣时会更有动力。

Discuss the extent to which you agree or disagree with the claim and the reason on which that claim is based.

思路参考

【题目的理由有合理性吗？】

- Interest is the best teacher for students' education.

【题目的推理过程有合理性吗？】

- Students will be more motivated to study when the courses interest them.

【题目的观点有合理性吗？】

- An educational system that could satisfy all individual demands and interests is a perfect one. It will help students to fully develop their potential and talent.

【题目的理由有问题吗？】

- 由于缺乏必要的阅历和经验，有些年轻学生在挖掘兴趣方面存在一些困难；另一些学生在对自己兴趣的认知方面可能会存在一定偏差，而且人的兴趣会随着时间的推移有所变化。在这种情况下，依靠兴趣决定课程的选择可能存在一定的盲目性。

【题目的观点有问题吗？】

- [从教育的主要目标来说] The primary goal of education should be the cultivation of the ability of critical thinking and logical reasoning, healthy personalities. Overemphasis on individual interest and demand will work against cultivating students to be well-rounded person.

而且，各学科知识是互相交融的，对各领域知识的全面了解有助于学生对所学内容融会贯通。这一点论述可以参考E类 `143` 的一些思路和素材。

- ［从可行性来说］Planning courses specifically according to every student's interest and demand would be unfeasible, due to the limited educational resources.

【发散】

- 学校在提供保证学生获得基本能力和知识、满足基本教育目标的必修课的基础上，应该尽量给有不同兴趣和需求的学生提供各学科、各领域的选修课程。

---

13. 教育 Educators should take students' interests into account when planning the content of the `90` courses they teach. ［claim→solution］

教育者在安排教学内容的时候应该把学生的兴趣考虑在内。

Discuss the extent to which you agree or disagree with the recommendation and describe specific circumstances in which adopting the recommendation would or would not be advantageous.

思路参考

【提出题目观点的理由可能是什么？】

- Interest is the best teacher for students' education.
- Students will be more motivated to study when the courses interest them.

【题目观点在什么情况下有合理性？】

- An educational system that could satisfy all individual demands and interests is a perfect one. It will help students to fully develop their potential and talent.

【题目观点在什么情况下可能有问题？】

- ［从得出观点的前提来说］由于缺乏必要的阅历和经验，有些年轻学生在挖掘兴趣方面存在一些困难；另一些学生在对自己兴趣的认知方面可能会存在一定偏差，而且人的兴趣会随着时间的推移有所变化。在这种情况下，依靠兴趣决定课程的选择可能存在一定的盲目性。
- ［从教育的主要目标来说］The primary goal of education should be the cultivation of the ability of critical thinking and logical reasoning, healthy personalities. Overemphasis on individual interest and demand will work against cultivating students to be well-rounded person.

  而且，各学科知识是互相交融的，对各领域知识的全面了解有助于学生对所学内容融会贯通。这一点论述可以参考E类 `143` 的一些思路和素材。
- ［从可行性来说］Planning courses specifically according to every student's interest and demand would be unfeasible, due to the limited educational resources.

【发散】

- 学校在提供保证学生获得基本能力和知识、满足基本教育目标的必修课的基础上，应该尽量给有不同兴趣和需求的学生提供各学科、各领域的选修课程。

---

14. 教育 Educators should find out what students want included in the curriculum and then offer it `47` to them. ［claim］

教育者应该找出课程当中学生希望学习的内容，并把这些课程提供给学生。

Discuss the extent to which you agree or disagree with the recommendation and describe specific circumstances in which adopting the recommendation would or would not be advantageous.

【提出题目观点的理由可能是什么？】

- Interest is the best teacher for students' education. Students will be more motivated to study when the courses interest them and meet their demands.

【题目观点在什么情况下有合理性？】

- An educational system that could satisfy all individual demands and interests is a perfect one. It will help students to fully develop their potential and talent.

【题目观点在什么情况下可能有问题？】

- ［从得出观点的前提来说］由于缺乏必要的阅历和经验，有些年轻学生在挖掘自己的天分和兴趣方面存在一些困难；另一些学生在对自己天分和兴趣的认知方面可能会存在一定偏差，而且人的兴趣会随着时间的推移有所变化。在这种情况下，依靠学生的需求决定课程的选择可能存在一定的盲目性。

- ［从教育的主要目标来说］The primary goal of education should be the cultivation of the ability of critical thinking and logical reasoning, healthy personalities. Overemphasis on students' demand will work against cultivating students to be well-rounded person.

  而且，各学科知识是互相交融的，对各领域知识的全面了解有助于学生对所学内容融会贯通。这一点论述可以参考E类 143 的一些思路和素材。

- ［从可行性来说］Planning courses to cater every student's demand would be unfeasible, due to the limited educational resources.

【发散】

学校在提供保证学生获得基本能力和知识、满足基本教育目标的必修课的基础上，应该尽量给有不同需求的学生提供各学科、各领域的选修课程。

---

15. 教育 Claim: Colleges and universities should specify all required courses and eliminate elective
142 courses in order to provide clear guidance for students.

Reason: College students—like people in general—prefer to follow directions rather than make their own decisions. ［reasoning→comparison/solution］

观点：大学应该明确指定所有必修课，并取消选修课来为学生提供更清晰的指导。

理由：大学生——和普通人一样——倾向于遵从指导而不是自己作决定。

Discuss the extent to which you agree or disagree with the claim and the reason on which that claim is based.

【题目的理由有合理性吗？】

- It is true that under certain circumstances people prefer to follow directions from others, due to their inertia or lack of ability of critical reasoning.

【题目的观点有合理性吗？】

- A clear-presented, appropriate and correct arrangement of courses could help students to understand the objectives of education.

【题目的理由有问题吗？】

- Most people would prefer the freedom of choice, particularly when choosing an education and the future paths of their careers.

【题目推理过程的前提有问题吗？】

- ［题目推理的前提：学校有能力制定绝对正确的教学指导］

  Although professors and other educators are more experienced and informed in education, they may not know what the students really want and what is best for them.

The so-called clear guidance may not be completely suitable and correct for helping students to fully develop their potential and talent and achieving the real goal of education.

【题目的推理过程有问题吗？】

- 即使学生希望学校给出明确指导：

  The proposal raised by the speaker might not be the best or the only solution.

  学校应该明确的是教育的根本目标，而不是具体到每门课程的安排。因此，学校在提供保证学生获得基本能力和知识、满足基本教育目标的必修课的基础上，应该尽量给有不同需求的学生提供各学科、各领域的选修课程。

【题目的观点有问题吗？】

- ［从教育的主要目标来说］The primary goal of education should be the cultivation of the ability of critical thinking and logical reasoning, healthy personalities. A rigid curriculum will work against cultivating students to be well-rounded person.

  而且，各学科知识是互相交融的，对于各领域知识的全面了解有助于学生对所学内容融会贯通，做出更大的成就。这一点论述可以参考E类 **143** 的一些思路和素材。

---

16. 社会 If a goal is worthy, then any means taken to attain it are justifiable. ［claim→reasoning］

53 如果目标值得争取，那么，任何实现它的手段都是合理的。

Discuss the extent to which you agree or disagree with the statement and consider ways in which the statement might or might not hold true.

思路参考

【思路提示】

- 本题可以从Domain的角度来举例论证，讨论不同领域目标的实现是否需要考虑手段的合理性。

【题目的观点有合理性吗？】

- ［从必要性来说］If a goal is in the interest of the entire human race, and will benefit the general welfare, it is necessary to make effort to attain it.

【题目推理的前提有问题吗？】

- How to judge whether a goal is really worthy? What may be worthy for one person may not be equally worthy for another, or even will be harmful for others.

【题目的推理过程有问题吗？】

- Even if a goal is truly worthy, it does not imply that one can attain it through whatever means.

  Rules and limitations are necessary lest individual behavior harms the interest of the whole society.

【题目的观点有问题吗？】

- ［从后果来说］Persisting in certain goals one defines as worthy, totally ignoring the negative effects of the means one takes, usually lead people down the wrong path to destruction.

【发散】

- Some universal value must be set and keep in mind when evaluating if a goal is truly worthy.
- To what extent certain means are justifiable should be determined case-by-case, through weighing the benefits of attaining the goal against the costs, or harm that might generate along the way.

17. 社会 Claim: Many problems of modern society cannot be solved by laws and the legal system.

89 Reason: Laws cannot change what is in people's hearts or minds. [reasoning→solution]

观点：很多现代社会的问题无法通过律法系统解决。

理由：法律无法改变人们内心和思想中的一些东西。

Discuss the extent to which you agree or disagree with the claim and the reason on which that claim is based.

思路参考

【题目的理由有道理吗？】

- Moral behavior cannot be legislated.
- ［从可行性来说］It is unfeasible to regulate every aspect of moral behavior through legislation. Furthermore, the enforcement of such law, if any, would be extremely difficult.
- There are inherent weaknesses in human nature, such as greed, pride, and sloth, which cannot be changed by external condition.

【题目的推理过程和观点有道理吗？】

- Problems related to human nature, such as war, oppression, exploitation, deceiving, violence, etc., cannot be solved merely by laws.

【题目的理由有问题吗？】

- A perfect legal system could be guidance for people to form correct values and appropriate behaviors.

【题目的推理过程有问题吗？】

- Although laws cannot change human nature, rules and limitations are still necessary in preventing further problems or even disasters.

【题目的观点有问题吗？】

- Although the legal systems of many countries are far from perfect, they have indeed solved many social problems successfully.

18. 社会 Unfortunately, in contemporary society, creating an appealing image has become more

93 important than the reality or truth behind that image. [claim→comparison]

很遗憾，在当代社会，塑造吸引人的形象远比形象背后的本体和真相重要。

Discuss the extent to which you agree or disagree with the statement and consider ways in which the statement might or might not hold true.

思路参考

【思路提示】

- 本题可以从Domain的角度展开分析和举例，分别讨论对于不同领域（如政治、文化、经济、科研等）的人来说形象和本质的重要程度。也可以讨论对于不同对象（如人、团体、产品、服务等）来说形象和本质的重要程度。

【提出题目观点的理由可能是什么？】

- ［从重要性来说］The first impression of an object is critical for one to accept the object.
  An appealing image could make the object more attractive, and make people to be ready to accept it.

【题目的观点有合理性吗？】

- In many societies, people often pay more attention to the appearance of, whether a person, a product, or a service.

【从上述理由足以推出题目观点吗？】

- The product, service or person will ultimately fail if there is no substance behind the image.

【题目的观点有问题吗？】

- The attention to appearance often reveals an inappropriate value system and mentally immaturity of the whole society.
- The significance of image wanes considerably in the long term.

【发散】

- 要让整个社会明白内在实质的重要性，而非只注重光鲜亮丽的外表，需要全社会确立和推广正确的价值体系，而这一点反过来也会促进社会的长远发展。

---

19. 社会 Some people believe that corporations have a responsibility to promote the well-being of
    130 the societies and environments in which they operate. Others believe that the only responsibility
    of corporations, provided they operate within the law, is to make as much money as possible.
    [comparison]
    一些人认为企业有责任提升所在社会和环境的福祉。另一些人认为公司在合法运营的前提下唯一的责任就是尽可能多地赚钱。

    Discuss which view more closely aligns with your own position and address both of the views presented.

思路参考

【第一种观点有合理性吗？】

- ［从必要性来说］As a social member, a corporation should maintain certain ethical standard, and must ensure that their process of making profits will not harm the general welfare of the society.
- ［从后果来说］A corporation can project a positive image through taking social responsibility, thereby benefiting the company in the long run.

【第一种观点有问题吗？】

- ［从后果来说］Imposing on businesses undue duties to the society will add to business expenses and lower profits, thereby preventing the business from creating more jobs and providing products and services with low prices.

【第二种观点有道理吗？】

- The primary goal of a corporation is to make profits. A corporation has a duty to maximize shareholder value.

【第二种观点有问题吗？】

- No legal system is flawless. There must be some loopholes in laws. Mere compliance with laws is not enough for operating a company.
- ［从后果来说］Acceptance of the view would lead some corporations to put its profits before the well-being of the general society.
- Regarding profits as the only goal of a company, totally ignoring social responsibility will be detrimental to the image of that company, which will in turn affect its profitability in the long run.

【两种观点有调和的可能性吗？】

- 首先，承担社会责任和获取利润并不矛盾。一个企业可以在维持企业道德准则、造福社会的同时获得发展和利润。
- 其次，坚持企业道德、造福社会和环境能够提升一家企业的形象，从而进一步提升企业的盈利能力。
- 再次，作为企业生存和发展的大环境，社会总体利益的提升也有助于企业的长远发展，形成良性循环。社会大环境遭到破坏之后，企业自身即使能够获取再多的利润也没有任何意义。

20. **社会** It is more harmful to compromise one's own beliefs than to adhere to them. [comparison]

141 妥协自己的信念比坚持信念更加有害。

Discuss the extent to which you agree or disagree with the statement and consider ways in which the statement might or might not hold true.

思路参考

【思路提示】

- 本题最好从Condition的角度来展开，即从不同情况下的信念出发，讨论坚持信念的重要性。如果信念符合客观规律和普遍价值，就值得我们坚守；但如果所谓信念只是一种个人化的固执己见，不符合客观规律，甚至对社会有害，那么，则应该及时纠正和妥协。

【坚持信念有什么意义？】

- ［从必要性来说］It is necessary for one's moral integrity.
- It could help us to achieve our goals and to overcome difficulties.

【坚持信念有什么问题吗？】

- ［从前提来说］If one's belief could represent truths and correct values, then it is worthy adhering to. But if the so-called belief is biased or fallacious, then adhering to it will lead to disastrous result.
- ［从后果来说］Undue adherence to certain belief would result in the lack of flexibility, which would be harmful for achieving one's purpose.

【妥协自己的信念有什么意义？】

- Other people's opinion and feedback could help us to make correct judgment and decision.
- It could prevent us from going too far in the wrong direction.

【妥协自己的信念有什么问题？】

- One who is easily and quickly influenced by the opinion of others will accomplish little.

21. **认知** True success can be measured primarily in terms of the goals one sets for oneself.

144 [solution]

真正的成功主要可以通过人们为自己设定的目标来衡量。

Discuss the extent to which you agree or disagree with the statement and consider ways in which the statement might or might not hold true.

思路参考

【提出题目观点的理由可能是什么？】

- Success is a process of unceasingly exceeding oneself. To some extent, success can be defined as achieving one's goals.

【题目观点有合理性吗？】

- One who is easily and quickly influenced by external values and opinions will accomplish little.

【题目观点有问题吗？】

- 每个人的价值观、世界观不可避免地存在一定的局限性，因而，对于自己设定的目标是否正确、是否值得努力可能缺乏公正、客观的判断能力。完全通过自己设定的目标衡量成功会过于主观。

【衡量成功能不能通过其他手段？】

- other people's evaluation and feedback:

  These could help us to evaluate whether our goals are correct and worthy.
- society's external reward:

Social reward is an approval for individual success, and could motivate people to achieve greater goals.

【发散】

- ［从真正成功的定义来说］True success should be measured by one's contribution on the development and progress of the entire human race, not individual fulfillment.

Ⓗ Convention and Innovation 传统与创新

1. **社会** Claim: In any field—business, politics, education, government—those in power should step down after five years.

Reason: The surest path to success for any enterprise is revitalization through new leadership.

［reasoning/solution］

观点：在任何领域——商业、政治、教育、政府——当权者都应该在5年以后退位。

理由：任何领域成功的最可靠途径是通过新的领导力。

Discuss the extent to which you agree or disagree with the claim and the reason on which that claim is based.

思路参考

【思路提示】

- 本题可以结合Domain来展开分析和举例，分别讨论不同领域（如政治、军事、商业、教育、科技等）要求当权者定期退位的合理性和必要性。此外，也可以结合Condition来展开，讨论要求当权者定期退位的前提条件。对题目的观点不能一刀切：假如前任当权者非常受人们爱戴和尊敬，也没有更合适的人选，那么强行采取题目的行为似乎没有必要；而如果前任当权者在任期内并没有表现出优秀的领导才能，或是对于某些发展变化较快的领域，采取题目的措施就存在合理性了。

【题目的理由有道理吗？】

- ［从后果来说］New leaders could bring new ideas of leading and managing, and could ensure the enterprise keeping up with the trends of the times.
- ［从合理性来说］New leaders can usually lead the enterprise without the constraints of established habits and attitudes, thereby ensuring the development and innovation of the enterprise.

【题目的观点有道理吗？】

- Success, fame and wealth may lead the leaders to corrupt and abuse their power. Long term tenure in leading positions may impede healthy development of an enterprise.

【题目的理由有问题吗？】

- ［要保证成功除了当权者更迭还有没有其他方法？］

The quality of the team, the communication and coordination between leaders and subordinates, and the management system are also key factors for the success of any enterprise.

【题目的推理过程有问题吗？】

- Granted that the change of leadership is necessary, are five years an appropriate period?

对于不同领域、不同企业，当权者的更迭周期似乎不应一概而论，而应根据运营情况和环境的变化具体考虑。

【题目的观点有问题吗？】

- The experience, knowledge, and connections of a reigning leader are equally important for the development of an enterprise.

- [从后果来说] Frequent replacement of leader might be harmful for subordinates to adapt to working conditions, for carrying out consistent policies, for the sustained development of the enterprise, and for achieving long term goals.

【总结】

- 当权者的经验可以保证一个团体不出现重大失误，其建立的关系、领导方法可以保证团体的效率和发展；而新当权者能带来创新和活力。想要确保成功应该能够兼收并蓄两方面的长处，而不是对任期或其他方面进行不加区分的硬性规定。
- 特殊情况下，一些能力出众、受下属以及社会爱戴和尊重的当权者，不一定非要受固定任期的限制。
- 保证领导层活力还可以通过其他途径，比如对当权者定期培训或建立完善的监督制约机制。
- 保证企业或团体成功也可以通过其他途径，比如建立完善有效的人才招募机制吸引高级人才、建立完善的沟通管理机制提高运行效率等等。

---

2. **社会** In any profession—business, politics, education, government—those in power should step `111` down after five years. [claim→solution]

在任何领域——商业、政治、教育、政府——当权者应该在5年后退位。

Discuss the extent to which you agree or disagree with the claim and address the most compelling reasons and/or examples that could be used to challenge your position.

思路参考

【思路提示】

〈略，参考 **8** 〉

【提出题目观点的理由可能是什么？】

- [从后果来说] New leaders could bring new ideas of leading and managing, and could ensure the enterprise keeping up with the trends of the times.
- Success, fame and wealth may lead the leaders to corrupt and abuse their power. Long term tenure in leading positions may impede healthy development of an enterprise.

【题目的观点有合理性吗？】

- New leaders can usually lead the enterprise without the constraints of established habits and attitudes, thereby ensuring the development and innovation of the enterprise.

【可能存在哪些不同看法？】

- Granted that the change of leadership is necessary, are five years an appropriate period?
  对于不同领域、不同企业，当权者的更迭周期不应一概而论，而应根据运营情况和环境的变化具体考虑。
- The experience, knowledge, and connections of a reigning leader are equally important for the development of an enterprise.
- [从后果来说] Frequent replacement of leader might be harmful for subordinates to adapt to working conditions, for carrying out consistent policies, for the sustained development of the enterprise, and for achieving long term goals.

【回应】

- 当权者的经验可以保证一个团体不出现重大失误，其建立的关系、领导方法可以保证团体的效率和发展；而新当权者能带来创新和活力。想要确保成功应该能够兼收并蓄两方面的长处，而不是对任期或其他方面进行不加区分的硬性规定。
- 特殊情况下，一些能力出众、受下属以及社会爱戴和尊重的当权者，不一定非要受固定任期的限制。

- 保证领导层活力还可以通过其他途径，比如对当权者定期培训或建立完善的监督制约机制。
- 保证企业或团体成功也可以通过其他途径，比如建立完善有效的人才招募机制吸引高级人才、建立完善的沟通管理机制提高运行效率等。

---

3. 社会 In any field—business, politics, education, government—those in power should be
149 required to step down after five years. [claim→comparison]

在任何领域——商业、政治、教育、政府——当权者应该在5年后退位。

Discuss your views on the policy and consider the possible consequences of implementing the policy.

思路参考

【思路提示】

〈略，参考 **8** 〉

【提出题目政策的理由可能是什么？】

- Success, fame and wealth may lead the leaders to corrupt and abuse their power. Long term tenure in leading positions may impede healthy development of an enterprise.

【采纳题目政策可能有哪些正面效果？】

- New leaders could bring new ideas of leading and managing, and could ensure the enterprise keeping up with the trends of the times.
- New leaders can usually lead the enterprise without the constraints of established habits and attitudes, thereby ensuring the development and innovation of the enterprise.

【题目的推理过程有问题吗？】

- Granted that the change of leadership is necessary, are five years an appropriate period?

  对于不同领域、不同企业，当权者的更迭周期不应一概而论，而应根据运营情况和环境的变化具体考虑。

【采纳题目政策可能导致哪些不良后果？】

- The experience, knowledge, and connections of a reigning leader are equally important for the development of an enterprise.
- Frequent replacement of leader might be harmful for subordinates to adapt to working conditions, for carrying out consistent policies, for the sustained development of the enterprise, and for achieving long term goals.

【总结】

- 特殊情况下，一些能力出众、受下属以及社会爱戴和尊重的当权者，不一定非要受固定任期的限制。
- 当权者的经验可以保证一个团体不出现重大失误，其建立的关系、领导方法可以保证团体的效率和发展；而新当权者能带来创新和活力。想要确保成功应该能够兼收并蓄两方面的长处，而不是对任期或其他方面进行不加区分的硬性规定。保证领导层活力还可以通过其他途径，比如对当权者定期培训、建立完善的监督制约机制等。
- The quality of the team, the communication and coordination between leaders and subordinates, and the management system are also key factors for the success of any enterprise.

  因而保证企业或团体成功也可以通过其他途径，比如建立完善有效的人才招募机制吸引高级人才、建立完善的沟通管理机制提高运行效率等。

4. **认知** In any field of endeavor, it is impossible to make a significant contribution without first being strongly influenced by past achievements within that field. [claim/solution]

9

在任何领域，如不首先受到该领域以往成果的强烈影响是不可能做出重大成就的。

Discuss the extent to which you agree or disagree with the statement and consider ways in which the statement might or might not hold true.

思路参考

【思路提示】

- 本题一般要结合Domain展开，分别讨论不同领域（如社会科学、自然科学、文化、艺术、教育等）要取得进步是否一定要受到以往成果的影响。

【提出题目观点的理由可能是什么？】

- In most fields, success is a step-by-step process. Former achievements provide foundation for future progress.

【题目观点有合理性吗？】

- 可以从自然科学、社会科学、政治、文化等方面举例说明以往成果对于该领域进步的作用。

【题目观点有问题吗？】

- [从不同领域来说]对于有些领域，特别是艺术方面的进步，更重要的是天分和灵感，这些领域的以往成就对未来发展的影响不是很大。
- 有些成就的意义就在于推翻了以往的陈旧观点（比如日心说、重力理论、相对论等）。
- Some discoveries are purely accidental, and have nothing to do with former establishments.

  这一点可以参考D类 56 的一些思路和素材。
- Limitations set by existing experiences and theories will sometimes impede creative activities.

【发散】

- [要做出成就有没有其他途径或条件？]

  Talents, imagination, and inspiration are also essential for making achievements.
- 以往的成就需要有选择性、有批判性地借鉴和吸收，同时也需要自身有创新意识。两者结合才能取得重大成就。

5. **教育** Formal education tends to restrain our minds and spirits rather than set them free. [claim/comparison]

17

正规教育趋向于限制我们的思想和精神而不是解放它们。

Discuss the extent to which you agree or disagree with the statement and consider ways in which the statement might or might not hold true.

思路参考

【思路提示】

- 本题可以结合Condition来展开分析，讨论在不同地区、不同情况下的正规教育体系有没有束缚思想和精神。假如教育制度和体系是开放的，符合学生心智发展的客观规律，那么正规教育未必一定限制学生思想；但如果教育的目标和方式有问题，比如应试教育和填鸭式教育，则有可能束缚学生的思想。

【提出题目观点的理由可能是什么？】

- Some contents of formal education, such as learning of common knowledge and basic skills, seem dull and tedious.
- Some educational systems tend to overemphasize memorizing facts and knowledge.

【题目观点有合理性吗？】

- ［从教育的前提和目标来说］The cultivation of the ability of critical thinking, logical reasoning, problem solving, and universal values might be more important than acquiring knowledge for college-education. An educational system which ignores the cultivation of these abilities may restrain students' creativity.

【题目观点有问题吗？】

- ［从必要性来说］Formal education provides students with basic skills, methodologies and knowledge, which are foundations for students' future development.
- An open and enlightened educational system, with appropriate goals and values of education, will promote students' mental and spiritual development.

【发散】

- 能否创新和进步更关键的是取决于学生自身的思考能力和学习意愿。
- 正规教育在给学生提供必要的基础知识技能方面是必须的，但我们也必须对正规教育体制的目标和方式不断加以完善和改进，使之符合人类社会发展的需求并能激发学生对人生的探索和思考。

---

6. **教育** Some people believe that the purpose of education is to free the mind and the spirit. 68 Others believe that formal education tends to restrain our minds and spirits rather than set them free. [comparison]

一些人认为教育的目的是解放思想和灵魂。另一些人认为正规教育趋向于限制我们的思想和灵魂而不是解放它们。

Discuss which view more closely aligns with your own position and address both of the views presented.

思路参考

【思路提示】

〈略，参考 17 〉

【第一种观点有合理性吗？】

- ［从合理性来说］One of the purposes of education is to enlighten students mentally and spiritually.
- ［从后果来说］Enlightenment of mankind could ensure true progress, and promote the general welfare of human being.

【第一种观点有问题吗？】

- ［从教育的其他功能来说］Formal education provides students with basic skills, methodologies and knowledge, which are foundations for students' future development.

【第二种观点有合理性吗？】

- Some contents of formal education, such as learning of common knowledge and basic skills, seem dull and tedious.
- Some educational systems tend to overemphasize memorizing facts and knowledge.
- ［从教育的前提和目标来说］The cultivation of the ability of critical thinking, logical reasoning, problem solving, and universal values might be more important than acquiring knowledge for college-education. An educational system which ignores the cultivation of these abilities may restrain students' creativity.

【第二种观点有问题吗？】

- An open and enlightened educational system, with appropriate goals and values of education, will promote students' mental and spiritual development.

【总结】

- 题目中的两种观点其实并不互斥。教育的目标之一确实是启蒙和解放思想，但这并不排除在现实中有些教育体系并不能实现这一目标。

- 正规教育对于为学生提供必要的基础知识技能是必须的，不能因为基础理论和基本技能的训练过程枯燥就否定它的意义。但我们也必须对正规教育体制的目标和教学方式不断加以完善和改进，使之符合人类社会发展的需求并能激发学生对人生的探索和思考。
- 另外，能否创新和进步更关键的是取决于学生自身的思考能力和学习意愿。

---

7. **认知** In any field of inquiry, the beginner is more likely than the expert to make important **27** contributions. [comparison]

在任何领域的探索中，新手比专家更有可能作出重大贡献。

Discuss the extent to which you agree or disagree with the statement and consider ways in which the statement might or might not hold true.

思路参考

【思路提示】

- 本题可以结合Domain或Condition来展开和举例，分别讨论在不同领域和不同学科中，新手做出成就的可能性和专家的必要性。此外，本题在论证时可以参考D类 **105** 的一些思路和素材。

【新手作出更大贡献的原因可能是什么？】

- Beginners, without the constraints of established habits and attitudes, are usually more imaginative and innovative, which could help them break previous rules and limitations.
- Beginners often try new things with intense curiosity and great courage, therefore they are more progressive.
- Beginners are often motivated by the willing of achieving success and becoming famous, therefore they are more efficient.

【新手在工作中的问题是什么？】

- Ideas of beginners who lack experience and expertise often fall into whimsicality or even fallacy. Their endeavors may turn into unpractical and unrealistic actions.
- 有些研究周期比较长的学科，其研究过程有很强的连贯性和延续性，通常需要长年的研究观察积累才能得到成果，这些领域的发现和突破往往是本领域的专家才能做出的。

【专家的经验和知识有重要性吗？】

- The experience, expertise, and in-depth views of experts are often key factors of discoveries and achievements.
- In most fields, achievement is a step-by-step process. The experience, expertise, and in-depth views of experts provide foundation for future progress.

【过分依赖专家的问题是什么？】

- Limitations set by existing experience and habits will sometimes impede creative activities.

【总结】

- 在一般领域中，新手的创新探索精神和专家的经验知识都是很重要的。仅仅倚重其中一方不利于做出重大成就——仅仅依靠新手会使研究探索过程存在很大的偶然性和随机性，而过分依靠专家又容易禁锢想象力和创造力。因此，要获得进步应该把两方面优势有效结合。

---

8. **认知** The main benefit of the study of history is to dispel the illusion that people living now are **57** significantly different from people who lived in earlier times. [solution]

研究历史的主要意义在于消除现代人和古代人明显不同的错觉。

Discuss the extent to which you agree or disagree with the statement and consider ways in which the statement might or might not hold true.

【思路提示】

- 本题可以结合Period和Domain来展开举例,分别讨论不同领域在不同时期的变化。

【提出题目观点的理由可能是什么?】

- Some basic human nature, such as desire, envy, greed, fear and other foibles, has remained constant over time.

【题目的观点有合理性吗?】

- The study of history could help us to discover the similarities between the past and the present. Many problems of human society（such as equality, oppression, exploitation, war, etc.）occur repeatedly merely in different forms.
- ［从后果来说］The cognition of this invariability could help us understand and be more tolerant of others, as well as develop compassionate responses to the problems and failings of others. These would be beneficial to how we live as a society.

【题目的观点有问题吗?】

- Many aspects of human lives, such as lifestyle, values, custom, culture, belief, etc., have changed significantly.
- Even the same kind of problem, for example, conflicts and wars, differs greatly in its form, process, and consequence in different time periods.
- An awareness of these evolutions helps us formulate informed, comprehensive, and enlightened values and ideals for our society.

【历史研究还有其他意义吗?】

- Learning about the stories of great persons inspires us to similar accomplishments and provides us precious experience about success.
- Learning about mistakes of past societies helps us avoiding similar ones.
- Learning about cultural heritage fosters a healthy sense of self and interest in preserving art and other cultural artifacts.

---

9. **认知** Knowing about the past cannot help people to make important decisions today. [claim]

74 了解过去并不能帮助人们在今天作出重要决策。

Discuss the extent to which you agree or disagree with the statement and consider ways in which the statement might or might not hold true.

【思路提示】

- 本题可以结合Domain来展开举例,分别讨论不同领域过去的经验对今天的借鉴作用。

【提出题目观点的理由可能是什么?】

- Many aspects of human lives, such as lifestyle, values, custom, culture, belief, etc., have changed significantly.
- Even the same kind of problem, for example, conflicts and wars, differs greatly in its form, process, and consequence in different time periods.

【从上述理由足以推出题目观点吗?】

- An awareness of these evolutions helps us formulate informed, comprehensive, and enlightened values and ideals for our society.

尽管社会生活很多方面都发生了变化，过去的经验不能直接用于今天；但对这些变化的研究和了解有助于我们从更全面的角度解决当下的社会问题。

【推出题目观点的前提存在问题吗？】

- Some basic human nature, such as desire, envy, greed, fear and other foibles, has remained constant over time.

【题目的观点存在问题吗？】

- ［从后果来说］The cognition of this invariability could help us understand and be more tolerant of others, as well as develop compassionate responses to the problems and failings of others. These would be beneficial to how we live as a society.

- The study of history provides us important references and experience for individuals and societies:
Learning about the stories of great persons inspires us to similar accomplishments and provides us precious experience about success.
Learning about mistakes of past societies helps us avoiding similar ones.
Learning about cultural heritage fosters a healthy sense of self and interest in preserving art and other cultural artifacts.

【总结】

- 研究过去为我们未来的发展提供了经验，但不能不加鉴别地完全照搬。必须要结合现代社会的变化和具体特点，才能作出正确的决策。

---

10. 社会/认知 Claim: Knowing about the past cannot help people to make important decisions
133 today.

Reason: The world today is significantly more complex than it was even in the relatively recent past. ［reasoning→solution］

观点：了解过去并不能帮助人们在今天作出重大决策。

理由：当代世界就算与并不很遥远的近代相比也要复杂得多。

Discuss the extent to which you agree or disagree with the claim and the reason on which that claim is based.

思路参考

【思路提示】

〈略，参考 **74** 〉

【题目的理由有道理吗？】

- Many aspects of human lives, such as lifestyle, values, custom, culture, belief, etc., have changed significantly and have become much more complex.
- Even the same kind of problem, for example, conflicts and wars, differs greatly in its form, process, and consequence in different time periods.

【题目的观点有道理吗？】

- 过去的情况、经验、方法当然不能一成不变地用于今天的决策。不加鉴别地照搬以往经验往往不能有效地解决今天的问题。必须要结合当前的实际情况和变化作出决策。

【题目的理由有问题吗？】

- Some basic human nature, such as desire, envy, greed, fear and other foibles, has remained constant over time.

- 即使当代世界发生了巨大变化：

An awareness of these evolutions helps us formulate informed, comprehensive, and enlightened values and ideals for our society.

【题目的观点存在问题吗？】

- ［从后果来说］The cognition of this invariability could help us understand and be more tolerant of others, as well as develop compassionate responses to the problems and failings of others. These would be beneficial to how we live as a society.

- The study of history provides us important references and experience for individuals and societies:

Learning about the stories of great persons inspires us to similar accomplishments and provides us precious experience about success.

Learning about mistakes of past societies helps us avoiding similar ones.

Learning about cultural heritage fosters a healthy sense of self and interest in preserving art and other cultural artifacts.

These factors altogether contribute to help us make correct decisions.

【总结】

〈略，参考 74 〉

---

11. 社会/认知 Claim: Knowing about the past cannot help people to make important decisions
134 today.

Reason: We are not able to make connections between current events and past events until we have some distance from both. [reasoning]

观点：了解过去并不能帮助人们在今天作出重大决策。

理由：我们无法在当前事件与过去事件之间建立联系，除非我们与两者之间都有一定距离。

Discuss the extent to which you agree or disagree with the claim and the reason on which that claim is based.

思路参考

【思路提示】

〈略，参考 74 〉

【题目的理由有道理吗？】

- ［从必要性来说］Certain distance from events is necessary for us to obtain deep and complete understanding of the connections between events.

【题目的观点有道理吗？】

- 过去的情况、经验、方法当然不能一成不变地用于今天的决策。不加鉴别地照搬以往经验往往不能有效解决今天的问题。必须要结合当前的实际情况和变化作出决策。

【题目的理由有问题吗？】

- Some basic human nature, such as desire, envy, greed, fear and other foibles, has remained unchanged over time. Many problems of human society could be explained by these factors. We can easily establish connections between past and current events related to these aspects.

- There are internal connections between events. We can still find laws behind these events although we are not distant from them.

【从题目理由足以推出题目观点吗？】

- 即使无法建立过去与今天的联系：

An awareness of these evolutions helps us formulate informed, comprehensive, and enlightened values and ideals for our society.

【题目的观点存在问题吗？】

- The study of history provides us important references and experience for individuals and societies:

Learning about the stories of great persons inspires us to similar accomplishments and provides us precious experience about success.

Learning about mistakes of past societies helps us avoiding similar ones.

Learning about cultural heritage fosters a healthy sense of self and interest in preserving art and other cultural artifacts.

These factors altogether contribute to help us make correct decisions.

【总结】

〈略，参考 74 〉

---

12. 社会 When old buildings stand on ground that modern planners feel could be better used for
119 modern purposes, modern development should be given precedence over the preservation of historic buildings. [reasoning/comparison/solution]

当现代规划人员觉得老建筑用地能更好地被用于现代用途时，现代发展应该优先于历史建筑保护加以考虑。

Discuss the extent to which you agree or disagree with the statement and consider ways in which the statement might or might not hold true.

思路参考

【思路提示】

- 本题建议从Condition来展开，讨论不同情况的老建筑应该保留还是让位于当前用途。有些毫无价值、破旧不堪、影响市容，甚至有一定危险性的建筑，将其拆除没有任何问题；而对于有一定价值的建筑，是否保留应经过充分论证。

【提出题目观点的出发点可能是什么？】

- Expansion and development are inevitable for a society. The function of cities and towns must meet the demand of modern society.
- ［从老建筑的状况来说］Some valueless old buildings could certainly be removed for modern purpose.

【题目的观点存在问题吗？】

- ［从老建筑的状况来说］

Some old buildings are of great cultural or historical value. They may uniquely represent a past era, or may play a critical role in the history, or may serve as the home of some famous people or the location of an important historical event. Some old buildings themselves are of aesthetic and architectural value. Understandably, preservation of these buildings should be given priority. Or at least we should weigh the advantage and disadvantage of removing these buildings carefully.

【发散】

- 老建筑保护和现代发展并不完全互斥。有些旧建筑在经过适当改造后本身就可以用于现代用途。另外，也可以通过其他方法来处理现代城市发展与历史建筑保护之间的矛盾，比如通过某些科技手段，或者从规划方面入手寻求其他解决方案。

本章从第二章的A、B、C、E、F类题目中各挑选了一道比较典型的题目，提供了5篇Issue参考文章，涵盖了对比型、问题解决型、推理型、观点型全部4种论证结构，涉及3种写作要求。

需要注意的是这些文章都不是在规定时间内完成的。为给考生提供更有参考价值的文字，所有文章均经过一定的修改打磨。而且，为给考生提供较为详尽的思路参考，多数文章的字数也大大超出了一般的写作要求。真正考试时不必强求字数，只要能在保证文章整体逻辑性的前提下围绕2~4个主要论点展开分析，字数达到420~450即可。

每道题目之后都附上了写作提纲，文章中间也加入了一些思路说明，主要目的是让考生通过这些提纲和结构体会第一、二章所介绍的写作素材搜集思路和文章构建方式。

SAMPLE 1

A 类
63
There is little justification for society to make extraordinary efforts—especially at a great cost in money and jobs—to save endangered animal or plant species.
Discuss the extent to which you agree or disagree with the statement and consider ways in which the statement might or might not hold true.

提　纲

【作者提出该观点的理由是什么？】
- The extinction of some species has nothing to do with human activities.
- The protection of some species is beyond human capability.
- Some urgent problems of human society have higher priority than to save endangered species.

【这些理由充分吗？】
- The extinctions of some species are caused by human activities, directly or indirectly.

【上述理由足以推出观点吗？】
- Human society has the responsibility to save those species even if they will be naturally extinct.

【题目行为本身有道理吗？】
- Some species possess great value to human race.

论证结构

Claim（观点型）

The claim that human societies need not make particular efforts to save endangered species implies that the potential extinction of those species neither is a result of human activities nor will pose any detrimental impact on the survival of human race. In my view, however, disastrous effects may follow should human societies underestimate the importance of saving endangered species.

首先分析题目提出不必拯救濒危物种的可能理由，整体作为让步。这道题正文完全可以构造成完全反对的直线型。正面内容可以完全不写，或简单陈述一下出题人提出题目观点的理由即可。

Admittedly, the statement holds certain merit in three aspects. First, the extinction of some species has nothing to do with human activities. Many species have already become extinct before human appeared on earth, only in a lower frequency. Therefore, it is not an obligation for societies to save them. Second, the protection of some species is beyond human capability. Imagine, for example, if dinosaurs still exist on earth, how could human ensure their survival? Furthermore, some urgent problems of human society have higher priority than to save endangered species. It might be inappropriate, or even cruel, to save animals and plants before the problems, such as poverty, famine and fatal diseases, are solved.

本题论证重点应该在负面，因为题目观点显然和主流价值判断相距较远。可以把提纲中的负面素材分2~3个正文段进行论述。首先可以分析题目观点的前提存在的问题。

The merits above, however, are far from sufficient for justifying the claim. Today, increasingly more species become extinct, which could be, at least partly, blamed on more intensive human activities. Human constructions destroy those species' habitat; industrial and other kinds of pollution ruin their living environment; and these factors all together result in vanishing of their food. Moreover, humans hunted many animal species, making them rare or even extinct. Numerous endangered or extinct species, such as wild elephant and dodo, could illustrate this point. Simply put, humans are responsible for most extinction.

其次可以分析推理过程的不充分性：即使有些物种的灭绝确实和人类活动没有关系，也不能由此推出人类不用理会这些物种的灭绝。

Granted that some species will become naturally extinct even without human interference, societies still have the responsibility to save those species, for humans are the governor of the world. One may remember the words appeared in *Genesis*, the *Holy Bible*: "... (humans should) have dominion over the fish of the sea, and over the birds of the air, and over every living thing that moves on the earth."

然后可以再从后果方面论述：假如人类真的对物种灭绝袖手旁观，可能会对社会发展造成哪些危害。

From a practical and utilitarian point of view, accepting the statement may jeopardize the development and survival of human society. Many species possess great value to human race, some of which are not realized by human yet. First, every species, whether ubiquitous or rare, is valuable to some extent. It plays an important role in the eco-system, therefore its extinction will trigger chain-reactions which will in turn affect bigger system. Some species could provide materials for scientific research or medical and industrial use. For example, if rubber trees had been endangered when humans discovered them and societies did not make any effort to save them—just as suggested in the statement, people at present time would not be able to enjoy many convenient products made with latex.

Although the issue of endangered-species protection is a complex one which involves moral duty and the comparative value of various life-forms, it would be irresponsible to hastily accept the statement that there is no need for societies to save endangered species. At least for the sake of our own survival, societies should pay attention to the condition of animals and plants around us. (*521 words*)

参考译文

人类社会不需做特别的努力拯救濒危物种的观点暗含了这样的假设：那些物种的灭绝既不是由人类活动导致，也不会对人类生存产生任何危害性影响。然而在我看来，如果人类社会低估了拯救濒危物种的重要性，可能会招致灾难性的影响。

诚然，题目观点在三方面有一定的意义。首先，有些物种的灭绝确实和人类活动没有关联。在人类出现之前地球上已经有很多物种灭绝，只不过灭绝的频率要低得多。因此，人类社会没有义务拯救这些物种。其次，有些物种的保护超出了人类的能力范畴。假如恐龙仍然在世，人类如何保证其生存？而且，与拯救濒危物种相比，人类社会存在一些更急需解决的问题。在贫困、饥荒、致命疾病等问题依旧存在的情况下，先拯救动植物可能是不合适的，甚至是残忍的。

但是，仅有以上正面因素远不足以支持题目观点。今天，越来越多的物种灭绝，这至少可以部分归因于日趋频繁的人类活动。人类的建设破坏了这些物种的栖居地；工业和其他形式的污染摧毁了他们的生存环境；这些因素共同导致了他们食物链的断裂。而且，人类对很多动物的猎捕直接导致了他们的濒危乃至灭绝。无数濒危或已经灭绝的物种，比如野象和渡渡鸟，都是很好的例证。简言之，人类对大多数物种的灭绝是负有责任的。

即使有些物种就算在不受人类活动干扰的情况下也会自然灭绝，但人类社会依然有责任拯救它们，因为人类是地球的管理者。有些人可能记得《圣经》创世纪中的话语："……（人类应该）管理海里的鱼、空中的鸟和陆地上各样行动的活物。"

从实用和功利的角度来看，接受题目观点也可能会危害人类社会的生存和发展。很多物种对人类都具有很高的价值，有些价值甚至迄今为止还没有被人类认识到。首先，任何物种，不论是不起眼的还是珍稀的，在某种程度上都有价值。它们在生态圈中起着重要作用，因此其灭绝可能引发某些连锁反应进而影响到更大的生态系统。有些物种能够为科研或医药及工业提供原材料。例如，假如人类发现橡胶树时它已濒临灭绝，而人类社会就像题目中提到的那样没有采取任何行动去拯救它们，那么，今天的人们就无法享用众多用橡胶制造的便利用品。

尽管濒危物种保护是一个涉及道德责任以及多种生命形式相对价值的复杂问题，草率接受社会无需拯救濒危物种的说法仍是不负责任的。至少从人类自身的生存角度来看，社会应该对我们周围的动植物生存环境给予关注。

SAMPLE 2

B 类
69
Some people believe it is often necessary, even desirable, for political leaders to withhold information from the public. Others believe that the public has a right to be fully informed.
Discuss which view more closely aligns with your own position and explain your reasoning for the position you take and you should address both of the views presented.

提 纲

【第一种观点的合理性：有些情况下信息必须控制】
- Withholding information could help to serve some strategic or political purposes.
- Disclosure of certain types of information would threaten national security.

【第二种观点的合理性：确保民众了解真相的必要性】
- To avoid unnecessary social disturbance and chaos, leaders should ensure the public to be informed.
- A gesture of sincerity and forthrightness is a demonstration of a concern for the broader interests of the public and the democratic system.

【第二种观点的必要性/第一种观点的问题：向公众隐瞒信息会导致社会危害】
- Undue information-control would raise public distrust or even hostility against the government.
- 有可能导致不受约束和监督的权力，从而导致腐败，甚至独裁专制。

【有些情况下信息必须公开】
- The settlement of some accidents requires instant information-publication.

Comparison(显性对比型)

Whether a piece of information should be withheld or be made public depends on the extent to which the information is related to the vital interest of the general public. Some information involving national strategy or security should be, or even must be kept secret. Otherwise, making public informed does nothing but benefit the social progress.

首先可以从必要性的角度分析第一种观点的正面因素：有些信息可以甚至必须控制。

The former claim is reasonable under certain circumstances. It should be acknowledged that withholding certain types of information from the public is necessary in that fully disclosing of such information would threaten national interest and even national security. Never would one country make public its military deployment in a skirmish, nor will a government publicize its real strategy in a trade war with other nations. These actions have nothing to do with honesty but reveal the naivety and inexperience of leaders on international politics.

第一种观点的负面因素可以结合第二种观点的正面因素讨论：首先，可以从必要性的角度分析向民众公开真相的重要意义；其次，从后果的角度分析控制信息的危害。

Although it is necessary to withhold information of the types cited above, public should be informed about information related to their immediate welfare or vital interests. Withholding such information would arouse public suspicions and rumors; social disturbance and chaos will thus follow. Furthermore, indiscriminate information-control often leads to more disastrous results. A gesture of sincerity and forthrightness of leaders to the general public is a demonstration of a concern for the broader interests of the public and for the democratization process. It is foreseeable that governmental monopoly of information will raise public distrust or even hostility against the government, or will result in undue government power which is free from public supervision and restraint—this will in turn result in corruption or even autarchy.

最后，可以再从Condition的角度讨论有些社会危机必须要通过及时公开信息才能妥善解决。

In addition, the settlement of some accidents requires instant information-disclosure. When the solution of certain social problem necessitates cooperation of the public, or withholding the information would be detrimental to people's livelihood, making public informed is not an option but a prerequisite for solving the problem.

In sum, making public informed is an effective method for leaders to communicate with citizens, and is essential for the advance of the process to democracy. Sincerity and forthrightness of leaders and government towards their people will ultimately benefit the well-being of the society. Thus, except for certain information related to national interest and security, as analyzed above, the public should be informed. (*402 words*)

【参考译文】

　　一条信息是应该控制还是应该公开取决于该信息与公众切身利益的相关程度。有些关系到国家战略或国家安全的信息应该甚至必须保密，除此以外，对公众公布真相对社会发展只有好处。

　　前一种观点在某些情况下是有道理的。可以肯定的是，对于某些类别的信息的控制是必要的，这类信息的完全公开可能会威胁国家利益甚至国家安全。没有任何一个国家在冲突中会公开自己的军事部署；也没有任何一个政府会在和别国的贸易战中公开自己的真正策略。这种行为和诚实与否无关，而是反映了领导者对于国际政治的无知和经验缺乏。

　　尽管对上述种类信息的控制是必要的，但和公众切身利益相关的信息应该对公众公开。控制这类信息将导致民众的猜疑和谣言，从而带来社会的动荡和混乱。而且，不加鉴别的信息控制往往会带来更多的灾难性后果。领导对公众开诚布公的姿态表达了其对更广泛的公众利益以及民主进程的关注。可以预见，政府对信息的垄断将造成公信力的下降，甚至是民众对政府的敌对情绪，或导致不受民众监督和制约的过度权力的产生，而这往往会带来腐败甚至独裁。

而且，有些事件的解决要依靠信息的及时披露。当某些社会问题的解决需要公众配合，或控制有些信息会危害民生的时候，告知公众真相就不是一个可有可无的选择，而是解决问题的必要前提了。

总而言之，对公众公开信息是领导和民众沟通的有效途径，也是推动民主进程的必要条件。领导和政府对其人民的真诚和坦率最终将有益于社会总体利益。因此，除了上文分析的某些和国家利益及安全相关的信息外，民众应该知道真相。

SAMPLE 3

C 类
64
The human mind will always be superior to machines because machines are only tools of human minds.

Discuss the extent to which you agree or disagree with the statement and consider ways in which the statement might or might not hold true.

提　纲

【思路提示】
- 本题可以围绕"superior"的定义展开，对于"superior"不同层面的理解，决定了对题目观点的不同判断。

【题目的理由有道理吗？】
- Machines are tools of human minds. No machine could exist unless humans invent it.

【题目的推理过程有道理吗？】
- Humans are superior in that, from ethical point of view, humans produce and dominate machines.

【题目的推理过程有问题吗？】
- Most tools are superior to human in their special use—that's why humans devise them.

【题目的观点有问题吗？】
- Machines can perform certain technical jobs with greater accuracy and speed than human minds ever could.

【题目的观点有道理吗？】
- On the basis of creative thinking and emotional sensitivity, human minds are superior, for no machines could develop the ability to think on their own, or develop so-called "emotional intelligence" so far.

论证结构

Reasoning（隐性推理）

One cannot deny that until now, machines are only tools that serve certain purposes designated by human. But whether one could confidently assert that human mind will always be superior to machines depends on how we define "superiority", and in what aspect do we look into the question.

首先，可以分析题目推理理由和推理过程的合理性：人类是机器的制造者和支配者，从伦理角度来说，支配者高于被支配者。

The premise of the claim that machines are only tools of human mind is obviously sound. Any machine so far is, and will be in the foreseeable future, devised by human and working for human. At any rate, no machine could exist unless humans invent it, and the meaning of the existence of a machine lies in that it can serve certain purpose. Even a seemingly meaningless little widget could be used to entertain somebody, or the process of its design and production could be a mind exercise for its designer. Thus, from ethical point of view, humans are superior in that machines are produced and dominated by humans.

接下来可以从Definition和Condition的角度分析推理过程的问题：人类是否优于机器取决于观察的角度和层面。首先，仅仅因为机器是人类的工具不足以得出人类一定在各方面都优于机器的结论；机器在其特定使用功能方面一般要优于人类。

However, does the fact that an object is a tool of its owner necessarily imply that the owner will be superior to that object at every aspect? In fact, most tools are superior to human in their special use, and that is the very reason why humans devise them: they are the extension of human capability and can do better jobs in certain fields. Can we find a human hand tougher than a hammer in nailing a nail? Similarly, hardly can we find anyone who can do numeric calculating faster than a calculator, although the latter is only a tool of human.

其次，在创造性、情感判断方面，机器显然还不具备这方面能力。

On the other hand, on the basis of creative thinking and emotional sensitivity, human minds are superior. No machine could develop the ability to think on its own, for any ability of thinking of machine is preset by human. Nor could machines develop so-called "emotional intelligence" so far. Machines with such ability are no more than science fictions. Even if machines of this kind could be and will be eventually designed and produced, humans will still be superior, at least to the extent that one can imagine at present, to those machines in these aspects.

对题目讨论的话题可以做一定的发散论述：无限度发展机器导致其不受控可能会对人类生存产生威胁。

Yet it would also be dangerous to claim that humans will always maintain the superior status over-confidently and optimistically. As people rely more and more on machines to solve problems, many abilities of human will deteriorate, including the ability of thinking, logical reasoning, and even emotional communicating. This would even threaten the survival of human societies, as described in many science fiction movies such as *The Matrix*, and *I, Robot*.

In conclusion, humans design, produce, and dominate machines, thus, machines can undoubtedly be defined as tools of human minds and the owner is deservedly superior to his tool from the ethical point of view. Also, humans are unique in independent thought, logical reasoning, subjective judgment, and emotional response, which cannot be performed by machines at least at present stage. Nevertheless, we should also admit that, in areas such as data storage, speed and accuracy in doing technical jobs, machines could surpass human beings. (*507 words*)

参考译文

不可否认，到目前为止，机器只是服务于人类所设定的某种目的的工具。然而人们是否有把握断言人脑将永远优于机器则取决于如何定义"优于"，以及从什么角度去看待这个问题。

题目观点中关于机器只是人脑的工具的前提显然是有道理的。目前为止任何机器都是，而且在可以预见的将来也将由人类设计并为人类工作。无论如何，除非人类发明，否则任何机器都不可能存在，而且机器存在的意义就在于它能服务于某种目标。即使一个看起来毫无意义的小器具也可以用于逗某人开心，或其设计制造过程可以作为其设计者的脑力练习。因此，从伦理角度来说，人类是要优于机器的，因为机器是由人类制造和支配的。

然而，某物体是其制造者的工具这一点是否足以说明制造者必然在所有方面都优于该物体呢？事实上，大多数工具在其特定功能方面都要优于人类，而这也是人类设计它们的原因：它们是人类能力的延伸，而且在特定领域能够更好地完成工作。人们能否找到钉钉子时比锤子更坚硬的手？同理，人们也很难找到在数字计算方面比计算器还要快的人，尽管计算器只是人类的工具。

另一方面，从创造性思维和情感认知层面，人脑更为优越。没有机器能够发展出独立思考的能力，任何机器的思考能力都是人类预设的。目前也没有机器能发展出所谓的"情感智能"。具有此类能力的机器还只存在于科幻小说中。即使此类机器最终将被设计并制造出来，至少从目前能够想象的程度来说，人类在这些方面依然会优于那些机器。

但是，过于自信和乐观地肯定人类将永远比机器更具优势也将有一定危险性。随着人们越来越多地依赖于机器解决问题，人类的很多能力将会退化，包括思考、逻辑推理，甚至情感交流的能力。这甚至可能会威胁到人类社会的存活，就像许多科幻电影所描述的那样，比如《黑客帝国》或《我，机器人》。

总而言之，人类设计、制造、支配机器，因而机器无疑可以被定义为人脑的工具，而从伦理角度来说，制造者当然要优于其工具。而且，人类在独立思考、逻辑推理、客观判断以及情感反应方面是独一无二的，至少当前的机器无法完成这些工作。但是，我们也要看到在数据存储以及进行某些技术工作的速度和精确性方面，机器可能胜过人类。

SAMPLE 4

E 类
55
In order for any work of art—for example, a film, a novel, a poem, or a song—to have merit, it must be understandable to most people.

Discuss the extent to which you agree or disagree with the statement and consider ways in which the statement might or might not hold true.

提　纲

【题目的说法有道理吗？】

- Arts are expressions of thoughts and feelings. It is reasonable to request arts to be understandable to people.
- The theme, technique, and means of expression of some great art works are so simple that almost everyone could understand them.

【题目的说法有问题吗？】

- Some art works are exclusive expressions of artists' inner feelings. Some great works contain ideas and thoughts that transcend the time. They often confront us with uncertainty and lack of reason.
- The fact that the majority of people could not understand them does not mean that those works are of no merit.

【有其他途径赋予艺术作品价值吗？】

- Art works that reveal otherwise hidden ideas and impulses could also have merit.
- Some art works hold merit through upsetting old ways of artistic creation.

论证结构

Solution（问题解决型）

The assertion that valuable art works must be widely understood reveals certain ignorance of the speaker towards the real value of art. A great art work might be easy to understand, however, being understandable to most people is neither sufficient nor necessary for an art work to hold merit.

这道题正文可以构造成完全反对的直线型。正面内容可以完全不写或用一段简单陈述即可。首先肯定一下题目观点的合理性，整体作为让步。

Admittedly, since art works are media which convey the thoughts and feelings of the artists, it is reasonable to request arts to be understandable to its audience. Otherwise, art creation will become sheer narcissism or self-appreciation. Also, the themes of many great art works have been presented in simple techniques, and almost everyone will find no difficulty in understanding them. Most narrative arts which depict an object or an event, such as portraits, operas, light literature, share this feature.

本题论证重点是在负面。首先可以分析题目观点存在的问题：很多伟大的艺术作品不能被大众接受，但不能因此否认其价值。

However, these examples could only illustrate that plainness and greatness could exist in one piece of art work simultaneously, but not that the former contributes to the latter. Not all great works are necessarily understandable to the general public. Some art works are exclusive expressions of the artists' inner feelings. Some great works contain ideas and thoughts that transcend the time. They often confront us with uncertainty and lack of reason. Many abstract arts, such as the cubism painting of Picasso, are clear examples. In other words, both artistic creation and appreciation are subjective processes. The result and feeling of aesthetic appreciation depends on many factors such as the experience, age and class of the audience. It is quite normal that some people cannot accept or enjoy some art works, but one cannot deny the value of them merely because the majority of people could not understand them.

其次，可以按Solution论证结构发散论证使艺术作品具有价值还有哪些其他途径。

On the contrary, many other ways could ensure the merit of an art work. Some art works that reveal otherwise hidden ideas and impulses of society are valuable in their criticism and reflection of the reality and absurdity of the world. For example, the reflection of the public's attitude toward the condition of politics in America at that time in the short satires of Mark Twain won them recognition. And the reflection of the impotence and struggle of a perplexed individual against his surrounding world in one of Pink Floyd's most highly-rated albums, *The Wall*, also made the album appreciated by modern people.

Other art works hold merit in that they upset old ways of artistic creation. Take Pink Floyd as example again, the melody, lyric, and effects in their famous album *The Dark Side of the Moon* are subversive to people's traditional understanding of music. Yet this could not prevent the album becoming a huge success: it stayed on the Billboard chart for unbelievable 741 weeks from 1973 to 1988, longer than any other album in history. Also, the significance of the deconstructivism architecture of Frank Gehry, Zaha Hadid, Rem Koolhaas lies in that they upset people's former understanding and request toward architecture.

Simply put, whether an art work holds merit almost has nothing to do with the extent to which the work is understood. One who knows the very essence of art will agree that the true value of an art work could be determined in many different ways. Furthermore, in accepting the statement we take the risk that artists may pander to public taste, which will surely hinder real artistic progress. (*550 words*)

参考译文

有价值的艺术作品必须要被广泛理解的观点反映了持此观点的人对艺术的真正价值一定程度的无知。一件伟大的艺术作品可能是易于理解的，然而，被大众理解既不能充分保证也不是唯此才能使一件艺术品具有价值。

应该承认，既然艺术作品是艺术家表达其思想和感受的媒介，那么，要求作品能够被其观众（或听众）理解也是合理的。否则艺术创作将演变成纯粹的自恋或自我欣赏。而且，很多伟大艺术作品主题的表达手法通俗易懂，几乎所有人都能理解。大多数描述某对象或某事件的叙述性艺术，比如肖像、歌剧、通俗文学等，都具有此类特点。

然而，这些例子只能说明通俗和伟大可以共存于同一作品中，但不能说明其通俗造就了其伟大。并不是所有伟大的作品都能被大众理解。有些艺术作品是艺术家内心感受的特定表达；有些伟大作品包含了超越时代的理念和思想。它们呈现在大众面前时往往具有不确定性和非理性。很多抽象艺术，比如毕加索的立体主义绘画，就是很明显的例子。换句话说，艺术创作和艺术欣赏都是主观过程，审美的结果和感受则取决于很多因素，比如欣赏者的审美经验、年龄、阶层等。有些人群无法接受或欣赏某些艺术作品是很正常的，但是不能仅仅因为大多数人不能理解这些作品就否认它们的价值。

另一方面，有很多其他方式也可以赋予艺术作品价值。有些揭示了社会深层观点和潮流的作品因其对世界的现状和荒谬性的批判和反映而获得价值。比如，马克·吐温的讽刺短篇中对美国民众对当时美国政治状况的意见的反映为其赢得声誉。平克·弗洛伊德在其著名专辑之一《迷墙》中对于一个彷徨无助的人对其周围世界的无奈和反抗的反映也使该专辑到今天依然广为流传。

还有些艺术作品因其推翻了以往的艺术创作手法而具有价值。还是以平克·弗洛伊德为例，其著名专辑《月之暗面》中的旋律、歌词和音效对于人们对音乐的传统理解来说都是颠覆性的。但这并不妨碍该专辑的巨大成功：它从1973年到1988年在《公告牌》排行榜上停留了难以置信的741周，比历史上任何其他专辑都要长。再比如，弗兰克·盖里、扎哈·哈迪德、雷姆·库哈斯的结构主义建筑的意义在于它们推翻了人们以往对于建筑的基本理解和要求。

简言之，一件艺术作品是否具有价值与其被大众理解的程度几乎是无关的。任何了解艺术本质的人都会承认艺术作品的真正价值可能取决于很多方面。而且，接受题目观点有可能会导致艺术家媚俗和迎合大众的危险，这显然将阻碍真正的艺术进步。

SAMPLE 5

> **F 类**
> **65**
> Every individual in a society has a responsibility to obey just laws and to disobey and resist unjust laws.
>
> *Discuss the extent to which you agree or disagree with the claim and address the most compelling reasons and/or examples that could be used to challenge your position.*

提　纲

【思路提示】

- 本题可以结合Condition来展开，分别讨论不同程度、不同情况下应该如何对待不公正法律。

【对于公正的法律】

- Laws must be absolutely obeyed if only they are fair, for laws are basic guidelines on the behavior of citizens.

【对于不公正的法律，题目提出的方案有合理性吗？】

- Unjust laws should be fought against only under some extreme circumstances.

【可能存在哪些相反观点？】

- To attain the goal of justice, any means to fight against unjust laws are desirable.

【回应】【对抗不公正法律存在哪些问题？】

- How to define just and unjust? People may have different criterion in their judgment.
- Disobedience of law may result in social disturbance and chaos.
- Disobedience and resistance of law might be infeasible for citizens.

【总结】

- 对于只是有些瑕疵，或立法者考虑不周而导致损害特定人群利益的法律，应该通过合理、合法且有利于社会发展的方式对其加以修正。

Solution(问题解决型)

I strongly agree that every individual should obey just laws unconditionally and that unjust laws must be amended as soon as possible. However, whether radical actions such as disobedience and resistance are an effective way to revise unjust laws is open to doubt.

对于题目中公正的法律方面可以一笔带过，对于不公正的法律则要分情况考虑：只有对极端不公正的法律可以采用题目提出的手段；而对于只是考虑不周的法律则应该通过其他方式来解决。

Anyone who wants the society to be truly civilized and to run in order will acknowledge that laws must be absolutely obeyed if only they are fair, for laws are the basic guidelines on the behavior of citizens. Yet one would also admit that there are certain unjust laws which will damage the well-being of society or will impede social progress. These laws should be revised through proper means. In my opinion, the solution raised in the claim—disobedience and resistance—is applicable only under certain extreme circumstances, for example, the anti-semitism clauses in German laws during the World War II, and the protection on slavery of the *American Constitution* before the Civil War. These laws are not only unjust but could be considered evil laws, which undoubtedly deserve resistance. But for other cases, treating unjust laws with these radical actions seems improper.

相反观点可能认为公正是法律的基本要义，因此为了公正的目的可以采取任何手段。

Some people may argue that the idea of justice is the very foundation of a legal system, thus, any laws that are found unfair or biased must be fought against through whatever means that are necessary. Such position sounds righteous and compelling, however, in-depth examination will reveal the following problems.

接下来可以从前提、后果、可行性等方面对相反观点作出回应。

First, how should we define just and unjust? People or social groups with different interests and values will surely have different criterion in their judgment. Consider, for example, the controversial issues of abortion and homosexuality. Any laws on these issues might be considered just by one group of people while be considered unjust by another. Second, laws, even those unjust ones, are basic disciplines that ensure the society run in order. Fighting laws through whatever means would probably result in social disturbance and chaos. Granted that radical actions are desirable for the purpose of justice, it would still be infeasible for citizens to resist laws. Imagine, for example, how could bare-handed masses fight with the law enforcement institutions of the government such as the armed police?

最后总结对于大多数不公正的法律应该如何处理。

Therefore, unjust laws which do not violate basic moral principles but only have minor flaws, or are inconsiderately legislated, should be modified with rational and reasonable approaches. For example, we can perfect the laws through perpetual improvement of the legislation system, or through the supervision of mass media. The Internet also provides us an effective and powerful way to stand for justice and reflect the demand of public.

On the whole, for those unjustified laws which violate the core values upon which a democratic society depends to thrive, and those which harm the well-being of the general public, people should do their very best to amend them. While for slightly flawed or biased rules and regulations, a step-by-step, moderate improvement might be more appropriate. (*486 words*)

　　我强烈赞同每个人都应该无条件遵守公正的法律，而且不公正的法律一定要及时修正。但是，像违反和对抗这类极端行为是否是纠正不公正法律的有效途径值得进一步讨论。

　　任何希望社会实现真正文明并有序运转的人都会承认公民应绝对遵守公正的法律，因为法律是人们行为的基本准则。但也应该承认确实有一些损害社会利益或会阻碍社会进步的不公正法律。这些法律应该通过恰当的手段修正。在我看来，题目中提到的方案——违反和对抗——只对某些极端情形适用，比如，二战期间德国法律中的反犹太条款；以及南北战争之前《美国宪法》对奴隶制的保护。这些法律不仅仅是不公正的，而且可以称之为邪恶的，这样的法律无疑应当抵制。但对于其他情形，以极端行为对抗不公正的法律似乎不甚妥当。

　　有些人可能会提出"正义是法律制度的基础"，因此，不公正的、有失偏颇的法律必须以任何必要手段加以反抗。这一观点看似充满正义感且理直气壮，但是，深入分析后将会发现以下问题。

　　首先，如何界定公正与不公正？利益和价值观不同的人或社会群体在判断时肯定会有不同标准。比如像堕胎、同性恋这些有争议的问题，任何对于这类问题的法律都会被某一人群视为公正而被另一人群视为不公正。其次，法律是维系社会秩序的基本规则，即使是不公正的法律也有同样的作用。不择手段地对抗法律很可能会导致社会动荡和混乱。即使承认为了正义的目的极端手段也是可取的，但对于普通公民来说，对抗法律依然是不可行的。想象一下，手无寸铁的群众如何能够对抗武警之类的执法机构？

　　因此，对于不违反基本道德准则且仅有微小瑕疵，或立法时考虑不周的不公正法律，应该通过合理和理性的手段修正。比如，可以通过不断改进立法体系或通过大众媒体的监督来完善法律。网络也给我们提供了伸张正义、反映大众呼声的有效和有力的途径。

　　总之，对于违背民主社会的繁荣所必需的核心价值，以及危害大众利益的不公正法律，人们应该尽其所能去修正它。而对于一些只有些微漏洞或考虑不周的条文规定，采取循序渐进的、温和的改进方式可能更为合适。

第四章　Argument写作思路简介

　　Argument写作需要考生结合写作要求评价题目推理过程的逻辑合理性，也就是作者的论据是否足以推出最终结论。

　　在准备Argument写作时可以分以下几个步骤展开：

　　一、分析题目结构。

　　二、找出论证过程中的主要假设和可能存在问题的环节。

　　三、构造针对每类主要问题的论证思路。

　　四、提纲结合模板，构造正文主体。

一　分析题目结构

　　Argument所有题目从逻辑本质来说，都是作者提供论据来支持结论的一个推理论证过程。因此，在分析题目结构时要完成的工作主要是两方面：分清论据和结论；看清推理关系。

❶ 结论的确定

　　不能简单认定最后一句就是结论。在Argument的所有题目中，有70%左右的结论确实是最后一句话；但还有10%左右是第一句话；出现在第二句和倒数第二句的共占10%左右；还有10%位置不确定。要判断作者最终支持和主张的结论，首先可以锁定一些标志性的词汇。一般来说，题目的结论会以therefore、thus、clearly等词汇引导，或者会出现一些情态动词如should、must等，也有些题目结论之前会有目的状语，如to do sth.、in order to do sth. 等等。当然最根本的还需要以推理逻辑的最终指向作为结论的判断依据，即所有论据、信息指向的、支持的就是作者的最终结论。

❷ 论据和推理结构的确定

　　作者在推理时有可能使用事实、统计数据、调查结果作为论据，并运用例证、类比、对比等论证手法来支持自己的结论。

　　找出作者使用的论据和要支持的结论后，考生应该在脑子里整理分析一下这些论据是如何一步一步推出结论的。这种对题目推理结构分析能力的训练十分必要，它有助于考生准确找出作者每个推理环节所包含的假设，也有助于考生合理安排正文段落的论证层次和顺序。

　　本书第五章给出了Argument作文题库每道题目的推理结构，考生可以参考这部分内容，把握每道题目的推理脉络和思路。

二　找出论证过程中的主要假设和可能存在问题的环节

　　首先要注意，Argument写作只要求考生对题目的推理过程进行分析和评价，而非要推翻原有的结论。因此只需要评价一下题目推理过程的每个环节是否具有必然性、是否环环相扣即可，而不要把写作目的理解成否定或驳斥原有的结论。

一般来说，题目推理出现的主要问题可以分成3大类、24小类。在论证时并不一定要先明确指出作者推理问题的类型才能展开论述。对常见问题进行分类有助于考生挖掘和认识题目中论证的环节，也有助于考生针对每类问题构建有针对性的论证模板。

下面开始对题目中经常论证的逻辑问题简单地介绍一下。

第1大类：论据中的问题，即作者提供的数据、事实、调查统计结果可能存在的漏洞。

❶ Survey 调查类问题

作者在题目中提供调查结果、统计数据作为论据时基于的最基本假设是该调查从过程到结果各个环节均是可靠的，只有作者认为调查结果可靠时才会用它作为论据支持结论。而一个调查在可靠性方面可能会出现8小类问题：

1）Selective sample 选择性样本

即作者在进行调查时没有研究全部应调查的子群体，而仅仅研究了一些特殊的、没有代表性的个案。论证时需要指出要得到更加全面有效的调查结果，作者应该在样本中包含更多、更广泛的子群体。

【典型例题】Argument 作文题库 66, 137

2）Quantity of the sample 样本数量不够充分

作者在进行调查时只研究了或提供了寥寥几个个案的情况，没有形成一定规模，因而调查结果也就没有代表性。这一点和选择性样本没有本质区别，假如样本数量太少那就必然是选择性样本。

【典型例题】Argument 作文题库 75, 113

3）Who conducted the survey? 调查机构不满足"中立"

要保证调查结果有效，首先应该保证调查机构或调查者是中立的，不会在调查结果中有利益关系。如果调查者可能从调查结果中获益或者受损，就有可能歪曲或误导调查结果。

【典型例题】Argument 作文题库 81

4）When was the survey conducted? 调查的时效性

文中提到的调查可能是在某一特殊时期进行的，或者是很久以前的调查结果，因而不能用来说明当前的情况。本质上说和"从过去推将来"的草率推广类似。

【典型例题】Argument 作文题库 85

5）What question was asked in the survey? 调查所问的问题与结论无关或无直接联系

调查时对被访对象提出的问题无关痛痒，不能直接说明结论。

【典型例题】Argument 作文题库 55

6）Are the respondents forthright when answering the questions? 回应者是否表达真实情况

如果回应者在回答问卷时出于某些原因不愿意或不敢表达自己的真实想法，那么调查本身就没有任何可信度，也就不能作为论据支持论证了。

【典型例题】Argument 作文题库 22

7）Are the respondents representative? 回应者是否有代表性

如果调查问卷不指定被访对象且不强行回收，则往往是对调查问题感兴趣的人更愿意回答问卷。

这样就有可能导致回应者形成一个选择性样本。

【典型例题】Argument 作文题库 43

8）Does the survey make any difference? 调查本身没有意义

作者进行调查的目标不明确；或调查过程无关痛痒；或调查内容不够充分全面；或调查本身没有问题，但和结论缺乏逻辑联系，不能充分支持结论。

【典型例题】Argument作文题库 81

❷ Data 数据信息问题

作者在题目中提供具体数字或关于某些事件的情况描述时会出现的信息不精确、不完整的情况。主要体现在两方面：

1）Vague data 模糊数据

最常见的形式是绝对总量和相对比例的混淆，即作者仅仅指出某种讨论对象总量很多或很少，但是没有考虑该对象所在区域的人口基数，因而无法说明该对象的人均拥有情况；或是没有提供具有某特征的对象所属群体的总数，因而无法判断该对象在总群体中所占的比例是高是低。在很多情况下，我们需要考虑"人均"或某事件的"发生率"、"拥有率"等数值才能精确判断题目的推理过程是否合理。

【典型例题】Argument 作文题库 25, 31

2）Incomplete information 信息不完整

作者在论述中仅提供了一部分和结论相关的信息，而没有提供评价推理过程所需的全部关键信息，因而无法对作者结论作出全面判断。

【典型例题】Argument 作文题库 73, 85

第2大类：推理过程的问题，即作者在用调查结果、数据、信息推出结论的过程中，在论证方法和思路上可能存在漏洞。主要有7类：

❶ False Analogy 错误类比

作者以个体A（该个体可能是个人、公司、城市等）来类推个体B，认为A如何B也应该如何，但是没有考虑到A与B两者之间可能存在很多差别，从而导致两者未必能够进行类比。

【典型例题】Argument 作文题库 97, 160

❷ Confusing Comparison and Variation 横向比较和纵向比较混淆

要说明结论，作者本来应该提供讨论对象和其他可参照群体的横向对比，但仅仅提供了该对象自身某方面的变化；或反之。

【典型例题】Argument 作文题库 46, 48

❸ Incomplete Comparison/Selective Comparison/Ex parte Information 不完整比较/选择性比较/单方面信息

作者在对比两个对象的时候没有把影响对比结果的因素全部加以衡量，而仅仅挑选了一些（可能对作者有利的）因素加以对比；或是作者仅仅提供了关于对比双方之中一方的描述，而另外一方情况如何无法判断，因而无法作出公正全面的比较。

【典型例题】Argument 作文题库 69, 78, 170

❹ Hasty Generalization 草率推广

作者在证据不充分的情况下，在两个没有必然逻辑联系的概念之间建立了推理关联，认为A必然能推出B。具体有3种表现形式：

1）Unrelated concepts 无关概念

作者进行推理的前后两个概念在逻辑上没有任何必然关联。比如看到某事物数量多，就认为该事物质量高；看到人们因为某种疾病去看医生的次数少，就认为该疾病的真正发病率也低，等等。

【典型例题】Argument 作文题库 10, 36, 109

2）Changing scopes 差异范围

从本质来说就是通常所说的"以偏概全"，即作者从一些特殊的、不具有代表性的个案推广出适用于更广泛对象的一般性原则和看法。但这里的覆盖面更广一些，包括作者从特殊个案推知一般原则；或是从一般性的、整体趋势推知个体情况。换言之，凡是作者前后讨论对象的限定范围存在差异的都归为此类问题。

【典型例题】Argument 作文题库 39, 47

3）Inferring a future condition from a past condition 从过去推知未来

作者把过去曾经发生或使用过的情况、经验、办法照搬到现在或未来，认为过去如何将来一样也可以如何，但没有考虑到很多关键因素会随着时间的推移发生变化。这些条件变化之后，过去的一些老办法、老经验在当前不再适用。

【典型例题】Argument 作文题库 33, 69

❺ Failing to Weigh the Advantage and Disadvantage Thoroughly 没有全面衡量正负得失

作者在进行某些评判时，片面强调了某事物带来的好处（或者坏处），但没有充分考虑另外一方面。比如作者仅看到某种行为可能带来的收入，但是没有考虑到实施这种行为必须要投入多少成本；或者仅看到某方案能解决一些问题，但没有看到它可能带来的负面影响。

【典型例题】Argument 作文题库 56, 58

❻ False Dilemma 非此即彼，极端选择

作者给一个本来有很多可能情况和解释的事件强加了一个非此即彼的选择，认为对这件事而言只有两种极端化的可能，但没有考虑到整个事件过程还可能存在很多中间状态和解释。

【典型例题】Argument 作文题库 15, 35

❼ Cause-effect Fallacy 因果关系问题

作者暗示A导致了B，但没有提供任何直接的或实质性的证据来证实A与B之间的因果联系。具体有4种表现形式：

1）Non-causal relationship 无因果

题目中提到的两个概念或行为A和B，无论从逻辑还是常识上都没有任何必然关联，但作者认为一定是A导致了B。

【典型例题】Argument 作文题库 4, 17

2）Confusing concurrence with causality 在同时发生的两事件之间建立因果联系

　　题目中提到的两个现象或行为A和B只是在同一时期发生，作者就认为是A导致了B。两个事件同时发生，有可能仅仅是巧合，或说明A与B两者之间有关联，但不一定能证明A与B两者之间存在因果联系。

　　【典型例题】Argument 作文题库 14, 36, 68

3）Post hoc, ergo propter hoc（After this, therefore because of this）在时间上先后发生的两个事件之间建立因果联系

　　题目中提到的两个事件A和B仅仅是在时间上先后发生，作者就认为是A导致了B。原因必然发生在结果之前，但不能说发生在前的就一定是原因。

　　【典型例题】Argument 作文题库 12, 71

4）Confusing the cause and the effect 混淆因果/因果倒置

　　作者认为是A导致B，而在现实中有可能是B导致了A。

　　【典型例题】Argument 作文题库 14, 40, 68

第3大类：结论的问题。对于结论要注意以下两方面：

❶ Sufficiency and Necessity of the Solution 对策的充分性和必要性

　　如果作者的结论是为解决某些问题、达到某种目标提出了一种方案，那么，可以从两方面分析：一、仅采取作者的方案是否足以解决问题，是否需要满足其他必要条件或完成其他重要工作。这是对该方案对于保证实现目标的充分性的分析；二、要达到作者的目的并解决问题，还有没有其他可以采取的手段和方式，换句话说，是否一定要采取作者提出的方案。这是对该方案对于保证实现目标的必要性的分析。

　　【典型例题】Argument 作文题库 42, 171

❷ Feasibility of the Conclusion 结论的可行性

　　作者在结论中提出的行为仅仅在理论上成立，在现实中因为存在某些障碍而无法操作。

　　【典型例题】Argument 作文题库 16, 27, 44

　　以上是Argument写作中比较常见的分析论证的逻辑问题。在准备Argument写作时最好做到对每种逻辑问题的表现形式、成因、特点和论证要点都能准确理解和把握。这有助于考生发现和认识需要论证的问题并有针对性地整理论证思路，同时确保写作速度、字数和论证的逻辑性、层次性。

（三）构造针对每类主要问题的论证思路

　　考生应该在上考场之前把要论证的每类常见问题的论证思路整理清楚，并构建针对每类问题的基本分析构架，也就是所谓的"模板"。具体来说，就是要把该问题分析清楚：第一句即段首句应如何描述；第二句是应该让步，还是递进解释；第三句应如何深入展开……语言基础好的考生只需把论证思路理清即可，语言基础欠佳的考生可根据自身情况把展开分析时所用的语言表达也思考一下。本书第六章列举了针对以上各个主要问题的参考模板，考生可以参考其中的语言和思路，再结合自己的思维特点和表达习惯构造自己的论证模板。

（四）提纲结合模板，构造正文主体

在看到题目后，考生应迅速回想之前准备这道题时找出的需要论证的主要环节（即提纲），再结合论证每个环节的展开思路（即模板）构造正文主体。

❶ 正文段落的数量

有些逻辑结构简单或很难挖掘论证点的题目，写2个正文段论证2个主要环节即可，但这种情况下对每个环节都需要有比较深入的分析展开。对于大多数题目，一般构造3~4个正文段比较合理。主要的正文段每段围绕一个问题展开，也可以把几个有逻辑关联的、如果单独论述没有太多语言展开空间的问题合成一段讨论。写作时并不要求考生分析题目中的所有问题，短短30分钟的写作时间也不可能把一道题目所有存在问题的环节都加以展开，因此只要选择题目推理过程中比较重要的、自己擅长论证的主要环节即可。

❷ 正文段落之间的逻辑衔接

在展开正文论述时还应注意所论证问题之间的逻辑关系。ETS在其官网关于Argument部分的说明中明确指出，这篇作文的考查要点之一就是要看考生作文的整体逻辑性。而这个整体逻辑性，指的就是所论证问题之间的论证顺序安排和有效的语言衔接。

1）论证顺序安排

正文段落的顺序建议根据题目本身的推理结构来确定。准备题目的第一步工作：分析题目结构的目的之一就在于帮助考生认清所分析问题之间的逻辑关系，从而确定论证顺序。

一般来说，如果题目所使用的论据相互之间是平行关系，即所有论据之间没有任何逻辑关联，那么，这种结构我们称之为"并列式推理"；这种题目在安排顺序的时候比较随意，可以按照所分析问题的逻辑重要性、对原文推理过程的破坏作用从重到轻来安排，即先写主要的、严重的，后写次要的、枝节性的。如果题目整个推理过程是环环相扣的，即A → B → C → conclusion，那么，这种题目结构我们称之为"递进式推理"；正文顺序可以按照题目推理的顺序一环接一环地展开，即先分析A推至B这一环节所包含的问题，再分析B推出C的问题等。

当然，题库中属于完全并列或完全递进结构的题目并不多，大多数题目属于混合型。但从根本来说，所有题目结构都是并列和递进两种基本结构的穿插组合。建议考生在写作时先分析几条论据之间的逻辑关系，再结合上述原则安排顺序。

2）段落之间的语言衔接

这一点主要是指如何在段首句体现出本段论述的问题和其他段落之间的逻辑关系。这也是保证文章整体逻辑性很重要的一环。很多考生仅把要论证的问题找出来罗列，但在具体分析论述时对这些问题之间的逻辑关系的表达不太在意，这样就容易导致阅卷者读文章时无法把握考生的总体思路。因此，最好在段首句选择恰当的语言把本段论述的内容和其他段落内容之间的关系表达清楚。

一般来说，如果两段所分析的内容A和B在逻辑上是递进的，即题目基于A进一步推出B，那么在论证第二个环节B时，段首句可以用让步来衔接：

例如，第一段段首句：In the first place, 环节A存在某些问题。

第二段段首句：Granted that 环节A不存在问题，we cannot ensure that 环节B可以被有效推出。

如果两段分析的内容是并列的，即A与B两个环节之间没有逻辑关系，那么第二段段首句用让步或递进都可以：

  例如：第一段段首句：In the first place, 环节A存在某些问题。

     第二段段首句：Furthermore, 环节B还存在某些问题。

举例来说，假如题目的推理结构是先由A推出B，再由B并列C推出结论，即

$$A \rightarrow B$$
$$\quad\;\; C \Big\} \rightarrow conclusion$$

正文分别讨论A、B、C三个环节出现的问题，那么段首句可以这样构造：

第一段：First, the author hastily assumes A.

第二段：Basing on the underlying assumption A, the author further implies B. However, B 存在某些问题。

或：Granted that assumption A could be substantiated, we cannot ensure that B is justified.

第三段：Moreover, the author's assumption C is open to doubt.

当然，这只是一些示意句式，考生在练习时要勤于思考，想清楚所论证问题之间的逻辑层次，并大量阅读经典范文、GRE Verbal部分的长阅读文章、外文期刊读物的论证文章来积累这类衔接语言的表达，在自己写作时灵活运用。

❸ 对写作要求的呼应

Argument写作对考生提出了7种不同的写作要求，分别是：

1）Write a response in which you examine the stated and/or unstated **assumptions** of the argument. Be sure to explain how the argument depends on these assumptions and what the implications for the graument are if the assumptions prove unwarranted.

2）Write a response in which you discuss what **questions** would need to be answered in order to decide whether the **recommendation** and the argument on which it is based are reasonable. Be sure to explain how the answers to these questions would help to evaluate the recommendation.

3）Write a response in which you discuss what **questions** would need to be answered in order to decide whether the **advice** and the argument on which it is based are reasonable. Be sure to explain how the answers to these questions would help to evaluate the advice.

4）Write a response in which you discuss what **questions** would need to be answered in order to decide whether the **prediction** and the argument on which it is based are reasonable. Be sure to explain how the answers to these questions would help to evaluate the prediction.

5）Write a response in which you discuss what **questions** would need to be answered to decide whether the **recommendation** is likely to have the **predicted result**. Be sure to explain how the answers to these questions would help to evaluate the recommendation.

6）Write a response in which you discuss what specific **evidence** is needed to evaluate the argument and explain how the evidence would weaken or strengthen the argument.

7）Write a response in which you discuss one or more **alternative explanations** that could rival the proposed explanation and explain how your explanation(s) can plausibly account for the facts presented in the argument.

其中，第2）、3）、4）、5）条要求没有本质区别，可以看作同一类。因此，这7种要求可以归纳为4大类：

前3类要求中Assumption是最根本的。只要能找到推理环节的假设，Question和Evidence的写作要求只要在论述语言上稍作调整即可对应。要评价题目推理需要回答什么问题呢？本质来说，就是要回答"文中假设是否成立？"要评价题目推理需要提供哪些证据呢？就是要提供证明文中假设成立与否的证据。

举例来说，题目中常出现的问题之一是错误类比（False Analogy），作者在A与B两者之间进行类推时必然包含的基本假设就是A与B双方应该是可比的，即：A and B are comparable. 如果AB之间存在很多差别而不可比，那么作者的类推就是不成立的。把这条假设改成问句，即：Are A and B comparable? 这就是要判断题目类比是否成立必须回答的问题，可以用来对应Question的写作要求。而凡是用来证实或有助于证实A与B之间可比性的信息和论据，就是要判断题目类比是否成立必须提供的论据和信息，可以用来对应Evidence的写作要求。

因此，只要能准确找出题目推理过程中的假设，其他几种写作要求在展开时的分析思路其实没有本质差别，只不过在段首句、第二句过渡句以及段落总结句的句式、语言表达方面略有不同而已。

比如，同样是论证错误类比，对于Assumption的写作要求可以这样展开：

In the argument the author suggests A to copy the policy of B, **while the inference based on an assumption that** A and B are comparable. However, A and B might be different in many aspects, for example... **Before the author could substantiate the critical assumption**, we cannot determine whether A could attain its objective through copying the policy of B.

对于Question的写作要求可以这样展开：

In the argument the author suggests A to copy the policy of B. **To evaluate the suggestion we should ask that** whether A and B are comparable. A and B might be different in many aspects, for example... Before the author could address this critical question, we cannot determine whether A could attain its objective through copying the policy of B.

对于Evidence的写作要求可以这样展开：

In the argument the author suggests A to copy the policy of B. **To make the suggestion logically sound the author should provide concrete evidence to illustrate** the comparability of A and B. A and B might be different in many aspects, for example... **Before evidence about** their comparability is **provided**, we cannot determine whether A could attain its objective through copying the policy of B.

这只是一个简单的例子，目的在于说明这三种写作要求之间的联系。具体写作时针对不同写作要求还有很多种展开形式和语言表达句式。总之，从上面的例子可以看到，这三种写作要求没有本质差别，展开分析时不必过于拘泥或纠结于写作要求，只需在一些关键性的位置在语言句式安排上有意地加以对应即可。

第四种写作要求（Alternative Explanation）稍微特殊一些，题库中这种要求的题目也比较少，一共10道。这些题目推理结构一般都是作者从一个现象，或一个实验、研究结果出发，推断了可能导致该结果或现象出现的原因。这类题目尽管论证难度较高而且论证点较少，但从写作要求来说反而比较单一。所谓Alternative Explanation就是分析推测一下导致题目所述结果和现象的原因，除了作者所分析的之外，还有其他哪些可能的原因或解释。

另外，对于不同的写作要求，在论证点的选择上会有一些差别。一道题目本身可能有10个主要问题，针对Assumption写作要求的时候可能会重点选择其中3个，针对Evidence写作要求时则可能会选择另外几个。

一般来说，针对Evidence的写作要求，凡是因为作者提供的信息不全面、不完整、缺乏关键证据而导致的问题可以重点分析。比如：

- incomplete information 信息不完整；
- vague data 模糊数据；
- incomplete comparison / selective comparison / ex parte information 不完整、选择性比较，单方面信息；
- confusing comparison and variation 横向比较和纵向比较混淆；
- failing to weigh the advantage and disadvantage thoroughly 未全面衡量正负得失；
- failing to consider the feasibility of the conclusion 未考虑结论的可行性。

这些都是作者需要提供更全面信息才能进一步支持推论的问题。

针对Assumption的写作要求，凡是因为作者作了不合理假设而导致的问题可以重点分析。比如：

- false analogy 错误类比（作者假定A和B必然可比）；
- hasty generalization 草率推广（作者假定A与B两概念之间存在必然联系，或特殊个案能够说明一般原则，或在过去一定时间段内影响推论的关键条件都没有发生变化）；
- false dilemma 非此即彼（作者假定除了AB两种极端情况之外没有其他可能）；
- cause-effect fallacy 因果关系问题（作者假定除了题目中提到的原因以外没有其他因素导致该结果）；
- sufficiency and necessity of the solution 对策的充分性和必要性（作者假定题目提出的方案对于解决问题是既充分又必要的）。

Question的写作要求对论证点的选择性不强。这种写作要求之下几乎所有问题都可以讨论，只要选择在推理过程中比较重要、自己擅长论证并且值得展开的环节分析即可；但要注意，对于前述第5种要求（要判断上文建议是否能达到预期效果，需要回答哪些问题），对策的必要性（necessity of the solution）这一点不要进行分析。因为写作要求是讨论题目的方案是否能达到目标，而对策必要性的论证思路是讨论要达到目标还有没有其他方案，与写作要求有一定矛盾，因而不要展开。

综上所述，在准备Argument写作时的两个最根本环节就是**逻辑思路**和**语言**，可以说Argument所有准备工作都是围绕以上两方面展开的。在逻辑上，要对每道题的推理过程加以分析，列出写作要点提纲。再针对每类典型常见问题构造思路和语言，即模板。本书第五、六两章列出了每道题目比较详细的论证点以及每类问题的模板，但考生只能作为参考，要结合自己的思维特点和语言论证习惯挖掘每道题目的论证角度，构造具有个人特色的论证结构。平时考生可以对每类要论述的问题进行默想，在脑子里对论证过程加以整理：即要思考如何把这类问题说清楚，应该如何一步一步展开解释。在语言上，还需要阅读大量范文、GRE Verbal部分的阅读文章、外文期刊中的社论等论证文章来提高语感。需要注意的是，阅读这些材料的目的并不是让考生在考试中生搬硬套其中的某些句式或表达，而是通过阅读逐渐积累语感。久而久之，考生就会对这些语言达到灵活应用的程度了。

第五章　Argument题目结构和论证要点详细分析

本章列出了Argument作文题库每道题目本身推理结构和写作论证点的分析。

每道题目的不同逻辑成分将用不同的字体或符号标出，帮助考生确认哪些部分是题目论述的背景信息，哪些是事实性的论据，哪些是作者的假设，哪些是结论。

1. 每道题目的逻辑成分包括以下4类：背景信息；一般论据；作者的假设；结论。题目文字的标志含义如下：

- 标有下划线的部分是该题目的背景信息，一般不存在逻辑问题；
- 没有任何标识的正常字体部分是该题目的一般论据；
- 斜体字部分是作者的假设，即作者认定或想当然认为必然成立，但在现实中未必真正存在的信息；
- 黑体字的部分是该题目的结论。

2. 题目中带括号的数字，如：(1)、(3)，是指这句话所包含的问题出现在下列提纲的第几条。

3. 题目后面的括号内容(former XX)是指这道题对应的是旧GRE Argument作文题库中的第几题；括号内容(≈/=XX)是指这道题目和新GRE Argument作文题库中的第几题相近或者相同。

4. 题目后面的星号(★)表示这道题目的逻辑复杂性或论证难度，星号越多表示题目逻辑复杂程度或写作论证难度越高。

5. 为节省篇幅，每道题目的写作要求在此都简化处理。

【推理结构】描述了作者的推理论证思路，即作者是如何一步一步从论据推出结论的。其中加边框的内容是作者的假设；加底纹的内容是事实性信息。对于推理结构的分析认识有助于在展开论证时准确找到作者推理过程中包含的假设；也有助于针对题目的推理结构合理安排所分析的每个点的论证顺序，从而选择恰当的衔接语言来表达不同论证点之间的逻辑关系。

【提纲】列出了每道题目几乎所有可能的论证点。这些论证点并不需要考生在写作时全部加以论证，只需挑选一些对题目推理过程影响力大的，或者自己比较擅长论证的、能够展现自己语言和论证水平的问题即可。提纲中每条论证点后面括号里的斜体字描述了该问题所属类型或性质，缩写含义如下：

adv:disadv: failing to weigh the advantage and disadvantage thoroughly 没有全面衡量正负得失

C.S.: changing scopes 差异范围草率推广

F.A.: false analogy 错误类比

F.D.: false dilemma 极端选择

I.C.: incomplete comparison 不完整比较/选择性比较

I.E.: insufficient evidence 论据不充分

I.I.: incomplete information 信息不完整

I.T.: incomplete thought 考虑问题不全面

N.C.R.: non causal relationship 无因果

P→F / P→C / C→F / C→P: inferring future (current/past) condition from past (current) condition 从过去推将来

提纲中每条论证要点后面的星号（★）表示这条论证点的重要程度和对原文推理的影响力度。星号越多表示该点和题目论证的相关性和破坏力越强，写文章时应该重点论证。

此外，Argment作文题库题目顺序已作调整，主题相同或相近的题目都排在一起。

---

1. Woven baskets characterized by a particular distinctive pattern have previously been found only in the immediate vicinity of the prehistoric village of Palea and therefore were believed to have been made only by the Palean people. Recently, however, archaeologists discovered such a "Palean" basket in Lithos, an ancient village across the Brim River from Palea. *The Brim River is very deep and broad(1), and so the ancient Paleans could have crossed it only by boat(2),* and no Palean boats have been found(3). **Thus it follows that the so-called Palean baskets were not uniquely Palean(4)**. （former 37）★ ★ ★

翻　译 一种具有独特花纹的编织篮子以前只在史前村庄Palea附近地区发现过，因而被认为只可能是由Palea居民编制的。然而最近，考古学家在一个与Palea隔着一条叫做Brim河的村庄Lithos发现了一个这样的Palea篮子。Brim河很深、很宽，所以古代Palea人只能坐船穿过它，但并没有发现过Palea人的船只。这表明这种所谓的Palea篮子并不是Palea人所独有的。

推理结构

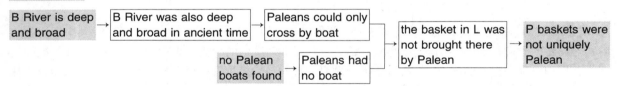

写作要求 *What specific **evidence** is needed to evaluate the argument?*

提　纲

我们需要作者提供论据证明3点：

1. The change of the condition of Brim River. If in Palean time, the Brim River was not as deep and broad as it currently is, then Paleans could have crossed it without boat. （C→P）★ ★ ★

2. If the Paleans could cross broad rivers by means other than boat. （I.T.）★ ★ ★ ★

3. How does the author know Paleans have no boats? The fact that no Palean boats were found hitherto does not necessarily indicate that Paleans have no boats at all. （*Does the survey make any difference?*）★ ★ ★ ★

同时，对于上文论证的情况，还存在以下可能性：

4. The Palean basket could have arrived in other places through many possible methods such as trade, flood, or boats possessed by other culture. （I.T.）★ ★ ★ ★

本题推理的最关键环节就在于被发现的篮子有没有可能是Palea人制造，后来通过其他渠道流传到其他地区的。因此，论证的主要环节就集中在作者提供的论据是否足以排除以上可能性上面。

---

2. The following appeared as part of a letter to the editor of a scientific journal.

② **"A recent study of eighteen rhesus monkeys provides clues as to the effects of birth order on an individual's levels of stimulation.** The study showed that in stimulating situations（such as an encounter with an unfamiliar monkey）, firstborn infant monkeys produce up to twice as much of the hormone cortisol, which primes the body for increased activity levels (1), as do their younger siblings. Firstborn humans also produce relatively high levels of cortisol in stimulating situations（such as the return of a parent after an absence）(2). The study also found that during pregnancy, first-time mother monkeys had higher levels of cortisol than did those who had had several offspring(3)." ★★★★★

翻　译 最近一次对于18只猕猴的研究在出生次序对于个体刺激程度的影响方面提供了线索。研究表明，当处于刺激环境下（比如遇到一只不认识的猴子），头胎幼猕猴所分泌的皮质醇（一种导致身体活动程度增加的物质）比它们的弟弟妹妹多一倍。头胎人类在刺激环境下（比如父母一方离开一段时间后回来）也会分泌相对更多的皮质醇。研究也发现，在怀孕期间，第一次生育的母猕猴皮质醇水平高于已经多次生育的猕猴。

推理结构

firstborn monkeys produce more cortisol in stimulating situation

firstborn humans also produce more cortisol in similar situation → birth order affects levels of stimulation through cortisol

first-time mother monkeys have higher levels of cortisol

写作要求 *alternative explanations*

提　纲

1. Although cortisol primes the body for increased activity levels, as the author mentioned, such activities might also result from other factors, such as the individual's gene, environment in which the individual was brought up, etc. (*confusing concurrence with causality*) ★★★★★

2. Granted that cortisol levels are closely related to the levels of stimulation, the study above only studied limited situations of stimulation（namely, encountering with unfamiliar monkeys, returning of parents）. Therefore, whether the level of cortisol secretion will also be different among siblings under other stimulating condition is open to doubt. The secretion of cortisol may only govern activities under certain stimulation. (*C.S.*) ★★★★

3. For the last piece of evidence, we could not find any relationship between mother monkeys' levels of cortisol and their offsprings' levels of activity under stimulation. (*N.C.R.*) ★★★

论证要点

本题结论为第一句，即：个体出生次序对个体受刺激时的反应有影响。题目要求对这一结论提出其他可能解释，也就是导致个体对刺激的不同反应除了出生次序以外的其他可能原因；对于其他可能诱因的分析是本题最核心的论证点。另外，该研究只研究了所谓"刺激环境"中有限的几种情形（遇到陌生个体、与双亲分离等），因而，出生次序对于其他种类的刺激环境是否也有影响未知，也可以针对这一差异范围草率推广加以质疑。而最后一条关于母体皮质醇水平的信息则和结论完全没有直接逻辑联系，写文章时基本无法深入展开，点到即可。

3. The following appeared as a letter to the editor from a Central Plaza store owner.

> <u>"Over the past two years, the number of shoppers in Central Plaza has been steadily decreasing while the popularity of skateboarding has increased dramatically(1)</u>. *Many Central Plaza store owners(2) believe that the decrease in their business is due to the number of skateboard users in the plaza.* There has also been a dramatic increase in the amount of litter and vandalism throughout the plaza. **Thus, we recommend that the city prohibit skateboarding in Central Plaza.** *If skateboarding is prohibited here, we predict that business in Central Plaza will return to its previously high levels(3,4)."* (former 227) ★★★

翻　译 过去2年中，到中央广场购物的人数逐渐减少，而玩滑板的人数显著增加。很多中央广场的商户相信他们生意的减少归因于在广场玩滑板的人数的增多。整个广场乱丢废弃物和破坏公物的现象也显著增加。因此，我们建议本市禁止在中央广场玩滑板。我们预计，如果这里禁止玩滑板，中央广场的贸易额将会恢复到以往的高水平。

推理结构

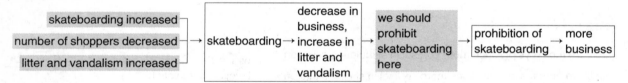

写作要求 What **questions** should be answered to decide whether the recommendation will have the predicted result?

提　纲

1. The author unfairly assumes that it is the presence of skateboarders that leads to the current situation of the plaza. Are there any other possible explanations? Is it possible that the recession of the plaza results in the increasing popularity of skateboarding here? (*N.C.R./confusing the cause and the effect*) ★★★★★

2. Downtown merchants' opinion might not be representative of all people. How about other citizens' attitude toward skateboarding? (*selective sample*) ★★★★

3. Would banning skateboarding in Central Plaza suffice for business returning to previous level? (*sufficiency of the solution*) ★★★★

4. Is it possible that skateboarding is actually helpful for achieving the city's objective of providing a fun and relaxing place for people to congregate? (*adv:disadv*) ★★★

论证要点

　　本题关键环节在于是否是因为玩滑板人数的增多导致了中央广场贸易额的减少？对于这一因果关系的疑问是本题作者需要回答的首要问题。首先，有可能存在其他原因；其次，有可能正因为这里日渐衰败所以才成为滑板活动场所。此外，当地商户这一选择性样本以及禁止滑板对于恢复广场繁荣的充分性也是作者需要考虑的问题。

4. The following appeared as a letter to the editor from the owner of a skate shop in Central Plaza.

171 "Two years ago the city voted to prohibit skateboarding in Central Plaza. They claimed that skateboard users were responsible for the litter and vandalism that were keeping other visitors from coming to the plaza. In the past two years, however, there has only been a small increase in the number of visitors to Central Plaza(1), and litter and vandalism are still problematic(2). Skateboarding is permitted in Monroe Park, however, and there is no problem with litter or vandalism there(3). In order to restore Central Plaza to its former glory(4), then, **we recommend that the city lift its prohibition on skateboarding in the plaza.**" (former 227, ≈3) ★★★

翻　译 2年前本市投票禁止在中央广场玩滑板。他们宣称乱扔垃圾和破坏公物现象是玩滑板的人造成的，而这些现象正是导致人们不去该广场的原因。而在过去2年中，去中央广场的游客数量仅有少量回升，乱扔垃圾和破坏公物的问题仍然存在。Monroe公园就允许玩滑板，但那里并没有乱扔垃圾和破坏公物的问题。为使中央广场重塑往日辉煌，我们建议本市解除该广场对玩滑板的限制。

推理结构

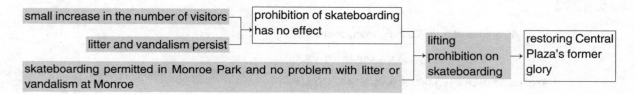

写作要求

*What **questions** should be answered to decide whether the recommendation and the argument are reasonable?*

提　纲

1. Isn't the increase, though small, an indication of the effectiveness of the prohibition? (*negative evidence*) ★★

2. Would the situation of litter and vandalism be even worse without the prohibition on skateboarding? (*lack of controlled study*) ★★★★

3. Are Central Plaza and Monroe Park comparable at every aspect? (*F.A.*) ★★★

4. Is skateboarding a contributing factor to Central Plaza's former glory? (*sufficiency/necessity of the solution*) ★★★★

论证要点

　　本题的主要问题是作者认为对滑板的限制没有起到效果，但在缺乏对比的情况下不能盲目认为该禁令一定无效。其次，Monroe公园中央广场未必可比，而且取消对滑板的限制也未必能保证广场的繁荣。

　　请注意本题和第3题的区别：第3题是作者认为滑板导致了广场的衰败而要求禁止玩滑板；而本题是作者认为滑板没有导致负面影响而要对玩滑板解禁。

5. The following appeared in a letter from a homeowner to a friend.

4 "*Of the two leading real estate firms in our town—Adams Realty and Fitch Realty—Adams is clearly superior*. Adams has 40 real estate agents; in contrast, Fitch has 25, many of whom work only part-time(1,2,3). Moreover, Adams' revenue last year(4) was twice as high as that of Fitch(5), and included home sales that averaged $168,000, compared to Fitch's $144,000(6). Homes listed with Adams sell faster as well: ten years ago, I listed my home with Fitch and it took more than four months to sell; last year, when I sold another home, I listed it with Adams, and it took only one month(7). **Thus, if you want to sell your home quickly and at a good price, you should use Adams.**"(former 4) ★★

翻　译　在本市两家最大的房地产经纪公司——Adams Realty和Fitch Realty——中，Adams显然更优秀。Adams有40名房地产经纪人，而Fitch只有25个，且很多是兼职者。而且，Adams去年的收入是Fitch的两倍，其平均房价为$168000，而Fitch仅为$144000。在Adams销售的房屋卖得也更快：10年前，我把我的房产交给Fitch，它用了4个多月才卖出去；去年，我在Adams卖了另一处房产，仅用1个月就售出了。因此，要想让你的房产卖得更快更好，你应该选择Adams。

推理结构

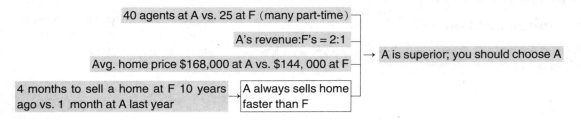

写作要求 *assumptions*

提　纲

1. The author hastily assumes that the quality of a real estate firm is directly proportional to the number of its agents or the number of hours per week that its agents work. (*U.C.*) ★★★

2. The author unfairly implies that most (or all) agents in Adams work full-time.(*ex parte information*) ★★

3. For lack of data concerning the average number of homes sold per agent, we cannot evaluate the actual performance of agents in the two firms.(*V.D.*) ★★

4. The assumption that last year's sales result could be representative of all time is obviously unwarranted. (*selective sample*) ★★★

5. The disparity in sales volume of the two companies can readily be explained by other factors, such as their serving areas and locations.(*N.C.R.*) ★★★★

6. The fact that the average sales price of a home sold by Adams is higher than that of a home sold by Fitch does not indicate that Adams is more effective in selling homes than Fitch.(*N.C.R.*)
Adams售出房屋平均价格高可能有其他因素，比如地段、档次、面积、装修情况等。★★★★

7. The disparity in the speed of the two sales could be explained by factors that would change through the time, or some critical differences of the two properties. (*F.A./I.C./P→F*) ★★★★★

本题最核心的假设在于Adams更加优秀，上述所有论证点全是围绕这一点展开的。员工数量、兼职或全职都和作为房产中介的能力没有直接联系。而去年两家公司的收入、平均房价以及两处房产的销售速度也都可以由其他因素解释；因而未必能证明是Adams更出色的能力导致了这些后果。

---

6. The following appeared in a letter to the editor of the *Balmer Island Gazette*.

5 "On Balmer Island, where mopeds serve as a popular form of transportation, the population increases to 100,000 during the summer months. **To reduce the number of accidents involving mopeds and pedestrians (4), the town council of Balmer Island should limit the number of mopeds rented by the island's moped rental companies (3) from 50 per day to 25 per day during the summer season (5).** *By limiting the number of rentals, the town council will attain the 50 percent annual reduction in moped accidents(4) that was achieved last year on the neighboring island of Seaville(2), when Seaville's town council enforced similar limits on moped rentals(1)."* (former 20) ★ ★ ★ ★

翻 译 在以机动自行车为主要交通方式之一的Balmer Island，其人口在夏季达到100000。为减少由机动自行车和行人引发的事故，Balmer Island市议会应在夏季把本岛机动自行车出租公司的自行车出租数量从每天50辆限制到每天25辆。通过限制出租数量，市议会将能够像去年邻岛Seaville市议会实施了类似的限制后一样，实现年度机动自行车事故减少50%的目标。

推理结构

50% reduction in moped accidents on Seaville after enforcing the limits	→	limits → reduction	→	Balmer should pose similar limits

写作要求 *What **questions** should be answered to decide whether the recommendation will have the predicted result?*

提 纲

1. Are there any other possible explanations（other than the limits）for the 50% decline in Seaville's moped accident rate last year?（*N.C.R.*）★ ★ ★ ★

2. Are Balmer Island and Seaville comparable?（*F.A.*）★ ★ ★ ★

3. What's the accurate data about the current number of mopeds rented by the companies per day? And how many accidents result from those rented mopeds?（*I.I.*）★ ★ ★

4. Would the restrictions that served to reduce the incidence of all "**moped accidents**" by 50% also serve to reduce the incidence of accidents involving "mopeds **and pedestrians**" by 50%?（*U.C.*）★ ★ ★

5. Will any of the conditions in Balmer that might affect the rate of moped-pedestrian accidents vary after the restrictions are enacted?（*P→F*）★ ★ ★

论证要点

本题主要推理手法就是Balmer和Seaville的类比。首先需要论证的就是，在Seaville，是否是因为出台了这些限制而使事故减少；其次，Seaville和Balmer是否可比。其他论证点，例如Balmer目前每家机动自行车公司的出租数量（也就是出租数量还有没有进一步减少的可能性和空间）、所有事故中由出租的机动自行车引发的事故所占比例，以及限制了机动自行车是否也能减少行人事故等，其不全面和概念模糊的问题可以辅助论证。

7. The following appeared in a letter to the editor of the *Balmer Island Gazette*.

159 "The population on Balmer Island increases to 100,000 during the summer months. To reduce the number of accidents involving mopeds and pedestrians（4）, the town council of Balmer Island plans to limit the number of mopeds rented by each of the island's six moped rental companies （3）from 50 per day to 30 per day during the summer season（5,6）. Last year, the neighboring island of Torseau（2）enforced similar limits on moped rentals（1）and saw a 50 percent reduction in moped accidents. **We predict that putting these limits into effect on Balmer Island will result in the same reduction in moped accidents.**"（former 20, ≈5）
★ ★ ★ ★

翻 译 Balmer Island的人口在夏季达到了100000。为减少由机动自行车和行人引发的事故，Balmer Island市议会计划把本岛6个机动自行车出租公司的自行车出租数量在夏季从每天50辆限制到每天30辆。去年，邻岛Torseau市在对机动自行车出租实施了类似的限制之后，机动自行车事故减少了50%。我们预计，在Balmer Island实施这些限制将带来减少机动自行车事故的同样效果。

推理结构

50% reduction in moped accidents on Torseau after enforcing the limits → limits → reduction → Balmer should pose similar limits

写作要求

*What **questions** should be answered to decide whether the prediction and the argument are reasonable?*

提 纲

1. Are there any other possible explanations for the 50% decline in Torseau's moped accident rate last year? （*N.C.R.*）★ ★ ★ ★

2. Are Balmer Island and Torseau comparable?（*F.A.*）★ ★ ★ ★

3. What percentage of mopeds in Balmer Island is rented by the six companies? What is the current number of mopeds rented by the six companies per day? How many accidents result from those rented mopeds?（*I.I.*）假如：①这6家公司所出租的机动自行车在Balmer所有机动自行车中占的比例很小；②这些公司当前每天出租的自行车数量并不比30辆多很多；③大多数事故都不是由这些出租的机动自行车造成的，那么实施作者所说的限制对于减少机动自行车事故不会有太大作用。★ ★ ★

4. Would the restrictions that served to reduce the incidence of all "**moped** accidents" by 50% also serve to reduce the incidence of accidents involving "mopeds and **pedestrians**" by 50%?（*U.C.*）★ ★ ★

5. Will any of the conditions in Balmer that might affect the rate of moped-pedestrian accidents vary after the restrictions are enacted?（*P→F*）★ ★ ★

6. Are there any other effective methods that could serve the author's purpose?（*necessity of the solution*）★ ★ ★

论证要点

本题主要推理方式就是Balmer和Torseau的类比。因此，首先需要论证的是，Torseau是否是因为出台了这些限制而使事故减少；其次，Torseau和Balmer是否可比。其他论证点，例如Balmer目前每家机动自行车公司的出租数量（也就是出租数量还有没有进一步减少的可能性和空间）、所有事故中由出租的机动自行车引发的事故所占比例，以及限制了机动自行车是否也能减少行人事故等，其不全面和概念模糊的问题可以辅助论证。

8. The following appeared in a letter to the editor of the *Balmer Island Gazette*.

173 "The population on Balmer Island doubles during the summer months. During the summer, then, the town council of Balmer Island should decrease the maximum number of moped rentals allowed at each of the island's six moped and bicycle rental companies（3）from 50 per day to 30 per day（5）. *This will significantly reduce the number of summertime accidents involving mopeds and pedestrians*（4）. The neighboring island of Torseau（2）actually saw a 50 percent reduction in moped accidents last year（1）when Torseau's town council enforced similar limits on moped rentals. **To help reduce moped accidents, therefore, we should also enforce these limitations during the summer months (6).**" (former 20, ≈5, 159) ★★★★

翻　译 Balmer Island的人口在夏季翻了番。因此，Balmer Island市议会应在夏季把本岛6个机动自行车和自行车出租公司每天的出租数量从50辆降低到30辆。这将显著减少在夏季与机动自行车和行人有关的事故。去年，邻岛Torseau市议会实施了类似的限制后机动自行车事故真的减少了50%。因此，为帮助减少机动自行车事故，我们也应该在夏季实施这些限制。

推理结构

50% reduction in moped accidents on Torseau after enforcing the limits	→	limits → reduction	→	Balmer should pose similar limits

写作要求 *assumptions*

提　纲

1. The author unfairly assumes that it is the limits on moped rentals that result in the 50% decline in Torseau's moped accidents rate last year. (*N.C.R.*) ★★★★

2. The author assumes that Balmer Island and Torseau are comparable. (*F.A.*) ★★★★

3. We need to know what percentage of mopeds in Balmer Island is rented by the six companies, the current number of mopeds rented by the six companies per day, and the number of accidents resulting from those rented mopeds to evaluate whether posing limits on the number of moped rented by the companies will have effect on reducing accident rate. (*I.I.*)

   假如：①这6家公司所出租的机动自行车在Balmer所有机动自行车中占的比例很小；②这些公司当前每天出租的自行车数量并不比30辆多很多；③大多数事故都不是由这些出租的机动自行车造成的，那么实施作者所说的限制对于减少机动自行车事故不会有太大作用。★★★

4. The author assumes that the restrictions that served to reduce the incidence of all "**moped** accidents" by 50% will also serve to reduce the incidence of accidents involving "mopeds and **pedestrians**" by 50%. (*U.C.*) ★★★

5. The author assumes that the conditions in Balmer that might affect the rate of moped-pedestrian accidents will remain unchanged after the restrictions are enacted. (*P→F*) ★★★

6. The author ignores other effective methods that could serve the purpose of reducing accidents. (*necessity of the solution*) ★★★

论证要点

　　本题的主要推理方式就是Balmer和Torseau的类比。因此，首先需要论证的是，Torseau是否是因为出台了这些限制而使事故减少；其次，Torseau和Balmer是否可比。其他论证点，例如Balmer目前每家机动自行车公司的出租数量（也就是出租数量还有没有进一步减少的可能性和空间）、所有事故中由出租的机动自行车引发的事故所占比例，以及限制了机动自行车是否也能减少行人事故等，其不全面和概念模糊的问题可以辅助论证。

9. Arctic deer live on islands in Canada's arctic regions. They search for food by moving over ice from island to island during the course of the year. Their habitat is limited to areas warm enough to sustain the plants on which they feed and cold enough, at least some of the year, for the ice to cover the sea separating the islands, allowing the deer to travel over it. Unfortunately, according to reports from local hunters(1), the deer populations are declining. Since these reports coincide with recent global warming trends(2) that have caused the sea ice to melt, **we can conclude that the purported decline in arctic deer populations is the result of the deer's being unable to follow their age-old migration patterns(4) across the frozen sea(3).** (former 45) ★★★★★

翻　译 北极鹿生活在加拿大极地区域的岛屿上。它们全年都通过冰块在岛屿间移动来寻找食物。它们的栖居地局限在那些温暖得足以维持它们赖以生存的植物的生长，并且在一年中至少某些时候冷到足以让岛屿间的海面结冰以使它们能够在岛屿间穿行的地方。不幸的是，根据当地猎人的报告，鹿的数量正在下降。由于这些报告正好与最近引起海洋冰面融化的全球变暖趋势同时发生，我们由此可以得出结论：北极鹿数量的下降是它们无法按由来已久的迁移习惯穿越结冰海面的结果。

推理结构

population of arctic deer declined

global warming trends

→ warming → ice melt → deer unable to migrate

写作要求 *What specific **evidence** is needed to evaluate the argument?*

提　纲

我们需要作者提供论据说明3点：

1. The accuracy and details about the reports from local hunters. (*selective sample*) ★★★
2. The actual area influenced by the global warming trends. The trends may have no effects on the specific region mentioned by the editorial. (*C.S.*) ★★★★
3. Alternative explanations that can account for the decline in arctic deer population.(*N.C.R.*) ★★★★

同时，对于上文论证的情况，还存在以下可能性：

4. The change in climate patterns does not inevitably cause the decline in deer populations; deer may adapt themselves to the new weather pattern through certain means. (*sufficiency of the claim/N.C.R.*) ★★★★

论证要点

本题论证点比较零散。猎人观察数据的准确性，全球变暖对于上述极地地区的影响，北极鹿对于气候变化的适应能力以及引起鹿数量下降的其他原因——这些都是影响作者结论比较关键的因素。

10. The following is a recommendation from the Board of Directors of Monarch Books.

"We recommend that Monarch Books open a café in its store(2). Monarch, having been in business at the same location for more than twenty years, has a large customer base because it is known for its wide selection of books on all subjects. *Clearly, opening the café would attract more customers(1).* **Space could be made for the café by discontinuing the children's book section(6),** *which will probably become less popular* given that the most recent national census(3) indicated a significant decline in the percentage of the population under age ten (4,5). *Opening a café will allow Monarch to attract more customers and better compete with Regal Books, which recently opened its own café.*" (former 44) ★★★

翻　译 我们建议Monarch书店在店内开设一家咖啡厅。Monarch已经在同一店址经营了20余年，因其广泛提供各类型图书而著名，并因此拥有庞大的消费者群体。显然，开设咖啡厅能吸引更多的顾客。咖啡厅的空间可以通过撤销儿童书籍的柜台获得。最近一次全国调查显示，10岁以下的儿童在总人口中所占比例显著下降，因此儿童书籍很可能将卖得不好。开设咖啡厅将使Monarch吸引更多消费者，并能更好地和最近开设了咖啡厅的Regal书店竞争。

推理结构

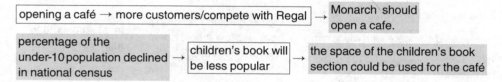

```
opening a café → more customers/compete with Regal  →  Monarch should
                                                        open a cafe.

percentage of the
under-10 population declined  →  children's book will  →  the space of the children's book
in national census               be less popular           section could be used for the café
```

写作要求 *What **questions** should be answered to decide whether the recommendation will have the predicted result?*

提　纲

1. Is there any guarantee that opening a café at Monarch will surely attract substantially more customers? (*I.E./ sufficiency of the solution*) ★★★

2. How much is the cost of opening the café? (*adv:disadv*) ★★★

3. Could the result of the national census be properly applied to the region where Monarch located? (*C.S.*) ★★★★

4. Although the percent of children in the general population has declined, the total number of children may increase. (*V.D.*) ★★★

5. Granted that the number of children who are under age ten has decreased, will the number of children who go to our bookstore, or the need for children's book also decline? (*N.C.R.*) ★★★

6. Are there any negative effects of cutting out children's book section and opening the café? (*adv:disadv*) ★★★★★

论证要点

　　本题有两个并行的结论：我们要开设咖啡厅以及儿童书籍柜台可以撤销。但针对本题写作要求"探讨建议是否能达到预期效果"，写作时主要论证的内容应该集中在讨论开设咖啡厅是否能保证我们吸引更多顾客且更好地与Regal竞争这一环节上面。因此，论证点主要围绕两方面展开：首先，开设咖啡厅未必能吸引顾客、提高竞争力——顾客未必对咖啡厅感兴趣；作者提到的全国调查也未必说明在这个书店儿童书籍销售量会受影响。其次，开设咖啡厅可能会带来不良影响，比如增加成本和运营投入、影响书店形象（取消儿童书籍正好和该书店广泛提供各类图书的声誉相矛盾，这一点可以用反证法来展开）。

---

11. The following is a recommendation from the business manager of Monarch Books.

98 "Since its opening in Collegeville twenty years ago, Monarch Books has developed a large customer base due to its reader-friendly atmosphere and wide selection of books on all subjects (5). Last month, Book and Bean, a combination bookstore and coffee shop, announced its intention(1) to open a Collegeville store(2,3). **Monarch Books should open its own in-store café (4) in the space currently devoted to children's books(5).** Given recent national census data(6) indicating a significant decline in the percentage of the population under age ten(7), *sales of children's books are likely to decline(8).* By replacing its children's books section with a café, *Monarch Books can increase profits and ward off competition from Book and Bean.*" (former 44, ≈7)

Monarch书店自从20年前在Collegeville开业以来，因其友好的阅读氛围以及广泛的图书选择而建立了广大客户群。上个月，结合了书店和咖啡店的Book and Bean综合商店宣布了在Collegeville开店的意愿。Monarch书店应该用现在陈列儿童图书的空间开设自己的店内咖啡厅。鉴于最近一次全国调查显示10岁以下的儿童在总人口中所占的比例显著下降，儿童书籍很可能将不再好卖。通过将儿童图书柜台改造为咖啡厅，Monarch将提高利润并能与Book and Bean展开竞争。

推理结构

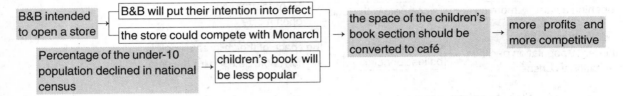

写作要求 *assumptions*

提　纲

1. No evidence could guarantee that B&B will actually put the intention into effect. (*U.A.*) ★★★

2. Without any detailed information about the proposed store (e.g. its scale, the scope of its business, etc.), the assumption that Monarch should take the store into account when formulating its business strategies is unfounded. (*I.I./necessity of the solution*) ★★★

3. The manager hastily assumes that the proposed store will be able to compete with Monarch. (*U.A.*) ★★★

4. The manager fails to provide any information about the cost of opening and running the café, thus the proposed profit increase is not guaranteed. (*I.I./adv:disadv*) ★★★★

5. The manager fails to consider the negative effects of cutting out children's book section to open the café. The action may pose negative impact on their reputation of providing wide selection of books on all subjects. (*adv:disadv*) ★★★★★

6. The result of a national census might not be properly applied to the region where Monarch located. (*C.S.*) ★★★★

7. Although the percent of children in the general population has declined, the total number of children may increase. (*V.D.*) ★★★

8. Granted that the number of children who are under age ten has decreased, the manager also assumes that the number of children who go to our bookstore, or the need for children's book will also decline. (*N.C.R.*) ★★★

论证要点

　　本题论证点主要围绕三方面展开：首先，B&B只是表达其开店意愿，但不能保证是否真的会开；而且就算开了也未必会对Monarch构成威胁。其次，Monarch开设咖啡厅未必能吸引顾客、提高竞争力——Monarch的顾客未必对咖啡厅感兴趣；作者提到的全国调查也未必说明在这个书店儿童书籍也将会滞销。而且，开设咖啡厅可能会带来不良影响，比如增加成本和运营投入、影响书店形象(取消儿童书籍柜台正好和该书店提供广泛的图书选择相矛盾，这一点可以用反证法来展开)。

12. The following is a recommendation from the business manager of Monarch Books.

99 <u>"Since its opening in Collegeville twenty years ago, Monarch Books has developed a large</u> <u>customer base due to its reader-friendly atmosphere and wide selection of books on all subjects(5).</u> <u>Last month, Book and Bean, a combination bookstore and coffee shop, announced its intention(1)</u> <u>to open a Collegeville store(2,3).</u> **Monarch Books should open its own in-store café(4) in the** **space currently devoted to children's books(5).** Given recent national census data(6) indicating a significant decline in the percentage of the population under age ten(7), *sales of children's books* *are likely to decline(8).* By replacing its children's books section with a café, *Monarch Books can* *increase profits and ward off competition from Book and Bean.*" (former 44, ≈7, =98))

翻 译 自从Monarch书店20年前在Collegeville开业以来,因其友好的阅读氛围以及广泛的图书选择而建立了广大客户群。上个月,结合了书店和咖啡店的Book and Bean综合商店宣布了在Collegeville开店的意愿。Monarch书店应该用现在陈列儿童图书的空间开设自己的店内咖啡厅。鉴于最近一次全国调查显示10岁以下的儿童在总人口中所占的比例显著下降,儿童书籍很可能将不再好卖。通过将儿童书籍柜台改造为咖啡厅,Monarch将提高利润并能与Book and Bean展开竞争。

推理结构

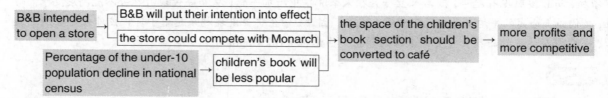

写作要求 *What specific **evidence** is needed to evaluate the argument?*

提 纲

作者需要提供能说明以下方面的论据或信息:

1. B&B will put the intention into effect. (*U.A.*) ★★★

2. Detailed information about the proposed store (e.g. its scale, the scope of its business, etc.). The assumption that Monarch should take the store into account when formulating its business strategies is unfounded. (*I.I./necessity of the solution*) ★★★

3. The proposed store will be able to compete with Monarch. (*U.A.*) ★★★★

4. The cost of opening and running the café. The proposed profit increase is not guaranteed. (*I.I./adv:disadv*) ★★★

5. The negative effects of cutting out children's book section to open the café. The action may just pose negative impact on their reputation of providing wide selection of books on all subjects. (*adv:disadv*)
   ★★★★★

6. The result of a national census could be properly applied to the region where Monarch located. (*C.S.*)
   ★★★★

对于上文论述还存在以下问题:

7. Although the percent of children in the general population has declined, the total number of children may increase. (*V.D.*) ★★★

8. Granted that the number of children who are under age ten has decreased, the manager still need to provide evidence to show that the number of children who go to our bookstore, or the need for children's book will also decline. (*N.C.R.*) ★★★

本题论证点主要围绕三方面展开：首先，B&B只是表达其开店意愿，但不能保证是否真的会开；而且就算开了也未必会对Monarch构成威胁。其次，Monarch开设咖啡厅未必能吸引顾客、提高竞争力——Monarch的顾客未必对咖啡厅感兴趣；作者提到的全国调查也未必说明在这个书店儿童书籍也将会滞销。而且，开设咖啡厅可能会带来不良影响，比如增加成本和运营投入、影响书店形象（取消儿童书籍柜台正好和该书店广泛提供各类图书的声誉相矛盾）。作者需要提供证据说明以上情况。

---

13. The following appeared in a memo from the director of student housing at Buckingham College.

"To serve the housing needs of our students, Buckingham College should build a number of new dormitory(6). Buckingham's enrollment is growing and, based on current trends(1), *will double over the next 50 years, thus making existing dormitory space inadequate.* Moreover, the average rent for an apartment in our town has risen(3) in recent years(2). *Consequently, students will find it increasingly difficult to afford off-campus housing. Finally, attractive new dormitories would make prospective students more likely to enroll at Buckingham (4,5).*" （former 240）★ ★ ★

翻　译 为满足学生的住宿需求，Buckingham学院应该建造一批新的宿舍。Buckingham的报名人数正在增加，而且按照现有趋势，报名人数将会在未来50年中增加一倍，从而导致现有宿舍不能满足要求。而且，我们镇上公寓的平均租金在近几年间上涨了。因此，学生将会发现越来越难于负担校外住宿费用。最后，一幢引人注目的新宿舍将会使未来的学生更愿意报考Buckingham。

推理结构

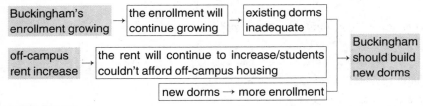

写作要求 *What specific **evidence** is needed to evaluate the argument?*

提　纲

我们需要作者提供论据证明以下几点：

1. The trends of increasing enrollment will continue in the future. （C→F）★ ★ ★

2. The rent for off-campus apartment will continue to increase in the following years. （C→F）★ ★ ★

3. Whether the average rent for off-campus apartment has increased to an extent that students cannot afford. （I.I./confusing comparison with variation）★ ★ ★

4. New dormitories will be both sufficient and necessary for attracting prospective students. （sufficiency/ necessity of the solution）★ ★ ★

5. More enrollment of prospective students will not conflict the director's purpose of solving the housing problem. （negative evidence）★ ★ ★

6. Current dormitories in Buckingham could not meet students' housing needs. （necessity of the solution）★ ★ ★

论证要点

本题论证点比较分散，与题目推理的相关性都没有太大差别。

14. Nature's Way, a chain of stores selling health food and other health-related products (4), is opening its next franchise in the town of Plainsville. **The store should prove to be very successful(8):** Nature's Way franchises tend to be most profitable in areas where residents lead healthy lives(6,7), *and clearly Plainsville is such an area.* Plainsville merchants report that sales of running shoes and exercise clothing are at all-time highs(1,3). The local health club has more members than ever, and the weight training and aerobics classes are always full (2,3). Finally, Plainsville's schoolchildren represent a new generation of potential customers: these schoolchildren are required to participate in a fitness-for-life program, which emphasizes the benefits of regular exercise at an early age(5). (former 1) ★★

翻　译 一家经营健康食品以及其他相关健康产品的连锁店Nature's Way打算在Plainsville开设一家新店。该店将会非常成功：Nature's Way连锁店在那些人们注重健康生活的地区赢利是最多的，Plainsville显然就是这样的地区。Plainsville的商家报告说运动鞋和运动衣的销售处于历史高点。当地一家康体俱乐部现在的会员比以往任何时候都多，减肥训练班和体操班总是满员。最后，Plainsville的学生将会是新的潜在客户群：这些在校学生被要求参加一个叫做"健康生活"的项目，它强调从小开始经常锻炼的好处。

推理结构

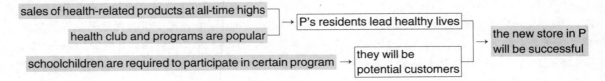

写作要求 *assumptions*

提　纲

1. Strong sales of exercise apparel do not necessarily indicate that Plainesville residents are interested in exercise, or that they would be interested in NW's products. (*U.C./N.C.R.*) ★★★

2. The popularity of the local health club is little indication that the residents in Plainsville now live much healthier lives. The fact could be explained by other factors. (*N.C.R.*)

3. The arguer fails to substantiate the assumption that this interest will continue in the foreseeable future. (*P→F*) ★★★★

4. Granted that Plainsville residents do exercise regularly, the assumption that people who exercise regularly are also interested in buying health food and health-related products is unwarranted. (*U.C.*) ★★★

5. For lack of details of the program, the mere fact that a certain fitness program is mandatory for Plainesville's schoolchildren accomplishes nothing toward bolstering the recommendation. (*I.I./N.C.R.*) ★★★

6. The arguer fails to consider other possible factors besides residents' interest in healthy lives that may determine the success of their existing stores. (*adv:disadv/confusing concurrence with causality*) ★★

7. The arguer assumes that their former experience could also be properly applied to future condition. (*P→F*) ★★★

8. The arguer unfairly assumes that Plainesville residents will prefer Nature's Way over other merchants that sell similar products. (*U.A./I.T.*) ★★

本题关键假设在于 Nature's Way 以往的成功经验在将来也同样适用，而且 Plainsville 的居民确实注重健康生活。本题主要论证都是围绕以往的经验、情况在未来未必延续，以及作者提供的信息不足以证明 Plainsville 居民注重健康生活这些关键环节展开的。

---

15. The following appeared in a memorandum written by the vice president of Health Naturally, a small but expanding chain of stores selling health food and other health-related products.

"<u>Our previous experience has been that our stores are most profitable in areas where residents are highly concerned with leading healthy lives (1,2)</u>. **We should therefore build one of our new stores in Plainsville (8),** *which clearly has many such residents (9).* Plainsville merchants report that sales of running shoes and exercise equipment are at all-time highs (3). The local health club, which nearly closed five years ago due to lack of business, has more members than ever, and the weight-training and aerobics classes are always full (4,5). *We can even anticipate a new generation of customers:* Plainsville's schoolchildren are required to participate in a program called Fitness for Life, which emphasizes the benefits of regular exercise at an early age (6,7)." (former 1, ≈9) ★ ★

翻　译 以往经验显示，我们的商店在那些居民对健康生活高度关注的地区赢利最多。因此我们应该在 Plainsville 开设一家新的连锁店，那里显然有很多这样的居民。Plainsville 的商家报告说运动鞋和运动设备的销售处于历史高点。当地一家 5 年前因缺乏客源而濒临倒闭的健康俱乐部现在的会员比以往任何时候都多，减肥训练班和体操班总是满员。我们还可以预见到新生代顾客群：Plainsville 的在校学生被要求参加一个叫做"健康生活"的项目，它强调从小开始经常锻炼的好处。

推理结构

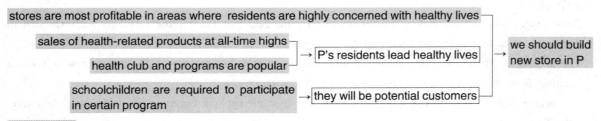

写作要求 *What specific **evidence** is needed to evaluate the argument?*

提　纲

作者需要提供说明以下情况的信息或论据：

1. Other factors besides residents' interest in healthy lives that may contribute to the success of their existing stores. (*confusing concurrence with causality*) ★ ★

2. Previous experience could be successfully applied to future condition. (*P→F*) ★ ★ ★
   对于上文论述还存在以下问题：

3. Strong sales of exercise apparel do not necessarily indicate that Plainesville residents are interested in exercise, or that these residents would be interested in HN's products. (*U.C.*) ★ ★ ★

4. The popularity of the local health club is little indication that the residents in Plainsville live much healthier lives now, and that HN will earn a profit from a store in Plainesville. (*N.C.R.*)

作者还需要提供信息或论据来说明：

5. This interest will continue in the foreseeable future. (P→F) ★★★★

6. People who exercise regularly are also interested in buying health food and health-related products. (U.C.) ★★★

7. Details of the program. The mere fact that a certain fitness program is mandatory for Plainesville's schoolchildren accomplishes nothing toward bolstering the recommendation. (N.C.R.) ★★★

8. The cost of building such a new store. We can not be convinced that the new store will be profitable. (adv: disadv) ★★

9. Plainesville residents will prefer HN over other merchants that sell similar products. (U.A./I.T.) ★★

论证要点

本题关键环节在于HN以往的成功经验在将来是否同样适用，以及Plainsville的居民是否确实注重健康生活。本题主要论证都是围绕以往的经验、情况在未来未必延续，以及作者提供的信息不足以证明Plainsville居民注重健康生活这些关键环节展开的。

---

16. The following appeared in a memorandum written by the vice president of Health Naturally, a small but expanding chain of stores selling health food and other health-related products.

〔90〕 "Our previous experience has been that our stores are most profitable in areas where residents are highly concerned with leading healthy lives(1,2). **We should therefore build one of our new stores in Plainsville (8),** *which clearly has many such residents(9).* Plainsville merchants report that sales of running shoes and exercise equipment are at all-time highs(3). The local health club, which nearly closed five years ago due to lack of business, has more members than ever, and the weight-training and aerobics classes are always full(4,5). *We can even anticipate a new generation of customers:* Plainsville's schoolchildren are required to participate in a program called Fitness for Life, which emphasizes the benefits of regular exercise at an early age(6,7)." (former 1, ≈9, =88) ★★

翻　　译 以往经验显示，我们的商店在那些居民对健康生活高度关注的地区赢利最多。因此我们应该在Plainsville开设一家新的连锁店，那里显然有很多这样的居民。Plainsville的商家报告说运动鞋和运动设备的销售处于历史高点。当地一家5年前因缺乏客源而濒临倒闭的健康俱乐部现在的会员比以往任何时候都多，减肥训练班和体操班总是满员。我们还可以预见到新生代顾客群：Plainsville的在校学生被要求参加一个叫做"健康生活"的项目，它强调从小开始经常锻炼的好处。

推理结构

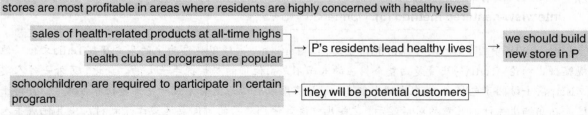

写作要求 *assumptions*

提　　纲

1. The vice president hastily assumes that no other factors besides residents' interest in healthy lives could

141

explain the success of their existing stores. (*confusing concurrence with causality*) ★★

2. The vice president also assumes that their previous experience could be applied to future condition and every specific region. (*P→F*) ★★★

3. Strong sales of exercise apparel do not necessarily indicate that Plainesville residents are interested in exercise, or that these residents would be interested in HN's products. (*U.C./N.C.R.*) ★★★

4. The popularity of the local health club is little indication that the residents in Plainsville live much healthier lives now, and that HN will earn a profit from a store in Plainesville. (*N.C.R.*)

5. The vice president fails to substantiate the assumption that this interest will continue in the foreseeable future. (*P→F*) ★★★★

6. The assumption that people who exercise regularly are also interested in buying health food and health-related products is open to doubt. (*U.C.*) ★★★

7. The mere fact that a certain fitness program is mandatory for Plainesville's schoolchildren accomplishes nothing toward bolstering the recommendation. We need more details of the program. (*N.C.R.*) ★★★

8. The arguer does not provide any information regarding the cost of building such a new store, therefore we can not be convinced that the new store will be profitable. (*adv:disadv*) ★★

9. The arguer unfairly assumes that Plainesville residents will prefer HN over other merchants that sell similar products. (*U.A./I.T.*) ★★

论证要点

　　本题关键环节在于HN以往的成功经验在将来是否同样适用,以及Plainsville的居民是否确实注重健康生活。本题主要论证都是围绕以往的经验、情况在未来未必延续,以及作者提供的信息不足以证明Plainsville居民注重健康生活这些关键环节展开的。

---

17. Twenty years ago(1), Dr. Field, a noted anthropologist, visited the island of Tertia. Using an observation-centered approach to studying Tertian culture, he concluded from his observations that children in Tertia were reared by an entire village rather than by their own biological parents. Recently another anthropologist, Dr. Karp, visited the group of islands that includes Tertia(2) and used the interview-centered method to study child-rearing practices. In the interviews that Dr. Karp conducted with children living in this group of islands, the children spent much more time talking about their biological parents(3) than about other adults in the village. **Dr. Karp decided that Dr. Field's conclusion about Tertian village culture must be invalid (4). Some anthropologists recommend that to obtain accurate information on Tertian child-rearing practices, future research on the subject should be conducted via the interview-centered method (5).** (former 36) ★★★★

翻　译 20年前,著名人类学家Field博士访问了Tertia岛,通过以观察为主的方式研究Tertia文化。他从观察得出结论:Tertia的儿童是由整个村庄的人而不是由他们的双亲抚养长大的。最近,另外一位人类学家Karp博士访问了包括Tertia在内的一组岛屿,并使用以对话为主的方式研究儿童抚养方式。Karp博士与这些在岛屿上生活的儿童的对话显示,这些儿童谈到他们双亲的时间要远多于谈到村庄中其他成年人的时间。Karp博士认为Field博士关于Tertia村庄文化的结论肯定是错误的,一些人类学家建议为获得关于Tertia儿童抚养方式的更精确信息,未来该课题研究应该采用以对话为主的方式。

Dr. F（using observation-centered approach）
concluded that T children were reared by entire village

Dr. K（using interviewing-centered method）found
out that T children talk more about their parents → T children were reared
by their parents → Dr. F's conclusion invalid

observation-centered
method invalid

写作要求 *What* **questions** *should be answered to decide whether the recommendation and the argument are reasonable?*

提　纲

1. Have there been any dramatic changes in nurturing patterns of Teria children during the past 20 years? （P→F）★★★

2. How many of the children interviewed by Dr. Karp were actually from island of Tertia? （I.I.）
    文中仅提及Dr. Karp研究了包括Tertia在内的岛屿，但不能确定其研究对象有多少真正来自Tertia。★★★

3. Could the fact that the children talk more about their biological parents effectively illustrate that those children were reared by their parents? （U.C.）★★★★★

4. Could the facts cited by Dr. Karp necessarily prove that the observation-centered method used by Dr. Field is invalid? （I.E.）★★★★

5. Granted that Dr. Field's claim is indeed invalid, will the observation-centered approach be no use in any other research of that field? （F.D.）★★★★★

论证要点

　　本题核心环节在于，Karp博士的研究结果并不能充分说明Tertia岛的儿童一定是由他们双亲抚养的；进而也就不能说明Field博士的观点和方法一定是无效的。上述论证点基本都围绕这一核心环节展开。

---

18. The following appeared in an article written by Dr. Karp, an anthropologist.

21 "Twenty years ago（1），Dr. Field, a noted anthropologist, visited the island of Tertia and concluded from his observations that children in Tertia were reared by an entire village rather than by their own biological parents. However, my recent interviews with children living in the group of islands that includes Tertia（2）show that these children spend much more time talking about their biological parents than about other adults in the village（3）. **This research of mine proves that Dr. Field's conclusion about Tertian village culture is invalid and thus that the observation-centered approach to studying cultures is invalid as well(4). The interview-centered method that my team of graduate students is currently using in Tertia will establish a much more accurate understanding of child-rearing traditions there and in other island cultures (5,6).**" (former 36, ≈10) ★★★★

翻　译 20年前，著名人类学家Field博士访问了Tertia岛，并从他的观察得出结论：Tertia的儿童是由整个村庄的人而不是由他们的双亲抚养长大的。然而，我最近对包括Tertia的一些岛屿上生活的儿童的采访显示，这些儿童谈到他们双亲的时间要远多于谈到村庄中其他成年人的时间。这个研究证实了Field博士关于Tertia村庄文化的结论是错误的，因而这种以观察为中心的研究文化的方法是无效的。我的研究生们在Tertia使用的以采访为中心的方式将对那里以及其他岛屿的儿童抚养传统建立更精确的了解。

Dr. F (using observation-centered approach) concluded that T children were reared by entire village

Dr. K (using interviewing-centered method) found out that T children talk more about their parents → Dr. F's conclusion invalid / observation-centered method invalid → interview-centered method → accurate understanding

写作要求 *What specific **evidence** is needed to evaluate the argument?*

提 纲

作者需要提供能说明以下方面问题的信息和论据：

1. Information about any dramatic changes in nurturing patterns of Teria children during the past 20 years. (*P→F*) ★★★

2. The number of children interviewed by Dr. Karp who were actually from island of Tertia. (*I.I.*)
文中仅提及Dr. Karp研究了包括Tertia在内的岛屿，但不能确定其研究对象有多少真正来自Tertia。★★★

另外，对于上文讨论的情况还存在以下可能：

3. The fact that talking more about their biological parents does not effectively illustrate that those children were not reared by the entire village. (*U.C.*) ★★★★★

此外，作者还需要提供论据来证明：

4. The observation-centered method used by Dr. Field is indeed invalid. (*I.E.*) ★★★★

5. The interview-centered method is indeed superior to observation-centered method. (*I.E./N.C.R.*) ★★★

6. The interview-centered method will also be effective in establishing accurate understanding of other island cultures. (*C.S.*) ★★★

论证要点

本题核心环节在于，Karp博士的研究结果并不能充分说明Tertia岛的儿童一定是由他们双亲抚养的；进而也不能说明Field博士的观点和方法一定是无效的。上述论证点基本都围绕这一核心环节展开。

---

19. The following appeared in an article written by Dr. Karp, an anthropologist.

23 "Twenty years ago (1), Dr. Field, a noted anthropologist, visited the island of Tertia and concluded from his observations that children in Tertia were reared by an entire village rather than by their own biological parents. However, my recent interviews with children living in the group of islands that includes Tertia(2) show that these children spend much more time talking about their biological parents than about other adults in the village(3). **This research of mine proves that Dr. Field's conclusion about Tertian village culture is invalid and thus that the observation-centered approach to studying cultures is invalid as well(4). The interview-centered method that my team of graduate students is currently using in Tertia will establish a much more accurate understanding of child-rearing traditions there and in other island cultures (5,6).**" (former 36, ≈ 10, =21) ★★★★

翻 译 20年前，著名人类学家Field博士访问了Tertia岛，并从他的观察得出结论：Tertia的儿童是由整个村庄的人而不是由他们的双亲抚养长大的。然而，我最近对包括Tertia的一些岛屿上生活的儿童的采访显示，这些儿童谈到他们双亲的时间要远多于谈到村庄中其他成年人的时间。这个研究证实了Field博士关于Tertia村庄文化的结论是错误的，因而这种以观察为中心的研究文化的方法是无效的。我的研究生们在Tertia使用的以采访为中心的方式将对那里以及其他岛屿的儿童抚养传统建立更精确的了解。

推理结构

Dr. F（using observation-centered approach）
concluded that T children were reared by entire village

Dr. K（using interviewing-centered method）found out that T children talked more about their parents → Dr. F's conclusion invalid / observation-centered method invalid → interview-centered method → accurate understanding

写作要求 *assumptions*

提　纲

1. Dr. Karp assumes without justification that no dramatic changes in nurturing patterns of Teria children have taken place during the past 20 years.（P→F）★★★

2. Dr. Karp fails to provide the number of children interviewed who were actually from island of Tertia. The result might not represent the situation at Tertia.（I.I./ C.S.）
   文中仅提及Dr.Karp研究了包括Tertia在内的岛屿，但不能确定其研究对象有多少真正来自Tertia。★★★

3. The fact that talking more about their biological parents does not effectively illustrate that those children were not reared by the entire village.（U.C.）★★★★★

4. No substantial evidence could illustrate that the observation-centered method used by Dr. Field is indeed invalid.（I.E.）★★★★

5. The assumption that the interview-centered method is superior to observation-centered method is unwarranted.（I.E./N.C.R.）★★★

6. Dr. Karp also generalizes without any evidence that the interview-centered method will be effective in establishing accurate understanding of other island cultures.（C.S.）★★★

论证要点

本题核心环节在于Karp博士的研究结果并不能充分说明Tertia岛的儿童一定是由他们双亲抚养的；进而也不能说明Field博士的观点和方法一定是无效的。上述论证点都围绕这一核心环节展开。

---

20. The council of Maple County, concerned about the county's becoming overdeveloped, is debating a proposed measure that would prevent the development of existing farmland in the county. *But the council is also concerned that such a restriction, by limiting the supply of new housing, could lead to significant increases in the price of housing in the county.* Proponents of the measure note that Chestnut County established a similar measure ten years ago, and its housing prices have increased only modestly since（1）. However, opponents of the measure note that Pine County adopted restrictions on the development of new residential housing fifteen years ago, and its housing prices have since more than doubled（2,3）. **The council currently predicts that the proposed measure, if passed, will result in a significant increase in housing prices in Maple County (4).** (former 109) ★★★★

翻　译 Maple County市议会考虑到该市过度开发的状况，正在讨论一项防止开发现有耕地的预案。但市议会也考虑到这样一项限制新住宅供应的措施会导致该市房价大幅上涨。该预案的支持者指出，10

年前Chestnut County出台了类似措施，随后其房价只有小幅上涨。然而，该预案的反对者指出Pine County15年前实施了对新建居民住宅发展的限制，从那以后其房价上涨了一倍多。当前，市议会预计该预案如果获得通过，将导致Maple County房价大幅上涨。

推理结构

housing price in Chestnut County increased modestly since establishing the measure

housing price in Pine County doubled since adopting similar restrictions → housing price in Maple County will increase if the measure passed

写作要求 *What **questions** should be answered to decide whether the prediction and the argument are reasonable?*

提 纲

1. Will the situation of Chestnut County take place in Maple County? (*I.I./I.C.*) ★★★
2. Did the increased housing prices in Pine County actually result from the limitations on new building construction? (*N.C.R.*) ★★★★
3. Are Pine County and Chestnut County comparable at every aspect? (*I.C.*) ★★
4. Will Maple County inevitably follow Pine County's pattern? (*F.A.*) ★★★★

论证要点

　　本题主要推理环节集中于两点：Pine County房价上升是因为对新建住宅的限制；Maple County的房价将会重现Pine County的轨迹而不是Chestnut County的。因而作者需要回答的主要问题，一是除了限制政策是否有其他因素导致Pine County房价上升；二是为什么Maple County的地产市场一定会重复Pine County的情形而不是Chestnut County的。

---

21. Fifteen years ago, Omega University implemented a new procedure that encouraged students
【12】to evaluate the teaching effectiveness of all their professors（1）. Since that time, Omega professors have begun to assign higher grades in their classes, and overall student grade averages at Omega have risen by 30 percent.（2）*Potential employers, looking at this dramatic rise in grades, believe the grades at Omega are inflated and do not accurately reflect student achievement; as a result, Omega graduates have not been as successful at getting jobs as have graduates from nearby Alpha University (3,4).* **To enable its graduates to secure better jobs, Omega University should terminate student evaluation of professors.(5,6,7)** (former 9)
　★★★

翻 译 15年前，Omega大学实施了一项新措施，鼓励学生对所有教授的教学效果进行评价。从那以后，Omega的教授开始给予学生更高的分数，而Omega的学生总平均成绩上升了30%。未来的雇主看到分数的显著上升，认为Omega的分数贬值了，且不能准确反映学生水平；这导致Omega毕业生找工作时没有邻近的Alpha大学毕业生顺利。为使毕业生找到好工作，Omega应停止学生对教授的评价。

推理结构

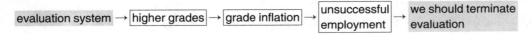

evaluation system → higher grades → grade inflation → unsuccessful employment → we should terminate evaluation

提 纲

作者需要提供能说明以下方面问题的信息或论据：

1. The number or percentage of Omega students who actually participated in the procedure. (*V.D.*) ★★
2. The grade-average increase is the result of the evaluation procedure—rather than some other factors. (*post hoc, ergo propter hoc*) ★★★★★
3. Evidence that could help establishing the relationship between grade inflation and the fact that Omega graduates are less successful than Alpha graduates in getting jobs. (*N.C.R.*) ★★★★
4. The graduates from the two universities are comparable. (*I.C.*) ★★
5. Other possible ways by which Omega can increase its job-placement record. (*necessity of the solution*) ★★
6. Terminating the evaluation system suffices to enable Omega's graduates to secure better jobs. (*sufficiency of the solution*) ★★★★
7. The positive effects of the evaluation system. (*adv:disadv*) ★★★★★

论证要点

本题核心环节在于Omega大学的就业情况是否是由于评价系统的存在而导致的。上述2、6两点都是围绕评价系统是否导致就业变差这一推理主线展开。此外，关于两学校的可比性以及参与评价学生的人数和比例可作为辅助论证。

---

22. In an attempt to improve highway safety, Prunty County last year（1）lowered its speed limit from 55 to 45 miles per hour on all county highways. *But this effort has failed:* the number of accidents has not decreased（2）, and, based on reports by the highway patrol, many drivers are exceeding the speed limit（3）. **Prunty County should instead undertake the same kind of road improvement project that Butler County completed five years ago(6): increasing lane widths, resurfacing rough highways, and improving visibility at dangerous intersections(7).** Today, major Butler County roads still have a 55 mph speed limit（4）, yet there were 25 percent fewer reported（5）accidents in Butler County this past year than there were five years ago. (former 18) ★★★★

翻 译 为改善高速公路安全性，去年Prunty County把镇上所有高速公路的限速从每小时55英里降到了每小时45英里。但这种努力失败了：事故数量并没有下降，而且基于高速巡逻队的报告，很多司机都超过了限速。Prunty County应该采取和Butler County 5年前所实施的同样的道路改善计划：增加车道宽度，重新填补不平整路面，改善危险路段视野。现在，Butler County主要道路仍然采用每小时55英里限速，而那里去年上报的事故比5年前减少了25%。

推理结构

写作要求 *What specific **evidence** is needed to evaluate the argument?*

提　纲

我们需要作者提供论据说明以下两点：

1. One year is long enough for determining the effectiveness of the limit on reducing the accident rate. (*I.E.*) ★★★

2. Other factors affecting highway accident rates have remained unchanged since the county lowered its speed limit. (*P→C*) ★★★

对于上文论述还存在以下可能性：

3. The fact that many drivers are exceeding the new speed limit may just prove that the limit will be effective if strictly executed. (*negative evidence / lack of controlled study*) ★★

作者还需要提供论据证明：

4. The higher speed limit in Butler County has not served to increase the incidence of road accidents in that county. (即，假如Butler降低其限速，其事故率将进一步降低。) (*lack of controlled experiment*) ★★★

另外：

5. The cited statistics involve only "reported" accidents in Butler County. We do not know the percentage of accidents which are going unreported in that county. (*I.I.*) ★★★

最后，我们还需要能说明以下两点的论据：

6. The comparability of Prunty County and Butler County. (*F.A.*) ★★★★

7. Road improvement will be both sufficient and necessary to guarantee fewer accidents in Prunty County. (*sufficiency/necessity of the solution*) ★★★★

论证要点

本题主要环节有两方面：Prunty County的限速不起作用；以及Butler County的改善措施确实有效而且可以应用到Prunty County。主要论证内容基本都集中在作者能否提供充分论据证明以上环节。

---

23. The following appeared as part of an article in a business magazine.

14 "*A recent study rating 300 male and female Mentian advertising executives(5) according to the average number of hours they sleep per night showed an association between the amount of sleep the executives need and the success of their firms.* Of the advertising firms studied, those whose executives reported needing no more than 6 hours of sleep per night had higher profit margins and faster growth(1,2,3). **These results suggest that if a business wants to prosper, it should hire only(6) people who need less than 6 hours of sleep per night (4).**" ★★★★

翻　译 最近的一项研究对300名Mentian男女广告经理的日平均睡眠时间进行了研究。研究发现经理所需的睡眠时间和其企业的成功存在联系。在被研究的公司中，那些报告说每天所需睡眠时间不超过6小时的经理所在的公司有更高的利润率和更快的增长速度。这些结果表明，如果一个企业要壮大，它应该只雇用那些每天所需睡眠不超过6小时的人。

推理结构

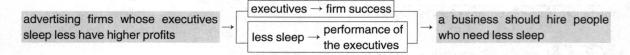

advertising firms whose executives sleep less have higher profits → executives → firm success / less sleep → performance of the executives → a business should hire people who need less sleep

写作要求 *assumptions*

提　　纲

1. The author falsely assumes that no other factors besides the performance of their executives could determine the firms' success. (*confusing concurrence with causality*) ★★★★★

2. The author fails to rule out the possibility that the fast growth and heavy business of those firms prevent their executives from getting more sleep. (*confusing the cause and the effect*) ★★★

3. Granted that the performance of executives is the key factor of those firms' success, the author also hastily assumes that it is the less sleep time that gives them the ability of business management. (*N.C.R.*) ★★★

4. Granted that the outstanding performance of those executives derives from their less sleeping time, we cannot ensure that other people who sleep less will also have such performance. (*C.S.*) ★★★★

5. The experience and situation in advertising industry may not apply to businesses in all other fields. (*C.S.*) ★★★

6. People who sleep more than 6 hours per night may have other characteristics which are necessary for a business to prosper. (*I.T.*) ★★★

论证要点

　　本题主要论证方向在于更少的睡眠时间和经理的管理能力是否存在联系；以及经理的能力是否是企业成功的决定因素。上述1~3点即讨论这些环节中存在的假设。此外，从这些经理到其他人、从广告行业到其他行业的草率推广也可以作为辅助论证。

---

24. The following appeared as part of an article in a business magazine.

118　"*A recent study rating 300 male and female advertising(5) executives according to the average number of hours they sleep per night showed an association between the amount of sleep the executives need and the success of their firms.* Of the advertising firms studied, those whose executives reported needing no more than six hours of sleep per night had higher profit margins and faster growth(1,2,3). **On the basis of this study, we recommend that businesses hire only (6) people who need less than six hours of sleep per night (4).**" (14) ★★★★

翻　　译 最近的一项研究对300名男女广告经理的日平均睡眠时间进行了研究。研究发现经理所需的睡眠时间和其企业成功存在联系。在被研究的公司中，那些报告说每天所需睡眠时间不超过6小时的经理所在公司有更高的利润率和更快的增长速度。基于这一研究，我们建议企业只雇用那些每天所需睡眠不超过6小时的人。

推理结构

firms whose executives sleep less have higher profits → less sleep → performance of the executives → firm success → business should hire people who need less sleep

写作要求 What *questions* should be answered to decide whether the recommendation and the argument are reasonable?

提　　纲

1. Are there any other factors besides the performance of their executives that could determine the firms' success? (*confusing concurrence with causality*) ★★★★★

2. Is there possibility that the fast growth and heavy business of those firms prevent their executives from getting more sleep? (*confusing the cause and the effect*) ★ ★ ★

3. Granted that the performance of executives is the key factor of those firms' success, does the ability of business management of these executives derive from the less sleep time? (*N.C.R.*) ★ ★ ★

4. Granted that the outstanding performance of those executives derives from their less sleeping time, will other people who sleep less also have such performance? (*C.S.*) ★ ★ ★ ★

5. Could the experience and situation in advertising industry apply to businesses in all other fields? (*C.S.*) ★ ★ ★

6. Do people who sleep more than 6 hours per night have other characteristics which are necessary for a business to prosper? (*I.T.*) ★ ★ ★

论证要点

本题主要论证方向在于更少的睡眠时间和经理的管理能力是否存在联系；以及经理的能力是否是企业成功的决定因素。上述1~3点即为要确定这些方面需要回答的问题。此外，4~6点则是要评价从这些经理到其他人以及从广告行业到其他行业的草率推广是否成立需要回答的问题。

---

25. The following memorandum is from the business manager of Happy Pancake House restaurants.

[15]

"Recently, butter has been replaced by margarine in Happy Pancake House restaurants throughout the southwestern United States. **This change, however, has had little impact on our customers.** In fact, only about 2 percent of customers have complained, *indicating that an average of 98 people out of 100 are happy with the change(1).* Furthermore, many(2) servers have reported that a number of(2) customers who ask for butter do not complain when they are given margarine instead. *Clearly, either these customers do not distinguish butter from margarine or they use the term 'butter' to refer to either butter or margarine(3).*" (former 182)

★ ★ ★

翻　　译 最近, Happy Pancake House在美国西南部餐厅用人造黄油代替了天然黄油。然而, 这一变化对消费者只有很小的影响。事实上, 只有大约2%的顾客曾经投诉, 这说明98%的人对这种替换是乐于接受的。而且, 很多服务生报告说一些点了天然黄油的顾客在得到人造黄油时并没有投诉。显然, 这些顾客或者不会区分天然黄油和人造黄油, 或者是用"天然黄油"这个词来统指天然黄油或人造黄油。

推理结构

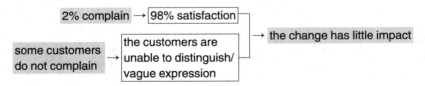

写作要求 *alternative explanations*

提　　纲

1. Some customers might be unhappy but didn't complain. (*F.D.*) ★ ★ ★ ★

2. The author fails to point out the actual number of server who reported, and what percentage of the whole server group do they make up. Also, the author does not tell us the percentage of customers who do not

complain, thus the conclusion that the change had little impact is unfounded. (*V.D.*) ★★★

3. The fact that few customers complain when they are given margarine might be explained by other factors, e.g, they may prefer the lower price of margarine, or they have no time or distain to argue with the restaurant. (*F.D.*) ★★★

论证要点

本题主要论证点集中在对"98%的顾客对于替换行为满意"以及"顾客不投诉或者是没有鉴别能力，或者是用词含混"这两条假设的其他解释上面。顾客不投诉有很多其他可能性，应推测一下顾客不去投诉的其他合理解释。

---

26. The following memorandum is from the business manager of Happy Pancake House
51 restaurants.

"Butter has now been replaced by margarine in Happy Pancake House restaurants throughout the southwestern United States. Only about 2 percent of customers have complained, *indicating that 98 people out of 100 are happy with the change(1)*. Furthermore, many (3) servers have reported that a number of (3) customers who ask for butter do not complain when they are given margarine instead. Clearly, *either these customers cannot distinguish butter from margarine or they use the term 'butter' to refer to either butter or margarine (2)*. **Thus, to avoid the expense of purchasing butter and to increase profitability (5), the Happy Pancake House should extend this cost-saving change to its restaurants in the southeast and northeast as well (4).**" (former 182, ≈15) ★★★

翻　　译 Happy Pancake House在美国西南部的餐厅用人造黄油代替了天然黄油。只有大约2%的顾客曾经投诉，这说明98%的人对于这种替换是乐于接受的。而且，很多服务生报告说一些点了天然黄油的顾客在得到人造黄油时并没有投诉。显然，这些顾客或者分不清天然黄油和人造黄油，或者是用"天然黄油"这个词统指天然黄油或人造黄油。因此，为节省购买天然黄油的花费并增加利润，Happy Pancake House应该把这项节省措施推广到东南部以及东北部的餐厅。

推理结构

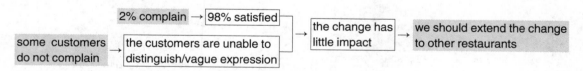

写作要求 *What **questions** should be answered to decide whether the recommendation will have the predicted result?*

提　　纲

1. Is it possible that some customers might be unhappy but didn't complain? (*F.D.*) ★★★★
2. Could the fact that few customers complain when they are given margarine be explained by other factors? e.g., they may prefer the lower price of margarine, or they have no time or distain to argue with the restaurant. (*F.D.*) ★★★
   1 & 2：如果对于上述情况还有其他可能的解释，那么该行为可能已经对餐厅造成一些负面影响，在其他地区推广这种行为将造成更大的损失。

3. What's the actual number of servers who reported, and what percentage of the whole server group do they make up? We cannot evaluate whether the fact cited above is significant. Also, the author does not tell us the percentage of customers who do not complain. (*V.D.*) ★★★

4. Will customers in other regions respond to the change similarly as southwestern customers? (*F.A.*) ★★★★

5. How about the actual change in the profit of Happy Pancake House after the replacement? We cannot evaluate the overall effect of the recommendation mentioned above. (*adv:disadv*) ★★★★

论证要点

本题主要问题在于，作者没有考虑该行为对餐厅利润的影响，以及将该行为推广到其他地区的可行性。另外，关于消费者"要么投诉，要么满意"、"要么分不清两种食品，要么用一个词指两个东西"的false dilemma也可以加以论述。

---

27. The following memorandum is from the business manager of Happy Pancake House 130 restaurants.

"Butter has now been replaced by margarine in Happy Pancake House restaurants throughout the southwestern United States. Only about 2 percent of customers have filed a formal complaint, *indicating that an average of 98 people out of 100 are happy with the change(1).* Furthermore, many(3) servers have reported that a number of(3) customers who ask for butter do not complain when they are given margarine instead. *Clearly, either these customers cannot distinguish butter from margarine or they use the term 'butter' to refer to either butter or margarine(2).* **Thus, to avoid the expense of purchasing butter(5), the Happy Pancake House should extend this cost-saving change to its restaurants throughout the rest of the country (4).**" (former 182, ≈15, =51) ★★★

翻译 Happy Pancake House在美国西南部餐厅用人造黄油代替了天然黄油。只有大约2%的顾客签署了正式的投诉文件，这说明98%的人对于这种替换是乐于接受的。而且，很多服务生报告说一些点了天然黄油的顾客在得到人造黄油时并没有投诉。显然，这些顾客或者分不清天然黄油和人造黄油，或者是用"天然黄油"这个词统指天然黄油或人造黄油。因此，为节省购买天然黄油的花费，Happy Pancake House应该把这项节省措施推广到其他地区的连锁店。

推理结构

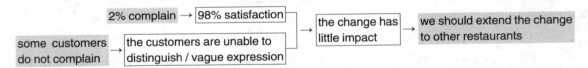

写作要求 *assumptions*

提纲

1. The manager hastily assumes that all customers who didn't complain are satisfied with the change. (*F.D.*) ★★★★

2. The manager assumes that no other factors could explain the fact that few customers complain when they are given margarine. e.g., they may prefer the lower price of margarine, or they have no time or distain to argue with the restaurant. (*F.D.*) ★★★

3. Without the actual number of servers who reported, and the percentage of the whole server group they make up, we cannot evaluate whether the fact cited above is significant. Also, the author does not tell us the percentage of customers who do not complain. (*V.D.*) ★★★

4. The manager assumes that customers in other regions will respond to the change similarly as southwestern customers. (*F.A.*) ★★★

5. The manager does not provide any information about the actual change in the profit of Happy Pancake House after the replacement, thus we cannot evaluate the overall effect of the recommendation mentioned above. (*adv:disadv*) ★★★★

论证要点

本题主要问题在于,作者对于该行为对餐厅利润的影响,以及将该行为推广到其他地区的可行性的假设都是有疑问的。另外,关于消费者"要么投诉,要么满意"、"要么分不清两种食品,要么用一个词指两个东西"的false dilemma也可以加以论述。

---

28. The following memorandum is from the business manager of Happy Pancake House
131 restaurants.

"Butter has now been replaced by margarine in Happy Pancake House restaurants throughout the southwestern United States. Only about 2 percent of customers have complained, *indicating that an average of 98 people out of 100 are happy with the change(1)*. Furthermore, many(3) servers have reported that a number of(3) customers who ask for butter do not complain when they are given margarine instead. *Clearly, either these customers cannot distinguish butter from margarine or they use the term 'butter' to refer to either butter or margarine(2)*. **Thus, we predict that Happy Pancake House will be able to increase profits dramatically (5) if we extend this cost-saving change to all our restaurants in the southeast and northeast as well (4).**" (former 182, ≈15, =51, 130) ★★★

翻　译 Happy Pancake House在美国西南部的餐厅用人造黄油代替了天然黄油。只有大约2%的顾客曾经投诉,这说明98%的人对于这种替换是乐于接受的。而且,很多服务生报告说一些点了天然黄油的顾客在得到人造黄油时并没有投诉。显然,这些顾客或者分不清天然黄油和人造黄油,或者是用"天然黄油"这个词统指天然黄油或人造黄油。因此,我们预计,如果Happy Pancake House把这项节省措施推广到东南部以及东北部的餐厅,那么,利润将得到极大提升。

推理结构

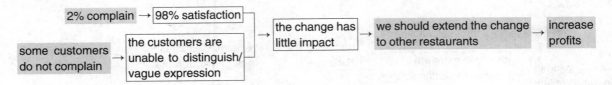

写作要求 What **questions** should be answered to decide whether the prediction and the argument are reasonable?

提　纲

1. Is it possible that some customers might be unhappy but didn't complain? (*F.D.*) ★★★★

2. Could the fact that few customers complain when they are given margarine be explained by other factors?

e.g., they may prefer the lower price of margarine, or they have no time or distain to argue with the restaurant. (*F.D.*) ★ ★ ★

3. What's the actual number of servers who reported, and what percentage of the whole server group do they make up? We cannot evaluate if the fact cited above is significant. Also, the author does not tell us the percentage of customers who do not complain. (*V.D.*) ★ ★ ★

4. Will customers in other regions respond to the change similarly as southwestern customers? (*F.A.*) ★ ★ ★

5. How about the actual change in the profit of Happy Pancake House after the replacement? We cannot evaluate the overall effect of the recommendation mentioned above. (*adv:disadv*) ★ ★ ★ ★

论证要点

本题主要问题在于，作者没有考虑该行为对餐厅利润的影响，以及将该行为推广到其他地区的可行性。另外，关于消费者"要么投诉，要么满意"、"要么分不清两种食品，要么用一个词指两个东西"的false dilemma也可以加以论述。

---

29. The following memorandum is from the business manager of Happy Pancake House
`133` restaurants.

"Butter has now been replaced by margarine in Happy Pancake House restaurants throughout the southwestern United States. Only about 2 percent of customers have complained, *indicating that an average of 98 people out of 100 are happy with the change(1).* Furthermore, many(3) servers have reported that a number of(3) customers who ask for butter do not complain when they are given margarine instead. *Clearly, either these customers cannot distinguish butter from margarine or they use the term 'butter' to refer to either butter or margarine(2).* **Thus, to avoid the expense of purchasing butter and to increase profitability(5), the Happy Pancake House should extend this cost-saving change to its restaurants in the southeast and northeast as well(4).**" (former 182, ≈15, = 51, 130, 131)
★ ★ ★

翻　　译 Happy Pancake House在美国西南部的餐厅用人造黄油代替了天然黄油。只有大约2%的顾客曾经投诉，这说明98%的人对于这种替换是乐于接受的。而且，很多服务生报告说一些点了天然黄油的顾客在得到人造黄油时并没有投诉。显然，这些顾客或者分不清天然黄油和人造黄油，或者是用"天然黄油"这个词统指天然黄油或人造黄油。因此，为节省购买天然黄油的花费并增加利润，Happy Pancake House应该把这项节省措施推广到东南部以及东北部的连锁店。

推理结构

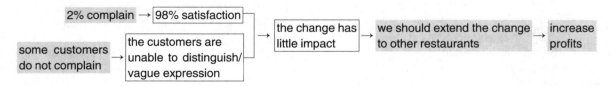

写作要求 *What specific **evidence** is needed to evaluate the argument?*

提　　纲

作者需要提供能说明以下方面问题的信息和论据：

1. All customers who didn't complain are satisfied with the change. (*F.D.*) ★ ★ ★ ★

2. Evidence to rule out other factors which could explain the fact that few customers complain when they are given margarine. e.g., they may prefer the lower price of margarine, or they have no time or distain to argue with the restaurant. (*F.D.*) ★ ★ ★

3. The actual number of servers who reported, and the percentage of the whole server group they make up. We cannot evaluate if the fact cited above is significant. Also, the author does not tell us the percentage of customers who do not complain. (*V.D.*) ★ ★ ★

4. Customers in other regions will respond to the change similarly as southwestern customers. (*F.A.*) ★ ★ ★

5. The actual change in the profit of Happy Pancake House after the replacement. We cannot evaluate the overall effect of the recommendation mentioned above. (*adv:disadv*) ★ ★ ★ ★

论证要点

本题主要问题在于，作者没有考虑该行为对餐厅利润的影响，以及将该行为推广到其他地区的可行性。另外，关于消费者"要么投诉，要么满意"、"要么分不清两种食品，要么用一个词指两个东西"的false dilemma也存在疑问。作者需要提供直接证据来说明以上方面。

30.
16 In surveys Mason City residents rank water sports(swimming, boating, and fishing)among their favorite recreational activities(1). The Mason River flowing through the city is rarely used for these pursuits, however, and the city park department devotes little of its budget to maintaining riverside recreational facilities. For years there have been complaints from residents about the quality of the river's water and the river's smell(2). In response, the state has recently announced plans to clean up Mason River(3). *Use of the river for water sports is, therefore, sure to increase(4).* **The city government should for that reason devote more money in this year's budget to riverside recreational facilities (5).** (former 137) ★ ★

翻　译 在调查中，Mason市居民把水上运动(游泳、划船和垂钓)列为他们最喜欢的休闲形式之一。然而流经该市的Mason河很少用于这些目的，而且本市园林部门用于维护河边休闲设施的预算也非常少。几年来曾经有居民对这条河的水质及味道进行投诉。作为回应，本州最近宣布了清理Mason河的计划。因此，该河被用于水上运动的几率肯定会大大增加。市政府应该因此增加用于河边休闲设施今年的预算。

推理结构

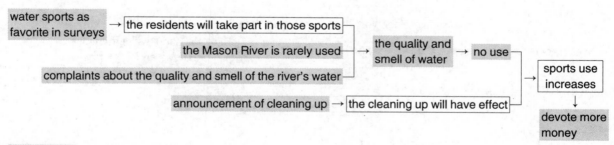

写作要求 *assumptions*

提　纲

1. The author hastily reasons from the survey that the residents will actually take part in water sports. (*U.C.*) ★ ★ ★

2. The author simply assumes that it is the quality and smell of the water in Mason River that prevent residents from using it for recreational activities. (*N.C.R.*) ★ ★ ★ ★

3. No evidence could illustrate the effectiveness of the proposed plan, and how much time would it take for the plan to be effective, thus we cannot ensure that recreational use of the river will automatically increase. (*I. I. /sufficiency of the solution*) ★ ★ ★ ★ ★

4. No evidence could illustrate that Mason River is suitable for those water sports favored by residents in Mason, even after the cleaning-up, and that residents are willing to use the river for recreational activities. (*feasibility of the conclusion*) ★ ★ ★

5. The author fails to demonstrate the necessity of increasing budget on riverside recreational facilities. (*necessity of the solution*) ★ ★ ★

论证要点

本题主要推理环节集中于两点：市民因为水质问题而不使用该河流；清淤措施必将产生效果，且市民会使用Mason河进行水上运动。上述1、2两点围绕第一个环节展开，3、4两点围绕第二个环节展开。

---

31. The following appeared in a memorandum from the manager of WWAC radio station.

17 "**To reverse a decline in listener numbers, our owners have decided that WWAC must change from its current rock-music format (1).** The decline has occurred despite population growth in our listening area, but that growth has resulted mainly from people moving here after their retirement. *We must make listeners of these new residents(2). We could switch to a music format tailored to their tastes, but a continuing decline in local sales of recorded music suggests limited interest in music(3).* **Instead we should change to a news and talk format, a form of radio that is increasingly popular in our area (4,5).**" (≈former 235) ★ ★ ★

翻　译 为了扭转听众人数锐减的局面，WWAC电台的所有者决定必须改变现有的摇滚乐节目形式。尽管我们收听范围内的人口增加了——其原因是退休后移居本地的人增多，但听众数量还是呈下降趋势。我们必须把这些新居民转化为听众。我们可以转向迎合这些人口味的音乐节目形式，但本地音乐专辑销量的持续下降表明居民对音乐兴趣有限。因此，我们应该向在本地区越来越受欢迎的新闻以及对话广播节目转变。

推理结构

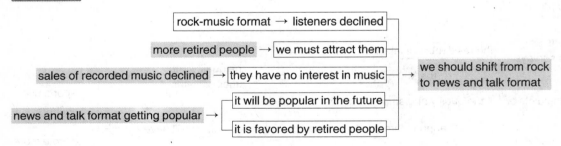

写作要求 What specific **evidence** is needed to evaluate the argument?

提　纲

作者需要提供能够说明以下方面的论据或信息：

1. It is the rock-music format, rather than other factors, that resulted in the decline. (*N.C.R.*) ★ ★ ★ ★ ★

2. If we have better ways, other than attracting those retired people, to reverse the decline. (*necessity of the solution*) ★ ★ ★ ★

3. The sales of recorded music are a good indication of people's interest in music. (*U.C.*) ★★★

4. The popularity of news and talk format will continue in the future. (*P→F*) ★★★

5. The group of people who actually favor news and talk format. Although the format is popular in the area, it is not necessarily preferred by the retired people. (*V.D./I.I.*) ★★★

论证要点

本题作者最主要的假设是我们必须以吸引退休人群为扭转颓势的手段,而且把节目转为新闻和对话就可以有效吸引这些人群。但首先,作者并不能充分证明一定是摇滚乐节目导致听众流失,也不能证明吸引退休人群是扭转听众流失的必要措施。其次,音乐专辑的销量能否说明听众对音乐兴趣的下降、退休人群是否也喜好新闻对话节目也值得讨论。

---

32. The following appeared in a memorandum from the manager of WWAC radio station.

[93] "**WWAC must change from its current rock-music format(1)** because the number of listeners has been declining, even though the population in our listening area has been growing. The population growth has resulted mainly from people moving to our area after their retirement, *and we must make listeners of these new residents (2). But they seem to have limited interest in music:* several local stores selling recorded music have recently closed(3). *Therefore, just changing to another kind of music is not going to increase our audience.* **Instead, we should adopt a news-and-talk format, a form of radio that is increasingly popular in our area (4,5,6).**" (former 235, ≈17) ★★★

翻　译 WWAC电台必须改变现有的摇滚乐节目形式,因为尽管我们收听范围内的人口增加了,但听众数量还是下降了。人口增加的主要原因是许多人退休后移居此地——我们必须把这些新居民转化为听众。但他们对音乐的兴趣似乎有限:本地一些出售音乐专辑的商店关门了。因此,仅仅改变音乐形式不能吸引更多听众。我们应该向在本地区越来越受欢迎的新闻以及对话广播节目转变。

推理结构

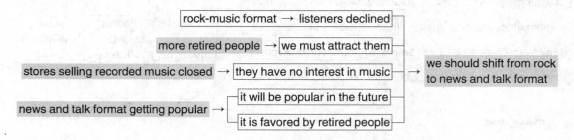

写作要求 *What **questions** should be answered to decide whether the recommendation and the argument are reasonable?*

提　纲

1. Is the rock-music format, rather than other factors, the real cause that resulted in the decline? (*N.C.R.*) ★★★★★

2. Do we have better ways, other than attracting those retired people, to reverse the decline? (*necessity of the solution*) ★★★★

3. Could the closure of these stores be explained by factors other than limited interest in music? (*U.C./N.C.R.*) ★★★★

4. Will the popularity of news and talk format continue in the future? (*P→F*) ★ ★ ★

5. What groups of people actually favor news and talk format? Although the format is popular in the area, it is not necessarily preferred by the retired people. (*V.D./I.I.*) ★ ★ ★

6. Is there any other radio format, other than music and news-and-talk, which can attract more listeners? (*F.D./necessity of the solution*) ★ ★ ★ ★

论证要点

本题作者最主要的假设是：一、摇滚乐节目导致电台收听率下降；二、我们必须吸引退休人群以扭转颓势；三、把节目转为新闻和对话就可以有效吸引这些人群。上述第1点是针对第一环节提出的问题；第2点是针对第二环节提出的问题；4~6是针对第三环节提出的问题。

---

33. The following appeared in a memorandum from the general manager of KNOW radio station.

109 "**Several factors indicate that radio station KNOW should shift its programming from rock-and-roll music to a continuous news format.** Consider, for example, that the number of people in our listening area over fifty years of age has increased dramatically(1), while our total number of listeners has declined(2). Also, music stores in our area report decreased sales of recorded music(3,4,5). Finally, continuous news stations in neighboring cities have been very successful(6,7). *The switch from rock-and-roll music to 24-hour news will attract older listeners(8) and secure KNOW radio's future(9).*" (former 235, ≈17) ★

翻　　译 若干因素表明KNOW电台应该把节目从摇滚乐转成连续的新闻节目形式。举例来说，我台收听范围内50岁以上的老年人数量显著增加，而总听众数量减少了。而且，我们地区的音像店报告说音乐专辑销量下降。最后，邻近城市的连续新闻节目非常成功。从摇滚乐节目转为24小时的新闻节目将吸引老年听众，并确保KNOW电台的持续发展。

推理结构

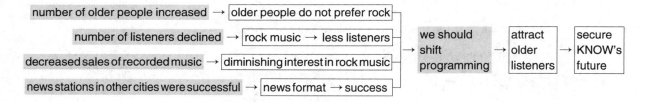

写作要求 *assumptions*

提　　纲

1. The arguer falsely assumes that older people do not prefer rock-and-roll but favor all-news programming. (*U.A.*) ★ ★ ★

2. The manager unfairly assumes that it is the rock music program that leads to the decline in their listeners. (*N.C.R.*) ★ ★ ★ ★

3. The sales of recorded music are not a good indication of people's interest in rock-and-roll. (*U.C.*) ★ ★ ★ ★

4. We do not know what types of music recordings actually experienced sales decline in the music stores, thus we cannot evaluate if the popularity of rock-and-roll is also diminishing. (*I.I.*) ★ ★ ★

5. The manager fails to illustrate that people who buy music recordings are basically the same group of people who listen to music on the radio. (*Are the respondents representative?*) ★ ★ ★

6. The assumption that the success of these news stations is due to their news program is unwarranted. (*N.C.R.*) ★★★

7. The fact that news stations in neighboring cities have been successful does not indicate that KNOW could also be successful through shifting its programming to a continuous news format. (*F.A.*) ★★★★

8. The manager assumes without justification that switching the program will not result in any loss of their existing and potential listeners. (*adv:disadv*) ★★★★

9. Taking the proposed action may not be sufficient for ensuring KNOW's future. (*sufficiency of the solution*) ★★★★

论证要点

本题主要问题在于作者提供的信息都不足以支持摇滚乐没有市场、新闻节目能吸引听众的核心假设。首先，老年人数量增加未必一定说明摇滚乐没有市场；其次，听众数量下降未必是摇滚乐节目导致的；再次，由于不知道销量下降的都是什么类型的音乐专辑，以及购买这些专辑的是哪些人群，因而不能说明对摇滚乐的兴趣在下降；最后，其他电台的成功未必归因于新闻节目，就算能，照搬他人经验未必能达到相同效果。

---

34. The following appeared in a memorandum from the manager of KNOW radio station.

110 "*Several factors indicate that KNOW radio can no longer succeed as a rock-and-roll music station.* Consider, for example, that the number of people in our listening area over fifty years of age has increased dramatically(1), while our total number of listeners has declined(2). Also, music stores in our area report decreased sales of rock-and-roll music(3,4). Finally, continuous news stations in neighboring cities have been very successful(5,6). **We predict that switching KNOW radio from rock-and-roll music to 24-hour news will allow the station to attract older listeners(7) and make KNOW radio more profitable than ever(8).**" (former 235, ≈17, 109) ★

翻　译 若干因素表明KNOW电台作为摇滚乐电台将无法继续获得成功。举例来说，我们收听范围内50岁以上的老年人数量显著增加，而总听众数量减少了。而且，我们地区音像店报告说摇滚乐的销量下降。最后，邻近城市的连续新闻节目非常成功。我们预计，从摇滚乐节目转为24小时新闻节目将吸引老年听众，并使KNOW获得更多利润。

推理结构

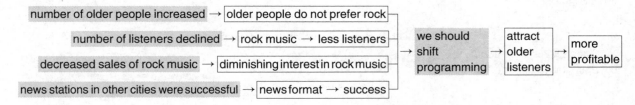

写作要求 *What **questions** should be answered to decide whether the prediction and the argument are reasonable?*

提　纲

1. Is the assumption that older people do not prefer rock-and-roll but favor all-news programming reasonable? (*U.A.*) ★★★

2. Does the decline in their listeners result from their rock music program? (*N.C.R.*) ★★★★

3. Are the sales of recorded music a good indication of people's interest in rock-and-roll? (*U.C.*) ★★★★

4. Are people who buy music recordings basically the same group of people who listen to music on the radio? (*Are the respondents representative?*) ★★★

5. Is the success of these news stations due to their news program? (*N.C.R.*) ★★★

6. Does the fact that news stations in neighboring cities have been successful indicate that KNOW could also be successful through shifting its programming? (*F.A.*) ★★★★

7. Will switching the program result in any loss of their existing and potential listeners? (*adv:disadv*) ★★★★

8. Is the proposed action sufficient for ensuring KNOW's profitability? (*sufficiency of the solution*) ★★★★

论证要点

本题主要问题在于作者提供的信息都不足以支持摇滚乐没有市场、新闻节目能吸引听众的核心假设。首先,老年人数量增加未必一定说明摇滚乐没有市场;其次,听众数量下降未必是摇滚乐节目导致的;再次,由于不知道购买音乐专辑的人群是什么,因此不能说明对摇滚乐的兴趣在下降;最后,其他电台的成功未必归因于新闻节目,就算能,照搬他人经验未必能达到相同效果。

---

35. The following is a memorandum from the business manager of a television station.

18 "Over the past year, our late-night news program has devoted increased time to national news and less time to weather and local news. During this period, most of the complaints(1,2) received from viewers were concerned with our station's coverage of weather and local news (3,4). In addition, local businesses that used to advertise during our late-night news program have canceled their advertising contracts with us(5). Therefore, **in order to attract more viewers to our news programs and to avoid losing any further advertising revenues, we should expand our coverage of weather and local news on all(7) our news programs (6).**" (former 135) ★★★

翻 译 去年,我们的夜间新闻节目在全国新闻上投入了越来越多的时间,而用较少的时间播放天气预报和地方新闻。在这一时期,我们从观众那里得到的投诉大部分是关于电视台对于天气和地方新闻播报的。而且,若干曾经在我们夜间新闻节目播放广告的地方企业也取消了和我们的广告合同。因此,为吸引更多的电视观众观看我们的新闻节目并避免失去更多的广告收入,我们应该在所有的新闻节目中增加天气和地方新闻的播报。

推理结构

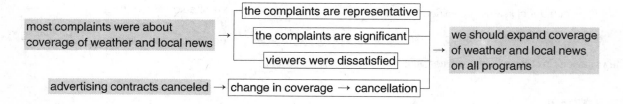

写作要求 *assumptions*

提 纲

1. The manager fails to provide the total number of complaints received before and after the coverage of news was changed. (*confusing comparison with variation/V.D.*) ★★★

2. The manager also fails to inform us the details of the complaints they received, thus we cannot evaluate whether these audience are dissatisfied with the quantity of weather and local news. (*I.I.*) ★ ★ ★ ★

1 & 2: 文中提及的投诉未必说明节目的问题很严重这一假设。

3. The manager simply assumes that those complaints are representative of the opinions of the entire audience. (*C.S.*) ★ ★ ★

4. The manager fails to analyze the actual attitude of the audience toward the late-night news program. The program might be welcome although there are a few complaints about it. (*I.I.*) ★ ★ ★ ★

5. The manager unjustifiably assumes that it is the change in the coverage of news that caused those businesses to cancel their ad contract. (*N.C.R.*) ★ ★ ★ ★

6. The manager ignores many other possible methods of attracting more viewers and increasing advertising revenues. (*necessity of the solution*) ★ ★ ★

7. The necessity of expanding the coverage of weather and local news on all news programs is open to doubt. (*C.S.*) ★ ★ ★

论证要点

本题核心假设有两条：一、听众投诉说明节目的问题已经很严重，必须采取措施；二、客户取消广告合同是因为节目的变化。但在不知道节目改革之前和之后接到的投诉数量对比以及投诉的具体内容的情况下，未必能说明观众对节目的变化存在很大意见。上述论证点中，1~4是围绕第一条假设的分析；第5条是围绕第二条假设的分析。

---

36. The following is a memorandum from the business manager of a television station.

[20] "Over the past year, our late-night news program has devoted increased time to national news and less time to weather and local news. During this time period, most of the complaints (1,2) received from viewers were concerned with our station's coverage of weather and local news (3,4). In addition, local businesses that used to advertise during our late-night news program have just canceled their advertising contracts with us (5). **Therefore, in order to attract more viewers to the program and to avoid losing any further advertising revenues, we should restore the time devoted to weather and local news to its former level (6).**" (former 135, =18) ★ ★ ★

翻　译 去年，我们的夜间新闻节目在全国新闻上投入了越来越多的时间，而用较少的时间播放天气预报和地方新闻。在这一时期，我们从观众那里得到的投诉大部分是关于电视台对于天气和地方新闻播报的。而且，若干曾经在我们夜间新闻节目播放广告的地方企业也取消了和我们的广告合同。因此，为吸引更多的电视观众观看我们的节目并避免流失更多的广告收入，我们应该把播放天气预报和本地新闻的时长恢复到以往的水平。

推理结构

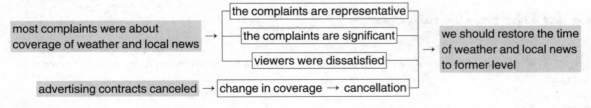

写作要求 *What specific **evidence** is needed to evaluate the argument?*

作者需要提供能说明以下方面的信息或论据：

1. Whether the total number of complaints received before and after the change in the coverage of news varied significantly. (*confusing comparison with variation/V.D.*) ★★★

2. The details of the complaints they received. We cannot evaluate if these audience are dissatisfied with the quantity of weather and local news. (*I.I.*) ★★★★

3. Whether those complaints are representative of the opinions of the entire audience. (*C.S.*) ★★★

4. The actual attitude of viewers toward the late-night news program. The program might be welcome although there are a few complaints about it. (*I.I.*) ★★★★

5. It is the change in the coverage of news that caused those businesses to cancel their ad contract. (*N.C.R.*) ★★★★

6. Other possible methods to attract more viewers and to increase advertising revenues. (*necessity of the solution*) ★★★

论证要点

　　本题核心假设有两条：一、听众投诉说明节目的问题已经很严重，必须采取措施；二、客户取消广告合同是因为节目的变化。但在不知道节目改革之前和之后接到的投诉数量对比以及投诉的具体内容的情况下，未必能说明观众对节目的变化存在很大意见。上述论证点中，1~4是围绕第一条假设的分析；第5条是围绕第二条假设的分析。

---

37. Two years ago(2), radio station WCQP in Rockville decided to increase the number of call-in advice programs that it broadcast; since that time, its share of the radio audience in the Rockville listening area has increased significantly(1). *Given WCQP's recent success with call-in advice programming*, and citing a nationwide survey indicating that many radio listeners are quite interested in such programs(3), **the station manager of KICK in Medway recommends that KICK include more call-in advice programs in an attempt to gain a larger audience share in its listening area (4,5,6).** ★

翻　　译　2年前，Rockville的电台WCQP决定增加其播放的电话咨询节目的数量；从那以后，它在Rockville所占的听众比例显著增加。鉴于WCQP最近在电话咨询节目方面的成功，以及一项指出很多广播听众对这类节目相当感兴趣的全国调查，Medway的KICK电台经理建议KICK播放更多的电话咨询节目，以期在其收听区域赢得更大的听众比例。

推理结构

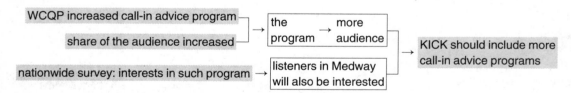

写作要求　*What **questions** should be answered to decide whether the recommendation and the argument are reasonable?*

提　纲

1. Is the introduction of the program a key factor that contributes to WCQP's increased share of audience?

(post hoc, ergo propter hoc) ★★★★

2. Granted that it is the program that contributed to the increase in share of audience, will copying the same action has the same effect two years later? ($P \rightarrow F$) ★★★

3. Could the interest mentioned in the national survey also be found in the region of Medway? (*C.S.*) ★★★

4. Are the situations of Rockville and Medway comparable? (*F.A.*) ★★★★★

5. Are there any other effective ways to gain more audience? (*sufficiency of the solution*) ★★★

6. Are there any other aspects of KICK that should be improved in order to attract more listeners? (*necessity of the solution*) ★★★

论证要点

本题主要论证点集中在WCQP听众数量增加是否是因为该电台播放了更多的电话咨询节目这一因果关系、WCQP和KICK是否具有可比性，以及全国调查结果是否能应用于Medway地区这三方面问题的分析上。

---

38. According to a recent report, cheating among college and university students is on the rise. [22] *However, Groveton College has successfully reduced student cheating by adopting an honor code*, which calls for students to agree(1) not to cheat in their academic endeavors and to notify a faculty member if they suspect that others have cheated(2). Groveton's honor code replaced a system in which teachers closely monitored students; under that system, teachers reported an average of thirty cases of cheating per year. In the first year the honor code was in place, students reported(5) twenty-one cases of cheating; five years later(6), this figure had dropped to fourteen(3,4). Moreover, in a recent survey, a majority of Groveton students said that they would be less likely to cheat with an honor code in place than without(7). **Thus, all colleges and universities should adopt honor codes (8) similar to Groveton's in order to decrease cheating among students (9,10).** (former 242) ★★

翻　译 根据最近的一份报告，大学生作弊现象呈上升趋势。然而，Groveton学院通过实施一种诚信制度成功减少了作弊，该制度要求学生同意在学业中不会作弊，并且当他们怀疑别人作弊时会告知老师。Groveton的诚信制度取代了老师严密监督学生的体制——在该体制中教师平均每年上报30起作弊现象。在诚信制度实施的第一年，学生上报了21起作弊现象；5年后，这一数字下降到了14。而且，在最近一次调查中，Groveton大部分学生说有了诚信制度他们更不可能作弊。因此，所有大学和学院都应该采取和Groveton类似的诚信制度以减少学生作弊现象。

推理结构

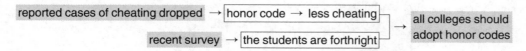

写作要求

*What **questions** should be answered to decide whether the recommendation and the argument are reasonable?*

提　纲

1. Will students keep their promises under the existence of the codes? (*U.A.*) ★★★★

2. Are Groveton students as capable of detecting cheating as teachers? Are these students likely to report

cheating whenever they observe it? (*U.A.*) ★★

3. Would the number of cases of cheating at Groveton be fewer without the honor code? (*lack of controlled experiment*) ★★★★

4. Are there any other factors that could explain the decreasing number of cases of cheating at Groveton? (*post hoc, ergo propter hoc*) ★★★★★

5. What's the number of cases of cheating which were not reported? (*I.I.*) ★★★★

6. How about the situation of cheating in the in-between and other years? (*I.I.*) ★★★

7. Are the students forthright under the circumstances in which the survey was set? (*Are the respondents being forthright when answering the questions?*) ★★★★

8. Are there any negative effects of adopting such honor codes? (*adv:disadv*) ★★★

9. Will the honor code be as effective at other colleges and universities as it was at Groveton? (*C.S.*) ★★★

10. Are there any other measures that could be taken to combat cheating? (*necessity of the solution*) ★★★

论证要点

本题最核心的问题是诚信制度是否有效减少了作弊现象，因而应重点论证的是第3和第4点，即该制度与作弊现象减少之间的因果关系。另外，学生在调查中表述的真实性以及上报作弊信息的全面性等可以作为辅助论证。

> 39. **Evidence suggests that academic honor codes, which call for students to agree not to**
> 119 **cheat in their academic endeavors and to notify a faculty member if they suspect that others have cheated(1), are far more successful than are other methods at deterring cheating among students at colleges and universities.** Several years ago, Groveton College adopted such a code and discontinued its old-fashioned system in which teachers closely monitored students. Under the old system, teachers reported an average of thirty cases of cheating per year. In the first year the honor code was in place, students reported(4) twenty-one cases of cheating; five years later(5), this figure had dropped to fourteen(2,3). Moreover, in a recent survey, a majority of Groveton students said that they would be less likely to cheat with an honor code in place than without(6). (former 242, ≈22) ★★★

翻 译 有证据表明，一种要求学生同意在学业中不会作弊，并且当他们怀疑别人作弊时会通知老师的所谓学术诚信制度，在震慑大学生作弊方面比其他方法都要成功得多。若干年前，Groveton实施了这种制度，并且停止了老师严密监控学生的旧体制。在旧体制中，教师平均每年上报30起作弊现象。在新制度实施后的第一年，学生上报了21起作弊现象；5年后，这一数字下降到了14。而且，在最近一次调查中，Groveton大部分学生说有了诚信制度他们更加不可能作弊。

推理结构

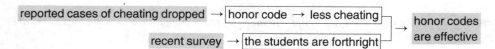

写作要求 *alternative explanations*

提 纲

1. Maybe Groveton students are not as capable of detecting cheating as faculty members, or they are not likely

164

to report their classmates' cheating when they observe it. (*U.A.*) ★★

2. Perhaps the number of cases of cheating at Groveton will be even lower without the honor code. (*lack of controlled experiment*) ★★★★

3. Other factors could also explain the decreasing number of cases of cheating at Groveton, such as the quality of the students, the difficulty of the academic works, etc. (*post hoc, ergo propter hoc*) ★★★★★

4. It is possible that many cases of cheating occurred but were not reported. (*I.I.*) ★★★★

5. The situation of one or two single years might be an unusual case. The problem of cheating might still be serious in other years. (*I.I.*) ★★★

6. The students might not be forthright under the circumstances in which the survey was set. (*Are the respondents being forthright when answering the questions?*) ★★★★

论证要点

本题主要应该对作弊减少的现象提出其他可能解释。比如,相对于教师,学生可能不太擅长发现或不愿意上报作弊现象;也可能学生素质提高、考试难度下降从而不需要作弊;抑或制度实施之后的第一年和第五年恰好是不具有代表性的年份;还有可能是被访学生没有表达他们的真实想法等。

---

40. Several years ago, Groveton College adopted an honor code, which calls for students to agree (1) not to cheat in their academic endeavors and to notify a faculty member if they suspect that others have cheated(2). Groveton's honor code replaced a system in which teachers closely monitored students. Under that system, teachers reported an average of thirty cases of cheating per year. *The honor code has proven far more successful:* in the first year it was in place, students reported(5) twenty-one cases of cheating; five years later(6), this figure had dropped to fourteen(3,4). Moreover, in a recent survey, a majority of Groveton students said that they would be less likely to cheat with an honor code in place than without(7). **Such evidence suggests that all colleges and universities should adopt honor codes similar to Groveton's(8).** *This change is sure to result in a dramatic decline in cheating among college students(9).* (former 242, ≈22, 119) ★★

翻　译　若干年前,Groveton学院推行了一种诚信制度,该制度要求学生同意在学业中不作弊,并且当他们怀疑别人作弊时会告知老师。Groveton的诚信制度代替了原有的老师严密监控学生的旧体制,在旧体制中教师平均每年上报30起作弊现象。该诚信制度被证明更成功:在它实施后的第一年,学生上报了21起作弊现象;5年后,这一数字下降到了14。而且,在最近一次调查中,Groveton大部分学生说有了诚信制度他们更加不可能作弊。这些证据说明所有大学都应该实施与Groveton类似的诚信制度。这一措施肯定能够使大学生作弊数量显著下降。

推理结构

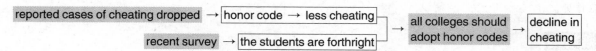

写作要求　What **questions** should be answered to decide whether the recommendation will have the predicted result?

提　纲

1. Will students keep their promise under the existence of the codes? (*U.A.*) ★★★★

2. Are Groveton students as capable of detecting cheating as faculty members? Are these students likely to report cheating whenever they observe it? (*U.A.*) ★★

3. Will the number of cases of cheating at Groveton be higher without the honor code? (*lack of controlled experiment*) ★★★★

4. Are there any other factors that could also explain the decreasing number of cases of cheating at Groveton? (*post hoc, ergo propter hoc*) ★★★★★

5. What's the number of cases of cheating which were not reported? (*I.I.*) ★★★★

6. How about the situation of cheating in other years? (*I.I.*) ★★★

7. Are the students forthright under the circumstances in which the survey was set? (*Are the respondents being forthright when answering the questions?*) ★★★★

8. Will the honor code be as effective at other colleges and universities as it was at Groveton? (*C.S.*) ★★★

9. Are there any other measures that could be taken to combat cheating? (*necessity of the solution*) ★★★

论证要点

本题最核心的问题是诚信制度是否有效减少了作弊，因而应重点论证的是第3和第4点，即该制度与作弊减少之间的因果关系。另外，学生在调查中表述的真实性以及上报作弊信息的全面性等可以作为辅助论证。

---

41. The following appeared as an editorial in the student newspaper of Groveton College.

`138` "To combat the recently reported dramatic rise in cheating among college students, colleges and universities should adopt honor codes (8) similar to Groveton's (9,10), which calls for students to agree (1) not to cheat in their academic endeavors and to notify a faculty member if they suspect that others have cheated (2). Groveton's honor code replaced an old-fashioned system in which teachers closely monitored students. Under that system, teachers reported an average of thirty cases of cheating per year. The honor code has proven far more successful: in the first year it was in place, students reported (5) twenty-one cases of cheating; five years later (6), this figure had dropped to fourteen (3,4). Moreover, in a recent survey conducted by the Groveton honor council (7), a majority of students said that they would be less likely to cheat with an honor code in place than without." (former 242, ≈22, 119, 120) ★★

翻　　译 为解决最近报道的大学生作弊现象显著增加的问题，大学院校应该采取和Groveton学院类似的诚信制度，该制度要求学生同意在学业中不作弊，并且当他们怀疑别人作弊时会告知老师。Groveton的诚信制度代替了老师严密监控学生的旧体制，在旧体制中教师平均每年上报30起作弊现象。新制度被证明成功得多：在它实施后的第一年，学生上报了21起作弊现象；5年后，这一数字下降到了14。而且，在最近一次由Groveton诚信委员会组织的调查中，大部分学生表示有了诚信制度他们更加不可能作弊。

推理结构

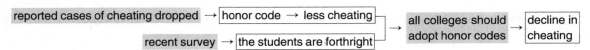

提　　纲

作者需要提供能说明以下方面问题的论据或信息：

1.　Students will keep their promise under the existence of the codes. (*U.A.*) ★★★★

2.　Groveton students are as capable of detecting cheating as faculty members, and are as likely to report cheating whenever they observe it. (*U.A.*) ★★

3.　The number of cases of cheating at Groveton would be higher if we did not adopt the honor code. (*lack of controlled experiment*) ★★★★

4.　Other factors that could explain the decreasing number of cases of cheating at Groveton. (*post hoc, ergo propter hoc*)

　　作弊数量减少有可能是由学生素质提高、学术风气改善，或是考试难度降低等因素导致。★★★★★

5.　The number of cases of cheating which were not reported. (*I.I.*) ★★★★

6.　The situation of cheating in other years. (*I.I.*)

　　文中仅提及制度实施后第一年和第五年的数据，我们需要其他年份的情况以观察作弊情况变化的趋势。★★★

7.　The students will be forthright under the circumstances in which the survey was set. (*Are the respondents being forthright when answering the questions?*) ★★★★

8.　The negative effects of adopting such honor codes. (*adv:disadv*) ★★★

9.　The honor code will be as effective at other colleges and universities as it was at Groveton. (*C.S.*) ★★★

10.　Other measures that could be taken to combat cheating. (*necessity of the solution*) ★★★

论证要点

　　本题最核心的问题是诚信制度是否有效减少了作弊，因而应重点论证的是第3和第4点，即该制度与作弊减少之间的因果关系。另外，学生在调查中表述的真实性以及上报作弊信息的全面性等可以作为辅助论证。

---

42. A recently issued twenty-year study on headaches suffered by the residents of Mentia
24 investigated the possible therapeutic effect of consuming salicylates. Salicylates are members of the same chemical family as aspirin, a medicine used to treat headaches(1). Although many foods are naturally rich in salicylates, food-processing companies also add salicylates to foods as preservatives. The twenty-year study found a correlation between the rise in the commercial use of salicylates and a steady decline in the average number of headaches reported by study participants(2). At the time when the study concluded, food-processing companies had just discovered that salicylates can also be used as flavor additives for foods, and, as a result, many companies plan to do so(3). **Based on these study results, some health experts predict that residents of Mentia will suffer even fewer headaches in the future (4).** (former 35) ★★★★

翻　　译 最近发表的一项关于Mentia居民头疼的为期20年的研究调查了食用水杨酸酯的可能疗效。水杨酸酯和用来治疗头痛的药物——阿司匹林是同一类化合物。尽管很多食品天然富含水杨酸酯，但食品加工公司也会在食品中加入它作为防腐剂。这项为期20年的研究发现，水杨酸酯越来越多的商业用途与研究对象所报告的头痛发病的平均数量下降是相关的。研究结束时，食品加工公司发现水杨酸酯也可

以被用作食品香料，因而很多公司计划将其用于此用途。根据这些研究结果，一些健康专家预言Mentia居民未来患头痛症的数量将会更少。

推理结构

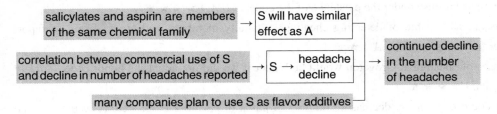

写作要求 *What **questions** should be answered to decide whether the prediction and the argument are reasonable?*

提　纲

1. Do salicylates have the same effect as aspirin in treating headaches? (*F.A.*) ★★★★
2. Are there any other factors that may lead to the decline in the number of headaches reported in the study mentioned above? (*N.C.R./ procedure of the survey/I.I.*) ★★★★★
3. Granted that salicylates are effective in treating headaches, what fraction of foods is consumed by citizens of Mentia contains salicylates, and how many citizens prefer such kind of foods? (*I.I.*) ★★★
4. Are there any factors that may result in the increase in the number of headaches suffered by citizens of Mentia, such as environment, lifestyle, etc.? (*I.T.*)
   假如影响头痛发病率的因素还有很多，那么水杨酸酯的大量使用未必带来头痛发病率的持续下降。
   ★★★

论证要点

　　本题主要问题有两方面：一是水杨酸酯是否和阿司匹林具有类似效果；二是研究中的头痛数量下降和水杨酸酯的使用是否具有因果联系。Mentia居民是否喜欢或会大量食用含这种物质的食品也会影响作者的结论。

---

43. The following appeared in the summary of a study on headaches suffered by the residents of
[26] Mentia.

"Salicylates are members of the same chemical family as aspirin, a medicine used to treat headaches(1). Although many foods are naturally rich in salicylates, for the past several decades, food-processing companies have also been adding salicylates to foods as preservatives. This rise in the commercial use of salicylates has been found to correlate with a steady decline in the average number of headaches reported by participants in our twenty-year study(2). Recently, food-processing companies have found that salicylates can also be used as flavor additives for foods(3). **With this new use for salicylates, we can expect a continued steady decline in the number of headaches suffered by the average citizen of Mentia(4).**" (former 35, ≈24) ★★★★

翻　译 水杨酸酯和用来治疗头痛的药物——阿司匹林是同一类化合物。尽管很多食品天然富含水杨酸酯，但过去几十年中，食品加工公司仍然在食品中加入它作为防腐剂。研究发现，水杨酸酯日渐增加的商业用途与我们为期20年的研究对象所报告的头痛发病平均数量下降是相关的。最近，食品加工公司

发现水杨酸酯也可以被用作食品香料。根据水杨酸酯的这种新用途，我们可以预期Mentia居民患头痛症的数量将会持续稳步下降。

推理结构

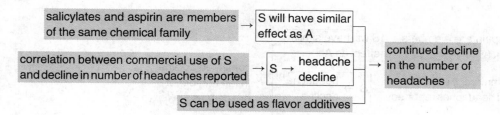

写作要求 *What specific **evidence** is needed to evaluate the argument?*

提　　纲

作者需要提供论据证明以下几点：

1. Salicylates have the same effect as aspirin in treating headaches.（*F.A.*）★★★★

2. No other factors could lead to the decline in the number of headaches reported in the study.（*N.C.R./procedure of the survey/I.I.*）★★★★★

3. Granted that salicylates are effective in treating headaches, we need to know what fraction of foods consumed by citizens of Mentia contains salicylates, and how many citizens prefer such kind of foods.（*I.I.*）★★★

4. No factors will result in the increase in the number of headaches suffered by citizens of Mentia, such as environment, lifestyle, etc.（*I.T.*）

   假如影响头痛发病率的因素还有很多，那么水杨酸酯的大量使用未必能带来头痛发病率的持续下降。★★★

论证要点

本题主要问题有两方面：一是水杨酸酯是否和阿司匹林具有类似效果；二是研究中的头痛数量下降和水杨酸酯的使用是否具有因果联系。Mentia居民是否喜欢或会大量食用含这种物质的食品也会影响作者的结论。

---

44. The following appeared in the summary of a study on headaches suffered by the residents of
[28] Mentia.

"Salicylates are members of the same chemical family as aspirin, a medicine used to treat headaches(1). Although many foods are naturally rich in salicylates, for the past several decades, food-processing companies have also been adding salicylates to foods as preservatives. This rise in the commercial use of salicylates has been found to correlate with a steady decline in the average number of headaches reported by participants in our twenty-year study(2). Recently, food-processing companies have found that salicylates can also be used as flavor additives for foods(3). **With this new use for salicylates, we can expect a continued steady decline in the number of headaches suffered by the average citizen of Mentia(4).**" （former 35, ≈24, =26）★★★★

翻　　译 水杨酸酯和用来治疗头痛的药物——阿司匹林是同一类化合物。尽管很多食品天然富含水杨酸酯，但过去几十年中食品加工公司仍然在食品中加入它作为防腐剂。研究发现，水杨酸酯日渐增加

169

的商业用途与我们为期20年的研究对象所报告的头痛发病平均数量下降是相关的。最近，食品加工公司发现水杨酸酯也可以被用作食品香料。根据水杨酸酯的这种新用途，我们可以预期Mentia居民患头痛症的数量将会持续稳步下降。

推理结构

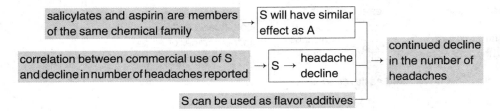

写作要求 *assumptions*

提　纲

1. Salicylates may not have the same effect as aspirin in treating headaches although they are members of the same chemical family.（*F.A.*）★★★★

2. The author assumes that no other factors could lead to the decline in the number of headaches reported in the study.（*N.C.R/ procedure of the survey/I.I.*）★★★★★

3. Granted that salicylates are effective in treating headaches, we need to know what fraction of foods consumed by citizens of Mentia contains salicylates, and how many citizens prefer such kind of foods.（*I.I.*）★★★

4. The argument also assumes that no factors will result in the increase in the number of headaches suffered by citizens of Mentia, such as environment, lifestyle, etc.（*I.T.*）
   假如影响头痛发病率的因素还有很多，那么水杨酸酯的大量使用未必带来头痛发病率的持续下降。
   ★★★

论证要点

　　本题主要问题有两方面：一是水杨酸酯是否和阿司匹林具有类似效果；二是研究中的头痛数量下降和水杨酸酯的使用是否具有因果联系。Mentia居民是否喜欢或会大量食用含这种物质的食品也会影响作者的结论。

---

45. The following was written as a part of an application for a small-business loan by a group of developers in the city of Monroe.

　　"**A jazz music club in Monroe would be a tremendously profitable enterprise.** Currently, the nearest jazz club is 65 miles away（1）; thus, *the proposed new jazz club in Monroe, the C-Note, would have the local market all to itself (2,8). Plus, jazz is extremely popular in Monroe:* over 100,000 people attended Monroe's annual jazz festival last summer（3）; several well-known jazz musicians live in Monroe（4）; and the highest-rated radio program in Monroe is 'Jazz Nightly,' which airs every weeknight at 7 P.M（5）. Finally, a nationwide study indicates that the typical jazz fan spends close to $1,000 per year on jazz entertainment（6,7）." （former 6）★★★

翻　译　在Monroe建立爵士乐俱乐部将是非常赢利的产业。目前，最近的爵士俱乐部也在65英里以外；因此，我们在此筹建的俱乐部C-Note将会占有本地全部市场。而且，爵士乐在Monroe非常流行：去年夏天，10万多人参加了Monroe的年度爵士音乐节；若干知名爵士音乐家居住在Monroe；Monroe获评价最

高的广播节目是工作日每晚7点播出的Jazz Nightly。最后，一项全国性研究表明，典型的爵士爱好者每年花费近1000元用于爵士娱乐。

推理结构

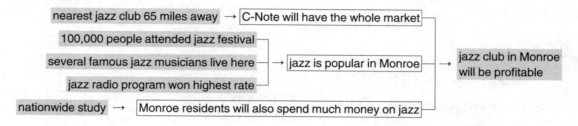

写作要求 *What specific **evidence** is needed to evaluate the argument?*

提　纲

上文讨论的问题存在以下可能性，作者需要提供论据说明：

1. If the demand for a jazz club in Monroe was as great as the applicant claims, why there isn't any such club in Monroe currently? (*negative evidence*) ★★★

2. Granted that jazz is extremely popular in Monroe, we need evidence to show that those jazz fans will attend the jazz club. (*U.A.*) ★★★

作者还需要提供论据说明以下几点：

3. What fraction of people who attended the jazz festival are Monroe residents, and for what purpose did those people attend? (*V.D./I.I.*) ★★★

4. The relationship between the fact that several well-known jazz musicians live here and Monroe residents' interest in jazz. (*I.E.*) ★★★

5. The high-rating of Monroe's jazz radio program results from the popularity of jazz at Monroe, but not other factors. (*N.C.R.*) ★★★★

6. Monroe residents are also willing to spend much money on jazz entertainment. (*C.S.*) ★★★★

7. The distribution of the $1,000, i.e., how much goes to club admission? (*V.D.*) ★★★

8. The scale of Monroe's jazz market, and the profitability of the proposed club. (*I.I.*) ★★★★

论证要点

本题3、4、5三点旨在说明作者提供的关于音乐节、音乐家、音乐节目的信息不足以说明本地居民对爵士乐有极高的兴趣。其他几点旨在说明即使本地居民对爵士乐的兴趣很高，爵士乐俱乐部的赢利能力仍然值得怀疑。

---

46. The following was written as a part of an application for a small-business loan by a group of
[100] developers in the city of Monroe.

"*Jazz music is extremely popular in the city of Monroe:* over 100,000 people attended Monroe's annual jazz festival last summer(1), and the highest-rated radio program in Monroe is 'Jazz Nightly', which airs every weeknight(2). Also, a number of well-known jazz musicians own homes in Monroe(3). Nevertheless, the nearest jazz club is over an hour away(4). Given the popularity of jazz in Monroe(5) and a recent nationwide study indicating that the typical jazz fan spends close to $1,000 per year on jazz entertainment(6,7), **a jazz music club in Monroe would be tremendously profitable (8).**" (former 6, ≈25)

爵士乐在Monroe非常受欢迎：去年夏天，10万多人参加了Monroe的年度爵士音乐节；Monroe获评价最高的广播节目是每周工作日夜晚播出的Jazz Nightly。而且，若干知名爵士音乐家在Monroe拥有住所。然而，现在最近的爵士俱乐部也在1小时车程以外。鉴于爵士乐在Monroe的受欢迎程度以及最近全国调查显示典型的爵士爱好者每年花费近1000元用于爵士娱乐，在Monroe建立爵士乐俱乐部将会非常赢利。

推理结构

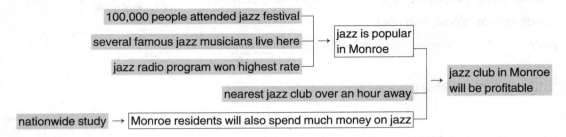

写作要求 *assumptions*

提　纲

1. We need to know what fraction of people who attended the jazz festival are Monroe residents, and for what purpose those people attended it. (*V.D./I.I.*) ★★★

2. The applicant hastily assumes that the high-rating of Monroe's jazz radio results from the popularity of jazz at Monroe, but not other factors. (*N.C.R.*) ★★★★

3. The fact that several well-known jazz musicians own homes here does not necessarily illustrate Monroe residents' interest in jazz music. (*I.E.*) ★★★

   1, 2, 3: The assumption that jazz music is extremely popular in Monroe is unwarranted.

4. If the demand for a jazz club in Monroe was as great as the applicant claims, it seems that Monroe would already have one or more such clubs. (*negative evidence*) ★★★

5. Granted that jazz is extremely popular in Monroe, we need evidence to show that those jazz fans will attend the jazz club. (*U.A.*) ★★★

6. The applicant hastily assumes that Monroe residents are also willing to spend much money on jazz entertainment. (*C.S.*) ★★★★

7. We need to know the distribution of the $1,000, i.e., how much goes to club admission. (*V.D.*) ★★★

8. Before further information about the scale of Monroe's jazz market, and the profitability of the proposed club are provided, the assumption that the jazz club will be profitable is untenable. (*I.I.*) ★★★★

论证要点

　　本题1、2、3三点旨在说明作者提供的关于音乐节、音乐家、音乐节目的信息不足以说明本地居民对爵士乐有极高的兴趣这一假设。其他几点旨在说明即使本地居民对爵士乐的兴趣很高，爵士乐俱乐部的赢利能力仍然值得怀疑。

---

47. The following was written as a part of an application for a small-business loan by a group of developers in the city of Monroe.

[102]

　　"*Jazz music is extremely popular in the city of Monroe*: over 100,000 people attended Monroe's annual jazz festival last summer(1), and the highest-rated radio program in Monroe is 'Jazz

Nightly', which airs every weeknight（2）. Also, a number of well-known jazz musicians own homes in Monroe（3）. Nevertheless, the nearest jazz club is over an hour away（4）. Given the popularity of jazz in Monroe（5）and a recent nationwide study indicating that the typical jazz fan spends close to $1,000 per year on jazz entertainment（6,7）, **we predict that our new jazz music club in Monroe will be a tremendously profitable enterprise (8).**"（former 6, ≈25, =100）

翻　　译 爵士乐在Monroe非常受欢迎：去年夏天，10多万人参加了Monroe的年度爵士音乐节；Monroe获评价最高的广播节目是每周工作日夜晚播出的Jazz Nightly。而且，若干知名爵士音乐家在Monroe拥有住所。然而，现在最近的爵士俱乐部也在1小时车程以外。鉴于爵士乐在Monroe的受欢迎程度以及最近全国调查显示典型的爵士爱好者每年花费近1000元用于爵士娱乐，在Monroe建立爵士乐俱乐部将会非常赢利。

推理结构

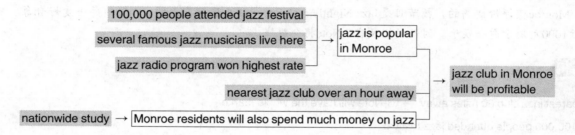

写作要求 *What **questions** should be answered to decide whether the prediction and the argument are reasonable?*

提　　纲

1. What fraction of people who attended the jazz festival are Monroe residents, and for what purpose did those people attend?（V.D./I.I.）★★★

2. Does the high-rating of Monroe's jazz radio result from the popularity of jazz at Monroe, but not other factors?（N.C.R.）★★★★

3. Does the fact that several well-known jazz musicians own homes here necessarily illustrate Monroe residents' interest in jazz music?（I.E.）★★★

4. If the demand for a jazz club in Monroe was as great as the applicant claims, why does Monroe have no such clubs running currently?（negative evidence）★★★

5. Granted that jazz is extremely popular in Monroe, will those jazz fans attend the jazz club?（U.A.）★★★

6. Are Monroe residents also willing to spend much money on jazz entertainment?（C.S.）★★★★

7. How about the distribution of the $1,000? i.e., how much goes to club admission?（V.D.）★★★

8. How about the scale of Monroe's jazz market, and the profitability of the proposed club?（I.I.）★★★★

论证要点

　　本题1、2、3三点旨在说明作者提供的关于音乐节、音乐家、音乐节目的信息不足以说明本地居民对爵士乐有极高的兴趣这一假设。其他几点旨在说明即使本地居民对爵士乐的兴趣很高，爵士乐俱乐部的赢利能力仍然值得怀疑。

48. The following was written by a group of developers in the city of Monroe.

164 "*A jazz music club in Monroe would be a tremendously profitable enterprise.* At present, the nearest jazz club is over 60 miles away from Monroe（1）; thus, *our proposed club, the C-Note, would have the local market all to itself (2,8).* In addition, *there is ample evidence of the popularity of jazz in Monroe:* over 100,000 people attended Monroe's jazz festival last summer （3）, several well-known jazz musicians live in Monroe（4）, and the highest-rated radio program in Monroe is 'Jazz Nightly.' （5） Finally, a nationwide study indicates that the typical jazz fan spends close to $1,000 per year on jazz entertainment （6,7）. **We therefore predict that the C-Note cannot help but make money.**" (former 6, ≈25, 100, 102) ★ ★

翻　　译　在Monroe建立爵士乐俱乐部将会是非常赢利的产业。目前,最近的爵士乐俱乐部也在60英里以外;因此,我们计划筹建的俱乐部C-Note将占有本地的全部市场。而且,大量证据表明爵士乐在Monroe非常受欢迎:去年夏天,10万多人参加了Monroe的爵士音乐节;若干知名爵士音乐家居住在Monroe;Monroe获评价最高的广播节目是Jazz Nightly。最后,一项全国研究表明,典型的爵士爱好者每年花费近1000元用于爵士娱乐。因而我们预言C Note将会赚钱。

推理结构

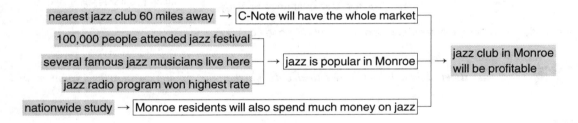

写作要求　*What **questions** should be answered to decide whether the prediction and the argument are reasonable?*

提　　纲

1. If the demand for a jazz club in Monroe was as great as the applicant claims, why there isn't any such club in Monroe currently? (*negative evidence*) ★ ★ ★

2. Granted that jazz is extremely popular in Monroe, will those jazz fans attend the jazz club? (*U.A.*) ★ ★ ★

3. What fraction of people who attended the jazz festival are Monroe residents, and for what purpose did those people attend? (*V.D./ I.I.*) ★ ★ ★

4. Is there any relationship between the fact that several well-known jazz musicians live here and Monroe residents' interest in jazz? (*I.E.*) ★ ★ ★

5. Does the high-rating of Monroe's jazz radio result from the popularity of jazz at Monroe, but not other factors? (*N.C.R.*) ★ ★ ★ ★

6. Are Monroe residents also willing to spend much money on jazz entertainment? (*C.S.*) ★ ★ ★ ★

7. How about the distribution of the $1,000? i.e., how much goes to club admission? (*V.D.*) ★ ★ ★

8. How about the scale of Monroe's jazz market, and the profitability of the proposed club? (*I.I.*) ★ ★ ★ ★

论证要点

本题3、4、5三点旨在说明作者提供的关于音乐节、音乐家、音乐节目的信息不足以说明本地居民对爵士乐有极高的兴趣。其他几点旨在说明即使本地居民对爵士乐的兴趣很高，爵士乐俱乐部的赢利能力仍然值得怀疑。

49. The following appeared in a letter to the editor of a local newspaper.

27 "Commuters complain that increased rush-hour traffic on Blue Highway between the suburbs and the city center has doubled their commuting time. The favored proposal of the motorists' lobby is to widen the highway, adding an additional lane of traffic. But last year's addition of a lane to the nearby Green Highway was followed by a worsening of traffic jams on it(1,2,3). **A better alternative is to add a bicycle lane to Blue Highway.** Many area residents are keen bicyclists(4). *A bicycle lane would encourage them to use bicycles to commute(5,6), and so would reduce rush-hour traffic rather than fostering an increase(7,8).*"（former 55）★★

翻　译 乘客抱怨说，郊区和市中心之间的Blue Highway在高峰时期日趋严重的交通拥堵使他们在路上所花的时间多了一倍。乘客最希望的是拓宽公路，增加一条机动车道。但去年，附近的Green Highway增加车道带来的是更严重的交通拥堵。较好的替代方案是在Blue Highway修建一条自行车道。很多市民是自行车爱好者。自行车道将会鼓励他们使用自行车出行，从而减少高峰时期的交通拥堵。

推理结构

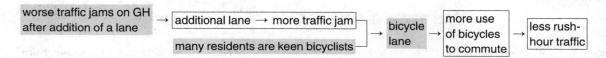

写作要求 *What specific **evidence** is needed to evaluate the argument?*

提　纲

作者需要提供论据说明以下几点：

1. If there are any other causes that could result in the increased traffic jams on Green Highway. （*post hoc, ergo propter hoc*）★★★★★

2. There will be less traffic jams on Green Highway without the additional lane. （*lack of controlled study*）Green Highway如果不增加车道，交通拥堵可能会更加严重。★★★★

3. Problems emerged on Green Highway would also take place on Blue Highway. （*F.A.*）★★★★

4. What percentage of the whole citizens here are keen bicyclists. （*V.D.*）★★★

5. Among those keen bicyclists, how many are using Blue Highway for commuting. （*V.D.*）★★★

6. The willingness and feasibility of those bicyclists to use the bicycle lane for commuting. （*feasibility of the conclusion*）★★★★

7. If there are any negative effects of building a bicycle lane. （*adv:disadv*）★★★★★

8. Other possible measures that could be used to solve the traffic problem. （*necessity of the solution*）★★★

论证要点

　　本题主要环节在于作者能否提供充分论据证明修建自行车道能更好地缓解拥堵，而修建机动车道则不能。首先，Green Highway的拥堵未必来自于机动车道的修建，而且假如不修建这条车道可能会更加拥堵；就算是Green Highway机动车道的修建导致了拥堵，同样的现象未必也会在Blue Highway发生。另外，很多居民是自行车爱好者并不能说明他们一定会用自行车通勤（他们可能只是把自行车用于休闲目的），更不一定说明他们会用Blue Highway通勤。

50. The following appeared in an editorial in a local newspaper.

29 "<u>Commuters complain that increased rush-hour traffic on Blue Highway between the suburbs and the city center has doubled their commuting time.</u> The favored proposal of the motorists' lobby is to widen the highway, adding an additional lane of traffic. Opponents note that last year's addition of a lane to the nearby Green Highway was followed by a worsening of traffic jams on it(1,2,3). **Their suggested alternative proposal is adding a bicycle lane to Blue Highway.** Many area residents are keen bicyclists(4). *A bicycle lane would encourage them to use bicycles to commute(5,6), it is argued, thereby reducing rush-hour traffic(7,8)*." (former 55, =27) ★★

翻 译 乘客抱怨说,郊区和市中心之间的Blue Highway在高峰时期日趋严重的交通拥堵使他们在路上所花的时间多了一倍。乘客最希望的是拓宽公路,增加一条机动车道。反对者指出,去年附近的Green Highway增加车道带来的是更严重的交通拥堵。他们提出的替代方案是在Blue Highway修建一条自行车道。很多市民是自行车爱好者。自行车道将会鼓励他们使用自行车出行,从而减少高峰时期的交通拥堵。

推理结构

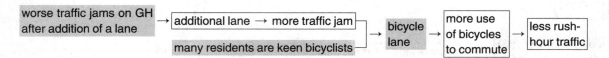

写作要求 *What **questions** should be answered to decide whether the recommendation and the argument are reasonable?*

提 纲

1. Are there any other factors that could result in the increased traffic jams on Green Highway? (*post hoc, ergo propter hoc*) ★★★★★

2. Will there be even more traffic jams on Green Highway without the additional lane? (*lack of controlled study*) ★★★★

3. Will the problems emerged on Green Highway also take place on Blue Highway? (*F.A.*) ★★★★

4. What percentage of the whole citizens here are keen bicyclists? (*V.D.*) ★★★

5. Among the keen bicyclists, how many are using Blue Highway for commuting? (*V.D.*) ★★★

6. How about the willingness and feasibility of those bicyclists to use the bicycle lane for commuting? (*feasibility of the conclusion*) ★★★★

7. Are there any negative effects of building a bicycle lane? (*adv:disadv*) ★★★★★

8. Are there any other possible measures that could be used to solve the traffic problem? (*necessity of the solution*) ★★★

论证要点

　　本题主要环节在于作者能否充分证明修建自行车道能更好地缓解拥堵,而修建机动车道则不能。首先,Green Highway的拥堵未必来自于机动车道的修建,而且假如不修建这条车道可能会更加拥堵;其次,就算是Green Highway机动车道的修建导致了拥堵,同样的现象未必也会在Blue Highway发生。另外,很多居民是自行车爱好者并不能说明他们一定会用自行车通勤(他们可能只是把自行车用于休闲目的),更不一定说明他们会用Blue Highway通勤。上述问题都是围绕这些推理环节提出的,回答了这些问题才能评判作者提出的方案是否合理。

51. The following appeared as a recommendation by a committee planning a ten-year budget for the city of Calatrava.

30

"The birthrate in our city is declining: in fact, last year's birthrate was only one-half that of five years ago. *Thus the number of students enrolled in our public schools will soon decrease dramatically(1),* **and we can safely reduce the funds budgeted for education during the next decade(2,3). At the same time, we can reduce funding for athletic playing fields and other recreational facilities(7).** As a result, we will have sufficient money to fund city facilities and programs used primarily by adults(5,6), *since we can expect the adult population of the city to increase(4).*" ★★

翻　译 我市出生率正在下降：事实上，去年出生率仅为5年前的一半。因而，我市公立学校的学生数量将很快显著下降，无疑我们可以在下一个10年减少教育经费预算。同时，我们可以减少运动场地和其他休闲设施的投入。从而，我们将会有充足的资金用于主要供成年人使用的城市设施和项目，因为我们可以预期本市成年人数量将会增加。

推理结构

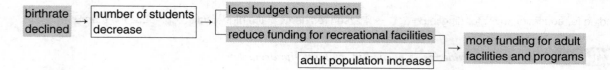

写作要求 *What specific **evidence** is needed to evaluate the argument?*

提　纲

作者需要提供论据来说明以下几点：

1. No factors would lead to the increase in the number of students enrolled in public schools. (*N.C.R. / I.T.*) ★★★★

2. The current funding for education is sufficient, and could be cut. (*feasibility of the conclusion*) ★★★★

3. There is no need for us to devote more money on education. (*I.T.*) ★★★

4. Why the adult population will surely increase. (*U.A.*) ★★★

5. The relationship between increased adult population and the need for more facilities and programs mentioned above. (*N.C.R. / necessity of the solution*) ★★★

6. Granted that the demand for adult facilities and programs will increase, we need further research on other possible methods that could provide funding for those facilities and programs. (*necessity of the solution*) ★★

7. Granted that the number of students will decrease, we need evidence to show that those playing fields and recreational facilities are used only by schoolchildren, and information about the negative effects of reducing funding for these facilities. (*adv:disadv*) ★★★★

论证要点

　　本题中提供的信息首先不能充分支持作者提出的学生数量一定会下降的假设，因而减少教育经费和减少运动休闲设施投入的观点也就不一定成立；其次，文章末尾关于成年人数量增加的看法没有任何论据支持。

52. The following appeared in a letter to the editor of Parson City's local newspaper.

31 "In our region of Trillura, the majority（1）of money spent on the schools that most students attend—the city-run public schools—comes from taxes that each city government collects. **The region's cities differ, however, in the budgetary priority they give to public education.** For example, both as a proportion of its overall tax revenues and in absolute terms, Parson City has recently（2）spent almost twice as much per year（3）as Blue City has for its public schools—even though both cities have about the same number of residents（4,5）. **Clearly, Parson City residents place a higher value on providing a good education in public schools than Blue City residents do.**"（former 214）★★★★

翻　译 在我们Trillura地区，大多数学生所上的市立学校教育开支大部分是从市政府税收而来的。然而，该地区不同城市对公共教育预算的优先级是不同的。举例而言，无论从占总税收的比例还是从绝对值来说，Parson市最近用于公立学校的预算几乎是Blue市的两倍，尽管两市居民数量基本相同。显然，Parson市的居民比Blue市居民更关注为公立学校提供良好教育。

推理结构

funding for education in P : funding in B =2:1　→　Parson residents place higher value on education than B

写作要求 *What specific **evidence** is needed to evaluate the argument?*

提　纲

作者需要提供关于以下两方面的信息：

1. The information about other sources of funding for public schools.（I.I.）★★
2. Former data of funding for education in the two cities.（C → P/C → F/selective sample）★★★
   上文推理还存在以下问题：
3. The city's budget for its public schools is neither an accurate indication of the value it places on public education, nor an indication of the residents' attitude towards public education.（U.C.）★★★★★
   此外，作者还需要提供关于以下方面的信息：
4. Other differences between Parson City and Blue City that may explain the differences in the amount of money they budget for their public schools.（I.C.）★★★
5. The number of students who go to public schools in the two cities.（I.I./V.D.）★★★★

论证要点

　　本题最关键的环节在于，首先在不知道两地区学生基数的情况下，无法判断平均到每名学生有多少教育投入（第5点），因而不能以此说明P市投入更多；其次，政府教育预算不能完全代表城市对教育的重视程度，也不能代表居民对教育的看法（第3点）（1、2、4几点是围绕第3点展开的）。

53. The following appeared in a memo from a vice president of Quiot Manufacturing.

32 "During the past year, Quiot Manufacturing had 30 percent more on-the-job accidents（1,2）than at the nearby Panoply Industries plant, where the work shifts are one hour shorter than ours（3,4）. Experts say that significant contributing factors in many on-the-job accidents are fatigue and sleep deprivation among workers. **Therefore, to reduce the number of on-the-job**

accidents at Quiot (5) and thereby increase productivity (7), we should shorten each of our three work shifts by one hour *so that employees will get adequate amounts of sleep(6).*"
(former 12) ★★

翻　译　在过去一年中，我们Quiot工厂的工伤事故比邻近的Panoply工厂多30%，Panoply每班的工作时间比我们的短1个小时。专家认为，导致很多工伤事故的重要因素就是工人的疲劳和睡眠不足。因此，为减少Quiot的工伤事故数量并提高生产率，我们应该把3个班次工作的时间都减少1小时，从而我们的雇员将得到更充足的睡眠。

推理结构

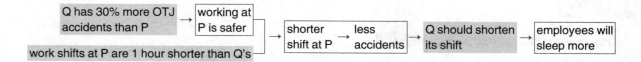

写作要求　*assumptions*

提　纲

1. The president assumes that at least some accidents at Quiot are caused by fatigue or sleep deprivation. (*U.A.*) ★★★★

2. The president fails to convince us that the safety record at Panoply is superior, for we do not know the total number of workers at each plant. The per-worker accident rate might reveal that Quiot is actually safer than Panoply. (*V.D.*) ★★★★★

3. Granted that working at Panoply is safer, we cannot ensure that it is the shorter shift that resulted in the differences in accident rate. (*N.C.R. / confusing concurrence with causality*) ★★★★★

4. The president fails to consider possible differences between Quiot and Panoply which may render them incomparable. (*F.A.*) ★★★★

5. The assumption that shortening the work shifts suffices to reduce the number of on-the-job accidents is open to doubt. (*sufficiency of the solution*) ★★★

6. The assumption that Quiot's workers will use the additional hour of free time to sleep or rest is open to doubt. (*U.A.*) ★★★

7. The president provides no evidence that overall worker productivity is attributable in part to the number of on-the-job accidents. (*N.C.R.*) ★★★

论证要点

　　本题题目推理结构十分清晰，因而针对它写出的论证文章结构也可以安排得十分清晰流畅。首先可以分析文中最根本假设：P未必比Q更加安全，因为我们不知道工厂规模和工人基数；其次，就算P更加安全，其安全纪录未必来自于更短的工作时间；再次，就算工作时间和事故率有关系，P与Q未必可比；最后，员工提前下班是否会用富余时间休息，以及这一点是否足以减少工伤事故，也不能保证。

54. The following appeared in a memo from a vice president of a manufacturing company.

104 "During the past year, workers at our newly opened factory reported 30 percent more on-the-job accidents（1,2）than workers at nearby Panoply Industries. Panoply produces products very similar to those produced at our factory, but its work shifts are one hour shorter than ours（3).

*Experts say that fatigue and sleep deprivation among workers are significant contributing factors in many on-the-job accidents. **Panoply's superior safety record can therefore be attributed to its shorter work shifts (2), which allow its employees to get adequate amounts of rest.**"* (former 12, ≈32) ★★★★

翻　译 在过去一年中，我们新工厂上报的工伤事故比邻近的Panoply工厂多30%。Panoply生产的产品和我们非常类似，但他们每班的工作时间比我们短1个小时。专家认为导致很多工伤事故的重要因素就是工人的疲劳和睡眠不足。因此，Panoply出色的安全纪律可以归因于其更短的工作班次，这使其员工得到充分休息。

推理结构

our factory has 30% more OTJ accidents than P	
work shifts at P are 1 hour shorter than ours	→ shorter shift at P → adequate rest → less accidents

写作要求 *alternative explanations*

提　纲

1. The greater amount of accidents at our factory may be explained by greater total number of workers at our factory. (*V.D.*) ★★★★★

2. The criteria on what kind of accidents should be reported might be different at the two factories. Perhaps only serious accidents were reported at Panoply while at our factory all accidents were reported. (*I.C.*) ★★★★

3. Granted that working at Panoply is safer, other factors may also contribute to the lower accident rate, e.g., the workers at Panoply are more experienced or well trained, or the equipements and devices at Panoply are more advanced and easy to operate. (*N.C.R.*) ★★★★★

论证要点

　　本题首先可以针对文中最根本假设"P更加安全"分析其他可能原因：我们工厂可能规模更大、工人数量更多，在事故概率相近的情况下，规模越大的工厂当然事故总数更多。因此，只要我们工厂的工人总数比P工人总数多30%以上，那么实际上我们工厂就更加安全；而且，两个工厂对于什么事故需要上报的标准可能也不一样。标准低的工厂当然事故数量多。其次，就算P更加安全，其原因未必由于更短的工作时间而可能有其他解释，比如工人更加训练有素、生产工艺和设备更加先进等。

55. The following appeared in a memo from the vice president of Butler Manufacturing.

[105] "During the past year, workers at Butler Manufacturing reported 30 percent more on-the-job accidents(1) than workers at nearby Panoply Industries, where the work shifts are one hour shorter than ours(2). A recent government study reports that fatigue and sleep deprivation among workers are significant contributing factors in many on-the-job accidents(3). **If we shorten each of our work shifts by one hour (4,5), we can improve Butler Manufacturing's safety record by ensuring that our employees are adequately rested(6).**" (former 12, ≈32, 104) ★★

翻　　译　在过去一年中，Butler工厂上报的工伤事故比邻近的Panoply工厂多30%，Panoply每班的工作时间比我们短1个小时。最近的一项政府研究报告说，导致很多工伤事故的重要因素就是工人的疲劳和睡眠不足。如果我们每个班次的工作时间都减少1小时，就可以通过保证员工得到充分休息而提高Butler的安全纪录。

推理结构

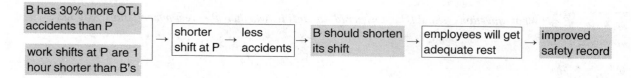

写作要求　*What specific **evidence** is needed to evaluate the argument?*

提　　纲

作者需要提供说明以下方面的信息或论据：

1.　The total number of workers at each company. The per-worker accident rate might reveal that working at Butler is actually safer than at Panoply.（*V.D.*）★★★★★

2.　The better safety record of Panoply could be attributed to their shorter working shift.（*N.C.R.*）★★★★★

3.　At least some accidents at Butler are caused by fatigue or sleep deprivation.（*I.I./U.A.*）★★★★

4.　Shortening the work shifts suffices to reduce the number of on-the-job accidents at Butler.（*sufficiency of the solution*）★★★

5.　Other differences between Butler and Panoply.（*F.A.*）★★★★

6.　Butler's workers would use the additional hour of free time to sleep or rest.（*U.A.*）★★★

论证要点

　　本题题目推理结构十分清晰，因而针对它写出的论证文章结构也可以安排得十分清晰流畅。首先可以分析文中的最根本假设"P未必比B更加安全"，因为我们不知道工厂规模和工人基数；其次，就算P更加安全，其原因未必来自于更短的工作时间；再次，就算工作时间和事故率有关系，P与B未必可比；最后，员工提前下班是否会用富余时间休息，以及这一点是否足以减少工伤事故，也不能保证。

---

56. The following appeared in a memo from the Board of Directors of Butler Manufacturing.

106 "During the past year, workers at Butler Manufacturing reported 30 percent more on-the-job accidents（1）than workers at nearby Panoply Industries, where the work shifts are one hour shorter than ours（2）. A recent government study reports that fatigue and sleep deprivation among workers are significant contributing factors in many on-the-job accidents（3）. **Therefore, we recommend that Butler Manufacturing**（5）**shorten each of its work shifts by one hour.** *Shorter shifts will allow Butler to improve its safety record(4) by ensuring that its employees are adequately rested(6).*"（former 12, ≈32, 104, 105）★★

翻　　译　在过去一年中，Butler工厂上报的工伤事故比邻近的Panoply工厂多30%，Panoply每班的工作时间比我们短1个小时。最近的一项政府研究报告说，导致很多工伤事故的重要因素就是工人疲劳和睡眠不足。因此，我们建议Butler把每个班次的工作时间都减少1小时。缩短工作班次可以通过保证员工得到充分休息而提高Butler的安全纪录。

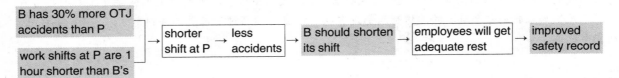

What **questions** should be answered to decide whether the recommendation will have the predicted result?

提　纲

1. How about the total number of workers at each company? The per-worker accident rate might reveal that working at Butler is actually safer than at Panoply. (*V.D.*) ★★★★★

2. Could the better safety record of Panoply be attributed to their shorter working shift? (*N.C.R.*) ★★★★★

3. Is any of the accidents at Butler caused by fatigue or sleep deprivation? (*I.I./U.A.*) ★★★★

4. Does shortening the work shifts suffice to reduce the number of on-the-job accidents? (*sufficiency of the solution*) ★★★

5. Are there any other differences between Butler and Panoply? (*F.A.*) ★★★★

6. Would Butler's workers use the additional hour of free time to sleep or rest? (*U.A.*) ★★★

论证要点

　　本题首先可以分析文中的最根本假设"P未必比B更加安全"，因为我们不知道工厂规模和工人基数；其次，就算P更加安全，其原因未必来自于更短的工作时间；再次，就算工作时间和事故率有关，P与B未必可比；最后，员工提前下班是否会用富余时间休息，以及这一点是否足以减少工伤事故，也不能保证。如果以上4点均无法确认，那么采纳作者的建议显然无助于提高B的安全纪录。

---

57. The following appeared in a memo from a vice president of Alta Manufacturing.

167 "During the past year, Alta Manufacturing had thirty percent more on-the-job accidents (1,2) than nearby Panoply Industries, where the work shifts are one hour shorter than ours (3). Experts believe that a significant contributing factor in many accidents is fatigue caused by sleep deprivation among workers. Therefore, to reduce the number of on-the-job accidents at Alta (4), **we recommend shortening each of our three work shifts by one hour.** *If we do this, our employees will get adequate amounts of sleep (5)."* (former 12, ≈32,104,105,106) ★★

翻　译 去年，Alta工厂的工伤事故比邻近的Panoply工厂多30%，Panoply的每班工作时间比我们短1个小时。专家认为导致很多工伤事故的重要因素就是工人的疲劳和睡眠不足。因此，为减少Alta的工伤事故，我们建议把3个班次的工作时间都减少1小时。这样做将使员工获得充足的睡眠。

推理结构

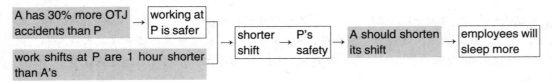

*What **questions** should be answered to decide whether the recommendation and the argument are reasonable?*

提　纲

1. How many accidents at Alta are caused by fatigue or sleep deprivation? (*U.A.*) ★★★★

2. How about the per-worker accident rate? Maybe working at Alta is actually safer than at Panoply, depending on the total number of workers at each company. (*V.D.*) ★★★★★

3. Are there any differences between Alta and Panoply which render them incomparable? (*F.A.*) ★★★★

4. Does shortening the work shifts suffice to reduce the number of on-the-job accidents? (*sufficiency of the solution*) ★★★

5. Will workers of Alta use the additional hour of free time to sleep or rest? (*U.A.*) ★★★

论证要点

本题首先可以分析文中的最根本假设"P未必比A更加安全",因为不知道工厂规模和工人基数;其次,就算P更加安全,其原因未必来自于更短的工作时间;再次,就算工作时间和事故率有关系,P与A未必可比;最后,员工提前下班是否会用富余时间休息,以及这一点是否足以减少工伤事故,也不能保证。

---

58. The following appeared in a memorandum from the planning department of an electric power
33 company.

"Several recent surveys indicate that home owners are increasingly eager to conserve energy (1,2). At the same time, manufacturers are now marketing many home appliances, such as refrigerators and air conditioners, that are almost twice as energy efficient as those sold a decade ago(3). Also, new technologies for better home insulation and passive solar heating are readily available to reduce the energy needed for home heating(3). **Therefore, the total demand for electricity in our area will not increase—and may decline slightly(4). Since our three electric generating plants in operation (6) for the past twenty years have always met our needs, construction of new generating plants will not be necessary(5)."**
(former 208) ★★★

翻　译 最近的几次调查表明,房主越来越强烈地希望节省能源。同时,生产商现在正在推出很多能效比10年前的电器几乎高一倍的家用电器,比如冰箱和空调。而且,更好的房屋隔热和被动式太阳能采暖的新技术已经可以用于减少家庭采暖所需的能源。因此,本地区的用电需求总量不会增加,而可能有轻微下降。已经运作了20年的三座发电站一直能够满足需求,因此,我们无需建造新的发电厂。

推理结构

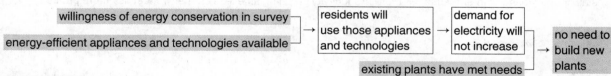

写作要求 *assumptions*

提　纲

1. The author assumes that home owners who are eager to conserve energy will purchase and use those energy-efficient home appliances. (*U.A.*) ★★★

2. The reliability of the survey is not guaranteed: people who are eager to conserve energy might be more willing to respond to the survey than other people. (*Are the respondents representative?*) ★ ★

3. We are not informed about the price of those energy-efficient home appliances and the cost of employing the new technologies, thus we could not predict whether residents could afford using them, and whether they are willing to pay for these technologies. (*adv:disadv/feasibility of the conclusion*) ★ ★ ★

4. The assumption that no other factors will lead to the increase in the demand for electricity in the future is apparently unwarranted. (*sufficiency of the conclusion/I.T./C→F*) ★ ★ ★ ★ ★

5. The author fails to rule out many possibilities which will render one or more additional generating plants necessary. (*C→F*) ★ ★ ★ ★ ★

6. The old plants might be less energy efficient than a new plant using new technology, or might have some negative effects on environment and economic. (*adv:disadv*) ★ ★ ★

论证要点

本题最主要问题在于最后两句关于用电需求和发电厂的判断明显属于没有考虑时间变化，4、5两点是围绕这方面展开的；其次是关于节能电器和技术的信息都不完整的问题：它们是否已经处于应用阶段，成本几何，消费者是否能负担以及是否有使用它们的意愿。

---

59. The vice president of human resources at Climpson Industries sent the following recommendation
34 to the company's president.

"In an effort to improve our employees' productivity(1), **we should implement electronic monitoring of employees' Internet use from their workstations.** Employees who use the Internet from their workstations(3) need to be identified and punished if we are to reduce the number of work hours spent on personal or recreational activities(2), such as shopping or playing games(4). *By installing software(5) to detect employees' Internet use on company computers, we can prevent employees from wasting time, foster a better work ethic(6) at Climpson, and improve our overall profits(7).*" (former 127) ★ ★ ★

翻　　译 为努力提高员工生产效率，我们应该在员工的终端上加装电子监控(设施)来监视员工的互联网使用情况。如果要减少(员工)用于私人以及娱乐活动，比如购物或玩游戏的工作时间，那么，(我们需要采取)在终端上使用互联网的员工要被确认并且受到惩罚(的措施)。通过在公司电脑上安装检测员工使用互联网情况的软件，我们可以防止员工浪费时间，培养Climpson更好的工作氛围，并提高我们的整体利润。

推理结构

installing monitoring of Internet use → more productivity / wasting time less / better work ethic / more profits

写作要求 *assumptions*

提　　纲

1. The vice president fails to provide any information about current performance and productivity of the employees, thus the assumption that their productivity should be and could be further improved is open to doubt. (*I.I./U.A./necessity of the solution*) ★ ★

2. The vice president unfairly assumes that at least some of the employees have already used Internet for personal or recreational activities. (*U.A./I.I./necessity of the solution*) ★ ★ ★

3. The vice president ignores the necessity for some employees to use the Internet in their work. (*adv: disadv*) ★★★★

4. Employees could still spend much time on personal or recreational activities even if the Internet access is banned. (*sufficiency of the solution*) ★★★★★

5. The vice president fails to consider possible negative effects of installing such software on the computers, and fails to analyze the cost of installing the software. (*adv:disadv*) ★★★

6. The vice president overlooks the negative effects of the proposed action on employees' morale, thus the better work ethic mentioned above is not guaranteed. (*adv:disadv*) ★★★★★

7. Since Climpson's profits are determined by many factors, adopting the proposal alone may not sufficiently ensure greater profits. (*sufficiency of the solution*) ★★★

论证要点

本题论证内容主要集中在两方面：安装上述系统带来的成本、员工情绪的负面影响；以及该方案的充分性和必要性。首先，Climpson的员工效率未必有进一步提高的空间；其次，副总裁也没有提供信息证明员工已经有人因私上网浪费时间并且影响了工作效率这一大前提；再次，就算安装了他所说的监控系统，也未必能保证员工不通过其他方式浪费时间，也就未必能保证Climpson公司利润上升。

---

60. The vice president for human resources at Climpson Industries sent the following
58 recommendation to the company's president.

"In an effort to improve our employees' productivity (1), **we should implement electronic monitoring of employees' Internet use from their workstations.** Employees who use the Internet inappropriately from their workstations (3) need to be identified and punished if we are to reduce the number of work hours spent on personal or recreational activities (2), such as shopping or playing games (4). **Installing software(5) on company computers to detect employees' Internet use is the best way(6) to prevent employees from wasting time on the job.** *It will foster a better work ethic(7)at Climpson and improve our overall profits(8)*."

(former 127, ≈34) ★★★

翻　　译 为提高员工生产效率，我们应该在员工的终端上加装电子监控(系统)来监视员工的互联网使用情况。如果要减少(员工)用于私人以及娱乐活动，比如购物或玩游戏的工作时间，那么，(我们需要采取)在终端上使用互联网的员工要被确认并且受到惩罚(的措施)。在公司电脑上安装软件检测员工使用互联网情况是防范员工浪费工作时间的最好办法。它可以培养Climpson更好的工作氛围并提高我们的整体利润。

推理结构

installing monitoring of Internet use → more productivity / wasting time less / better work ethic / more profits

写作要求 *What specific **evidence** is needed to evaluate the argument?*

提　　纲

作者需要提供能说明以下问题的信息或论据：

1. Current performance and productivity of the employees. The assumption that their productivity should be and could be further improved is open to doubt. (*I.I./U.A./necessity of the solution*) ★★

2. At least some of the employees have already used Internet for personal or recreational activities. (*U.A./I.I./*

necessity of the solution) ★★★

1、2两点都是上文论证的大前提。如果员工没有上网浪费时间，那么，其效率也就没有提高空间，进而作者的论述就没有任何意义。

3. The necessity for some employees to use the Internet in their work. (*adv: disadv*) ★★

4. Employees will not spend time on personal or recreational activities once the Internet access is banned. (*sufficiency of the solution*) ★★★★★

5. Negative effects of installing such software on the computers, and the cost of installing the software. (*adv: disadv*) ★★★

6. Other ways to prevent employees from wasting working time. (*necessity of the solution*) ★★★

7. Negative effects of the proposed activity on employees' morale. The better work ethic mentioned above is not guaranteed. (*adv: disadv*) ★★★★★

8. Other factors that determine Climpson's profits. Adopting the proposal may not sufficiently ensure greater profits. (*sufficiency of the solution*) ★★★

论证要点

本题论证内容主要集中在两方面：安装上述系统带来的成本、员工情绪的负面影响；以及副总裁提出的方案的充分性和必要性。首先，Climpson的员工效率未必有进一步提高的空间；其次，副总裁也没有提供信息证明员工已经有人因私上网浪费时间并且影响了工作效率这一大前提；再次，就算安装了上述监控系统，也未必能保证员工不通过其他方式浪费时间，也就未必能保证Climpson公司利润上升。

---

61. The vice president of human resources at Climpson Industries sent the following recommendation
⟨94⟩ to the company's president.

"A recent national survey(1) found that the majority of workers with access to the Internet at work had used company computers for personal or recreational activities, such as banking or playing games. In an effort to improve our employees' productivity （2,3）, **we should implement electronic monitoring of employees' Internet use from their workstations.** *Using electronic monitoring software is the best way (4) to reduce the number of hours Climpson employees spend on personal or recreational activities(5). We predict that installing software(6) to monitor employees' Internet use (7) will allow us to prevent employees from wasting time, thereby increasing productivity(8) and improving overall profits(9)."* （former 127, ≈34, 58）★★★

翻　译 最近的一项全国调查发现，大多数工作时能上网的员工都会将公司电脑用于私人或娱乐用途，比如理财和玩游戏。为努力提高我们员工的生产效率，我们应该在员工的终端上加装电子监控（系统)来监视员工的互联网使用情况。使用电子监控软件是减少Climpson员工私人及娱乐行为时间的最好办法。我们预计，在公司电脑上安装软件监测员工对互联网的使用可以帮助我们防止员工浪费时间，从而提高生产率和整体利润。

推理结构

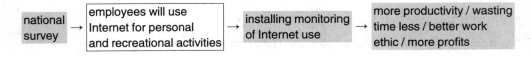

national survey → employees will use Internet for personal and recreational activities → installing monitoring of Internet use → more productivity / wasting time less / better work ethic / more profits

提　纲

1. Could the result of the national survey be applied to C's workers? (*C.S.*) ★★★

2. How about current performance and productivity of the employees? The assumption that their productivity should be and could be improved is open to doubt. (*I.I./U.A./necessity of the solution*) ★★

3. Is the premise that at least some of the employees have already used Internet for personal or recreational activities justified? (*U.A./I.I./necessity of the solution*) ★★★

4. Are there any other solutions that could reduce the number of hours spent on personal or recreational activities, if any? (*necessity of the solution*) ★★★★

5. Do employees have other means to spend time on personal or recreational activities even if the Internet access is banned? (*sufficiency of the solution*) ★★★★★

6. Are there any negative effects of installing such software on the computers? How much is the cost of installing the software? (*adv:disadv*) ★★★

7. Are there any employees who must use Internet in their daily works? (*adv:disadv*) ★★★★

8. Are there any negative effects of the proposed action on employees' morale? The better work ethic mentioned above is not guaranteed. (*adv:disadv*) ★★★★★

9. Will adopting the proposal sufficiently ensure greater profits? (*sufficiency of the solution*) ★★★

论证要点

本题论证内容主要集中在两方面：安装上述系统带来的成本、员工情绪的负面影响；以及副总裁提出的方案的充分性和必要性。首先，Climpson的员工效率未必有进一步提高的空间；其次，仅有一条全国调查也不能说明员工已经有人因私上网浪费时间并且影响了工作效率这一大前提；再次，就算安装了他所说的监控系统也未必能保证员工不通过其他方式浪费时间，也就未必能保证Climpson公司利润上升。

---

62. The following appeared in a letter from the owner of the Sunnyside Towers apartment complex `35` to its manager.

"One month ago, all the showerheads in the first three buildings of the Sunnyside Towers complex were modified to restrict maximum water flow to one-third of what it used to be. Although actual readings of water usage before and after the adjustment are not yet available（3）, *the change will obviously result in a considerable savings for Sunnyside Corporation*, since the corporation must pay for water each month. Except for a few complaints about low water pressure（4,5）, no problems with showers（2）have been reported since the adjustment（1）. **I predict that modifying showerheads to restrict water flow throughout all twelve buildings(7) in the Sunnyside Towers(6) complex will increase our profits even more dramatically(8).**" （former 185）★★

翻　译 1个月前，Sunnyside综合楼的头3栋楼所有淋浴喷头的最大水流被调节成只有以前的三分之一。尽管调节前后用水量的确切读数还没有出来，但这种变革显然将为Sunnyside公司节省大量的花费，因为公司必须每月为所用的水付费。除了关于低水压的几起投诉外，在调节之后没有发生关于淋浴问题的报告。我预计，Sunnyside综合楼的所有12栋楼都限制水流将会显著增加我们的利润。

no big problem with shower reported after the adjustment ┐
                                                          ├→ we should restrict water flow in all complex → more profits
we must pay for water ┘

写作要求 *What **questions** should be answered to decide whether the prediction and the argument are reasonable?*

提　纲

1. Is one month a time period long enough for negative effects to emerge? (*reliability of the survey*) ★★★★

2. What is the usage of the first three buildings of the complex? Perhaps water flow will not be a problem here no matter how we restrict the flow. (*I.I./selective sample*) ★★★

3. What are the actual readings of water usage before and after the adjustment? We cannot evaluate whether the modification could actually save water without such information. (*I.I.*) ★★★

4. Does the fact that a few people complained about water pressure necessarily indicate that all other clients are satisfied with the modification? (*F.D.*) ★★★

5. What's the detail about these complaints? They might be significant although there are only a few. (*I.I.*) ★★★

6. Are there any negative effects of restricting the water flow? (*adv:disadv*) ★★★★

7. Could the restriction on water flow be successfully carried out to all other buildings in the complex? (*C.S.*) ★★★★★

8. Does adopting the owner's suggestion alone suffice to ensure increased profits? (*sufficiency of the solution*) ★★★

论证要点

本题论证点主要是3方面：首先，由于不知道前3栋楼的用途、投诉的具体内容、代表性和严重性，因此，根据作者提供的信息未必说明水流调节没有带来问题。其次，就算在前3栋楼没有问题，未必在其他楼座也没有问题。再次，限制水流也未必就能显著节省花费从而使利润增加。

---

63. The following appeared in a letter from the owner of the Sunnyside Towers apartment building **52** to its manager.

"One month ago, all the showerheads on the first five floors of Sunnyside Towers were modified to restrict the water flow to approximately one-third of its original flow. Although actual readings of water usage before and after the adjustment are not yet available(3), *the change will obviously result in a considerable savings for Sunnyside Corporation*, since the corporation must pay for water each month. Except for a few complaints about low water pressure(4,5), no problems with showers(2) have been reported since the adjustment(1). **Clearly, restricting water flow throughout all the twenty floors(7) of Sunnyside Towers(6) will increase our profits further (8).**" (former 185, ≈35) ★★

翻　译 1个月前，Sunnyside综合楼最低5层的所有淋浴喷头的水流被调节成只有以前的大约三分之一。尽管调节前后用水量的确切读数还没有出来，但这种变革显然将为Sunnyside公司节省大量的花费，因为公司必须每月为所用的水付费。除了关于低水压的几起投诉外，在调节之后没有发生关于淋浴问题的报告。显然，Sunnyside综合楼所有的20层都限制水压将会进一步增加我们的利润。

no big problem with shower reported after the adjustment
we must pay for water → we should restrict water flow in all floors → more profits

写作要求 *What **questions** should be answered to decide whether the recommendation will have the predicted result?*

提　　纲

1. Is one month a time period long enough for negative effects to emerge? (*reliability of the survey*) ★★★

2. What is the usage of the first five floors of the building? Perhaps water flow will not be a problem here no matter how we restrict the flow. (*I.I./selective sample*) ★★★

3. What are the actual readings of water usage before and after the adjustment? We cannot evaluate if the modification could indeed save water without such information. (*I.I.*) ★★★

4. Does the fact that a few people complained about water pressure necessarily indicate that all other clients are satisfied with the modification. (*F.D.*) ★★★

5. What's the detail about these complaints? They might be significant although there are only a few. (*I.I.*) ★★★

6. Are there any negative effects of restricting the water flow? (*adv:disadv*) ★★★★
   1~6: 调节水流的行为未必没有问题。

7. Could the restriction on water flow be successfully carried out to all other floors in the building? (*C.S.*)
   如果其他楼层的用途、客户群显著不同，那么在其他楼层推广这种行为未必也没有问题。★★★★★

8. Does adopting the owner's suggestion alone suffice to ensure increased profits? (*sufficiency of the solution*) ★★★

论证要点

　　本题论证点主要是3方面：首先，由于不知道这5层楼的用途、投诉的具体内容、代表性和严重性，因此，根据作者提供的信息未必说明水流调节没有带来问题。其次，就算在这5层楼没有问题，未必在其他楼层限制水压也没有问题。再次，限制水流也未必就能显著节省花费从而使利润增加。

---

64. The following appeared in a letter from the owner of the Sunnyside Towers apartment complex
128 to its manager.

"One month ago, all the showerheads in the first three buildings of the Sunnyside Towers complex were modified to restrict maximum water flow to one-third of what it used to be. Although actual readings of water usage before and after the adjustment are not yet available (3), *the change will obviously result in a considerable savings for Sunnyside Corporation*, since the corporation must pay for water each month. Except for a few complaints about low water pressure (4,5), no problems with showers (2) have been reported since the adjustment (1). **Clearly, modifying showerheads to restrict water flow throughout all twelve buildings(7) in the Sunnyside Towers complex(6) will increase our profits further(8)."** (former 185, ≈ 52, =35) ★★

翻　　译　1个月前，Sunnyside综合楼头3栋楼的所有淋浴喷头的最大水流被调节成只有以前的三分之一。尽管调节前后用水量的确切读数还没有出来，但这种变革显然将为Sunnyside公司节省大量的花费，因为公司必须每月为所用的水付费。除了关于低水压的几起投诉外，在调节之后没有发生关于淋浴问题的报告。显然，Sunnyside综合楼所有12栋楼的喷头都限制水流将会进一步增加我们的利润。

no big problem with shower reported after the adjustment ┐
we must pay for water ┘ → we should restrict water flow in all complex → more profits

写作要求 *What specific **evidence** is needed to evaluate the argument?*

提 纲

作者需要提供能说明以下问题的信息或论据：

1. One month is a time period long enough for negative effects to emerge. (*reliability of the survey*) ★★★★

2. Detailed information about the usage of the first three buildings of the complex, perhaps water flow will not be a problem here no matter how we restrict it. (*I.I./selective sample*) ★★★

3. Actual readings of water usage before and after the adjustment. We cannot evaluate whether the modification could actually save water. (*I.I.*) ★★★

4. All other clients are satisfied with the modification. (*F.D.*) ★★★

5. The detail about these complaints. They might be significant although there are only a few. (*I.I.*) ★★★

6. Negative effects of restricting the water flow. (*adv:disadv*) ★★★★

7. The restriction on water flow could be successfully carried out to all other buildings in the complex. (*C.S.*) ★★★★★

8. Adopting the owner's suggestion alone suffices to ensure increased profits. (*sufficiency of the solution*) ★★★

论证要点

本题论证点主要是3方面：首先，由于不知道前3栋楼的用途、投诉的具体内容、代表性和严重性，因此，根据作者提供的信息未必说明水流调节没有带来问题。其次，就算在前3栋楼没有问题，未必在其他楼座也没有问题。再次，限制水流也未必就能显著节省花费从而使利润增加。作者需要提供实质论据说明以上方面。

---

65. The following appeared in a letter from the owner of the Sunnyside Towers apartment complex
129 to its manager.

"Last week, all the showerheads in the first three buildings of the Sunnyside Towers complex were modified to restrict maximum water flow to one-third of what it used to be. Although actual readings of water usage before and after the adjustment are not yet available(3), *the change will obviously result in a considerable savings for Sunnyside Corporation*, since the corporation must pay for water each month. Except for a few complaints about low water pressure(4,5), no problems with showers(2) have been reported since the adjustment(1). **Clearly, modifying showerheads to restrict water flow throughout all twelve buildings(7) in the Sunnyside Towers complex(6) will increase our profits further(8).**" (former 185, ≈52, =35, 128) ★★

翻 译 上周，Sunnyside综合楼头3栋楼的所有淋浴喷头的最大水流被调节成只有以前的三分之一。尽管调节前后用水量的确切读数还没有出来，但这种变革显然将为Sunnyside公司节省大量的花费，因为公司必须每月为所用的水付费。除了关于低水压的几起投诉外，在调节之后没有发生关于淋浴问题的报告。显然，Sunnyside综合楼所有12栋楼的喷头都限制水流将会进一步增加我们的利润。

no big problem with shower reported after the adjustment ┐
we must pay for water ┘ → we should restrict water flow in all complex → more profits

写作要求 *assumptions*

提　　纲

1. The owner assumes that one week is a time period long enough for negative effects to emerge. (*reliability of the survey*) ★★★★

2. We do not have any information about the usage of the first three buildings of the complex. Perhaps water flow will not be a problem here no matter how we restrict it. (*I.I./selective sample*) ★★★

3. Without actual readings of water usage before and after the adjustment, we cannot evaluate if the modification could actually save water. (*I.I.*) ★★★

4. The fact that a few people complained about water pressure does not necessarily indicate that all other clients are satisfied with the modification. (*F.D.*) ★★★

5. The owner unfairly implies that these complaints are insignificant without providing the detail about them. They might be significant although there are only a few. (*I.I.*) ★★★

6. The owner ignores the negative effects of restricting the water flow. (*adv:disadv*) ★★★★

7. The owner assumes without justification that the restriction on water flow could be successfully carried out to all other buildings in the complex. (*C.S.*) ★★★★★

8. The owner assumes that adopting the suggestion alone suffices to ensure increased profits. (*sufficiency of the solution*) ★★★

论证要点

　　本题论证点主要是3方面：首先，在不知道前3栋楼的用途、投诉的具体内容、代表性和严重性的情况下，作者就认为水流调节不会带来问题。其次，就算在前3栋楼没有问题，未必在其他楼座也没有问题。再次，限制水流能显著节省花费从而使利润增加的假设也值得怀疑。

---

66. The following report appeared in the newsletter of the West Meria Public Health Council.

36 "An innovative treatment has come to our attention that promises to significantly reduce absenteeism in our schools and workplaces. A study reports that in nearby East Meria(3), where fish consumption is very high, people visit the doctor only once or twice per year for the treatment of colds(1). *Clearly, eating a substantial amount of fish can prevent colds(2).* Since colds represent the most frequently given reason(6) for absences from school and work, **we recommend the daily use of Ichthaid(4,5)—a nutritional supplement derived from fish oil—as a good way to prevent colds and lower absenteeism.**" (former 38) ★★★

翻　　译 我们注意到一种确保可以显著减少学校和工作场所缺勤的创新方法。一项研究报告说，在附近鱼消费量很高的East Meria，人们每年因为治感冒而去看医生的次数只有一或两次。显然，吃大量的鱼可以预防感冒。由于感冒是学校和工作缺勤的最常见原因，因此，我们建议每天服用一种从鱼油中提取的营养物质Ichthaid作为预防感冒和减少缺勤的有效措施。

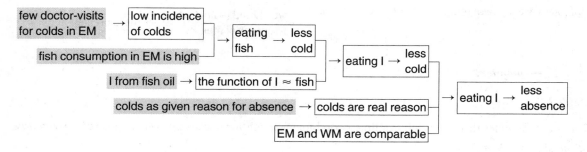

What specific evidence is needed to evaluate the argument?

提 纲

1. The number of doctor-visit for the treatment of colds is not a good indication of incidence of colds. (*U.C.*)
   作者应该提供关于EM感冒发病率更直接有效的信息。★★★★
   作者还需要提供论据说明以下几点：

2. The causal relationship between high level of fish consumption and the low incidence of cold in East Meria. (*confusing concurrence with causality*) ★★★★★

3. The comparability of East and West Meria. (*F.A.*) ★★★

4. Ichthaid has the same function in preventing colds as fish. (*F.A.*) ★★★★

5. The cost, and any possible side effects of Ichthaid. (*adv:disadv*) ★★★★

6. How many absences from school and work were actually caused by colds. (*I.I.*) ★★

论证要点

本题首先需要论证的就是吃鱼预防感冒这一因果关系，上述1、2两点围绕因果关系展开；其次，Ichthaid未必和鱼有相同功能；而且，由于不知道EM和WM的可比性，以及WM缺勤的真正原因，那么，服用Ichthaid未必能在WM有效减少缺勤。

---

67. The following memo appeared in the newsletter of the West Meria Public Health Council.

163 "An innovative treatment has come to our attention that promises to significantly reduce absenteeism in our schools and workplaces. A study reports that in nearby East Meria（3），where consumption of the plant beneficia is very high, people visit the doctor only once or twice per year for the treatment of colds（1）. *Clearly, eating a substantial amount of beneficia can prevent colds(2)*. Since colds are the reason most frequently given（6）for absences from school and work, **we recommend the daily use of nutritional supplements derived from beneficia(4,5). We predict this will dramatically reduce absenteeism in our schools and workplaces.**"（former 38, ≈36）★★★

翻 译 我们注意到一种确保可以显著减少学校和工作场所缺勤的创新方法。一项研究报告说，在附近beneficia消费量很高的East Meria，人们每年因为治感冒而去看医生的次数只有一或两次。显然，吃大量的beneficia可以预防感冒。由于感冒被认为是学校和工作缺勤的最常见原因，因此，我们建议每天服用从beneficia中提取的营养物质。我们预计这将显著减少学校和工作场所的缺勤。

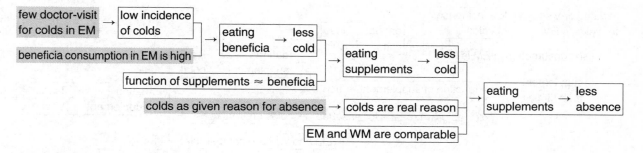

*What **questions** should be answered to decide whether the recommendation will have the predicted result?*

提　纲

1. Is the number of doctor-visit for the treatment of colds a good indication of incidence of colds? (*U.C.*) ★★★★

2. Is there any causal relationship between high level of beneficia consumption and the low incidence of cold in East Meria? (*confusing concurrence with causality*) ★★★★★

3. Are East and West Meria comparable? (*F.A.*) ★★★

4. Will the supplements have the same function in preventing colds as beneficia? (*F.A.*) ★★★★

5. How about the cost of the supplements? Are there any side effects of the supplements? (*adv:disadv*) ★★★★

6. How many absences from school and work were actually caused by colds? (*I.I.*) ★★★

论证要点

　　本题首先需要论证的就是吃beneficia预防感冒这一因果关系，上述1、2两点围绕因果关系展开；其次，该营养物质未必和beneficia有相同功能；而且，由于不知道EM和WM的可比性，以及WM缺勤的真正原因，那么，服用该营养物质未必能在WM有效减少缺勤。

---

68. The following memo appeared in the newsletter of the West Meria Public Health Council.

166 "An innovative treatment has come to our attention that promises to significantly reduce absenteeism in our schools and workplaces. A study reports that in nearby East Meria(3), where fish consumption is very high, people visit the doctor only once or twice per year for the treatment of colds(1). *This shows that eating a substantial amount of fish can clearly prevent colds(2).* Furthermore, since colds are the reason most frequently given(6) for absences from school and work, *attendance levels will improve.* **Therefore, we recommend the daily use of a nutritional supplement derived from fish oil(4,5) as a good way to prevent colds and lower absenteeism.**" (former 38, ≈163, =36) ★★★

翻　译　我们注意到一种确保可以显著减少学校和工作场所缺勤的创新方法。一项研究报告说，在附近鱼消费量很高的East Meria，人们每年因为治感冒而去看医生的次数只有一或两次。这显然表明吃大量的鱼可以预防感冒。而且，由于感冒被认为是学校和工作缺勤的最常见原因，（这样做的话）出勤率将会提高。因此，我们建议每天服用一种从鱼油中提取的营养物质作为预防感冒和减少缺勤的有效措施。

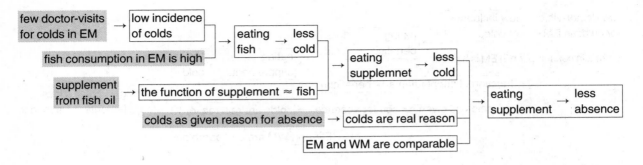

*What **questions** should be answered to decide whether the recommendation and the argument are reasonable?*

1. Is the number of doctor-visit for the treatment of colds a good indication of incidence of colds? (*U.C.*) ★★★★

2. Is there any causal relationship between high level of fish consumption and the low incidence of cold in East Meria? (*confusing concurrence with causality*) ★★★★★

3. Are East and West Meria comparable? (*F.A.*) ★★★

4. Does the supplement have the same function in preventing colds as fish? (*F.A.*) ★★★★

5. How much is the cost of the supplement? Is there any side effect of it? (*adv:disadv*) ★★★★

6. How many absences from school and work were actually caused by colds? (*I.I.*) ★★

本题首先需要论证的就是吃鱼预防感冒这一因果关系,上述1、2两点就是要求作者回答的问题: EM地区感冒发病率是否确实很低;有没有其他可能原因导致EM感冒少;其次,文中提到的营养物质未必和鱼有相同功能;而且,由于不知道EM和WM的可比性,以及WM缺勤的真正原因,那么,服用该营养物质未必能在WM有效减少缺勤。

---

69. The following appeared in a recommendation from the planning department of the city of
37 Transopolis.

"Ten years ago(3), as part of a comprehensive urban renewal program, the city of Transopolis adapted for industrial use a large area of severely substandard housing near the freeway. Subsequently, several factories were constructed there, crime rates in the area declined, and property tax revenues for the entire city(2) increased(1). To further revitalize the city(7), **we should now take similar action in a declining residential area on the opposite side of the city(4,5,6,8,9)**. Since some houses and apartments in existing nearby neighborhoods are currently unoccupied, *alternate housing for those displaced by this action will be readily available(10)*." (former 230) ★★

翻 译 10年前,作为综合城市改造项目的一部分,Transopolis市在快速路旁改造了一大片严重低于标准的住房用于工业用途。随后,那里建立了若干工厂,犯罪率降低了,全市资产税收入增加。为进一步使城市重新繁荣,我们应该在城市另一侧正在衰落的居住区采取类似的行动。由于现有邻近社区的一些住宅和公寓无人居住,那么,这一行动产生的搬迁户的住所将有所保障。

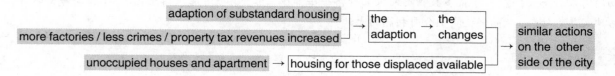

*What specific **evidence** is needed to evaluate the argument?*

提　纲

作者需要提供能说明以下方面的信息或论据：

1. The prosperity of the area indeed results from the industrial adaptation. (*post hoc, ergo propter hoc*)
   ★★★★★

2. The detailed distribution of the tax revenue: increase in overall property-tax revenue does not necessarily indicate an increase in tax revenue from properties in the freeway area. (*C.S.*) ★★★

3. Factors that would influence the effectiveness of the action would not have changed during the past decade. (*P→C*) ★★★★

4. The residential area on the opposite side of the city is suitable for industrial use. (*feasibility of the conclusion*) ★★★★

5. The comparability of the two areas. Taking similar action on the opposite side of the city may not generate the same good effects. (*F.A.*) ★★★★

6. The necessity of adapting more area for industrial use. (*necessity of the solution*) ★★

7. Taking the same action in the area could sufficiently revitalize the city. (*sufficiency of the solution*) ★★★

8. Other possible solutions that could be used to revitalize the city. (*necessity of the solution*) ★★★

9. The cost of the proposed action, and whether the city could afford it. (*adv:disadv*) ★★★

10. The willingness of residents in the area to be allocated to those houses and apartments. (*feasibility of the conclusion*) ★★★

论证要点

　　本题主要问题有两方面：一、快速路旁区域的改造是否是使该地区繁荣的直接原因（1、2）；二、在城市另一侧实施相同改造是否具有可行性与必要性，以及改造对于区域复兴的充分性（3~10）。

---

70. The following appeared in a memo from the new vice president of Sartorian, a company that
[38] manufactures men's clothing.

"Five years ago, at a time when we had difficulties in obtaining reliable supplies of high quality wool fabric, we discontinued production of our alpaca overcoat. Now that we have a new fabric supplier(1), **we should resume production(6).** *This coat should sell very well:* since we have not offered an alpaca overcoat for five years and since our major competitor no longer makes an alpaca overcoat(2), *there will be pent-up customer demand.* Also, since the price of most types of clothing has increased in each of the past five years(3,4), *customers should be willing to pay significantly higher prices for alpaca overcoats than they did five years ago(5), and our company profits will increase.*" (former 21) ★★★

翻　译 5年前，当我们在获取高质量羊毛毛料的可靠渠道方面存在困难的时候，我们停止了高档羊毛外套的生产。现在有了新的毛料供应商，我们应该重新开始生产。这种外套应该卖得很好：因为我们已

经5年没有供应羊毛外套了,而且由于我们的主要竞争对手已不再生产羊毛外套,因此,消费者将有很迫切的需求。而且,过去5年中多数种类的服装价格每年都在上涨,消费者应该愿意花比5年前高得多的价格购买羊毛外套,从而促使我们公司利润的上升。

推理结构

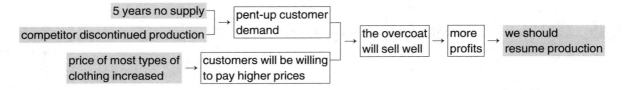

写作要求 *What specific **evidence** is needed to evaluate the argument?*

提　纲

作者需要提供论据来说明:

1. The quality of the fabric they supply, and that the new fabric supplier will be a reliable supplier of wool fabric.（U.A./I.I.）★★★★

对于上文论述还存在以下可能性:

2. The fact that competitor stopped making alpaca coats may just indicate diminishing consumer demand for them.（negative evidence）★★★

作者还需要提供关于以下方面的信息:

3. The changes of other factors that would determine the company's profits during the past five years.（P→F）★★★

4. The phrase "most types" is too vague. We need the information about prices and market for clothes similar to those alpaca overcoats.（V.D./ I.I.）★★★

5. The assumption that consumers will be willing to pay significant higher prices for alpaca overcoats is unwarranted.（U.A.）★★★

6. The possible cost of resuming production.（adv:disadv）★★★★

论证要点

本题主要问题在于文中的论据基本全都是作者想当然的一些假设,因此作者需要提供充分证据证明:一、恢复生产是可行的(1、6);二、该服装确实会有市场并可以带来利润(2、3、4、5)。

---

71. The following appeared in a memo from the new vice president of Sartorian, a company that
⑨⑤ manufactures men's clothing.

"Five years ago, at a time when we had difficulty obtaining reliable supplies of high-quality wool fabric, we discontinued production of our popular alpaca overcoat. Now that we have a new fabric supplier(1), **we should resume production(6)**. Given the outcry from our customers when we discontinued this product(2) and the fact that none of our competitors offers a comparable product(3), *we can expect pent-up consumer demand for our alpaca coats*. This demand and the overall increase in clothing prices(4,5) will make *Sartorian's alpaca overcoats more profitable than ever before(7)*."（former 21, ≈38）★★★

5年前，当我们在获取高质量羊毛毛料的可靠渠道方面存在困难的时候，我们停止了当时很受欢迎的羊毛外套的生产。现在有了新的毛料供应商，我们应该重新开始生产。鉴于我们停产该外套时顾客的呼声以及我们的主要竞争对手都已不再生产类似产品的事实，我们可以预期消费者对于羊毛外套的迫切消费需求。这种需求和服装价格的总体上涨将会使Sartorian羊毛外套比以往任何时候都赚钱。

推理结构

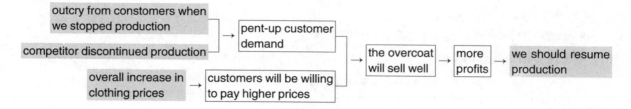

写作要求 *assumptions*

提　纲

1. The vice president fails to substantiate the assumption that the new fabric supplier will be a reliable supplier of wool fabric, and fails to provide any information about the quality of the fabric they supply. (*U.A./I.I.*) ★★★★

2. The vice president assumes that customers will also favor the overcoat today as they did five years ago. (*P→C*) ★★★★

3. The fact that competitors stopped making alpaca coats may just indicate diminishing consumer demand for them. (*negative evidence*) ★★★

4. The vice president fails to consider the changes of other factors during the past five years. (*P→F*) ★★★

5. The phrase "overall increase" is too vague. We need the information about prices and market for clothes similar to those alpaca overcoats. (*V.D./I.I.*) ★★★

6. The vice president fails to consider the possible cost of resuming production. (*adv:disadv*) ★★★★

7. The vice president's claim that the company's overall profits would increase is unwarranted. (*U.A.*) ★★★

论证要点

　　本题主要问题在于文中的论据基本全都是作者的假设：一、恢复生产是可行的(1、6)；二、该服装确实会有市场并带来利润(2、3、4、5、7)。

---

72. The following appeared in a memo from the new vice president of Sartorian, a company that
[96] manufactures men's clothing.

"Five years ago, at a time when we had difficulty obtaining reliable supplies of high-quality wool fabric, we discontinued production of our popular alpaca overcoat. Now that we have a new fabric supplier(1), **we should resume production(6).** Given the outcry from our customers when we discontinued this product(2) and the fact that none of our competitors offers a comparable product(3), *we can expect pent-up consumer demand for our alpaca coats.* Due to this demand and the overall increase in clothing prices(4,5), **we can predict that Sartorian's alpaca overcoats will be more profitable than ever before(7).**" (former 21, ≈ 38, =95) ★★★

翻　译 5年前，当我们在获取高质量羊毛毛料的可靠渠道方面存在困难的时候，我们停止了当时很受欢迎的羊毛外套的生产。现在有了新的毛料供应商，我们应该重新开始生产。鉴于我们停产该外套时顾客的呼声以及我们的主要竞争对手都已不再生产类似产品的事实，我们可以预期消费者对于羊毛外套的迫切消费需求。这种需求和服装价格的总体上涨将会使Sartorian羊毛外套比以往任何时候都赚钱。

推理结构

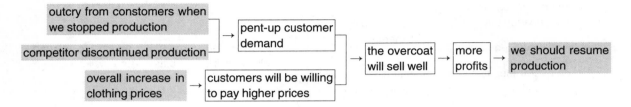

写作要求 What **questions** should be answered to decide whether the prediction and the argument are reasonable?

提　纲

1. Will the new fabric supplier be a reliable supplier of wool fabric? How about the quality of the fabric they supply? (*U.A./I.I.*) ★★★★
2. Will customers still favor the overcoat today as they did five years ago? (*P→C*) ★★★★
3. May the fact that competitors stopped making alpaca coats just indicate diminishing consumer demand for the coats? (*negative evidence*) ★★★
4. Are there any changes of other factors during the past five years? (*P→F*) ★★★
5. The phrase "overall increase" is too vague. How about prices and market for clothes similar to those alpaca overcoats? (*V.D./I.I.*) ★★★
6. How about the cost of resuming production? (*adv:disadv*) ★★★★
7. Is the vice president's claim that the company's overall profits would increase justified? (*U.A.*) ★★★

论证要点

　　本题主要问题在于文中的论据基本全都是作者的假设，因此我们需要作者回答：一、恢复生产是否可行（1、6）？ 二、该服装是否确实会有市场并带来利润（2、3、4、5、7）？

---

73. A recent sales study indicates that consumption of seafood dishes in Bay City restaurants has
39 increased by 30 percent during the past five years（1,2,3）. Yet there are no currently operating city restaurants whose specialty is seafood. Moreover, the majority of families in Bay City are two-income families, and a nationwide study（4）has shown that such families eat significantly fewer home-cooked meals than they did a decade ago but at the same time express more concern about healthful eating（5,6,7,8）. **Therefore, the new Captain Seafood restaurant that specializes in seafood should be quite popular and profitable (9).** (former 23) ★★

翻　译 最近的销量调查显示Bay City餐馆的海鲜菜肴消费在过去5年增加了30%。而现在该市还没有专门经营海鲜菜的餐厅。而且，Bay City的大多数家庭是双收入家庭，一次全国性调查显示这类家庭在家做饭的次数比10年前显著减少，同时他们更关注饮食健康。因此，新开张的专营海鲜菜的Captain Seafood餐馆将会非常受欢迎而且有利可图。

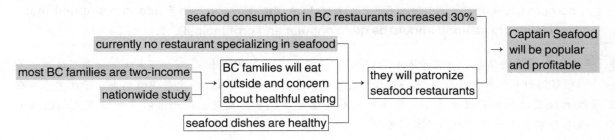

*What specific **evidence** is needed to evaluate the argument?*

提　纲

作者需要提供能说明以下方面的信息或论据：

1. The base amount of seafood consumption in Bay City five years ago. The 30% increase might be insignificant. (*V.D.*) ★★

2. Seafood consumption will continue to increase in the future. (*P→F*) ★★★
   对于上文信息，还存在以下可能情况：

3. The increase in the consumption of seafood dishes in normal restaurants does not indicate that a restaurant specializing in seafood will be profitable. (*I.E./C.S.*) ★★
   作者还需要提供论据说明以下几点：

4. The nationwide study showing trends among two-income families could reflect the situation of Bay City. (*C.S.*) ★★★

5. Detailed data concerning the number of home-cooked meals these two-income families eat currently and formerly, and the actual level of their concern about eating healthily. We cannot evaluate whether these families are a key factor in determining the profitability of a restaurant specializing in seafood without such information. Other families may eat even fewer home-cooked meals and are concerned more about eating healthily. (*confusing comparison and variation / lack of comparison*) ★★★★
   对于上文论述内容还存在以下问题：

6. The author assumes without any warrant that seafood dishes will be considered healthy. (*U.A.*) ★★★

7. The fact that two-income families express more concern about eating healthily does not indicate that they will necessarily patronize a new seafood restaurant. (*U.C.*) ★★★★

8. The fact that two-income families eat fewer home-cooked meals may lead to the popularity of catering services, delivered meals, but not necessarily that of a sit-down restaurant. (*U.A.*) ★★★
   此外，作者还需要以下方面信息：

9. The expense of establishing such a restaurant. (*adv:disadv*) ★★★

论证要点

本题主要论证环节集中在两方面：首先，海鲜菜未必持续受欢迎（1~3）；其次，全国调查结果未必能有效反映该地区情况，而且该结果也未必说明专营海鲜的餐厅将会受欢迎（4~8）。

---

74. A recent sales study indicates that consumption of seafood dishes in Bay City restaurants has
174 increased by 30 percent during the past five years（1,2,3）. Yet there are no currently operating city restaurants whose specialty is seafood. Moreover, the majority of families in Bay City are two-income families, and a nationwide study（4）has shown that such families eat significantly

fewer home-cooked meals than they did a decade ago but at the same time express more concern about healthful eating(5,6,7). **Therefore, the new Captain Seafood restaurant that specializes in seafood should be quite popular and profitable(8).** (former 23, =39) ★★

翻 译 最近的销量调查显示Bay City餐馆的海鲜菜肴消费在过去5年增加了30%。而现在该市还没有专门经营海鲜菜的餐厅。而且，Bay City的大多数家庭是双收入家庭，一次全国性调查显示这类家庭在家做饭的次数比10年前显著减少，同时他们更关注健康饮食。因此，新开张的专营海鲜菜的Captain Seafood餐馆将会非常受欢迎而且有利可图。

推理结构

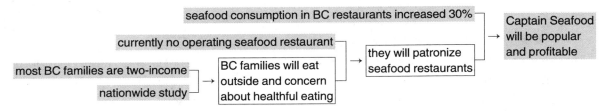

写作要求 *What **questions** should be addressed to decide whether the conclusion and the argument are reasonable?*

提 纲

1. What is the base amount of seafood consumption in Bay City? The 30% increase might be insignificant. (*V.D.*) ★★

2. Will seafood consumption in Bay City continue to increase in the future? (*P→F*) ★★★

3. Does the increase in the consumption of seafood dishes in normal restaurants indicate that a restaurant specializing in seafood will be profitable? (*I.E./C.S.*) ★★

4. Could the result of the nationwide study showing trends among two-income families also reflect the situation of Bay City? (*C.S.*) ★★★

5. Does the fact that two-income families express more concern about eating healthily indicate that they will necessarily patronize a new seafood restaurant? (*U.C.*) ★★★★

6. What is the number of home-cooked meals these two-income families eat currently and formerly? What is the actual level of their concern about eating healthily? We cannot evaluate whether these families are a key factor in determining the profitability of a restaurant specializing in seafood without such information. Other families may eat even fewer home-cooked meals and are concerned more about eating healthily. (*confusing comparison and variation / lack of comparison*) ★★★★

7. Will the fact that two-income families eat fewer home-cooked meals necessarily lead to the popularity of a sit-down restaurant? (*U.A.*) ★★★

8. How much is the expense of establishing such a restaurant? (*adv:disadv*) ★★★

论证要点

本题主要论证环节集中在两方面：首先，海鲜菜未必持续受欢迎(1~3)；其次，全国调查结果未必能有效反映该地区情况，而且该结果也未必说明专营海鲜的餐厅将会受欢迎(4~8)。

75. Milk and dairy products are rich in vitamin D and calcium—substances essential for building
40 and maintaining bones. Many people therefore say that a diet rich in dairy products can help
prevent osteoporosis, a disease that is linked to both environmental and genetic factors and
that causes the bones to weaken significantly with age. But a long-term study of a large number
of people found that those who consistently consumed dairy products throughout the years of
the study have a higher rate of bone fractures than any other participants in the study(1, 2).
Since bone fractures are symptomatic of osteoporosis(3), this study result shows that a
diet rich in dairy products may actually increase, rather than decrease, the risk of
osteoporosis. (former 34) ★ ★ ★

翻　译 牛奶和奶制品富含维生素D和钙，这是骨骼生长和维持所需的物质。因此很多人相信多吃
奶制品有助于预防骨质疏松症，这是一种与环境和基因因素相关且导致骨骼随年龄增长而显著弱化的疾
病。但是一项对大量人群的长期研究发现，那些在研究期间经常食用奶制品的人骨折发病率比其他参加
研究的人要高。由于骨折是骨质疏松症的症状之一，因此，这一研究结果表明富含奶制品的饮食实际上
会增加而不是减少患骨质疏松症的危险。

推理结构

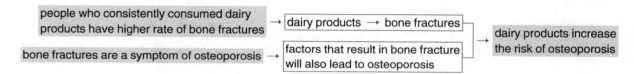

写作要求 *What specific **evidence** is needed to evaluate the argument?*

提　纲

作者应该提供：

1. Detailed information about the studied people who consistently consume dairy products and those who do
not. Other reasons, such as aging, genetic factors, lifestyle, etc. may also account for the higher rate of bone
fractures of the people mentioned in the study. (*Are the respondents representative?/I.C.*) ★ ★ ★ ★
对于上文讨论的问题存在以下可能性：

2. People who consistently consume dairy products in the study may do so just because they are more likely to
suffer from bone fractures. (*confusing the cause and the effect*)
作者需要提供证据排除这种可能性。 ★ ★ ★ ★ ★

3. Granted that a diet rich in dairy products increases the risk of bone fracture, osteoporosis may well result
from other causes. (*U.C.*)
即，按文中描述，骨折只是骨质疏松的一种症状，也就是两者之间存在关联性。就算奶制品确实导致
骨折，未必也导致与之相关联的骨质疏松。作者应该提供证据证明奶制品和骨质疏松之间的切实联
系。★ ★ ★ ★ ★

论证要点

　　本题最核心的环节在于食用奶制品造成骨折的因果关系是否成立。首先，导致骨折可能有其他因
素；其次，有可能这些人正因为容易骨折且为了预防才多吃奶制品。此外，该调查的范围、样本人群的代
表性、全面性和可靠性可以作为辅助论证。

76. The following appeared in a health newsletter.

41 "A ten-year nationwide study of the effectiveness of wearing a helmet while bicycling indicates that ten years ago, approximately 35 percent of all bicyclists reported wearing helmets, whereas today that number is nearly 80 percent. Another study, however, suggests that during the same ten-year period, the number of bicycle-related accidents(1,3) has increased 200 percent(2). *These results demonstrate that bicyclists feel safer because they are wearing helmets(4), and they take more risks as a result(5).* Thus, to reduce the number of serious injuries from bicycle accidents(7), **the government should concentrate more on educating people about bicycle safety(6) and less on encouraging or requiring bicyclists to wear helmets(8).**" (former 120) ★★

翻　译 一项为期10年的对于骑自行车时戴头盔的作用的全国性研究显示，10年前，所有骑车人中约有35%报告说他们戴头盔，而现在这个比例接近80%。然而，另外一项调查显示，在相同的10年期间，与自行车相关的事故数量增加了200%。这些结果说明骑车人因为戴着头盔而感到更安全，结果导致他们更加冒险。因此，为减少自行车事故中严重伤害的数量，政府应该更多地致力于对大众的自行车安全教育，并减少鼓励或要求骑车人戴头盔。

推理结构

写作要求 *assumptions*

提　纲

1. For lack of data concerning the accident rates and total number of bicyclists, the assumption that wearing helmets increased bicyclists' risks is open to doubt. (*V.D.*)
   事故总数增加未必意味着事故率上升。★★★★★

2. Other factors may also result in the increase in the number of accidents. (*N.C.R.*) ★★★★★

3. The author fails to point out how many bicyclists involved in accidents are wearing helmets. (*I.I.*)
   如果发生事故的骑车人都没有佩戴头盔，则作者的假设显然不能成立。★★★★

4. The author unfairly assumes that wearing helmets will necessarily create false senses of safety in bicyclists. (*U.A./N.C.R.*) ★★★

5. The assumption that bicyclists will take more risks once they feel safe is unfounded. (*U.A.*) ★★★

6. The author falsely assumes that educating people about bicycle safety will be effective in reducing the number of serious injuries. (*N.C.R./U.A./sufficiency of the solution*) ★★★

7. The author fails to consider accidents caused by other vehicles and the severity of injuries; the proposed education may not be sufficient for ensuring safety of bicyclists.
   如果大部分事故都是由自行车以外的其他车辆引发的，那么仅仅加强对于骑车人的安全教育未必足以减少事故率。(*I.I./U.C./sufficiency of the solution*) ★★★

8. Requiring bicyclists to wear helmets would still be necessary to ensure bicyclists' safety. (*I.T.*) ★★★★

论证要点

由于数据的模糊和信息的不完整，作者提供的数据未必说明骑车的危险性在增加(1~3)；其他几条基本都是作者没有任何根据的假设。

202

77. The following appeared in a health newsletter.

123 "A ten-year nationwide study of the effectiveness of wearing a helmet while bicycling indicates that ten years ago, approximately 35 percent of all bicyclists reported wearing helmets, whereas today that number is nearly 80 percent. Another study, however, suggests that during the same ten-year period, the number of accidents caused by bicycling(1,3) has increased 200 percent(2). *These results demonstrate that bicyclists feel safer because they are wearing helmets(4), and they take more risks as a result(5).* **Thus, there is clearly a call for the government to strive to reduce the number of serious injuries from bicycle accidents (6,7) by launching an education program that concentrates on the factors other than helmet use (8) that are necessary for bicycle safety.**" (former 120, ≈41) ★ ★

翻 译 一项为期10年的对于在骑自行车时戴头盔的作用的全国性研究显示,10年前,所有骑车人中大约有35%报告说他们戴头盔,而现在这个比例接近80%。然而,另外一项调查显示,在相同的10年期间,由骑车引起的事故数量增加了200%。这些结果说明骑车人因为戴着头盔而感到更安全,结果导致他们更加冒险。因此,政府显然应该通过集中介绍除头盔以外的其他骑车安全必要因素的教育项目来努力减少在行车事故中的严重伤害。

推理结构

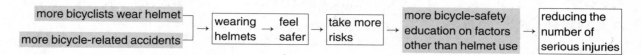

写作要求 *What **questions** should be answered to decide whether the recommendation and the argument are reasonable?*

提 纲

1. How about the accident rates and total number of bicyclists? The assumption that wearing helmets actually increased bicyclists' risks is open to doubt. (*V.D.*)
   如果骑车人数大幅增加,自行车事故肯定会增加。需要对比事故率才能判断作者结论。★ ★ ★ ★ ★

2. Are there any other factors that may also result in the increase in the number of accidents? (*N.C.R.*)
   ★ ★ ★ ★ ★

3. How many bicyclists involved in accidents are wearing helmets? (*I.I.*)
   如果发生事故的骑车人都没有佩戴头盔,那就说明作者的看法没有依据。★ ★ ★ ★

4. Is the assumption that wearing helmets will necessarily create false senses of safety in bicyclists justified? (*U.A./N.C.R.*) ★ ★ ★

5. Is the assumption that bicyclists will take more risks once they feel safe? (*U.A.*) ★ ★ ★

6. Will the proposed education program be effective in reducing the number of serious injuries? (*N.C.R./U.A./ sufficiency of the solution*) ★ ★ ★

7. How about accidents caused by other vehicles? How about the severity of bicyclists' injuries in these accidents? (*I.I./U.C./sufficiency of the solution*)
   如果大部分事故都是由自行车以外的其他车辆引发的,那么仅仅加强对于骑车人的安全教育未必可以减少事故率。★ ★ ★

8. Is helmet use insignificant in ensuring bicyclists' safety? (*I.T.*) ★ ★ ★ ★

由于自行车事故率数据的模糊和事故原因信息的不完整，作者提供的数据未必说明骑车的危险性在增加；即使增加，也未必是佩戴头盔导致的(1~3)；其他几条基本都是作者没有任何根据的假设。

---

78. The following appeared in a health newsletter.

125 "A ten-year nationwide study of the effectiveness of wearing a helmet while bicycling indicates that ten years ago, approximately 35 percent of all bicyclists reported wearing helmets, whereas today that number is nearly 80 percent. Another study, however, suggests that during the same ten-year period, the number of accidents caused by bicycling(1,3) has increased 200 percent(2). *These results demonstrate that bicyclists feel safer because they are wearing helmets(4), and they take more risks as a result(5).* **Thus there is clearly a call for the government to strive to reduce the number of serious injuries from bicycle accidents (6,7) by launching an education program that concentrates on the factors other than helmet use(8) that are necessary for bicycle safety.**" (former 120, ≈41, =123) ★★

翻　译　一项为期10年的对在骑自行车时戴头盔的作用的全国性研究显示，10年前，所有骑车人中大约有35%报告说他们戴头盔，而现在这个比例接近80%。然而，另外一项调查显示，在相同的10年期间，由骑车引起的事故数量增加了200%。这些结果说明骑车人因为戴着头盔而感到更安全，结果导致他们更加冒险。因此，政府显然应该通过集中介绍除头盔以外的其他骑车安全必要因素的教育项目来努力减少在行车事故中的严重伤害。

推理结构

写作要求　*What specific **evidence** is needed to evaluate the argument?*

提　纲

作者需要提供能够说明以下方面问题的信息或论据：

1. The accident rates and total number of bicyclists. The assumption that wearing helmets actually increased bicyclists' risks is open to doubt.（*V.D.*）
   如果骑车人数大幅增加，自行车事故肯定会增加。需要对比事故率才能判断作者结论。★★★★★

2. Other factors that may also result in the increase in the number of accidents.（*N.C.R.*）★★★★★

3. The number of bicyclists involved in accidents who are wearing helmets.（*I.I.*）
   如果发生事故的骑车人都没有佩戴头盔，那就说明作者的看法没有依据。★★★★

4. Wearing helmets will necessarily create false senses of safety in bicyclists.（*U.A./N.C.R.*）★★★

5. Bicyclists will take more risks once they feel safe.（*U.A.*）★★★

6. The proposed education program will be effective in reducing the number of serious injuries.（*N.C.R./U.A./ sufficiency of the solution*）★★★

7. Information about accidents caused by other vehicles and the severity of bicyclists' injuries in these accidents.（*I.I./U.C./sufficiency of the solution*）

如果大部分事故都是由自行车以外的其他车辆引发的，那么仅仅加强对于骑车人的安全教育未必足以减少事故率。★★★

8.　Helmet use is of no significant importance in ensuring bicyclists' safety. (*I.T.*) ★★★★

论证要点

由于自行车事故率数据的模糊和事故原因信息的不完整，作者提供的数据未必说明骑车的危险性在增加；即使增加，也未必是佩戴头盔导致的(1~3)；其他几条基本都是作者没有任何根据的假设。作者需要提供论据证明以上几点。

---

79. The following is a letter to the head of the tourism bureau on the island of Tria.

42 "Erosion of beach sand along the shores of Tria Island is a serious threat to our island and our tourist industry. **In order to stop the erosion(1), we should charge people for using the beaches(6,7,8).** Although this solution may annoy a few tourists in the short term, *it will raise money for replenishing the sand(9). Replenishing the sand*, as was done to protect buildings on the nearby island of Batia(3), *will help protect buildings along our shores(2), thereby reducing these buildings' risk of additional damage from severe storms (4). And since beaches and buildings in the area will be preserved, Tria's tourist industry will improve over the long term (5).*" (former 152) ★★★

翻　　译　Tria岛海岸沙滩的侵蚀对于我们岛和旅游业是个严重的威胁。为阻止侵蚀，我们应该对使用海滩的人收费。尽管这一解决方案会在短期内触怒少量游客，但它能够增加补充沙子的资金。像附近的Batia岛一样为保护建筑补充沙子将会有助于对我们沿岸建筑的保护，从而减少这些建筑在大风暴中受损的危险。随着该地区海滩和建筑得到保护，Tria的旅游业将会得到更长远地发展。

推理结构

写作要求　*What specific **evidence** is needed to evaluate the argument?*

提　　纲

作者需要提供有关以下方面的信息或证据：

1.　The extent of erosion in Tria. We cannot evaluate whether any measures are necessary to resolve the problem. (*necessity of the solution*) ★★★

2.　The buildings along our shores need to be protected. (*necessity of the solution*) ★★★
　　对于上文论述还存在以下问题：

3.　The fact that replenishing beach sand has served to protect shoreline buildings on Batia does not indicate that Tria could also achieve its goals by following Batia's example. (*F.A.*) ★★★
　　作者还需要提供证据来说明以下方面：

4.　Replenishing sand would suffice to reduce the buildings' risk of damage from severe storms. (*sufficiency of the solution*) ★★★

5.　Adopting the actions proposed by the author is sufficient for improving Tria's tourist industry in the long

205

term.（*sufficiency of the solution*）★ ★ ★

6. Other possible methods to stop the erosion.（*necessity of the solution*）★ ★

7. Charging people for using the beach could effectively stop the erosion.（*sufficiency of the solution*）★ ★ ★

8. Negative effects of the charging policy.（*adv:disadv*）★ ★ ★ ★

9. How much money we should charge to ensure raising enough money for replenishing the sand, and whether the charge is feasible.（*I.I./feasibility of the conclusion*）★ ★ ★

论证要点

本题主要分析环节就是对游客收费和补充沙子对于保护海滩和建筑的充分性和必要性。首先，保护海滩和建筑不一定非要通过补充沙子；其次，就算一定要补充沙子，经费也不一定非要通过向游客收费获得；再次，补充沙子之后也未必足以保证建筑能够抵御风暴并确保旅游业的长远发展。

---

80. The following appeared in a memorandum written by the chairperson of the West Egg Town **43** Council.

"Two years ago, consultants predicted that West Egg's landfill, which is used for garbage disposal, would be completely filled within five years（7）. During the past two years（6）, however, the town's residents have been recycling twice as much material as they did in previous years（1,2）. *Next month the amount of recycled material—which includes paper, plastic, and metal—should further increase*, since charges for pickup of other household garbage will double（4）. Furthermore, over 90 percent of the respondents to a recent survey （5）said that they would do more recycling in the future. *Because of our town's strong commitment to recycling,* **the available space in our landfill should last for considerably longer than predicted (3,6).**"（former 11）★ ★ ★

翻　译 2年前，顾问预言，West Egg用于投放垃圾的填埋地将在5年内完全被填满。然而在过去的2年中，市民循环再利用的材料数量比以前翻了一番。下个月循环再利用的材料（包括纸张、塑料和金属）数量将进一步增加，因为其他家庭垃圾的处理费用将会加倍。而且，最近一次调查中超过90%的回应者表示他们将会在未来做更多的循环再利用工作。由于居民对循环再利用的有力支持，我们填埋地的使用时间将比预期的长得多。

推理结构

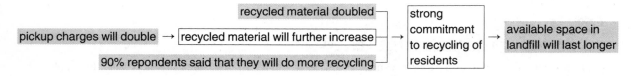

写作要求 *What specific **evidence** is needed to evaluate the argument?*

提　纲

作者需要提供关于以下方面的信息或证据：

1. The actual amount of recycled garbage in previous years. The doubling may be insignificant.（*V.D.*）★ ★ ★
   对于上文论述还存在以下问题：

2. An increase in the amount of recycled materials does not necessarily indicate a decrease in the total amount of trash deposited in the city's landfill.（*U.C.*）★ ★ ★ ★

3. The recycling habit of West Egg residents is not the only factor determining how quickly the landfill will reach its capacity. (*I.T.*) ★★★★

4. The assumption that increased charges for trash pickup will serve to slow the rate at which the landfill reaches its capacity is unwarranted. (*U.A.*) ★★★

作者还需要提供信息和论据说明以下方面：

5. The survey's respondents are representative of the overall group of people whose trash goes to the city's landfill. (*Are the respondents representative?*) ★★★★

6. Other factors that related to the garbage-disposal behavior and the lasting time of the landfill will not change in the future. (*P→F*) ★★★★★

对于上文论述还存在以下可能性：

7. The consultants may have already taken the recycling factors into consideration when they made the prediction. If so, the assumption that the available space in the landfill will last for longer than predicted is unfounded. (*U.A.*) ★★

论证要点

本题主要问题在于决定垃圾场填满速度的因素不只有垃圾循环使用这一条(2、3、6)。即使垃圾循环再利用是决定垃圾场寿命的主要因素，作者提供的数据和信息也不足以证明本地居民一定会进行更多再生工作(4、5)。

---

81. The following appeared in a letter to the editor of a journal on environmental issues.

44 "Over the past year, the Crust Copper Company（CCC）has purchased over 10,000 square miles of land in the tropical nation of West Fredonia(2,3). Mining copper on this land will inevitably result in pollution and, since West Fredonia is the home of several endangered animal species, in environmental disaster(1,8). **But such disasters can be prevented if consumers simply refuse to purchase products(4) that are made with CCC's copper(5) unless the company abandons its mining plans(6,7).**" (former 141) ★★

翻 译 去年，Crust Copper Company(CCC)在热带国家West Fredonia购买了上万平方英里的土地。在这些地方采矿将不可避免地导致污染和环境灾害，因为West Fredonia是很多濒危物种的栖居地。但只要消费者拒绝购买用CCC所生产的铜制造的产品，那么，只要CCC公司放弃它的采矿计划就可以避免这种灾害。

推理结构

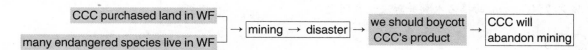

写作要求 *assumptions*

提 纲

1. CCC's mining activities do not necessarily lead to pollution and environmental disaster. (*N.C.R./I.I.*) ★★★★★

2. We do not know what portion of CCC's land is inhabited by endangered animals. (*I.I.*) ★★★

3. We do not know what fraction of the 10,000 square miles of land will be used for CCC's mining activities. (*V.D.*) ★★★

2&3：CCC的采矿活动未必一定导致作者暗示的灾害性影响。

4. The author fails to demonstrate the critical assumption that most consumers can reliably distinguish products that are made with CCC's copper. (*feasibility of the conclusion*) ★ ★ ★

5. The author fails to consider whether most consumers are willing to cooperate in the boycott. (*feasibility of the conclusion*) ★ ★ ★

6. The author ignores the possibility that other measures could also be taken to prevent the harmful result. (*necessity of the solution*) ★ ★ ★

7. The author hastily assumes that the proposed boycott will sufficiently prevent pollution and environmental disaster. (*sufficency of the solution*) ★ ★ ★

8. The definition of the term "disaster" is very vague. We cannot evaluate whether the disastrous results implied by the author will necessarily emerge. (*definition of the term "disaster"*) ★ ★

论证要点

本题核心假设在于CCC的采矿活动必然导致灾害性影响的因果关系，前三点都围绕其展开。其次，作者方案的可行性（即消费者是否有能力区分CCC的铜制品，以及消费者是否愿意共同抵制CCC的铜制品）、充分性、必要性也可以加以论述。

---

82. The following is part of a memorandum from the president of Humana University.

45 "Last year the number of students who enrolled in online degree programs offered by nearby Omni University increased by 50 percent (1,2). During the same year, Omni showed a significant decrease from prior years in expenditures for dormitory and classroom space, *most likely because instruction in the online programs takes place via the Internet (3).* In contrast, over the past three years, enrollment at Humana University has failed to grow, and the cost of maintaining buildings has increased (4) along with our budget deficit. To address these problems, Humana University will begin immediately to create and actively promote online degree programs like those at Omni (5,6,7). **We predict that instituting these online degree programs will help Humana both increase its total enrollment and solve its budget problems (8).**" (former 39) ★ ★ ★

翻　译 去年报名参加附近Omni大学在线教学项目的学生人数上升了50%。同年，Omni用于宿舍和教室的开支比前些年显著下降，这很可能是因为在线教学项目通过网络来授课。相比而言，在过去3年中，Humana大学的报名人数没有增长，而用于建筑维护的费用上升了，且出现了预算赤字。为解决这些问题，Humana将马上开始设置并积极推广和Omni类似的在线教学项目。我们预计，开设这些在线教学项目将有助于增加Humana的报名人数并解决预算问题。

推理结构

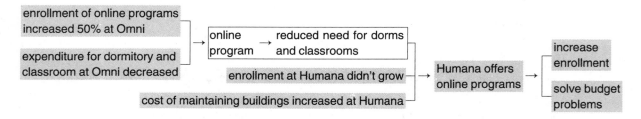

写作要求 *What **questions** should be answered to decide whether the prediction and the argument are reasonable?*

提　　纲

1. What's the actual number of students who enrolled in long-distance programs at Omni University the year before last? The 50% increase might be insignificant. (*V.D.*) ★★★

2. What's the total number of enrollment, and actual tuition income of Omni last year? (*I.I.*) ★★★

3. Are there any other factors that may explain the decrease in expenditures for dormitory and classroom space at Omni? (*N.C.R.*) ★★★

4. What fraction of the expenditures is used on buildings related to teaching? (*V.D.*)
   如果这些开支主要是用于一些教学以外的辅助用房，那么就算开设了在线教学项目也解决不了这部分的预算问题。★★★

5. Are Omni and Humana comparable at every aspect? (*F.A.*) ★★★★

6. What's the cost and requirements of installing such a program? (*adv:disadv/feasibility of the conclusion*) ★★★★

7. Are there any other methods that could be applied to solve the problem? (*necessity of the solution*) ★★★

8. Are there other possible causes that may result in the enrollment and budget problems? (*N.C.R.*) ★★★

论证要点

　　本题论证内容主要是两条线：一、Omni的在线教学未必起到了作者想象的良好效果(1~3)；二、就算Omni的在线教学确实非常好，Humana开设同样的课程未必能保证同样的效果(4~8)。

---

83. The following is part of a memorandum from the president of Humana University.

49 "Last year the number of students who enrolled in online degree programs offered by nearby Omni University increased by 50 percent (1,2). During the same year, Omni showed a significant decrease from prior years in expenditures for dormitory and classroom space, *most likely because online instruction takes place via the Internet (3)*. In contrast, over the past three years, enrollment at Humana University has failed to grow and the cost of maintaining buildings has increased (4). **Thus, to increase enrollment and solve the problem of budget deficits at Humana University(8), we should initiate and actively promote online degree programs like those at Omni (5,6,7).**" (former 39, ≈45) ★★★

翻　　译 去年报名参加附近Omni大学在线教学项目的学生人数上升了50%。同年，Omni用于宿舍和教室的开支比前些年显著下降，很可能是因为在线教学通过网络来授课。相比而言，在过去3年中，Humana大学的报名人数没有增长，而且用于建筑维护的费用上升了。为增加Humana的报名人数并解决预算赤字问题，我们应该开始设置并积极推广和Omni那些类似的在线教学项目。

推理结构

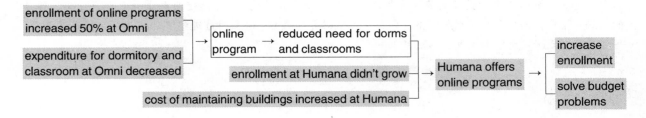

提　纲

1. We do not know the actual number of students who enrolled in long-distance programs at Omni University the year before last. The 50% increase might be insignificant. (*V.D.*) ★★★

2. We do not know the total number of enrollment, and actual tuition income at Omni last year. (*I.I.*) ★★★
    1 & 2: The online programs at Omni might not be as successful as the president implies.

3. The president assumes that no other factors could explain the decrease in expenditures for dormitory and classroom space at Omni. (*N.C.R.*) ★★★

4. We need to know what fraction of the expenditures of Humana is used on buildings related to teaching. (*V.D.*)
    如果这些开支主要是用于一些教学以外的辅助用房，那么就算开设了在线教学项目也解决不了这部分的预算问题。★★★

5. The president assumes that Omni and Humana are comparable at every aspect. (*F.A.*) ★★★★

6. The president does not provide any information about the cost and requirements of installing such a program. (*adv:disadv/feasibility of the conclusion*) ★★★★

7. The president overlooks other methods that could be applied to solve the problem. (*necessity of the solution*) ★★★

8. The president assumes that no other causes may result in the enrollment and budget problems. (*N.C.R./ sufficiency of the solution*) ★★★

论证要点

　　本题论证内容主要是两条线：一、Omni的在线教学未必起到了作者想象的良好效果（1~3）；二、就算Omni的在线教学确实非常好，Humana开设同样的课程未必能保证同样的效果（4~8）。

---

84. The following appeared in a health magazine published in Corpora.

46 "Medical experts say that only one-quarter of Corpora's citizens meet the current standards for adequate physical fitness, even though twenty years ago, one-half of all of Corpora's citizens met the standards as then defined(1). *But these experts are mistaken when they suggest that spending too much time using computers has caused a decline in fitness.* Since overall fitness levels are highest in regions of Corpora where levels of computer ownership(2) are also highest(3,4), *it is clear that using computers has not made citizens less physically fit.* Instead, as shown by this year's unusually low expenditures on fitness-related products and services (5), **the recent decline in the economy is most likely the cause(6), and fitness levels will improve when the economy does (7).**" (former 48) ★★★

翻　　译　医学专家指出，Corpora市民中只有四分之一达到当前的健康标准，而20年前，Corpora的市民有一半都达到了当时定义的标准。但专家关于长时间使用电脑导致健康状况下降的观点是错误的。因为在Corpora，电脑拥有量最高的地区也是总体健康水平最高的地区，显然使用电脑并没有导致市民体质的下降。相反，今年用于健身产品和服务的花费低得异乎寻常，这表明最近经济的衰退最可能是其原因。当经济复苏之后，健康水平也会随之提高。

fitness levels in regions with high computer ownership are highest → computer using has not caused a decline in fitness

low expenditures on fitness-related products →

decline in economy led to less fitness

→ better economy → better fitness levels

写作要求 *assumptions*

提　　纲

1. The standard for fitness may vary during past 20 years. (P→F)
   这是上文推理的大前提。如果健康标准发生了变化(比20年前更加严格),则未必说明居民的健康状况在下降。★★★★

2. Although the regions mentioned by the author have relatively highest fitness levels, it is still possible that their fitness levels are declining compared with themselves. (*confusing variation and comparison*)
   专家观点是使用电脑导致健康水平下降,而这条论据是说使用电脑后健康水平仍然比别人高,这是属于对比参照系选择的失误。★★★★

3. High levels of computer ownership do not indicate that citizens of these regions will spend more time on using computers. (U.C.) ★★★

4. It is possible that using computer does result in the decline in the fitness levels, while the decline was offset by certain factors which could promote the fitness levels, such as better environment, working condition, and health care, etc. (I.T.) ★★★★

5. The low expenditures on fitness-related products and services may not result in low level of fitness. (N.C.R.) ★★★★

6. The low expenditures on fitness-related products do not necessarily result from the decline in the economy. (N.C.R.) ★★★

7. The author fails to provide evidence to show that once the economy improves, people will spend more money on fitness-related products and services, and their fitness levels will therefore be improved. (*sufficiency of the conclusion*) ★★★★

论证要点

　　首先,本题推理的大前提"居民健康状况下降"未必成立,因为作者衡量健康状况用的是不同的标准。其次,由于2、3、4三点缺乏纵向比较、概念缺乏必然联系以及不全面思维的问题,导致作者提出的信息不足以推翻专家观点。最后,作者对于经济衰退导致健康状况下降的因果关系假设也没有任何依据。

---

85. The following appeared in a memorandum from the owner of Movies Galore, a chain of movie-rental stores.

`47`

"*Because of declining profits, we must reduce operating expenses at Movies Galore's ten movie-rental stores. Raising prices is not a good option(1),* since we are famous for our low prices. **Instead, we should reduce our operating hour**s. Last month (2) our store in downtown Marston(3) reduced its hours by closing at 6:00 p.m. rather than 9:00 p.m. and reduced its overall inventory by no longer stocking any DVD released more than five years ago. Since we have received very few customer complaints(4) about these new policies(5), **we should now adopt them(6) at all other Movies Galore stores as our best strategies(7) for improving profits.**" (former 213) ★★★

翻　　译 由于利润下降，我们必须压缩Movies Galore10家录像租赁店的营业开支。涨价并不是一个好选择，因为我们就是因低价知名的。相应地，我们应该缩短营业时间。上个月我们位于闹市区Marston的店结业时间从以前的晚9点改为下午6点，并通过不再保留发行5年以上的DVD来减少总库存量。我们很少接到关于这些新政策的客户投诉，因此，我们应该在Movie Galore的所有商店实施这些政策，作为增加利润的最好策略。

推理结构

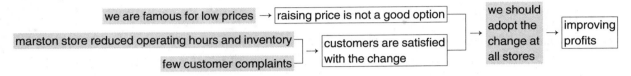

写作要求 *What specific **evidence** is needed to evaluate the argument?*

提　　纲

作者需要提供论据以说明：

1. Why raising prices would not be a good solution for improving profits. (*I.E.*) ★★★

对于上文讨论的情况，还存在以下问题，需要作者提供论据加以排除：

2. The new policies were implemented only one month ago; the situation of a single month might not be representative of that of the whole year, or the negative effects might not have fully emerged yet. (*P→F/reliability of the survey*) ★★★★

3. The success of the new policies at one store does not ensure that adopting them would be successful at all other stores. (*C.S.*) ★★★★

4. The fact that few customer complaints were received does not indicate that most customers are satisfied with these policies. (*F.D.*) ★★★

作者还需要提供关于以下方面的信息：

5. The possible change in the profits of the store in Marston after the policies were adopted. We cannot evaluate whether we should adopt them at all other stores. (*I.I.*) ★★★★

6. Any negative effects of the new policies. (*adv:disadv*) ★★★

7. Other possible measures we can adopt to improve profits. (*necessity of the solution*) ★★★

论证要点

本题的论证可以这样展开思路：首先，Marston的新措施未必没有问题(2、4、5)；其次，就算没有问题，该措施未必能成功推广到其他连锁店(3、6)；再次，就算能推广，也可能存在其他解决方案(1、7)。

---

86. The following appeared in a memorandum from the owner of Movies Galore, a chain of movie-

`111` rental stores.

"*In order to stop the recent decline in our profits, we must reduce operating expenses at Movies Galore's ten movie-rental stores.* Since we are famous for our special bargains, *raising our rental prices is not a viable way to improve profits*(1). Last month(2) our store in downtown Marston(4) significantly decreased its operating expenses by closing at 6:00 P.M. rather than 9:00 P.M. and by reducing its stock by eliminating all movies released more than five years ago (3,5). **By implementing similar changes in our other stores(4), Movies Galore can increase profits(6) without jeopardizing our reputation for offering great movies at low prices**." (former 213, ≈47) ★★★

翻　译 为阻止最近出现的利润下滑，我们必须压缩Movies Galore10家录像租赁店的营业开支。由于我们是因低价而知名的，因此，上涨租赁价格并不是增加利润的可行方案。上个月，我们位于闹市区Marston的店通过将结业时间从以前的晚9点改为下午6点，并通过不再保留发行5年以上的电影来减少总库存量，从而显著减少了运营开支。通过在其他店实施类似办法，Movies Galore可以在不影响我们提供低价大片的声誉的前提下增加利润。

推理结构

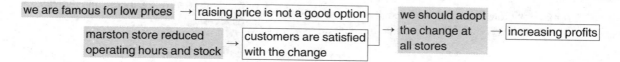

写作要求 *assumptions*

提　纲

1. The claim that raising prices is not a good solution for improving profits is unjustified. (*U.A.*) ★★★

2. The new policies were implemented only one month ago; the situation of this month might not be representative of that of the whole year, or the negative effects might not have emerged yet. (*P→F/ reliability of the survey*) ★★★★

3. For lack of the feedback from customers and information about the change in MG's profits, we cannot evaluate whether the policies are successful. (*I.I./U.A.*) ★★★

   2 &3: The assumption that the new policy has been successfully carried out is open to doubt.

4. The success of the new policies at one store does not ensure that adopting them would necessarily be successful at all other stores. (*C.S.*) ★★★★

5. The manager falsely assumes that those old movies are of no market value, and eliminating those movies will not have any impact on their business and reputation. (*U.A.*) ★★★★

6. The manager assumes that the proposed changes are sufficient and necessary for ensuring profits. (*sufficiency/necessity of the solution*) ★★★

论证要点

本题的论证展开思路：首先，Marston的新措施未必没有问题（2、3、5）；其次，就算没有问题，该措施也未必能成功推广到其他连锁店（4）；再次，就算能推广，也可能存在其他解决方案（1、6）。

---

87. The following appeared in a memorandum from the owner of Movies Galore, a chain of movie-
112 rental stores.

"In order to reverse the recent decline in our profits, *we must reduce operating expenses at Movies Galore's ten movie-rental stores. Since we are famous for our special bargains, raising our rental prices is not a viable way to improve profits(1).* Last month(2) our store in downtown Marston(3) significantly decreased its operating expenses by closing at 6:00 p.m. rather than 9:00 p.m. and by reducing its stock by eliminating all movies released more than five years ago (4,5). **Therefore, in order to increase profits(6) without jeopardizing our reputation for offering great movies at low prices, we recommend implementing similar changes in our other nine Movies Galore stores(3).**" (former 213, ≈47, 111)

翻　译 为扭转最近出现的利润下滑，我们必须压缩Movies Galore10家录像租赁店的营业开支。由于

我们是因低价而知名的，因此，上涨租赁价格并不是增加利润的可行方案。上个月，我们位于闹市区Marston的店通过将结业时间从以前的晚9点改为下午6点，并通过不再保留发行5年以上的电影来减少总库存量，从而显著减少了运营开支。为在不影响我们提供低价大片的声誉的前提下增加利润，我们建议在Movies Galore其他9家店实施类似办法。

推理结构

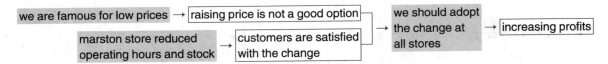

写作要求

What **questions** should be answered to decide whether the recommendation and the argument are reasonable?

提　纲

1. Is the claim that raising prices is not a good solution for improving profits justified? (*U.A.*) ★★★

2. The new policies were implemented only one month ago; is the situation of this month representative of that of the whole year? Have the possible negative effects fully emerged? (*P→F /reliability of the survey*) ★★★★

3. Could the success of the changes at one store ensure that adopting them would necessarily be successful at all other stores? (*C.S.*) ★★★★

4. What are the feedback and response of customers toward the changes? How about the change in MG's profits? We cannot evaluate if the changes are successful without such information. (*I.I./U.A.*) ★★★

5. Do those old movies have any market value? Will eliminating those movies have any impact on their business and reputation? (*U.A.*) ★★★★

6. Are the proposed changes sufficient and necessary for ensuring profits? (*sufficiency/necessity of the solution*) ★★★

论证要点

本题的论证可以这样展开思路：首先，Marston的新措施未必没有问题（2、3、5）；其次，就算没有问题，该措施未必能成功推广到其他连锁店（4）；再次，就算能推广，也可能存在其他解决方案（1、6）。

---

88. The following appeared in a magazine article about planning for retirement.

48 "**Clearview should be a top choice for anyone seeking a place to retire (9)**, because it has spectacular natural beauty and a consistent climate. Another advantage is that housing costs in Clearview have fallen(1) significantly during the past year(2), and taxes remain lower than those in neighboring towns(3). Moreover, Clearview's mayor promises(4) many new programs to improve schools, streets, and public services(5). And best of all, *retirees in Clearview can also expect excellent health care as they grow older*, since the number of physicians(6) in the area is far greater than the national average(7,8)." (former 216) ★

翻　译　Clearview的天然景色与温和气候使其成为那些为退休后寻找生活地的人的首选。另一个优点是Clearview的房价在去年显著下降，税率一直比邻近城镇低。而且，Clearview的市长承诺了很多新方案来改善学校、街道和公共服务。最棒的是，Clearview的退休人员也可以在老年时享受到出色的医疗服务，因为该地区的医生数量远高于全国平均水平。

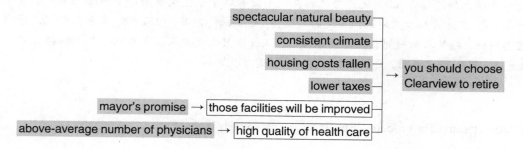

*What specific **evidence** is needed to evaluate the argument?*

提　纲

作者需要提供论据说明以下几方面：

1. The housing costs in Clearview compared with other silimar cities, and whether we can afford the costs even after the decrease. The variation in the housing costs does not indicate that Clearview has advantage in housing costs. (*confusing comparison and variation*) ★★★★

2. Housing costs in Clearview will not increase in the future. ($P \rightarrow F$) ★★

3. The average tax rates of the whole nation; non-neighboring cities might enjoy even lower taxes. (*I.C.*) ★★★★

4. If the mayor can keep his promise, and how long it will take for those improvements to be accomplished. (*U.A.*) ★★★

对于上文推理还存在以下问题：

5. The mayor's promise might just indicate that those facilities are in bad condition now. (*negative evidence*) ★★★

6. The number of physicians does not necessarily indicate the quality of health care. (*U.C.*) ★★★★

7. Although the number of physicians in Clearview is relatively high, the per capita number might be relatively low. (*V.D.*) ★★★

8. This fact may well illustrate that there are some special medical demands in this region. (*negative evidence*) ★★

作者还需要提供关于以下方面的信息：

9. Other conditions in Clearview which would influence retirees' decisions, such as consumer price, transportation, etc. (*I.I.*) ★★★★★

论证要点

本题论据完全平行并列，论证时可以针对房价、税收、公共设施、医疗以及其他生活条件逐条展开。

---

89. **An ancient, traditional remedy for insomnia—the scent of lavender flowers—has now**
[50] **been proved effective.** In a recent study, 30 volunteers(1,2) with chronic insomnia slept each night for three weeks on lavender-scented pillows in a controlled room where their sleep was monitored electronically(8). During the first week, volunteers continued to take their usual sleeping medication. They slept soundly but wakened feeling tired. At the beginning of the second week, the volunteers discontinued their sleeping medication. During that week, they slept less soundly than the previous week and felt even more tired. During the third week, the volunteers slept longer and more soundly than in the previous two weeks(3,4,5). *Therefore, the study proves that lavender cures insomnia within a short period of time (6,7).* (former 167) ★★★

一种治疗失眠的古老传统疗法——薰衣草花香——现在被证明是有效的。在一次最近的调查中，30名患有慢性失眠症的志愿者在3周之内每晚都在一个带有电子监控设备的房屋内睡在带薰衣草花香的枕头上。在第1周，志愿者继续服用他们常用的安眠药。他们睡得很沉，但醒来时觉得很累。第2周开始，他们不再服用药物。结果与前一周相比他们睡得不那么沉并且感觉更累。在第3周，他们睡得比前2周时间更长而且更深。这一研究证明，薰衣草在短时间内治愈了失眠。

推理结构

30 volunteers with chronic insomnia sleep longer in the study → the remedy is effective

写作要求 *What specific **evidence** is needed to evaluate the argument?*

提　纲

对于上文研究存在以下问题：

1. 30 volunteers are too small a sample to be representative. (*quantity of the sample*) ★★★
   作者需要提供有关以下方面的信息或论据：

2. Detailed information about the 30 volunteers, e.g. the severity of their insomnia, their physical condition. We could not evaluate whether they are representative. (*Are the respondents representative?*) ★★★★

3. The volunteers' sleep patterns prior to the experiment. (*I.C./ex parte information/lack of comparison*) ★★★

4. How the volunteers felt after the third week. We could not evaluate the actual effect of lavender flowers on their sleeping. (*I.I.*) ★★★
   上文论述还存在以下问题：

5. How soundly or how long a person sleeps, or how tired a person feels after sleep, is irrelevant to whether the person suffers from insomnia. (*U.C./definition of the term "insomnia"*) ★★★

6. Granted that the volunteers' sleep was improved through the three weeks, we cannot ensure it is the lavender that caused the result. Other factors could also account for the improvement. (*N.C.R.*) ★★★

7. The author cannot hastily conclude that the volunteers' insomnia has been thoroughly cured without any follow-up studies. (*C→F*) ★★★★

8. The study should include another group of people with similar sleeping problems who do not sleep on such pillows as counterparts. (*lack of controlled experiment*) ★★★★

论证要点

本题主要论证环节集中在：一、研究样本的代表性；二、缺乏研究对象和自身之前睡眠情况的纵向比较以及和参照对象的横向比较；三、没有考虑除了枕头以外，导致睡眠情况变化的其他因素。第5条对于失眠定义的攻击以及第7条对于该方法长期效果的质疑可作为辅助论证。

90. The following appeared in a health magazine.

53 "**The citizens of Forsythe have adopted more healthful lifestyles (7)**. Their responses to a recent survey(1) show that in their eating habits they conform more closely to government nutritional recommendations(2) than they did ten years ago(3). Furthermore, there has been a fourfold increase in sales of food products containing kiran(5), a substance that a scientific study has shown reduces cholesterol(4). This trend is also evident in reduced sales of sulia, a food that few of the most healthy citizens regularly eat(6)." (former 201) ★★★

Forsythe的居民选择了更健康的生活方式。他们对于最近一项调查的回答显示，他们的饮食习惯比10年前更加贴近政府的营养建议。而且，含有kiran的食品销量增长了4倍，在一次科学研究中发现，kiran是一种能够降低胆固醇水平的物质。这种趋势同样也被sulia的销量下降所证实，而健康的居民很少有人经常食用sulia。

推理结构

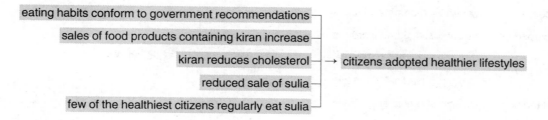

eating habits conform to government recommendations
sales of food products containing kiran increase
kiran reduces cholesterol → citizens adopted healthier lifestyles
reduced sale of sulia
few of the healthiest citizens regularly eat sulia

写作要求 *What specific **evidence** is needed to evaluate the argument?*

提　纲

作者需要提供关于以下方面的信息或论据：

1. The reliability of the recent survey, who responded and the number of respondents. (*Are the respondents representative?*) ★★

2. The details of government nutritional recommendations. They do not necessarily represent standards of healthy lifestyles. (*U.C.*) ★★★

3. Any change about the government nutritional recommendations during the past decade. (*C→P*) ★★★

4. Other reasons that lead people to purchase food products containing kiran. The increase in sales of these food products does not necessarily indicate that the citizens are leading healthier lives. (*U.C./N.C.R.*) ★★★★

5. If there are any unhealthy ingredients in those food products which contain kiran. (*adv:disadv*) ★★★

对于上文论述，还存在以下问题：

6. The fact that few of the healthiest citizens regularly eat sulia does not demonstrate that sulia is unhealthy. (*U.C.*) ★★★★

作者还需要提供以下方面信息：

7. Other factors that could be used to evaluate whether people are having healthier lives. (*sufficiency of the evidence/I.E.*) ★★★★★

论证要点

本题论证点首先是政府的营养建议是否能代表真正的健康标准以及在过去十年间有没有发生变化；其次是kiran和sulia两种食品的销量和居民的健康程度之间没有必然的逻辑联系。

---

91. **The citizens of Forsythe have adopted more healthful lifestyles (7)**. Their responses to a
144 recent survey(1) show that in their eating habits they conform more closely to government nutritional recommendations(2) than they did ten years ago (3). Furthermore, there has been a fourfold increase in sales of food products containing kiran(5), a substance that a scientific study has shown reduces cholesterol(4). This trend is also evident in reduced sales of sulia, a food that few of the healthiest citizens regularly eat(6). (former 201, =53) ★★★

翻　译 Forsythe的居民选择了更健康的生活方式。他们对于最近一项调查的回答显示，他们的饮食习惯比10年前更加贴近政府的营养建议。而且，含有kiran的食品销量增长了4倍，在一次科学研究中发现，kiran是一种能够降低胆固醇水平的物质。这种趋势同样也被sulia的销量下降所证实，而sulia是那些健康的居民极少食用的食品。

推理结构

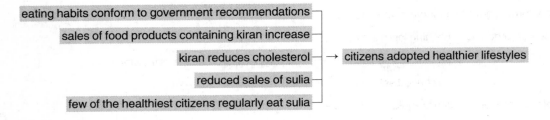

写作要求 *assumptions*

提　纲

1. In the absence of details about the procedure of the survey (e.g. who responded, the number of respondents), the reliability of the survey is open to doubt. (*Are the respondents representative?*) ★★

2. The author does not provide any details about the government nutritional recommendations; the recommendations do not necessarily represent standards of healthy lifestyles. (*U.C.*) ★★★

3. The author assumes that there are no fundamental changes in the government nutritional recommendations during the past decade. (*C→P*)
    如果营养建议发生变化，那么居民饮食习惯更加贴近建议的现象只是因为建议变了，而非居民的饮食习惯变了。★★★

4. The increase in the sales of these food products containing kiran does not necessarily indicate that the citizens are leading healthier lives; they may purchase them for other reasons. (*U.C./N.C.R.*) ★★★★

5. We need to know if there are any unhealthy ingredients in those food products which contain kiran. (*adv: disadv*) ★★★

6. The fact that few of the healthiest citizens regularly eat sulia does not demonstrate that sulia is unhealthy. (*U.C.*) ★★★★

7. The author ignores other factors that could be used to evaluate whether people are having healthier lives. (*sufficiency of the evidence/I.E.*) ★★★★★

论证要点

　　本题论证点首先是政府的营养建议是否能代表真正的健康标准以及在过去十年间有没有发生变化；其次是kiran和sulia两种食品的销量和居民的生活方式是否健康没有必然的逻辑联系。

---

92. *Benton City residents have adopted healthier lifestyles(7)*. A recent survey of city residents(1) **[151]** shows that the eating habits of city residents conform more closely to government nutritional recommendations(2) than they did ten years ago(3). During those ten years, local sales of food products containing kiran(5), a substance that a scientific study has shown reduces cholesterol, have increased fourfold(4), while sales of sulia, a food rarely eaten by the healthiest residents, have declined dramatically(6). **Because of these positive changes in the eating habits of Benton City residents, we predict that the obesity rate in the city will soon be well below the national average(8).** (former 201, ≈53, 144) ★★

Benton市居民选择了更健康的生活方式。最近一次市民调查显示，他们的饮食习惯比10年前更加贴近政府的营养建议。在这10年中，含有kiran的食品销量增长了4倍，在一次科学研究中发现，kiran是一种能够降低胆固醇水平的物质。而健康居民很少食用的sulia销量显著下降。基于这些Benton居民饮食习惯中的积极变化，我们预计本市的肥胖率会很快低于全国平均水平。

推理结构

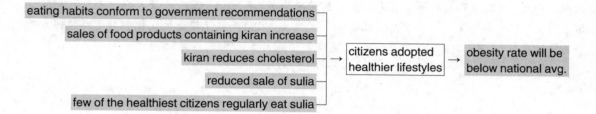

写作要求 *What **questions** should be answered to decide whether the prediction and the argument are reasonable?*

提　纲

1. Is the reliability of the survey guaranteed? (*Are the respondents representative?*) ★★

2. Do the government nutritional recommendations represent standards of healthy lifestyles? (*U.C.*) ★★★

3. Are there any fundamental changes in the government nutritional recommendations during the past decade? (*C→P*)

   如果营养建议发生变化，那么居民饮食习惯更加贴近建议的现象只是因为建议变了，而非居民的饮食习惯变了。★★★

4. Does the increase in the sales of these food products containing kiran necessarily indicate that the citizens are leading healthier lives? They may purchase them for other reasons. (*U.C./N.C.R.*) ★★★★

5. Are there any unhealthy ingredients in those food products which contain kiran? (*adv:disadv*) ★★★

6. Does the fact that few of the healthiest citizens regularly eat sulia sufficiently demonstrate that sulia is unhealthy? (*U.C.*) ★★★★

7. Are there other factors that could be used to evaluate whether people are living healthier lives? (*sufficiency of the evidence/I.E.*) ★★★★★

8. Are there other factors, other than eating habits, that also contribute to obesity? (*sufficiency of the claim*) ★★★★

论证要点

本题论证点首先是政府的营养建议是否能代表真正的健康标准以及在过去十年间有没有发生变化；其次是kiran和sulia两种食品的销量和居民的生活方式是否健康没有必然的逻辑联系。而且，仅仅是饮食习惯更加健康并不足以保证肥胖率的下降。

---

93. Humans arrived in the Kaliko Islands about 7,000 years ago, and within 3,000 years most of the
54 large mammal species that had lived in the forests of the Kaliko Islands had become extinct. *Yet humans cannot have been a factor in the species' extinctions (2)*, because there is no evidence that the humans had any significant contact with the mammals (1). Further, archaeologists have discovered numerous sites (3) where the bones of fish had been

discarded, but they found no such areas containing the bones of large mammals, so the humans cannot have hunted the mammals (4). **Therefore, some climate change or other environmental factor must have caused the species' extinctions (5).** (former 202) ★★★

翻　译　大约7000年前人类到达了Kaliko岛，在3000年内曾经生活在Kaliko岛树林中的大型哺乳动物绝大多数已经灭绝。然而人类并不是导致这些物种灭绝的因素，因为没有证据表明人类与这些哺乳动物有明显接触。而且，考古学家发现很多有大量废弃鱼骨的场所，而他们并没有发现存在大型哺乳动物骨头的类似场所，因而人类并没有猎杀这些哺乳动物。因此，一定是一些气候上的变化或其他环境因素导致了这些物种的灭绝。

推理结构

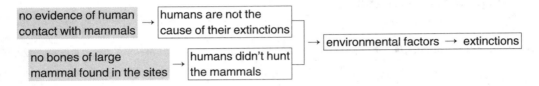

写作要求　*assumptions*

提　纲

1. The fact that no evidence showing significant contact between humans and the mammals has been found does not sufficiently prove that there was no any such contact at all.

    The argument treats a lack of proof that humans might be responsible for the extinctions as constituting sufficient proof that they were not. (*Does the study make any difference?/I.E.*)

    没有证据表明人类与动物有接触并不能充分证明人类与它们确实没有接触的假设。★★★★

2. Even if humans had no significant contact with mammals, human activities might pose negative effects on mammals in different ways. Human activities might have caused the species' extinctions indirectly. (*I.T.*)
    ★★★★★

3. The author fails to prove that those discovered sites were inhabited by humans. (*U.A.*) ★★★

4. The fact that no areas containing the bones of large mammals were found does not sufficiently demonstrate that humans have not hunted those mammals. (*I.T.*)

    与第1点类似，没有发现类似场地并不能充分证明这种场地一定不存在。而且即使真的不存在这种场地，也不能以此充分证明人类没有猎杀这些动物，因为对它们的骨头可能存在其他处理方式。
    ★★★★

5. The author ignores other factors besides climate change and environmental ones that could also explain the extinctions. (*F.D./N.C.R.*) ★★★★

论证要点

　　本题首先要论证的是人类与这些动物没有接触的假设；其次，就算确实没有接触，人类可能通过间接方式造成动物死亡；再次，文中考古学家的发现也不足以证明人类没有猎杀这些动物。

94. Humans arrived in the Kaliko Islands about 7,000 years ago, and within 3,000 years most of the [165] large mammal species that had lived in the forests of the Kaliko Islands were extinct. Previous archaeological findings have suggested that early humans generally relied on both fishing and

翻　译　大约7000年前人类到达了Kaliko岛，在3000年内曾经生活在Kaliko岛的树林中的大型哺乳动物绝大多数已经灭绝了。以前的考古发现说明早期人类通常依赖打渔和捕猎获取食物；由于考古学家在Kaliko岛发现了很多有废弃鱼骨的场所，很有可能人类也捕猎哺乳动物。而且，研究人员也发现了能用于捕猎的简单工具，比如石刀。唯一清楚的解释就是，是人类的过度捕猎导致了这些哺乳动物的灭绝。

推理结构

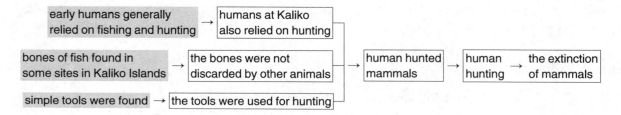

写作要求 *alternative explanations*

提　纲

1. No evidence could indicate that Kaliko people also relied on fishing and hunting for food; they might have other sources of food. (*C.S.*) ★★★

2. The bones of fish could be discarded by other predators. (*U.A.*) ★★★★

3. The author treats a lack of proof that humans at Kaliko did not hunt the mammals as sufficient proof that they did hunt them. (*Does the study make any difference?/I.E.*) ★★★★

4. The humans at Kaliko may use the tools for other purposes, although the tools are capable of hunting. (*U.A.*) ★★★

5. The extinction could be explained by other factors, such as the change in the climate, or some geological factors. (*U.A.*) ★★★★★

论证要点

　　本题主要问题在于作者提出的古代人类通常依靠打渔和捕猎为生、鱼骨场所的发现、简单工具的发现都不足以证明Kaliko岛的人类也捕猎哺乳动物。该岛居民有可能有其他食物来源、被发现的场所的鱼骨有可能是其他食肉动物丢弃的、被发现的工具尽管可以用来捕猎但Kaliko居民制造它们的目的未必在此等，都是对作者推理过程的其他可能解释。

　　请注意本题和Argument作文题库54题的区别：54题的结论是人类没有导致这些动物的灭绝；而这道题正好相反，认为人类捕猎导致了这些动物的灭绝。

95. The following appeared in an editorial in a business magazine.

55 "Although the sales of Whirlwind video games have declined（1）over the past two years, *a recent survey of video-game players suggests that this sales trend is about to be reversed*. The survey asked video-game players what features they thought were most important in a video game（2）. According to the survey, players prefer games that provide lifelike graphics, which require the most up-to-date computers（3）. Whirlwind has just introduced several such games with an extensive advertising campaign directed at people ten to twenty-five years old（4）, the age-group most likely to play video games. **It follows, then, that the sales of Whirlwind video games are likely to increase(5) dramatically in the next few months.**"（former 147）
★★★

翻　译 尽管Whirlwind公司的游戏销量在过去2年下降了，但最近一次对于电子游戏玩家的调查显示这种销售趋势可能会逆转。该调查询问游戏玩家，他们认为对于一个游戏来说最重要的特征是什么。根据调查结果，玩家倾向于那些需要最先进的电脑的、具有栩栩如生图像的游戏。Whirlwind刚刚通过广告活动向10~25岁的人群大力推广若干此类游戏，而10~25岁是最喜欢玩游戏的年龄层。这说明Whirlwind公司的游戏销量将会在未来几个月猛增。

推理结构

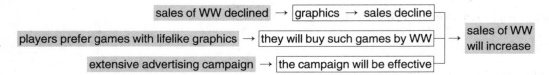

写作要求 *assumptions*

提　纲

1. The author unfairly assumes that it is the graphics that lead to the decline in their sales of video games.（*N.C.R.*）★★★

2. Many other questions that are directly related to the conclusion are ignored by the author.（*What question was asked in the survey?*）
   该调查所问的问题只能说明玩家喜欢图像逼真的游戏，但并不一定说明他们一定会买WW制作的游戏。其他决定游戏销量与质量的因素，比如市场、价格等等，作者都没有考虑。★★★★

3. The author fails to analyze how many players have access to such most up-to-date computers.（*I.I./ feasibility of the conclusion*）★★★

4. No evidence could indicate that players 10−25 years old will also value graphics as the most important feature.（*C.S.*）★★★

5. Sales of video games are determined by many factors. The author hastily assumes that improving graphics alone could ensure the increase in sales, ignoring other features that may also influence the overall quality of a game.（*I.T. /sufficiency of the solution*）★★★

论证要点

　　本题论证点首先是调查所问的问题和作者的判断有些脱节，被调查玩家把图像看做游戏的第一重要因素并不一定说明玩家会愿意购买WW新推出的游戏。其次，作者所说的广告策略未必一定能起到他所想象的良好效果。另外,由于没有深入分析导致公司销售疲软的真正原因,作者所说的策略未必一定足以保证销量上升。

---

96. The following appeared in a memo from the vice president of marketing at Dura-Sock, Inc.

56 "*A recent study of our customers suggests that our company is wasting the money it spends on its patented Endure manufacturing process (1)*, which ensures that our socks are strong enough to last for two years. We have always advertised our use of the Endure process, but the new study shows that despite our socks' durability, our average customer actually purchases new Dura-Socks every three months. Furthermore, our customers surveyed in our largest market, northeastern United States cities (2), say that they most value Dura-Socks' stylish appearance and availability in many colors (3). **These findings suggest that we can increase our profits (4,6) by discontinuing use of the Endure manufacturing process (5).**" (former 111) ★★★

翻　译 最近一次对顾客的调查表明,我们公司花在专利工艺Endure上的钱是浪费的,这种工艺使我们生产的袜子足以使用2年。我们一直在做广告宣传使用Endure工艺,但这次新调查显示,尽管我们的袜子很耐穿,但顾客一般每3个月就会买新的Dura-Sock袜子。而且,在我们最大的市场——美国东北部城市——回应调查的Dura-Sock消费者说他们最欣赏Dura-Sock时尚的外观和众多的颜色选择。这些发现说明,我们可以通过停止使用Endure工艺来增加赢利。

推理结构

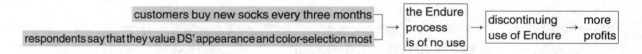

写作要求 *assumptions*

提　纲

1. The vice president fails to rule out the possibility that the customers purchase new Dura-Socks frequently just because they favor the Endure process. (*I.T.*) ★★★★

2. The customers surveyed in northeastern United States cities may not be representative of all customers. (*Are the respondents representative?*) ★★★

3. The study cited by the president does not imply that our customers no longer care about the durability of socks. (*I.E.*) ★★★★

4. The vice president fails to inform us the cost of using Endure process, thus we cannot evaluate the vice president's conclusion. (*adv:disadv*)
   如果该工艺的投入并不大,那么停止使用该工艺就没有太大意义,也不能显著节约成本。★★★

5. The vice president fails to consider the negative effect of discontinuing use of the process. (*adv: disadv*) ★★★★

6. The vice president fails to consider and analyze other factors that would influence the profits. (*sufficiency of the solution*) ★★

上述1~3三点都旨在说明作者认为Endure工艺已经没有吸引力的假设不一定成立。4、5两点主要是论证停止使用这种工艺的可能影响。

---

97. The following appeared in a memo from the vice president of marketing at Dura-Sock, Inc.

57 *"A recent study of our customers suggests that our company is wasting the money it spends on its patented Endure manufacturing process(1)*, which ensures that our socks are strong enough to last for two years. We have always advertised our use of the Endure process, but the new study shows that despite our socks' durability, our average customer actually purchases new Dura-Socks every three months. Furthermore, our customers surveyed in our largest market, northeastern United States cities(2), say that they most value Dura-Socks' stylish appearance and availability in many colors(3). **These findings suggest that we can increase our profits (4,6) by discontinuing use of the Endure manufacturing process (5).**"

(former 111, =56) ★★★

翻　译 最近一次对于顾客的调查表明，我们公司花在专利工艺Endure上的钱是浪费的，这种工艺使我们生产的袜子足以使用2年。我们一直在做广告宣传使用Endure工艺，但这次新调查显示，尽管我们的袜子很耐穿，但顾客一般每3个月就会购买新的Dura-Sock袜子。而且，在我们最大的市场——美国东北部城市——回应调查的Dura-Sock消费者说他们最欣赏Dura-Sock时尚的外观和众多的颜色选择。这些发现说明，我们可以通过停止使用Endure工艺来增加赢利。

推理结构

customers buy new socks every three months

respondents say that they value DS' appearance and color-selection most

→ the Endure process is of no use → discontinuing use of Endure → more profits

---

写作要求 *What specific **evidence** is needed to evaluate the argument?*

提　纲

作者需要提供能用于排除以下情况的证据：

1.　The possibility that customers purchase new Dura-Socks frequently just because they favor the Endure process. (*I.T.*) ★★★★

作者还需要提供证据来证明：

2.　The customers surveyed in northeastern United States cities are representative of all their customers. (*Are the respondents representative?*) ★★★

对于上文论述还存在以下问题：

3.　The study cited by the vice president does not imply that our customers no longer care about the durability of socks. (*I.E.*) ★★★★

4.　We cannot evaluate the vice president's prediction without knowing the cost of using Endure process. (*adv: disadv*)

如果该工艺的投入并不大，那么停止使用该工艺就没有太大意义，也不能显著节约成本。★★★

作者还需要提供关于以下方面的信息：

5.　The negative effect of discontinuing the use of the process. (*adv: disadv*) ★★★★

6.　Other factors that influence their profits. (*sufficiency of the solution*) ★★

上述1~3三点旨在说明Endure工艺未必已经没有吸引力；4、5两点主要是论证停止使用这种工艺的可能影响。

---

98. The following appeared in a memo from the vice president of marketing at Dura-Socks, Inc.

[82] *"A recent study of Dura-Socks customers suggests that our company is wasting the money it spends on its patented Endure manufacturing process (1), which ensures that our socks are strong enough to last for two years. We have always advertised our use of the Endure process, but the new study shows that despite the socks' durability, our customers, on average, actually purchase new Dura-Socks every three months. Furthermore, customers surveyed in our largest market—northeastern United States cities (2)—say that they most value Dura-Socks' stylish appearance and availability in many colors (3).* **These findings suggest that we can increase our profits (4,6) by discontinuing use of the Endure manufacturing process (5)."**
(former 111, =56, 57) ★★★

翻　译 最近一次对于Dura-Socks顾客的调查表明，我们公司花在专利工艺Endure上的钱是浪费的，这种工艺使我们生产的袜子足以使用2年。我们一直在做广告宣传使用Endure工艺，但这次新调查显示，尽管我们的袜子很耐穿，但顾客一般每3个月就会买新的Dura-Sock袜子。而且，在我们最大的市场——美国东北部城市——回应调查的Dura-Sock消费者说，他们最欣赏Dura-Sock时尚的外观和众多的颜色选择。这些发现说明，我们可以通过停止使用Endure工艺来增加赢利。

推理结构

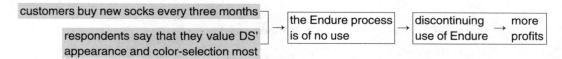

写作要求 What **questions** should be answered to decide whether the recommendation and the argument are reasonable?

提　纲

1. Is there possibility that the customers purchase new Dura-Socks frequently just because they favor the Endure process? (*I.T.*) ★★★★

2. Are the customers surveyed in northeastern United States cities representative of all customers? (*Are the respondents representative?*) ★★★

3. Does the study cited by the vice president necessarily imply that customers no longer care about the durability of socks? (*I.E.*) ★★★★

4. How about the cost of using Endure process? (*adv:disadv*)
   如果该工艺的投入并不大，那么停止使用该工艺就没有太大意义，也不能显著节约成本。★★★

5. Are there any negative effects of discontinuing the use of the process? (*adv:disadv*) ★★★★

6. Are there other factors that would influence the profits? (*sufficiency of the solution*) ★★

上述1~3三点旨在分析作者认为Endure工艺已经没有吸引力的假设；4、5两点主要是分析停止使用这种工艺的可能影响。

---

99. The following appeared in a memo from the president of Bower Builders, a company that constructs new homes.

59

"A nationwide survey(1) reveals that the two most-desired home features(2) are a large family room and a large, well-appointed kitchen. A number of homes in our area built by our competitor Domus Construction have such features and have sold much faster and at significantly higher prices than the national average(3,4,5). **To boost sales and profits(6), we should increase the size of the family rooms and kitchens in all the homes we build and should make state-of-the-art kitchens a standard feature(7,8).** Moreover, our larger family rooms and kitchens can come at the expense of the dining room, since many of our recent buyers(9) say they do not need a separate dining room for family meals (10)." (former 94) ★★

翻　译 一项全国调查发现，人们最想拥有的两项家庭设施就是大型家庭室和设备齐全的大型厨房。我们的竞争对手Domus Construction在本地区开发的一些新住宅提供了这些设施，这些住宅的销售速度和售价显著高于全国平均水平。为增加我们的销售和利润，我们应该在我们所建的住宅中增加家庭室面积并将先进厨房作为标准配置。而且，这些更大的家庭室和厨房可以通过牺牲餐厅来获得，因为我们最近的很多顾客说他们不需要家庭用餐的独立餐厅。

推理结构

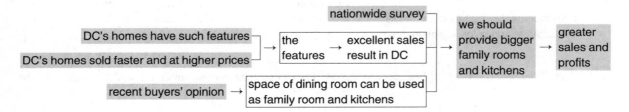

写作要求 *assumptions*

提　纲

1. The result of the nationwide survey does not necessarily apply to all specific regions. (*C.S.*) ★★★★

2. Many other features are also important for consumers when they make the decision of buying a house. (*sufficiency of the solution*) ★★★

3. The president unfairly assumes that it is those features that resulted in the fast selling and higher price of the homes built by Domus. (*N.C.R.*) ★★★★★

4. The president fails to provide any information about the profits Domus gained from the mentioned development. (*I.I.*)
    如果这些住宅仅仅售价高、卖得快，但利润并不高，那么借鉴Domus的做法就没有太多意义。★★★

5. There may be significant differences between Bower and Domus. (*F.A.*) ★★★

6. Merely including the new features in new homes may not sufficiently ensure our sales and profits to increase. (*sufficiency of the solution*) ★★

7. The president fails to illustrate the necessity of including the features in all new homes. (*C.S./necessity of the solution*) ★★

8. The president fails to consider the possible cost of providing these features, thus we cannot ensure the increase in profits. (*adv:disadv*) ★★★

9. The feedback from the recent buyers may not be representative of all consumers. (*C.S.*) ★★★

10. The fact that recent buyers did not care about separate dining rooms does not indicate there will not be any such demand in the future. (*C→F*) ★★★

论证要点

主要论证环节：一、全国调查结果未必说明各地区情况；二、Domus的销售业绩未必是因为提供了上述设施带来的；三、最近的顾客的意见未必能代表将来的趋势以及所有潜在客户的看法。

---

100. The following appeared in a letter from a firm providing investment advice for a client.

60 "<u>Most homes in the northeastern United States, where winters are typically cold, have traditionally used oil as their major fuel for heating.</u> Last heating season that region experienced 90 days with below-normal temperatures, and climate forecasters（1）predict that this weather pattern will continue for several more years. Furthermore, many new homes are being built in the region in response to recent population growth（2）. Because of these trends, **we predict an increased demand for heating oil (3,4) and recommend investment in Consolidated Industries(5)**, one of whose major business operations is the retail sale of home heating oil."
(former 66) ★★★★

翻　译 在冬季寒冷的美国东北部的多数家庭，传统上使用油料作为主要的采暖燃料。上一个采暖季，该地区经历了90天低于平均水平的气温，并且气象预报预测这样的气候还会持续很多年。而且，该地区去年针对最近的人口增长新建了很多住宅。基于这些趋势，我们预测对于采暖用油料的需求将会增加，因此建议对Consolidated Industries进行投资，它的主营业务之一是家用采暖油料的零售。

推理结构

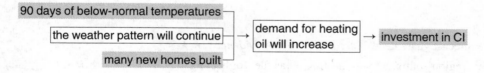

写作要求 *assumptions*

提　纲

1. The accuracy of the prediction is open to doubt. (*credibility of the evidence*) ★★★

2. No evidence could guarantee that new homes in this region will continue to use heating oil as fuel for heating. (*U.A./P→F*) ★★★

3. Other new heating fuel or heating methods may be available currently or in the near future. (*I.T.*) ★★★

4. The author does not provide any information about the actual amount of heating oil used due to the cold weather last year, thus we cannot evaluate the argument. (*I.I.*) ★★★★

5. Granted that the demand for heating oil will increase, we cannot guarantee that investing in Consolidated Industries will be profitable. (*C.S./sufficiency of the solution*) ★★★★

本题主要假设：一、低温天气确实会持续；二、持续低温确实导致油料使用增加；三、新建住宅仍会使用油料采暖；四、使用油料采暖的家庭会购买CI的产品；五、决定公司业绩的其他关键因素不会产生不利变化。

101. The following appeared in a memo to the board of directors of a company that specializes in the delivery of heating oil.
145

"Most homes in the northeastern United States, where winters are typically cold, have traditionally used oil as their major fuel for heating. Last heating season, that region experienced 90 days with below-normal temperatures, and climate forecasters（1）predict that this weather pattern will continue for several more years. Furthermore, many new homes are being built in the region in response to recent population growth（2）. Because of these trends, **we can safely predict that this region will experience an increased demand（3,4）for heating oil during the next five years.**"（former 66, ≈60）★ ★ ★

翻 译 在冬季寒冷的美国东北部大多数家庭，传统上使用油料作为主要采暖燃料。上一个采暖季，该地区经历了90天低于平均水平的气温，并且气象预报预测这样的气候还会持续很多年。而且，该地区为最近的人口增长新建了很多住宅。基于这些趋势，我们有把握预见，该地区在未来5年将出现采暖油料需求的增加。

推理结构

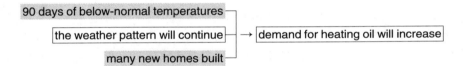

写作要求 *What questions should be answered to decide whether the prediction and the argument are reasonable?*

提 纲

1. Is the accuracy of the forecast guaranteed?（*credibility of the evidence*）★ ★ ★
2. Will new homes in this region continue to use heating oil as fuel for heating?（*U.A./P→F*）★ ★ ★
3. Are other new heating fuels or heating methods available currently or in the near future?（*I.T.*）★ ★ ★
4. What is the actual amount of heating oil used due to the cold weather last year?（*I.I.*）★ ★ ★ ★

论证要点

本题主要需要论证的环节在于：一、低温天气是否确实会持续；二、新建住宅是否仍会使用油料采暖；三、在未来是否有其他替代能源；四、持续低温是否确实导致油料使用增加。作者需要回答以上问题才能更好地评价上文论述。

102. The following appeared in a memo to the board of directors of a company that specializes in the delivery of heating oil.
146

"Most homes in the northeastern United States, where winters are typically cold, have traditionally used oil as their major fuel for heating. Last heating season, that region experienced 90 days with below-normal temperatures, and climate forecasters(1) predict that this weather pattern will continue for several more years. Furthermore, many new homes are being built in the region in response to recent population growth(2). Because of these trends, **we can safely predict that this region will experience an increased demand (3,4) for heating oil during the next five years.**" (former 66, ≈60, =145) ★ ★ ★

翻　译　在冬季寒冷的美国东北部大多数家庭，传统上使用油料作为主要的采暖燃料。上一个采暖季，该地区经历了90天低于平均水平的气温，并且气象预报预测这样的气候还会持续很多年。而且，该地区为最近的人口增长新建了很多住宅。基于这些趋势，我们有把握预见，该地区在未来5年将出现采暖油料需求的增加。

推理结构

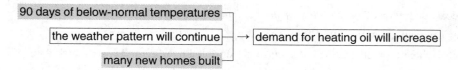

写作要求　*What specific **evidence** is needed to evaluate the argument?*

提　纲　作者需要提供能够说明以下方面问题的信息或论据：

1. The accuracy of the forecast. (*credibility of the evidence*) ★ ★ ★
2. Information about the heating method used by the new homes in this region. (*U.A./P→F*) ★ ★ ★
3. Information about the availability and application of other new heating fuels or heating methods. (*I.T.*) ★ ★ ★
4. The actual amount of heating oil used due to the cold weather last year. (*I.I.*) ★ ★ ★ ★

论证要点

　　本题主要需要论证的环节在于：一、低温天气是否确实会持续；二、新建住宅是否仍会使用油料采暖；三、在未来是否有其他替代能源；四、持续低温是否确实导致油料使用增加。作者需要提供论据来说明以上问题。

103. The following appeared in a letter from a firm providing investment advice to a client.

[150] "Homes in the northeastern United States, where winters are typically cold, have traditionally used oil as their major fuel for heating. Last year that region experienced 90 days with below-average temperatures, and climate forecasters(1) at Waymarsh University predict that this weather pattern will continue for several more years. Furthermore, many new homes have been built in this region during the past year(2). *Because these developments will certainly result in an increased demand for heating oil* (3,4), **we recommend investment in Consolidated Industries(5), one of whose major business operations is the retail sale of home heating oil.**" (former 66, ≈60, 145, 146) ★ ★ ★

翻　译　在冬季寒冷的美国东北部家庭，传统上使用油料作为主要的采暖燃料。去年该地区经历了90天低于平均水平的气温，并且Waymarsh大学气象预报预测这样的气候还会持续很多年。而且，该地区在去年新建了很多住宅。由于这些变化肯定会导致采暖油料需求的增加，因此，我们建议对Consolidated Industries进行投资，其主要业务之一就是家用采暖油料的零售。

推理结构

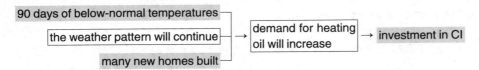

写作要求

What **questions** should be answered to decide whether the recommendation and the argument are reasonable?

提　纲

1. Is the accuracy of the forecast guaranteed? (*credibility of the evidence*) ★★★
2. Will new homes in this region continue to use oil as fuel for heating? (*U.A./P→F*) ★★★
3. Are other new heating fuels or heating methods available currently or in the near future? (*I.T.*) ★★★
4. What is the actual amount of heating oil used due to the cold weather last year? (*I.I.*) ★★★★
5. Granted that the demand for heating oil will increase, will investing in Consolidated Industries be profitable? (*C.S.*) ★★★★

论证要点

本题主要需要论证的环节在于：一、低温天气是否确实会持续；二、新建住宅是否仍会使用油料采暖；三、在未来是否有其他替代能源；四、持续低温是否确实导致油料使用增加；五、采暖油料需求增加是否一定能保证CI的业绩上升。

---

104. The following appeared in a letter from a firm providing investment advice to a client.

154 "Homes in the northeastern United States, where winters are typically cold, have traditionally used oil as their major fuel for heating. Last year that region experienced twenty days with below-average temperatures, and local weather forecasters (1) throughout the region predict that this weather pattern will continue for several more years. Furthermore, many new homes have been built in this region during the past year (2). Based on these developments, *we predict a large increase in the demand for heating oil (3,4)*. **Therefore, we recommend investment in Consolidated Industries (5)**, one of whose major business operations is the retail sale of home heating oil." (former 66, ≈60, 145, 146, 150) ★★★

翻　译 在冬季寒冷的美国东北部家庭，传统上使用油料作为主要的采暖燃料。去年该地区经历了20天低于平均水平的气温，并且整个地区的气象预报预测这样的气候还会持续很多年。而且，该地区在去年新建了很多住宅。基于这些变化，我们预计采暖油料的需求将大幅增加。因此，我们建议对Consolidated Industries进行投资，其主要业务之一就是家用采暖油料的零售。

推理结构

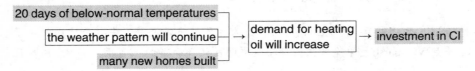

提　纲

1. Is the accuracy of the forecast guaranteed? (*credibility of the evidence*) ★★★
2. Will new homes in this region continue to use oil as fuel for heating? (*U.A./P→F*) ★★★
3. Are other new heating fuels or heating methods available currently or in the near future? (*I.T.*) ★★★
4. What is the actual amount of heating oil used due to the cold weather last year? (*I.I.*) ★★★★
5. Granted that the demand for heating oil will increase, will investing in Consolidated Industries be profitable? (*C.S.*) ★★★★

论证要点

本题主要需要论证的环节在于：一、低温天气是否确实会持续；二、新建住宅是否仍会使用油料采暖；三、在未来是否有其他替代能源；四、持续低温是否确实导致油料使用增加；五、采暖油料需求增加是否一定能保证CI的业绩上升。

---

105. The following appeared in a letter from a firm providing investment advice to a client.

[155] "Homes in the northeastern United States, where winters are typically cold, have traditionally used oil as their major fuel for heating. Last year that region experienced twenty days with below-average temperatures, and local weather forecasters (1) throughout the region predict that this weather pattern will continue for several more years. Furthermore, many new homes have been built in this region during the past year (2). Because of these developments, **we predict an increased demand for heating oil (3, 4) and recommend investment in Consolidated Industries (5)**, one of whose major business operations is the retail sale of home heating oil." (former 66, ≈60, 145, 146, 150, 154) ★★★

翻　译 在冬季寒冷的美国东北部家庭，传统上使用油料作为主要的采暖燃料。去年该地区经历了20天低于平均水平的气温，并且整个地区的气象预报预测这样的气候还会持续很多年。而且，该地区在去年新建了很多住宅。基于这些变化，我们预计采暖油料的需求将大幅增加，因此建议对Consolidated Industries进行投资，其主要业务之一就是家用采暖油料的零售。

推理结构

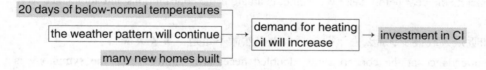

写作要求 *What specific **evidence** is needed to evaluate the argument?*

提　纲

作者需要提供能说明以下方面问题的信息或论据：

1. The accuracy of the forecast. (*credibility of the evidence*) ★★★
2. Information about the heating method used by new homes in this region. (*U.A./P→F*) ★★★
3. Information about the availability and application of other new heating fuels or heating methods. (*I.T.*) ★★★

4. The actual amount of heating oil used due to the cold weather last year. (*I.I.*) ★★★★

5. Investing in Consolidated Industries will be profitable. (*C.S.*) ★★★★

论证要点

本题主要需要论证的环节在于：一、低温天气是否确实会持续；二、新建住宅是否仍会使用油料采暖；三、在未来是否有其他替代能源；四、持续低温是否确实导致油料使用增加；五、采暖油料需求增加是否一定能保证CI的业绩上升。

---

106. The following appeared in an article in the *Grandview Beacon*.

61 "For many years the city of Grandview has provided annual funding for the Grandview Symphony. Last year, however, private contributions to the symphony increased by 200 percent(1) and attendance at the symphony's concerts-in-the-park series doubled(1,2,3). The symphony has also announced an increase in ticket prices for next year (4). Given such developments, *some city commissioners argue that the symphony can now be fully self-supporting,* and **they recommend that funding for the symphony be eliminated from next year's budget (5).**" (former 68) ★★★

翻　译 很多年来，Grandview市都按年度资助Grandview交响乐团。然而去年，对乐团的个人资助增加了200%，乐团的公园音乐会系列演出听众人数也翻了一番。乐团还宣布明年票价将会提高。鉴于这些变化，一些市委成员辩称乐团现在完全能够自给自足，并建议在下一年的预算中停止对乐团的资助。

推理结构

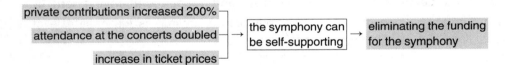

写作要求 *What **questions** should be answered to decide whether the recommendation and the argument are reasonable?*

提　纲

1. What's the base amount of private contributions to the symphony the year before last? What's the actual attendance at the concerts the year before last? We cannot evaluate if the contributions and attendance were significant. (*V.D.*)
   如果前年的资助和听众人数很少，那么去年即使翻番也仍然微不足道。★★★★

2. Does the fact that attendance at the concert series doubled necessarily indicate that the symphony is operating successfully? (*U.C.*) ★★★

3. Will the phenomena cited by the planner, including the increased private contributions, popularity of concert series, recur in the following years? (*P→F*) ★★★★

4. How much will the ticket prices actually increase? (*I.I.*) ★★

5. Will there be any negative effects of eliminating the funding? (*adv:disadv*) ★★★

论证要点

本题主要论证环节在于，作者提供的数据和信息都不足以说明乐团现在能够自给自足，因而取消资助可能会对乐队运作造成困难或其他不利影响。

107. The following appeared in a memo from a budget planner for the city of Grandview.

139 "Our citizens are well aware of the fact that while the Grandview Symphony Orchestra was struggling to succeed, our city government promised annual funding to help support its programs. Last year, however, private contributions to the symphony increased by 200 percent (1), and attendance at the symphony's concerts-in-the-park series doubled (2,3). The symphony has also announced an increase in ticket prices for next year (4). *Such developments indicate that the symphony can now succeed without funding from city government and we can eliminate that expense from next year's budget.* **Therefore, we recommend that the city of Grandview eliminate its funding for the Grandview Symphony from next year's budget.** *By doing so, we can prevent a city budget deficit without threatening the success of the symphony (5).*" (former 68, ≈61) ★★★

翻 译 我们的市民都注意到，当Grandview管弦乐团为其维持做斗争的时候，市政府承诺每年提供资助来支持乐团的计划。然而去年，对乐团的个人资助增加了200%，乐团的公园音乐会系列演出听众人数翻了一番。乐团还宣布明年票价将会提高。这些事实说明，乐团可以不依靠市政府的资助就能维持，因此，我们可以取消来年预算中这项支出。因而，我们建议Grandview市从来年预算中取消对Grandview管弦乐团的资助。这样做肯定能够在不影响乐团成功的前提下防止本市预算赤字。

推理结构

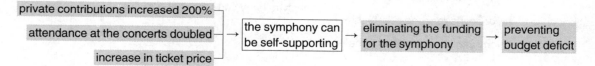

写作要求 *What **questions** should be answered to decide whether the recommendation will have the predicted result?*

提 纲

1. What's the base amount of private contributions to the symphony the year before last? What's the actual attendance at the concerts the year before last? We cannot evaluate if the contributions and attendance were significant. (*V.D.*)
   如果前年的资助和听众人数很少，就算去年翻番也仍然微不足道。★★★★

2. Does the fact that attendance at the concert series doubled necessarily indicate that the symphony is operating successfully? (*U.C.*) ★★★

3. Will the phenomena cited by the planner, including the increased private contributions, popularity of concert series, recur in the following years? (*P→F*) ★★★★

4. How much will the ticket prices actually increase? (*I.I.*) ★★

5. Is eliminating the funding for the symphony alone sufficient for preventing a budget deficit? (*sufficiency of the solution*) ★★★★

论证要点

本题主要论证环节在于，作者提供的数据和信息不足以说明乐队现在能够自给自足，因而取消资助可能会对乐队运作造成困难或其他不利影响。

108. The following appeared in a memo to the board of the Grandview Symphony.

141 "The city of Grandview has provided annual funding for the Grandview Symphony since the symphony's inception ten years ago. Last year the symphony hired an internationally known conductor, who has been able to attract high-profile guest musicians to perform with the symphony（1）. Since then, private contributions to the symphony have doubled（2）and attendance at the symphony's concerts-in-the-park series has reached new highs（3,4）. *Now that the Grandview Symphony is an established success, it can raise ticket prices (5).* **Increased revenue from larger audiences and higher ticket prices will enable the symphony to succeed without funding from the city government (6).**"（former 68, ≈ 61,139）★ ★ ★

翻　译 Grandview市从10年前Grandview交响乐团设立时开始每年对其提供资助。去年乐团雇用了一名国际知名指挥，他有能力吸引著名音乐家和乐团客串演出。从那以后，乐团获得的私人捐助翻了一番，乐团的公园音乐会系列演出的听众人数也创下新高。Grandview乐团获得了成功，因此它可以提高票价。更多由听众带来的收入和更高的票价将能使乐团在没有市政府资助的情况下成功运作。

推理结构

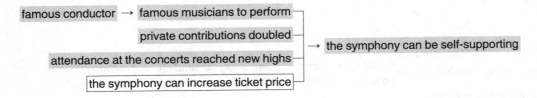

写作要求 *What specific **evidence** is needed to evaluate the argument?*

提　纲
作者需要提供能说明以下方面问题的信息和论据：

1. The conductor is able to continue attracting famous musicians to perform with the symphony.（P→F）★ ★ ★ ★

2. The base amount of private contributions to the symphony the year before last, and the actual attendance at the concerts. We cannot evaluate whether the contributions and attendance were significant.（V.D.）
    如果前年的私人捐助数量很少，那么，去年即使捐助翻番也仍然微不足道。★ ★ ★ ★

3. The attendance at the concert series could indicate the success in the symphony's operation.（U.C.）★ ★ ★

4. The situation cited, including the increased private contributions, popularity of concert series, will recur in the following years.（P→F）★ ★ ★ ★

5. The negative impact of raising ticket price on the symphony's reputation and operation.（I.I.）★ ★

6. Further information about negative effects of eliminating government funding.（adv:disadv）★ ★ ★

论证要点
本题主要论证环节在于，作者提供的数据和信息不足以说明乐队现在能够自给自足，而且也未必能保证这些成功的现象在将来依然会持续。因而，乐队的运作仍然可能在一定程度上需要依靠政府资助。

109. The following appeared in a memo from a budget planner for the city of Grandview.

143 "When the Grandview Symphony was established ten years ago, the city of Grandview agreed to provide the symphony with annual funding until the symphony became self-sustaining. Two years ago, the symphony hired an internationally known conductor, who has been able to attract high-profile guest musicians to perform with the symphony（1）. Since then, private contributions to the symphony have tripled（2）and attendance at the symphony's outdoor summer concert series has reached record highs（3,4,5）. *Now that the symphony has succeeded in finding an audience,* **the city can eliminate its funding of the symphony (6).**"
（former 68, ≈61,139, 141）★ ★ ★

翻　译 10年前当Grandview交响乐团成立的时候，Grandview市同意在乐团能够自给自足之前按年度给予资助。2年前，乐团雇用了一名国际知名指挥，他能够吸引著名音乐家来乐团客串演出。从那以后，对乐队的个人资助增加了两倍，乐队夏季户外系列音乐会的听众人数也创下历史纪录。由于Grandview乐团已能够成功吸引听众，因此，本市可以取消对乐团的资助。

推理结构

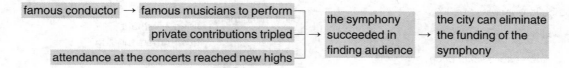

写作要求 *assumptions*

提　纲

1. The planner hastily assumes that the conductor will be able to continue attracting famous musicians to perform with the symphony.（P→F）★ ★ ★ ★

2. Without knowing the base amount of private contributions to the symphony the year before last, and the actual attendance at the concerts, we cannot evaluate whether the contributions and attendance were significant.（V.D.）
如果前年的个人资助数额很少，那么，去年即使资助增加两倍仍然微不足道。★ ★ ★ ★

3. The tripled attendance at the concert series does not necessarily indicate the success in the symphony's operation.（U.C.）★ ★ ★

4. The planner hasilty assumes that the situation cited above, including the increased private contributions, popularity of concert series, will recur in the following years.（P→F）★ ★ ★ ★

5. The attendance at the concert series is not sufficient for illustrating the symphony's ability of attracting audience.（C.S.）★ ★

6. The planner fails to consider the negative effects of eliminating government funding.（adv:disadv）★ ★ ★

论证要点
　　本题主要论证环节在于，作者提供的数据和信息不足以说明乐队现在能够自给自足，而且也未必能保证这些成功的现象在将来依然会持续。因而，乐队的运作仍然可能在一定程度上需要依靠政府资助。

110. The following appeared in a memo from a budget planner for the city of Grandview.

162 "*It is time for the city of Grandview to stop funding the Grandview Symphony Orchestra.* It is true that the symphony struggled financially for many years, but last year private contributions to the symphony increased by 200 percent(1) and attendance at the symphony's concerts-in-the-park series doubled(2,3,4). In addition, the symphony has just announced an increase in ticket prices for next year(5). **For these reasons, we recommend that the city eliminate funding for the Grandview Symphony Orchestra from next year's budget. We predict that the symphony will flourish in the years to come even without funding from the city (6).**" (former 68, ≈61, 139, 141, 143) ★ ★ ★

翻 译 现在是Grandview市停止对Grandview管弦乐团进行资助的时候了。很多年来,乐团确实在经济上存在困难,但去年对乐团的个人资助增加了200%,乐团的公园音乐会系列演出的听众人数翻番。而且,乐团刚刚宣布明年提高票价。由于这些原因,我们建议本市在明年的预算中取消对乐团的资助。我们预计,在没有本市资助的情况下,乐团能够在随后几年中保持繁荣。

推理结构

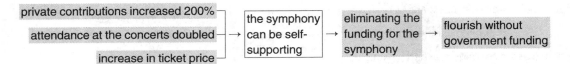

写作要求 *What **questions** should be answered to decide whether the recommendation will have the predicted result?*

提 纲

1. What's the base amount of private contributions to the symphony the year before last? What's the actual attendance at the concerts the year before last? We cannot evaluate whether the contributions and attendance were significant. (*V.D.*)
   如果前年的个人资助数额和听众人数很少,那么去年就算翻番也仍然微不足道。★ ★ ★ ★

2. Does the fact that attendance at the concert series doubled necessarily indicate that the symphony is operating successfully? (*U.C.*) ★ ★ ★

3. Could the attendance at the concert series sufficiently illustrate the symphony's ability of attracting audience? (*C.S.*) ★ ★

4. Will the phenomena cited by the planner, including the increased private contributions, popularity of concert series, recur in the following years? (*P→F*) ★ ★ ★ ★

5. How much will the ticket prices actually increase? (*I.I.*) ★ ★

6. Will there be any negative effects of eliminating the funding? (*adv:disadv*) ★ ★ ★

论证要点

本题主要论证环节在于,作者提供的数据和信息都不足以说明乐队现在能够自给自足。因而,取消资助可能会对乐队运作造成困难或其他不利影响。

111. The following appeared in a memo from the director of a large group of hospitals.

62 "In a laboratory study（1）of liquid antibacterial hand soaps, a concentrated solution of UltraClean produced a 40 percent greater（2）reduction in the bacteria population than did the liquid hand soaps currently used in our hospitals. During a subsequent test of UltraClean at our hospital in Workby, that hospital reported significantly fewer cases of patient infection（3）than did any of the other hospitals in our group（4）. **Therefore, to prevent serious patient infections（5）, we should supply UltraClean（8,9）at all（6）hand-washing stations throughout our hospital system（7）.**" (former 98) ★★

翻　译 在一次对抗菌洗手液的实验研究中，UltraClean浓缩液比我们医院现在使用的洗手液能多杀灭40%的细菌。在我们Workby医院随后所做的对UltraClean的测试中，该医院上报的患者感染数量显著少于我们集团的其他医院。因此，为防止严重交叉感染，我们应该在整个医院系统所有的洗手站提供UltraClean。

推理结构

UC produced 40% greater bacteria-reduction ┐
　　　　　　　　　　　　　　　　　　　　　├→ supply UC at all
W hospital reported fewer cases of infection → | UC → less infection | ┘　hand-washing stations

写作要求 *assumptions*

提　纲

1. The result of the laboratory study may not properly apply to **normal hospital environment**.（C.S.）★★★
2. The director fails to inform us whether the bacteria killed by UltraClean are all harmful.（I.I.）★★★
3. The director unfairly assumes that it is UltraClean that resulted in the fewer cases of patient infection at the tested hospital.（N.C.R.）★★★★
4. There may be many other differences between the tested hospital and its counterparts.（I.C.）★★★★★
5. The director fails to differentiate between the severity of infections at the tested hospital, thus we cannot ensure that UltraClean can effectively prevent **serious** infections.（I.T./C.S.）★★★★
   1~5：作者关于UltraClean杀菌效果出众的假设未必成立。
6. The success of UltraClean at the tested hospital, if any, does not necessarily recur at other hospitals.（C.S.）★★★
7. Granted that UltraClean is very effective in killing bacteria, the director does not demonstrate the necessity of supplying it at **all** hospitals.（*necessity of the solution*）★★★
8. The director overlooks other effective measures of preventing patient infections.（I.T.）★★
9. The director assumes that UltraClean will not have any side effect.（*adv:disadv*）★★

论证要点

　　本题主要问题在于文中提供的实验结果、对比测试未必说明作者认定的UC在杀灭有害细菌、预防严重感染方面非常有效的假设；其次，就算UC确实十分有效，是否有必要在所有医院使用UC，以及有没有其他办法来抗菌也都值得讨论。

112. The following appeared in a memo from the director of a large group of hospitals.

121 "In a controlled laboratory study (1) of liquid hand soaps, a concentrated solution of extra strength UltraClean hand soap produced a 40 percent greater reduction in harmful bacteria than did the liquid hand soaps currently used in our hospitals. During our recent test of regular-strength UltraClean with doctors, nurses, and visitors at our hospital in Worktown, the hospital reported significantly fewer cases of patient infection (2) (a 20 percent reduction) than did any of the other hospitals in our group (3). **Therefore, to prevent serious patient infections(5), we should supply UltraClean(7,8) at all(4) hand-washing stations, including those used by visitors, throughout our hospital system (6).**" (former 98, ≈62) ★★

翻　译 在一次对洗手液的对比实验研究中，UltraClean超强浓缩洗手液比我们医院现在使用的洗手液能多杀灭40%的有害细菌。在我们最近和Worktown医院的医生、护士和参观者共同进行的对UltraClean常规洗手液的测试中，医院报告的交叉感染的数量比我们集团其他任何医院都少得多（减少了20%）。因此，为防止严重的交叉感染，我们应该在我们整个医院系统所有的洗手站都提供UltraClean，包括那些参观者使用的洗手站。

推理结构

UC produced 40% greater bacteria-reduction

W hospital reported 20% fewer infection → UC → less infection → supply UC at all hand-washing stations

写作要求 *assumptions*

提　纲

1. The result of the **laboratory study** may not properly apply to **normal hospital environment**. (*C.S.*) ★★★

2. The director unfairly assumes that it is UltraClean that resulted in the fewer cases of patient infection at the tested hospital. (*N.C.R.*) ★★★★

3. There may be many other differences between the tested hospital and its counterparts. (*I.C.*) ★★★★★

4. The success of UltraClean at the tested hospital, if any, does not necessarily recur at other hospitals. (*C.S.*) ★★★

5. The director fails to differentiate between the severity of infections at the tested hospital, thus we cannot ensure that UltraClean can effectively prevent **serious** infections. (*I.T./C.S.*)
   如果UC杀灭的都是轻微感染，那么根据作者提供的信息未必说明UC能预防严重感染的结论。★★★★

6. Granted that UltraClean is very effective in killing bacteria, the director does not demonstrate the necessity of supplying it at **all** hospitals. (*necessity of the solution*) ★★★

7. The director overlooks other effective measures of preventing patient infections. (*I.T.*) ★★

8. The director fails to consider if UltraClean has any side effect. (*adv:disadv*) ★★

论证要点

文中提供的实验结果、对比测试未必说明UC在杀灭有害细菌、预防严重感染方面非常有效；其次，就算UC确实十分有效，是否有必要在所有医院使用UC，以及有没有其他办法来抗菌也都值得讨论。

113. The following appeared in a memo from the director of a large group of hospitals.

122 "In a controlled laboratory study of liquid hand soaps, a concentrated solution of extra strength UltraClean hand soap produced a 40 percent greater reduction in harmful bacteria than did the liquid hand soaps currently used in our hospitals. During our recent test of regular-strength UltraClean with doctors, nurses, and visitors at our hospital in Worktown, the hospital reported significantly fewer cases of patient infection(1)(a 20 percent reduction) than did any of the other hospitals in our group(2). **The explanation for the 20 percent reduction in patient infections is the use of UltraClean soap.**" (former 98, ≈62, 121) ★★★

翻　译 在一次对洗手液的对比实验研究中, UltraClean超强浓缩液比我们医院现在使用的洗手液能多杀灭40%的有害细菌。在我们最近和Worktown医院的医生、护士和参观者共同进行的对UltraClean常规洗手液的测试中, 医院报告的交叉感染的数量比我们集团其他任何医院都少得多(减少了20%)。这20%交叉感染减少的解释就是UltraClean洗手液的使用。

推理结构

UC produced 40% greater bacteria-reduction

W hospital reported 20% fewer infection

} → | UC → less infection |

写作要求 *alternative explanations*

提　纲

1. The fewer cases of patient infection at the tested hospital do not necessarily result from the using of UltraClean. Other factors, such as other effective anti-infection procedure, the experience of doctors and nurses, could also help to reduce the incidence of infection. (*N.C.R.*) ★★★★

2. There may be many other differences between the tested hospital and its counterparts, for example, the type and severity of patients' disease, other hospital facilities, environmental factors(e.g. temperature, humidity). (*I.C.*) ★★★★★

论证要点

　　对于上文被测试医院20%感染下降的其他解释主要是两方面:一、未必是洗手液导致感染数量少, 其他抗菌措施, 如医生护士的经验和能力等, 也可能是感染数量少的原因;二、被测试医院和其他医院的情况未必可比, 患者感染的严重性、环境因素都有可能导致其他医院感染数量多。

114. The following appeared in a memo from the director of a large group of hospitals.

124 "In a controlled laboratory study(1) of liquid hand soaps, a concentrated solution of extra strength UltraClean hand soap produced a 40 percent greater reduction in harmful bacteria than did the liquid hand soaps currently used in our hospitals. During our recent test of regular-strength UltraClean with doctors, nurses, and visitors at our hospital in Worktown, the hospital reported significantly fewer cases of patient infection(2) (a 20 percent reduction) than did any of the other hospitals in our group(3). **Therefore, to prevent serious patient infections (5), we should supply UltraClean(7,8) at all(4) hand-washing stations, including those used by visitors, throughout our hospital system(6).**" (former 98, ≈62,122, =121) ★★

多杀灭40%的有害细菌。在我们最近和Worktown医院的医生、护士和参观者共同进行的对UltraClean常规
洗手液的测试中，医院报告的交叉感染的数量比我们集团其他任何医院都少得多（减少了20%）。因此，
为防止严重交叉感染，我们应该在整个医院系统所有洗手站提供UltraClean，包括那些参观者使用的洗
手站。

推理结构

UC produced 40% greater bacteria-reduction

W hospital reported 20% fewer infection → UC → less infection → supply UC at all hand-washing stations

写作要求 *What specific **evidence** is needed to evaluate the argument?*

提　纲

作者需要提供能说明以下情况的信息或论据：

1. The result of the **laboratory study** could properly apply to **normal hospital environment**. (*C.S.*) ★ ★ ★
2. It is UltraClean that resulted in the fewer cases of patient infection at the tested hospital. (*N.C.R.*) ★ ★ ★ ★
3. Other differences between the tested hospital and its counterparts. (*I.C.*) ★ ★ ★ ★ ★
4. The success of UltraClean at the tested hospital, if any, will recur at other hospitals. (*C.S.*) ★ ★ ★
5. The severity of infections at the tested hospital. We cannot ensure that UltraClean can effectively prevent **serious** infections. (*I.T./C.S.*)

   如果UC杀灭的都是轻微感染，那么根据作者提供的信息未必说明UC能预防严重感染的结论。
   ★ ★ ★ ★

对于上文论述还存在以下问题：

6. Granted that UltraClean is very effective in killing bacteria, the director does not demonstrate the necessity of supplying it at **all** hospitals. (*necessity of the solution*) ★ ★ ★

   作者还需要提供能说明以下情况的信息或论据：

7. Other effective measures of preventing patient infections. (*I.T.*) ★ ★
8. The side effects of using UltraClean. (*adv:disadv*) ★ ★

论证要点

本题主要问题在于文中提供的实验结果、对比测试未必说明UC在杀灭有害细菌、预防严重感染方面非常有效；其次，就算UC确实十分有效，是否有必要在所有医院使用UC，以及有没有其他办法来抗菌也存在疑问。作者需要提供实质证据来说明以上关键环节。

---

115. The following appeared in a letter to the editor of the *Parkville Daily* newspaper.

63 "Throughout the country（1）last year, as more and more children below the age of nine participated in youth-league sports（2）, over 40,000 of these young players（3）suffered injuries（4,5,6）. When interviewed for a recent study, youth-league soccer players（7）in several major cities also reported psychological pressure（8）exerted by coaches and parents to win games. Furthermore, *education experts say that long practice sessions for these sports take away time that could be used for academic activities (9, 10)*. Since the disadvantages outweigh any advantages（11）, **we in Parkville should discontinue organized athletic competition (2) for children under nine.**" （former 206）★ ★

去年在全国范围内，随着越来越多9岁以下的儿童参加少年运动队，这些儿童选手中有超过40000人受伤。在最近一次研究所做的采访中，很多大城市的少年足球选手报告说存在来自教练和家长要求赢得比赛的心理压力。而且，教育专家指出这些运动项目长时间的训练占据了本应用于专业学习的时间。由于不利因素明显超过了有利因素，我们Parkville应该停止9岁以下儿童的有组织的体育比赛。

推理结构

40,000 young players injured

psychological pressure reported　→　discontinue athletic competition

practice sessions affect academic activities

写作要求 *assumptions*

提　纲

1.　The fact that many young players suffered injuries **throughout the country** does not necessarily indicate that **Parkville** should discontinue athletic competition.（*C.S.*）★★★

2.　Without information about in playing what kind of sports did those young players suffer injuries, we cannot evaluate whether **all** athletic competitions should be banned.（*I.I.*）★★★★

3.　Without the total number of children who participated in the competitions we could not evaluate the situation.（*V.D.*）
　　没有参赛儿童总数就无法判断受伤率，从而无法判断问题是否严重。★★★

4.　The author does not differentiate the severity of injuries.（*I.I.*）★★★

5.　We need to know the injury-rate of those young players compared with children who do not participate in these games.（*lack of controlled experiment*）★★★

6.　We do not know the rate of injuries before children participated in these games, thus could not determine if the situation are getting worse.（*confusing comparison and variation*）★★
　　3～6: The assumption that the youth-league sports are dangerous is unwarranted.

7.　The players in the recent study might not be representative of all young players.（*Are the respondents representative?*）★★★

8.　The young players at Parkville do not necessarily also suffer psychological pressure as the players do in those major cities.（*C.S.*）★★★★

9.　The author unfairly assumes that children would use the time for academic activities if they did not take part in those games.（*U.A.*）★★★

10.　No information about the academic performance of the children who participated in youth-leagues is provided, thus we could not judge whether we need to discontinue athletic competition to guarantee more time for academic activities of these students.（*I.I./necessity of the solution*）
　　如果这些儿童学习成绩和表现已然不错，则没有必要为了增加学习时间而取消体育运动。★★

11.　The author fails to consider the positive effects of athletic competition.（*adv:disadv*）★★★★

论证要点

　　本题可质疑的假设首先是作者认为这种少年体育比赛十分危险，但根据作者提供的数据未必能说明这一点。其次，由于缺乏导致儿童受伤的具体项目类型的信息，作者关于应全面禁止所有体育比赛的结论也存在问题。再次，作者又以全国或其他大城市的情况来类推P城市，但没有考虑P城市可能存在特殊性因而不会产生上述问题。

116. Collectors prize the ancient life-size clay statues of human figures made on Kali Island but have long wondered how Kalinese artists were able to depict bodies with such realistic precision. Since archaeologists have recently discovered molds of human heads and hands on Kali(1), **we can now conclude that the ancient Kalinese artists used molds of actual bodies, not sculpting tools and techniques, to create these statues(2,3).** *This discovery explains why Kalinese miniature statues were abstract and entirely different in style: molds could be used only for life-size sculptures(4). It also explains why few ancient Kalinese sculpting tools have been found(5,6).* **In light of this discovery, collectors predict that the life-size sculptures will decrease in value while the miniatures increase in value (7,8).** (former 56) ★★★★★

翻 译 收藏家很欣赏Kali岛出产的古代等身黏土人物雕像,但长期以来不清楚Kali的艺术家何以能够如此精确地刻画人体。考古学家最近在Kali发现了人类头部和手的模具,因此我们现在可以得出结论:古代Kali艺术家使用真人的模子,而不是雕刻工具和技艺来塑造这些雕像。这一发现解释了为什么Kali的缩微雕像是抽象的而且风格迥异:模子只能被用于等身雕像。它也同样解释了为什么很少发现Kali的雕刻工具。受该发现的影响,收藏家预计等身雕像将会贬值,而缩微雕像将会升值。

推理结构

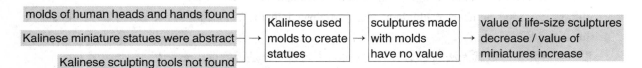

写作要求 *What **questions** should be answered to decide whether the prediction and the argument are reasonable?*

提 纲

1. Were the molds of human heads and hands used by Kalinese artists for sculpting? (*U.A.*) ★★★★

2. Granted that those molds were used for sculpting purposes, did Kalinese artists use molds to create **all** life-size statues? (*C.S.*) ★★★★

3. Is there any evidence to prove that Kalinese artists did not use any sculpting tools and techniques to create life-size statue? (*I.E.*) ★★★

4. Were there any other factors that would lead to the differences between miniature statues and life-size statures? (*I.C.*) ★★★★

5. Are there any alternative explanations that could explain why few ancient Kalinese sculpting tools have been found? (*N.C.R.*) ★★★

6. Does the fact that no sculpting tools found hitherto sufficiently illustrate that there wasn't any such tool existed? (*Does the information make any difference?*) ★★★★

7. Will the sculptures made by molds, or the molding technics themselves have certain artistic value? (*U.A.*) ★★★★

8. Do the discoveries and theories above have anything to do with the value of miniature statues? (*U.A./N.C.R.*) ★★★★

论证要点

本题关键环节在于模具的发现并不足以证明等身雕像一定是用模具制作的。同时,缩微雕像的不同风格以及没有发现Kali雕刻工具的事实也存在其他可能解释。最后，即使该雕像是用模具制作，但这种雕像以及该工艺本身仍然可能具有一定的艺术价值。

---

117. <u>When Stanley Park first opened, it was the largest, most heavily used public park in town.</u> It is [65] still the largest park, but it is no longer heavily used. Video cameras mounted in the park's parking lots last month（2）revealed *the park's drop in popularity:* the recordings showed an average of only 50 cars per day（1,3）. In contrast, tiny Carlton Park in the heart of the business district is visited by more than 150 people on a typical weekday（4,5）. An obvious difference is that Carlton Park, unlike Stanley Park, provides ample seating（6）. **Thus, if Stanley Park is ever to be as popular with our citizens as Carlton Park, the town will obviously need to provide more benches, thereby converting some of the unused open areas into spaces suitable for socializing (7,8).** (former 63) ★★★

翻　译 当Stanley公园首次开放的时候，它是本市最大、使用频率最高的公园。现在它仍是最大的，但使用频率已经不再高了。上个月在公园停车场架设的摄像头发现公园的受欢迎度下降：录像显示平均每天只有50辆车。与之相比，位于商业区中心地带的Carlton小公园在工作日每天游客超过150人。Carlton公园与Stanley公园一个很明显的差别就是前者提供充足的座椅。因此，如果Stanley公园想要和Carlton公园同样受欢迎的话，相关部门显然需要提供更多的长椅，从而把一些未加利用的开阔地转化成适于人们交往的空间。

推理结构

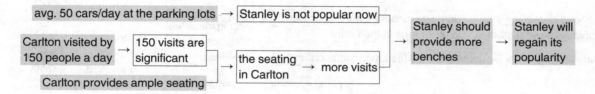

写作要求 *assumptions*

提　纲

1.　The number of cars at the park's parking lots may not be a good indication of the park's popularity. (*U.C.*) ★★★★

2.　There might be some special reasons last month that resulted in the dropped popularity of Stanley Park. (*selective sample*) ★★★★

3.　The author does not provide information concerning the number of visitors at Stanley before the cameras were mounted. (*confusing comparison with variation*) ★★★
　　1~3: The assumption that Stanley is no longer popular now is unfounded.

4.　The assumption that 150 visits per day are a significant indication of Carlton's popularity is open to doubt. (*U.C./I.I.*) ★★★

5.　Many other differences may render the two parks not comparable. (*I.C./F.A.*) ★★★

6.　The author fails to convince us that it is the ample seating that makes Carlton so popular. (*N.C.R.*) ★★★★

7.　The author fails to consider the possible negative effects of converting unused open areas into public social spaces. (*adv:disadv*) ★★★

8.　The author hastily assumes that there are no other better ways to attract visitors. (*necessity of the solution*) ★★★

论证要点

首先，作者提供的录像信息未必说明Stanley一定不再受欢迎了（1~3）；其次，文中信息也未必说明Carlton受欢迎（4）；而且把Carlton的一些特点照搬到Stanley未必能产生相同效果（5、6）。

---

118. The following appeared in a memo from the owner of a chain of cheese stores located throughout the United States.

66

"For many years all the stores in our chain have stocked a wide variety of both domestic and imported cheeses. Last year(1), however, all of the five best-selling cheeses at our newest store(2) were domestic cheddar cheeses from Wisconsin. Furthermore, a recent survey by *Cheeses of the World* magazine indicates an increasing preference for domestic cheeses among its subscribers(3). Since our company can reduce expenses by limiting inventory, **the best way(4) to improve profits(5) in all(2) of our stores is to discontinue stocking many of our varieties of imported cheese(6) and concentrate primarily on domestic cheeses.**"

（former 65）★ ★ ★

翻　　译 多年来，我们所有连锁店都储备了很多种类的国产奶酪和进口奶酪。然而去年，我们最新的店里5种销量最高的奶酪都是威斯康星州出产的cheddar奶酪。而且，最近一次由*Cheeses of the World*杂志进行的调查显示，其订阅者对于国产奶酪的倾向性越来越高。既然我们公司可以通过限制库存来减少开支，那么，在我们所有连锁店增加赢利的最好方式就是停止储备过多的进口奶酪而集中储备国产奶酪。

推理结构

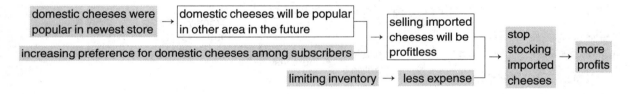

写作要求　*What **questions** should be answered to decide whether the recommendation will have the predicted result?*

提　　纲

1.　Is the situation last year a normal phenomenon? It does not indicate that domestic cheddar cheeses will also be popular in the future. (*P→F*) ★ ★ ★

2.　Is the situation at the newest store representative of all stores? (*selective sample / C.S.*) ★ ★ ★ ★

3.　The owner does not provide any information about the subscribers of *Cheese of the World*; are they representative of United States consumers? (*selective sample/Are the respondents representative?*) ★ ★ ★ ★

4.　Are there any other better ways available to improve profits? (*necessity of the solution*) ★ ★ ★

5.　Are there any negative effects of discontinuing the inventory of imported cheeses? (*adv:disadv*) ★ ★ ★ ★

6.　How about the actual profit of domestic and imported cheese respectively? We cannot estimate the change in profits without such information. (*I.I.*)
如果进口奶酪销量少但利润高，那么停止储存进口奶酪不一定有提升公司利润的作用。★ ★ ★ ★ ★

论证要点

本题关键环节在于作者认为本地奶酪将会受欢迎，但作者选取的去年、最新商店、杂志的订阅者都

244

是选择性样本，不能说明本地奶酪在所有地区、所有时间段都会有好的销量。另外，4~6三点则集中讨论停止储存进口奶酪对于增加利润的充分性和必要性以及可能带来的负面影响。

> **119.** The following appeared in a memo from the business manager of a chain of cheese stores
> 〔107〕 located throughout the United States.
>
> "For many years all the stores in our chain have stocked a wide variety of both domestic and imported cheeses. Last year（1）, however, all of the five best-selling cheeses at our newest store（2）were domestic cheddar cheeses from Wisconsin. Furthermore, a recent survey by *Cheeses of the World* magazine indicates an increasing preference for domestic cheeses among its subscribers（3）. Since our company can reduce expenses by limiting inventory, **the best way（4）to improve profits（5）in all of our stores（2）is to discontinue stocking many of our varieties of imported cheese（6）and concentrate primarily on domestic cheeses.**"
> （former 65, =66）★★★

翻　译　多年来，我们所有连锁店都储备了很多种类的国产奶酪和进口奶酪。然而去年，我们最新的店里5种销量最高的奶酪都是威斯康星州出产的cheddar奶酪。而且，最近一次由*Cheeses of the World*杂志进行的调查显示，其订阅者对于国产奶酪的倾向性越来越高。既然我们公司可以通过限制库存来减少开支，那么，在我们所有连锁店增加赢利的最好方式就是停止储备过多品种的进口奶酪而集中储备国产奶酪。

推理结构

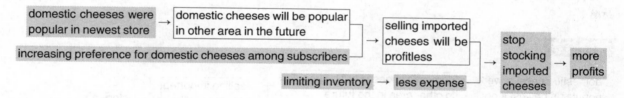

写作要求 *assumptions*

提　纲

1. Last year's sales result does not indicate that domestic cheddar cheeses will also be popular in the future. （*P→F*）★★★
2. The situation at the newest store might not be representative of all stores. （*selective sample/C.S.*）★★★★
3. The manager does not provide any information about the subscribers of *Cheese of the World*; they may not be representative of all United States consumers. （*selective sample/Are the respondents representative?*）★★★★

    1~3: The assumption that domestic cheeses will be popular in all over the country in the future is open to doubt.

4. The manager hastily assumes that no other better ways could be used to improve profits. （*necessity of the solution*）★★★
5. The assumption that discontinuing the inventory of imported cheeses will not bring about any negative effect is open to doubt. （*adv:disadv*）★★★★
6. The manager does not provide any information concerning the actual profit of domestic and imported cheese respectively. The assumption that the proposed action will ensure increase in profits is unwarranted. （*I.I.*）★★★★★

论证要点

　　本题关键环节在于作者认定本地奶酪将会受欢迎，但作者选取的去年、最新商店、杂志的订阅者都是选择性样本，不能说明本地奶酪在所有地区、所有时间段都会有好的销量。另外，4~6三点则集中讨论停止储存进口奶酪对于增加利润的充分性和必要性以及可能带来的负面影响。

---

120. The following appeared in a memo from the owner of a chain of cheese stores located
[108] throughout the United States.

　　"For many years all the stores in our chain have stocked a wide variety of both domestic and imported cheeses. Last year(1), however, all of the five best-selling cheeses at our newest store(2) were domestic cheddar cheeses from Wisconsin. Furthermore, a recent survey by *Cheeses of the World* magazine indicates an increasing preference for domestic cheeses among its subscribers(3). Since our company can reduce expenses by limiting inventory, **the best way(4) to improve profits(5) in all of our stores is to discontinue stocking many of our varieties of imported cheese(6) and concentrate primarily on domestic cheeses.**"

　　(former 65, =66, 107) ★★★

翻　译　多年来，我们所有连锁店都储备了很多种类的国产奶酪和进口奶酪。然而去年，我们最新的店里5种销量最高的奶酪都是威斯康星州出产的cheddar奶酪。而且，最近一次由*Cheese of the World*杂志进行的调查显示，国产奶酪越来越受到该杂志订阅者的青睐。既然我们公司可以通过限制库存来减少开支，那么，在我们所有连锁店增加赢利的最好方式就是停止储备过多品种的进口奶酪而集中储备国产奶酪。

推理结构

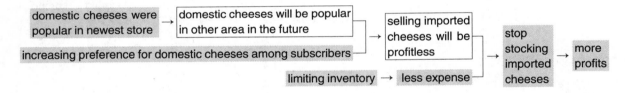

写作要求　*What specific **evidence** is needed to evaluate the argument?*

提　纲

　　作者需要提供关于以下方面的信息或论据：

1. Last year's sales result was not an abnormal case. (*P→F*) ★★★
2. The situation at the newest store could be representative of all stores. (*selective sample/C.S.*) ★★★★
3. Information about the subscribers of *Cheese of the World*. Are they representative of United States' consumers? (*selective sample/Are the respondents representative?*) ★★★★
4. Other better ways available to improve profits. (*necessity of the solution*) ★★★
5. Negative effects of discontinuing the inventory of imported cheeses. (*adv:disadv*) ★★★★
6. The actual profit of domestic and imported cheese, respectively. We cannot estimate the change in profits without such information. (*I.I.*) ★★★★★

论证要点

　　本题关键环节在于作者认定本地奶酪将会受欢迎，但作者选取的去年、最新商店、杂志的订阅者都是选择性样本，不能说明本地奶酪在所有地区、所有时间段都会有好的销量。另外，4~6三点则集中讨论停止储存进口奶酪对于增加利润的充分性和必要性以及可能带来的负面影响。

---

121. The following appeared as part of a business plan developed by the manager of the Rialto
🔲67 Movie Theater.

"Despite its downtown location, the Rialto Movie Theater, a local institution for five decades, must make big changes or close its doors forever. **It should follow the example of the new Apex Theater in the mall outside of town(1).** When the Apex opened last year, it featured a video arcade, plush carpeting and seats, and a state-of-the-art sound system(2,3). Furthermore, in a recent survey, over 85 percent of respondents(4) reported that the high price of newly released movies prevents them from going to the movies more than five times per year(5). **Thus, if the Rialto intends to hold on to its share of a decreasing pool of moviegoers, it must (9) offer the same features as Apex (6,7,8).**" (former 43) ★★★

翻　译 位于本地已成立50余年的Rialto剧院尽管地处闹市，但它必须采取重大变革，否则将关门大吉。它应该借鉴城外商业街上新的Apex剧院的例子。Apex去年开业的时候，拥有视听走廊、豪华地毯和座椅，以及最先进的音响系统。而且，在近期一次调查中，超过85%的受访者报告说新发行影片的过高票价致使他们看电影的次数每年不超过5次。因此，如果Rialto想在电影观众减少的情况下保持市场份额，它必须提供和Apex相同的设施和服务。

推理结构

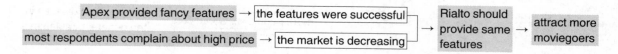

写作要求 *What **questions** should be answered to decide whether the recommendation will have the predicted result?*

提　纲

1.　Are the two theaters comparable? (*F.A.*) ★★★

2.　How about the actual profit and the number of moviegoers of Apex since its opening? (*I.I.*) ★★★★

3.　Did the success of Apex, if any, result from those new features mentioned above? (*N.C.R.*) ★★★★★

4.　Is there any guarantee about the reliability of the survey on which the argument bases? (*Are the respondents representative?*) ★

5.　Is there any substantial evidence to show that the pool of moviegoers is indeed diminishing? (*I.I.*) ★★★

6.　How about the cost of these fashionable features? (*adv:disadv/feasibility of the conclusion*) ★★★

7.　How much will be the price of Rialto after providing such features? Will it further prevent viewers from going to theaters? (*negative evidence*) ★★★

8.　Do the consumers in the region where Rialto located care about those features? (*I.I./F.A.*) ★★★

9.　Are there other solutions that can be used to achieve the manager's goal? (*necessity of the solution*) ★★★

论证要点

　　本题作者仅仅指出Apex开业的时候提供了很多先进设施，但话只说了半截，Apex开业之后的经营、利润情况我们并不知道，因而无法判断这些设施带来的效果。其次，就算这些设施确实使Apex获得成功，但Apex和Rialto是否可比、这些设施在Rialto能否成功复制以及提供这些设施之后会不会存在一些负面影响都可以进行分析。

---

122. A recent study reported that pet owners have longer, healthier lives on average than do people who own no pets (1,2). Specifically, dog owners tend to have a lower incidence of heart disease. In light of these findings, **Sherwood Hospital should form a partnership with Sherwood Animal Shelter to institute an adopt-a-dog program (3,5).** The program would encourage dog ownership for patients recovering from heart disease (4,7), *which should reduce these patients' chance of experiencing continuing heart problems and also reduce their need for ongoing treatment (6). As a further benefit, the publicity about the program would encourage more people(9) to adopt pets(8) from the shelter. And that will reduce the incidence of heart disease in the general population(7,10).* (former 129) ★★

翻　译　一项最近的研究报告说，平均而言，养宠物的人比不养宠物的人活得更长、更健康。特别是，养狗的人心脏病发病率更低。根据这些发现，Sherwood医院应该和Sherwood动物收养所合作建立一个"收养狗"的计划。这一计划将鼓励正在治疗心脏病的患者养狗，这将减少这些患者持续发生心脏问题的可能性，同样也会减少他们继续治疗的需求。进一步的好处是，对于这一计划的宣传将鼓励更多的人从收养所领养宠物，这将减少整个人群患心脏病的危险。

推理结构

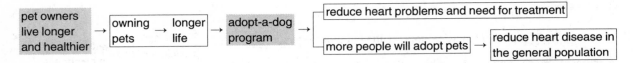

写作要求　*assumptions*

提　纲

1. No causal relationship between owning pets and healthier lives of the pet owners is established. (*confusing concurrence with causality/confusing the cause and the effect*) ★★★★★

2. There may be other differences between people who own pets and those who do not. (*I.C.*) ★★★★

3. Pets could cause other health problems. (*adv:disadv*) ★★★★

4. The author fails to illustrate that owning a dog would have the same positive effects on recovery of heart disease as it has on preventing heart disease. (*U.C./C.S.*)
养狗的人心脏病发病率低只能说明养狗有一定预防心脏病的作用，但养狗能否促进心脏病康复则不能保证。★★★

   1~4: The assumption that owning a dog promotes health status is open to doubt.

5. Some patients may not be willing to adopt a dog, or be capable of owning dogs, or could afford raising a dog. (*feasibility of the conclusion*) ★★★

6. The patients may suffer from other health problems, thus their need for ongoing treatment would not necessarily decrease even if owning a dog could indeed lower the risk of heart disease. (*sufficiency of the solution/U.A.*) ★★★

7. The author unfairly assumes that at least a significant number of people who adopt pets from the shelter will have risks of heart disease. (*U.A.*) ★★

8. The author fails to illustrate that adopting other pets would have the same effect on preventing heart disease as owning a dog has. (*C.S.*) ★★★

9. The author hastily assumes that the proposed program would be appealing to the general public. (*feasibility of the conclusion*) ★★★

10. Since the risk of heart disease in the general population might be determined by many factors, implementing the program alone may not sufficiently reduce the risk. (*sufficiency of the solution/U.A.*) ★★★

论证要点

本题最关键环节在于养宠物和心脏病发病率低之间的因果关系没有任何实质论据支持。其次，作者的提案对于减少心脏问题、减少治疗需求以及降低公众整体心脏病危险的充分性、必要性和可行性可以作为辅助论证。

---

123. The following appeared in a memo from a vice president of a large, highly diversified company.

[69] "Ten years ago (4) our company had two new office buildings constructed as regional headquarters for two regions. The buildings were erected by different construction companies—Alpha and Zeta. Although the two buildings had identical floor plans, the building constructed by Zeta cost 30 percent more to build. However, that building's expenses for maintenance last year (2) were only half those of Alpha's. In addition, the energy consumption of the Zeta building has been lower than that of the Alpha building every year since its construction (1,3). Given these data, plus the fact that Zeta has a stable workforce with little employee turnover (5,6), **we recommend using Zeta rather than Alpha (8) for our new building project (7)**, even though Alpha's bid promises lower construction costs."

翻　译 10年前我们公司在两个不同的地区建造了两座新办公楼作为区域总部。它们由两家建筑公司——Alpha和Zeta分别建造。尽管两座建筑的平面布局基本相同，但由Zeta所建造的建筑造价高出了30%。然而，该建筑去年的维护费用仅是由Alpha建的楼的一半。而且，Zeta大楼建成以来每年的能耗都比Alpha大楼低。鉴于这些数据，再加上Zeta公司拥有稳定的员工队伍且雇员流动性很小的事实，我们建议使用Zeta建筑公司而不是Alpha来建造我们的新项目，尽管Alpha的标书承诺更低的造价。

推理结构

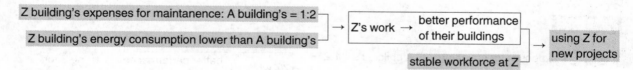

写作要求 *What **questions** should be answered to decide whether the recommendation and the argument are reasonable?*

提　纲

1. Are there any differences between the two regions and the two buildings? (*I.C.*) ★★★★★

2. Are the lower expenses for maintenance of the Zeta building last year an unusual case? Will the expenses keep low in the future? (*P→F*) ★★★

3. Could the outstanding performance of Zeta building be attributed to the superior working-quality of Zeta? (*N.C.R.*) ★★★★★

4. Granted that the fact above could illustrate Zeta's superior work quality in those years, will their working quality still be superior to that of Alpha today as decades ago? (*P→F*) ★★★★

5. Does a stable workforce with little employee turnover sufficiently indicate the construction quality of a construction company? (*I.E./U.C.*) ★★★

6. How about the stability and turnover at Alpha? (*ex parte information*) ★★★

7. What is the type of the proposed new building? Does Zeta have advantages over Alpha in constructing this type of building? (*C.S.*) ★★★★★

8. Are there any other competent construction companies besides Alpha and Zeta? (*F.D.*) ★★★

论证要点

首先，因为不知道两座建筑的具体使用情况，因此，作者提供的建筑项目的对比未必能说明Z的建筑技术更高超(1~3)，作者需要回答以上问题才能评价Z的建筑水平；其次，就算Z当年的建筑技术更好，但毕竟是10年前的项目，很多重要因素和条件在今天都可能发生变化(4)；再次，由于不知道该公司新项目的具体建筑类型，因此，我们也无法判断Z在建造这类建筑方面是否也比A更有优势(7)。

---

124. The following appeared in a memo from a vice president of a large, highly diversified company.

[70] "Ten years ago（4） our company had two new office buildings constructed as regional headquarters for two regions. The buildings were erected by different construction companies—Alpha and Zeta. Although the two buildings had identical floor plans, the building constructed by Zeta cost 30 percent more to build. However, that building's expenses for maintenance last year（2） were only half those of Alpha's. Furthermore, the energy consumption of the Zeta building has been lower than that of the Alpha building every year since its construction（1,3）. **Such data indicate that we should use Zeta rather than Alpha(6) for our contemplated new building project (5)**, even though Alpha's bid promises lower construction costs." (former 93, ≈69) ★★

翻 译 10年前我们公司在两个不同地区建造了两座新办公楼作为区域总部。它们由两家建筑公司——Alpha和Zeta分别建造。尽管两座建筑的平面布局基本相同，但由Zeta所建造的建筑造价高出了30%。然而，该建筑去年的维护费用仅是由Alpha建的楼的一半。而且，Zeta大楼建成以来每年的能耗都比Alpha大楼低。这些数据表明我们应该使用Zeta建筑公司而不是Alpha来建造我们的新项目，尽管Alpha的标书承诺更低的造价。

推理结构

| Z building's expenses for maintanence: A building's = 1:2 | → | Z's work | → | better performance of their buildings | → | using Z for new projects |
| Z building's energy consumption lower than A building's | | | | | | |

写作要求
*What specific **evidence** is needed to evaluate the argument?*

提 纲

作者需要提供能说明以下方面的论据或信息：

1. Differences between the two regions and the two buildings. (*I.C.*) ★★★★★

2. The lower expenses for maintenance of the Zeta building last year were not an unusual case. (*P→F*) ★★★

3. The outstanding performance of Zeta building could be attributed to superior working-quality of Zeta. (*N.C.R.*) ★★★★★

4. Granted that Zeta's work was superior in the past years, we need proof that their working quality is still

superior to that of Alpha today as decades ago. (P→F) ★★★★

5. The type of the proposed new building, and whether Zeta has advantages over Alpha in constructing this type of building. (C.S.) ★★★★★

6. Other competent construction companies besides Alpha and Zeta. (F.D.) ★★★

论证要点

首先，因为不知道两座建筑的具体使用情况，因此，作者提供的建筑项目的对比未必能说明Z的建筑技术更高超（1~3）；其次，就算Z当年建筑技术更好，但毕竟是10年前的项目，很多重要因素和条件在今天都可能发生变化（4）；再次，由于不知道该公司新项目的具体建筑类型，因此，我们也无法判断Z在建造这类建筑方面是否也比A更有优势（5）。我们需要作者提供更多、更充分的论据来说明以上情况。

---

125. The following appeared in a memo from a vice president of a large, highly diversified company.

115 "Ten years ago（4）our company had two new office buildings constructed as regional headquarters for two different regions. The buildings were erected by two different construction companies—Alpha and Zeta. Even though the two buildings had identical floor plans, the building constructed by Zeta cost 30 percent more to build, and its expenses for maintenance last year were twice those of the building constructed by Alpha（2）. Furthermore, the energy consumption of the Zeta building has been higher than that of the Alpha building every year since its construction（1,3）. Such data, plus the fact that Alpha has a stable workforce with little employee turnover（5,6）, indicate that **we should use Alpha rather than Zeta（8）for our contemplated new building project (7).**" (former 93, ≈ 69, 70)

翻　译 10年前我们公司在两个不同地区建造了两座新办公楼作为区域总部。它们由两家建筑公司——Alpha和Zeta分别建造。尽管两座建筑的平面布局相同，但由Zeta所建造的建筑造价高出了30%，而且去年其维护费用是由Alpha建的楼的2倍。此外，Zeta大楼建成以来每年能耗都高于Alpha大楼。这些数据，再加上Alpha公司拥有稳定的员工队伍且雇员流动性很小的事实，说明我们应该使用Alpha而不是Zeta来建造我们的新项目。

推理结构

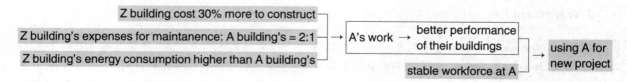

写作要求 *assumptions*

提　纲

1. The vice president unfairly assumes that the two buildings are comparable at every aspect. Many differences between the two regions and the two buildings may result in the different cost and expenses. (I.C.) ★★★★★

2. The vice president assumes that the high expenses for maintenance of the Zeta building last year were not an unusual case, and will continue in the future. (P→F) ★★★

3. The vice president hastily attributes the outstanding performance of Alpha building to the superior working quality of Alpha. (N.C.R.) ★★★★★

4. The vice president unfairly assumes that the working quality of Alpha is still superior, if ever, to that of Zeta today as decades ago. (*P→F*) ★ ★ ★ ★

5. A stable workforce with little employee turnover tells nothing about the construction quality of a construction company. (*I.E./U.C.*) ★ ★ ★

6. The vice president unfairly implies that the workforce of Zeta is not stable, and with high turnover. (*ex parte information*) ★ ★ ★

7. The facts cited by the vice president do not necessarily indicate that Alpha will have advantages over Zeta in constructing the new project. (*C.S.*) ★ ★ ★ ★ ★

8. The vice president fails to consider other competent construction companies besides Alpha and Zeta. (*F.D.*) ★ ★ ★

论证要点

首先，因为不知道两座建筑的具体使用情况，因此，作者提供的建筑项目的对比未必能说明A的建筑技术更高超(1~3)；其次，就算A当年建筑技术更好，但毕竟是10年前的项目，很多重要因素和条件在今天都可能发生变化(4)；再次，由于不知道该公司新项目的具体建筑类型，因此，我们也无法判断A在建造这类建筑方面是否也比Z更有优势(7)。

请注意本题和Argument69、70两题的区别：69、70的作者认为Zeta建造的楼更节能且维护费用更低，而本题作者认为Alpha的建筑质量更好。

---

126. The following is a letter to the editor of the *Waymarsh Times*.

71 "*Traffic here in Waymarsh is becoming a problem*. Although just three years ago a state traffic survey showed that the typical driving commuter took 20 minutes to get to work, the commute now takes closer to 40 minutes(1,2), according to the survey just completed. Members of the town council already have suggested more road building to address the problem, but as well as being expensive, *the new construction will surely disrupt some of our residential neighborhoods (3,4)*. **It would be better to follow the example of the nearby city of Garville.** Last year Garville implemented a policy that rewards people who share rides to work, giving them coupons for free gas(9). Pollution levels in Garville have dropped since the policy was implemented(5), and people from Garville(6) tell me that commuting times have fallen considerably. There is no reason why a policy like Garville's shouldn't work equally well in Waymarsh(7,8)." (former 119) ★ ★

翻　译 Waymarsh的交通越来越成问题。仅仅3年前一项全州交通调查显示，普通驾车人在路上花20分钟上班，根据刚完成的调查，现在几乎需要40分钟。一些市委成员建议多修路以解决问题，但除了花费高以外，新的建设也肯定会扰民。借鉴我们临近城市Garville的例子可能是更好的办法。去年，Garville实施了一项政策，向那些拼车上下班的人发放免费汽油券作为奖励。政策实施之后Garville的污染水平下降了，一些Garville居民告诉我通勤时间显著下降。类似Garville的政策一定会在Waymarsh产生同样的效果。

推理结构

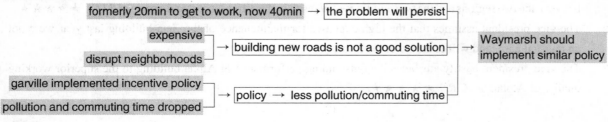

提　纲

作者需要提供说明以下方面的信息或证据：

1. The situation cited by the author is not an unusual case. (*C.S.*) ★★★★
2. The current situation will continue in the future. (*C→F*) ★★★
3. Why the proposed construction will surely disrupt residential neighborhood. (*U.A.*) ★★★
4. Evidence to fully demonstrate the effectiveness of building new roads on solving the traffic problem. (*I.I./U.A.*) ★★★★
5. The causal relationship between implementing the policy and the drop of pollution levels in Garville. (*post hoc, ergo propter hoc*) ★★★★
6. Those people are representative of all Garville residents. (*selective sample/C.S.*) ★★★
7. Implementing the policy similar to Garville's will be equally effective in Waymarsh. (*F.A.*) ★★★★★
8. The actual level of pollution in Waymarsh and the causes for the pollution. Implementing the policy may not necessarily improve Waymarsh's traffic and environment. (*I.I./N.C.R.*)

   如果Waymarsh的污染主要是其他原因导致的，比如工业污染，那么实施上述政策显然无助于改善环境。★★★★
9. Negative effects that may result from the proposed reward policy. (*adv:disadv*) ★★★

论证要点

本题论证点主要集中于几个环节：一、论证大前提未必成立，即交通问题可能只是特殊情况，在将来未必持续（1、2）；二、作者没有提供实质证据说明为什么修路一定会扰民而且不是很好的解决途径（3、4）；三、Garville的情况改善（如果有的话）未必是因为出台这些政策，而且这些政策在Waymarsh未必同样有效（5~8）。

---

127. The following appeared as a letter to the editor of a national newspaper.

72 "Your recent article on corporate downsizing* in Elthyria maintains that the majority of competent workers who have lost jobs as a result of downsizing face serious economic hardship, often for years, before finding other suitable employment. **But this claim is undermined by a recent report on the Elthyrian economy(5)**, which found that since 1999 far more jobs(1,2) have been created than have been eliminated, bringing the unemployment rate in Elthyria to its lowest level in decades. Moreover, two-thirds of these newly created jobs have been in industries that tend to pay above-average wages(4), and the vast majority of these jobs are full-time(3)." (former 143) ★★★

*Downsizing is the process whereby corporations deliberately make themselves smaller, reducing the number of their employees.

翻　译 你们最近关于Elthyria公司缩编*的文章认为，大多数因裁员而失业的有能力的工人在找到合适的工作之前经常连续几年面临严重的经济困难。但这一观点被最近一项关于Elthyria经济的报告推翻，报告发现自1999年以来新增就业机会数量远超过消失的岗位数量，使Elthyria失业率达到几十年来的最低水平。而且，新增就业机会中有三分之二是那些付高于平均水平薪酬的企业提供的，而且这些岗位绝大多数是全职工作。

*缩编是指企业蓄意减少员工数量以缩减企业规模的过程。

new jobs created > jobs eliminated → unemployment rate at lowest level ┐

most new jobs are in highly-paid industries ┐

most new jobs are full-time ┘ → the laid-off workers could find these jobs → the purported difficulties of laid-off workers are unfounded

写作要求 *What specific **evidence** is needed to evaluate the argument?*

提　纲

作者需要提供能够说明以下方面的信息或证据：

1. The actual number of new jobs created. Perhaps the number is still lower than the total number of laid-off workers although it is higher than the number of jobs eliminated. (*V.D.*) ★★★

2. The newly created jobs are suitable for those workers downsized by corporations. (*I.I./feasibility of the conclusion*) ★★★★

3. How many laid-off workers engaged in those highly paid and full-time jobs mentioned above. (*I.I.*) ★★★
对于上文论述还存在以下问题：

4. The fact that many new jobs are in industries that tend to pay high wages does not necessarily guarantee that these new jobs are also highly paid. (*U.C.*) ★★★

5. The statistics cited by the author still do not rule out the possibility that many laid-off workers do face serious economic hardship before they find new jobs. (*I.E.*) ★★★

论证要点

　　本题论证点比较零散。新增就业岗位数量能否满足下岗工人需求、是否适合这些工人、有多少下岗员工能够获得这些高薪全职工作等等都可以加以分析。另外，即使这些员工能够获得这些就业机会，作者提供的信息依然不能说明这些员工能得到很高的薪酬，也不能排除很多下岗员工在再就业之前依然会面临经济困难的可能性。

---

128. The following appeared on the Mozart School of Music Web site.

[73] "**The Mozart School of Music should be the first choice(8) for parents considering enrolling their child in music lessons(7).** First of all, the Mozart School welcomes youngsters at all ability and age levels; there is no audition to attend the school. Second, the school offers instruction in nearly all musical instruments as well a wide range of styles and genres from classical to rock(1). Third, the faculty includes some(2) of the most distinguished musicians in the area(3). Finally, many(4)Mozart graduates have gone on to become well-known and highly paid(6) professional musicians(5)." (former 172) ★

翻　译 Mozart音乐学校应该是想把孩子送去学音乐的家长的首选。首先，Mozart学校欢迎所有起点和所有年龄段的青少年，入学也无需面试。其次，学校提供几乎所有乐器以及从古典到摇滚多种音乐风格种类的教学。第三，其教职员工包括一些该地区最著名的音乐家。最后，很多Mozart的毕业生已经成为非常著名的、收入颇高的职业音乐家。

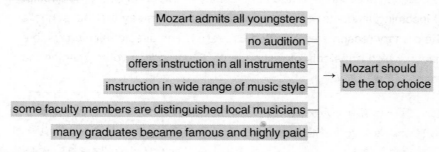

assumptions

提　　纲

1. The fact that Mozart admits all youngsters and offers instruction in all instruments and music styles may just indicate that the school is not professional and dedicated enough. (*negative evidence*)

2. We are not informed about the performance of other faculty members; students are not necessarily taught by those distinguished music teachers. (*I.I.*) ★★★★

3. Other music schools may also have famous teachers and attractive features. (*ex parte information*) ★★★
   2 & 3: The assumption that Mozart's faculty and instructions are outstanding is open to doubt.

4. The argument fails to provide information concerning the **general** employment condition of the school's graduates, and information about what fraction of their graduates get highly paid and become famous. (*I.I./C.S./V.D.*) ★★

5. The author unfairly attributes the graduates' success to the education they received in Mozart School. (*N.C.R.*) ★★★★★

6. The argument simply equates being best known and highly paid with musical achievements. (*U.C.*) ★★★
   4~6: The assumption that attending Mozart could guarantee a prosperous future is open to doubt.

7. The author does not inform us the amount of tuition charged by Mozart Music School, and if the parents could afford it. (*I.I./feasibility of the conclusion*) ★★★★

8. Other music schools may be more suitable for some students. (*necessity of the solution*) ★★★★
   7 & 8: The assumption that Mozart is the top choice, and parents could afford attending the school is open to doubt.

论证要点

　　本题主要论据完全平行并列。可以展开论证的主要集中在最后两条关于师资和就业前景的论据。首先，关于师资的信息不完整，我们不知道除了这些知名音乐家以外的其他教职员水平如何；其次，其他音乐学校未必就没有这类知名音乐家。关于就业，一方面也是信息不完整，我们不知道该校毕业生的总体就业情况，而且成名和高收入也不能作为衡量音乐教育水平的指标；就算这些毕业生确实非常成功，他们的成功也未必来自于在Mozart接受的音乐教育，可能有其他原因。关于课程设置是否过于庞杂导致不够专业、与其他学校的对比不够全面、以及学费情况不清楚等可以作为辅助论证。

---

129. The president of Grove College has recommended that the college abandon its century-old tradition of all-female education and begin admitting men. Pointing to other all-female colleges that experienced an increase in applications after adopting coeducation（1）, *the president argues that coeducation would lead to a significant increase in applications and enrollment(2,3).* However, the director of the alumnae association opposes the plan（7）.

> Arguing that all-female education is essential to the very identity of the college(3), the director cites annual surveys of incoming students(4,5) in which these students say that the school's all-female status was the primary reason they selected Grove(6). The director also points to a survey of Grove alumnae in which a majority of respondents(5) strongly favored keeping the college all female. (former 174) ★ ★ ★

翻　译 Grove学院院长建议，废除已有百年历史的女校传统，开始录取男性。鉴于其他女校采取了男女同校政策后申请数量上升，院长认为男女同校将使申请报名数量大幅增加。然而，校友会主任反对该计划。主任认为女校教育是学院的基本特点，并指出，每年对于刚入学的学生所做的调查表明，学校的女校形式是他们选择Grove的主要原因。主任还指出，一次对Grove校友的调查表明大多数回应者强烈支持学院保持女校形式。

推理结构

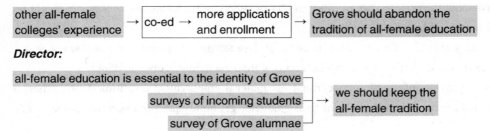

President:

other all-female colleges' experience → co-ed → more applications and enrollment → Grove should abandon the tradition of all-female education

Director:

all-female education is essential to the identity of Grove
surveys of incoming students → we should keep the all-female tradition
survey of Grove alumnae

写作要求 *What **questions** should be answered to decide whether the recommendation and the argument are reasonable?*

提　纲

1. Did the increase in applications result from the coeducation policy? (*N.C.R.*) ★ ★ ★ ★ ★
2. Granted that the increase was the result of coeducation policy, will the increase also occur in Grove College? (*F.A.*) ★ ★ ★ ★
3. Which goal is more important for Grove? More applications and enrollment or the identification as an all-female college? (*I.I.*) ★ ★ ★ ★ ★
4. Are those incoming students representative of all students? Did they change their attitude in the following years? (*selective sample*) ★ ★ ★
5. Will students and alumnae who favor all-female education be more likely to respond to the survey? (*Are the respondents representative?*) ★ ★ ★
6. Will the coeducation policy attract other groups of students? (*I.I./I.T.*) ★ ★ ★
7. Are there any positive effects of introducing coeducation? (*adv:disadv*) ★ ★ ★ ★ ★

论证要点

本题结构比较特殊，提出了两方观点。题目要求是讨论需回答哪些问题能评价上文建议是否合理。文中的建议应该是指院长的观点，因此结论应该是第一句话。但在写作时不用考虑是要反对院长还是支持主任，只要讨论一下要评价院长和主任的观点分别需要回答哪些问题就可以了。对于院长的建议，主要需要考虑的问题是：其他院校的申请人数上升是否是因为采取了同校政策？即使是，同样的政策是否在Grove会产生相同效果？而对于主任的观点，主要要考虑的问题是：文中提到的调查结果是否有代表性？采取同校政策会不会有其他方面的好处？

130. The following recommendation was made by the president and administrative staff of Grove
147 College, a private institution, to the college's governing committee.

"**We recommend that Grove College preserve its century-old tradition of all-female
education rather than admit men into its programs(3).** It is true that a majority of faculty
members voted in favor of coeducation, arguing that it would encourage more students to apply
to Grove. But 80 percent of the students responding to a survey(1) conducted by the student
government wanted the school to remain all female, and over half of the alumnae who
answered a separate survey(1,2) also opposed coeducation. *Keeping the college all female
will improve morale among students(4) and convince alumnae to keep supporting the college
financially(5).*"（former174, ≈74）★ ★ ★

翻　　译 我们建议Grove学院保留其已有百年历史的女校传统，不允许录取男性。确实有大部分员工
投票赞成男女同校，认为这会使更多的学生申请Grove。但学生组织的一次调查显示，有80%的被访学
生要求学校维持女校形式，并且另一个调查表明，校友中超过一半的人也反对男女同校。维持女校形式
将鼓舞学生的士气并且让校友继续对学院进行财政资助。

推理结构

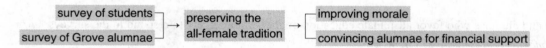

写作要求 *What specific **evidence** is needed to evaluate the argument?*

提　　纲

对于上文论述存在以下问题：

1. Students and alumnae who favor all-female education might be more likely to respond to the surveys. (*Are
   the respondents representative?*) ★ ★ ★

作者需要提供能够说明以下方面问题的信息或论据：

2. The reliability of the second survey. (*reliability of the survey*) ★ ★

3. The positive effects of introducing coeducation. (*adv:disadv*) ★ ★ ★ ★ ★

4. Preserving all-female education will suffice to improve morale among students. (*U.A.*) ★ ★ ★

5. We cannot attract other sources of financial supporting, or alumnae will stop or decrease their financial
   supporting once we do not keep all-female education. (*I.I./U.A.*) ★ ★ ★ ★

论证要点

本题需要论证的主要问题在于：一、两次调查回应者的代表性：很有可能是赞成男女同校的学生和
校友更倾向于回应调查；二、作者没有考虑采取同校形式可能带来的好处；三、鼓舞学生的士气、获得资
助可以通过其他途径，未必非要通过保持女校传统。

131. The following recommendation was made by the president and administrative staff of Grove
148 College, a private institution, to the college's governing committee.

"**We recommend that Grove College preserve its century-old tradition of all-female
education rather than admit men into its programs(3).** It is true that a majority of faculty
members voted in favor of coeducation, arguing that it would encourage more students to

apply to Grove. But 80 percent of the students responding to a survey(1) conducted by the student government wanted the school to remain all female, and over half of the alumnae who answered a separate survey(2) also opposed coeducation. *Keeping the college all female will improve morale among students(4) and convince alumnae to keep supporting the college financially(5)."* （former174, ≈74, =147）★ ★

翻　译 我们建议Grove学院保留其已有百年历史的女校传统，不允许录取男性。确实有大部分员工投票赞成男女同校，认为这会使更多的学生申请Grove。但学生会组织的一次调查显示，有80%的被访学生要求学校维持女校形式，并且另一个调查表明，校友中超过一半的人也反对男女同校。维持女校形式将鼓舞学生的士气并且让校友继续对学院进行财政资助。

推理结构

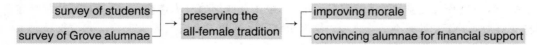

写作要求 *assumptions*

提　纲

1. Students and alumnae who favor all-female education might be more likely to respond to the surveys. (*Are the respondents representative?*) ★ ★ ★

2. The result of the second survey might not be reliable. (*reliability of the survey*) ★ ★
   1 & 2: 文中提到的调查结果未必说明多数学生和校友都支持保留女校形式的假设。

3. The author assumes that the positive effects of introducing coeducation will not exceed the negative ones. (*adv:disadv*) ★ ★ ★ ★ ★

4. The assumption that preserving all-female education will suffice to improve morale among students is unjustified. (*U.A.*) ★ ★ ★

5. The author hastily assumes that alumnae will stop or decrease their financial supporting, and that we cannot attract other sources of financial supporting once we discontinue all-female education. (*I.I./U.A.*) ★ ★ ★ ★

论证要点

　　本题需要论证的主要假设在于：一、两次调查的回应者的看法能代表所有学生和校友的意见，但很有可能是赞成男女同校的学生和校友更倾向于回应调查；二、采取同校形式可能带来的好处不会超过其负面影响；三、采取男女同校一定会影响学生的士气、并对学校获得资助造成障碍。

132. The following recommendation was made by the president and administrative staff of Grove
149 College, a private institution, to the college's governing committee.

　　"We recommend that Grove College preserve its century-old tradition of all-female education rather than admit men into its programs(3). It is true that a majority of faculty members voted in favor of coeducation, arguing that it would encourage more students to apply to Grove. But 80 percent of the students responding to a survey(1) conducted by the student government wanted the school to remain all female, and over half of the alumnae who answered a separate survey(2) also opposed coeducation. *Keeping the college all female will improve morale among students(4) and convince alumnae to keep supporting the college financially(5)."* （former174, ≈74, =147, 148）★ ★ ★

推理结构

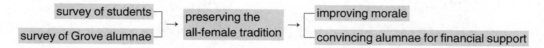

写作要求 *What **questions** should be answered to decide whether the recommendation will have the predicted result?*

提　　纲

1. Will students and alumnae who favor all-female education be more likely to respond to the surveys? (*Are the respondents representative?*) ★★★

2. Is the result of the second survey reliable? (*reliability of the survey*) ★★

3. Will the positive effects of introducing coeducation not exceed the negative ones? (*adv:disadv*) ★★★★★

4. Will preserving all-female education suffice to improve morale among students? (*U.A.*) ★★★

5. Will alumnae stop or decrease their financial supporting once we discontinue all-female education? Can we attract other sources of financial supporting? (*I.I./U.A.*) ★★★★

论证要点

　　本题需要论证的主要问题在于：一、两次调查的回应者是否有代表性——很有可能是赞成男女同校的学生和校友更倾向于回应调查；二、作者没有考虑采取同校形式可能带来的好处；三、鼓舞学生的士气、获得资助是否可以通过其他途径。我们需要作者回答以上问题才能够更好地评价上文论述。

---

133. The following recommendation was made by the president and administrative staff of Grove
156　College, a private institution, to the college's governing committee.

　　"Recently, there have been discussions about ending Grove College's century-old tradition of all-female education by admitting male students into our programs(3). At a recent faculty meeting, a majority of faculty members voted in favor of coeducation, arguing that it would encourage more students to apply to Grove. However, *Grove students, both past and present, are against the idea of coeducation.* Eighty percent of the students responding to a survey(1) conducted by the student government wanted the school to remain all female, and over half of the alumnae who answered a separate survey(2) also opposed coeducation. **Therefore, we recommend maintaining Grove College's tradition of all-female education. We predict that keeping the college all-female will improve morale among students　(4) and convince alumnae to keep supporting the college financially (5).**" (former174, ≈74, 147, 148, 149) ★★★

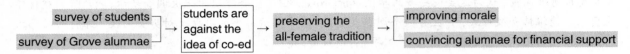

写作要求 What **questions** should be answered to decide whether the recommendation will have the *predicted result?*

提　纲

1. Will students and alumnae who favor all-female education be more likely to respond to the surveys? (*Are the respondents representative?*) ★★★

2. Is the result of the second survey reliable? (*reliability of the survey*) ★★

3. Will the positive effects of introducing coeducation not exceed the negative ones? (*adv:disadv*) ★★★★★

4. Will preserving all-female education suffice to improve morale among students? (*U.A.*) ★★★

5. Will alumnae stop or decrease their financial supporting once we discontinue all-female education? Can we attract other sources of financial supporting? (*I.I./U.A.*) ★★★★

论证要点

　　本题需要论证的主要问题在于：一、两次调查的回应者是否有代表性——很有可能是赞成男女同校的学生和校友更倾向于回应调查；二、作者没有考虑采取同校形式可能带来的好处；三、鼓舞学生的士气、获得资助是否可以通过其他途径。我们需要作者回答以上问题才能够更好地评价上文论述。

---

134. The following appeared in a letter to the editor of a Batavia newspaper.

75 "The department of agriculture in Batavia reports that the number of dairy farms(1) throughout the country is now 25 percent greater than it was 10 years ago. During this same time period, however, the price of milk at the local Excello Food Market(2,3) has increased from $1.50 to over $3.00 per gallon(4,5,6). To prevent *farmers from continuing to receive excessive profits on an apparently increased supply of milk,* **the Batavia government should begin to regulate retail milk prices (7).** *Such regulation is necessary to ensure fair prices for consumers.*" (former 10) ★★

翻　译 Batavia农业部报告说全国乳牛场的数量比10年前增加了25%。然而在同一时期，当地Excello Food Market的奶价从每加仑1.5美元上涨到了3.0美元。为防止农场主在牛奶明显增产的情况下获取过多的利润，Batavia政府应开始限制牛奶的零售价。这种限价对于为消费者保证公平的价格是必需的。

推理结构

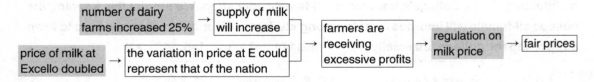

写作要求 What **questions** should be answered to decide whether the recommendation will have the predicted *result?*

1. Could the number of dairy farms indicate the supply of milk? (*U.C.*) ★ ★ ★ ★

2. Could Excello's milk prices reflect those throughout Batavia? (*C.S./quantity of the sample*) ★ ★ ★ ★

3. Granted that the production of milk in the country increased in general, did the production in the area where Excello locates also increase? (*C.S.*) ★ ★ ★

4. How much did the price of milk actually increase after adjustment for inflation? (*I.T.*) ★ ★ ★

5. How about the variation in the demand of milk? (*I.T./I.I.*) ★ ★ ★

6. How about the variation in the cost of running farms and producing milk? (*I.I.*) ★ ★ ★

7. Will the proposed regulation lead to undesirable consequences? (*I.T./unexpected consequences*) ★ ★ ★ ★ ★

论证要点

　　本题根本假设在于作者认为农场主在牟取暴利。这一假设基于的前提是牛奶增产了。而作者之所以认为牛奶增产，是因为看到农场数量增加。但是，农场数量增加未必带来牛奶供应量增加（1）；其次就算全国牛奶供应量整体增加，Excello所在地区的供应量未必也增加，并且由于通货膨胀、需求增加、成本上涨等因素（4~6），Excello奶价上涨可能是合理的（3）；就算不合理，这一市场的价格也不能代表整个Batavia的价格趋势（2）。考虑并回答这些问题之后，才能判断作者提出的限价能否达到平抑奶价的效果。

---

135. The following appeared in a newsletter offering advice to investors.

76　"Over 80 percent of the respondents to a recent survey indicated a desire to reduce their intake of foods containing fats and cholesterol（1,2,3）, and today low-fat products abound in many food stores（4）. Since many（5）of the food products currently（6）marketed by Old Dairy Industries are high in fat and cholesterol, *the company's sales are likely to diminish greatly and company profits will no doubt decrease(7)*. **We therefore advise Old Dairy stockholders to sell their shares(8,9), and other investors not to purchase stock in this company(10).**"
(former 15) ★ ★ ★ ★

翻　译　近来的一次调查显示，超过80%的回应者表达了他们想减少饮食中脂肪和胆固醇摄入量的愿望，现在很多食品商店都提供丰富的低脂肪食品。由于Old Dairy Industries当前生产的很多产品都有很高的脂肪和胆固醇含量，因此，该公司的销量有可能严重下降，其赢利无疑会减少。因而我们建议Old Dairy的股票持有者抛出他们所持的股票，其他投资者也不应购买该公司的股票。

推理结构

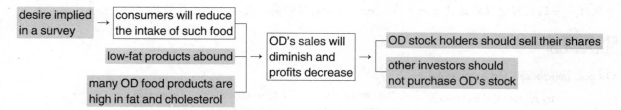

写作要求　What **questions** should be answered to decide whether the advice and the argument are reasonable?

1. Does the result of the survey accurately reflect the desires of most consumers? Could the result accurately predict consumer behavior? (*Are the respondents representative?*) ★ ★

2. Will those consumers who desired to reduce the intake of unhealthy food really do so? (*U.A.*) ★★★

3. Are there any other key factors that influence the consumers' decision in choosing food products? (*I.T.*) ★★★

4. Does the fact that low-fat foods are in abundant supply necessarily indicate an increasing demand for low-fat dairy products or a diminishing demand for high-fat dairy products? (*N.C.R./U.C.*) ★★★★★

5. What fraction of food products marketed by OD are high in fat and cholesterol? Does OD have other competitive low-fat food products? (*V.D./I.I.*)
   如果高脂、高胆固醇食品只占OD产品的一小部分，或OD还有其他低脂、低胆固醇产品，那么OD的业绩未必会受到很大影响。★★★★

6. Will Old Dairy change its strategy and main product in the future? (*P→F*) ★★★

7. Is there any concrete evidence to show that Old Dairy's sales and profits will decline? (*U.A.*) ★★★

8. Are there any negative effects of selling OD's stock immediately? (*adv:disadv*) ★★★

9. Could the mere fact that many Old Dairy's food products are high in fat and cholesterol necessarily prove that their stock is not worth investing? (*I.T.*) ★★★★

10. Are there any factors that will lead the price of OD's stock to increase in the future? (*adv:disadv/C→F*) ★★★★

论证要点

文章提及的调查结果在可靠性和代表性方面存在一些问题，而对于OD产品的描述信息又不够全面完整，因而仅有上文信息并不能说明OD的产品一定没有市场。而且决定抛出或持有股票还有很多其他因素，现在就决定抛售并不再投资OD股票可能过于草率。

---

136. The following recommendation appeared in a memo from the mayor of the town of Hopewell.

77 "Two years ago（3）, the nearby town of Ocean View built a new municipal golf course and resort hotel. During the past two years, tourism in Ocean View has increased, new businesses have opened there, and Ocean View's tax revenues have risen by 30 percent（1,2）. Therefore, **the best way（6）to improve Hopewell's economy — and generate additional tax revenues—is to build a golf course and resort hotel similar to those in Ocean View(4,5).**"
（former 25）★

翻 译 2年前，临近城市Ocean View建了一个新的市高尔夫球场和度假旅店。在过去2年中，Ocean View的旅客增加了，开设了很多新的商业，而且税收增加了30%。因此，改善Hopewell的经济——带来更多税收——的最好途径就是建立一个和Ocean View类似的高尔夫球场和度假旅店。

推理结构

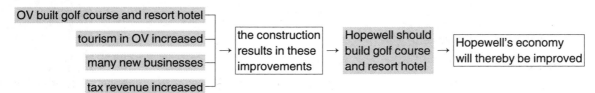

写作要求 *assumptions*

提 纲

1. The 30 percent increase in tax revenues of Ocean View does not indicate that its economic condition is

better than Hopewell's, because we do not know the base amount of tax revenues to begin with. (*V.D.*) ★★

2. Granted that the improvement of Ocean View's economy is significant, the arguer fails to point out how the golf course and resort hotel actually contributed to the economy of Ocean View. (*post hoc, ergo propter hoc*) ★★★★

3. Granted that it is the construction of golf course and resort hotel that lead to Ocean View's prosperity, the mayor assumes too hastily that similar constructions will continue to benefit Hopewell's overall economy in the future. (*P→F*) ★★★★

4. The argument relies on an unwarranted premise that Hopewell lacks golf course and resort hotel, or that the existing ones are not attractive enough. (*U.A.*) ★

5. Ocean View and Hopewell may not be comparable. (*F.A.*) ★★★★★

6. The arguer ignores other possible methods that may improve Hopewell's economy more efficiently. (*necessity of the solution*) ★★★

论证要点

本题论证过程比较清晰。首先，文中数据未必说明OV的经济有显著改善(1)；其次就算OV经济确实发展了，但未必是这些建设项目带来的(2)；第三，就算这些建设促进了经济发展，其对于Hopewell未来的经济发展未必产生相同的效果(3、5)；最后，就算这些建设对于H也有效，但可能还有其他更好的促进经济发展的途径(6)。

---

137. The following appeared in a memo from the mayor of Brindleburg to the city council.

169 "Two years ago(4), the town of Seaside Vista opened a new municipal golf course and resort hotel. Since then, the Seaside Vista Tourism Board has reported a 20% increase in visitors(1). In addition, local banks reported a steep rise in the number of new business loan applications they received this year (2). The amount of tax money collected by Seaside Vista has also increased, allowing the town to announce plans to improve Seaside Vista's roads and bridges (3). **We recommend building a similar golf course and resort hotel in Brindleburg(5). We predict that this project will generate additional tax revenue that the city can use to fund much-needed public improvements.**" (former 25, ≈77) ★★

翻　译 2年前，Seaside Vista开设了新的市高尔夫球场和度假旅店。从那以后，Seaside Vista旅游协会上报游客量增加了20%。而且，当地银行报告今年他们接到的新商业贷款申请数量激增。Seaside Vista的税收也在增加，使得该市得以出台改善城市道路和桥梁的方案。我们建议在Brindleburg建立类似的高尔夫球场和度假旅店。我们预计这一项目将带来很多税收进而得以资助急需改善的公共设施。

推理结构

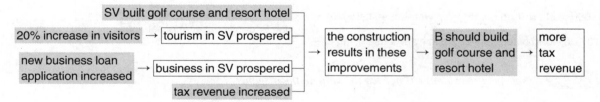

写作要求 *What **questions** should be answered to decide whether the recommendation will have the predicted result?*

1. What's the purpose of these visitors to visit Seaside Vista? Were they attracted by the golf course or the hotel? (*I.I./N.C.R.*) ★★★

2. Did the rise in the number of applications result from a prosperous business at SV? Are there any other explanations? (*N.C.R.*) ★★★

3. Granted that SV's economy was indeed prosperous, how the golf course and resort hotel actually contributed to the economy of SV? (*post hoc, ergo propter hoc*) ★★★★

4. Granted that it is the construction of golf course and resort hotel that resulted in SV's prosperity, will similar constructions continue to benefit Brindleburg's overall economy in the future? (*P→F*) ★★★★

5. Are Seaside View and Brindleburg comparable? (*F.A.*) ★★★★★

论证要点

本题首先需要讨论的就是作者提供的信息是否能说明SV旅游业的繁荣。假如游客、贷款申请和税收的增加是因为去年某些特殊情况导致的，那就未必说明SV的经济会持续繁荣。其次，SV的经济大幅改善得益于高尔夫球场和旅店这一因果关系也未必成立。再次，就算是球场和旅店的建设使SV经济繁荣，2年后在B开展同样的建设是否能得到和当年在SV一样的效果也值得怀疑。

---

138. The following appeared in a memo from the vice president of a food distribution company with food storage warehouses in several cities.

[78] "Recently, we signed a contract with the Fly-Away Pest Control Company to provide pest control services at our fast-food warehouse in Palm City, but last month we discovered that over $20,000 worth of food there had been destroyed by pest damage. Meanwhile, the Buzzoff Pest Control Company, which we have used for many years, continued to service our warehouse in Wintervale, and last month only $10,000 worth of the food stored there (1) had been destroyed by pest damage (2). Even though the price charged by Fly-Away is considerably lower (3), **our best(6) means of saving money is to return to Buzzoff(5) for all (4) our pest control services.**" (former 41) ★★

翻　译 最近我们和Fly-Away Pest Control公司签了一项合同为我们在Palm City的快餐食品仓库提供害虫控制服务，但上个月我们发现，那里有价值超过20000美元的食品被害虫破坏。同时，我们合作多年的Buzzoff Pest Control公司继续在Wintervale的仓库服务，上个月那里只有价值10000美元的食品被害虫破坏。尽管Fly-Away的收费低得多，但我们节省花费的最好方式就是重新使用Buzzoff公司来为我们提供所有的害虫控制服务。

推理结构

$20,000 worth of food damaged in warehouse using FA ⎤
$10,000 worth of food damaged in warehouse using B ⎦ → use B for all pest control services → | save money |

写作要求 *What specific **evidence** is needed to evaluate the argument?*

提　纲

作者需要提供说明以下方面的信息或论据：

1. Total value of food products stored in each warehouse. We cannot evaluate the loss at which warehouse is heavier. (*V.D.*)

不知道每个仓库存货受害的比例，无法判断哪个仓库的害虫控制更有效。★★★★

2. The situations in Palm City and Wintervale are not quite different. (*I.C.*)

   如果两地区环境、气候、虫害严重性不同，那么，两仓库根本无法比较。★★★★★

3. The actual price charged by each company. We can not determine whether adopting the vice president's advice will save money. (*lack of comparison/I.I.*)

   在比较两家公司的收费与避免的损失的差值之后，才能判断用哪家公司更经济。★★★★

4. Detailed information about the differences between the specialties of the two companies on pest-control. It is too hasty to use Buzzoff for **all** pest-control services. (*C.S.*) ★★★★

5. Information about other pest-control companies which can do even better than the two companies. (*F.D.*) ★★★

6. Other methods that can be applied to achieve the vice president's purpose of saving money. (*necessity of the solution*) ★★

论证要点

本题最核心的论证点在于两家公司服务的仓库的不完整比较。在没有对比两仓库的损失率、环境气候、虫害严重性以及使用两家公司的成本收益比的情况下，不能草率判断哪家公司更适合。此外，B是否能在所有地区、所有仓库都有出色表现，以及是否有其他更好的公司和更好的防虫手段也可以分析讨论。

---

139. The following appeared in a memo from the vice president of a food distribution company with

114 food storage warehouses in several cities.

"Recently, we signed a contract with the Fly-Away Pest Control Company to provide pest control services at our warehouse in Palm City, but last month we discovered that over $20,000 worth of food there had been destroyed by pest damage. Meanwhile, the Buzzoff Pest Control Company, which we have used for many years in Palm City, continued to service our warehouse in Wintervale, and last month only $10,000 worth of the food stored there(1) had been destroyed by pest damage(2). Even though the price charged by Fly-Away is considerably lower(3), **our best(6) means of saving money is to return to Buzzoff(5) for all (4) our pest control services.**" (former 41, =78) ★★

翻　译 最近我们和Fly-Away Pest Control公司签订了一项合同为我们在Palm City的仓库提供害虫控制服务，但上个月我们发现，那里有价值超过20000美元的食品被害虫破坏。同时，我们在Palm City使用多年的Buzzoff Pest Control公司继续在Wintervale的仓库服务，上个月那里只有价值10000美元的食品被害虫破坏。尽管Fly-Away收费低得多，但我们节省花费的最好方式就是重新使用Buzzoff公司来为我们提供所有的害虫控制服务。

推理结构

$20,000 worth of food damaged in warehouse using FA ┐
$10,000 worth of food damaged in warehouse using B ┘ → use B for all pest control services → save money

写作要求 What **questions** should be answered to decide whether the recommendation and the argument are reasonable?

提　纲

1. How much is the total value of food products stored in each warehouse? We cannot evaluate the loss at which warehouse is heavier. (*V.D.*)

不知道每个仓库存货受害的比例，无法判断哪个仓库的害虫控制更有效。★ ★ ★

2. Are the situations in Palm City and Wintervale comparable? (*F.A.*)

   如果两地区环境、气候、虫害严重性不同，那么，两仓库根本无法比较。★ ★ ★ ★ ★

3. How much is the actual price charged by each company? We can not determine whether adopting the vice president's advice will save money. (*lack of comparison/I.I.*)

   在比较两家公司的收费与避免的损失的差值之后，才能判断用哪家公司更经济。★ ★ ★ ★

4. What are the differences between the specialties of the two companies on pest-control? It is too hasty to use Buzzoff for all pest-control services. (*C.S.*) ★ ★ ★ ★

5. Are there any other pest-control companies which can do even better than the two companies? (*F.D.*) ★ ★ ★

6. Are there any other methods that can be applied to achieve the vice president's purpose of saving money? (*necessity of the solution*) ★ ★

论证要点

本题最核心的论证点在于两家公司服务的仓库的不完整比较。在没有对比两仓库的损失率、环境气候、虫害严重性以及使用两家公司的成本收益比的情况下，不能草率判断哪家公司更适合。此外，B是否能在所有地区、所有仓库都有出色表现，以及是否有其他更好的公司和更好的防虫手段也可以分析讨论。

---

140. The following appeared in a memo from the vice president of a food distribution company with
〔116〕 food storage warehouses in several cities.

"Recently, we signed a contract with the Fly-Away Pest Control Company to provide pest control services at our warehouse in Palm City, but last month we discovered that over $20,000 worth of food there had been destroyed by pest damage. Meanwhile, the Buzzoff Pest Control Company, which we have used for many years in Palm City, continued to service our warehouse in Wintervale, and last month only $10,000 worth of the food stored there (1) had been destroyed by pest damage (2). **This difference in pest damage is best explained by the negligence of Fly-Away.**" (former 41, ≈78, 114) ★ ★ ★ ★

翻 译

最近我们和Fly-Away Pest Control公司签了一项合同为我们在Palm City的仓库提供害虫控制服务，但上个月我们发现，那里有价值超过20000美元的食品被害虫破坏。同时，我们在Palm City使用多年的Buzzoff Pest Control公司继续在Wintervale的仓库服务，上个月那里只有价值10000美元的食品被害虫破坏。这一虫害差别的最好解释就是Fly-Away的疏忽。

推理结构

$20,000 worth of food damaged in warehouse using FA ─┐
                                                       ├→ negligence of FA → damage
$10,000 worth of food damaged in warehouse using B ─┘

写作要求 *alternative explanations*

提 纲

1. Maybe the total value of food products stored in each warehouse is different. If the worth of food in Palm is more than twice of that in Wintervale, then the loss at Wintervale is actually heavier. (*V.D.*) ★ ★ ★ ★

2. The difference could also be explained by different situation in Palm City and Wintervale, such as climate, environment, the severity of insect pest, etc. (*I.C.*) ★ ★ ★ ★ ★

对于两个仓库的损失情况，除了作者所说的疏忽之外，还可能受到仓库规模、存货总量和总价值的影响。在虫害发生率一定的情况下，仓库越大，货值越多，虫害损失肯定越大。另外，两仓库所在地区的环境、气候、虫害严重性也可能解释损失上的差别。

---

141. The following appeared in a memo from the vice president of a food distribution company with
117 food storage warehouses in several cities.

"Recently, we signed a contract with the Fly-Away Pest Control Company to provide pest control services at our warehouse in Palm City, but last month we discovered that over $20,000 worth of food there had been destroyed by pest damage. Meanwhile, the Buzzoff Pest Control Company, which we have used for many years in Palm City, continued to service our warehouse in Wintervale, and last month only $10,000 worth of the food stored there（1）had been destroyed by pest damage（2）. Even though the price charged by Fly-Away is considerably lower（3）, **our best(6) means of saving money is to return to Buzzoff(5) for all (4) our pest control services.**"（former 41, =78, 114, ≈116）

翻　译 最近我们和Fly-Away Pest Control公司签了一项合同为我们在Palm City的仓库提供害虫控制服务，但上个月我们发现，那里有价值超过20000美元的食品被害虫破坏。同时，我们在Palm City使用多年的Buzzoff Pest Control公司继续在Wintervale的仓库服务，上个月那里只有价值10000美元的食品被害虫破坏。尽管Fly-Away的收费低得多，但我们节省花费的最好方式就是重新使用Buzzoff公司来为我们提供所有的害虫控制服务。

推理结构

$20,000 worth of food damaged in warehouse using FA ⎤
$10,000 worth of food damaged in warehouse using B ⎦ → use B for all pest control services → save money

---

写作要求 *assumptions*

提　纲

1. The vice president does not provide any information about the total value of food products stored in each warehouse, thus the assumption that the loss at Palm City is heavier is open to doubt.（*V.D.*）
   不知道每个仓库存货受害的比例，无法判断哪个仓库的害虫控制更有效。★★★★

2. The vice president fails to consider other differences between the two cities; they may not be comparable at other aspects.（*F.A.*）
   如果两地区环境、气候、虫害严重性不同，那么，两仓库根本无法比较。★★★★★

3. Lacking information about the actual price charged by each company; the assumption that the company can save money by adopting the vice president's advice is unjustified.（*lack of comparison/I.I.*）
   在比较两家公司的收费与避免的损失的差值之后，才能判断用哪家公司更经济。★★★★

4. The specialties of the two companies on pest-control may be different. It is too hasty to claim that Buzzoff is suitable for all pest-control services.（*C.S.*）★★★★

5. The vice president fails to consider other pest-control companies which can do even better than the two companies.（*F.D.*）★★★

6. The vice president ignores other methods that can be applied to achieve the purpose of saving money.（*necessity of the solution*）★★

本题最核心的论证点在于两家公司服务的仓库的不完整比较。在没有对比两仓库的损失率、环境气候、虫害严重性以及使用两家公司的成本收益比的情况下，不能草率判断哪家公司更适合。此外，B是否能在所有地区、所有仓库都有出色表现，以及是否有其他更好的公司和更好的防虫手段也可以分析讨论。

---

142. Since those issues of *Newsbeat* magazine that featured political news on their front cover were **79** the poorest-selling issues over the past three years (1), **the publisher of *Newsbeat* has recommended that the magazine curtail its emphasis on politics (4) to focus more exclusively on economics and personal finance (3).** She points to a recent survey of readers of general interest magazines (2) that indicates greater reader interest in economic issues (3) than in political ones. *Newsbeat's* editor, however, opposes the proposed shift in editorial policy, pointing out that very few magazines offer extensive political coverage anymore (5). （former 173）★ ★ ★

翻　　译 由于过去3年在封面上刊登了政治新闻的那几期*Newsbeat*杂志是销量最低的几期，因此，*Newsbeat*出版商建议杂志减少对政治的关注而更多致力于经济以及个人理财。她指出最近一项对于大众杂志读者的调查表明，和政治问题相比，读者对经济问题更感兴趣。然而，*Newsbeat*的编辑反对这一编排政策的转变，指出很少有杂志还提供大量的政治报道。

推理结构

Publisher:

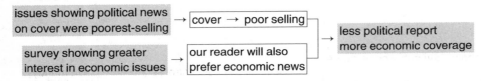

Editor:

few magazines offer extensive political coverage → there will be advantage if we do not change

写作要求 *What **questions** should be answered to decide whether the recommendation and the argument are reasonable?*

提　　纲

1. Do the poor sales of these issues result from featuring international news stories on magazines' front covers? (*confusing concurrence with causality*) ★ ★ ★ ★ ★

2. What groups of people are subscribing these magazines? Could they be representative of readers of *Newsbeat*? (*Are the respondents representative?*) ★ ★ ★

3. Does the interest in **economic issues** indicate an interest in **personal finance**? (*U.C.*) ★ ★ ★

4. Granted that featuring political news on the **front covers** did cause problems, does this fact sufficiently justify that the magazine should decrease the amount of political news in the **content**? (*U.C.*) ★ ★ ★ ★

5. May the fact that few magazines offer political coverage just indicate decreased interest in political news of readers? (*negative evidence*) ★ ★ ★

论证要点

本题结构类似于 **74**，提出了出版商和编辑的两方观点。题目同样要求讨论需回答哪些问题能评价上文建议，这个建议还是指出版商的观点，因此结论应该是第一句的后半句。论证时同样不用考虑赞同谁反对谁，只要讨论一下要评价双方看法都需要回答哪些问题就可以了。对于出版商的建议，主要应考虑封面故事与杂志销量的因果关系、调查结果的代表性问题；对于编辑的看法，主要应考虑导致其他杂志缩减政治报道原因的因果关系问题。

143. The following is taken from a memo from the advertising director of the Super Screen Movie
⑧ Production Company.

"According to a recent report from our marketing department, during the past year, fewer people attended Super Screen-produced movies than in any other year（1）. And yet the percentage of positive reviews by movie reviewers about specific Super Screen movies actually increased during the past year（2,3）. *Clearly, the contents of these reviews are not reaching enough of our prospective viewers(4). Thus, the problem lies not with the quality of our movies (5) but with the public's lack of awareness that movies of good quality are available(6).* **Super Screen should therefore allocate a greater share of its budget next year to reaching the public through advertising(7).**"

翻　译 根据我们市场部最近的一份报告，去年，观看Super Screen拍摄的电影的人比以往任何一年都少，而去年影评对于特定的Super Screen电影的正面评价比例实际上提高了。显然，这些影评内容并没有被我们的潜在观众看到。因此，问题不在于我们电影的质量，而在于公众不知道我们推出了高质量电影。因此Super Screen应该把下一年预算的更大份额用于广告以提升公众认识度。

推理结构

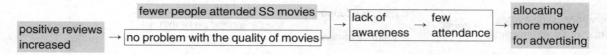

写作要求 *What **questions** should be answered to decide whether the recommendation and the argument are reasonable?*

提　纲

1. Is the report from marketing department accurate enough to reflect the real situation?（*U.A.*）★★
2. Could the opinion of those reviewers reflect the attitude of general moviegoers and the quality of movies?（*U.C./selective sample*）★★★★
3. What is the detailed and comprehensive evaluation of SS's movies?（*I.I./confusing comparison and variation*）
   仅仅是正面评价增加并不能说明SS的电影评价很高。也许之前评价很差，就算有些提高总体来说也比较低。★★★★
4. To what extent will viewers refer to these reviews when choosing a movie?（*I.I./U.A.*）★★★
5. Is there any substantial evidence to illustrate that there is no problem with the quality of the movies?（*U.A./I.I.*）★★★★
6. Are there any other factors that prevent people from attending Super Screen-produced movies?（*N.C.R.*）★★★★
7. Is increasing the budget for advertising sufficient and necessary for attracting public attention and solving the whole problem?（*sufficiency/necessity of the solution*）★★★

论证要点

本题主要论证环节在于文中提到的影评在多大程度上能反映电影的真实质量和代表观众的意见；以及观众在选择电影的时候在多大程度上会参考这些影评。另外，除了关于影评的信息，作者没有任何实质证据来说明他们的电影在质量上确实没有问题。

---

144. The following appeared in a business magazine.

[81] "As a result of numerous complaints of dizziness and nausea on the part of consumers of Promofoods tuna, the company requested that eight million cans of its tuna(1) be returned for testing. **Promofoods concluded that the canned tuna did not, after all, pose a health risk.** This conclusion is based on tests performed on samples of the recalled cans(2) by chemists(3) from Promofoods; the chemists found that of the eight food chemicals(4) most commonly blamed for causing symptoms of dizziness and nausea, five were not found(5) in any of the tested cans. The chemists did find small amounts of the three remaining suspected chemicals but pointed out that these occur naturally in all canned foods(6)." (former 165) ★★★

翻 译 由于有大量Promofoods金枪鱼的消费者投诉说产生了眩晕和恶心，Promofoods公司召回了800万罐金枪鱼罐头进行检测。Promofoods下结论说这些罐头根本不会产生健康威胁。这一结论基于Promofoods的化学家对回收的罐头样本进行的检测；化学家发现在8种最受指责的导致眩晕和恶心症状的化学物质中，有5种没有在任何被测试的罐头中发现。化学家确实发现剩下3种受怀疑的化学物质有少量存在，但他们指出这些物质在所有罐头食品中都有。

推理结构

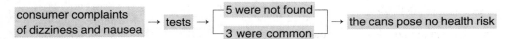

consumer complaints of dizziness and nausea → tests → [5 were not found / 3 were common] → the cans pose no health risk

---

写作要求 *What **questions** should be addressed to decide whether the conclusion and the argument are reasonable?*

提 纲

1. How many tuna cans did Promofoods sell in total? We do not know whether the eight million returned cans are among the batch which caused the problems.(*I.I./V.D.*) ★★★

2. How many cans were tested? Are they representative? (*selective sample*) ★★

3. The test was performed by chemists from Promofoods; is the result reliable?(*Who conducted the survey?*) ★★★★

4. Are there other chemicals or substances that could cause dizziness and nausea?(*Do the tests make any difference?*) ★★★★★

5. Does the fact that the chemicals were not found so far necessarily indicate that there isn't any such chemical in the cans? (*Do the tests make any difference?*)
   *were not found*只能表示到目前为止没有发现，但并不能以此断定一定不存在这种物质。★★★
   4 & 5: The argument treats a lack of proof that the tuna cans may pose some extent of health risk as sufficient proof that the cans were not responsible for any of the sickness.

6. How much of these chemicals are there in canned food products produced by other companies? And how much of them are dangerous? (*I.I./lack of comparison*) ★★★★

本题主要问题在于该公司进行的测试没有实质意义：除了这8种常见有害物质以外，有没有其他可能导致上述症状的物质没有被检测出；在被检测的8种物质中有5种没有找到，从语言表述来说，没找到不等于绝对没有。对于另外3种，small amounts这一描述过于模糊。含量达到多少是危险的？其他罐头食品里含多少？文中检测的样本数量、代表性、可信度都值得怀疑。

---

145. The following is a letter to the editor of an environmental magazine.

[83] "In 1975 a wildlife census (1) found that there were seven species of amphibians in Xanadu National Park, with abundant numbers of each species. However, in 2002 (1) only four species of amphibians were observed in the park, and the numbers of each species were drastically reduced. There has been a substantial decline in the numbers of amphibians worldwide, and global pollution of water and air is clearly implicated. **The decline of amphibians in Xanadu National Park, however, almost certainly has a different cause(2): in 1975, trout—which are known to eat amphibian eggs—were introduced into the park(3).**" (former 150) ★ ★ ★ ★

翻 译 1975年一次野生动物调查发现，Xanadu国家公园有7种两栖动物，每种数量都很丰富。然而到了2002年，在公园中只观察到4种两栖动物，并且每种动物的数量都显著下降。全世界两栖动物数量都在大幅下降，全球水质和空气污染显然与之相关。然而，Xanadu国家公园两栖动物的减少几乎可以断定是另一不同的原因导致的：1975年鲑鱼——我们知道鲑鱼捕食两栖动物的卵——被放养到该公园。

推理结构

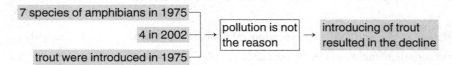

写作要求 *What specific **evidence** is needed to evaluate the argument?*

提 纲

作者需要提供能说明以下情况的信息或论据：

1. The results of the two censuses are reliable; the information provided was complete and accurate. (*reliability of the survey*) ★ ★ ★

2. Direct evidence to show that pollution was not responsible for the decline of amphibians in Xanadu. (*I.E./N.C.R.*) ★ ★ ★ ★ ★

3. Substantial evidence to show that introducing of trout is the real reason of the decline, such as the amount of trout, the regions where they were introduced, and natural enemies of trout there, etc. (*I.E.*) ★ ★ ★ ★ ★

论证要点

本题论证点主要有三方面：一、文中调查的结果能否准确反映实际情况；二、关于鲑鱼的信息并不足以排除污染导致两栖动物数量下降；三、能否确实建立鲑鱼与两栖动物数量下降之间的因果关系。

---

146. The following is a letter to the editor of an environmental magazine.

[84] *"Two studies (1) of amphibians in Xanadu National Park confirm a significant decline in the numbers of amphibians. In 1975 there were seven species of amphibians in the park, and there*

were abundant numbers of each species. However, in 2002 only four species of amphibians were observed in the park, and the numbers of each species were drastically reduced. **One proposed explanation is that the decline was caused by the introduction of trout into the park's waters, which began in 1975(2).** (Trout are known to eat amphibian eggs.)" (former 150, ≈83) ★★★★★

翻　　译　两项对于Xanadu国家公园两栖动物的调查证实了该物种数量的显著下降。1975年公园中共有7种两栖动物，每种数量都很丰富。然而到了2002年在公园中只观察到4种两栖动物，并且每种动物的数量都显著下降。一种解释是数量下降是由1975年开始放养到公园水域的鲑鱼导致的（我们知道鲑鱼捕食两栖动物的卵）。

推理结构

```
7 species of amphibians in 1975 ─┐
               4 in 2002 ────────┼─→  introduction of trout
                                 │    resulted in the decline
   trout were introduced in 1975 ─┘
```

写作要求 *alternative explanations*

提　　纲

1. We do not have any information about the procedure of the studies. The information provided by the two studies might be incomplete and may not accurately reflect the actual situation at Xanadu. (*reliability of the survey*) ★★★

2. Other factors, such as pollution of air and water, destruction of natural habitats, more visits and other increasingly intensive human activities might also lead to the decline. (*N.C.R.*) ★★★★★

论证要点

　　本题论证难度较大。对于文中"鲑鱼导致两栖动物数量下降"这一结论的其他可能解释主要是两方面：一、文中调查得到的数据不准确，不能反映真实的情况。也就是两栖动物的数量并没有下降，而是因为观察方法或其他方面的原因没有观察到；二、除了鲑鱼以外还可能有其他因素导致数量下降，列举其他可能原因。

---

147. In a study of the reading habits of Waymarsh citizens conducted by the University of
85 Waymarsh, most respondents(1) said that they preferred literary classics as reading material. However, a second study(4,5) conducted by the same researchers found that the type of book most frequently checked out of each of the public libraries(2,6) in Waymarsh was the mystery novel(3). **Therefore, it can be concluded that the respondents in the first study had misrepresented their reading habits (7).** (former 161) ★★★

翻　　译　一项由Waymarsh大学开展的关于Waymarsh居民阅读习惯的调查显示，多数回应者说他们倾向于阅读古典文学。然而，由相同的研究人员随后进行的调查发现，Waymarsh所有公共图书馆中最经常被借阅的书是神秘小说。因此，我们可以得出结论，第一次调查的回应者错误地表达了他们的阅读习惯。

```
                        respondents said that they prefer classics
mystery novels were most  →  the situation in libraries could  →  respondents of the first study
frequently checked out         reflect people's reading habit        misrepresented their reading habits
                        literary classics and mystery novels do not overlap
```

写作要求 *What specific **evidence** is needed to evaluate the argument?*

提 纲

作者需要提供关于以下方面的信息或论据：

1. How many, and what groups of citizens responded to the survey? The representativeness of the result is open to doubt. (*Are the respondents representative?*) ★★★

对于上文论述还存在以下问题：

2. The frequency of certain type of book being checked out from the public libraries is not a good indication of whether that type was preferred by citizens. (*U.C.*) ★★★★

作者还需要提供能说明以下方面问题的信息或论据：

3. Analysis about to what extent the literary classics and mystery novels mentioned in the argument overlap. (*I.I.*)

   如果所谓的神秘小说和古典文学有一定的重叠，那么作者的看法就不一定准确。★★★★

4. The result of the follow-up study is representative of all-time reading habits of Waymarsh citizens. (*C→F*) ★★★

5. The interim period between the two studies. Many conditions may change after a long period of time. (*P→C*) ★★★★

6. The assumption that the respondents in the first study borrow most of their reading materials from public libraries is open to doubt. (*U.A.*) ★★★

7. Other explanations that could explain the discrepancy between the respondents' answer and the result of the follow-up study, e.g. if the respondents were forthright, if they correctly understood the survey's question, etc. (*necessity of the solution*) ★★★

论证要点

本题主要论证点是公共图书馆图书借阅情况并不一定能反映民众的阅读习惯(2~6)。此外，文中调查回应者的代表性以及调查结果的真实性(1、7)可以辅助论证。

---

148. In a study of the reading habits of Waymarsh citizens conducted by the University of
87 Waymarsh, most respondents(1) said they preferred literary classics as reading material. However, a second study(4,5) conducted by the same researchers found that the type of book most frequently checked out of each of the public libraries(2,6) in Waymarsh was the mystery novel(3). **Therefore, it can be concluded that the respondents in the first study had misrepresented their reading preferences(7).** (former 161, =85) ★★★

翻 译 一项由Waymarsh大学进行的关于Waymarsh居民阅读习惯的调查显示，多数回应者说他们倾向于阅读古典文学。然而，由相同的研究人员随后进行的调查发现，Waymarsh所有公共图书馆中最经常被借阅的书是神秘小说。因此，我们可以得出结论，第一次调查的回应者错误地表达了他们的阅读习惯。

respondents said that they prefer classics

mystery novels were most frequently checked out → the situation in libraries could reflect people's reading habit → respondents of the first study misrepresented their reading habits

literary classics and mystery novels do not overlap

写作要求 *assumptions*

提　纲

1. We do not know how many, and what kind of citizens responded to the survey. The representativeness of the result is open to doubt. (*Are the respondents representative?*) ★ ★ ★

2. The frequency of certain type of book being checked out from the public libraries is not a good indication of whether that type was preferred by citizens. (*U.C.*) ★ ★ ★ ★

3. The author assumes without justification that the literary classics and mystery novels mentioned in the argument do not overlap. (*I.I.*)
   如果所谓的神秘小说和古典文学有一定的重叠，那么作者的看法就不一定准确。★ ★ ★ ★

4. The author fails to provide evidence to show that the result of the follow-up study is representative of all-time reading habits of Waymarsh citizens. (*C→F*) ★ ★ ★

5. We do not know how long is the interim period between the two studies: many conditions may change after a long period of time.(*P→C*) ★ ★ ★ ★

6. The author unfairly assumes that the respondents in the first study borrow most of their reading materials from public libraries. (*U.A.*) ★ ★ ★

7. The author fails to consider other explanations that could explain the discrepancy between the respondents' answer and the result of the follow-up study, e.g. if the respondents were forthright, if they correctly understood the survey's question, etc. (*necessity of the solution*) ★ ★ ★

论证要点

本题主要假设是公共图书馆图书借阅情况能反映民众的阅读习惯(2~6)。此外，文中调查回应者的代表性以及调查结果的真实性(1、7)可以辅助论证。

---

149. The following appeared in a memo at XYZ company.

86 "When XYZ lays off employees, it pays Delany Personnel Firm to offer those employees assistance in creating résumés and developing interviewing skills, if they so desire. *Laid-off employees have benefited greatly from Delany's services:* last year those who used Delany found jobs much more quickly than did those who did not(1). Recently, it has been proposed that we use the less expensive Walsh Personnel Firm in place of Delany. **This would be a mistake** because eight years ago, when XYZ was using Walsh, only half of the workers we laid off at that time found jobs within a year(2,3,4,5). Moreover, *Delany is clearly superior*, as evidenced by its bigger staff(7) and larger number of branch offices(6). After all, last year(10) Delany's clients took an average of six months to find jobs, whereas Walsh's clients took nine (8,9)." (former 241) ★ ★

当XYZ裁员的时候，它雇用了Delany人事公司在这些下岗员工有需要的时候为他们在写简历和提高面试技巧方面提供帮助。下岗员工从Delany的服务中受益极大：去年获得了Delany帮助的员工在找工作方面比没有接受Delany帮助的员工快得多。最近，有提案提出用收费较少的Walsh人事公司代替Delany。这将是一个错误，因为8年前XYZ使用的就是Walsh，我们当时裁减的员工中只有一半在1年之内找到了工作。而且，Delany显然更好，理由是它的员工更多，分支机构也更多。不论如何，去年Delany的客户平均用6个月时间找到工作，而Walsh的客户平均用了9个月。

推理结构

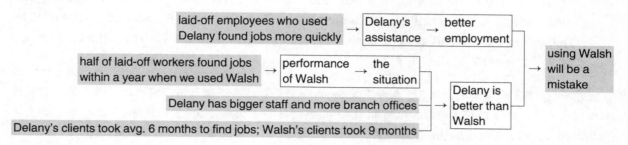

写作要求 *What specific **evidence** is needed to evaluate the argument?*

提　纲

作者需要提供能说明以下方面问题的信息或论据：

1. The successful employment result of the laid-off employees who used Delany could be attributed to Delany's assistance. (*N.C.R.*) ★★★★

2. The poor re-employment result could be blamed on ineffectiveness of Walsh. (*N.C.R./I.C.*)
   可能有其他因素导致使用Walsh的员工花更多的时间再就业，比如总体就业形势等。★★★★

3. Other factors that could explain the differences between the employment results of using different companies. (*I.C.*) ★★★★

4. Comparative data to determine whether the re-employment situation of workers who use Walsh eight years ago is poor. (*lack of comparison/I.I.*)
   当年使用Walsh的员工花了多少时间找到工作？找到的工作具体岗位情况如何？★★

5. Conditions that may have changed during the past eight years. (*P→C*) ★★★
   对于上文论述还存在以下问题：

6. The size of staff and the number of branch offices do not necessarily indicate the quality and effectiveness of a company's service. (*U.C.*) ★★★★

7. A bigger staff may just indicate that the efficiency at Delany is lower. (*negative evidence*) ★★
   作者还需要提供能说明以下方面的信息或论据：

8. The difference between finding job within six months and within nine months is significant. (*I.E.*) ★★

9. Detailed description of Delany's clients and Walsh's clients, and description of jobs their clients get respectively. (*I.I./I.C.*) ★★★★

10. A single year's placement statistics suffice to draw the conclusions. (*selective sample/P→F*) ★★★

论证要点

本题主要论证环节在于D和W两家公司的不完整比较。作者比较的时期不同、就业市场情况不同，因而不具可比性。而且，作者也没有提供寻求两家公司帮助的员工的具体信息以及他们找到的工作好坏的具体信息，因而无法判断D是否比W更有优势。

150. The following appeared in a memo at XYZ company.

89 "When XYZ lays off employees, it pays Delany Personnel Firm to offer those employees assistance in creating résumés and developing interviewing skills, if they so desire. *Laid-off employees have benefited greatly from Delany's services:* last year those who used Delany found jobs much more quickly than did those who did not(1). Recently, it has been proposed that we use the less expensive Walsh Personnel Firm in place of Delany. **This would be a mistake** because eight years ago, when XYZ was using Walsh, only half of the workers we laid off at that time found jobs within a year(2,3,4,5). Moreover, *Delany is clearly superior*, as evidenced by its bigger staff(7) and larger number of branch offices(6). After all, last year(10) Delany's clients took an average of six months to find jobs, whereas Walsh's clients took nine (8,9)." (former 241, =86) ★★

翻　译 当XYZ裁员的时候，它雇用了Delany人事公司在这些下岗员工有需要的时候为他们在写简历和提高面试技巧方面提供帮助。下岗员工从Delany的服务中获益良多：去年获得了Delany帮助的员工在找工作方面比没有接受Delany帮助的员工快得多。最近，有提案提出用收费较少的Walsh人事公司代替Delany。这将是一个错误，因为8年前XYZ使用的就是Walsh，我们当时裁减的员工中只有一半在1年之内找到了工作。而且，Delany显然更好，理由是它的员工更多，分支机构也更多。不论如何，去年Delany的客户平均用6个月时间找到工作，而Walsh的客户平均用了9个月。

推理结构

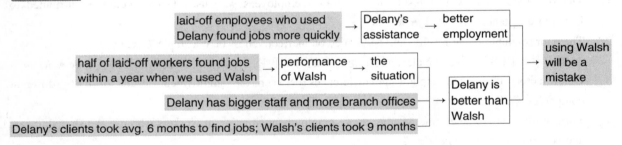

写作要求 *assumptions*

提　纲

1. The author unfairly attributes the successful employment result of the laid-off employees who used Delany to Delany's assistance. (*N.C.R.*) ★★★★

2. The poor re-employment result may not result from ineffectiveness of Walsh. (*N.C.R./I.C.*) ★★★★

3. The author fails to consider many other factors that could explain the differences between the employment results of using different companies. (*I.C.*) ★★★★

4. Without any comparative data, we cannot determine whether the re-employment situation of workers who use Walsh eight years ago is poor. (*lack of comparison/I.I.*)
    当年使用Walsh的员工花了多少时间找到工作？找到的工作具体岗位情况如何？ ★★

5. Many conditions would have changed during the past eight years. (*P→C*) ★★★

6. The size of staff and number of branch offices do not necessarily indicate the quality and effectiveness of a company's service. (*U.C.*) ★★★★

7. A bigger staff may just indicate that the efficiency at Delany is lower. (*negative evidence*) ★★

8. There is no significant difference between finding job within six months and within nine months. (*I.E.*) ★★

9. Without detailed description of Delany's clients and Walsh's clients, and description about the jobs their clients found respectively, we cannot evaluate which company is more effective. (*I.I./I.C.*) ★★★★

10. A single year's placement statistics hardly suffice to draw any firm conclusions. (*selective sample/P→F*) ★★★

论证要点

本题主要论证环节在于D和W两家公司的不完整比较。作者比较的时期不同、就业市场情况不同，因而不具可比性。而且，作者也没有提供寻求两家公司帮助的员工的具体情况以及他们找到的工作好坏的具体信息，因而无法判断D是否比W更有优势。

---

151. <u>Three years ago, because of flooding at the Western Palean Wildlife Preserve, 100 lions and</u> **91** <u>100 western gazelles were moved to the East Palean Preserve, an area that is home to most of the same species that are found in the western preserve, though in larger numbers, and to the eastern gazelle, a close relative of the western gazelle. The only difference in climate(1) is that the eastern preserve typically has slightly less rainfall(3). Unfortunately, after three years in the eastern preserve, the imported western gazelle population has been virtually eliminated.</u> *Since the slight reduction in rainfall cannot be the cause of the virtual elimination of western gazelle,* **their disappearance must have been caused by the larger number of predators in the eastern preserve(2,4).** ★★★★★

翻　　译　3年前由于西Palean野生动物保护区的洪水，100只狮子和100只西部瞪羚被迁移到东Palean保护区，这里是大多数与西部保护区所发现的动物相同的物种的栖居地，而数量比西部更多一些，而且也是东部瞪羚（一种西部瞪羚的近亲）的栖居地。气候上的唯一差别就是东部保护区通常降雨略少。然而，3年后东部保护区那些迁移来的西部瞪羚已近乎绝迹。由于降雨量的些微差别不会是导致西部瞪羚绝迹的原因，那么，它们的消失一定是由东部保护区的大量食肉动物导致的。

推理结构

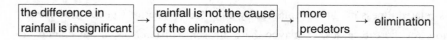

| the difference in rainfall is insignificant | → | rainfall is not the cause of the elimination | → | more predators | → | elimination |

写作要求　*What specific **evidence** is needed to evaluate the argument?*

提　　纲

作者需要提供能说明以下情况的信息或论据：

1. The differences between East and West Palean in aspects other than climate, such as the environment, vegetation (especially the amount of the food of gazelles), geological conditions, etc. (*I.C./I.I.*) ★★★★

2. The variation in the number of other similar species, such as the eastern gazelle, and other vegetarians. (*lack of controlled study/lack of comparison*)
   如果东部瞪羚和其他食草动物数量也在下降，则说明除了食肉动物以外还有其他未查明的主要原因。★★★

3. The detailed difference in the amount of rainfall. Perhaps the slight reduction in rainfall suffices for the elimination of western gazelles. (*I.I./N.C.R.*) ★★★

4. Detailed information of the predators mentioned above. Their actual number, what kind of animals do they prey on, and if they are capable of preying on gazelles. (*I.I./N.C.R.*) ★★★★

本题论证难度较高，主要集中在两点：一、是否有充分证据证明降雨量减少一定不是原因；二、是否有直接证据证明文中所说的食肉动物确实捕食了这些瞪羚，而且除了食肉动物以外没有其他因素导致瞪羚灭绝。

---

152. Workers in the small town of Leeville take fewer sick days than workers in the large city of Masonton(1), 50 miles away. Moreover, relative to population size, the diagnosis of stress-related illness(2) is proportionally much lower(3) in Leeville than in Masonton. **According to the Leeville Chamber of Commerce, these facts can be attributed to the health benefits of the relatively relaxed pace of life in Leeville(4).** (former 234) ★ ★ ★ ★

翻　译 小镇Leeville的工人病假天数比50里外的大城市Masonton要少。而且，相对于人口规模，Leeville诊断出的与压力相关疾病的发病率比Masonton低得多。根据Leeville商会的说法，这些现象可以归因于Leeville相对更为悠闲的生活节奏给健康带来的好处。

推理结构

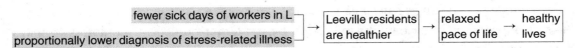

fewer sick days of workers in L ┐
proportionally lower diagnosis of stress-related illness ┘ → Leeville residents are healthier → relaxed pace of life → healthy lives

写作要求 *alternative explanations*

提　纲

1. The number of days of sick leave does not necessarily indicate workers' health status. The fewer sick days may result from other factors such as more strict restrictions and harsher punishment on absenteeism, or the workers' unwillingness of being absent from work. (*U.C./N.C.R.*) ★ ★ ★ ★

2. The diagnosis of stress-related illness may not necessarily reflect the actual level of stress of people, let alone the actual level of health. (*U.C.*) ★ ★ ★

3. The fewer diagnosis of stress-related illness might be explained by other factors; perhaps people in Leeville are not willing to visit doctors for these diseases, or maybe there are some differences in the diagnostic criteria of the disease in the two cities.(*N.C.R.*) ★ ★ ★ ★

4. Granted that Leeville workers are healthier, there are many other factors that could explain the situation, such as better working condition, healthier life style, better environment, and better physical condition of the workers. (*I.C./N.C.R.*) ★ ★ ★ ★ ★

论证要点

本题主要问题在于作者提出的病假天数、压力疾病发病率等信息并不能说明Leeville居民更加健康。病假少、诊断率低都有除了居民本身健康之外的其他可能原因。其次，就算L居民确实更加健康，导致他们健康的也可能有其他因素，而非题目分析的生活节奏。

---

153. **There is now evidence that the relaxed pace of life in small towns promotes better health and greater longevity than does the hectic pace of life in big cities.** Businesses in the small town of Leeville(5) report fewer days of sick leave(1) taken by individual workers than do businesses in the nearby large city of Masonton(5). Furthermore, Leeville has only one physician(2) for its one thousand residents(3), but in Masonton the proportion of physicians to residents is five times as high. Finally, the average age of Leeville residents is significantly higher(4) than that of Masonton residents. **These findings suggest that people seeking longer and healthier lives should consider moving to small communities(6,7).** (former 234, ≈92) ★★

翻　　译 现有证据表明，在小镇的悠闲生活比在大城市的快节奏生活更有利于健康和长寿。小城镇Leeville的商业行业上报的员工病假天数比邻近大城市Masonton要少。而且，Leeville每千人只有1名医生，而Masonton市医生的比例是Leeville的5倍。最后，Leeville居民的平均年龄显著高于Masonton居民。这些发现表明寻求更健康、更长寿生活的人应该考虑移居到小型社区。

推理结构

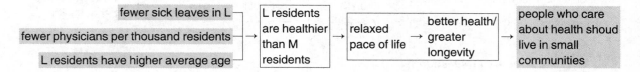

写作要求 *assumptions*

提　　纲

1. The number of days of sick leave taken by workers does not necessarily indicate their health status. (*U.C.*) ★★★★

2. The ratio of physicians to residents is not a good indication of the health level of citizens. (*U.C.*) ★★★★

3. The fact that Leeville has lower ratio of physicians to residents may just suggest that residents here have difficulties in finding adequate health care. (*negative evidence*) ★★★★

4. The author ignores many other differences that would contribute to the higher average age of Leeville residents. (*I.C./N.C.R.*) ★★★★

   1~4: The assumption that Leeville residents are healthier than Masonton residents is open to doubt.

5. Leeville and Masonton are not necessarily representative of all small towns and big cities. (*C.S.*) ★★★★

6. Granted that living in small towns does promote better health and greater longevity, we cannot hastily claim that living at small communities would have the same advantages. (*U.C.*) ★★★★

7. The author fails to consider the disadvantages and inconveniences of living in small towns. (*adv:disadv*) ★★★★

论证要点

本题首要环节是根据作者提供的病假天数、医生比例、平均年龄不能推出Leeville居民更加健康的假设。其次，就算L居民确实健康，Leeville和Masonton也不能代表所有的小城镇和大城市。最后，就算生活在小城镇确实对健康有好处，也不能推出生活在小型社区也会有相同好处的结论。

154. **There is now evidence that the relaxed pace of life in small towns promotes better health and greater longevity than does the hectic pace of life in big cities.** Businesses in the small town of Leeville(5) report fewer days of sick leave(1) taken by individual workers than do businesses in the nearby large city of Masonton(5). Furthermore, Leeville has only one physician for its one thousand residents(2), but in Masonton the proportion of physicians to residents is five times as high. Finally, the average age of Leeville residents is significantly higher(3) than that of Masonton residents. *These findings suggest that the relaxed pace of life in Leeville allows residents to live longer, healthier lives(4).* (former 234, ≈92, 101) ★★

翻　译　现有证据表明，在小镇的悠闲生活比在大城市的快节奏生活更有利于健康和长寿。小镇Leeville的商业行业上报的员工病假天数比邻近大城市Masonton要少。而且，Leeville每千人只有1名医生，而Masonton市医患的比例是Leeville的5倍。最后，Leeville居民的平均年龄显著高于Masonton居民。这些发现说明Leeville的悠闲生活方式使其居民更长寿、生活更健康。

推理结构

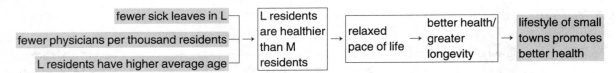

写作要求　*alternative explanations*

提　纲

1. The number of days of sick leave does not necessarily indicate workers' health status. The fewer sick days may result from other factors such as more strict restrictions and harsher punishment on absenteeism, or the workers' unwillingness of being absent from work. (*U.C./N.C.R.*) ★★★★

2. The ratio of physicians to residents is not a good indication of the health level of citizens. Perhaps Leeville is just unable to attract enough physicians to serve the residents. (*U.C.*) ★★★★

3. Many other differences would contribute to the higher average age of Leeville residents. (*I.C./N.C.R.*) ★★★★

4. Granted that Leeville residents are healthier than Masonton residents, the fact could be explained by other factors, such as better working condition, healthier life style, better environment. (*N.C.R.*) ★★★★

5. It is possible that Leeville and Masonton are exceptional cases; they may not necessarily be representative of all small towns and big cities. (*C.S.*) ★★★★

论证要点

　　本题首要环节是根据作者提供的病假天数、医生比例、平均年龄不能推出Leeville居民更加健康的假设。病假天数少可能是因为管理制度更加严格、缺勤惩罚更严厉；医生少可能正因为Leeville无法吸引足够的医生；平均年龄高可能是基因问题、L老龄化比较严重或L大量年轻人群外出打工经商等。其次，就算L居民确实健康，这一现象也可能是由于当地的水土环境、工作条件等因素导致，而且Leeville和Masonton也不能代表所有的小城镇和大城市。

155. The following appeared in an e-mail sent by the marketing director of the Classical
[97] Shakespeare Theatre of Bardville.

"Over the past ten years, there has been a 20 percent decline(1) in the size of the average audience at Classical Shakespeare Theatre productions. In spite of increased advertising, we are attracting fewer and fewer people to our shows, causing our profits to decrease significantly. *We must take action to attract new audience members. The best way(4) to do so is by instituting a 'Shakespeare in the Park' program this summer.* Two years ago the nearby Avon Repertory Company started a 'Free Plays in the Park' program, and its profits have increased 10 percent since then(2,3). **If we start a 'Shakespeare in the Park' program, we can predict that our profits will increase, too(1,5).**" ★★

翻　译　过去10年，Classical Shakespeare剧院平均观众数量减少了20%。尽管增加了广告投入，我们所能吸引的观众越来越少，导致利润显著下滑。我们必须采取措施吸引新的观众。最好的办法就是在今年夏天开展"公园里的莎士比亚"活动。2年前，附近的Avon Repertory公司开展了"公园免费演出"活动，其利润随后增加了10%。如果开展"公园莎士比亚"活动，可以预见我们的利润也会增加。

推理结构

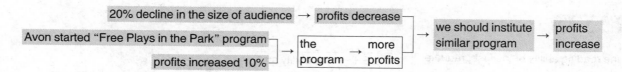

写作要求　*What **questions** should be answered to decide whether the recommendation will have the predicted result?*

提　纲

1. What is the actual cause of the decline in the size of the audience and in the overall profits? (*U.A./I.I./N.C.R.*) ★★★★

2. Does the 10 percent increase in Avon's profits result from the "Free Plays in the Park" program? (*post hoc, ergo propter hoc*) ★★★★

3. Are Classical Shakespeare Theater and Avon Repertory Company comparable at every critical aspect? (*F.A.*) ★★★★

4. Are there other ways to attract new audience members and to increase profits? （*necessity of the solution*） ★★★

5. Is there any other necessary work to be accomplished to ensure the increase in profits? (*sufficiency of the solution*) ★★★

论证要点

　　本题主要问题在于作者提出的活动未必保证利润上升。首先，作者应该分析导致Shakespeare剧院听众减少、利润下滑的真正原因再对症下药；其次，Avon的公园演出未必是带来他们利润上升的真正原因；而且就算是，照搬别人的做法也未必同样会带来Shakespeare的利润上升。

156. The following is a recommendation from the personnel director to the president of Acme
113 Publishing Company.

　　"Many other companies(1) have recently stated that having their employees take the Easy Read Speed-Reading Course has greatly improved productivity. One graduate of the course was able to read a 500-page report in only two hours(2,3); another graduate(5) rose from an assistant manager to vice president of the company in under a year(4). *Obviously, the faster you can read, the more information you can absorb in a single workday.* Moreover,

Easy Read would cost Acme only $500 per employee—*a small price (6) to pay when you consider the benefits.* Included in this fee is a three-week seminar in Spruce City and a lifelong subscription to the Easy Read newsletter. **Clearly, to improve productivity (8), Acme should require all of our employees (7) to take the Easy Read course.**" (former 180) ★★

翻　译 最近，很多其他公司指出他们的员工参加了Easy Read的速读课程之后生产效率显著提高。这个课程的一名毕业生能够在2个小时之内读完长达500页的报告，另一名毕业生在1年内从助理经理升到了副总裁。显然，阅读速度越快，在1天之内能吸收的信息就越多。而且，Easy Read的学费只有每人500元，当考虑到它给Acme带来的效益时这就是个小数目。这个费用包括参加在Spruce City举行的为期3周的研讨会和Easy Read新闻刊物的终身订阅。显然，为提高生产率，Acme应要求所有员工参加Easy Read课程。

推理结构

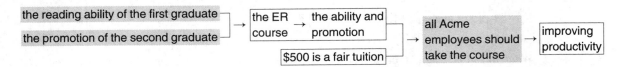

写作要求 *What **questions** should be answered to decide whether the advice and the argument are reasonable?*

提　纲

1. Are these companies and Acme comparable? (*F.A.*) ★★★★
2. How about the reading speed of the first graduate before taking the course? (*confusing comparison and variation*) ★★★
3. What kind of reading material did the first graduate read? (*I.I.*) ★★★
4. Is there any causal relationship between taking the Easy Read course and the reading ability of the first graduate, and the promotion of the second graduate as well? (*post hoc, ergo propter hoc*) ★★★★★
5. Could the two individual cases illustrate the actual effect of the course? (*quantity of the sample*) ★★★★
6. How about the prices of other similar courses? The assumption that 500 dollars is a cheap tuition is open to doubt. (*lack of comparison*) ★★★
7. Do all employees at Acme Publishing Company need to improve their reading speed? Not every worker has to attain a lot of information in their workplace. (*C.S.*) ★★★
8. Will the benefits of the course outweigh its costs? (*adv:disadv*) ★★★★

论证要点

　　本题首先要解决的问题就是文中两个毕业生的个案能否说明课程效果。在不知道第一名毕业生之前的阅读能力和他阅读材料的具体内容以及第二名毕业生的背景的情况下，不能认定是参加课程带来了作者所说的惊人效果。其次，只有这两个特殊个案不能说明其他公司员工都能从参加课程中获益。另外，就算该课程确实非常不错，是否有必要让所有员工都参加课程也值得怀疑。

157. The following is a recommendation from the personnel director to the president of Acme 126 Publishing Company.

　　"Many other companies (1) have recently stated that having their employees take the Easy

Read Speed-Reading Course has greatly improved productivity. One graduate of the course was able to read a 500-page report in only two hours(2,3); another graduate(5) rose from an assistant manager to vice president of the company in under a year(4). *Obviously, the faster you can read, the more information you can absorb in a single workday.* Moreover, Easy Read would cost Acme only $500 per employee—*a small price(6) to pay when you consider the benefits.* Included in this fee is a three-week seminar in Spruce City and a lifelong subscription to the Easy Read newsletter. **Clearly, Acme would benefit greatly(8) by requiring all of our employees(7) to take the Easy Read course.**" (former 180, =113) ★★

翻　译 最近，很多其他公司指出他们的员工参加了Easy Read的速读课程之后生产效率显著提高。这个课程的一名毕业生能够在2个小时内读完长达500页的报告，另一名毕业生在1年内从助理经理升到了副总裁。显然，阅读速度越快，在1天之内所能吸收的信息就越多。而且，Easy Read的学费只有每人500元，当考虑到它给Acme带来的效益时这就是个小数目。这个费用包括参加在Spruce City举行的为期3周的研讨会和Easy Read新闻刊物的终身订阅。显然，Acme通过要求所有员工参加Easy Read的课程将会极大地受益。

推理结构

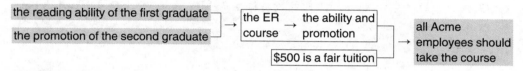

写作要求 *What specific **evidence** is needed to evaluate the argument?*

提　纲

作者需要提供能说明以下方面问题的信息或论据：

1. These companies and Acme are comparable. (*F.A.*) ★★★★
2. The reading speed of the first graduate before taking the course. (*confusing comparison and variation*) ★★★
3. What kind of reading material did the first graduate read? (*I.I.*) ★★★
4. The causal relationship between taking the Easy Read course and the reading ability of the first graduate, and the promotion of the second graduate as well. (*post hoc, ergo propter hoc*) ★★★★★
5. The two individual cases could sufficiently demonstrate the effect of the course. (*quantity of the sample*) ★★★★
6. The prices of other similar courses. The assumption that 500 dollars is a cheap tuition is open to doubt. (*lack of comparison*) ★★★
7. All employees at Acme Publishing Company need to improve their reading speed. (*C.S.*) ★★★
8. Further analysis on benefits and costs of the course. (*adv:disadv*) ★★★★

论证要点

　　本题首先需要论证的就是文中两个毕业生的个案能否说明课程效果。在不知道第一名毕业生之前的阅读能力和他阅读材料的具体内容以及第二名毕业生背景的情况下，不能认定是参加课程带来了作者所说的惊人效果。其次，只有这两个特殊个案不能说明其他公司员工都能从参加课程中获益。另外，就算该课程确实非常不错，是否有必要让所有员工都参加课程也值得怀疑。作者需要提供进一步实质论据证明以上方面。

158. The following is a recommendation from the personnel director to the president of Acme 127 Publishing Company.

"Many other companies(1) have recently stated that having their employees take the Easy Read Speed-Reading Course has greatly improved productivity. One graduate of the course was able to read a 500-page report in only two hours(2,3); another graduate(5) rose from an assistant manager to vice president of the company in under a year(4). *Obviously, the faster you can read, the more information you can absorb in a single workday.* Moreover, Easy Read would cost Acme only $500 per employee—*a small price(6) to pay when you consider the benefits.* Included in this fee is a three-week seminar in Spruce City and a lifelong subscription to the Easy Read newsletter. **Clearly, to improve overall productivity (8), Acme should require all of our employees(7) to take the Easy Read course.**" (former 180, =113, 126) ★★

翻 译 最近，很多其他公司指出他们的员工参加了Easy Read的速读课程之后生产效率显著提高。这个课程的一名毕业生能够在2个小时内读完长达500页的报告，另一名毕业生在1年内从助理经理升到副总裁。显然，阅读速度越快，在1天之内所能吸收的信息就越多。而且，Easy Read的学费只有每人500元，当考虑到它给Acme带来的效益时这就是个小数目。这个费用包括参加在Spruce City举行的为期3周的研讨会和Easy Read新闻刊物的终身订阅。显然，为提高整体生产率，Acme应要求所有员工参加Easy Read课程。

推理结构

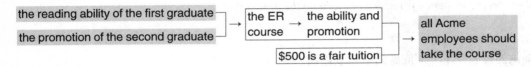

写作要求 *What* **questions** *should be answered to decide whether the recommendation and the argument are reasonable?*

提 纲

1. Are these companies and Acme comparable? (*F.A.*) ★★★★
2. How about the reading speed of the first graduate before taking the course? (*confusing comparison and variation*) ★★★
3. What kind of reading material did the first graduate read? (*I.I.*) ★★★
4. Is there any causal relationship between taking the Easy Read course and the reading ability of the first graduate, and the promotion of the second graduate as well? (*post hoc, ergo propter hoc*) ★★★★★
5. Could the two individual cases illustrate the actual effect of the course? (*quantity of the sample*) ★★★★
6. How about the prices of other similar courses? The assumption that 500 dollars is a cheap tuition is open to doubt. (*lack of comparison*) ★★★
7. Do all employees at Acme Publishing Company need to improve their reading speed? Not every worker has to attain a lot of information in their workplace. (*C.S.*) ★★★
8. Will the benefits of the course outweigh its costs? (*adv:disadv*) ★★★★

论证要点

本题首先需要论证的就是文中两个毕业生的个案能否说明课程效果。在不知道第一名毕业生之前的阅读能力和他阅读材料的具体内容以及第二名毕业生背景的情况下，不能认定是参加课程带来了作者所说的惊人效果。其次，只有这两个特殊个案不能说明其他公司员工都能从参加课程中获益。另外，就算该课程确实非常不错，是否有必要让所有员工都参加课程也值得怀疑。

---

159. The following is a recommendation from the personnel director to the president of Acme
161 Publishing Company.

"Many other companies(1) have recently stated that having their employees take the Easy Read Speed-Reading Course has greatly improved productivity. One graduate of the course was able to read a 500-page report in only two hours(2,3); another graduate(5) rose from an assistant manager to vice president of the company in under a year(4). *Obviously, the faster you can read, the more information you can absorb in a single workday.* Moreover, Easy Read would cost Acme only $500 per employee—*a small price(6) to pay when you consider the benefits.* Included in this fee is a three-week seminar in Spruce City and a lifelong subscription to the Easy Read newsletter. **Clearly, Acme would benefit greatly(8) by requiring all of our employees(7) to take the Easy Read course.**" (former 180, =113, 126, 127) ★★

翻 译 最近，很多其他公司指出他们的员工参加了Easy Read的速读课程之后生产效率显著提高。这个课程的一名毕业生能够在2小时内读完长达500页的报告，另一名毕业生在1年内从助理经理升到副总裁。显然，阅读速度越快，1天内能吸收的信息就越多。而且，Easy Read的学费只有每人500元，当考虑到它给Acme带来的效益时这就是个小数目。这个费用包括参加在Spruce City举行的为期3周的研讨会和Easy Read新闻刊物的终身订阅。显然，Acme通过要求所有员工参加Easy Read的课程将会极大地受益。

推理结构

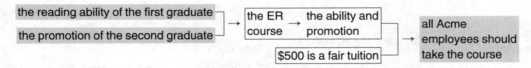

写作要求 *assumptions*

提 纲

1. The director assumes that these companies and Acme are comparable. (*F.A.*) ★★★★

2. The director does not provide any information concerning the reading speed of the first graduate before taking the course. (*confusing comparison and variation*) ★★★

3. We need to know what kind of reading material the first graduate read. (*I.I.*) ★★★
   2 & 3: The assumption that the first graduate benefits from the course is open to doubt.

4. The director fails to establish the causal relationship between taking the Easy Read course and the reading ability of the first graduate, and the promotion of the second graduate as well. (*post hoc, ergo propter hoc*)
   ★★★★★

5. The two individual cases could hardly illustrate the actual effect of the course. (*quantity of the sample*)
   ★★★★

6. Without information about the prices of other similar courses, the assumption that 500 dollars is a cheap tuition is open to doubt. (*lack of comparison*) ★★★

7. The director fails to convince us that all employees at Acme Publishing Company need to improve their reading speed. Not every worker has to attain a lot of information in their workplace. (*C.S.*) ★★★

8. The director hastily assumes that the benefits of the course will outweigh its costs. (*adv:disadv*) ★★★★

本题首先需要论证的就是文中两名毕业生的个案能否说明课程效果。在不知道第一名毕业生之前的阅读能力和他阅读材料的具体内容以及第二名毕业生的背景的情况下，作者所认定的参加课程带来了上述惊人效果的假设是没有依据的。其次，只有这两个特殊个案不能说明其他公司员工都能从参加课程获益的假设。另外，就算该课程确实非常不错，是否有必要让所有员工都参加也值得怀疑。

---

160. The following appeared in a letter to the school board in the town of Centerville.

132 "**All(1) students should be required to take the driver's education course at Centerville High School.** In the past two years, several accidents（2,3）in and around Centerville have involved teenage drivers. Since a number of（6）parents in Centerville have complained that they are too busy to teach their teenagers to drive（5）, *some other instruction is necessary to ensure that these teenagers are safe drivers*. Although there are two driving schools in Centerville, parents on a tight budget（6）cannot afford to pay for driving instruction. **Therefore an effective and mandatory program sponsored by the high school(8,9) is the only(7) solution to this serious problem (4).**"（former 175）★ ★

翻　　译 所有学生都应该参加Centerville高中的驾驶教育课程。在过去2年中，Centerville及其周围有几起交通事故涉及青少年驾驶者。由于Centerville一些家长抱怨说他们太忙、没有时间教他们的孩子驾驶，因此，必须有一些其他课程来保证这些孩子成为安全驾驶者。尽管Centerville已经有2所驾校，但手头不宽裕的家长无法负担驾校学费。因此，由学校组织的、有效的强制性课程是解决这一严重问题的唯一方案。

推理结构

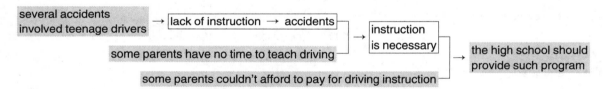

写作要求 *assumptions*

提　　纲

1. The author's assumption that **all** students in Centerville need to take the course is open to doubt.（*C.S.*）★ ★ ★

2. The author fails to describe the severity of accidents, and who actually caused these accidents.（*I.I./necessity of the solution*）★ ★ ★ ★

3. In the absence of comparative accident rates during earlier years, we cannot evaluate if the situation is getting worse and if the program is necessary.（*lack of comparison*）★ ★ ★
   2 & 3: The assumption that teenager driving is a serious problem and we must take steps to solve it is unjustified.

4. The high accident rate might be caused by many factors, so implementing the program alone may not suffice to ensure a lower accident rate.（*sufficiency of the solution*）★ ★ ★

5. Having no time to teach their children to drive does not necessarily imply that the parents are unable to ensure their children to be safe drivers. The safe-driving course is not equal to driving instruction.（*U.C./necessity of the solution*）★ ★ ★

6. The author fails to inform us the percentage of parents who have no time to teach their children to drive and who are on tight budgets. (*V.D.*) ★★★

5 & 6: The assumption that additional driving instructions are necessary is unwarranted.

7. The proposed program sponsored by the high school may not be the only solution to the problem. (*F.D.*) ★★★★

8. The author fails to consider whether the high school is qualified to offer the program. (*feasibility of the conclusion*) ★★★

9. The author fails to consider wether the high school has the responsibility and enough funding to sponsor the program, and whether students will accept it. (*feasibility of the conclusion*) ★★★★

7~9: The assumption that the school could and must carry out such program is unfounded.

论证要点

本题论证的主要环节在于作者提供的关于事故的信息不完整,不能证明作者所暗示的青少年驾驶事故问题已经很严重的假设,从而采取上文措施的必要性也就不一定能保证。此外,学校是否有能力、财力和责任来开设该课程,以及这种课程是否是解决问题的唯一方案也值得怀疑。

---

161. The following appeared in a letter to the school board in the town of Centerville.

134 "**All(1) students should be required to take the driver's education course at Centerville High School.** In the past two years, several accidents(2,3) in and around Centerville have involved teenage drivers. Since a number of(6) parents in Centerville have complained that they are too busy to teach their teenagers to drive(5), *some other instruction is necessary to ensure that these teenagers are safe drivers.* Although there are two driving schools in Centerville, parents on a tight budget(6) cannot afford to pay for driving instruction. **Therefore an effective and mandatory program sponsored by the high school(8,9) is the only(7) solution to this serious problem(4).**" (former 175, =132) ★★

翻　译 所有学生都应该参加Centerville高中的驾驶教育课程。在过去2年中,Centerville及其周围有几起交通事故涉及青少年驾驶者。由于Centerville一些家长抱怨说他们太忙、没有时间教他们的孩子驾驶,因此,必须有一些其他课程来保证这些孩子成为安全驾驶者。尽管Centerville已经有2所驾校,但手头不宽裕的家长无法负担驾校学费。因此,由学校组织的、有效的强制性课程是解决这一严重问题的唯一方案。

推理结构

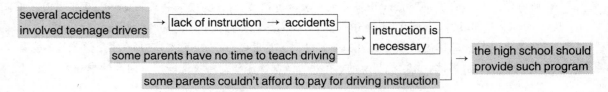

写作要求 *What specific **evidence** is needed to evaluate the argument?*

提　纲

作者需要提供能说明以下方面问题的信息或论据:

1. The necessity for **all** students in Centerville to take the course. (*C.S.*) ★★★

2. The severity of accidents and injuries, if any, and who actually caused these accidents. (*I.I./necessity of the solution*) ★ ★ ★ ★

3. Comparative accident rates during earlier years. We cannot evaluate whether the situation is getting worse and whether the program is necessary. (*lack of comparison*) ★ ★ ★

上文论述还存在以下问题：

4. The high accident rate might be caused by many factors, so implementing the program alone may not suffice to ensure a lower accident rate. (*sufficiency of the solution*) ★ ★ ★

5. Having no time to teach their children to drive does not necessarily imply that the parents are unable to ensure their children to be safe drivers. The safe-driving course is not equal to driving instruction. (*U.C./ necessity of the solution*) ★ ★ ★

作者还需要提供能说明以下方面问题的信息或论据：

6. The percentage of parents who have no time to teach their children to drive and who are on tight budgets. (*V.D.*) ★ ★ ★

7. Other possible solutions to solve the problem. (*F.D.*) ★ ★ ★ ★

8. The high school is qualified to offer the program. (*feasibility of the conclusion*) ★ ★ ★

9. The high school has the responsibility and enough funding to sponsor the program, and students will accept it. (*feasibility of the conclusion*) ★ ★ ★ ★

论证要点

本题论证的主要环节在于作者提供的关于事故的信息不完整，不能说明该地区青少年驾驶事故问题已经很严重，因而采取上文措施的必要性也就不一定能保证。此外，学校是否有能力、财力和责任来开设该课程，以及这种课程是否是解决问题的唯一方案也值得怀疑。作者需要提供实质论据来证明以上问题。

---

162. The following appeared in a letter to the school board in the town of Centerville.

136 **"All(1) students should be required to take the driver's education course at Centerville High School.** In the past two years, several accidents(2,3) in and around Centerville have involved teenage drivers. Since a number of(6) parents in Centerville have complained that they are too busy to teach their teenagers to drive(5), some other instruction is necessary to ensure that these teenagers are safe drivers. Although there are two driving schools in Centerville, parents on a tight budget(6) cannot afford to pay for driving instruction. **Therefore an effective and mandatory program sponsored by the high school(8,9) is the only(7) solution to this serious problem(4)."** (former 175, =132, 134) ★ ★

翻　译 所有学生都应该参加Centerville高中的驾驶教育课程。在过去2年中，Centerville及其周围有几起交通事故涉及青少年驾驶者。由于Centerville一些家长抱怨说他们太忙、没有时间教他们孩子驾驶，因此，必须有一些其他课程来保证这些孩子成为安全驾驶者。尽管Centerville已经有2所驾校，但手头不宽裕的家长无法负担驾校学费。因此，由学校组织的、有效的强制性课程是解决这一严重问题的唯一方案。

推理结构

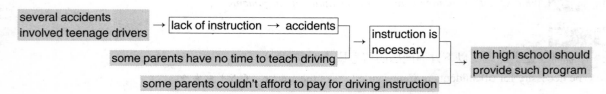

288

提　纲

1. Is there necessity for all students in Centerville to take the course? (*C.S.*) ★★★

2. How about the severity of accidents and injuries, if any, and who actually caused these accidents? (*I.I./ necessity of the solution*) ★★★★

3. How about the comparative accident rates during earlier years? We cannot evaluate whether the situation is getting worse and whether the program is necessary. (*lack of comparison*) ★★★

4. Does implementing the program alone suffice to ensure a lower accident rate? The high accident rate might be caused by many factors. (*sufficiency of the solution*) ★★★

5. Does the fact that parents have no time to teach their children to drive necessarily imply that the parents are unable to ensure their children to be safe drivers? The safe-driving course is not equal to driving instruction. (*U.C./necessity of the solution*) ★★★

6. What is the percentage of parents who have no time to teach their children to drive and who are on tight budgets? (*V.D.*) ★★★

7. Are there other possible solutions to solve the problem? (*F.D.*) ★★★★

8. Is the high school qualified to offer the program? (*feasibility of the conclusion*) ★★★

9. Does the high school have the responsibility and enough funding to sponsor the program? Will students accept it? (*feasibility of the conclusion*) ★★★★

论证要点

本题论证的主要环节在于作者提供的关于事故的信息不完整，不能说明该地区青少年驾驶事故问题已经很严重，因而采取上文措施的必要性也就不一定能保证。此外，学校是否有能力、财力和责任来开设该课程，以及这种课程是否是解决问题的唯一方案也值得怀疑。

---

163. The data from a survey of high school math and science teachers(1) show that in the district of
135 Sanlee many of these teachers reported assigning daily homework, whereas in the district of Marlee(6), most science and math teachers reported assigning homework no more than two or three days per week(2). Despite receiving less frequent homework assignments, Marlee students earn better grades overall and are less likely to be required to repeat a year of school (3) than are students in Sanlee(4,5,9). *These results call into question the usefulness of frequent homework assignments. Most likely the Marlee students have more time to concentrate on individual assignments than do the Sanlee students who have homework every day.* **Therefore teachers in our high schools should assign homework no more than twice(7) a week(8).** (former 193) ★★

翻　译 一项对于高中数理化教师的调查数据表明，在Sanlee地区很多数理化教师报告说他们每天布置作业，而在Marlee地区大多数这类教师报告说他们每周布置作业不超过2或3次。尽管被布置的作业少，但Marlee地区的学生综合成绩比Sanlee地区的学生更好，而且留级现象也更少。这些结果对于经常布置作业的作用提出质疑。很可能Marlee地区的学生比每天都有作业的Sanlee学生有更多时间专注于个人发展。因此，我们的高中教师每周布置作业不应该超过2次。

many Sanlee teachers assign daily homework; Marlee teachers assign homework no more than 2–3 days/week	→	less homework	→	more time on individual assignment	→	homework no more than twice a week
Marlee students perform better						

写作要求 *What specific* **evidence** *is needed to evaluate the argument?*

提 纲

作者需要提供能说明以下方面问题的论据或信息：

1. The situation about teachers in other subjects. (*selective sample*) ★★★

2. Information about the respective **total amount** of homework assigned each time in Sanlee and Marlee. (*U.C./I.I.*) ★★★

3. Evidence to establish the causal relationship between homework frequency and students' performance. (*N.C.R.*) ★★★★★

4. Other differences between Sanlee and Marlee which could explain the differences in their students' grades and likelihood to repeat a year of school. (*I.C.*) ★★★★★

5. The students' grades and likelihood to repeat a year of school could accurately reflect the quality of education. (*U.C.*) ★★★★

6. The two districts are representative of the state's school districts overall. (*C.S.*) ★★★

7. Why we should assign homework no more than **twice** a week, but no more and no less. (*I.E.*) ★

8. Negative effects of assigning inadequate homework. (*adv:disadv*) ★★★

9. Evidence to substantiate the assumption that any educational activity is valuable only to the extent that it enhances overall grades. (*I.T.*) ★★★

论证要点

本题主要问题在于Sanlee和Marlee两地区学生分数和升级的差异不一定是作业次数导致的；其次，文中调查对象"数理化教师"是选择性样本，不一定能说明所有科目布置作业的作用；另外，作业布置不充分会不会对学校教育和学生的培养产生负面影响也可以进行论证。

---

164. While the Department of Education in the state of Attra recommends that high school students

137 be assigned homework every day, *the data from a recent statewide survey of high school math and science teachers(1) give us reason to question the usefulness of daily homework.* In the district of Sanlee, 86 percent of the teachers reported assigning homework three to five times a week, whereas in the district of Marlee(6), less than 25 percent of the teachers reported assigning homework three to five times a week(2). Yet the students in Marlee earn better grades overall and are less likely to be required to repeat a year of school(3) than are the students in Sanlee(4,5,9). **Therefore, all teachers in our high schools should assign homework no more than twice(7) a week(8).** (former 193, ≈135) ★★

翻 译 尽管Attra州教育部建议高中学生应该每天都被布置家庭作业，但最近一项对于全州的数理化高中教师的调查数据使我们有理由对每天布置家庭作业的作用提出疑问。在Sanlee地区，86%的教师报告说每周布置3~5次家庭作业，而在Marlee地区，只有不到25%的教师报告说每周布置3~5次家庭作业。而Marlee地区的学生综合成绩更好，而且与Sanlee的学生相比留级现象也更少。因此，我们高中的所有教师每周布置作业都不应该超过2次。

86% Sanlee teachers assign homework 3–5 times/week;
25% Marlee teachers assign homework 3–5 times/week → less homework → better performance → homework no more than twice a week

Marlee students perform better

写作要求 *assumptions*

提 纲

1. The result of the survey lacks credibility because many teachers in other subjects were actually excluded from the survey. (*selective sample*) ★★★

2. The author provides no information about the respective total amount of homework assigned each time in Sanlee and Marlee. (*U.C./I.I.*)
作者仅仅提供了两地区布置作业的次数，但是每次布置的作业量没有提及。★★★

3. The author fails to establish the causal relationship between homework frequency and students' performance. (*N.C.R.*) ★★★★★

4. Many other differences between Sanlee and Marlee could explain the differences in their students' grades and their likelihood to repeat a year of school. (*I.C.*) ★★★★★

   1~4: The assumption that the lower homework frequency at Marlee results in better performance of their students is unjustifiable.

5. The students' grades and likelihood to repeat a year of school are not a good indication of the quality of education. (*U.C.*) ★★★★

6. The two districts may not be representative of the state's school districts overall. (*C.S.*) ★★★

7. The author fails to illustrate why we should assign homework no more than **twice** a week, but no more or no less. (*I.E.*) ★

8. The author ignores some negative effects of assigning inadequate homework. (*adv:disadv*) ★★★

9. The author unfairly assumes that any educational activity is valuable only to the extent that it enhances overall grades. (*I.T.*) ★★★

论证要点

本题主要问题在于Sanlee和Marlee两地区学生分数和升级的差异不一定是作业次数导致的；其次，文中调查对象"数理化教师"是选择性样本，不一定能说明所有科目布置作业的作用；另外，作业布置不充分会不会对学校教育和学生的培养产生负面影响也可以进行论证。

---

165. While the Department of Education in the state of Attra suggests that high school students be
140 assigned homework every day, *the data from a recent statewide survey of high school math and science teachers(1) give us reason to question the usefulness of daily homework*. In the district of Sanlee(6), 86 percent of the teachers reported assigning homework three to five times a week, whereas in the district of Marlee, less than 25 percent of the teachers reported assigning homework three to five times a week(2). Yet the students in Marlee earn better grades overall and are less likely to be required to repeat a year of school(3) than are the students in Sanlee (4,5,9). **Therefore, we recommend that all teachers in our high schools should assign homework no more than twice(7) a week(8).** (former 193, ≈ 135, =137) ★★

尽管Attra州教育部建议高中学生应该每天都被布置家庭作业，但最近一项对于全州的数理化高中教师的调查数据使我们有理由对每天布置家庭作业的作用提出疑问。在Sanlee地区，86%的教师报告说每周布置3~5次家庭作业，而在Marlee地区，只有不到25%的教师报告说每周布置3~5次家庭作业。而Marlee地区的学生综合成绩更好，而且与Sanlee的学生相比留级现象也更少。因此，我们建议高中的所有教师每周布置作业都不应该超过2次。

推理结构

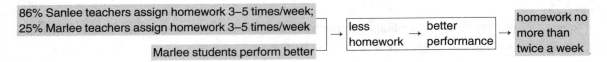

写作要求　*What **questions** should be answered to decide whether the recommendation and the argument are reasonable?*

提　　纲

1. Is the result of the survey reliable? Many teachers in other subjects were actually excluded from the survey. (*selective sample*) ★★★

2. How about the respective total amount of homework assigned each time in Sanlee and Marlee? (*U.C./I.I.*) 文中仅提及两地区布置作业的次数，但每次布置的作业量没有提及。★★★

3. Is there a causal relationship between homework frequency and students' performance? (*N.C.R.*) ★★★★★

4. Are there other differences between Sanlee and Marlee that could explain the differences in their students' grades and likelihood to repeat a year of school? (*I.C.*) ★★★★★

5. Are the students' grades and likelihood to repeat a year of school a good indication of the quality of education? (*U.C.*) ★★★★

6. Are the two districts representative of the state's school districts overall? (*C.S.*) ★★★

7. Why should we assign homework no more than twice a week, but no more or no less? (*I.E.*) ★

8. Are there any negative effects of assigning inadequate homework? (*adv:disadv*) ★★★

9. Is educational activity valuable only to the extent that it enhances overall grades? (*I.T.*) ★★★

论证要点

本题主要问题在于Sanlee和Marlee两地区学生分数和升级的差异不一定是作业次数导致的；其次，文中调查对象"数理化教师"是选择性样本，不一定能说明所有科目布置作业的作用；另外，作业布置不充分会不会对学校教育和学生的培养产生负面影响也可以进行论证。

---

166. *Hospital statistics regarding people who go to the emergency room after roller-skating* **142** *accidents indicate the need for more protective equipment.* Within that group of people, 75 percent（1）of those who had accidents in streets or parking lots（2）had not been wearing any protective clothing（helmets, knee pads, etc.）or any light-reflecting material（clip-on lights, glow-in-the-dark wrist pads, etc.）（3）. **Clearly, the statistics indicate that by investing in high-quality（4）protective gear and reflective equipment, roller skaters will greatly（5）reduce their risk of being severely（6）injured in an accident.**

翻　　译　医院对于滚轴溜冰事故后去急诊室的人的统计表明我们需要更多保护装备。在这些人当中，在街道或停车场发生事故的人有75%没有穿戴任何保护服装（头盔、护膝等）或任何反光材料（小灯、夜光护腕等）。显然，这些数据表明，通过购买高质量保护装置和反光设备，溜冰者将能极大地降低他们在事故中受到严重伤害的危险。

推理结构

75% of those who had accidents did not wear equipments → no gear → injury → wearing gears → less risk of injury

写作要求 *assumptions*

提 纲

1. The author unfairly assumes that the percent of skaters who do not wear those gears in the general skater population is lower than 75%. (*lack of comparison/controlled study*)
   如果不穿保护装置的溜冰者在所有溜冰人群中的比例高于75%，那就未必说明穿戴保护装置能够降低受伤率。★★★

2. The author assumes that the hospital statistics at these relatively dangerous places are representative of the condition of general roller-skaters. (*C.S./selective sample*) ★★★

3. The author assumes that it is the lack of gears and equipments, rather than other factors, that contributes to the high accident rate. (*confusing concurrence with causality*) ★★★★★

4. No evidence could indicate that skaters must invest in **high-quality** gears to serve the purpose of reducing risk of injury. (*U.A.*) ★★★

5. Without further information about the actual cause of the accidents, the assumption that wearing gears could greatly reduce the risk of injury is unwarranted. (*I.I.*) ★★★★

6. The author does not differentiate the severity of injuries, thus we cannot evaluate if adopting the author's proposal could be sufficient for reducing the risk of being **severely** injuried. (*I.I./sufficiency of the solution*) ★★★

论证要点

本题最关键环节在于因为数据对比的不全面以及没有考虑导致受伤的其他可能因素，未必能充分说明是因为缺乏保护装置而导致事故中的受伤这一假设。而且，作者选取的街道和停车场这些相对比较危险的地区的情况未必能说明在其他地区溜冰的危险性。另外，溜冰者是否必须购买高质量装置以及佩戴这些装置是否足以避免所有严重伤害也值得讨论。

---

167. The following appeared in a memo to the board of directors of Bargain Brand Cereals.

`152` "One year ago（3）we introduced our first product, Bargain Brand breakfast cereal. Our very low prices quickly drew many customers away from the top-selling cereal companies（1）. Although the companies producing the top brands have since tried to compete with us by lowering their prices and although several plan to introduce their own budget brands（4）, not once have we needed to raise our prices to continue making a profit（2）. Given *our success in selling cereal*, **we recommend that Bargain Brand now expand its business and begin marketing other low-priced food products（5）as quickly as possible.**" (former 171) ★★★

翻 译 1年前我们推出了第一种产品Bargain Brand早餐麦片，我们非常低廉的价格迅速从一些销量最大的麦片厂商那里吸引了大量客户。尽管这些生产顶级品牌的厂商曾经试图通过降低价格来与我们竞

争，并且有一些公司打算推出他们自己的廉价品牌，但我们从不需要通过涨价来维持赢利。基于销售麦片的成功，我们建议Bargain Brand尽快扩展业务，开始推出其他的廉价食品。

推理结构

| low prices → success of BB |
| no pressure of competition → no need to raise price |

→ expand business/marketing other low-priced products

写作要求 *What **questions** should be answered to decide whether the recommendation and the argument are reasonable?*

提 纲

1. Did the low price of Bargain Brand attract those customers? (*N.C.R.*) ★ ★ ★ ★
2. How about the actual profit of the company after Bargain Brand cereal was introduced? (*I.I.*) ★ ★ ★
3. Will the strong sales of Bargain Brand breakfast cereal last year continue in the following years? (*P→F*) ★ ★ ★
4. Why do other companies' strategies constitute no threat to our company? (*I.E.*) ★ ★ ★
5. Could the company succeed in selling other food products through the low-price strategy? (*C.S.*) ★ ★ ★ ★

论证要点

本题问题首先在于作者并没有提供公司推出BB之后利润方面的信息，因而无法判断BB的推出除了吸引客户之外还有没有其他意义。其次，就算BB的推出十分成功，是否是受益于低价策略也不能保证。另外，BB的低价策略是否能应用于其他食品也存在问题。

---

168. The following appeared in a memo to the board of directors of Bargain Brand Cereals.

153 "One year ago(3) we introduced our first product, Bargain Brand breakfast cereal. Our very low prices quickly drew many customers away from the top-selling cereal companies(1). Although the companies producing the top brands have since tried to compete with us by lowering their prices and although several plan to introduce their own budget brands(4), not once have we needed to raise our prices to continue making a profit(2). Given *our success in selling cereal*, **we recommend that Bargain Brand now expand its business and begin marketing other low-priced food products(5) as quickly as possible.**" (former 171, =152) ★ ★ ★

翻 译 1年前我们推出了第一种产品Bargain Brand早餐麦片，我们低廉的价格迅速从一些销量最大的麦片厂商那里吸引了大量客户。尽管这些厂商曾经试图通过降低价格来与我们竞争，并且有一些公司打算推出他们自己的廉价品牌，但我们从不需要通过涨价来维持赢利。基于销售麦片的成功，我们建议Bargain Brand尽快扩展业务，开始推出其他的廉价食品。

推理结构

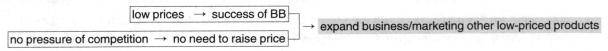

| low prices → success of BB |
| no pressure of competition → no need to raise price |

→ expand business/marketing other low-priced products

写作要求 *assumptions*

1. The director unfairly assumes that it is the low price of Bargain Brand that attracted those customers. (*N.C.R.*) ★★★★

2. The argument contains no information concerning the actual profits of the company after Bargain Brand cereal was introduced, thus we cannot evaluate whether the cereal selling strategy was successful. (*I.I.*) ★★★

3. The director over-optimistically assumes that the strong sales of Bargain Brand breakfast cereal last year will continue in the following years. (*P→F*) ★★★

4. The director fails to provide any substantial evidence to show why other companies' strategies constitute no threat to our company. (*I.E.*) ★★★

5. The director hastily assumes that the company will succeed in selling other food products through their low-price strategy. (*C.S.*) ★★★★

论证要点

本题问题首先在于作者没有提供公司推出BB之后利润方面的信息，因而无法判断BB的推出除了吸引客户之外还有没有其他意义。其次，就算BB的推出十分成功，是否是得益于低价策略也不能保证。另外，BB的低价策略可以应用于其他食品的假设也存在问题。

---

169. The following appeared in a memo from the marketing director of Top Dog Pet Stores.

157 "Five years ago(2) Fish Emporium started advertising in the magazine *Exotic Pets Monthly*. Their stores saw sales increase by 15 percent after their ads began appearing in the magazine. The three Fish Emporium stores in Gulf City saw an even greater increase than that(1). Because Top Dog Pet Stores is based in Gulf City, **it seems clear that we should start placing our own ads in Exotic Pets Monthly(3).** *If we do so, we will be sure to reverse the recent trend of declining sales and start making a profit again(4)."* ★

翻 译 5年前Fish Emporium开始在*Exotic Pets Monthly*杂志上做广告。广告刊登后其商店销售量增加了15%。Gulf市的三家Fish Emporium商店销售量增加更多。由于Top Dog Pet商店植根于Gulf市，显然我们应该开始在*Exotic Pets Monthly*上面刊登广告。这样做肯定能够使我们扭转最近销量下降的局面，并开始重新赢利。

推理结构

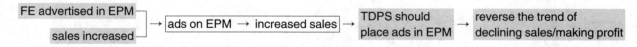

写作要求 *assumptions*

提 纲

1. The director unfairly assumes that it is the ads on EPM that resulted in the increased sales of Fish Emporium stores. (*post hoc, ergo propter hoc*) ★★★★★

2. The director also assumes that the strategies 5 years ago will also be effective at present time. (*P→C*) ★★★★

3. The assumption that FE and TDPS are comparable is unwarranted. (*F.A.*) ★★★★

4. The director assumes that placing ads in EPM is sufficient and necessary to ensure increasing sales and making profit. (*sufficiency/necessity of the solution*) ★★★

本题论证结构比较清晰，也比较简单。首先，作者假定FE销量上升是因为在EPM刊登了广告；其次，作者还认定5年前有效的策略和方案在今天依然适用，而且对FE有效的方法对TDPS也同样有效；此外，作者还假定在EPM刊登广告对于保证销量上升、增加赢利既是充分的也是必要的。

---

170. The following appeared in a memo from the marketing director of Top Dog Pet Stores.

158 "Five years ago(2), Fish Emporium started advertising in the magazine *Exotic Pets Monthly*. Their stores saw sales increase by 15 percent. The three Fish Emporium stores in Gulf City saw an even greater increase than that(1). Because Top Dog has some of its largest stores in Gulf City, **it seems clear that we should start placing our own ads in *Exotic Pets Monthly* (3)**. *If we do so, we will be sure to reverse the recent trend of declining sales and start making a profit again(4).*" （=157） ★

翻　译 5年前Fish Emporium开始在*Exotic Pets Monthly*杂志上做广告。广告刊登后其商店销售量增加了15%。Gulf市的三家Fish Emporium商店销售量增加更多。由于Top Dog几家最大的商店都位于Gulf市，显然我们应该开始在*Exotic Pets Monthly*上面刊登广告。这样做肯定能够使我们扭转最近销量下降的局面，并开始重新赢利。

推理结构

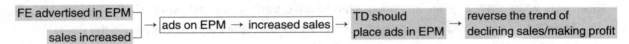

FE advertised in EPM / sales increased → ads on EPM → increased sales → TD should place ads in EPM → reverse the trend of declining sales/making profit

写作要求 *What specific **evidence** is needed to evaluate the argument?*

提　纲

作者需要提供能够说明以下方面问题的论据或信息：

1. It is the ads on EPM that resulted in the increased sales of Fish Emporium stores. (*post hoc, ergo propter hoc*) ★★★★★

2. The strategies 5 years ago will also be effective at present time. (*P→C*) ★★★★

3. FE and TDPS are comparable. (*F.A.*) ★★★★

4. Placing ads in EPM is sufficient and necessary to ensure increasing sales and making profit. (*sufficiency/necessity of the solution*) ★★★

本题论证结构比较清晰，也比较简单。首先，作者需要提供证据证明FE销量上升是因为在EPM刊登了广告；其次，就算广告导致销量上升，5年前的策略和方案在今天未必适用，而且FE和TDPS未必可比；此外，在EPM刊登广告对于保证销量上升、增加赢利的充分性和必要性也需要作者论证。

---

171. The following appeared in a recommendation from the president of the Amburg Chamber of 160 Commerce.

"Last October, the city of Belleville installed high-intensity lighting in its central business district, and vandalism there declined almost immediately(1). The city of Amburg, on the other hand, recently instituted police patrols on bicycles in its business district(2, 3). However, the rate of vandalism here remains constant. *Since high-intensity lighting is clearly the most effective way (5) to combat crime(8)*, **we recommend using the money that is currently being spent on bicycle patrols to install such lighting throughout(7) Amburg(4,6).** *If we install this high-intensity lighting, we will significantly reduce crime rates in Amburg."* (former 205) ★★★

翻　译 去年10月，Belleville市在其中央商业区安装了高照度灯，立即显著减少了那里破坏公物的行为。另一方面，Amburg市最近开始在商业区安排警察骑自行车巡逻，但破坏公物的发生率并没有变化。由于高照度灯光显然是震慑犯罪的最有效途径，因此我们建议把现在用于自行车巡逻的经费用于在Amburg全市安装这种灯。如果安装这种高照度灯，Amburg市的犯罪率将显著减少。

推理结构

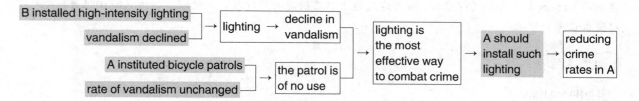

写作要求 *What **questions** should be answered to decide whether the recommendation will have the predicted result?*

提　纲

1. Is the installation of high-intensity lighting the primary cause of the decline in vandalism in Belleville? (*post hoc, ergo propter hoc*) ★★★★

2. In what places does most vandalism at Amburg take place? We cannot evaluate whether the police patrols are ineffective. (*I.I./U.A.*)
    如果A市主要的破坏公物行为并非发生在商业区，那么，作者提供的信息就不能说明警察巡逻完全没有作用。★★★

3. Would the rate of vandalism be even higher if the bicycle patrols were not instituted? (*lack of controlled study*) ★★★

4. Are Belleville and Amburg comparable? (*F.A.*) ★★★★

5. Are there other effective ways to combat crime? (*F.D.*) ★★★★

6. What is the cost of installing high-intensity lighting throughout Amburg? Could we afford it? (*adv:disadv/feasibility of the conclusion*) ★★★

7. Granted that installing such lighting could reduce vandalism, is it necessary to install the lighting all over Amburg? (*C.S.*) ★★★★

8. Granted that installing such lighting could reduce vandalism, would the lighting deter other types of crimes? For vandalism might not be the only type of crime in Amburg. (*C.S.*) ★★★★

论证要点

　　本题最根本的环节在于作者认为安装高照度灯非常有效，而警察巡逻无效。但在不知道A市破坏公物行为的主要发生地区和缺乏比较数据的情况下，警察巡逻是否完全没有效果是存在疑问的。另一方面，B市安装这种照明是否是那里破坏公物行为减少的主要原因也需要作者证实。此外，就算安装照明确实有效、警察巡逻确实无效，在A市也安装这种照明未必能起到相同的效果。最后，有没有必要以及有没有足够经费在A全市都安装这种照明，以及安装以后是否能降低整体犯罪率依然值得讨论。

172. The following appeared in a recommendation from the president of Amburg's Chamber of
172 Commerce.

"Last October the city of Belleville installed high-intensity lighting in its central business district,
and vandalism there declined within a month (1). The city of Amburg has recently begun police
patrols on bicycles in its business district (2, 3), but the rate of vandalism there remains
constant. **We should install high-intensity lighting throughout (7) Amburg (4,6)**, then,
*because doing so is a more effective way to combat crime (5,8). By reducing crime in this way,
we can revitalize the declining neighborhoods in our city (9)."* (former 205, ≈160) ★★★

翻　译　去年10月，Belleville市在其中央商业区安装了高照度灯，1个月后那里破坏公物的行为减少
了。Amburg市最近开始在其商业区安排警察骑自行车巡逻，但破坏公物的发生率并没有变化。因而，我们
应该在Amburg全市安装高照度灯，因为这是防止犯罪的更有效途径。通过以这种方式减少犯罪，我们可
以使本市重新繁荣起来。

推理结构

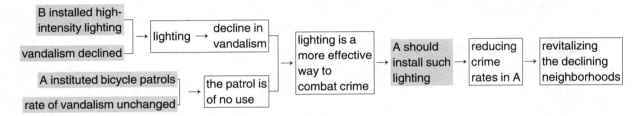

写作要求　*What specific **evidence** is needed to evaluate the argument?*

提　纲

作者需要提供能说明以下方面问题的信息或论据：

1. It is the installation of high-intensity lighting that resulted in the decline in vandalism in Belleville. (*post hoc, ergo propter hoc*) ★★★★

2. The places where most vandalism at Amburg takes place. We cannot evaluate whether the police patrols are ineffective. (*I.I./U.A.*)
   如果A市主要的破坏公物行为并非发生在商业区，那么，作者提供的信息就不能说明警察巡逻完全
   没有作用。★★★

3. The rate of vandalism would not be higher if the bicycle patrols were not instituted. (*lack of controlled study*) ★★★

4. Belleville and Amburg are comparable at every aspect. (*F.A.*) ★★★★

5. Other effective ways to combat crime. (*F.D.*) ★★★★

6. The cost of installing high-intensity lighting throughout Amburg and if we could afford it. (*adv:disadv/ feasibility of the conclusion*) ★★★

7. (Granted that installing such lighting could reduce vandalism) the necessity of installing the lighting **all over** Amburg. (*C.S.*) ★★★★

8. (Granted that installing such lighting could reduce vandalism) evidence to guarantee that it would deter other types of crimes, since vandalism is not the only type of crime in Amburg. (*C.S.*) ★★★★

9. The proposed actions would sufficiently guarantee revitalization of city neighborhoods. (*sufficiency of the solution*) ★★★

本题最根本的环节在于作者认为安装高照度灯非常有效，而警察巡逻无效。但在不知道A市破坏公物的主要发生地区和缺乏比较数据的情况下，警察巡逻是否完全没有效果是存在疑问的。另一方面，B市安装这种照明是否是那里破坏公物行为减少的主要原因也需要作者证实。此外，就算安装照明确实有效、警察巡逻确实无效，在A市也安装这种照明未必能起到相同的效果。最后，有没有必要以及有没有足够经费在A全市都安装这种照明，以及安装以后是否能降低整体犯罪率并使城市重新繁荣也值得讨论。

---

173. The following is a letter that recently appeared in the *Oak City Gazette*, a local newspaper.

168 "The primary function of the Committee for a Better Oak City is to advise the city government on how to make the best use of the city's limited budget. However, at some of our recent meetings we failed to make important decisions because of the foolish objections raised by committee members who are not even residents of Oak City(1). *People who work in Oak City but who live elsewhere cannot fully understand the business and politics of the city(2).* After all, only Oak City residents pay city taxes, *and therefore only residents understand how that money could best be used to improve the city(3).* **We recommend, then, that the Committee for a Better Oak City vote to restrict its membership to city residents only. We predict that, without the interference of non-residents(4), the committee will be able to make Oak City a better place in which to live and work.**" (former 177) ★ ★ ★

翻　译 For a Better Oak City委员会的主要职能是在如何最好地使用有限的城市预算方面给予市政府建议。然而，最近几次会议中一些甚至并不是Oak City居民的委员提出的愚蠢反对意见致使我们未能作出任何重要决策。在Oak City工作但在别的地方居住的人无法真正理解本城市的政治和经济。毕竟，只有Oak City居民付城市税，因而也只有他们才知道这些钱如何使用才能最好地促进城市发展。因此，我们建议委员会投票把成员资格仅仅限制在本地居民。我们预计，在没有外地人干扰的情况下，委员会有能力使Oak City成为更美好的适于工作和生活的地方。

推理结构

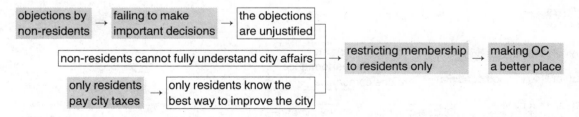

写作要求 *What **questions** should be answered to decide whether the recommendation will have the predicted result?*

提　纲

1. Are the objections raised by non-residents reasonable? Is there any evidence to prove that the so-called "important decision" was indeed justified? (*I.I./U.A.*)
   在不知道决策的具体内容的情况下，我们不能判断这些外地委员的反对一定是无理的。★ ★ ★

2. Is the assumption that residents necessarily understand the business and politics of the city better than non-residents justifiable? (*U.A.*) ★ ★ ★ ★

3. Is paying city taxes sufficient or necessary for one to understand the best way to improve the city? (*U.A./*

sufficiency/necessity of the solution）★ ★ ★

4. Are there any negative effects of excluding non-residents from the committee? The non-residents might have great contributions to Oak City's business and economy, or they might be able to give more valuable suggestions just because they live in elsewhere. (*I.T.*) ★ ★ ★ ★ ★

论证要点

本题的论据基本全都是作者想当然的假设。首先，如何保证外地委员反对的决议一定是正当的？假如决议本身确实有问题，那就不能说明外地委员阻碍了城市发展。其次，本地居民一定能更好地理解城市事务，以及只有本地居民才知道如何更好地使用财政经费的假设也没有任何依据。最后，把外地委员排除在外会不会对城市发展有不利影响也值得讨论。

---

174. The following appeared in a memo from the vice president of a company that builds shopping malls around the country.

"The surface of a section of Route 101（1）, paved just two years ago by Good Intentions Roadways, is now badly cracked with a number of dangerous potholes. In another part of the state, a section of Route 40, paved by Appian Roadways more than four years ago, is still in good condition（2）. In a demonstration of *their continuing commitment to quality*, Appian Roadways recently purchased state-of-the-art paving machinery and hired a new quality-control manager（3,4,5）. **Therefore, I recommend hiring Appian Roadways to construct the access roads(6) for all our new shopping malls. I predict that our Appian access roads will not have to be repaired for at least four years.**"（former 233）★

翻　译 2年前由Good Intentions筑路公司修筑的101公路的一段路面现已严重开裂，并出现危险的坑注。在同一州另一个地区，4年多以前由Appian筑路公司修筑的40公路的一段现在依然状况良好。作为其不懈追求质量的证明，Appian公司最近购买了最先进的筑路机械，并雇用了一名新的质量监控经理。因此，我建议雇用Appian公司为我们所有新商业街修筑通道。我预计Appian修筑的通道至少4年不用修理。

推理结构

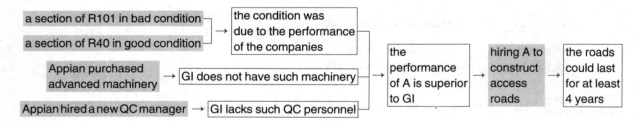

写作要求 *What **questions** should be answered to decide whether the recommendation will have the predicted result?*

提　纲

1. Is the condition of the **sections** of the two roads representative of the condition of **all roads** built by the two companies?（*I.C./selective sample/selective comparison*）★ ★ ★ ★

2. Has the vice president taken into account other factors that would influence the condition of a road?（*I.C.*）★ ★ ★ ★ ★

3. Does Good Intentions have similar advanced machinery and quality-control personnel? (*ex parte information*) ★★★

4. How about the performance of the new quality-control manager at Appian? (*I.I.*) ★★★

5. Has the vice president taken into account other factors besides equipment and on-site management that would also affect the quality of a pavement job? (*I.C.*) ★★★★

6. Granted that the quality of routes paved by Appian is superior, could Appian also do an excellent job in constructing the access roads for shopping malls? (*U.C./F.A.*) ★★★

论证要点

本题最核心问题在于对两家筑路公司工程质量的不完整比较。首先，作者只对比了两家公司修的一条路的一段，至于这一段路的状况能否代表两家公司的整体筑路质量根本无法保证；其次，就在对比这一段路的时候作者又仅考虑了影响道路状况的诸多因素中的一个：道路修筑质量，还有很多决定道路状况的因素作者没有综合对比；再次，仅凭作者提供的A公司购买先进机械、雇用质监经理的信息也不能推断出GI公司缺乏这种机械和人员；最后，就算A公司修公路水平确实高，他们是否愿意修商业街通道以及他们修的通道是否也能具备和公路一样的质量也依然不能保证。

Argument写作需要论证的问题一般可细分为约20类。为保证考场上的写作速度、论证层次和逻辑性，最好把每类经常讨论的问题的展开思路事先整理清楚，即：要把这类问题说明白，第一句该说什么，第二句该说什么。整理思路的工作是作文考取高分的前提，千万不要上考场之后再临时构建论证思路，这样文章字数和论证逻辑层次都很难保证。思路整理完成之后再根据自己的语言基础进行判断：假如基础不错就不用事先斟酌论证语言，可以到了考场上再遣词造句；但如果基础一般，事先不斟酌语言的话就难以保证文章字数、论证层次的准确性和逻辑性。

但要注意，模板只是一种思路提示的工具，其作用是提示考生要论证这类问题思路上应如何展开。因此，如要事先选定论证语言，那么，考生只需要选择一些最基本的衔接、过渡词汇和句式，保证在考场上知道这类问题应如何一步一步深入分析即可。千万不要把模板理解成凑字数的工具，不要期望通过模板可以把大部分的语言句式固定下来，这样写出的文章肯定会流于空泛而且有雷同的危险。因此，选定的模板语句在整个段落所占的比例一定不要过高，一般以不超过20%为宜。而且语言要有一定灵活性，要使用替换和改造的方法。

另外，在构造模板时也要考虑到针对不同写作要求的语言对应。前面也阐述过，Assumption、Question和Evidence三种问法存在内在联系，没有本质区别，因而在展开论证时要分析的基本内容是一致的，只是在段首句、第二句过渡句、段落总结句的表达上会有所变化。比如，对于错误类比问题（False Analogy），针对这三种写作要求的段首句可以用完全一样的句式：

In the argument the author recommends A to copy the actions of B.

第二句过渡句可以有所区别：

Assumption：This recommendation relies on a basic assumption that A and B are comparable at every critical aspect.

Question：To evaluate the recommendation we should ask that whether A and B are comparable at every critical aspect.

Evidence：To substantiate the recommendation the author should provide evidence to illustrate that A and B are comparable at every critical aspect.

接下来的展开思路基本类似，即都是展开分析A和B之间有哪些具体差别从而导致A与B两者可能不可比。

最后的总结句也可以体现出对写作要求的呼应：

Assumption：Before the author could substantiate the critical assumption that A and B are comparable, we should not hastily adopt the recommendation.

Question：Before the author addresses the critical question above, we could not sufficiently evaluate whether A could attain its objective through copying B's actions.

Evidence：For lack of critical evidence to illustrate the comparability of A and B, we should not hastily adopt the recommendation.

以下部分提供了针对每类主要论证问题的参考模板。为了让考生看清论证展开的思路，以下使用的固定语言成分所占比例较高。在实际操作时，应尽量降低固定语言所占的比例。而且，这里所列的只是对该类问题的其中一种展开思路，考生应该结合自己的思维和语言特点整理自己的论证模板。

下文中：

【**表现形式**】是指这类问题在题目中出现的常见形式；

【**基本假设**】是指论证中出现这类问题时作者所做的基本假设；

【**可参考**】是指这类问题与另外哪些问题相似或存在内在联系，可以互相参考甚至共用同样的论证模板；

【**分析思路**】是分析这类问题时的主要展开思路和要做的工作。

1. Selective Sample 选择性样本

【**表现形式**】

To sample only part of sub-groups in the whole general population.

作者仅研究了总群体中某些特殊子群体。

【**基本假设**】

The sample is randomly selected and is representative of the general group.

调查样本应随机选取且能代表总群体。

【**可参考**】

Quantity of the sample, are the respondents representative, changing scopes.

【**分析思路**】

To point out that the current sample is not randomly selected and could not represent the general group, or that the survey studies only special groups of subjects while many other sub-groups have been ignored.

指出样本的选取不符合随机性原则，或作者仅研究了某些特殊群体，因而不能代表总体研究对象。

【**参考模板**】

（针对Assumption的写作要求）

段首句：(*pointing out that the current sample is not representative*)

The author implies that the sample studied in the survey could present (*the general group*),

递进解释：but the author considers only...(*selective sub-groups*).

让步/转折：Although (*the sub-groups studied*) do constitute a significant part of (*the general population*), however, (*many other sub-groups*) are actually excluded from the survey.

论证展开：(*The conditions/situation of other sub-groups might be quite different.*)

段落小总结：Without ruling out the above possibilities, the author could not make any general conclusion about (*the general population*) merely based on (*the selective sub-groups*).

【**论证要点**】

调查的选择性样本问题和样本数量问题、差异范围草率推广问题本质相近，都是从一些特殊的、不具有代表性的个案推断出更广泛群体的特征。论证时应主要解释清楚作者所选取的样本和想要研究的总群体之间有什么可能差别，为什么样本不一定能代表整个群体。

2. Quantity of the Sample 样本的数量

【**表现形式**】

The size of the sample is insignificant to be statistically representative.

调查研究的对象数量不够充足。

【**基本假设**】

The quantity of the sample is sufficient to be representative.

样本的规模足以保证其代表性。

【可参考】

Selective sample, are the respondents representative, changing scopes.

【分析思路】

To point out that the current sample is not sufficient in size, and might not represent all other sub-groups.

指出样本数量不够充分，而且不足以代表总群体。

【参考模板】

（针对Assumption的写作要求）

段首句：（*pointing out that the current sample is too small in size*）

（*The fact cited by the author*）could hardly illustrate the assumption that...,

递进解释: because the author provides only N samples of (*the general population*).

论证展开：(*The sample studied might be special case(s), and is too limited to be representative.*)

段落小总结: We cannot accept the author's implication that...before more statistic data about(*the situation of other sub-groups*) are provided.

【论证要点】

样本数量问题和选择性样本问题没有本质差别。如果调查选取的样本太少，那就必然是选择性样本了。展开时需要分析指出调查样本数量太少，一些特殊的个案不能代表要研究的总体人群。

3. Do the statistics make any difference? 调查是否有意义？

【表现形式】

The purpose or the result of the survey is insignificant in supporting the final conclusion.

调查目标不明确，调查过程无关痛痒，或调查内容不充分，因而不足以支持结论。

【基本假设】

The result of the survey should be related to and could support the conclusion.

调查结果应与推理过程相关且足以支持结论。

【可参考】

What question was asked in the survey, insufficient evidence.

【分析思路】

To point out that the result of the study could not give strong and sufficient support to the final conclusion, or even has nothing to do with the conclusion.

指出调查结果不足以支持结论，或与推理过程没有逻辑关联。

【参考模板】

（针对Evidence的写作要求）

段首句：（*pointing out that the result of the survey is insignificant*）

The information provided by the author is insufficient for illustrating (*the conclusion or assumption*).

递进解释：The survey only studies the situation of...(*an (some) insignificant case(s)*),

转折: however, many more critical cases (*related to the final conclusion*) were ignored in the survey.

论证展开：To evaluate the argument, we need the author to provide information concerning (*the condition of some other cases about which we care more/the current case studied in the survey makes little sense on the final conclusion; the author should provide more important information about other subjects*).

段落小总结：Lacking further studies on these important issues, the author could not hastily conclude that... merely based on the insignificant study.

所谓"调查没有意义"指的是作者所做的调查从过程或内容来说无关痛痒,不能给予结论有效支持。论证时应主要分析作者调查过程做得不够充分的地方,或指出为什么调查本身不足以支持结论。

4. What question was asked in the survey? 调查所问的问题是否恰当?

【表现形式】

The question asked in the survey is not directly related to the final conclusion, or the question itself may have some misleading effects.

调查中针对被访对象所问的问题与最终结论没有直接联系,或可能存在误导性。

【基本假设】

The question asked in the survey should be directly related to the argument/conclusion.

调查所问的问题应能够直接支持结论。

【可参考】

Do the statistics make any difference, insufficient evidence.

【分析思路】

To point out that there are logical gaps between the question asked in the survey and the final conclusion, or some other critical questions should be asked in the survey.

指出调查所问的问题与最终结论之间存在脱节的地方,或指出要支持结论应该调查其他更关键的问题。

【参考模板】

(针对Evidence的写作要求)

段首句:(*pointing out that the question asked in the survey is insignificant*)

Another problem is the question asked in the survey about...

递进解释: Merely this question could not lend strong support to the author's conclusion that...

论证展开:(*The question has no direct relation to the final conclusion; some other critical questions should be asked in the survey to get more valuable information.*)

段落小总结: The result cited above could hardly support the conclusion before the author could provide substantial evidence to illustrate that ...

【论证要点】

这一点指的是调查所问的问题对于支持最终结论没有什么直接作用,或调查问题本身就有一定的误导性或倾向性。论证的时候主要应分析调查问题和最终结论之间有哪些逻辑跳跃,或要支持结论应该问哪些更直接的问题。

5. Who conducted the survey? 调查机构是否中立?

【表现形式】

The institution who conducted the survey may have vested interest in the result, or it may affect the reliability of the result.

调查机构可能在调查结果中存在利益关系,或有可能影响调查结果的可靠性。

【基本假设】

The institution who conducts the survey should be neutral, and has no vested interest in the result.

调查机构应具有中立性,与调查结果没有任何利益关系。

【分析思路】

To point out that the institution may have vested interest in the result and may distort the actual opinions of respondents.

指出调查机构可能在结果中有利益关系，并可能歪曲或误导调查结果。

【参考模板】

（针对Assumption的写作要求）

段首句：(*pointing out that the result of the survey may not be reliable because of the institution or individuals who conducted the survey*)

The reliability of the survey is also open to doubt due to the organization who conducted the survey.

递进解释：(*The organization*) has vested interest in the final decision/conclusion which was based on the result of the survey, and thus might distort the actual answers of the respondents.

论证展开：(*How the institution/individuals who conducted the survey may benefit from the result if the result was as currently interpreted?*)

段落小总结: The author should cite a survey which is conducted by an independent institution to convince us that (*the assumption*).

【论证要点】

要保证调查结果有效，首先应保证调查机构或调查者是中立的。假如调查者在调查结果中有某些利益关系，则有可能故意歪曲或误导数据。这一点在展开时应着重分析调查机构可能在调查结果中有哪些利益关系，因而导致结果不一定可信。

6. When was the survey conducted? 调查的时效性

【表现形式】

The survey was conducted during a special period, or was conducted a long time ago; the result could not represent the current or future conditions.

调查在某一特殊时期进行，或是在很久以前进行，从而其结果不能反映当前或未来情况。

【基本假设】

There is no fundamental change after the survey was conducted.

至今，调查各方面情况没有发生重大变化。

【可参考】

Inferring a future condition from a past condition.

【分析思路】

To point out that the result of the survey which was conducted during a special period may not accurately reflect current trends or opinions.

指出特殊时期的调查结果未必准确反映当前趋势。

【参考模板】

（针对Evidence的写作要求）

段首句：(*pointing out that the result of the survey may not be representative of current situation due to the date when the survey was conducted*)

The effectiveness of the survey cited as main evidence is also open to doubt.

递进解释: The survey was conducted (*during a special period, or a long time ago*), thus may not reflect the current situations accurately.

让步: It is true that (*the survey may reflect the opinions or situations of respondents at the time when it was conducted*).

转折: The author needs to provide evidence that people's opinion toward (*the subject surveyed*) has not changed greatly during the past time (*or, the result alone could not sufficiently illustrate that (the general group) will...all the time*).

论证展开：(*Many factors that could influence the validity of the survey will change in the future, or respondents may act differently after the survey was conducted, so the result of the survey could not represent the all-time situation.*)

段落小总结: A more recent survey, if necessary at all, should be provided to sufficiently illustrate the assumption that...

【论证要点】

调查时效性问题和从过去推将来的草率推广问题本质相近，都是作者没有考虑时间变化，过去特定时间的调查结果未必能用来说明今天或将来的情况。论证时应主要分析调查进行时期的特殊性，或者调查进行的日期到今天有哪些重要因素会发生变化从而导致过去的调查结果在今天不再适用。

7. Are the respondents forthright when answering the questions?
回应者在回答调查时是否诚实?

【表现形式】

The respondents may not express their actual feeling or situation due to the circumstances in which the survey was conducted.

出于某些原因，回应者可能没有表达其真实想法。

【基本假设】

The information provided by the respondents should be accurate and authentic.

回应者提供的信息应真实、准确。

【可参考】

Credibility of the evidence.

【分析思路】

To point out that some settings of the survey might be improper to obtain true information from respondents, or the respondents might be unwilling to tell the truth for some reason.

指出某些调查设置可能不利于得到真实信息，或出于某些原因回应者可能不愿意表达其真实状况。

【参考模板】

（针对Assumption的写作要求）

段首句：(*pointing out that the information provided by the respondents might be inaccurate*)

The reliability of the respondents' answers is not sufficiently justified.

递进解释: There is possibility that the respondents may not tell the truth about...

论证展开：(*Answering the questions honestly may lead to some undesirable consequences for the respondents, so they may evade the crucial point, or even lie in their answers.*)

段落小总结: Under such circumstances, it is almost impossible to expect the respondents to provide accurate information about...

【论证要点】

回应者不说真话这一点比较容易理解。如果回应者表达的根本不是真实情况，那么调查就没有任何意义。论证时应主要说明调查的设置情况（如调查环境、调查问题、调查者、是否匿名、是否保密等）有可能导致被访对象不愿意表达真实情况和意愿。

8. Are the respondents representative? 回应者是否有代表性?

【表现形式】

The respondents could not represent the general population, or the respondents constitute a selective sample due to certain reasons.

回应者不能代表总群体，或由于某种原因回应者形成了选择性样本。

【基本假设】

The respondents should be representative of the general group.

回应者应能代表总体研究对象。

【可参考】

Selective sample, quantity of the sample, changing scopes.

【分析思路】

To point out that the respondents might not be randomly selected, or people who are interested in the subject of the survey are more likely to respond to the survey than are other people and therefore inherently form a selective sample.

指出回应者的选择可能不具有随机性；或对调查问题感兴趣的人往往更愿意回答调查问卷，从而形成选择性样本。

【参考模板】

（针对Evidence的写作要求）

段首句：（*pointing out that people who responded to the survey might not be representative of the general group*）

We should also notice that the respondents may not represent the general group of...

递进解释: We all know that in many cases, people who are interested in...might be generally more likely to respond to the survey than other people, or more willing to express their opinions and positions on the issue of...

论证展开：（*Other people who did not respond may hold a totally different position toward the issue, and the author should include those people in the study to present a more convincing result.* ）

段落小总结: Without considering the attitudes of other groups of people, the result of the survey in itself could not justifiably illustrate that...

【论证要点】

如果调查问卷不指定被访对象且不强行回收，则往往是对调查问题感兴趣的人更愿意回答问卷。这样就有可能导致回应者形成一个选择性样本。论证时可以通过分析以上因素来指出回应者可能不能代表全体。

9. Vague Data 模糊数据

【表现形式】

The data or information provided in the argument are too vague to make thorough and justified evaluation about the actual situation.

文中提供的数据和信息过于笼统，不足以对真实情况作出全面判断。

【基本假设】

The data or information provided as evidence should be accurate enough.

作为论据的数据和信息应精确，且足以支持推理。

Incomplete information.

To point out that the data or information provided are misleadingly vague. We need more accurate data, or in many cases, more information about the base amount or corresponding fraction of the sample in its general group.

指出文中信息过于笼统。要评价结论，需要更精确、更全面的信息；或在一些情况下，需要作者提供讨论对象相对应的总群体基数或其在总群体中所占的比例。

（针对Evidence的写作要求）

段首句：（*pointing out that the data cited in the analysis are too vague*）

The information concerning...is not accurate enough to evaluate (*the actual condition*).

1）lack of base amount

递进解释: The author only informs us that (*the percentage/fraction of sub-groups in the general group*),

转折: but we do not know the base amount of (*the general group*).

2）lack of fraction

递进解释: The author only informs us that many/few (*sub-groups*)...,

转折: however, we need to know what fraction of (*the general group*) actually...

论证展开: (*If the base amount or corresponding fractions vary, the conclusion would be different.*)

段落小总结: For lack of detailed information about (*the base amount/fraction of*)..., we can hardly assess...

所谓模糊数据最常见的形式就是作者仅仅指出某对象总量很多或很少，而没有考虑人口基数或该对象所属的总群体的基数。在很多情况下，我们需要考虑"人均"或某事件的"发生率"、"拥有率"等数值才能精确判断题目的推理过程。

10. Incomplete Information 信息不完整

The information provided in the argument is incomplete to make thorough and justified evaluation about the actual situation.

文中信息不够完整，不足以对真实情况作出全面判断。

此类问题一般不包含假设。

Vague data, incomplete comparison/selective comparison/ex parte information, confusing comparison and variation, failing to weigh the advantage and disadvantage thoroughly, failing to consider the feasibility of the conclusion, insufficient evidence.

To point out that the information provided by the author is incomplete. We need more accurate information about the cases studied, or some other information that is more pertinent to the argument should be provided to assess the conclusion.

指出文中信息不够完整。要评价结论，需要提供与讨论对象相关的更精确、更全面的信息。

【参考模板】

（针对Evidence的写作要求）

段首句：（*pointing out that the information provided is not sufficient*）

The author does not provide complete information concerning...

递进解释: The author only informs us that...,

转折: but what we care more is that..., which is not mentioned by the author.

论证展开：（*Other substantial information is needed to assess the soundness of the argument, and the conclusion would vary greatly when other conditions varied.*）

段落小总结: For lack of detailed information about..., we can hardly evaluate...

【论证要点】

信息不完整是指作者在论述中没有提供全部和结论相关的关键信息，因而无法对作者结论作出全面判断。分析时应着重讨论作者需要提供哪些和判断结论相关但又没有提供的信息。

11. False Analogy 错误类比

【表现形式】

The author recommends an institution（city, company, etc.）to copy the actions or policies of another institution, while actually the two institutions are not comparable.

作者建议某对象（城市、公司等）照搬另一对象的做法，但实际上两者并不可比。

【基本假设】

The two institutions are comparable at every critical aspect.

类比双方在各个关键环节都类似、可比。

【可参考】

Incomplete comparison, changing scopes.

【分析思路】

To point out that there might be many differences between the two institutions, and copying the actions（or policies, solutions, etc.）of other city（or company, college, etc.）indiscriminately may not bring about expected results.

指出两对象之间可能存在差别，盲目照搬另一对象的做法未必带来预想效果。

【参考模板】

（针对Question的写作要求）

段首句：（*pointing out that the two institutions might not be comparable*）

In the argument the author recommends A to carry out the same（*policies, actions, solutions on ...*）as B,

递进解释: but we may ask that whether A and B are similar enough at every aspect and are indeed comparable.

让步: While it is true that A and B share some common grounds on...,

转折: there are still some obvious differences between them.

论证展开：（*Many differences exist between A and B and these differences may render the policies（actions, solutions, etc.）which are proved to be effective for B ineffective for A.*）

段落小总结：Before A decides to copy B's experience, the author should take these differences into account and make careful study on the comparability of the two（*cities, companies, colleges, etc.*）.

【论证要点】

错误类比的表现形式和论证思路都比较简单，论证的时候应主要分析作者进行类比的双方有哪些显著差异，而这些差异将会导致对其中一方起作用的方案、政策对另外一方可能会不起作用。

12. Incomplete Comparison/Selective Comparison/ex parte Information 不完整比较/选择性比较/单方面信息

【表现形式】

The argument compares two subjects through only limited or selective aspects, while other important factors that would influence the result are ignored./The argument provides information only about one of the two subjects being compared, thus we could not make thorough and justified evaluation.

作者在对比两个对象时，仅对比了有选择性的或有限的方面，而忽略了影响对比结果的其他重要因素。/作者在对比时，仅提供了对比双方中一方的情况，从而无法作出全面比较。

【基本假设】

All critical aspects that would influence the comparison should be compared thoroughly.

所有影响对比结果的关键方面都应进行对比。

【可参考】

Incomplete information, false analogy.

【分析思路】

To point out that the author compares only selective aspects of the two subjects, or provides information about only one side, and we need to know if other factors that would influence the result are equal in each case, or more detailed information about the other side.

指出作者仅对比了双方的某些选择性层面，或仅提供了一方的情况；要评价推理需要了解影响对比结果的其他方面是否存在差异，或需要关于另外一方的更详细信息。

【参考模板】

（针对Evidence的写作要求）

段首句：（*pointing out that the comparison between the subjects might be incomplete or selective*）

The author hastily implies that A is superior to B in..., but the comparison between A and B is incomplete.

递进解释：The author only compares...,

转折：however, there are myriad of factors which, if differ in these cases, would bring about totally different result for the comparison.

论证展开：To fully evaluate the...of A and B, the author should provide more concrete evidence about (*other factors that would influence the result while ignored by the author in the argument*).

段落小总结：Without any further consideration about these factors, the author could not convince us that (*A is better than B in...*) merely based on an incomplete comparison.

【论证要点】

对于这一点应主要分析要得到A与B两者的全面对比结果，作者还应该考虑和对比哪些关键方面。

13. Confusing Comparison and Variation 横向比较和纵向比较的混淆

【表现形式】

The author provides only the variation about certain subject on certain aspect, while in fact, the comparison between the subject and its counterparts is needed to evaluate the argument, or vice versa.

作者仅提供了某对象某方面的变化，而要评价推理，我们需要的是该对象和其他参照物的横向比较，或反之。

【基本假设】

此类问题一般不包含假设。

【可参考】

Lack of controlled experiment, incomplete information.

【分析思路】

To point out that to substantiate the conclusion, the author should provide information about the comparison between those entities (companies, schools, cities, etc.) instead of the variation on certain aspect of one entity, or vice versa.

指出要支持结论,作者应提供对象和参照物之间的对比,而非该对象某方面的变化;或反之。

【参考模板】

(针对Evidence的写作要求)

段首句:(*pointing out that the author provides only the variation of certain subject, or vice versa*)

The author provides the variation in...to illustrate that...

让步: Although the (*variation in...*) could partly indicate...,

转折: we all know that to demonstrate...the comparison between A and B is actually more convincing and necessary.

论证展开:(*The author should provide the comparison between those entities to illustrate the conclusion.*)

段落小总结: Lacking comparison between..., we could not assess if...

【论证要点】

对于这一点首先应明确要支持作者的结论,应该提供某物体自身某方面的变化还是它和其他类似参照群体的比较,也就是对比参照系应如何选择。如果作者选择的参照系不合适,比如应该用比较却用了变化,或应该用变化而用了比较,那么应该要求作者提供能更准确支持结论的信息。

14. Unrelated Concepts 无关概念

【表现形式】

The author uses term A to infer term B while actually there is no direct logical relationship between the two terms.

作者用概念A推出概念B,而A与B两概念之间没有必然逻辑关联。

【基本假设】

Term A and term B are logically related, or B could be necessarily inferred from A.

A与B两概念应具有逻辑关联,或B必然能由A推知。

【可参考】

Non-causal relationship.

【分析思路】

To point out that there are critical differences or logical gaps between term A and term B; term A could not necessarily indicate term B.

指出A与B两者之间存在差别或在逻辑上不存在直接联系,A不能必然推知B。

【参考模板】

(针对Assumption的写作要求)

段首句:(*pointing out that B could not be properly inferred from A*)

In illustrating the assumption that...the author commits a fallacy of hasty generalization.

递进解释: The author mentions A,

转折: however, A is not a good indication of B.

论证展开:(*There are fundamental differences between A and B, thus A could not be used to properly illustrate B.*)

段落小总结: The author ought to make careful and clear differentiation between A and B before we could evaluate if the inference that...is justified.

【论证要点】

无关概念是指作者进行推理的两个概念没有必然逻辑联系，比如某物体的数量和该物体的质量。论证时应主要解释为什么概念A不能用来推知概念B，两者之间有什么逻辑差别；或者指出要推知概念B，作者应该提供哪些更实质性的信息。

15. Changing Scopes 差异范围

【表现形式】

The argument generalizes from the condition of some individual cases to a general principal or conclusion which is intended to be applied to a wider range of subjects, or reversely, applies the condition or characteristics of a certain general group to some individual case(s) in that group.

作者从一些特殊个案推知针对更广范围整体对象的原则，或反之，将某总群体的总体特征应用于某特殊个体。

【基本假设】

The condition of individual case(s) could be representative of the general group, or the general trends could be properly applied to all individuals in that group.

个体情况能代表总群体特征；或整体趋势能够恰当应用于整体中的所有个体。

【可参考】

Selective sample, quantity of the sample, are the respondents representative, false analogy.

【分析思路】

To point out that the condition of specific case(s) may not be representative, and could not be used to generalize a general principal for a wider range of subjects; or reversely, the general situation or condition or characteristic of an entire group may not be properly applied to every single case among that group.

指出个体情况未必具有代表性，不能用于推知整体情况；或反之，整体特征不能有效说明群体中每个个体的特殊情况。

【参考模板】

（针对Question的写作要求）

段首句：(*pointing out that the author studies only limited or special case(s), while improperly draws a conclusion concerning a wider range of subjects*)

To fully evaluate the argument we may well ask that whether the (*condition of an individual case*) could sufficiently illustrate the condition of (*a larger group of subjects*).

让步: Although the author's inference that...might be true for some cases, for example, ...

转折: unfortunately, this is not true of every individual (*in the general group*).

论证展开: (*Other subjects may have totally different situation thus the author's inference could not be properly applied to them.*)

段落小总结: Unless the author can demonstrate that (*the condition of other subjects is similar to that of the case studied*), the conclusion cannot be reached basing on special and limited cases.

【论证要点】

所谓差异范围本质上就是通常所说的以偏概全，但这里覆盖的面稍微广泛一些。从特殊个案推知一般原则，或是从一般性的、整体趋势推知个体情况都称为"差异范围草率推广"。换言之，凡是作者前后讨论的对象限定范围有差异的都归为此类问题。论证时主要应分析作者讨论的个案的特殊性，即为什么不能用该个案推知整体情况；或反之，说明整体原则为什么不能应用于该个案。

16. Inferring a Future Condition From a Past Condition 从过去推知将来

【表现形式】

The author announces that we could implement solutions which had successfully solved past problems to solve current problems, while in fact, those old-fashioned ways might be ineffective due to some changing conditions.

作者认为在过去有效的行为在当前依然有效，而实际上，有很多条件可能随时间变化，从而导致过去的方法在今天可能不再起作用。

【基本假设】

There will be no fundamental changes during the time period discussed by the author.

在作者讨论的时间区间内各方面情况都没有发生重大变化。

【可参考】

When was the survey conducted.

【分析思路】

To point out that many factors or conditions may vary during the past years, thus a solution which was successful in the past might not also be successful in present time or in the future.

指出在过去，很多关键因素可能发生变化，因此，在过去有效的做法在今天或未来未必同样有效。

【参考模板】

（针对Assumption的写作要求）

段首句：(*pointing out that the author suggests to use former effective methods to solve current or future problems*)

The author suggests that we can (*solve current problems or achieve current goals*) through methods which successfully solved the same kind of problems in the past.

递进解释: A hidden assumption behind the argument is that all conditions and factors upon which the effectiveness of (*the method*) depends have remained unchanged during the past (*N years*).

转折: However, many factors could have been changed.

论证展开: (*Many conditions and factors could have varied, which might render the solutions which were proved to be effective in the past ineffective in present time or in the future.*)

段落小总结: Without taking into account all these changing factors, the author could not convince us that the proposed solution could be effective in solving current problems.

【论证要点】

对于这一点应主要分析在作者讨论的时间区间内有哪些影响结论的关键因素可能发生变化，而这些条件、因素变化之后，过去有效的一些行为、方法、政策在今天或将来可能不再适用。

17. Failing to Weigh the Advantage and Disadvantage Thoroughly 没有全面衡量正负得失

【表现形式】

The author overemphasizes the advantage (or, reversely, the disadvantage) of certain action, while ignores the opposite effect. Specifically, the author hastily advocates adopting certain actions, while in fact, that series of actions might bring about undesirable consequences; or the author hastily proposes to abandon certain actions, while those actions might actually bring about benefits.

作者在论证时过分强调了某行为可能带来的好处(或坏处)，而忽视了另外一方面。具体来说，即作者建议采取某种行为，而事实上，该行为可能导致不良后果；或作者建议禁止某行为，而事实上该行为可能会带来一定益处。

【基本假设】

The author has weighed the advantage(s) and disadvantage(s) thoroughly when putting forward his/her proposal.

作者在提出提案时应全面衡量正负得失。

【可参考】

Incomplete information, ex parte information, feasibility of the conclusion.

【分析思路】

To point out that adopting the author's proposal may actually bring about undesirable effects (if the author overemphasizes the advantage of taking the actions, or vice versa).

指出采纳作者建议将带来不良后果(如果作者过分强调采取某行为的好处,或反之)。

【参考模板】

(针对Evidence的写作要求)

段首句：(*pointing out that the author might ignore the disadvantage of the proposal*)

In claiming that..., the author needs to do comprehensive research on both positive and negative effects of the proposal.

让步: Although the proposal could (*solve the problem*) to a certain degree,

转折: carrying out the proposal may actually bring about more harmful effects.

论证展开: (*possible harmful effects ignored by the author*)

段落小总结: Under such scenario, adopting the author's proposal would harm, rather than benefit, (*the author's purpose*).

【论证要点】

针对这类问题展开时应主要分析被作者遗忘的好处(或坏处),指出采纳作者的建议可能会适得其反。

18. False Dilemma 非此即彼，极端选择

【表现形式】

The author falsely insists that we have only two extreme and mutually exclusive choices (or possibilities, explanations) in solving certain problem (or in explaining certain phenomenon), while in fact, there are many other choices (or possibilities, explanations).

作者认定解决某问题或解释某现象时只存在两种极端且互斥的可能,而实际上,对于该问题或现象还存在很多其他可能性。

【基本假设】

There are no other choices or explanations except the extreme ones implied by the author.

对于该现象,除了作者提供的极端解释外不存在其他可能情况。

【可参考】

Necessity of the solution.

【分析思路】

To point out that there are many other choices for us to solve the problem, or many other explanations towards certain result, not necessarily the two either-or choices suggested by the author.

指出要解决问题还有其他很多选择,或对于某结果还有很多其他解释,而并非只有作者提出的两种极端。

（针对Assumption的写作要求）

段首句：（*pointing out that the author unfairly imposes an either-or choice between two courses of action*）

In explaining..., the author is presenting a false dilemma.

递进解释: The author simply assumes that（*the situation would be either A or B*）, while the two...are not necessarily mutually exclusive.

论证展开：（*Many other solutions/explanations could exist, or could be more reasonable.*）

段落小总结: Before ruling out all the possibilities above, the author could not convince us that there are only two possible explanations for us to accept.

【论证要点】

针对这类问题应主要分析说明题目讨论的现象并不是只有作者提出的两种极端情况或解释，而可能还存在其他可能性。

19. Non-causal Relationship 无因果

【表现形式】

The author implies that A is the reason for B, while in fact there is no essential relation between the two facts.

作者认为A导致了B，而事实上，两者之间不存在本质联系。

【基本假设】

No other causes will result in B.

没有其他原因导致B。

【可参考】

Unrelated concepts, incomplete information.

【分析思路】

To point out that there is no logical relation between the cause and the effect suggested by the author, or to point out that there are many other alternative explanations which could also explain the result, or to point out that the comparison（or controlled experiment）between counterparts should be conducted to substantiate the causal relationship.

指出作者暗示的原因和结果之间不存在逻辑关联；或指出对于某结果还有其他可能解释；或指出要证实两者的因果关联，应该进行相应的比较或对比试验。

【参考模板】

（针对Assumption的写作要求）

段首句：（*pointing out that the causal relationship implied by the author is open to doubt*）

The author unfairly assumes that it is...that resulted in...

转折: But we find no concrete evidence to substantiate the inevitable relationship between...and...

论证展开：（*Many other factors could also lead to the result/the author should conduct controlled study to demonstrate the causal relationship.*）

段落小总结: In short, the author could not hastily conclude that...is the only possible reason for...before taking the above factors into account.

【论证要点】

针对因果关系问题展开讨论时一般是两种方式：一是列举他因，即分析还有哪些其他原因也会导致作者所说的结果；另一种是指出论证过程缺乏相应的对比试验，即需要对比研究对象和参照物的情况差别才能断定作者所暗示的原因和结果之间是否存在联系。

20. Confusing the Cause and the Effect 混淆因果

【表现形式】

The author implies that A is the reason for B, while in fact it is B that results in A.

作者认为A导致了B，而事实上，是B决定了A。

【基本假设】

There is no other explanation for the relationship between A and B except the one implied by the author.

A与B之间除了作者所暗示的因果关系以外不存在其他可能。

【分析思路】

To point out that actually it is B that results in A, rather than the reversed relationship implied by the author.

指出现实中可能是B决定A，而不是A导致了B。

【参考模板】

（针对Assumption的写作要求）

段首句：（*pointing out that the causal relationship implied by the author is open to doubt*）

In the process of reasoning the author implies that A is the reason for B.

转折: However, the author may confuse the cause and the effect.

论证展开: （*There is possibility that it is B that actually causes A.*）

The author fails to rule out the possibility that（*B results in A*）.

段落小总结: Without adequately taking this possibility into account, the assumption that...is untenable.

【论证要点】

展开时应主要分析在现实中有"B导致了A"这种可能性的存在。

21. Confusing Concurrence with Causality 同时性混淆为因果关系

【表现形式】

The author implies that A is the reason for B, basing on the mere fact that A and B occur simultaneously.

作者仅仅看到A与B两者同时发生，就认为A导致了B。

【基本假设】

No other causes will result in B.

没有其他原因导致B。

【可参考】

Non-causal relationship.

【分析思路】

To point out that there is no substantial evidence which could prove the causal relationship, or to point out that there are many other alternative explanations which could also explain the result, or to point out that the comparison（or controlled experiment）between counterparts should be conducted to substantiate the causal relationship.

指出作者没有提供实质证据证实A与B两者之间的因果关系；或指出对于该结果还有其他可能解释；或指出要证实两者的因果关联，应该进行相应的比较或对比试验。

【参考模板】

（针对Assumption的写作要求）

段首句：（*pointing out that the causal relationship implied by the author is open to doubt*）

The most important problem is the underlying assumption that it is...that resulted in...

递进解释: The author only points out that the two events occurred during the same period,

转折: however, we all know that merely a coincidence of two events could not sufficiently demonstrate a causal relationship between them.

论证展开: (*Many other factors could also lead to the result/the author should conduct controlled study to demonstrate the causal relationship.*)

Many other factors could also lead to..., which might include...

段落小总结: Without ruling out such factors, we could not be convinced that...is the actual cause of...

【论证要点】

针对因果关系问题展开时一般是两种方式: 一是列举他因, 即分析还有哪些其他原因也会导致作者所说的结果; 另一种是指出论证过程缺乏相应的对比试验, 即需要对比研究对象和参照物的情况差别才能断定作者所暗示的原因和结果之间是否存在联系。

22. Post hoc, ergo propter hoc 把时间上先后发生的事认定为因果关系

【表现形式】

The author implies that A is the reason for B, basing on the mere fact that B occurs after A.

作者仅仅看到A发生在B之前, 就认为A导致了B。

【基本假设】

No other causes will result in B.

没有其他原因导致B。

【可参考】

Non-causal relationship.

【分析思路】

To point out that there is no substantial evidence which could prove the causal relationship, or to point out that there are many other alternative explanations which could also explain the result, or to point out that the comparison (or controlled experiment) between counterparts should be conducted to substantiate the causal relationship.

指出没有实质证据证实A与B两者之间的因果关系; 或指出对于该结果还有其他可能解释; 或指出要证实两者的因果关联, 应该进行相应的比较或对比试验。

【参考模板】

(针对Assumption的写作要求)

段首句: (*pointing out that the causal relationship implied by the author is open to doubt*)

The author assumes that...is responsible for...,

递进解释: basing on the mere fact that...occurred after...

转折: however, the sequence of the two events in itself does not sufficiently prove that the former caused the later.

论证展开: (*Many other factors could also lead to the result/the author should conduct controlled study to demonstrate the causal relationship.*)

...might have resulted from other factors, such as...

段落小总结: Without ruling out these possible scenarios, the author could not establish a causal relationship between...and...

【论证要点】

针对因果关系问题展开时一般是两种方式: 一是列举他因, 即分析还有哪些其他原因也会导致作者所说的结果; 另一种是指出论证过程缺乏相应的对比试验, 即需要对比研究对象和参照物的情况差别才能断定作者所暗示的原因和结果之间是否存在联系。

【表现形式】

The author proposes a solution to attain certain objective while in fact the solution is neither sufficient nor necessary for that purpose.

作者提出实现某目标的方案，而事实上，该方案对于实现目标来说既不充分也不必要。

【基本假设】

Adopting the proposal alone, with no need to take any other actions, will be sufficient to attain the author's objective./The objective could not be attained without adopting the proposal.

仅采取作者的方案，无需附加其他条件，就足以实现目标。/不采取作者的方案将肯定无法实现该目标。

【可参考】

Incomplete information, incomplete thoughts, non-causal relationship.

【分析思路】

1）To point out that adopting the author's proposal alone could not solve the problem sufficiently. To attain the author's objective, many other important conditions must be fulfilled.

对充分性：指出采纳作者方案不足以解决问题。要实现作者的目标，还需满足其他重要条件。

2）To point out that many other effective methods could also be used to attain the author's objective, thus the proposed actions may not be necessary.

对必要性：指出要实现作者目标还可以通过其他有效途径，而并非必须采取作者的方案。

【参考模板】

（针对Assumption的写作要求）

段首句：（*pointing out that the author's proposal is neither sufficient nor necessary for solving the problem*）

The author assumes that the proposed actions are both sufficient and necessary for（*attaining certain objective*）.

转折：Adopting the actions alone, however, may not ensure（*solving the problem*）.

递进解释（1）：To attain the author's objective, many other fundamental requirements must be fulfilled.

论证展开：（*Many other important works must be done.*）

递进解释（2）：Furthermore, other available methods besides（*the author's proposal*）could also be used to achieve the same goal.

论证展开：（*Many other effective methods could be adopted.*）

段落小总结：Before the author makes thorough comparison between the effectiveness of his own proposal and other possible methods, the author's proposal should not be hastily carried out.

【论证要点】

针对题目方案的充分性，论证时主要应指出要实现作者的目的，仅仅采取作者提出的行为是不够的，我们还需要满足其他的重要条件或完成其他的重要工作；针对必要性，主要应指出要实现作者的目的还有其他有效手段，因而不采取作者的方法也能解决问题。

24. Failing to Consider the Feasibility of the Conclusion 未考虑结论的可行性

【表现形式】

The solution could not be smoothly carried out due to some obstacles.

作者方案仅在理论上完美，但在现实中存在某些障碍导致其无法操作。

【基本假设】

The solution should be practically feasible.

作者方案在现实中应该可行。

【可参考】

Incomplete information, sufficiency of the solution.

【分析思路】

To point out that there are many obstacles to the implementing of the solution, or some critical premise could not be fulfilled, thus the proposal could not be successfully carried out.

指出在方案实施过程中可能存在某些障碍，或某些关键条件无法满足，从而导致方案无法顺利实施。

【参考模板】

（针对Assumption的写作要求）

段首句：（*pointing out that the author's proposal might be practically unfeasible*）

The feasibility of the arguer's proposal can also be cast doubt on.

递进解释: The proposal relies on an assumption that（*the proposal could be successfully carried out*），

转折: however, the assumption might be unwarranted（*due to some obstacles*）.

论证展开：（*possible obstacles in implementing the solution*）

段落小总结: Unless the author could demonstrate that those obstacles could be effectively overcome, the proposal might be practically unfeasible.

【论证要点】

针对可行性应主要讨论作者的方案在实施过程中可能存在哪些障碍，或存在哪些可能无法满足的前提，从而导致作者的方案无法操作。

前24类已在第四章给出例题，本章不再单独列出。以下第25~31类不属于第四章所列的基本逻辑问题，但也是Argument经常分析的环节，每类列出典型题目供参考。

25. Insufficient Evidence 论据不充分

【表现形式】

The evidence provided by the author is insufficient to demonstrate the assumption/conclusion.

作者提供的论据和信息不足以支持其假设或结论。

【基本假设】

此类问题不包含假设。

【可参考】

Incomplete information, do the statistics make any difference, non-causal relationship.

【分析思路】

To point out that the evidence/information provided is insufficient, we need more substantial evidence to evaluate the argument.

指出文中的论据和信息不够充分，要评价论证作者需提供更多实质证据。

【参考模板】

（针对Evidence的写作要求）

段首句：（*pointing out that the evidence provided is insignificant or that no related evidence is provided at all to illustrate the assumption*）

The evidence provided by the author is insufficient to reach the conclusion.

递进解释：The author treats a lack of proof that...as constituting sufficient proof that..., for the author only points out that...

让步: Although (*the information provided by the author*) may have little relation with...

转折: this piece of information in itself is far from sufficient to demonstrate the assumption that...

论证展开: (*We need more important information about the case studied.*)

【论证要点】

分析这一点时需指出作者在提出某种观点或假设时提供的论据不够充足，或根本没有提供任何论据。展开时应分析作者还需要提供哪些关键信息才能支持结论。这一点和调查无意义、信息不完整比较类似。

【典型例题】

题库 `10` , `47` , `54`

---

26. Unwarranted Assumption/Credibility of the Evidence
没有根据的假设/论据没有可信度

【表现形式】

The evidence in the argument lacks credibility, or the author provides no effective evidence to substantiate the assumption.

文中使用的论据缺乏可信度，或作者提出某假设时没有提供有效论据支持。

【基本假设】

此类问题不包含假设。

【可参考】

Incomplete information, unrelated concepts, non-causal relationship.

【分析思路】

To point out that the evidence provided might be unreliable, or that the author's assumption might be unwarranted.

指出文中的论据可能不可信，或作者的假设可能没有根据。

【参考模板】

（针对Assumption的写作要求）

段首句：(*pointing out that the assumption is unwarranted*)

The assumption that...is open to doubt,

递进解释: since the author does not provide any evidence to substantiate the assumption.

论证展开: (*Many other possibilities might render the assumption suspect.*)

段落小总结: Given other possibilities about..., the author could not hastily assume that...

【论证要点】

这一点是指作者在没有任何证据的情况下就盲目认定某些假设必然成立，或作者提供的论据的可信度值得怀疑。

【典型例题】

题库 `64` , `165`

---

27. Definition Critique 定义攻击

【表现形式】

The definition of certain critical term in the argument is vague, or the term has no essential logical relation with the conclusion.

作者对于文中关键概念的定义和理解不够清晰准确；或该概念和结论不存在本质逻辑联系。

【基本假设】

此类问题不包含假设。

【可参考】

Unrelated concepts, incomplete information, vague data.

【分析思路】

To point out that the author's understanding of some critical term in the argument might be different from what we commonly consider the term to be, or that the definition is vague, so that we could not sufficiently evaluate the argument.

指出作者在文中对于某些关键概念的理解和人们通常的理解存在差别；或对其定义含混不清，从而使我们无法充分评价论证。

【参考模板】

（针对Question的写作要求）

段首句：（*pointing out that the definition of certain critical term is vague*）

One problem involves how the author defines...

论证展开：（*The definition might be different from what we commonly consider the term to be.*）

As we commonly accept, (*the term*) usually means (*a meaning other than the author's understanding*). Therefore, if (*the term*) is defined as (*other ways*), (*the evidence cited by the author*) is irrelevant to (*the author's conclusion*).

段落小总结：In one word, without a clear definition of..., it is impossible to assess the strength of the argument.

【论证要点】

定义攻击是围绕作者在论证过程中对于某些关键概念的定义含混不清的现象展开讨论，即作者没有对某些关键概念进行清晰的界定，因而我们无法评价推理的力度。

【典型例题】

题库 44 , 50

28. Negative Evidence 反证法

【表现形式】

The evidence provided by the author actually contradicts the conclusion.

作者提供的论据实际上会削弱其结论。

【基本假设】

此类问题不包含假设。

【分析思路】

To point out that the information provided by the author could be used to refute the author's conclusion.

指出文中的论据可以用于说明和作者相反的观点。

【参考模板】

（针对Evidence的写作要求）

段首句：（*pointing out that there may be some problems with the information provided by the author*）

The author cites the evidence that...to convince us that...

转折/论证展开：（*The information provided by the author could be used to refute the author's conclusion.*）

However, this piece of evidence may well prove (*an opposite situation*), and could serve to refute the author's assumption.

段落小总结: The author should provide more convincing evidence to reconcile this apparent self-contradictory claim.

【论证要点】

反证法的主要思路是指出作者提供的论据不能支持自己的结论，而是正好说明和作者相反的观点。

【典型例题】

题库 **25** , **38** , **79** , **101**

---

29. Profit-cost Analysis 成本收益分析

【表现形式】

The author hastily claims that we could earn great profits by adopting certain proposal, but fails to analyze the possible cost of doing so.

作者认定采取某些行为可以增加利润，但是没有考虑这样做的成本。

【基本假设】

The revenue should exceed the cost to make a profit.

产出应大于投入才能赢利。

【可参考】

Incomplete information, failing to weigh the advantage and disadvantage thoroughly, feasibility of the conclusion.

【分析思路】

To point out that the author should take the possible cost into account when assuming that carrying out certain proposal will make great profits.

指出作者在提出某方案将赢利的同时应考虑可能的投入。

【参考模板】

（针对Assumption的写作要求）

段首句：(*pointing out that profits may not necessarily follow by carrying out the author's proposal*)

Even if the author's proposal could be carried out effectively, we still could not hastily assume that...will necessarily earn a substantial profit, as the author predicted.

递进解释: To evaluate the profitability of...we should consider the function of both revenue and expense.

转折: However, the author does not provide any information about the possible cost of (*carrying out the author's proposal*).

论证展开: (*Many key steps of the proposal may involve great expense; if the cost of carrying out the proposal exceeds projected revenue, the proposal would be profitless.*)

段落小总结: Without more information about production costs, it is impossible to assess whether (*carrying out the author's proposal will be profitable*).

【论证要点】

当作者认定采取某种策略必然会带来巨额利润的时候，可以深入分析投入与产出之间的关系。

【典型例题】

题库 **38** , **45** , **56**

30. Lack of Controlled Experiment/Comparison 缺乏对比实验/缺乏横向比较

【表现形式】

The author ought to conduct controlled experiment/or to make comparison between the subject and its counterparts to illustrate the causal relationship between two events, but no such evidence is provided.

作者在论证两者之间的因果关系时应该进行相应的比较或对比试验。

【基本假设】

此类问题不包含假设。

【可参考】

Non-causal relationship, confusing concurrence with causality, post hoc, ergo propter hoc, confusing comparison and variation.

【分析思路】

To point out that the author should conduct controlled experiment to make the conclusion more convincing.

指出要使论证更有说服力,作者应该进行对比试验。

【参考模板】

(针对Evidence的写作要求)

段首句:(*pointing out that the causal relationship implied by the author is open to doubt*)

The author unfairly assumes that it is...that resulted in...

递进解释: The causal relationship is convincing only if the author could demonstrate that all other factors that might affect (*the result*) remained constant during the same period.

论证展开:(*pointing out that corresponding controlled experiment is needed, or explaining how the experiment should be conducted*)

Specifically, we need to know (*the experiment result of one group of the subjects*), while at the same time, we also need to find out (*the situation of the counterpart*).

段落小总结: Without appropriate comparison between (*one group*) and (*its counterpart*), the assumption that...is unwarranted.

【论证要点】

这一点在针对推理过程中的因果关系展开分析时可以使用。要证明A是否是B的原因,我们需要对比实验对象在受到A的影响和不受到A的影响两种情况下在B的产生方面存在的差异,以断定A和B之间是否存在必然联系。

【典型例题】

题库 13 , 50 , 63

31. Economic Factors 对于经济因素的论证

【表现形式】

The author fails to take the inflation rate into account, or fails to analyze the relationship between the demand and the supply of certain product when drawing economics-related conclusion.

在论证经济相关问题时,作者没有考虑通胀;或没有考虑供需关系。

【基本假设】

此类问题不包含假设。

【分析思路】

To point out that the author should consider how much does the price of certain product increase after adjustment for inflation, or should analyze the demand and the supply of the product before reaching the conclusion.

指出作者在论证时应考虑扣除通胀因素之后的价格变化，或应分析某产品的供需关系。

【参考模板】

（针对Question的写作要求）

段首句：(*pointing out that the reasoning might be weak due to some economic factors*)

Also, some economic factors should be taken into account in the argument.

递进解释（1）: First, we need to know how much did the price of...actually increase after adjustment for inflation.

论证展开（1）: (*If the rate of inflation exceeds the increase in the price of the product, then the increase is reasonable.*)

递进解释（2）: Second, the author fails to consider the variation in the demand for...during the same period.

论证展开（2）: If the supply of...falls short of demand, then there is good reason for the increased price of...

段落小总结: The soundness of the speaker's claim is significantly weakened for lack of economic consideration.

【论证要点】

这一点通常在作者论述经济现象、公司运作的时候可以使用，特别是作者认为某种商品的涨价不合理的时候，需要衡量通货膨胀、供需关系的影响。

【典型例题】

题库 `75`

第七章 Argument参考范文

本章提供了5篇Argument参考文章，覆盖了Assumption、Evidence、Question和Alternative Explanation 4种主要写作要求。

考生需要注意的是，这些文章都不是在规定时间内完成的。为给考生提供更有参考价值的文字，以下文章皆经过一定的修改润色。而且，为了提供较为详尽的参考思路，第1、2、4篇文章的篇幅也超出一般写作要求。真正考试时只要保证围绕3个左右主要环节进行深入分析论证、字数达到420~450左右即可。

SAMPLE 1

1. Woven baskets characterized by a particular distinctive pattern have previously been found only in the immediate vicinity of the prehistoric village of Palea and therefore were believed to have been made only by the Palean people. Recently, however, archaeologists discovered such a "Palean" basket in Lithos, an ancient village across the Brim River from Palea. The Brim River is very deep and broad, and so the ancient Paleans could have crossed it only by boat, and no Palean boats have been found. Thus it follows that the so-called Palean baskets were not uniquely Palean.

Write a response in which you discuss what specific evidence is needed to evaluate the argument and explain how the evidence would weaken or strengthen the argument.

In this argument the author employs a variety of evidence about Paleans, including their geographical isolation and the discovery of a basket, to argue that Palean baskets could have been made by non-Palean cultures. We may accept part of the author's claim regarding the Paleans, but in the absence of some critical evidence, we cannot accept the conclusion that the Paleans have no means of transporting one of their baskets to other regions.

In the first place, the author assumes that the Paleans could not have reached Lithos because no Palean boat has been found. However, the author is treating a lack of proof that the Paleans could have possessed some kind of boat as sufficient proof that they did not possess any such vehicles at all. From the passage we are only informed that Palean boats "were not found", but the mere fact that no boat found currently could not fully illustrate that the Paleans did not have boats. We need concrete evidence to show that the Paleans did not master the skill of shipbuilding.

Granted that the Paleans did possess no boats, we still need evidence to prove that the basket could not have arrived in Lithos by other means. Although the Brim River is deep and broad at present, it might be shallower and narrower at Palean time, or at least some sections of the river were less deep and broad at that time. If so, the Paleans could have crossed the river without boat. Some archaeological and geological records or documents about the condition of the Brim River at ancient time might be useful for evaluating the argument.

Assuming that the river was also deep and broad in ancient time and can be crossed only by boat, there is a possibility that some vehicles were in the possession of a second culture with whom the Palean people kept in contact. The second culture might have brought the discovered basket to Lithos during trading or other activities.

Also possibly, the basket may have been brought to Lithos by some other people latterly after the disappearance of the Paleans, or may have drifted to the site due to geological accidents such as a flood. The author should provide evidence to show that Paleans had no significant contact with other cultures who possessed boats, and that the basket could not be carried to the site through other methods such as trading or some accidents. We still cannot rule out the possibility that the baskets were unique to Palean culture without such information.

In sum, the conclusion is hastily reached. Before the claim that other cultures could have produced so-called Palean baskets is accepted, the author should provide concrete evidence to show that Paleans were never capable of building boats. The author also needs to rule out other possible ways by which the basket could travel to other places. (478 words)

参考译文

上文论述中，作者引述了若干关于Palea人的论据，包括其地理孤立性以及一个篮子的发现，以证实所谓的Palea篮子有可能是由Palea以外的文化制造的。我们能够接受作者关于Palea人的部分观点，但由于缺乏某些关键证据，我们不能接受关于Palea人没有办法把他们的其中一只篮子运送到其他地区的结论。

首先，因为没有发现Palea人的船只，作者就假定Palea人不可能到达Lithos。然而，作者把用以证明Palea人有可能拥有某种类型船只的证据的缺乏，当成用以证明Palea人肯定没有任何这类交通工具的充分证据。从上文我们只能得知"没有找到"Palea人的船只，但仅有"当前没有找到这类船只"的事实并不能充分说明Palea人没有船只。我们需要更加明确的证据来证明Palea人没有掌握造船技术。

即使承认Palea人确实没有船只，我们依然需要证据来证明文中提到的篮子不会通过其他方式到达Lithos。尽管Brim河当前又深又宽，但在Palea年代它可能更浅、更窄一些，或至少该河流的某些流域在当时不那么宽和深。如果是这样，那么Palea人不需要船只也可以穿过河流。关于Brim河当时状况的考古或地质纪录及文献对于评价上文论述可能是有用的。

即便假定这条河流在当时也又宽又深，且只能用船只通过，也依然存在一种可能性，即：与Palea人有联系的另一种文化拥有船只。这第二种文化可能在贸易或其他行为中将文中发现的篮子带到了Lithos。也可能是Palea人消失之后由其他人把该篮子带到了Lithos；或可能该篮子随某些地质事件，比如洪水，漂流到该地区。作者应提供证据证明Palea人没有和其他拥有船只的文化的显著接触，以及该篮子不可能是通过贸易或一些偶然事件等方式到达它被发现的场所的。没有这样的信息，我们依然不能排除这种篮子仍然为Palea人所独有的可能性。

总之，上文结论过于草率。在我们接受其他文化可能制造了所谓的Palea篮子的观点之前，作者应该提供切实证据证明Palea人从未有能力制造船只。作者还需要排除该篮子流传到其他地区的其他可能途径。

SAMPLE 2

44. The following appeared in a letter to the editor of a journal on environmental issues.

"Over the past year, the Crust Copper Company (CCC) has purchased over 10,000 square miles of land in the tropical nation of West Fredonia. Mining copper on this land will inevitably result in pollution and, since West Fredonia is the home of several endangered animal species, in environmental disaster. But such disasters can be prevented if consumers simply refuse to purchase products that are made with CCC's copper unless the company abandons its mining plans."

Write a response in which you examine the stated and/or unstated assumptions of the argument. Be sure to explain how the argument depends on these assumptions and what the implications are for the argument if the assumptions prove unwarranted.

In the argument the arguer points out that Crust Copper Company (CCC) has purchased a vast of land in West Fredonia and that mining here will inevitably lead to tremendous pollution. To avoid such environmental problems, the arguer suggests that boycott towards products produced by CCC will be an effective measure. Well-intentioned the arguer may be, several unwarranted assumptions may render the boycott unnecessary or ineffective.

First, the underlying assumption that the deterioration of environment and disturbance to endangered animals will inevitably occur is open to doubt. Ten thousand square miles are, without any doubt, so large an area that almost make up the total territory of New York City; there is likelihood that only a very small proportion of the land is used for mining. Furthermore, with the advanced technology of waste disposal and environmental-friendly recycling, the pollution, if any, can be so insignificant that almost has no negative effect to the environment. Even if the exploitation is heavy, the arguer does not inform us to what extent the mining areas and the habitat of endangered species overlap. If they locate far away from each other, the mining would have little effect to local animals. Without taking these factors into consideration, the arguer could not successfully convince us that CCC's mining process will bring about horrible results, and the boycott would be totally unnecessary in this case.

Second, the feasibility of the arguer's proposal can also be cast doubt on. The proposal could be smoothly carried out only if the consumers can reliably distinguish products that are made with CCC's copper. We all know that only the brand of the final producer will be engraved to a product. For instance, if a copper lock is manufactured, consumers can only identify the brand of the lock company. It is unlikely that a nonprofessional consumer can tell the material supplier of a certain product. Even assuming that consumers can effectively recognize copper products made with CCC's copper, and that the vast majority of such consumers can be gathered by certain means, whether all of them are willing to cooperate in the boycott is still not guaranteed. It is highly possible that most consumers care more about the quality and cost of a product while little about environmental problems. If the consumers cannot distinguish products using CCC's copper, or they have no interest in the boycott, the proposal would be meaningless at all, let alone prevent environmental problems.

In conclusion, the argument is unpersuasive and the arguer should provide additional information to demonstrate that CCC will cause a disastrous effect on the environment of West Fredonia once its mining plan is carried out. The arguer also needs to prove that the proposed boycott is not only practically feasible, but also sufficient and necessary for the arguer's purpose. (466 words)

参考译文

在上文论述中，作者指出Crust Copper Company(CCC)在West Fredonia购买了大片土地，并指出在此采矿将不可避免地造成严重污染。为防止出现环境问题，作者提出对CCC的产品加以抵制将会是有效策略。尽管作者可能出于好意，但若干未经证实的假设会导致该抵制不必要甚至无效。

首先，关于在这里将不可避免地发生对环境的破坏和对濒危动物的干扰的假设是值得怀疑的。毫无疑问，1万平方英里幅员广阔，几乎等同于纽约市的总面积，因此很有可能这片土地只有很小比例用于采矿。而且，由于有非常先进的垃圾处理和有利于环保的回收技术，即使产生一些污染也会非常轻微，甚至几乎不会对环境产生任何负面影响。即使对这片土地的开发非常严重，作者也没能告诉我们采矿地和濒危动物栖居地在多大程度上重合。如果两块地离得很远，那么采矿过程对当地动物产生的影响极其微小。在没有考虑这些因素的情况下，作者不能成功地使我们相信CCC的采矿活动将会带来可怕后果；在这种情况下，文中提出的抵制也就完全不必要了。

其次，作者提案的可行性也值得怀疑。只有当消费者能够分辨出CCC的铜生产的产品时，该提案才能顺利实施。我们都知道，只有最终生产商的商标会被印在产品上。举例来说，一个铜锁制造完成后，消费者只能分辨出铜锁厂商的商标。对于不具有专业知识的消费者来说很难区分某一产品的原材料供应商。即使消费者能够有效分辨CCC的铜生产的产品，而且大多数这样的消费者能够以某种方式集合起来，这些人是否愿意进行联合抵制依然不能保证。很可能多数消费者更关心产品的质量和价格，而对环境问题不太关注。如果消费者不能分辨出用CCC的铜生产的产品，或对抵制行为没有兴趣，文中提案将毫无意义，更谈不上能防止环境问题了。

总而言之，上文论证不太有说服力。作者应该提供额外信息论述一旦CCC采矿计划实施，将必然对West Fredonia的环境造成灾难性的影响。作者还需要证明文中提到的抵制不仅现实可行，而且对于达到目的来说既是充分也是必要的。

SAMPLE 3

67. The following appeared as part of a business plan developed by the manager of the Rialto Movie Theater.

"Despite its downtown location, the Rialto Movie Theater, a local institution for five decades, must make big changes or close its doors forever. It should follow the example of the new Apex Theater in the mall outside of town. When the Apex opened last year, it featured a video arcade, plush carpeting and seats, and a state-of-the-art sound system. Furthermore, in a recent survey, over 85 percent of respondents reported that the high price of newly released movies prevents them from going to the movies more than five times per year. Thus, if the Rialto intends to hold on to its share of a decreasing pool of moviegoers, it must offer the same features as Apex."

Write a response in which you discuss what questions would need to be answered in order to decide whether the recommendation is likely to have the predicted result. Be sure to explain how the answers to these questions would help to evaluate the recommendation.

In this argument the manager suggests that Rialto must offer same features as Apex, a newly opened theater, to attract moviegoers. The manager describes many fancy functions featured by Apex and the dissatisfaction of moviegoers about the high price of new movies. However, merely these facts could not prove that the proposed action will guarantee Rialto's share of the market.

A foremost question is: whether Apex was really a great success? We are not informed about the actual profit and the number of moviegoers of Apex. It is possible that the costs of these fashionable features are so high that the ticket prices of Apex are higher than other theaters, which will further prevent moviegoers on a tight budget from going to it, or that the ticket income of Apex remains low although it had featured those functions.

Granted that Apex has gained great profits, we may still ask that whether the success resulted from those new features. Many other factors would also influence people's choice on a theater. For example, people would be concerned more about the distance of the theater from their houses. Meanwhile, whether the lack of these features has caused a decreased share of moviegoers for Rialto is open to doubt. Perhaps the total number of residents in downtown area was decreasing recently, and therefore Rialto could not attract as many people as before.

Another question that should be addressed is the comparability of the two theaters. As we know, many factors would make them quite different from each other: their locations, the types of movie they mainly feature, the ticket price, etc. Any one of these factors would make the measures less effective in Rialto as in Apex. The manager cannot convince us that Rialto could gain profits by simply copying the features of Apex.

Furthermore, we may question the reliability of the survey. We could not be sure if the respondents of the survey are representative of the overall population of the city and constitute a large number of people. Besides, granted that the respondents' opinion could represent that of our general residents, Rialto could take other actions as response, such as featuring some formerly-released movies with lower price.

It is understandable that a theater should struggle for its survival. But before the manager could provide complete information about the actual profits of Apex, and show clear evidence that Apex has attracted many moviegoers because of its new features, we could not hastily conclude that providing these features at Rialto would secure its future prosper. (421 words)

参考译文

在上文论述中，经理指出Rialto必须提供和新开业的Apex一样的设施来吸引观众。经理描述了诸多Apex提供的新颖设施以及观众对于新发行影片票价过高的不满。然而，仅有这些事实并不能证明经理提出的措施能保证Rialto的市场份额。

一个最主要的问题是：Apex确实取得成功了吗？我们并不知晓Apex的实际利润和观众数量。有可能Apex提供的这些新颖设施成本高昂从而导致Apex票价高于其他影院，进一步导致手头比较紧张的观众无法负担Apex观影的巨额费用；也可能尽管Apex提供了这些设施，但影票收入依然不高。

姑且承认Apex获得了巨额利润，我们仍然需要确定这一成功是否就是得益于那些新设施。影响人们选择影院的因素还有很多。比如，人们可能更关心影院到他们家的距离。同时，我们也不能肯定Rialto是否是因为没有提供这些设施而导致观众数量的减少。有可能市中心区的居民总数最近减少了，因而Rialto无法像以前一样吸引很多观众。

另一个需要回答的问题是两家影院的可比性。我们知道有很多因素都可能导致他们之间存在差别：位置、主要放映的影片类型以及票价等等。这些因素中的任何一个都有可能导致在Rialto提供这些设施不会像在Apex那样有效。经理不能证明Rialto通过简单照搬Apex的设施就能赢利。

而且，我们还可以对文中调查的可信度提出疑问。我们无法确定调查的回应者是否能代表城市的总体人群，以及该调查是否囊括了足够多的研究对象。另外，就算这些回应者的看法能够代表总体居民的意见，Rialto也可以采取其他手段解决问题，比如以低价提供一些早期影片。

一个影院为生存谋求出路是可以理解的。但在经理提供Apex真实利润的完整信息，并提供论据证明Apex是因为提供了这些设施而吸引了大量观众之前，我们不能草率认定在Rialto提供这些设施后一定能保证影院的发展。

SAMPLE 4

75. The following appeared in a letter to the editor of a Batavia newspaper.

"The department of agriculture in Batavia reports that the number of dairy farms throughout the country is now 25 percent greater than it was 10 years ago. During this same time period, however, the price of milk at the local Excello Food Market has increased from $1.50 to over $3.00 per gallon. To prevent farmers from continuing to receive excessive profits on an apparently increased supply of milk, the Batavia government should begin to regulate retail milk prices. Such regulation is necessary to ensure fair prices for consumers."

Write a response in which you discuss what questions would need to be answered in order to decide whether the recommendation is likely to have the predicted result. Be sure to explain how the answers to these questions would help to evaluate the recommendation.

Basing on the assumption that farmers are receiving excessive profits on increased supply of milk, the author recommends Batavia government to regulate retail milk prices. Admittedly, it is the responsibility of the government to ensure the stability of the market, however, several questions must be addressed before we could determine whether the regulation will be necessary and effective for lowering milk price.

A critical assumption of the argument is that the farmers are receiving unreasonable profits, which is unwarranted before several factors have been considered. A foremost question is that whether the number of dairy farms could accurately reflect the supply of milk, for there is no necessary relationship between them. It is possible that the average milk supply of each single farm has dropped and therefore the total supply would not increase. It is also possible that a great proportion of milk produced has been processed to other dairy products or has been exported. The milk supply on market will decrease in these cases.

Granted that the supply of milk did increase during the past decade, we may well ask that whether the prices of milk are increasing all over the country. The author provides only one sample—the Excello market to illustrate the variation of milk price, but many factors may render the situation at the market unrepresentative of the national trends. Perhaps the supply of milk in the region where the market locates was relatively lower than national average, or the milk production is much more costly here due to some geographic factors. Any one of these possibilities would make the higher milk price in Excello totally a normal phenomenon.

Even if the prices of milk were also doubled throughout the country, just as happened in Excello, the author overlooks a myriad of economic factors that would result in the increase. Consider, for example, the cost of milk production and transportation might have increased as well during the same period, or perhaps the supply of milk could not meet the demand in spite of an increased supply. The author also needs to inform us how much did the price of milk actually increase after adjustment for inflation. Without accounting for these factors, the author could not convince us that farmers have received excessive profits and that the regulation is indeed necessary.

Finally, even if the author can successfully address all the questions foregoing, it is unjustifiable to conclude that the regulation of retail milk prices could ensure an adequate supply of milk and therefore, a fair price. It is likely that the regulation would reduce the profits of farmers; they might be less interested in producing milk, or will produce less milk as a response. If so, adopting the author's recommendation will actually lead to inadequate supply of milk rather than the optimistic result expected by the author.

Undoubtedly, the author's intention of keeping the market stable and ensuring fair price of milk is justified. But to convince us that the regulation is necessary to ensure a reasonable milk price and adequate supply, the author must substantiate the assumption that the profits received by farmers are undeserved and that the regulation is sufficient for ensuring lower price. Hastily carrying out such regulation would actually pose negative effects on the supply of milk. (545 words)

参考译文

基于农场主在牛奶增产的情况下牟取过度利润的假设，作者建议Batavia政府限制牛奶零售价。诚然，保证市场稳定是政府职责之一，但在确定限价政策对于平抑奶价是否必要及有效之前首先要解决若干问题。

上文论述的一个关键假设就是农场主在获取不合理利润。在没有充分考虑若干关键因素的情况下该假设不一定合理。一个首要问题就是奶牛农场数量是否能够准确反映牛奶供应量，因为两者之间并没有必然联系。有可能每个农场的平均产奶量下降，从而导致总产奶量并没有上升；也可能出产的牛奶很大一部分被加工成其他奶制品或出口了。在这些情况下，牛奶的市场供应量都将下降。

即使过去10年牛奶供应量确实增加了，我们还要问一问全国奶价是否都在上升。作者在文中仅提供了一个样本——Excello市场来说明奶价变化，但很多因素可能会导致该市场的情况并不能代表全国趋势。有可能该市场所在的区域牛奶供应量低于全国平均水平，或由于一些地理原因在该地生产牛奶的成本更高。在这种情况下，Excello奶价高完全属于正常现象。

即使全国奶价确实也像Excello市场一样翻番，作者还忽略了很多导致奶价上升的经济因素。比如，牛奶的生产运输成本可能在同期上涨，或可能牛奶供应量上升但依然不能满足需求。作者还需要告知我们扣除通胀因素之后奶价的实际涨幅是多少。在没有考虑这些因素的情况下，作者不能让我们相信农场主在牟取过度利润以及文中提到的限价确实是必要的。

最后，即使作者能有效解决以上所有问题，要得出限制牛奶零售价将保证充足牛奶供应以及合理价格的结论依然是不充分的。有可能该限价措施会压缩农场主的利润空间，从而导致他们不再有兴趣生产牛奶，或减少牛奶产量。如果是这样的话，采纳作者的建议实际上会导致牛奶供应不足，而不是作者预想的美好结局。

显然，作者关于维持市场稳定以及保证公平奶价的出发点是值得肯定的。但要使我们相信要保证合理奶价和充足供应必须进行限价的结论，作者必须证实农场主在获取不合理利润以及该限价足以保证更低奶价的假设。草率出台这类限价实际上会对牛奶供应产生负面影响。

SAMPLE 5

92. Workers in the small town of Leeville take fewer sick days than workers in the large city of Masonton, 50 miles away. Moreover, relative to population size, the diagnosis of stress-related illness is proportionally much lower in Leeville than in Masonton. According to the Leeville Chamber of Commerce, these facts can be attributed to the health benefits of the relatively relaxed pace of life in Leeville.

Write a response in which you discuss one or more alternative explanations that could rival the proposed explanation and explain how your explanation(s) can plausibly account for the facts presented in the argument.

The fewer sick days and lower diagnosis of stress-related illness in Leeville may, to some extent, indicate better health status of residents. But the situation could also be explained by many other factors. It is too hasty for the Chamber of Commerce to conclude that it is the relaxed pace of life that brings those health benefits.

First of all, the Chamber implies that Leeville residents are in satisfying health condition, which serves as a foremost premise of the argument. However, the number of sick days and the diagnosis of stress-related illness do not necessarily indicate the health condition of residents. The fewer sick days may result from strict restrictions on sick leaves at Leeville factories; or perhaps the workers will receive harsher punishment once they take too many sick leaves, thus they will be unable to take more sick leaves as a result. Another explanation is that the workers might be unwilling to be absent from work for certain reasons. Similarly, the fewer diagnosis of stress-related illness could also be explained by other reasons. It is possible that people in Leeville are not willing to visit doctors for these diseases, or maybe there are some differences in the diagnostic criteria of the disease in the two cities. If the criterion or definition of the disease is more rigorous in Leeville than in Masonton, then it is conceivable that the incidence of such disease in Masonton will be higher. In this case, the diagnosis of this illness could not accurately reflect the actual level of stress of residents, let alone their actual level of health.

Granted that Leeville residents are living healthier lives, physically and mentally, there are still many other factors, rather than the relaxed pace of life suggested by the Chamber, that could contribute to the situation. The myriad factors might include better environment and weather, healthier life style in Leeville, which will lead to good health condition and less illness. It is also possible that the working condition and work ethic in Leeville factories are better than those in Masonton, or Leeville has harmonious neighborhoods, which could explain the lower level of mental stress.

As commonly known, a relaxed pace of life often promotes peoples' health status, but we cannot conclude that the better health of Leeville residents is also the result of their pace of life. The Chamber should consider and rule out all other possibilities before we could be convinced that the relaxed lifestyle is the actual and only explanation for the health condition of Leeville residents. (422 words)

参考译文

　　Leeville更少的病假天数和更低的与压力相关疾病的确诊率可能在一定程度上说明其居民较好的健康状况。但这一情形也同样可以通过很多其他因素解释。商会现在就下结论认为悠闲的生活节奏带来了这些健康好处过于草率。

　　首先，商会认为Leeville居民处于理想的健康状况，这是上文论证的重要前提。但是，病假天数和压力相关疾病确诊率并不能必然说明居民的健康程度。较少的病假天数可能是由于Leeville工厂严格的病假制度造成的；也可能工人休过多病假会受到较为严厉的惩罚，从而导致他们无法请更多的病假。另一种解释是工人可能出于某些原因不愿意缺勤。与之类似，更少的压力相关疾病确诊率也可能有其他解释。有可能Leeville居民不愿意因为这些疾病看医生，也可能两城市对于此类疾病的诊断标准有些差别。如果Leeville对疾病的诊断标准或定义比Masonton更加严格，那么，可以想见Masonton疾病的发生率将会更高。这样的话，疾病的诊断率就不能准确反映居民的真正压力水平，更不用说反映他们的健康水平了。

　　就算Leeville居民身心都更健康，但除了商会提出的悠闲生活节奏以外还有很多其他因素会导致这种情况。这些因素可能包括Leeville更好的环境和气候，或其居民更健康的生活方式——这些都会带来更好的健康状况和更少的疾病。也可能Leeville工厂的工作条件和氛围要好于Masonton工厂，或Leeville的邻里关系更加和睦，这些都能够解释精神压力小的现象。

　　众所周知，悠闲的生活节奏通常能提升人们的健康状况，但我们不能认定Leeville居民更好的健康状况也是他们生活节奏的结果。商会在说服我们相信悠闲的生活方式就是Leeville居民健康状况的真正且唯一的解释之前应该考虑并排除以上种种可能情况。

附录一 Issue 作文题库

This page contains the Issue topics for the Analytical Writing section of the GRE® revised General Test. When you take the test, you will be presented with one Issue topic from this pool.

Each Issue topic consists of an issue statement or statements followed by specific task instructions that tell you how to respond to the issue. The wording of some topics in the test might vary slightly from what is presented here. Also, because there may be multiple versions of some topics with similar or identical wording but with different task instructions, it is very important to read your test topic and its specific task directions carefully and respond to the wording as it appears in the actual test.

1. As people rely more and more on technology to solve problems, the ability of humans to think for themselves will surely deteriorate.

    Write a response in which you discuss the extent to which you agree or disagree with the statement and explain your reasoning for the position you take. In developing and supporting your position, you should consider ways in which the statement might or might not hold true and explain how these considerations shape your position.

2. To understand the most important characteristics of a society, one must study its major cities.

    Write a response in which you discuss the extent to which you agree or disagree with the statement and explain your reasoning for the position you take. In developing and supporting your position, you should consider ways in which the statement might or might not hold true and explain how these considerations shape your position.

3. Educational institutions have a responsibility to dissuade students from pursuing fields of study in which they are unlikely to succeed.

    Write a response in which you discuss the extent to which you agree or disagree with the claim. In developing and supporting your position, be sure to address the most compelling reasons and/or examples that could be used to challenge your position.

4. Scandals are useful because they focus our attention on problems in ways that no speaker or reformer ever could.

    Write a response in which you discuss the extent to which you agree or disagree with the claim. In developing and supporting your position, be sure to address the most compelling reasons and/or examples that could be used to challenge your position.

5. Claim: Governments must ensure that their major cities receive the financial support they need in order to thrive.

Reason: It is primarily in cities that a nation's cultural traditions are preserved and generated.

Write a response in which you discuss the extent to which you agree or disagree with the claim and the reason on which that claim is based.

6. A nation should require all of its students to study the same national curriculum until they enter college.

Write a response in which you discuss the extent to which you agree or disagree with the recommendation and explain your reasoning for the position you take. In developing and supporting your position, describe specific circumstances in which adopting the recommendation would or would not be advantageous and explain how these examples shape your position.

7. Some people believe that government funding of the arts is necessary to ensure that the arts can flourish and be available to all people. Others believe that government funding of the arts threatens the integrity of the arts.

Write a response in which you discuss which view more closely aligns with your own position and explain your reasoning for the position you take. In developing and supporting your position, you should address both of the views presented.

8. Claim: In any field—business, politics, education, government—those in power should step down after five years.
Reason: The surest path to success for any enterprise is revitalization through new leadership.

Write a response in which you discuss the extent to which you agree or disagree with the claim and the reason on which that claim is based.

9. In any field of endeavor, it is impossible to make a significant contribution without first being strongly influenced by past achievements within that field.

Write a response in which you discuss the extent to which you agree or disagree with the statement and explain your reasoning for the position you take. In developing and supporting your position, you should consider ways in which the statement might or might not hold true and explain how these considerations shape your position.

10. Nations should pass laws to preserve any remaining wilderness areas in their natural state, even if these areas could be developed for economic gain.

Write a response in which you discuss your views on the policy and explain your reasoning for the position you take. In developing and supporting your position, you should consider the possible consequences of implementing the policy and explain how these consequences shape your position.

11. People's behavior is largely determined by forces not of their own making.

Write a response in which you discuss the extent to which you agree or disagree with the statement and explain your reasoning for the position you take. In developing and supporting your position, you should consider ways in which the statement might or might not hold true and explain how these considerations shape your position.

12. Governments should offer a free university education to any student who has been admitted to a university but who cannot afford the tuition.

    Write a response in which you discuss your views on the policy and explain your reasoning for the position you take. In developing and supporting your position, you should consider the possible consequences of implementing the policy and explain how these consequences shape your position.

13. Universities should require every student to take a variety of courses outside the student's field of study.

    Write a response in which you discuss the extent to which you agree or disagree with the claim. In developing and supporting your position, be sure to address the most compelling reasons and/or examples that could be used to challenge your position.

14. A nation should require all of its students to study the same national curriculum until they enter college.

    Write a response in which you discuss your views on the policy and explain your reasoning for the position you take. In developing and supporting your position, you should consider the possible consequences of implementing the policy and explain how these consequences shape your position.

15. Educational institutions should actively encourage their students to choose fields of study that will prepare them for lucrative careers.

    Write a response in which you discuss the extent to which you agree or disagree with the claim. In developing and supporting your position, be sure to address the most compelling reasons and/or examples that could be used to challenge your position.

16. Some people believe that in order to be effective, political leaders must yield to public opinion and abandon principle for the sake of compromise. Others believe that the most essential quality of an effective leader is the ability to remain consistently committed to particular principles and objectives.

    Write a response in which you discuss which view more closely aligns with your own position and explain your reasoning for the position you take. In developing and supporting your position, you should address both of the views presented.

17. Formal education tends to restrain our minds and spirits rather than set them free.

    Write a response in which you discuss the extent to which you agree or disagree with the statement and explain your reasoning for the position you take. In developing and supporting your position, you should consider ways in which the statement might or might not hold true and explain how these considerations shape your position.

18. The well-being of a society is enhanced when many of its people question authority.

    Write a response in which you discuss the extent to which you agree or disagree with the statement and explain your reasoning for the position you take. In developing and supporting your position, you should consider ways in which the statement might or might not hold true and explain how these considerations shape your position.

19. Governments should focus on solving the immediate problems of today rather than on trying to solve the anticipated problems of the future.

Write a response in which you discuss the extent to which you agree or disagree with the recommendation and explain your reasoning for the position you take. In developing and supporting your position, describe specific circumstances in which adopting the recommendation would or would not be advantageous and explain how these examples shape your position.

20. Some people believe that college students should consider only their own talents and interests when choosing a field of study. Others believe that college students should base their choice of a field of study on the availability of jobs in that field.

Write a response in which you discuss which view more closely aligns with your own position and explain your reasoning for the position you take. In developing and supporting your position, you should address both of the views presented.

21. Laws should be flexible enough to take account of various circumstances, times, and places.

Write a response in which you discuss the extent to which you agree or disagree with the statement and explain your reasoning for the position you take. In developing and supporting your position, you should consider ways in which the statement might or might not hold true and explain how these considerations shape your position.

22. The best way to understand the character of a society is to examine the character of the men and women that the society chooses as its heroes or its role models.
Reason: Heroes and role models reveal a society's highest ideals.

Write a response in which you discuss the extent to which you agree or disagree with the claim and the reason on which that claim is based.

23. Governments should place few, if any, restrictions on scientific research and development.

Write a response in which you discuss the extent to which you agree or disagree with the recommendation and explain your reasoning for the position you take. In developing and supporting your position, describe specific circumstances in which adopting the recommendation would or would not be advantageous and explain how these examples shape your position.

24. The best way to teach is to praise positive actions and ignore negative ones.

Write a response in which you discuss the extent to which you agree or disagree with the statement and explain your reasoning for the position you take. In developing and supporting your position, you should consider ways in which the statement might or might not hold true and explain how these considerations shape your position.

25. Governments should offer college and university education free of charge to all students.

Write a response in which you discuss the extent to which you agree or disagree with the recommendation and explain your reasoning for the position you take. In developing and supporting your position, describe specific circumstances in which adopting the recommendation would or would not be advantageous and explain how these examples shape your position.

26. The luxuries and conveniences of contemporary life prevent people from developing into truly strong and independent individuals.

Write a response in which you discuss the extent to which you agree or disagree with the statement and explain your reasoning for the position you take. In developing and supporting your position, you should consider ways in which the statement might or might not hold true and explain how these considerations shape your position.

27. In any field of inquiry, the beginner is more likely than the expert to make important contributions.

Write a response in which you discuss the extent to which you agree or disagree with the statement and explain your reasoning for the position you take. In developing and supporting your position, you should consider ways in which the statement might or might not hold true and explain how these considerations shape your position.

28. The surest indicator of a great nation is represented not by the achievements of its rulers, artists, or scientists, but by the general welfare of its people.

Write a response in which you discuss the extent to which you agree or disagree with the statement and explain your reasoning for the position you take. In developing and supporting your position, you should consider ways in which the statement might or might not hold true and explain how these considerations shape your position.

29. The best way to teach—whether as an educator, employer, or parent—is to praise positive actions and ignore negative ones.

Write a response in which you discuss the extent to which you agree or disagree with the claim. In developing and supporting your position, be sure to address the most compelling reasons and/or examples that could be used to challenge your position.

30. Teachers' salaries should be based on their students' academic performance.

Write a response in which you discuss the extent to which you agree or disagree with the claim. In developing and supporting your position, be sure to address the most compelling reasons and/or examples that could be used to challenge your position.

31. Society should make efforts to save endangered species only if the potential extinction of those species is the result of human activities.

Write a response in which you discuss your views on the policy and explain your reasoning for the position you take. In developing and supporting your position, you should consider the possible consequences of implementing the policy and explain how these consequences shape your position.

32. College students should base their choice of a field of study on the availability of jobs in that field.

Write a response in which you discuss the extent to which you agree or disagree with the claim. In developing and supporting your position, be sure to address the most compelling reasons and/or examples that could be used to challenge your position.

33. As we acquire more knowledge, things do not become more comprehensible, but more complex and mysterious.

Write a response in which you discuss the extent to which you agree or disagree with the statement and explain your reasoning for the position you take. In developing and supporting your position, you should consider ways in which the statement might or might not hold true and explain how these considerations shape your position.

34. In any situation, progress requires discussion among people who have contrasting points of view.

Write a response in which you discuss the extent to which you agree or disagree with the statement and explain your reasoning for the position you take. In developing and supporting your position, you should consider ways in which the statement might or might not hold true and explain how these considerations shape your position.

35. Educational institutions should dissuade students from pursuing fields of study in which they are unlikely to succeed.

Write a response in which you discuss your views on the policy and explain your reasoning for the position you take. In developing and supporting your position, you should consider the possible consequences of implementing the policy and explain how these consequences shape your position.

36. Governments should not fund any scientific research whose consequences are unclear.

Write a response in which you discuss the extent to which you agree or disagree with the recommendation and explain your reasoning for the position you take. In developing and supporting your position, describe specific circumstances in which adopting the recommendation would or would not be advantageous and explain how these examples shape your position.

37. Society should identify those children who have special talents and provide training for them at an early age to develop their talents.

Write a response in which you discuss the extent to which you agree or disagree with the recommendation and explain your reasoning for the position you take. In developing and supporting your position, describe specific circumstances in which adopting the recommendation would or would not be advantageous and explain how these examples shape your position.

38. It is primarily through our identification with social groups that we define ourselves.

Write a response in which you discuss the extent to which you agree or disagree with the statement and explain your reasoning for the position you take. In developing and supporting your position, you should consider ways in which the statement might or might not hold true and explain how these considerations shape your position.

39. College students should be encouraged to pursue subjects that interest them rather than the courses that seem most likely to lead to jobs.

Write a response in which you discuss the extent to which you agree or disagree with the recommendation and explain your reasoning for the position you take. In developing and supporting your position, describe specific circumstances in which adopting the recommendation would or would not be advantageous and explain how these examples shape your position.

40. Claim: When planning courses, educators should take into account the interests and suggestions of their students.
Reason: Students are more motivated to learn when they are interested in what they are studying.

Write a response in which you discuss the extent to which you agree or disagree with the claim and the reason on which that claim is based.

41. The greatness of individuals can be decided only by those who live after them, not by their contemporaries.

Write a response in which you discuss the extent to which you agree or disagree with the statement and explain your reasoning for the position you take. In developing and supporting your position, you should consider ways in which the statement might or might not hold true and explain how these considerations shape your position.

42. Students should always question what they are taught instead of accepting it passively.

Write a response in which you discuss the extent to which you agree or disagree with the statement and explain your reasoning for the position you take. In developing and supporting your position, you should consider ways in which the statement might or might not hold true and explain how these considerations shape your position.

43. The increasingly rapid pace of life today causes more problems than it solves.

Write a response in which you discuss the extent to which you agree or disagree with the statement and explain your reasoning for the position you take. In developing and supporting your position, you should consider ways in which the statement might or might not hold true and explain how these considerations shape your position.

44. Claim: It is no longer possible for a society to regard any living man or woman as a hero.
Reason: The reputation of anyone who is subjected to media scrutiny will eventually be diminished.

Write a response in which you discuss the extent to which you agree or disagree with the claim and the reason on which that claim is based.

45. Competition for high grades seriously limits the quality of learning at all levels of education.

Write a response in which you discuss the extent to which you agree or disagree with the statement and explain your reasoning for the position you take. In developing and supporting your position, you should consider ways in which the statement might or might not hold true and explain how these considerations shape your position.

46. Universities should require every student to take a variety of courses outside the student's field of study.

Write a response in which you discuss the extent to which you agree or disagree with the recommendation and explain your reasoning for the position you take. In developing and supporting your position, describe specific circumstances in which adopting the recommendation would or would not be advantageous and explain how these examples shape your position.

47. Educators should find out what students want included in the curriculum and then offer it to them.

Write a response in which you discuss the extent to which you agree or disagree with the recommendation and explain your reasoning for the position you take. In developing and supporting your position, describe specific circumstances in which adopting the recommendation would or would not be advantageous and explain how these examples shape your position.

48. Educators should teach facts only after their students have studied the ideas, trends, and concepts that help explain those facts.

Write a response in which you discuss the extent to which you agree or disagree with the recommendation and explain your reasoning for the position you take. In developing and supporting your position, describe specific circumstances in which adopting the recommendation would or would not be advantageous and explain how these examples shape your position.

49. Claim: We can usually learn much more from people whose views we share than from those whose views contradict our own.
Reason: Disagreement can cause stress and inhibit learning.

Write a response in which you discuss the extent to which you agree or disagree with the claim and the reason on which that claim is based.

50. Government officials should rely on their own judgment rather than unquestioningly carry out the will of the people they serve.

Write a response in which you discuss the extent to which you agree or disagree with the recommendation and explain your reasoning for the position you take. In developing and supporting your position, describe specific circumstances in which adopting the recommendation would or would not be advantageous and explain how these examples shape your position.

51. Young people should be encouraged to pursue long-term, realistic goals rather than seek immediate fame and recognition.

Write a response in which you discuss the extent to which you agree or disagree with the recommendation and explain your reasoning for the position you take. In developing and supporting your position, describe specific circumstances in which adopting the recommendation would or would not be advantageous and explain how these examples shape your position.

52. The best way to teach is to praise positive actions and ignore negative ones.

Write a response in which you discuss the extent to which you agree or disagree with the recommendation and explain your reasoning for the position you take. In developing and supporting your position, describe specific circumstances in which adopting the recommendation would or would not be advantageous and explain how these examples shape your position.

53. If a goal is worthy, then any means taken to attain it are justifiable.

   Write a response in which you discuss the extent to which you agree or disagree with the statement and explain your reasoning for the position you take. In developing and supporting your position, you should consider ways in which the statement might or might not hold true and explain how these considerations shape your position.

54. In order to become well-rounded individuals, all college students should be required to take courses in which they read poetry, novels, mythology, and other types of imaginative literature.

   Write a response in which you discuss the extent to which you agree or disagree with the recommendation and explain your reasoning for the position you take. In developing and supporting your position, describe specific circumstances in which adopting the recommendation would or would not be advantageous and explain how these examples shape your position.

55. In order for any work of art—for example, a film, a novel, a poem, or a song—to have merit, it must be understandable to most people.

   Write a response in which you discuss the extent to which you agree or disagree with the statement and explain your reasoning for the position you take. In developing and supporting your position, you should consider ways in which the statement might or might not hold true and explain how these considerations shape your position.

56. Many important discoveries or creations are accidental: it is usually while seeking the answer to one question that we come across the answer to another.

   Write a response in which you discuss the extent to which you agree or disagree with the statement and explain your reasoning for the position you take. In developing and supporting your position, you should consider ways in which the statement might or might not hold true and explain how these considerations shape your position.

57. The main benefit of the study of history is to dispel the illusion that people living now are significantly different from people who lived in earlier times.

   Write a response in which you discuss the extent to which you agree or disagree with the statement and explain your reasoning for the position you take. In developing and supporting your position, you should consider ways in which the statement might or might not hold true and explain how these considerations shape your position.

58. Learning is primarily a matter of personal discipline; students cannot be motivated by school or college alone.

   Write a response in which you discuss the extent to which you agree or disagree with the statement and explain your reasoning for the position you take. In developing and supporting your position, you should consider ways in which the statement might or might not hold true and explain how these considerations shape your position.

59. Scientists and other researchers should focus their research on areas that are likely to benefit the greatest number of people.

Write a response in which you discuss the extent to which you agree or disagree with the recommendation and explain your reasoning for the position you take. In developing and supporting your position, describe specific circumstances in which adopting the recommendation would or would not be advantageous and explain how these examples shape your position.

60. Politicians should pursue common ground and reasonable consensus rather than elusive ideals.

Write a response in which you discuss the extent to which you agree or disagree with the recommendation and explain your reasoning for the position you take. In developing and supporting your position, describe specific circumstances in which adopting the recommendation would or would not be advantageous and explain how these examples shape your position.

61. People should undertake risky action only after they have carefully considered its consequences.

Write a response in which you discuss the extent to which you agree or disagree with the recommendation and explain your reasoning for the position you take. In developing and supporting your position, describe specific circumstances in which adopting the recommendation would or would not be advantageous and explain how these examples shape your position.

62. Leaders are created by the demands that are placed on them.

Write a response in which you discuss the extent to which you agree or disagree with the statement and explain your reasoning for the position you take. In developing and supporting your position, you should consider ways in which the statement might or might not hold true and explain how these considerations shape your position.

63. There is little justification for society to make extraordinary efforts—especially at a great cost in money and jobs—to save endangered animal or plant species.

Write a response in which you discuss the extent to which you agree or disagree with the statement and explain your reasoning for the position you take. In developing and supporting your position, you should consider ways in which the statement might or might not hold true and explain how these considerations shape your position.

64. The human mind will always be superior to machines because machines are only tools of human minds.

Write a response in which you discuss the extent to which you agree or disagree with the statement and explain your reasoning for the position you take. In developing and supporting your position, you should consider ways in which the statement might or might not hold true and explain how these considerations shape your position.

65. Every individual in a society has a responsibility to obey just laws and to disobey and resist unjust laws.

   Write a response in which you discuss the extent to which you agree or disagree with the claim. In developing and supporting your position, be sure to address the most compelling reasons and/or examples that could be used to challenge your position.

66. People who are the most deeply committed to an idea or policy are also the most critical of it.

   Write a response in which you discuss the extent to which you agree or disagree with the statement and explain your reasoning for the position you take. In developing and supporting your position, you should consider ways in which the statement might or might not hold true and explain how these considerations shape your position.

67. Some people believe that society should try to save every plant and animal species, despite the expense to humans in effort, time, and financial well-being. Others believe that society need not make extraordinary efforts, especially at a great cost in money and jobs, to save endangered species.

   Write a response in which you discuss which view more closely aligns with your own position and explain your reasoning for the position you take. In developing and supporting your position, you should address both of the views presented.

68. Some people believe that the purpose of education is to free the mind and the spirit. Others believe that formal education tends to restrain our minds and spirits rather than set them free.

   Write a response in which you discuss which view more closely aligns with your own position and explain your reasoning for the position you take. In developing and supporting your position, you should address both of the views presented.

69. Some people believe it is often necessary, even desirable, for political leaders to withhold information from the public. Others believe that the public has a right to be fully informed.

   Write a response in which you discuss which view more closely aligns with your own position and explain your reasoning for the position you take. In developing and supporting your position, you should address both of the views presented.

70. Claim: Universities should require every student to take a variety of courses outside the student's major field of study.
   Reason: Acquiring knowledge of various academic disciplines is the best way to become truly educated.

   Write a response in which you discuss the extent to which you agree or disagree with the claim and the reason on which that claim is based.

71. Young people should be encouraged to pursue long-term, realistic goals rather than seek immediate fame and recognition.

   Write a response in which you discuss the extent to which you agree or disagree with the statement and explain your reasoning for the position you take. In developing and supporting your position, you should consider ways in which the statement might or might not hold true and explain how these considerations shape your position.

72. Governments should not fund any scientific research whose consequences are unclear.

Write a response in which you discuss your views on the policy and explain your reasoning for the position you take. In developing and supporting your position, you should consider the possible consequences of implementing the policy and explain how these consequences shape your position.

73. Colleges and universities should require all faculty to spend time working outside the academic world in professions relevant to the courses they teach.

Write a response in which you discuss your views on the policy and explain your reasoning for the position you take. In developing and supporting your position, you should consider the possible consequences of implementing the policy and explain how these consequences shape your position.

74. Knowing about the past cannot help people to make important decisions today.

Write a response in which you discuss the extent to which you agree or disagree with the statement and explain your reasoning for the position you take. In developing and supporting your position, you should consider ways in which the statement might or might not hold true and explain how these considerations shape your position.

75. In this age of intensive media coverage, it is no longer possible for a society to regard any living man or woman as a hero.

Write a response in which you discuss the extent to which you agree or disagree with the statement and explain your reasoning for the position you take. In developing and supporting your position, you should consider ways in which the statement might or might not hold true and explain how these considerations shape your position.

76. We can usually learn much more from people whose views we share than from people whose views contradict our own.

Write a response in which you discuss the extent to which you agree or disagree with the statement and explain your reasoning for the position you take. In developing and supporting your position, you should consider ways in which the statement might or might not hold true and explain how these considerations shape your position.

77. The most effective way to understand contemporary culture is to analyze the trends of its youth.

Write a response in which you discuss the extent to which you agree or disagree with the statement and explain your reasoning for the position you take. In developing and supporting your position, you should consider ways in which the statement might or might not hold true and explain how these considerations shape your position.

78. People's attitudes are determined more by their immediate situation or surroundings than by society as a whole.

   Write a response in which you discuss the extent to which you agree or disagree with the statement and explain your reasoning for the position you take. In developing and supporting your position, you should consider ways in which the statement might or might not hold true and explain how these considerations shape your position.

79. Claim: The best test of an argument is its ability to convince someone with an opposing viewpoint. Reason: Only by being forced to defend an idea against the doubts and contrasting views of others does one really discover the value of that idea.

   Write a response in which you discuss the extent to which you agree or disagree with the claim and the reason on which that claim is based.

80. Nations should suspend government funding for the arts when significant numbers of their citizens are hungry or unemployed.

   Write a response in which you discuss the extent to which you agree or disagree with the recommendation and explain your reasoning for the position you take. In developing and supporting your position, describe specific circumstances in which adopting the recommendation would or would not be advantageous and explain how these examples shape your position.

81. All parents should be required to volunteer time to their children's schools.

   Write a response in which you discuss the extent to which you agree or disagree with the recommendation and explain your reasoning for the position you take. In developing and supporting your position, describe specific circumstances in which adopting the recommendation would or would not be advantageous and explain how these examples shape your position.

82. Colleges and universities should require their students to spend at least one semester studying in a foreign country.

   Write a response in which you discuss the extent to which you agree or disagree with the recommendation and explain your reasoning for the position you take. In developing and supporting your position, describe specific circumstances in which adopting the recommendation would or would not be advantageous and explain how these examples shape your position.

83. Teachers' salaries should be based on the academic performance of their students.

   Write a response in which you discuss the extent to which you agree or disagree with the recommendation and explain your reasoning for the position you take. In developing and supporting your position, describe specific circumstances in which adopting the recommendation would or would not be advantageous and explain how these examples shape your position.

84. It is no longer possible for a society to regard any living man or woman as a hero.

   Write a response in which you discuss the extent to which you agree or disagree with the claim. In developing and supporting your position, be sure to address the most compelling reasons and/or examples that could be used to challenge your position.

85. Some people believe that in order to thrive, a society must put its own overall success before the well-being of its individual citizens. Others believe that the well-being of a society can only be measured by the general welfare of all its people.

    Write a response in which you discuss which view more closely aligns with your own position and explain your reasoning for the position you take. In developing and supporting your position, you should address both of the views presented.

86. Some people believe that government officials must carry out the will of the people they serve. Others believe that officials should base their decisions on their own judgment.

    Write a response in which you discuss which view more closely aligns with your own position and explain your reasoning for the position you take. In developing and supporting your position, you should address both of the views presented.

87. Claim: Any piece of information referred to as a fact should be mistrusted, since it may well be proven false in the future.
    Reason: Much of the information that people assume is factual actually turns out to be inaccurate.

    Write a response in which you discuss the extent to which you agree or disagree with the claim and the reason on which that claim is based.

88. Claim: Nations should suspend government funding for the arts when significant numbers of their citizens are hungry or unemployed.
    Reason: It is inappropriate—and, perhaps, even cruel—to use public resources to fund the arts when people's basic needs are not being met.

    Write a response in which you discuss the extent to which you agree or disagree with the claim and the reason on which that claim is based.

89. Claim: Many problems of modern society cannot be solved by laws and the legal system.
    Reason: Laws cannot change what is in people's hearts or minds.

    Write a response in which you discuss the extent to which you agree or disagree with the claim and the reason on which that claim is based.

90. Educators should take students' interests into account when planning the content of the courses they teach.

    Write a response in which you discuss the extent to which you agree or disagree with the recommendation and explain your reasoning for the position you take. In developing and supporting your position, describe specific circumstances in which adopting the recommendation would or would not be advantageous and explain how these examples shape your position.

91. The primary goal of technological advancement should be to increase people's efficiency so that they have more leisure time.

Write a response in which you discuss the extent to which you agree or disagree with the statement and explain your reasoning for the position you take. In developing and supporting your position, you should consider ways in which the statement might or might not hold true and explain how these considerations shape your position.

92. Educators should base their assessment of students' learning not on students' grasp of facts but on the ability to explain the ideas, trends, and concepts that those facts illustrate.

Write a response in which you discuss the extent to which you agree or disagree with the recommendation and explain your reasoning for the position you take. In developing and supporting your position, describe specific circumstances in which adopting the recommendation would or would not be advantageous and explain how these examples shape your position.

93. Unfortunately, in contemporary society, creating an appealing image has become more important than the reality or truth behind that image.

Write a response in which you discuss the extent to which you agree or disagree with the statement and explain your reasoning for the position you take. In developing and supporting your position, you should consider ways in which the statement might or might not hold true and explain how these considerations shape your position.

94. The effectiveness of a country's leaders is best measured by examining the well-being of that country's citizens.

Write a response in which you discuss the extent to which you agree or disagree with the claim. In developing and supporting your position, be sure to address the most compelling reasons and/or examples that could be used to challenge your position.

95. All parents should be required to volunteer time to their children's schools.

Write a response in which you discuss the extent to which you agree or disagree with the claim. In developing and supporting your position, be sure to address the most compelling reasons and/or examples that could be used to challenge your position.

96. A nation should require all of its students to study the same national curriculum until they enter college.

Write a response in which you discuss the extent to which you agree or disagree with the claim. In developing and supporting your position, be sure to address the most compelling reasons and/or examples that could be used to challenge your position.

97. Colleges and universities should require their students to spend at least one semester studying in a foreign country.

Write a response in which you discuss the extent to which you agree or disagree with the claim. In developing and supporting your position, be sure to address the most compelling reasons and/or examples that could be used to challenge your position.

98. Educational institutions should actively encourage their students to choose fields of study in which jobs are plentiful.

Write a response in which you discuss your views on the policy and explain your reasoning for the position you take. In developing and supporting your position, you should consider the possible consequences of implementing the policy and explain how these consequences shape your position.

99. People's behavior is largely determined by forces not of their own making.

Write a response in which you discuss the extent to which you agree or disagree with the claim. In developing and supporting your position, be sure to address the most compelling reasons and/or examples that could be used to challenge your position.

100. Colleges and universities should require their students to spend at least one semester studying in a foreign country.

Write a response in which you discuss your views on the policy and explain your reasoning for the position you take. In developing and supporting your position, you should consider the possible consequences of implementing the policy and explain how these consequences shape your position.

101. Although innovations such as video, computers, and the Internet seem to offer schools improved methods for instructing students, these technologies all too often distract from real learning.

Write a response in which you discuss the extent to which you agree or disagree with the statement and explain your reasoning for the position you take. In developing and supporting your position, you should consider ways in which the statement might or might not hold true and explain how these considerations shape your position.

102. Universities should require every student to take a variety of courses outside the student's field of study.

Write a response in which you discuss your views on the policy and explain your reasoning for the position you take. In developing and supporting your position, you should consider the possible consequences of implementing the policy and explain how these consequences shape your position.

103. The best ideas arise from a passionate interest in commonplace things.

Write a response in which you discuss the extent to which you agree or disagree with the statement and explain your reasoning for the position you take. In developing and supporting your position, you should consider ways in which the statement might or might not hold true and explain how these considerations shape your position.

104. To be an effective leader, a public official must maintain the highest ethical and moral standards.

Write a response in which you discuss the extent to which you agree or disagree with the claim. In developing and supporting your position, be sure to address the most compelling reasons and/or examples that could be used to challenge your position.

105. Claim: Imagination is a more valuable asset than experience.

Reason: People who lack experience are free to imagine what is possible without the constraints of established habits and attitudes.

Write a response in which you discuss the extent to which you agree or disagree with the claim and the reason on which that claim is based.

106. In most professions and academic fields, imagination is more important than knowledge.

Write a response in which you discuss the extent to which you agree or disagree with the statement and explain your reasoning for the position you take. In developing and supporting your position, you should consider ways in which the statement might or might not hold true and explain how these considerations shape your position.

107. To be an effective leader, a public official must maintain the highest ethical and moral standards.

Write a response in which you discuss the extent to which you agree or disagree with the statement and explain your reasoning for the position you take. In developing and supporting your position, you should consider ways in which the statement might or might not hold true and explain how these considerations shape your position.

108. Critical judgment of work in any given field has little value unless it comes from someone who is an expert in that field.

Write a response in which you discuss the extent to which you agree or disagree with the statement and explain your reasoning for the position you take. In developing and supporting your position, you should consider ways in which the statement might or might not hold true and explain how these considerations shape your position.

109. Some people believe that scientific discoveries have given us a much better understanding of the world around us. Others believe that science has revealed to us that the world is infinitely more complex than we ever realized.

Write a response in which you discuss which view more closely aligns with your own position and explain your reasoning for the position you take. In developing and supporting your position, you should address both of the views presented.

110. Critical judgment of work in any given field has little value unless it comes from someone who is an expert in that field.

Write a response in which you discuss the extent to which you agree or disagree with the claim. In developing and supporting your position, be sure to address the most compelling reasons and/or examples that could be used to challenge your position.

111. In any profession—business, politics, education, government—those in power should step down after five years.

Write a response in which you discuss the extent to which you agree or disagree with the claim. In developing and supporting your position, be sure to address the most compelling reasons and/or examples that could be used to challenge your position.

112. Requiring university students to take a variety of courses outside their major fields of study is the best way to ensure that students become truly educated.

Write a response in which you discuss the extent to which you agree or disagree with the statement and explain your reasoning for the position you take. In developing and supporting your position, you should consider ways in which the statement might or might not hold true and explain how these considerations shape your position.

113. Claim: The surest indicator of a great nation is not the achievements of its rulers, artists, or scientists.
Reason: The surest indicator of a great nation is actually the welfare of all its people.

Write a response in which you discuss the extent to which you agree or disagree with the claim and the reason on which that claim is based.

114. Any leader who is quickly and easily influenced by shifts in popular opinion will accomplish little.

Write a response in which you discuss the extent to which you agree or disagree with the statement and explain your reasoning for the position you take. In developing and supporting your position, you should consider ways in which the statement might or might not hold true and explain how these considerations shape your position.

115. Government officials should rely on their own judgment rather than unquestioningly carry out the will of the people whom they serve.

Write a response in which you discuss the extent to which you agree or disagree with the statement and explain your reasoning for the position you take. In developing and supporting your position, you should consider ways in which the statement might or might not hold true and explain how these considerations shape your position.

116. A nation should require all of its students to study the same national curriculum until they enter college.

Write a response in which you discuss the extent to which you agree or disagree with the statement and explain your reasoning for the position you take. In developing and supporting your position, you should consider ways in which the statement might or might not hold true and explain how these considerations shape your position.

117. It is primarily in cities that a nation's cultural traditions are generated and preserved.

Write a response in which you discuss the extent to which you agree or disagree with the statement and explain your reasoning for the position you take. In developing and supporting your position, you should consider ways in which the statement might or might not hold true and explain how these considerations shape your position.

118. We can learn much more from people whose views we share than from people whose views contradict our own.

Write a response in which you discuss the extent to which you agree or disagree with the statement and explain your reasoning for the position you take. In developing and supporting your position, you should consider ways in which the statement might or might not hold true and explain how these considerations shape your position.

119. When old buildings stand on ground that modern planners feel could be better used for modern purposes, modern development should be given precedence over the preservation of historic buildings.

Write a response in which you discuss the extent to which you agree or disagree with the statement and explain your reasoning for the position you take. In developing and supporting your position, you should consider ways in which the statement might or might not hold true and explain how these considerations shape your position.

120. Claim: The surest indicator of a great nation must be the achievements of its rulers, artists, or scientists.
Reason: Great achievements by a nation's rulers, artists, or scientists will ensure a good life for the majority of that nation's people.

Write a response in which you discuss the extent to which you agree or disagree with the claim and the reason on which that claim is based.

121. Some people claim that you can tell whether a nation is great by looking at the achievements of its rulers, artists, or scientists. Others argue that the surest indicator of a great nation is, in fact, the general welfare of all its people.

Write a response in which you discuss which view more closely aligns with your own position and explain your reasoning for the position you take. In developing and supporting your position, you should address both of the views presented.

122. The best way to understand the character of a society is to examine the character of the men and women that the society chooses as its heroes or its role models.

Write a response in which you discuss the extent to which you agree or disagree with the claim. In developing and supporting your position, be sure to address the most compelling reasons and/or examples that could be used to challenge your position.

123. The best way for a society to prepare its young people for leadership in government, industry, or other fields is by instilling in them a sense of cooperation, not competition.

Write a response in which you discuss the extent to which you agree or disagree with the claim. In developing and supporting your position, be sure to address the most compelling reasons and/or examples that could be used to challenge your position.

124. All college and university students would benefit from spending at least one semester studying in a foreign country.

Write a response in which you discuss the extent to which you agree or disagree with the statement and explain your reasoning for the position you take. In developing and supporting your position, you should consider ways in which the statement might or might not hold true and explain how these considerations shape your position.

125. Some people claim that a nation's government should preserve its wilderness areas in their natural state. Others argue that these areas should be developed for potential economic gain.

Write a response in which you discuss which view more closely aligns with your own position and explain your reasoning for the position you take. In developing and supporting your position, you should address both of the views presented.

126. In most professions and academic fields, imagination is more important than knowledge.

Write a response in which you discuss the extent to which you agree or disagree with the claim. In developing and supporting your position, be sure to address the most compelling reasons and/or examples that could be used to challenge your position.

127. The surest indicator of a great nation is not the achievements of its rulers, artists, or scientists, but the general well-being of all its people.

Write a response in which you discuss the extent to which you agree or disagree with the claim. In developing and supporting your position, be sure to address the most compelling reasons and/or examples that could be used to challenge your position.

128. Some people argue that successful leaders in government, industry, or other fields must be highly competitive. Other people claim that in order to be successful, a leader must be willing and able to cooperate with others.

Write a response in which you discuss which view more closely aligns with your own position and explain your reasoning for the position you take. In developing and supporting your position, you should address both of the views presented.

129. College students should base their choice of a field of study on the availability of jobs in that field.

Write a response in which you discuss the extent to which you agree or disagree with the recommendation and explain your reasoning for the position you take. In developing and supporting your position, describe specific circumstances in which adopting the recommendation would or would not be advantageous and explain how these examples shape your position.

130. Some people believe that corporations have a responsibility to promote the well-being of the societies and environments in which they operate. Others believe that the only responsibility of corporations, provided they operate within the law, is to make as much money as possible.

Write a response in which you discuss which view more closely aligns with your own position and explain your reasoning for the position you take. In developing and supporting your position, you should address both of the views presented.

131. Claim: Researchers should not limit their investigations to only those areas in which they expect to discover something that has an immediate, practical application.

Reason: It is impossible to predict the outcome of a line of research with any certainty.

Write a response in which you discuss the extent to which you agree or disagree with the claim and the reason on which that claim is based.

132. Some people believe that our ever-increasing use of technology significantly reduces our opportunities for human interaction. Other people believe that technology provides us with new and better ways to communicate and connect with one another.

Write a response in which you discuss which view more closely aligns with your own position and explain your reasoning for the position you take. In developing and supporting your position, you should address both of the views presented.

133. Claim: Knowing about the past cannot help people to make important decisions today.

Reason: The world today is significantly more complex than it was even in the relatively recent past.

Write a response in which you discuss the extent to which you agree or disagree with the claim and the reason on which that claim is based.

134. Claim: Knowing about the past cannot help people to make important decisions today.

Reason: We are not able to make connections between current events and past events until we have some distance from both.

Write a response in which you discuss the extent to which you agree or disagree with the claim and the reason on which that claim is based.

135. Educational institutions should actively encourage their students to choose fields of study that will prepare them for lucrative careers.

Write a response in which you discuss your views on the policy and explain your reasoning for the position you take. In developing and supporting your position, you should consider the possible consequences of implementing the policy and explain how these consequences shape your position.

136. Educational institutions should actively encourage their students to choose fields of study in which jobs are plentiful.

Write a response in which you discuss the extent to which you agree or disagree with the claim. In developing and supporting your position, be sure to address the most compelling reasons and/or examples that could be used to challenge your position.

137. Educational institutions have a responsibility to dissuade students from pursuing fields of study in which they are unlikely to succeed.

Write a response in which you discuss the extent to which you agree or disagree with the statement and explain your reasoning for the position you take. In developing and supporting your position, you should consider ways in which the statement might or might not hold true and explain how these considerations shape your position.

138. Some people believe that competition for high grades motivates students to excel in the classroom. Others believe that such competition seriously limits the quality of real learning.

Write a response in which you discuss which view more closely aligns with your own position and explain your reasoning for the position you take. In developing and supporting your position, you should address both of the views presented.

139. Claim: Major policy decisions should always be left to politicians and other government experts.
Reason: Politicians and other government experts are more informed and thus have better judgment and perspective than do members of the general public.

Write a response in which you discuss the extent to which you agree or disagree with the claim and the reason on which that claim is based.

140. Some people believe that universities should require every student to take a variety of courses outside the student's field of study. Others believe that universities should not force students to take any courses other than those that will help prepare them for jobs in their chosen fields.

Write a response in which you discuss which view more closely aligns with your own position and explain your reasoning for the position you take. In developing and supporting your position, you should address both of the views presented.

141. It is more harmful to compromise one's own beliefs than to adhere to them.

Write a response in which you discuss the extent to which you agree or disagree with the statement and explain your reasoning for the position you take. In developing and supporting your position, you should consider ways in which the statement might or might not hold true and explain how these considerations shape your position.

142. Claim: Colleges and universities should specify all required courses and eliminate elective courses in order to provide clear guidance for students.
Reason: College students—like people in general—prefer to follow directions rather than make their own decisions.

Write a response in which you discuss the extent to which you agree or disagree with the claim and the reason on which that claim is based.

143. No field of study can advance significantly unless it incorporates knowledge and experience from outside that field.

Write a response in which you discuss the extent to which you agree or disagree with the statement and explain your reasoning for the position you take. In developing and supporting your position, you should consider ways in which the statement might or might not hold true and explain how these considerations shape your position.

144. True success can be measured primarily in terms of the goals one sets for oneself.

Write a response in which you discuss the extent to which you agree or disagree with the statement and explain your reasoning for the position you take. In developing and supporting your position, you should consider ways in which the statement might or might not hold true and explain how these considerations shape your position.

145. The general welfare of a nation's people is a better indication of that nation's greatness than are the achievements of its rulers, artists, or scientists.

Write a response in which you discuss the extent to which you agree or disagree with the claim. In developing and supporting your position, be sure to address the most compelling reasons and/or examples that could be used to challenge your position.

146. The best test of an argument is the argument's ability to convince someone with an opposing viewpoint.

Write a response in which you discuss the extent to which you agree or disagree with the statement and explain your reasoning for the position you take. In developing and supporting your position, you should consider ways in which the statement might or might not hold true and explain how these considerations shape your position.

147. The effectiveness of a country's leaders is best measured by examining the well-being of that country's citizens.

Write a response in which you discuss the extent to which you agree or disagree with the statement and explain your reasoning for the position you take. In developing and supporting your position, you should consider ways in which the statement might or might not hold true and explain how these considerations shape your position.

148. Nations should pass laws to preserve any remaining wilderness areas in their natural state.

Write a response in which you discuss the extent to which you agree or disagree with the claim. In developing and supporting your position, be sure to address the most compelling reasons and/or examples that could be used to challenge your position.

149. In any field—business, politics, education, government—those in power should be required to step down after five years.

Write a response in which you discuss your views on the policy and explain your reasoning for the position you take. In developing and supporting your position, you should consider the possible consequences of im—plementing the policy and explain how these consequences shape your position.

附录二 Argument作文题库

This page contains the Argument topics for the Analytical Writing section of the GRE® revised General Test. When you take the test, you will be presented with one Argument topic from this pool.

Each Argument topic consists of a passage that presents an argument followed by specific task instructions that tell you how to analyze the argument. The wording of some topics in the test might vary slightly from what is presented here. Also, because there may be multiple versions of some topics with similar or identical wording but with different task instructions, it is very important to read your test topic and its specific task directions carefully and respond to the wording as it appears in the actual test.

1. Woven baskets characterized by a particular distinctive pattern have previously been found only in the immediate vicinity of the prehistoric village of Palea and therefore were believed to have been made only by the Palean people. Recently, however, archaeologists discovered such a "Palean" basket in Lithos, an ancient village across the Brim River from Palea. The Brim River is very deep and broad, and so the ancient Paleans could have crossed it only by boat, and no Palean boats have been found. Thus it follows that the so-called Palean baskets were not uniquely Palean.

   Write a response in which you discuss what specific evidence is needed to evaluate the argument and explain how the evidence would weaken or strengthen the argument.

2. The following appeared as part of a letter to the editor of a scientific journal.

   "A recent study of eighteen rhesus monkeys provides clues as to the effects of birth order on an individual's levels of stimulation. The study showed that in stimulating situations (such as an encounter with an unfamiliar monkey), firstborn infant monkeys produce up to twice as much of the hormone cortisol, which primes the body for increased activity levels, as do their younger siblings. Firstborn humans also produce relatively high levels of cortisol in stimulating situations (such as the return of a parent after an absence). The study also found that during pregnancy, first-time mother monkeys had higher levels of cortisol than did those who had had several offspring."

   Write a response in which you discuss one or more alternative explanations that could rival the proposed explanation and explain how your explanation(s) can plausibly account for the facts presented in the argument.

3. The following appeared as a letter to the editor from a Central Plaza store owner.

   "Over the past two years, the number of shoppers in Central Plaza has been steadily decreasing while the popularity of skateboarding has increased dramatically. Many Central Plaza store owners believe that the decrease in their business is due to the number of skateboard users in the plaza. There has also been a dramatic increase in the amount of litter and vandalism throughout the plaza. Thus, we recommend that the city prohibit skateboarding in Central Plaza. If skateboarding is prohibited here, we predict that business in Central Plaza will return to its previously high levels."

357

Write a response in which you discuss what questions would need to be answered in order to decide whether the recommendation is likely to have the predicted result. Be sure to explain how the answers to these questions would help to evaluate the recommendation.

4. The following appeared in a letter from a homeowner to a friend.

"Of the two leading real estate firms in our town—Adams Realty and Fitch Realty—Adams Realty is clearly superior. Adams has 40 real estate agents; in contrast, Fitch has 25, many of whom work only part-time. Moreover, Adams' revenue last year was twice as high as that of Fitch and included home sales that averaged $168,000, compared to Fitch's $144,000. Homes listed with Adams sell faster as well: ten years ago I listed my home with Fitch, and it took more than four months to sell; last year, when I sold another home, I listed it with Adams, and it took only one month. Thus, if you want to sell your home quickly and at a good price, you should use Adams Realty."

Write a response in which you examine the stated and/or unstated assumptions of the argument. Be sure to explain how the argument depends on these assumptions and what the implications are for the argument if the assumptions prove unwarranted.

5. The following appeared in a letter to the editor of the *Balmer Island Gazette*.

"On Balmer Island, where mopeds serve as a popular form of transportation, the population increases to 100,000 during the summer months. To reduce the number of accidents involving mopeds and pedestrians, the town council of Balmer Island should limit the number of mopeds rented by the island's moped rental companies from 50 per day to 25 per day during the summer season. By limiting the number of rentals, the town council will attain the 50 percent annual reduction in moped accidents that was achieved last year on the neighboring island of Seaville, when Seaville's town council enforced similar limits on moped rentals."

Write a response in which you discuss what questions would need to be answered in order to decide whether the recommendation is likely to have the predicted result. Be sure to explain how the answers to these questions would help to evaluate the recommendation.

6. Arctic deer live on islands in Canada's arctic regions. They search for food by moving over ice from island to island during the course of the year. Their habitat is limited to areas warm enough to sustain the plants on which they feed and cold enough, at least some of the year, for the ice to cover the sea separating the islands, allowing the deer to travel over it. Unfortunately, according to reports from local hunters, the deer populations are declining. Since these reports coincide with recent global warming trends that have caused the sea ice to melt, we can conclude that the purported decline in deer populations is the result of the deer's being unable to follow their age-old migration patterns across the frozen sea.

Write a response in which you discuss what specific evidence is needed to evaluate the argument and explain how the evidence would weaken or strengthen the argument.

7. The following is a recommendation from the Board of Directors of Monarch Books.

"We recommend that Monarch Books open a café in its store. Monarch, having been in business at the same location for more than twenty years, has a large customer base because it is known for its wide selection of books on all subjects. Clearly, opening the café would attract more customers. Space could be made for the café by discontinuing the children's book section, which will probably become less popular given that the most recent national census indicated a significant decline in the percentage of the population under age ten. Opening a café will allow Monarch to attract more customers and better compete with Regal Books, which recently opened its own café."

Write a response in which you discuss what questions would need to be answered in order to decide whether the recommendation is likely to have the predicted result. Be sure to explain how the answers to these questions would help to evaluate the recommendation.

8.   The following appeared in a memo from the director of student housing at Buckingham College.

"To serve the housing needs of our students, Buckingham College should build a number of new dormitories. Buckingham's enrollment is growing and, based on current trends, will double over the next 50 years, thus making existing dormitory space inadequate. Moreover, the average rent for an apartment in our town has risen in recent years. Consequently, students will find it increasingly difficult to afford off-campus housing. Finally, attractive new dormitories would make prospective students more likely to enroll at Buckingham."

Write a response in which you discuss what specific evidence is needed to evaluate the argument and explain how the evidence would weaken or strengthen the argument.

9.   Nature's Way, a chain of stores selling health food and other health-related products, is opening its next franchise in the town of Plainsville. The store should prove to be very successful: Nature's Way franchises tend to be most profitable in areas where residents lead healthy lives, and clearly Plainsville is such an area. Plainsville merchants report that sales of running shoes and exercise clothing are at all-time highs. The local health club has more members than ever, and the weight training and aerobics classes are always full. Finally, Plainsville's schoolchildren represent a new generation of potential customers: these schoolchildren are required to participate in a fitness-for-life program, which emphasizes the benefits of regular exercise at an early age.

Write a response in which you examine the stated and/or unstated assumptions of the argument. Be sure to explain how the argument depends on these assumptions and what the implications are for the argument if the assumptions prove unwarranted.

10.   Twenty years ago, Dr. Field, a noted anthropologist, visited the island of Tertia. Using an observation-centered approach to studying Tertian culture, he concluded from his observations that children in Tertia were reared by an entire village rather than by their own biological parents. Recently another anthropologist, Dr. Karp, visited the group of islands that includes Tertia and used the interview-centered method to study child-rearing practices. In the interviews that Dr. Karp conducted with children living in this group of islands, the children spent much more time talking about their biological parents than about other adults in the village. Dr. Karp decided that Dr. Field's conclusion about Tertian village culture must be invalid. Some anthropologists recommend that to obtain accurate information on Tertian child-rearing practices, future research on the subject should be conducted via the interview-centered method.

Write a response in which you discuss what questions would need to be answered in order to decide whether the recommendation and the argument on which it is based are reasonable. Be sure to explain how the answers to these questions would help to evaluate the recommendation.

11. The council of Maple County, concerned about the county's becoming overdeveloped, is debating a proposed measure that would prevent the development of existing farmland in the county. But the council is also concerned that such a restriction, by limiting the supply of new housing, could lead to significant increases in the price of housing in the county. Proponents of the measure note that Chestnut County established a similar measure ten years ago, and its housing prices have increased only modestly since. However, opponents of the measure note that Pine County adopted restrictions on the development of new residential housing fifteen years ago, and its housing prices have since more than doubled. The council currently predicts that the proposed measure, if passed, will result in a significant increase in housing prices in Maple County.

Write a response in which you discuss what questions would need to be answered in order to decide whether the prediction and the argument on which it is based are reasonable. Be sure to explain how the answers to these questions would help to evaluate the prediction.

12. Fifteen years ago, Omega University implemented a new procedure that encouraged students to evaluate the teaching effectiveness of all their professors. Since that time, Omega professors have begun to assign higher grades in their classes, and overall student grade averages at Omega have risen by 30 percent. Potential employers, looking at this dramatic rise in grades, believe that grades at Omega are inflated and do not accurately reflect student achievement; as a result, Omega graduates have not been as successful at getting jobs as have graduates from nearby Alpha University. To enable its graduates to secure better jobs, Omega University should terminate student evaluation of professors.

Write a response in which you discuss what specific evidence is needed to evaluate the argument and explain how the evidence would weaken or strengthen the argument.

13. In an attempt to improve highway safety, Prunty County last year lowered its speed limit from 55 to 45 miles per hour on all county highways. But this effort has failed: the number of accidents has not decreased, and, based on reports by the highway patrol, many drivers are exceeding the speed limit. Prunty County should instead undertake the same kind of road improvement project that Butler County completed five years ago: increasing lane widths, resurfacing rough highways, and improving visibility at dangerous intersections. Today, major Butler County roads still have a 55 mph speed limit, yet there were 25 percent fewer reported accidents in Butler County this past year than there were five years ago.

Write a response in which you discuss what specific evidence is needed to evaluate the argument and explain how the evidence would weaken or strengthen the argument.

14. The following appeared as part of an article in a business magazine.

"A recent study rating 300 male and female Mentian advertising executives according to the average number of hours they sleep per night showed an association between the amount of sleep the executives need and the success of their firms. Of the advertising firms studied, those whose executives reported needing no more than 6 hours of sleep per night had higher profit margins and faster growth. These results suggest that if a business wants to prosper, it should hire only people who need less than 6 hours of sleep per night."

Write a response in which you examine the stated and/or unstated assumptions of the argument. Be sure to explain how the argument depends on these assumptions and what the implications are for the argument if the assumptions prove unwarranted.

15. The following memorandum is from the business manager of Happy Pancake House restaurants.

"Recently, butter has been replaced by margarine in Happy Pancake House restaurants throughout the southwestern United States. This change, however, has had little impact on our customers. In fact, only about 2 percent of customers have complained, indicating that an average of 98 people out of 100 are happy with the change. Furthermore, many servers have reported that a number of customers who ask for butter do not complain when they are given margarine instead. Clearly, either these customers do not distinguish butter from margarine or they use the term 'butter' to refer to either butter or margarine."

Write a response in which you discuss one or more alternative explanations that could rival the proposed explanation and explain how your explanation(s) can plausibly account for the facts presented in the argument.

16. In surveys Mason City residents rank water sports (swimming, boating, and fishing) among their favorite recreational activities. The Mason River flowing through the city is rarely used for these pursuits, however, and the city park department devotes little of its budget to maintaining riverside recreational facilities. For years there have been complaints from residents about the quality of the river's water and the river's smell. In response, the state has recently announced plans to clean up Mason River. Use of the river for water sports is, therefore, sure to increase. The city government should for that reason devote more money in this year's budget to riverside recreational facilities.

Write a response in which you examine the stated and/or unstated assumptions of the argument. Be sure to explain how the argument depends on these assumptions and what the implications are for the argument if the assumptions prove unwarranted.

17. The following appeared in a memorandum from the manager of WWAC radio station.

"To reverse a decline in listener numbers, our owners have decided that WWAC must change from its current rock-music format. The decline has occurred despite population growth in our listening area, but that growth has resulted mainly from people moving here after their retirement. We must make listeners of these new residents. We could switch to a music format tailored to their tastes, but a continuing decline in local sales of recorded music suggests limited interest in music. Instead we should change to a news and talk format, a form of radio that is increasingly popular in our area."

Write a response in which you discuss what specific evidence is needed to evaluate the argument and explain how the evidence would weaken or strengthen the argument.

18. The following is a memorandum from the business manager of a television station.

"Over the past year, our late-night news program has devoted increased time to national news and less time to weather and local news. During this period, most of the complaints received from viewers were concerned with our station's coverage of weather and local news. In addition, local businesses that used to advertise during our late-night news program have canceled their advertising contracts with us. Therefore, in order to attract more viewers to our news programs and to avoid losing any further advertising revenues, we should expand our coverage of weather and local news on all our news programs."

Write a response in which you examine the stated and/or unstated assumptions of the argument. Be sure to explain how the argument depends on these assumptions and what the implications are for the argument if the assumptions prove unwarranted.

19. Two years ago, radio station WCQP in Rockville decided to increase the number of call-in advice programs that it broadcast; since that time, its share of the radio audience in the Rockville listening area has increased significantly. Given WCQP's recent success with call-in advice programming, and citing a nationwide survey indicating that many radio listeners are quite interested in such programs, the station manager of KICK in Medway recommends that KICK include more call-in advice programs in an attempt to gain a larger audience share in its listening area.

Write a response in which you discuss what questions would need to be answered in order to decide whether the recommendation and the argument on which it is based are reasonable. Be sure to explain how the answers to these questions would help to evaluate the recommendation.

20. The following is a memorandum from the business manager of a television station.

"Over the past year, our late-night news program has devoted increased time to national news and less time to weather and local news. During this time period, most of the complaints received from viewers were concerned with our station's coverage of weather and local news. In addition, local businesses that used to advertise during our late-night news program have just canceled their advertising contracts with us. Therefore, in order to attract more viewers to the program and to avoid losing any further advertising revenues, we should restore the time devoted to weather and local news to its former level."

Write a response in which you discuss what specific evidence is needed to evaluate the argument and explain how the evidence would weaken or strengthen the argument.

21. The following appeared in an article written by Dr. Karp, an anthropologist.

"Twenty years ago, Dr. Field, a noted anthropologist, visited the island of Tertia and concluded from his observations that children in Tertia were reared by an entire village rather than by their own biological parents. However, my recent interviews with children living in the group of islands that includes Tertia show that these children spend much more time talking about their biological parents than about other adults in the village. This research of mine proves that Dr. Field's conclusion about Tertian village culture is invalid and thus that the observation-centered approach to studying cultures is invalid as well. The interview-centered method that my team of graduate students is currently using in Tertia will establish a much more accurate understanding of child-rearing traditions there and in other island cultures."

Write a response in which you discuss what specific evidence is needed to evaluate the argument and explain how the evidence would weaken or strengthen the argument.

22. According to a recent report, cheating among college and university students is on the rise. However, Groveton College has successfully reduced student cheating by adopting an honor code, which calls for students to agree not to cheat in their academic endeavors and to notify a faculty member if they suspect that others have cheated. Groveton's honor code replaced a system in which teachers closely monitored students; under that system, teachers reported an average of thirty cases of cheating per year. In the first year the honor code was in place, students reported twenty-one cases of cheating; five years later, this figure had dropped to fourteen. Moreover, in a recent survey, a majority of Groveton students said that they would be less likely to cheat with an honor code in place than without. Thus, all colleges and universities should adopt honor codes similar to Groveton's in order to decrease cheating among students.

Write a response in which you discuss what questions would need to be answered in order to decide whether the recommendation and the argument on which it is based are reasonable. Be sure to explain how the answers to these questions would help to evaluate the recommendation.

23. The following appeared in an article written by Dr. Karp, an anthropologist.

"Twenty years ago, Dr. Field, a noted anthropologist, visited the island of Tertia and concluded from his observations that children in Tertia were reared by an entire village rather than by their own biological parents. However, my recent interviews with children living in the group of islands that includes Tertia show that these children spend much more time talking about their biological parents than about other adults in the village. This research of mine proves that Dr. Field's conclusion about Tertian village culture is invalid and thus that the observation-centered approach to studying cultures is invalid as well. The interview-centered method that my team of graduate students is currently using in Tertia will establish a much more accurate understanding of child-rearing traditions there and in other island cultures."

Write a response in which you examine the stated and/or unstated assumptions of the argument. Be sure to explain how the argument depends on these assumptions and what the implications are for the argument if the assumptions prove unwarranted.

24. A recently issued twenty-year study on headaches suffered by the residents of Mentia investigated the possible therapeutic effect of consuming salicylates. Salicylates are members of the same chemical family as aspirin, a medicine used to treat headaches. Although many foods are naturally rich in salicylates, food-processing companies also add salicylates to foods as preservatives. The twenty-year study found a correlation between the rise in the commercial use of salicylates and a steady decline in the average number of headaches reported by study participants. At the time when the study concluded, food-processing companies had just discovered that salicylates can also be used as flavor additives for foods, and, as a result, many companies plan to do so. Based on these study results, some health experts predict that residents of Mentia will suffer even fewer headaches in the future.

Write a response in which you discuss what questions would need to be answered in order to decide whether the prediction and the argument on which it is based are reasonable. Be sure to explain how the answers to these questions would help to evaluate the prediction.

25. The following was written as a part of an application for a small-business loan by a group of developers in the city of Monroe.

"A jazz music club in Monroe would be a tremendously profitable enterprise. Currently, the nearest jazz club is 65 miles away; thus, the proposed new jazz club in Monroe, the C-Note, would have the local market all to itself. Plus, jazz is extremely popular in Monroe: over 100,000 people attended Monroe's annual jazz festival last summer; several well-known jazz musicians live in Monroe; and the highest-rated radio program in Monroe is 'Jazz Nightly,' which airs every weeknight at 7 P.M. Finally, a nationwide study indicates that the typical jazz fan spends close to $1,000 per year on jazz entertainment."

Write a response in which you discuss what specific evidence is needed to evaluate the argument and explain how the evidence would weaken or strengthen the argument.

26. The following appeared in the summary of a study on headaches suffered by the residents of Mentia.

"Salicylates are members of the same chemical family as aspirin, a medicine used to treat headaches. Although many foods are naturally rich in salicylates, for the past several decades, food-processing companies have also been adding salicylates to foods as preservatives. This rise in the commercial use of salicylates has been found to correlate with a steady decline in the average number of headaches reported by participants in our twenty-year study. Recently, food-processing companies have found that salicylates can also be used as flavor additives for foods. With this new use for salicylates, we can expect a continued steady decline in the number of headaches suffered by the average citizen of Mentia."

Write a response in which you discuss what specific evidence is needed to evaluate the argument and explain how the evidence would weaken or strengthen the argument.

27. The following appeared in a letter to the editor of a local newspaper.

"Commuters complain that increased rush-hour traffic on Blue Highway between the suburbs and the city center has doubled their commuting time. The favored proposal of the motorists' lobby is to widen the highway, adding an additional lane of traffic. But last year's addition of a lane to the nearby Green Highway was followed by a worsening of traffic jams on it. A better alternative is to add a bicycle lane to Blue Highway. Many area residents are keen bicyclists. A bicycle lane would encourage them to use bicycles to commute, and so would reduce rush-hour traffic rather than fostering an increase."

Write a response in which you discuss what specific evidence is needed to evaluate the argument and explain how the evidence would weaken or strengthen the argument.

28. The following appeared in the summary of a study on headaches suffered by the residents of Mentia.

"Salicylates are members of the same chemical family as aspirin, a medicine used to treat headaches. Although many foods are naturally rich in salicylates, for the past several decades, food-processing companies have also been adding salicylates to foods as preservatives. This rise in the commercial use of salicylates has been found to correlate with a steady decline in the average number of headaches reported by participants in our twenty-year study. Recently, food-processing companies have found that salicylates can also be used as flavor additives for foods. With this new use for salicylates, we can expect a continued steady decline in the number of headaches suffered by the average citizen of Mentia."

Write a response in which you examine the stated and/or unstated assumptions of the argument. Be sure to explain how the argument depends on these assumptions and what the implications are for the argument if the assumptions prove unwarranted.

29. The following appeared in an editorial in a local newspaper.

"Commuters complain that increased rush-hour traffic on Blue Highway between the suburbs and the city center has doubled their commuting time. The favored proposal of the motorists' lobby is to widen the highway, adding an additional lane of traffic. Opponents note that last year's addition of a lane to the nearby Green Highway was followed by a worsening of traffic jams on it. Their suggested alternative proposal is adding a bicycle lane to Blue Highway. Many area residents are keen bicyclists. A bicycle lane would encourage them to use bicycles to commute, it is argued, thereby reducing rush-hour traffic."

Write a response in which you discuss what questions would need to be answered in order to decide whether the recommendation and the argument on which it is based are reasonable. Be sure to explain how the answers to these questions would help to evaluate the recommendation.

30. The following appeared as a recommendation by a committee planning a ten-year budget for the city of Calatrava.

"The birthrate in our city is declining: in fact, last year's birthrate was only one-half that of five years ago. Thus the number of students enrolled in our public schools will soon decrease dramatically, and we can safely reduce the funds budgeted for education during the next decade. At the same time, we can reduce funding for athletic playing fields and other recreational facilities. As a result, we will have sufficient money to fund city facilities and programs used primarily by adults, since we can expect the adult population of the city to increase."

Write a response in which you discuss what specific evidence is needed to evaluate the argument and explain how the evidence would weaken or strengthen the argument.

31. The following appeared in a letter to the editor of Parson City's local newspaper.

"In our region of Trillura, the majority of money spent on the schools that most students attend—the city-run public schools—comes from taxes that each city government collects. The region's cities differ, however, in the budgetary priority they give to public education. For example, both as a proportion of its overall tax revenues and in absolute terms, Parson City has recently spent almost twice as much per year as Blue City has for its public schools—even though both cities have about the same number of residents. Clearly, Parson City residents place a higher value on providing a good education in public schools than Blue City residents do."

Write a response in which you discuss what specific evidence is needed to evaluate the argument and explain how the evidence would weaken or strengthen the argument.

32. The following appeared in a memo from a vice president of Quiot Manufacturing.

"During the past year, Quiot Manufacturing had 30 percent more on-the-job accidents than at the nearby Panoply Industries plant, where the work shifts are one hour shorter than ours. Experts say that significant contributing factors in many on-the-job accidents are fatigue and sleep deprivation among workers. Therefore, to reduce the number of on-the-job accidents at Quiot and thereby increase productivity, we should shorten each of our three work shifts by one hour so that employees will get adequate amounts of sleep."

Write a response in which you examine the stated and/or unstated assumptions of the argument. Be sure to explain how the argument depends on these assumptions and what the implications are for the argument if the assumptions prove unwarranted.

33. The following appeared in a memorandum from the planning department of an electric power company.

"Several recent surveys indicate that home owners are increasingly eager to conserve energy. At the same time, manufacturers are now marketing many home appliances, such as refrigerators and air conditioners, that are almost twice as energy efficient as those sold a decade ago. Also, new technologies for better home insulation and passive solar heating are readily available to reduce the energy needed for home heating. Therefore, the total demand for electricity in our area will not increase—and may decline slightly. Since our three electric generating plants in operation for the past twenty years have always met our needs, construction of new generating plants will not be necessary."

Write a response in which you examine the stated and/or unstated assumptions of the argument. Be sure to explain how the argument depends on these assumptions and what the implications are for the argument if the assumptions prove unwarranted.

34. The vice president of human resources at Climpson Industries sent the following recommendation to the company's president.

"In an effort to improve our employees' productivity, we should implement electronic monitoring of employees' Internet use from their workstations. Employees who use the Internet from their workstations need to be identified and punished if we are to reduce the number of work hours spent on personal or recreational activities, such as shopping or playing games. By installing software to detect employees' Internet use on company computers, we can prevent employees from wasting time, foster a better work ethic at Climpson, and improve our overall profits."

Write a response in which you examine the stated and/or unstated assumptions of the argument. Be sure to explain how the argument depends on these assumptions and what the implications are for the argument if the assumptions prove unwarranted.

35. The following appeared in a letter from the owner of the Sunnyside Towers apartment complex to its manager.

"One month ago, all the showerheads in the first three buildings of the Sunnyside Towers complex were modified to restrict maximum water flow to one-third of what it used to be. Although actual readings of water usage before and after the adjustment are not yet available, the change will obviously result in a considerable savings for Sunnyside Corporation, since the corporation must pay for water each month. Except for a few complaints about low water pressure, no problems with showers have been reported since the adjustment. I predict that modifying showerheads to restrict water flow throughout all twelve buildings in the Sunnyside Towers complex will increase our profits even more dramatically."

Write a response in which you discuss what questions would need to be answered in order to decide whether the prediction and the argument on which it is based are reasonable. Be sure to explain how the answers to these questions would help to evaluate the prediction.

36. The following report appeared in the newsletter of the West Meria Public Health Council.

"An innovative treatment has come to our attention that promises to significantly reduce absenteeism in our schools and workplaces. A study reports that in nearby East Meria, where fish consumption is very high, people visit the doctor only once or twice per year for the treatment of colds. Clearly, eating a substantial amount of fish can prevent colds. Since colds represent the most frequently given reason for absences from school and work, we recommend the daily use of Ichthaid—a nutritional supplement derived from fish oil— as a good way to prevent colds and lower absenteeism."

Write a response in which you discuss what specific evidence is needed to evaluate the argument and explain how the evidence would weaken or strengthen the argument.

37. The following appeared in a recommendation from the planning department of the city of Transopolis.

"Ten years ago, as part of a comprehensive urban renewal program, the city of Transopolis adapted for industrial use a large area of severely substandard housing near the freeway. Subsequently, several factories were constructed there, crime rates in the area declined, and property tax revenues for the entire city increased. To further revitalize the city, we should now take similar action in a declining residential area on the opposite side of the city. Since some houses and apartments in existing nearby neighborhoods are currently unoccupied, alternate housing for those displaced by this action will be readily available."

Write a response in which you discuss what specific evidence is needed to evaluate the argument and explain how the evidence would weaken or strengthen the argument.

38. The following appeared in a memo from the new vice president of Sartorian, a company that manufactures men's clothing.

"Five years ago, at a time when we had difficulties in obtaining reliable supplies of high quality wool fabric, we discontinued production of our alpaca overcoat. Now that we have a new fabric supplier, we should resume production. This coat should sell very well: since we have not offered an alpaca overcoat for five years and since our major competitor no longer makes an alpaca overcoat, there will be pent-up customer demand. Also, since the price of most types of clothing has increased in each of the past five years, customers should be willing to pay significantly higher prices for alpaca overcoats than they did five years ago, and our company profits will increase."

Write a response in which you discuss what specific evidence is needed to evaluate the argument and explain how the evidence would weaken or strengthen the argument.

39. A recent sales study indicates that consumption of seafood dishes in Bay City restaurants has increased by 30 percent during the past five years. Yet there are no currently operating city restaurants whose specialty is seafood. Moreover, the majority of families in Bay City are two-income families, and a nationwide study has shown that such families eat significantly fewer home-cooked meals than they did a decade ago but at the same time express more concern about healthful eating. Therefore, the new Captain Seafood restaurant that specializes in seafood should be quite popular and profitable.

Write a response in which you discuss what specific evidence is needed to evaluate the argument and explain how the evidence would weaken or strengthen the argument.

40. Milk and dairy products are rich in vitamin D and calcium—substances essential for building and maintaining bones. Many people therefore say that a diet rich in dairy products can help prevent osteoporosis, a disease that is linked to both environmental and genetic factors and that causes the bones to weaken significantly with age. But a long-term study of a large number of people found that those who consistently consumed dairy products throughout the years of the study have a higher rate of bone fractures than any other participants in the study. Since bone fractures are symptomatic of osteoporosis, this study result shows that a diet rich in dairy products may actually increase, rather than decrease, the risk of osteoporosis.

Write a response in which you discuss what specific evidence is needed to evaluate the argument and explain how the evidence would weaken or strengthen the argument.

41. The following appeared in a health newsletter.

"A ten-year nationwide study of the effectiveness of wearing a helmet while bicycling indicates that ten years ago, approximately 35 percent of all bicyclists reported wearing helmets, whereas today that number is nearly 80 percent. Another study, however, suggests that during the same ten-year period, the number of bicycle-related accidents has increased 200 percent. These results demonstrate that bicyclists feel safer because they are wearing helmets, and they take more risks as a result. Thus, to reduce the number of serious injuries from bicycle accidents, the government should concentrate more on educating people about bicycle safety and less on encouraging or requiring bicyclists to wear helmets."

Write a response in which you examine the stated and/or unstated assumptions of the argument. Be sure to explain how the argument depends on these assumptions and what the implications are for the argument if the assumptions prove unwarranted.

42. The following is a letter to the head of the tourism bureau on the island of Tria.

"Erosion of beach sand along the shores of Tria Island is a serious threat to our island and our tourist industry. In order to stop the erosion, we should charge people for using the beaches. Although this solution may annoy a few tourists in the short term, it will raise money for replenishing the sand. Replenishing the sand, as was done to protect buildings on the nearby island of Batia, will help protect buildings along our shores, thereby reducing these buildings' risk of additional damage from severe storms. And since beaches and buildings in the area will be preserved, Tria's tourist industry will improve over the long term."

Write a response in which you discuss what specific evidence is needed to evaluate the argument and explain how the evidence would weaken or strengthen the argument.

43. The following appeared in a memorandum written by the chairperson of the West Egg Town Council.

"Two years ago, consultants predicted that West Egg's landfill, which is used for garbage disposal, would be completely filled within five years. During the past two years, however, the town's residents have been recycling twice as much material as they did in previous years. Next month the amount of recycled material—which includes paper, plastic, and metal—should further increase, since charges for pickup of other household garbage will double. Furthermore, over 90 percent of the respondents to a recent survey said that they would do more recycling in the future. Because of our town's strong commitment to recycling, the available space in our landfill should last for considerably longer than predicted."

Write a response in which you discuss what specific evidence is needed to evaluate the argument and explain how the evidence would weaken or strengthen the argument.

44. The following appeared in a letter to the editor of a journal on environmental issues.

"Over the past year, the Crust Copper Company (CCC) has purchased over 10,000 square miles of land in the tropical nation of West Fredonia. Mining copper on this land will inevitably result in pollution and, since West Fredonia is the home of several endangered animal species, in environmental disaster. But such disasters can be prevented if consumers simply refuse to purchase products that are made with CCC's copper unless the company abandons its mining plans."

Write a response in which you examine the stated and/or unstated assumptions of the argument. Be sure to explain how the argument depends on these assumptions and what the implications are for the argument if the assumptions prove unwarranted.

45. The following is part of a memorandum from the president of Humana University.

"Last year the number of students who enrolled in online degree programs offered by nearby Omni University increased by 50 percent. During the same year, Omni showed a significant decrease from prior years in expenditures for dormitory and classroom space, most likely because instruction in the online programs takes place via the Internet. In contrast, over the past three years, enrollment at Humana University has failed to grow, and the cost of maintaining buildings has increased along with our budget deficit. To address these problems, Humana University will begin immediately to create and actively promote online degree programs like those at Omni. We predict that instituting these online degree programs will help Humana both increase its total enrollment and solve its budget problems."

Write a response in which you discuss what questions would need to be answered in order to decide whether the prediction and the argument on which it is based are reasonable. Be sure to explain how the answers to these questions would help to evaluate the prediction.

46. The following appeared in a health magazine published in Corpora.

"Medical experts say that only one-quarter of Corpora's citizens meet the current standards for adequate physical fitness, even though twenty years ago, one-half of all of Corpora's citizens met the standards as then defined. But these experts are mistaken when they suggest that spending too much time using computers has caused a decline in fitness. Since overall fitness levels are highest in regions of Corpora where levels of computer ownership are also highest, it is clear that using computers has not made citizens less physically fit. Instead, as shown by this year's unusually low expenditures on fitness-related products and services, the recent decline in the economy is most likely the cause, and fitness levels will improve when the economy does."

Write a response in which you examine the stated and/or unstated assumptions of the argument. Be sure to explain how the argument depends on these assumptions and what the implications are for the argument if the assumptions prove unwarranted.

47. The following appeared in a memorandum from the owner of Movies Galore, a chain of movie-rental stores.

"Because of declining profits, we must reduce operating expenses at Movies Galore's ten movie-rental stores. Raising prices is not a good option, since we are famous for our low prices. Instead, we should reduce our operating hours. Last month our store in downtown Marston reduced its hours by closing at 6:00 p.m. rather than 9:00 p.m. and reduced its overall inventory by no longer stocking any DVD released more than five years ago. Since we have received very few customer complaints about these new policies, we should now adopt them at all other Movies Galore stores as our best strategies for improving profits."

Write a response in which you discuss what specific evidence is needed to evaluate the argument and explain how the evidence would weaken or strengthen the argument.

48. The following appeared in a magazine article about planning for retirement.

"Clearview should be a top choice for anyone seeking a place to retire, because it has spectacular natural beauty and a consistent climate. Another advantage is that housing costs in Clearview have fallen significantly during the past year, and taxes remain lower than those in neighboring towns. Moreover, Clearview's mayor promises many new programs to improve schools, streets, and public services. And best of all, retirees in Clearview can also expect excellent health care as they grow older, since the number of physicians in the area is far greater than the national average."

Write a response in which you discuss what specific evidence is needed to evaluate the argument and explain how the evidence would weaken or strengthen the argument.

49. The following is part of a memorandum from the president of Humana University.

"Last year the number of students who enrolled in online degree programs offered by nearby Omni University increased by 50 percent. During the same year, Omni showed a significant decrease from prior years in expenditures for dormitory and classroom space, most likely because online instruction takes place via the Internet. In contrast, over the past three years, enrollment at Humana University has failed to grow and the cost of maintaining buildings has increased. Thus, to increase enrollment and solve the problem of budget deficits at Humana University, we should initiate and actively promote online degree programs like those at Omni."

Write a response in which you examine the stated and/or unstated assumptions of the argument. Be sure to explain how the argument depends on these assumptions and what the implications are for the argument if the assumptions prove unwarranted.

50. An ancient, traditional remedy for insomnia—the scent of lavender flowers—has now been proved effective. In a recent study, 30 volunteers with chronic insomnia slept each night for three weeks on lavender-scented pillows in a controlled room where their sleep was monitored electronically. During the first week, volunteers continued to take their usual sleeping medication. They slept soundly but wakened feeling tired. At the beginning of the second week, the volunteers discontinued their sleeping medication. During that week, they slept less soundly than the previous week and felt even more tired. During the third week, the volunteers slept longer and more soundly than in the previous two weeks. Therefore, the study proves that lavender cures insomnia within a short period of time.

Write a response in which you discuss what specific evidence is needed to evaluate the argument and explain how the evidence would weaken or strengthen the argument.

51. The following memorandum is from the business manager of Happy Pancake House restaurants.

"Butter has now been replaced by margarine in Happy Pancake House restaurants throughout the southwestern United States. Only about 2 percent of customers have complained, indicating that 98 people out of 100 are happy with the change. Furthermore, many servers have reported that a number of customers who ask for butter do not complain when they are given margarine instead. Clearly, either these customers cannot distinguish butter from margarine or they use the term 'butter' to refer to either butter or margarine. Thus, to avoid the expense of purchasing butter and to increase profitability, the Happy Pancake House should extend this cost-saving change to its restaurants in the southeast and northeast as well."

Write a response in which you discuss what questions would need to be answered in order to decide whether the recommendation is likely to have the predicted result. Be sure to explain how the answers to these questions would help to evaluate the recommendation.

52. The following appeared in a letter from the owner of the Sunnyside Towers apartment building to its manager.

"One month ago, all the showerheads on the first five floors of Sunnyside Towers were modified to restrict the water flow to approximately one-third of its original flow. Although actual readings of water usage before and after the adjustment are not yet available, the change will obviously result in a considerable savings for Sunnyside Corporation, since the corporation must pay for water each month. Except for a few complaints about low water pressure, no problems with showers have been reported since the adjustment. Clearly, restricting water flow throughout all the twenty floors of Sunnyside Towers will increase our profits further."

Write a response in which you discuss what questions would need to be answered in order to decide whether the recommendation is likely to have the predicted result. Be sure to explain how the answers to these questions would help to evaluate the recommendation.

53. The following appeared in a health magazine.

"The citizens of Forsythe have adopted more healthful lifestyles. Their responses to a recent survey show that in their eating habits they conform more closely to government nutritional recommendations than they did ten years ago. Furthermore, there has been a fourfold increase in sales of food products containing kiran, a substance that a scientific study has shown reduces cholesterol. This trend is also evident in reduced sales of sulia, a food that few of the most healthy citizens regularly eat."

Write a response in which you discuss what specific evidence is needed to evaluate the argument and explain how the evidence would weaken or strengthen the argument.

54. Humans arrived in the Kaliko Islands about 7,000 years ago, and within 3,000 years most of the large mammal species that had lived in the forests of the Kaliko Islands had become extinct. Yet humans cannot have been a factor in the species' extinctions, because there is no evidence that the humans had any significant contact with the mammals. Further, archaeologists have discovered numerous sites where the bones of fish had been discarded, but they found no such areas containing the bones of large mammals, so the humans cannot have hunted the mammals. Therefore, some climate change or other environmental factor must have caused the species' extinctions.

Write a response in which you examine the stated and/or unstated assumptions of the argument. Be sure to explain how the argument depends on these assumptions and what the implications are for the argument if the assumptions prove unwarranted.

55. The following appeared in an editorial in a business magazine.

"Although the sales of Whirlwind video games have declined over the past two years, a recent survey of video-game players suggests that this sales trend is about to be reversed. The survey asked video-game players what features they thought were most important in a video game. According to the survey, players prefer games that provide lifelike graphics, which require the most up-to-date computers. Whirlwind has just introduced several such games with an extensive advertising campaign directed at people ten to twenty-five years old, the age-group most likely to play video games. It follows, then, that the sales of Whirlwind video games are likely to increase dramatically in the next few months."

Write a response in which you examine the stated and/or unstated assumptions of the argument. Be sure to explain how the argument depends on these assumptions and what the implications are for the argument if the assumptions prove unwarranted.

56. The following appeared in a memo from the vice president of marketing at Dura-Sock, Inc.

"A recent study of our customers suggests that our company is wasting the money it spends on its patented Endure manufacturing process, which ensures that our socks are strong enough to last for two years. We have always advertised our use of the Endure process, but the new study shows that despite our socks' durability, our average customer actually purchases new Dura-Socks every three months. Furthermore, our customers surveyed in our largest market, northeastern United States cities, say that they most value Dura-Socks' stylish appearance and availability in many colors. These findings suggest that we can increase our profits by discontinuing use of the Endure manufacturing process."

Write a response in which you examine the stated and/or unstated assumptions of the argument. Be sure to explain how the argument depends on these assumptions and what the implications are for the argument if the assumptions prove unwarranted.

57. The following appeared in a memo from the vice president of marketing at Dura-Sock, Inc.

"A recent study of our customers suggests that our company is wasting the money it spends on its patented Endure manufacturing process, which ensures that our socks are strong enough to last for two years. We have always advertised our use of the Endure process, but the new study shows that despite our socks' durability, our average customer actually purchases new Dura-Socks every three months. Furthermore, our customers surveyed in our largest market, northeastern United States cities, say that they most value Dura-Socks' stylish appearance and availability in many colors. These findings suggest that we can increase our profits by discontinuing use of the Endure manufacturing process."

Write a response in which you discuss what specific evidence is needed to evaluate the argument and explain how the evidence would weaken or strengthen the argument.

58. The vice president for human resources at Climpson Industries sent the following recommendation to the company's president.

"In an effort to improve our employees' productivity, we should implement electronic monitoring of employees' Internet use from their workstations. Employees who use the Internet inappropriately from their workstations need to be identified and punished if we are to reduce the number of work hours spent on personal or recreational activities, such as shopping or playing games. Installing software on company computers to detect employees' Internet use is the best way to prevent employees from wasting time on the job. It will foster a better work ethic at Climpson and improve our overall profits."

Write a response in which you discuss what specific evidence is needed to evaluate the argument and explain how the evidence would weaken or strengthen the argument.

59. The following appeared in a memo from the president of Bower Builders, a company that constructs new homes.

"A nationwide survey reveals that the two most-desired home features are a large family room and a large, well-appointed kitchen. A number of homes in our area built by our competitor Domus Construction have such features and have sold much faster and at significantly higher prices than the national average. To boost sales and profits, we should increase the size of the family rooms and kitchens in all the homes we build and should make state-of-the-art kitchens a standard feature. Moreover, our larger family rooms and kitchens can come at the expense of the dining room, since many of our recent buyers say they do not need a separate dining room for family meals."

Write a response in which you examine the stated and/or unstated assumptions of the argument. Be sure to explain how the argument depends on these assumptions and what the implications are for the argument if the assumptions prove unwarranted.

60. The following appeared in a letter from a firm providing investment advice for a client.

"Most homes in the northeastern United States, where winters are typically cold, have traditionally used oil as their major fuel for heating. Last heating season that region experienced 90 days with below-normal temperatures, and climate forecasters predict that this weather pattern will continue for several more years. Furthermore, many new homes are being built in the region in response to recent population growth. Because of these trends, we predict an increased demand for heating oil and recommend investment in Consolidated Industries, one of whose major business operations is the retail sale of home heating oil."

Write a response in which you examine the stated and/or unstated assumptions of the argument. Be sure to explain how the argument depends on these assumptions and what the implications are for the argument if the assumptions prove unwarranted.

61. The following appeared in an article in the *Grandview Beacon*.

"For many years the city of Grandview has provided annual funding for the Grandview Symphony. Last year, however, private contributions to the symphony increased by 200 percent and attendance at the symphony's concerts-in-the-park series doubled. The symphony has also announced an increase in ticket prices for next year. Given such developments, some city commissioners argue that the symphony can now be fully self-supporting, and they recommend that funding for the symphony be eliminated from next year's budget."

Write a response in which you discuss what questions would need to be answered in order to decide whether the recommendation and the argument on which it is based are reasonable. Be sure to explain how the answers to these questions would help to evaluate the recommendation.

62. The following appeared in a memo from the director of a large group of hospitals.

"In a laboratory study of liquid antibacterial hand soaps, a concentrated solution of UltraClean produced a 40 percent greater reduction in the bacteria population than did the liquid hand soaps currently used in our hospitals. During a subsequent test of UltraClean at our hospital in Workby, that hospital reported significantly fewer cases of patient infection than did any of the other hospitals in our group. Therefore, to prevent serious patient infections, we should supply UltraClean at all hand-washing stations throughout our hospital system."

Write a response in which you examine the stated and/or unstated assumptions of the argument. Be sure to explain how the argument depends on these assumptions and what the implications are for the argument if the assumptions prove unwarranted.

63. The following appeared in a letter to the editor of the *Parkville Daily* newspaper.

"Throughout the country last year, as more and more children below the age of nine participated in youth-league sports, over 40,000 of these young players suffered injuries. When interviewed for a recent study, youth-league soccer players in several major cities also reported psychological pressure exerted by coaches and parents to win games. Furthermore, education experts say that long practice sessions for these sports take away time that could be used for academic activities. Since the disadvantages outweigh any advantages, we in Parkville should discontinue organized athletic competition for children under nine."

Write a response in which you examine the stated and/or unstated assumptions of the argument. Be sure to explain how the argument depends on these assumptions and what the implications are for the argument if the assumptions prove unwarranted.

64. Collectors prize the ancient life-size clay statues of human figures made on Kali Island but have long wondered how Kalinese artists were able to depict bodies with such realistic precision. Since archaeologists have recently discovered molds of human heads and hands on Kali, we can now conclude that the ancient Kalinese artists used molds of actual bodies, not sculpting tools and techniques, to create these statues. This discovery explains why Kalinese miniature statues were abstract and entirely different in style: molds could be used only for life-size sculptures. It also explains why few ancient Kalinese sculpting tools have been found. In light of this discovery, collectors predict that the life-size sculptures will decrease in value while the miniatures increase in value.

Write a response in which you discuss what questions would need to be answered in order to decide whether the prediction and the argument on which it is based are reasonable. Be sure to explain how the answers to these questions would help to evaluate the prediction.

65. When Stanley Park first opened, it was the largest, most heavily used public park in town. It is still the largest park, but it is no longer heavily used. Video cameras mounted in the park's parking lots last month revealed the park's drop in popularity: the recordings showed an average of only 50 cars per day. In contrast, tiny Carlton Park in the heart of the business district is visited by more than 150 people on a typical weekday. An obvious difference is that Carlton Park, unlike Stanley Park, provides ample seating. Thus, if Stanley Park is ever to be as popular with our citizens as Carlton Park, the town will obviously need to provide more benches, thereby converting some of the unused open areas into spaces suitable for socializing.

Write a response in which you examine the stated and/or unstated assumptions of the argument. Be sure to explain how the argument depends on these assumptions and what the implications are for the argument if the assumptions prove unwarranted.

66. The following appeared in a memo from the owner of a chain of cheese stores located throughout the United States.

"For many years all the stores in our chain have stocked a wide variety of both domestic and imported cheeses. Last year, however, all of the five best-selling cheeses at our newest store were domestic cheddar cheeses from Wisconsin. Furthermore, a recent survey by *Cheeses of the World* magazine indicates an increasing preference for domestic cheeses among its subscribers. Since our company can reduce expenses by limiting inventory, the best way to improve profits in all of our stores is to discontinue stocking many of our varieties of imported cheese and concentrate primarily on domestic cheeses."

Write a response in which you discuss what questions would need to be answered in order to decide whether the recommendation is likely to have the predicted result. Be sure to explain how the answers to these questions would help to evaluate the recommendation.

67. The following appeared as part of a business plan developed by the manager of the Rialto Movie Theater.

"Despite its downtown location, the Rialto Movie Theater, a local institution for five decades, must make big changes or close its doors forever. It should follow the example of the new Apex Theater in the mall outside of town. When the Apex opened last year, it featured a video arcade, plush carpeting and seats, and a state-of-the-art sound system. Furthermore, in a recent survey, over 85 percent of respondents reported that the high price of newly released movies prevents them from going to the movies more than five times per year. Thus, if the Rialto intends to hold on to its share of a decreasing pool of moviegoers, it must offer the same features as Apex."

Write a response in which you discuss what questions would need to be answered in order to decide whether the recommendation is likely to have the predicted result. Be sure to explain how the answers to these questions would help to evaluate the recommendation.

68. A recent study reported that pet owners have longer, healthier lives on average than do people who own no pets. Specifically, dog owners tend to have a lower incidence of heart disease. In light of these findings, Sherwood Hospital should form a partnership with Sherwood Animal Shelter to institute an adopt-a-dog program. The program would encourage dog ownership for patients recovering from heart disease, which should reduce these patients' chance of experiencing continuing heart problems and also reduce their need for ongoing treatment. As a further benefit, the publicity about the program would encourage more people to adopt pets from the shelter. And that will reduce the incidence of heart disease in the general population.

Write a response in which you examine the stated and/or unstated assumptions of the argument. Be sure to explain how the argument depends on these assumptions and what the implications are for the argument if the assumptions prove unwarranted.

69. The following appeared in a memo from a vice president of a large, highly diversified company.

"Ten years ago our company had two new office buildings constructed as regional headquarters for two regions. The buildings were erected by different construction companies—Alpha and Zeta. Although the two buildings had identical floor plans, the building constructed by Zeta cost 30 percent more to build. However, that building's expenses for maintenance last year were only half those of Alpha's. In addition, the energy consumption of the Zeta building has been lower than that of the Alpha building every year since its construction. Given these data, plus the fact that Zeta has a stable workforce with little employee turnover, we recommend using Zeta rather than Alpha for our new building project, even though Alpha's bid promises lower construction costs."

Write a response in which you discuss what questions would need to be answered in order to decide whether the recommendation and the argument on which it is based are reasonable. Be sure to explain how the answers to these questions would help to evaluate the recommendation.

70. The following appeared in a memo from a vice president of a large, highly diversified company.

"Ten years ago our company had two new office buildings constructed as regional headquarters for two regions. The buildings were erected by different construction companies—Alpha and Zeta. Although the two buildings had identical floor plans, the building constructed by Zeta cost 30 percent more to build. However, that building's expenses for maintenance last year were only half those of Alpha's. Furthermore, the energy consumption of the Zeta building has been lower than that of the Alpha building every year since its construction. Such data indicate that we should use Zeta rather than Alpha for our contemplated new building project, even though Alpha's bid promises lower construction costs."

Write a response in which you discuss what specific evidence is needed to evaluate the argument and explain how the evidence would weaken or strengthen the argument.

71. The following is a letter to the editor of the *Waymarsh Times*.

"Traffic here in Waymarsh is becoming a problem. Although just three years ago a state traffic survey showed that the typical driving commuter took 20 minutes to get to work, the commute now takes closer to 40 minutes, according to the survey just completed. Members of the town council already have suggested more road building to address the problem, but as well as being expensive, the new construction will surely disrupt some of our residential neighborhoods. It would be better to follow the example of the nearby city of Garville. Last year Garville implemented a policy that rewards people who share rides to work, giving them coupons for free gas. Pollution levels in Garville have dropped since the policy was implemented, and people from Garville tell me that commuting times have fallen considerably. There is no reason why a policy like Garville's shouldn't work equally well in Waymarsh."

Write a response in which you discuss what specific evidence is needed to evaluate the argument and explain how the evidence would weaken or strengthen the argument.

72. The following appeared as a letter to the editor of a national newspaper.

"Your recent article on corporate downsizing* in Elthyria maintains that the majority of competent workers who have lost jobs as a result of downsizing face serious economic hardship, often for years, before finding other suitable employment. But this claim is undermined by a recent report on the Elthyrian economy, which found that since 1999 far more jobs have been created than have been eliminated, bringing the unemployment rate in Elthyria to its lowest level in decades. Moreover, two-thirds of these newly created jobs have been in industries that tend to pay above-average wages, and the vast majority of these jobs are full-time."

*Downsizing is the process whereby corporations deliberately make themselves smaller, reducing the number of their employees.

Write a response in which you discuss what specific evidence is needed to evaluate the argument and explain how the evidence would weaken or strengthen the argument.

73. The following appeared on the Mozart School of Music Web site.

"The Mozart School of Music should be the first choice for parents considering enrolling their child in music lessons. First of all, the Mozart School welcomes youngsters at all ability and age levels; there is no audition to attend the school. Second, the school offers instruction in nearly all musical instruments as well a wide range of styles and genres from classical to rock. Third, the faculty includes some of the most distinguished musicians in the area. Finally, many Mozart graduates have gone on to become well-known and highly paid professional musicians."

Write a response in which you examine the stated and/or unstated assumptions of the argument. Be sure to explain how the argument depends on these assumptions and what the implications are for the argument if the assumptions prove unwarranted.

74. The president of Grove College has recommended that the college abandon its century-old tradition of all-female education and begin admitting men. Pointing to other all-female colleges that experienced an increase in applications after adopting coeducation, the president argues that coeducation would lead to a significant increase in applications and enrollment. However, the director of the alumnae association opposes the plan. Arguing that all-female education is essential to the very identity of the college, the director cites annual surveys of incoming students in which these students say that the school's all-female status was the primary reason they selected Grove. The director also points to a survey of Grove alumnae in which a majority of respondents strongly favored keeping the college all female.

Write a response in which you discuss what questions would need to be answered in order to decide whether the recommendation and the argument on which it is based are reasonable. Be sure to explain how the answers to these questions would help to evaluate the recommendation.

75. The following appeared in a letter to the editor of a Batavia newspaper.

"The department of agriculture in Batavia reports that the number of dairy farms throughout the country is now 25 percent greater than it was 10 years ago. During this same time period, however, the price of milk at the local Excello Food Market has increased from $1.50 to over $3.00 per gallon. To prevent farmers from continuing to receive excessive profits on an apparently increased supply of milk, the Batavia government should begin to regulate retail milk prices. Such regulation is necessary to ensure fair prices for consumers."

Write a response in which you discuss what questions would need to be answered in order to decide whether the recommendation is likely to have the predicted result. Be sure to explain how the answers to these questions would help to evaluate the recommendation.

76. The following appeared in a newsletter offering advice to investors.

"Over 80 percent of the respondents to a recent survey indicated a desire to reduce their intake of foods containing fats and cholesterol, and today low-fat products abound in many food stores. Since many of the food products currently marketed by Old Dairy Industries are high in fat and cholesterol, the company's sales are likely to diminish greatly and company profits will no doubt decrease. We therefore advise Old Dairy stockholders to sell their shares, and other investors not to purchase stock in this company."

Write a response in which you discuss what questions would need to be answered in order to decide whether the advice and the argument on which it is based are reasonable. Be sure to explain how the answers to these questions would help to evaluate the advice.

77. The following recommendation appeared in a memo from the mayor of the town of Hopewell.

"Two years ago, the nearby town of Ocean View built a new municipal golf course and resort hotel. During the past two years, tourism in Ocean View has increased, new businesses have opened there, and Ocean View's tax revenues have risen by 30 percent. Therefore, the best way to improve Hopewell's economy—and generate additional tax revenues—is to build a golf course and resort hotel similar to those in Ocean View."

Write a response in which you examine the stated and/or unstated assumptions of the argument. Be sure to explain how the argument depends on these assumptions and what the implications are for the argument if the assumptions prove unwarranted.

78. The following appeared in a memo from the vice president of a food distribution company with food storage warehouses in several cities.

"Recently, we signed a contract with the Fly-Away Pest Control Company to provide pest control services at our fast-food warehouse in Palm City, but last month we discovered that over $20,000 worth of food there had been destroyed by pest damage. Meanwhile, the Buzzoff Pest Control Company, which we have used for many years, continued to service our warehouse in Wintervale, and last month only $10,000 worth of the food stored there had been destroyed by pest damage. Even though the price charged by Fly-Away is considerably lower, our best means of saving money is to return to Buzzoff for all our pest control services."

Write a response in which you discuss what specific evidence is needed to evaluate the argument and explain how the evidence would weaken or strengthen the argument.

79. Since those issues of *Newsbeat* magazine that featured political news on their front cover were the poorest-selling issues over the past three years, the publisher of *Newsbeat* has recommended that the magazine curtail its emphasis on politics to focus more exclusively on economics and personal finance. She points to a recent survey of readers of general interest magazines that indicates greater reader interest in economic issues than in political ones. *Newsbeat*'s editor, however, opposes the proposed shift in editorial policy, pointing out that very few magazines offer extensive political coverage anymore.

Write a response in which you discuss what questions would need to be answered in order to decide whether the recommendation and the argument on which it is based are reasonable. Be sure to explain how the answers to these questions would help to evaluate the recommendation.

80. The following is taken from a memo from the advertising director of the Super Screen Movie Production Company.

"According to a recent report from our marketing department, during the past year, fewer people attended Super Screen-produced movies than in any other year. And yet the percentage of positive reviews by movie reviewers about specific Super Screen movies actually increased during the past year. Clearly, the contents of these reviews are not reaching enough of our prospective viewers. Thus, the problem lies not with the quality of our movies but with the public's lack of awareness that movies of good quality are available. Super Screen should therefore allocate a greater share of its budget next year to reaching the public through advertising."

Write a response in which you discuss what questions would need to be answered in order to decide whether the recommendation and the argument on which it is based are reasonable. Be sure to explain how the answers to these questions would help to evaluate the recommendation.

81. The following appeared in a business magazine.

"As a result of numerous complaints of dizziness and nausea on the part of consumers of Promofoods tuna, the company requested that eight million cans of its tuna be returned for testing. Promofoods concluded that the canned tuna did not, after all, pose a health risk. This conclusion is based on tests performed on samples of the recalled cans by chemists from Promofoods; the chemists found that of the eight food chemicals most commonly blamed for causing symptoms of dizziness and nausea, five were not found in any of the tested cans. The chemists did find small amounts of the three remaining suspected chemicals but pointed out that these occur naturally in all canned foods."

Write a response in which you discuss what questions would need to be addressed in order to decide whether the conclusion and the argument on which it is based are reasonable. Be sure to explain how the answers to the questions would help to evaluate the conclusion.

82. The following appeared in a memo from the vice president of marketing at Dura-Socks, Inc.

"A recent study of Dura-Socks customers suggests that our company is wasting the money it spends on its patented Endure manufacturing process, which ensures that our socks are strong enough to last for two years. We have always advertised our use of the Endure process, but the new study shows that despite the socks' durability, our customers, on average, actually purchase new Dura-Socks every three months. Furthermore, customers surveyed in our largest market—northeastern United States cities—say that they most value Dura-Socks' stylish appearance and availability in many colors. These findings suggest that we can increase our profits by discontinuing use of the Endure manufacturing process."

Write a response in which you discuss what questions would need to be answered in order to decide whether the recommendation and the argument on which it is based are reasonable. Be sure to explain how the answers to these questions would help to evaluate the recommendation.

83. The following is a letter to the editor of an environmental magazine.

"In 1975 a wildlife census found that there were seven species of amphibians in Xanadu National Park, with abundant numbers of each species. However, in 2002 only four species of amphibians were observed in the park, and the numbers of each species were drastically reduced. There has been a substantial decline in the numbers of amphibians worldwide, and global pollution of water and air is clearly implicated. The decline of amphibians in Xanadu National Park, however, almost certainly has a different cause: in 1975, trout—which are known to eat amphibian eggs—were introduced into the park."

Write a response in which you discuss what specific evidence is needed to evaluate the argument and explain how the evidence would weaken or strengthen the argument.

84. The following is a letter to the editor of an environmental magazine.

"Two studies of amphibians in Xanadu National Park confirm a significant decline in the numbers of amphibians. In 1975 there were seven species of amphibians in the park, and there were abundant numbers of each species. However, in 2002 only four species of amphibians were observed in the park, and the numbers of each species were drastically reduced. One proposed explanation is that the decline was caused by the introduction of trout into the park's waters, which began in 1975. (Trout are known to eat amphibian eggs.)"

Write a response in which you discuss one or more alternative explanations that could rival the proposed explanation and explain how your explanation(s) can plausibly account for the facts presented in the argument.

85. In a study of the reading habits of Waymarsh citizens conducted by the University of Waymarsh, most respondents said that they preferred literary classics as reading material. However, a second study conducted by the same researchers found that the type of book most frequently checked out of each of the public libraries in Waymarsh was the mystery novel. Therefore, it can be concluded that the respondents in the first study had misrepresented their reading habits.

Write a response in which you discuss what specific evidence is needed to evaluate the argument and explain how the evidence would weaken or strengthen the argument.

86. The following appeared in a memo at XYZ company.

"When XYZ lays off employees, it pays Delany Personnel Firm to offer those employees assistance in creating résumés and developing interviewing skills, if they so desire. Laid-off employees have benefited greatly from Delany's services: last year those who used Delany found jobs much more quickly than did those who did not. Recently, it has been proposed that we use the less expensive Walsh Personnel Firm in place of Delany. This would be a mistake because eight years ago, when XYZ was using Walsh, only half of the workers we laid off at that time found jobs within a year. Moreover, Delany is clearly superior, as evidenced by its bigger staff and larger number of branch offices. After all, last year Delany's clients took an average of six months to find jobs, whereas Walsh's clients took nine."

Write a response in which you discuss what specific evidence is needed to evaluate the argument and explain how the evidence would weaken or strengthen the argument.

87. In a study of the reading habits of Waymarsh citizens conducted by the University of Waymarsh, most respondents said they preferred literary classics as reading material. However, a second study conducted by the same researchers found that the type of book most frequently checked out of each of the public libraries in Waymarsh was the mystery novel. Therefore, it can be concluded that the respondents in the first study had misrepresented their reading preferences.

Write a response in which you examine the stated and/or unstated assumptions of the argument. Be sure to explain how the argument depends on these assumptions and what the implications are for the argument if the assumptions prove unwarranted.

88. The following appeared in a memorandum written by the vice president of Health Naturally, a small but expanding chain of stores selling health food and other health-related products.

"Our previous experience has been that our stores are most profitable in areas where residents are highly concerned with leading healthy lives. We should therefore build one of our new stores in Plainsville, which clearly has many such residents. Plainsville merchants report that sales of running shoes and exercise equipment are at all-time highs. The local health club, which nearly closed five years ago due to lack of business, has more members than ever, and the weight-training and aerobics classes are always full. We can even anticipate a new generation of customers: Plainsville's schoolchildren are required to participate in a program called Fitness for Life, which emphasizes the benefits of regular exercise at an early age."

Write a response in which you discuss what specific evidence is needed to evaluate the argument and explain how the evidence would weaken or strengthen the argument.

89. The following appeared in a memo at XYZ company.

"When XYZ lays off employees, it pays Delany Personnel Firm to offer those employees assistance in creating résumés and developing interviewing skills, if they so desire. Laid-off employees have benefited greatly from Delany's services: last year those who used Delany found jobs much more quickly than did those who did not. Recently, it has been proposed that we use the less expensive Walsh Personnel Firm in place of Delany. This would be a mistake because eight years ago, when XYZ was using Walsh, only half of the workers we laid off at that time found jobs within a year. Moreover, Delany is clearly superior, as evidenced by its bigger staff and larger number of branch offices. After all, last year Delany's clients took an average of six months to find jobs, whereas Walsh's clients took nine."

Write a response in which you examine the stated and/or unstated assumptions of the argument. Be sure to explain how the argument depends on these assumptions and what the implications are for the argument if the assumptions prove unwarranted.

90. The following appeared in a memorandum written by the vice president of Health Naturally, a small but expanding chain of stores selling health food and other health-related products.

"Our previous experience has been that our stores are most profitable in areas where residents are highly concerned with leading healthy lives. We should therefore build one of our new stores in Plainsville, which clearly has many such residents. Plainsville merchants report that sales of running shoes and exercise equipment are at all-time highs. The local health club, which nearly closed five years ago due to lack of business, has more members than ever, and the weight-training and aerobics classes are always full. We can even anticipate a new generation of customers: Plainsville's schoolchildren are required to participate in a program called Fitness for Life, which emphasizes the benefits of regular exercise at an early age."

Write a response in which you examine the stated and/or unstated assumptions of the argument. Be sure to explain how the argument depends on these assumptions and what the implications are for the argument if the assumptions prove unwarranted.

91. Three years ago, because of flooding at the Western Palean Wildlife Preserve, 100 lions and 100 western gazelles were moved to the East Palean Preserve, an area that is home to most of the same species that are found in the western preserve, though in larger numbers, and to the eastern gazelle, a close relative of the western gazelle. The only difference in climate is that the eastern preserve typically has slightly less rainfall. Unfortunately, after three years in the eastern preserve, the imported western gazelle population has been virtually eliminated. Since the slight reduction in rainfall cannot be the cause of the virtual elimination of western gazelle, their disappearance must have been caused by the larger number of predators in the eastern preserve.

Write a response in which you discuss what specific evidence is needed to evaluate the argument and explain how the evidence would weaken or strengthen the argument.

92. Workers in the small town of Leeville take fewer sick days than workers in the large city of Masonton, 50 miles away. Moreover, relative to population size, the diagnosis of stress-related illness is proportionally much lower in Leeville than in Masonton. According to the Leeville Chamber of Commerce, these facts can be attributed to the health benefits of the relatively relaxed pace of life in Leeville.

Write a response in which you discuss one or more alternative explanations that could rival the proposed explanation and explain how your explanation(s) can plausibly account for the facts presented in the argument.

93. The following appeared in a memorandum from the manager of WWAC radio station.

"WWAC must change from its current rock-music format because the number of listeners has been declining, even though the population in our listening area has been growing. The population growth has resulted mainly from people moving to our area after their retirement, and we must make listeners of these new residents. But they seem to have limited interest in music: several local stores selling recorded music have recently closed. Therefore, just changing to another kind of music is not going to increase our audience. Instead, we should adopt a news-and-talk format, a form of radio that is increasingly popular in our area."

Write a response in which you discuss what questions would need to be answered in order to decide whether the recommendation and the argument on which it is based are reasonable. Be sure to explain how the answers to these questions would help to evaluate the recommendation.

94. The vice president of human resources at Climpson Industries sent the following recommendation to the company's president.

"A recent national survey found that the majority of workers with access to the Internet at work had used company computers for personal or recreational activities, such as banking or playing games. In an effort to improve our employees' productivity, we should implement electronic monitoring of employees' Internet use from their workstations. Using electronic monitoring software is the best way to reduce the number of hours Climpson employees spend on personal or recreational activities. We predict that installing software to monitor employees' Internet use will allow us to prevent employees from wasting time, thereby increasing productivity and improving overall profits."

Write a response in which you discuss what questions would need to be answered in order to decide whether the prediction and the argument on which it is based are reasonable. Be sure to explain how the answers to these questions would help to evaluate the prediction.

95. The following appeared in a memo from the new vice president of Sartorian, a company that manufactures men's clothing.

"Five years ago, at a time when we had difficulty obtaining reliable supplies of high-quality wool fabric, we discontinued production of our popular alpaca overcoat. Now that we have a new fabric supplier, we should resume production. Given the outcry from our customers when we discontinued this product and the fact that none of our competitors offers a comparable product, we can expect pent-up consumer demand for our alpaca coats. This demand and the overall increase in clothing prices will make Sartorian's alpaca overcoats more profitable than ever before."

Write a response in which you examine the stated and/or unstated assumptions of the argument. Be sure to explain how the argument depends on these assumptions and what the implications are for the argument if the assumptions prove unwarranted.

96. The following appeared in a memo from the new vice president of Sartorian, a company that manufactures men's clothing.

"Five years ago, at a time when we had difficulty obtaining reliable supplies of high-quality wool fabric, we discontinued production of our popular alpaca overcoat. Now that we have a new fabric supplier, we should resume production. Given the outcry from our customers when we discontinued this product and the fact that none of our competitors offers a comparable product, we can expect pent-up consumer demand for our alpaca coats. Due to this demand and the overall increase in clothing prices, we can predict that Sartorian's alpaca overcoats will be more profitable than ever before."

Write a response in which you discuss what questions would need to be answered in order to decide whether the prediction and the argument on which it is based are reasonable. Be sure to explain how the answers to these questions would help to evaluate the prediction.

97. The following appeared in an e-mail sent by the marketing director of the Classical Shakespeare Theatre of Bardville.

"Over the past ten years, there has been a 20 percent decline in the size of the average audience at Classical Shakespeare Theatre productions. In spite of increased advertising, we are attracting fewer and fewer people to our shows, causing our profits to decrease significantly. We must take action to attract new audience members. The best way to do so is by instituting a 'Shakespeare in the Park' program this summer. Two years ago the nearby Avon Repertory Company started a 'Free Plays in the Park' program, and its profits have increased 10 percent since then. If we start a 'Shakespeare in the Park' program, we can predict that our profits will increase, too."

Write a response in which you discuss what questions would need to be answered in order to decide whether the recommendation is likely to have the predicted result. Be sure to explain how the answers to these questions would help to evaluate the recommendation.

98. The following is a recommendation from the business manager of Monarch Books.

"Since its opening in Collegeville twenty years ago, Monarch Books has developed a large customer base due to its reader-friendly atmosphere and wide selection of books on all subjects. Last month, Book and Bean, a combination bookstore and coffee shop, announced its intention to open a Collegeville store. Monarch Books should open its own in-store café in the space currently devoted to children's books. Given recent national census data indicating a significant decline in the percentage of the population under age ten, sales of children's books are likely to decline. By replacing its children's books section with a café, Monarch Books can increase profits and ward off competition from Book and Bean."

Write a response in which you examine the stated and/or unstated assumptions of the argument. Be sure to explain how the argument depends on these assumptions and what the implications are for the argument if the assumptions prove unwarranted.

99. The following is a recommendation from the business manager of Monarch Books.

"Since its opening in Collegeville twenty years ago, Monarch Books has developed a large customer base due to its reader-friendly atmosphere and wide selection of books on all subjects. Last month, Book and Bean, a combination bookstore and coffee shop, announced its intention to open a Collegeville store. Monarch Books should open its own in-store café in the space currently devoted to children's books. Given recent national census data indicating a significant decline in the percentage of the population under age ten, sales of children's books are likely to decline. By replacing its children's books section with a café, Monarch Books can increase profits and ward off competition from Book and Bean."

Write a response in which you discuss what specific evidence is needed to evaluate the argument and explain how the evidence would weaken or strengthen the argument.

100. The following was written as a part of an application for a small-business loan by a group of developers in the city of Monroe.

"Jazz music is extremely popular in the city of Monroe: over 100,000 people attended Monroe's annual jazz festival last summer, and the highest-rated radio program in Monroe is 'Jazz Nightly,' which airs every weeknight. Also, a number of well-known jazz musicians own homes in Monroe. Nevertheless, the nearest jazz club is over an hour away. Given the popularity of jazz in Monroe and a recent nationwide study indicating that the typical jazz fan spends close to $1,000 per year on jazz entertainment, a jazz music club in Monroe would be tremendously profitable."

Write a response in which you examine the stated and/or unstated assumptions of the argument. Be sure to explain how the argument depends on these assumptions and what the implications are for the argument if the assumptions prove unwarranted.

101. There is now evidence that the relaxed pace of life in small towns promotes better health and greater longevity than does the hectic pace of life in big cities. Businesses in the small town of Leeville report fewer days of sick leave taken by individual workers than do businesses in the nearby large city of Masonton. Furthermore, Leeville has only one physician for its one thousand residents, but in Masonton the proportion of physicians to residents is five times as high. Finally, the average age of Leeville residents is significantly higher than that of Masonton residents. These findings suggest that people seeking longer and healthier lives should consider moving to small communities.

Write a response in which you examine the stated and/or unstated assumptions of the argument. Be sure to explain how the argument depends on these assumptions and what the implications are for the argument if the assumptions prove unwarranted.

102. The following was written as a part of an application for a small-business loan by a group of developers in the city of Monroe.

"Jazz music is extremely popular in the city of Monroe: over 100,000 people attended Monroe's annual jazz festival last summer, and the highest-rated radio program in Monroe is 'Jazz Nightly,' which airs every weeknight. Also, a number of well-known jazz musicians own homes in Monroe. Nevertheless, the nearest jazz club is over an hour away. Given the popularity of jazz in Monroe and a recent nationwide study indicating that the typical jazz fan spends close to $1,000 per year on jazz entertainment, we predict that our new jazz music club in Monroe will be a tremendously profitable enterprise."

Write a response in which you discuss what questions would need to be answered in order to decide whether the prediction and the argument on which it is based are reasonable. Be sure to explain how the answers to these questions would help to evaluate the prediction.

103. There is now evidence that the relaxed pace of life in small towns promotes better health and greater longevity than does the hectic pace of life in big cities. Businesses in the small town of Leeville report fewer days of sick leave taken by individual workers than do businesses in the nearby large city of Masonton. Furthermore, Leeville has only one physician for its one thousand residents, but in Masonton the proportion of physicians to residents is five times as high. Finally, the average age of Leeville residents is significantly higher than that of Masonton residents. These findings suggest that the relaxed pace of life in Leeville allows residents to live longer, healthier lives.

Write a response in which you discuss one or more alternative explanations that could rival the proposed explanation and explain how your explanation(s) can plausibly account for the facts presented in the argument.

104. The following appeared in a memo from a vice president of a manufacturing company.

"During the past year, workers at our newly opened factory reported 30 percent more on-the-job accidents than workers at nearby Panoply Industries. Panoply produces products very similar to those produced at our factory, but its work shifts are one hour shorter than ours. Experts say that fatigue and sleep deprivation among workers are significant contributing factors in many on-the-job accidents. Panoply's superior safety record can therefore be attributed to its shorter work shifts, which allow its employees to get adequate amounts of rest."

Write a response in which you discuss one or more alternative explanations that could rival the proposed explanation and explain how your explanation(s) can plausibly account for the facts presented in the argument.

105. The following appeared in a memo from the vice president of Butler Manufacturing.

"During the past year, workers at Butler Manufacturing reported 30 percent more on-the-job accidents than workers at nearby Panoply Industries, where the work shifts are one hour shorter than ours. A recent government study reports that fatigue and sleep deprivation among workers are significant contributing factors in many on-the-job accidents. If we shorten each of our work shifts by one hour, we can improve Butler Manufacturing's safety record by ensuring that our employees are adequately rested."

Write a response in which you discuss what specific evidence is needed to evaluate the argument and explain how the evidence would weaken or strengthen the argument.

106. The following appeared in a memo from the Board of Directors of Butler Manufacturing.

"During the past year, workers at Butler Manufacturing reported 30 percent more on-the-job accidents than workers at nearby Panoply Industries, where the work shifts are one hour shorter than ours. A recent government study reports that fatigue and sleep deprivation among workers are significant contributing factors in many on-the-job accidents. Therefore, we recommend that Butler Manufacturing shorten each of its work shifts by one hour. Shorter shifts will allow Butler to improve its safety record by ensuring that its employees are adequately rested."

Write a response in which you discuss what questions would need to be answered in order to decide whether the recommendation is likely to have the predicted result. Be sure to explain how the answers to these questions would help to evaluate the recommendation.

107. The following appeared in a memo from the business manager of a chain of cheese stores located throughout the United States.

"For many years all the stores in our chain have stocked a wide variety of both domestic and imported cheeses. Last year, however, all of the five best-selling cheeses at our newest store were domestic cheddar cheeses from Wisconsin. Furthermore, a recent survey by Cheeses of the World magazine indicates an increasing preference for domestic cheeses among its subscribers. Since our company can reduce expenses by limiting inventory, the best way to improve profits in all of our stores is to discontinue stocking many of our varieties of imported cheese and concentrate primarily on domestic cheeses."

Write a response in which you examine the stated and/or unstated assumptions of the argument. Be sure to explain how the argument depends on these assumptions and what the implications are for the argument if the assumptions prove unwarranted.

108. The following appeared in a memo from the owner of a chain of cheese stores located throughout the United States.

"For many years all the stores in our chain have stocked a wide variety of both domestic and imported cheeses. Last year, however, all of the five best-selling cheeses at our newest store were domestic cheddar cheeses from Wisconsin. Furthermore, a recent survey by *Cheeses of the World* magazine indicates an increasing preference for domestic cheeses among its subscribers. Since our company can reduce expenses by limiting inventory, the best way to improve profits in all of our stores is to discontinue stocking many of our varieties of imported cheese and concentrate primarily on domestic cheeses."

Write a response in which you discuss what specific evidence is needed to evaluate the argument and explain how the evidence would weaken or strengthen the argument.

109. The following appeared in a memorandum from the general manager of KNOW radio station.

"Several factors indicate that radio station KNOW should shift its programming from rock-and-roll music to a continuous news format. Consider, for example, that the number of people in our listening area over fifty years of age has increased dramatically, while our total number of listeners has declined. Also, music stores in our area report decreased sales of recorded music. Finally, continuous news stations in neighboring cities have been very successful. The switch from rock-and-roll music to 24-hour news will attract older listeners and secure KNOW radio's future."

Write a response in which you examine the stated and/or unstated assumptions of the argument. Be sure to explain how the argument depends on these assumptions and what the implications are for the argument if the assumptions prove unwarranted.

110. The following appeared in a memorandum from the manager of KNOW radio station.

"Several factors indicate that KNOW radio can no longer succeed as a rock-and-roll music station. Consider, for example, that the number of people in our listening area over fifty years of age has increased dramatically, while our total number of listeners has declined. Also, music stores in our area report decreased sales of rock-and-roll music. Finally, continuous news stations in neighboring cities have been very successful. We predict that switching KNOW radio from rock-and-roll music to 24-hour news will allow the station to attract older listeners and make KNOW radio more profitable than ever."

Write a response in which you discuss what questions would need to be answered in order to decide whether the prediction and the argument on which it is based are reasonable. Be sure to explain how the answers to these questions would help to evaluate the prediction.

111. The following appeared in a memorandum from the owner of Movies Galore, a chain of movie-rental stores.

"In order to stop the recent decline in our profits, we must reduce operating expenses at Movies Galore's ten movie-rental stores. Since we are famous for our special bargains, raising our rental prices is not a viable way to improve profits. Last month our store in downtown Marston significantly decreased its operating expenses by closing at 6:00 P.M. rather than 9:00 P.M. and by reducing its stock by eliminating all movies released more than five years ago. By implementing similar changes in our other stores, Movies Galore can increase profits without jeopardizing our reputation for offering great movies at low prices."

Write a response in which you examine the stated and/or unstated assumptions of the argument. Be sure to explain how the argument depends on these assumptions and what the implications are for the argument if the assumptions prove unwarranted.

112. The following appeared in a memorandum from the owner of Movies Galore, a chain of movie-rental stores.

"In order to reverse the recent decline in our profits, we must reduce operating expenses at Movies Galore's ten movie-rental stores. Since we are famous for our special bargains, raising our rental prices is not a viable way to improve profits. Last month our store in downtown Marston significantly decreased its operating expenses by closing at 6:00 p.m. rather than 9:00 p.m. and by reducing its stock by eliminating all movies released more than five years ago. Therefore, in order to increase profits without jeopardizing our reputation for offering great movies at low prices, we recommend implementing similar changes in our other nine Movies Galore stores."

Write a response in which you discuss what questions would need to be answered in order to decide whether the recommendation and the argument on which it is based are reasonable. Be sure to explain how the answers to these questions would help to evaluate the recommendation.

113. The following is a recommendation from the personnel director to the president of Acme Publishing Company.

"Many other companies have recently stated that having their employees take the Easy Read Speed-Reading Course has greatly improved productivity. One graduate of the course was able to read a 500-page report in only two hours; another graduate rose from an assistant manager to vice president of the company in under a year. Obviously, the faster you can read, the more information you can absorb in a single workday. Moreover, Easy Read would cost Acme only $500 per employee—a small price to pay when you consider the benefits. Included in this fee is a three-week seminar in Spruce City and a lifelong subscription to the Easy Read newsletter. Clearly, to improve productivity, Acme should require all of our employees to take the Easy Read course."

Write a response in which you discuss what questions would need to be answered in order to decide whether the advice and the argument on which it is based are reasonable. Be sure to explain how the answers to these questions would help to evaluate the advice.

114. The following appeared in a memo from the vice president of a food distribution company with food storage warehouses in several cities.

"Recently, we signed a contract with the Fly-Away Pest Control Company to provide pest control services at our warehouse in Palm City, but last month we discovered that over $20,000 worth of food there had been destroyed by pest damage. Meanwhile, the Buzzoff Pest Control Company, which we have used for many years in Palm City, continued to service our warehouse in Wintervale, and last month only $10,000 worth of the food stored there had been destroyed by pest damage. Even though the price charged by Fly-Away is considerably lower, our best means of saving money is to return to Buzzoff for all our pest control services."

Write a response in which you discuss what questions would need to be answered in order to decide whether the recommendation and the argument on which it is based are reasonable. Be sure to explain how the answers to these questions would help to evaluate the recommendation.

115. The following appeared in a memo from a vice president of a large, highly diversified company.

"Ten years ago our company had two new office buildings constructed as regional headquarters for two different regions. The buildings were erected by two different construction companies—Alpha and Zeta. Even though the two buildings had identical floor plans, the building constructed by Zeta cost 30 percent more to build, and its expenses for maintenance last year were twice those of the building constructed by Alpha. Furthermore, the energy consumption of the Zeta building has been higher than that of the Alpha building every year since its construction. Such data, plus the fact that Alpha has a stable workforce with little employee turnover, indicate that we should use Alpha rather than Zeta for our contemplated new building project."

Write a response in which you examine the stated and/or unstated assumptions of the argument. Be sure to explain how the argument depends on these assumptions and what the implications are for the argument if the assumptions prove unwarranted.

116. The following appeared in a memo from the vice president of a food distribution company with food storage warehouses in several cities.

"Recently, we signed a contract with the Fly-Away Pest Control Company to provide pest control services at our warehouse in Palm City, but last month we discovered that over $20,000 worth of food there had been destroyed by pest damage. Meanwhile, the Buzzoff Pest Control Company, which we have used for many years in Palm City, continued to service our warehouse in Wintervale, and last month only $10,000 worth of the food stored there had been destroyed by pest damage. This difference in pest damage is best explained by the negligence of Fly-Away."

Write a response in which you discuss one or more alternative explanations that could rival the proposed explanation and explain how your explanation(s) can plausibly account for the facts presented in the argument.

117. The following appeared in a memo from the vice president of a food distribution company with food storage warehouses in several cities.

"Recently, we signed a contract with the Fly-Away Pest Control Company to provide pest control services at our warehouse in Palm City, but last month we discovered that over $20,000 worth of food there had been destroyed by pest damage. Meanwhile, the Buzzoff Pest Control Company, which we have used for many years in Palm City, continued to service our warehouse in Wintervale, and last month only $10,000 worth of the food stored there had been destroyed by pest damage. Even though the price charged by Fly-Away is considerably lower, our best means of saving money is to return to Buzzoff for all our pest control services."

Write a response in which you examine the stated and/or unstated assumptions of the argument. Be sure to explain how the argument depends on these assumptions and what the implications are for the argument if the assumptions prove unwarranted.

118. The following appeared as part of an article in a business magazine.

"A recent study rating 300 male and female advertising executives according to the average number of hours they sleep per night showed an association between the amount of sleep the executives need and the success of their firms. Of the advertising firms studied, those whose executives reported needing no more than six hours of sleep per night had higher profit margins and faster growth. On the basis of this study, we recommend that businesses hire only people who need less than six hours of sleep per night."

Write a response in which you discuss what questions would need to be answered in order to decide whether the recommendation and the argument on which it is based are reasonable. Be sure to explain how the answers to these questions would help to evaluate the recommendation.

119. Evidence suggests that academic honor codes, which call for students to agree not to cheat in their academic endeavors and to notify a faculty member if they suspect that others have cheated, are far more successful than are other methods at deterring cheating among students at colleges and universities. Several years ago, Groveton College adopted such a code and discontinued its old-fashioned system in which teachers closely monitored students. Under the old system, teachers reported an average of thirty cases of cheating per year. In the first year the honor code was in place, students reported twenty-one cases of cheating; five years later, this figure had dropped to fourteen. Moreover, in a recent survey, a majority of Groveton students said that they would be less likely to cheat with an honor code in place than without.

Write a response in which you discuss one or more alternative explanations that could rival the proposed explanation and explain how your explanation(s) can plausibly account for the facts presented in the argument.

120. Several years ago, Groveton College adopted an honor code, which calls for students to agree not to cheat in their academic endeavors and to notify a faculty member if they suspect that others have cheated. Groveton's honor code replaced a system in which teachers closely monitored students. Under that system, teachers reported an average of thirty cases of cheating per year. The honor code has proven far more successful: in the first year it was in place, students reported twenty-one cases of cheating; five years later, this figure had dropped to fourteen. Moreover, in a recent survey, a majority of Groveton students said that they would be less likely to cheat with an honor code in place than without. Such evidence suggests that all colleges and universities should adopt honor codes similar to Groveton's. This change is sure to result in a dramatic decline in cheating among college students.

Write a response in which you discuss what questions would need to be answered in order to decide whether the recommendation is likely to have the predicted result. Be sure to explain how the answers to these questions would help to evaluate the recommendation.

121. The following appeared in a memo from the director of a large group of hospitals.

"In a controlled laboratory study of liquid hand soaps, a concentrated solution of extra strength UltraClean hand soap produced a 40 percent greater reduction in harmful bacteria than did the liquid hand soaps currently used in our hospitals. During our recent test of regular-strength UltraClean with doctors, nurses, and visitors at our hospital in Worktown, the hospital reported significantly fewer cases of patient infection (a 20 percent reduction) than did any of the other hospitals in our group. Therefore, to prevent serious patient infections, we should supply UltraClean at all hand-washing stations, including those used by visitors, throughout our hospital system."

Write a response in which you examine the stated and/or unstated assumptions of the argument. Be sure to explain how the argument depends on these assumptions and what the implications are for the argument if the assumptions prove unwarranted.

122. The following appeared in a memo from the director of a large group of hospitals.

"In a controlled laboratory study of liquid hand soaps, a concentrated solution of extra strength UltraClean hand soap produced a 40 percent greater reduction in harmful bacteria than did the liquid hand soaps currently used in our hospitals. During our recent test of regular-strength UltraClean with doctors, nurses, and visitors at our hospital in Worktown, the hospital reported significantly fewer cases of patient infection (a 20 percent reduction) than did any of the other hospitals in our group. The explanation for the 20 percent reduction in patient infections is the use of UltraClean soap."

Write a response in which you discuss one or more alternative explanations that could rival the proposed explanation and explain how your explanation(s) can plausibly account for the facts presented in the argument.

123. The following appeared in a health newsletter.

"A ten-year nationwide study of the effectiveness of wearing a helmet while bicycling indicates that ten years ago, approximately 35 percent of all bicyclists reported wearing helmets, whereas today that number is nearly 80 percent. Another study, however, suggests that during the same ten-year period, the number of accidents caused by bicycling has increased 200 percent. These results demonstrate that bicyclists feel safer because they are wearing helmets, and they take more risks as a result. Thus, there is clearly a call for the government to strive to reduce the number of serious injuries from bicycle accidents by launching an education program that concentrates on the factors other than helmet use that are necessary for bicycle safety."

Write a response in which you discuss what questions would need to be answered in order to decide whether the recommendation and the argument on which it is based are reasonable. Be sure to explain how the answers to these questions would help to evaluate the recommendation.

124. The following appeared in a memo from the director of a large group of hospitals.

"In a controlled laboratory study of liquid hand soaps, a concentrated solution of extra strength UltraClean hand soap produced a 40 percent greater reduction in harmful bacteria than did the liquid hand soaps currently used in our hospitals. During our recent test of regular-strength UltraClean with doctors, nurses, and visitors at our hospital in Worktown, the hospital reported significantly fewer cases of patient infection (a 20 percent reduction) than did any of the other hospitals in our group. Therefore, to prevent serious patient infections, we should supply UltraClean at all hand-washing stations, including those used by visitors, throughout our hospital system."

Write a response in which you discuss what specific evidence is needed to evaluate the argument and explain how the evidence would weaken or strengthen the argument.

125. The following appeared in a health newsletter.

"A ten-year nationwide study of the effectiveness of wearing a helmet while bicycling indicates that ten years ago, approximately 35 percent of all bicyclists reported wearing helmets, whereas today that number is nearly 80 percent. Another study, however, suggests that during the same ten-year period, the number of accidents caused by bicycling has increased 200 percent. These results demonstrate that bicyclists feel safer because they are wearing helmets, and they take more risks as a result. Thus there is clearly a call for the government to strive to reduce the number of serious injuries from bicycle accidents by launching an education program that concentrates on the factors other than helmet use that are necessary for bicycle safety."

Write a response in which you discuss what specific evidence is needed to evaluate the argument and explain how the evidence would weaken or strengthen the argument.

126. The following is a recommendation from the personnel director to the president of Acme Publishing Company.

"Many other companies have recently stated that having their employees take the Easy Read Speed-Reading Course has greatly improved productivity. One graduate of the course was able to read a 500-page report in only two hours; another graduate rose from an assistant manager to vice president of the company in under a year. Obviously, the faster you can read, the more information you can absorb in a single workday. Moreover, Easy Read would cost Acme only $500 per employee—a small price to pay when you consider the benefits. Included in this fee is a three-week seminar in Spruce City and a lifelong subscription to the Easy Read newsletter. Clearly, Acme would benefit greatly by requiring all of our employees to take the Easy Read course."

Write a response in which you discuss what specific evidence is needed to evaluate the argument and explain how the evidence would weaken or strengthen the argument.

127. The following is a recommendation from the personnel director to the president of Acme Publishing Company.

"Many other companies have recently stated that having their employees take the Easy Read Speed-Reading Course has greatly improved productivity. One graduate of the course was able to read a 500-page report in only two hours; another graduate rose from an assistant manager to vice president of the company in under a year. Obviously, the faster you can read, the more information you can absorb in a single workday. Moreover, Easy Read would cost Acme only $500 per employee—a small price to pay when you consider the benefits. Included in this fee is a three-week seminar in Spruce City and a lifelong subscription to the Easy Read newsletter. Clearly, to improve overall productivity, Acme should require all of our employees to take the Easy Read course."

Write a response in which you discuss what questions would need to be answered in order to decide whether the recommendation and the argument on which it is based are reasonable. Be sure to explain how the answers to these questions would help to evaluate the recommendation.

128. The following appeared in a letter from the owner of the Sunnyside Towers apartment complex to its manager.

"One month ago, all the showerheads in the first three buildings of the Sunnyside Towers complex were modified to restrict maximum water flow to one-third of what it used to be. Although actual readings of water usage before and after the adjustment are not yet available, the change will obviously result in a considerable savings for Sunnyside Corporation, since the corporation must pay for water each month. Except for a few complaints about low water pressure, no problems with showers have been reported since the adjustment. Clearly, modifying showerheads to restrict water flow throughout all twelve buildings in the Sunnyside Towers complex will increase our profits further."

Write a response in which you discuss what specific evidence is needed to evaluate the argument and explain how the evidence would weaken or strengthen the argument.

129. The following appeared in a letter from the owner of the Sunnyside Towers apartment complex to its manager.

"Last week, all the showerheads in the first three buildings of the Sunnyside Towers complex were modified to restrict maximum water flow to one-third of what it used to be. Although actual readings of water usage before and after the adjustment are not yet available, the change will obviously result in a considerable savings for Sunnyside Corporation, since the corporation must pay for water each month. Except for a few complaints about low water pressure, no problems with showers have been reported since the adjustment. Clearly, modifying showerheads to restrict water flow throughout all twelve buildings in the Sunnyside Towers complex will increase our profits further."

Write a response in which you examine the stated and/or unstated assumptions of the argument. Be sure to explain how the argument depends on these assumptions and what the implications are for the argument if the assumptions prove unwarranted.

130. The following memorandum is from the business manager of Happy Pancake House restaurants.

"Butter has now been replaced by margarine in Happy Pancake House restaurants throughout the southwestern United States. Only about 2 percent of customers have filed a formal complaint, indicating that an average of 98 people out of 100 are happy with the change. Furthermore, many servers have reported that a number of customers who ask for butter do not complain when they are given margarine instead. Clearly, either these customers cannot distinguish butter from margarine or they use the term 'butter' to refer to either butter or margarine. Thus, to avoid the expense of purchasing butter, the Happy Pancake House should extend this cost-saving change to its restaurants throughout the rest of the country."

Write a response in which you examine the stated and/or unstated assumptions of the argument. Be sure to explain how the argument depends on these assumptions and what the implications are for the argument if the assumptions prove unwarranted.

131. The following memorandum is from the business manager of Happy Pancake House restaurants.

"Butter has now been replaced by margarine in Happy Pancake House restaurants throughout the southwestern United States. Only about 2 percent of customers have complained, indicating that an average of 98 people out of 100 are happy with the change. Furthermore, many servers have reported that a number of customers who ask for butter do not complain when they are given margarine instead. Clearly, either these customers cannot distinguish butter from margarine or they use the term 'butter' to refer to either butter or margarine. Thus, we predict that Happy Pancake House will be able to increase profits dramatically if we extend this cost-saving change to all our restaurants in the southeast and northeast as well."

Write a response in which you discuss what questions would need to be answered in order to decide whether the prediction and the argument on which it is based are reasonable. Be sure to explain how the answers to these questions would help to evaluate the prediction.

132. The following appeared in a letter to the school board in the town of Centerville.

"All students should be required to take the driver's education course at Centerville High School. In the past two years, several accidents in and around Centerville have involved teenage drivers. Since a number of parents in Centerville have complained that they are too busy to teach their teenagers to drive, some other instruction is necessary to ensure that these teenagers are safe drivers. Although there are two driving schools in Centerville, parents on a tight budget cannot afford to pay for driving instruction. Therefore an effective and mandatory program sponsored by the high school is the only solution to this serious problem."

Write a response in which you examine the stated and/or unstated assumptions of the argument. Be sure to explain how the argument depends on these assumptions and what the implications are for the argument if the assumptions prove unwarranted.

133. The following memorandum is from the business manager of Happy Pancake House restaurants.

"Butter has now been replaced by margarine in Happy Pancake House restaurants throughout the southwestern United States. Only about 2 percent of customers have complained, indicating that an average of 98 people out of 100 are happy with the change. Furthermore, many servers have reported that a number of customers who ask for butter do not complain when they are given margarine instead. Clearly, either these customers cannot distinguish butter from margarine or they use the term 'butter' to refer to either butter or margarine. Thus, to avoid the expense of purchasing butter and to increase profitability, the Happy Pancake House should extend this cost-saving change to its restaurants in the southeast and northeast as well."

Write a response in which you discuss what specific evidence is needed to evaluate the argument and explain how the evidence would weaken or strengthen the argument.

134. The following appeared in a letter to the school board in the town of Centerville.

"All students should be required to take the driver's education course at Centerville High School. In the past two years, several accidents in and around Centerville have involved teenage drivers. Since a number of parents in Centerville have complained that they are too busy to teach their teenagers to drive, some other instruction is necessary to ensure that these teenagers are safe drivers. Although there are two driving schools in Centerville, parents on a tight budget cannot afford to pay for driving instruction. Therefore an effective and mandatory program sponsored by the high school is the only solution to this serious problem."

Write a response in which you discuss what specific evidence is needed to evaluate the argument and explain how the evidence would weaken or strengthen the argument.

135. The data from a survey of high school math and science teachers show that in the district of Sanlee many of these teachers reported assigning daily homework, whereas in the district of Marlee, most science and math teachers reported assigning homework no more than two or three days per week. Despite receiving less frequent homework assignments, Marlee students earn better grades overall and are less likely to be required to repeat a year of school than are students in Sanlee. These results call into question the usefulness of frequent homework assignments. Most likely the Marlee students have more time to concentrate on individual assignments than do the Sanlee students who have homework every day. Therefore teachers in our high schools should assign homework no more than twice a week.

Write a response in which you discuss what specific evidence is needed to evaluate the argument and explain how the evidence would weaken or strengthen the argument.

136. The following appeared in a letter to the school board in the town of Centerville.

"All students should be required to take the driver's education course at Centerville High School. In the past two years, several accidents in and around Centerville have involved teenage drivers. Since a number of parents in Centerville have complained that they are too busy to teach their teenagers to drive, some other instruction is necessary to ensure that these teenagers are safe drivers. Although there are two driving schools in Centerville, parents on a tight budget cannot afford to pay for driving instruction. Therefore an effective and mandatory program sponsored by the high school is the only solution to this serious problem."

Write a response in which you discuss what questions would need to be answered in order to decide whether the recommendation and the argument on which it is based are reasonable. Be sure to explain how the answers to these questions would help to evaluate the recommendation.

137. While the Department of Education in the state of Attra recommends that high school students be assigned homework every day, the data from a recent statewide survey of high school math and science teachers give us reason to question the usefulness of daily homework. In the district of Sanlee, 86 percent of the teachers reported assigning homework three to five times a week, whereas in the district of Marlee, less than 25 percent of the teachers reported assigning homework three to five times a week. Yet the students in Marlee earn better grades overall and are less likely to be required to repeat a year of school than are the students in Sanlee. Therefore, all teachers in our high schools should assign homework no more than twice a week.

Write a response in which you examine the stated and/or unstated assumptions of the argument. Be sure to explain how the argument depends on these assumptions and what the implications are for the argument if the assumptions prove unwarranted.

138. The following appeared as an editorial in the student newspaper of Groveton College.

"To combat the recently reported dramatic rise in cheating among college students, colleges and universities should adopt honor codes similar to Groveton's, which calls for students to agree not to cheat in their academic endeavors and to notify a faculty member if they suspect that others have cheated. Groveton's honor code replaced an old-fashioned system in which teachers closely monitored students. Under that system, teachers reported an average of thirty cases of cheating per year. The honor code has proven far more successful: in the first year it was in place, students reported twenty-one cases of cheating; five years later, this figure had dropped to fourteen. Moreover, in a recent survey conducted by the Groveton honor council, a majority of students said that they would be less likely to cheat with an honor code in place than without."

Write a response in which you discuss what specific evidence is needed to evaluate the argument and explain how the evidence would weaken or strengthen the argument.

139. The following appeared in a memo from a budget planner for the city of Grandview.

"Our citizens are well aware of the fact that while the Grandview Symphony Orchestra was struggling to succeed, our city government promised annual funding to help support its programs. Last year, however, private contributions to the symphony increased by 200 percent, and attendance at the symphony's concerts-in-the-park series doubled. The symphony has also announced an increase in ticket prices for next year. Such developments indicate that the symphony can now succeed without funding from city government and we can eliminate that expense from next year's budget. Therefore, we recommend that the city of Grandview eliminate its funding for the Grandview Symphony from next year's budget. By doing so, we can prevent a city budget deficit without threatening the success of the symphony."

Write a response in which you discuss what questions would need to be answered in order to decide whether the recommendation is likely to have the predicted result. Be sure to explain how the answers to these questions would help to evaluate the recommendation.

140. While the Department of Education in the state of Attra suggests that high school students be assigned homework every day, the data from a recent statewide survey of high school math and science teachers give us reason to question the usefulness of daily homework. In the district of Sanlee, 86 percent of the teachers reported assigning homework three to five times a week, whereas in the district of Marlee, less than 25 percent of the teachers reported assigning homework three to five times a week. Yet the students in Marlee earn better grades overall and are less likely to be required to repeat a year of school than are the students in Sanlee. Therefore, we recommend that all teachers in our high schools should assign homework no more than twice a week.

Write a response in which you discuss what questions would need to be answered in order to decide whether the recommendation and the argument on which it is based are reasonable. Be sure to explain how the answers to these questions would help to evaluate the recommendation.

141. The following appeared in a memo to the board of the Grandview Symphony.

"The city of Grandview has provided annual funding for the Grandview Symphony since the symphony's inception ten years ago. Last year the symphony hired an internationally known conductor, who has been able to attract high-profile guest musicians to perform with the symphony. Since then, private contributions to the symphony have doubled and attendance at the symphony's concerts-in-the-park series has reached new highs. Now that the Grandview Symphony is an established success, it can raise ticket prices. Increased revenue from larger audiences and higher ticket prices will enable the symphony to succeed without funding from the city government."

Write a response in which you discuss what specific evidence is needed to evaluate the argument and explain how the evidence would weaken or strengthen the argument.

142. Hospital statistics regarding people who go to the emergency room after roller-skating accidents indicate the need for more protective equipment. Within that group of people, 75 percent of those who had accidents in streets or parking lots had not been wearing any protective clothing （helmets, knee pads, etc.）or any light-reflecting material （clip-on lights, glow-in-the-dark wrist pads, etc.）. Clearly, the statistics indicate that by investing in high-quality protective gear and reflective equipment, roller skaters will greatly reduce their risk of being severely injured in an accident.

Write a response in which you examine the stated and/or unstated assumptions of the argument. Be sure to explain how the argument depends on these assumptions and what the implications are for the argument if the assumptions prove unwarranted.

143. The following appeared in a memo from a budget planner for the city of Grandview.

"When the Grandview Symphony was established ten years ago, the city of Grandview agreed to provide the symphony with annual funding until the symphony became self-sustaining. Two years ago, the symphony hired an internationally known conductor, who has been able to attract high-profile guest musicians to perform with the symphony. Since then, private contributions to the symphony have tripled and attendance at the symphony's outdoor summer concert series has reached record highs. Now that the symphony has succeeded in finding an audience, the city can eliminate its funding of the symphony."

Write a response in which you examine the stated and/or unstated assumptions of the argument. Be sure to explain how the argument depends on these assumptions and what the implications are for the argument if the assumptions prove unwarranted.

144. The citizens of Forsythe have adopted more healthful lifestyles. Their responses to a recent survey show that in their eating habits they conform more closely to government nutritional recommendations than they did ten years ago. Furthermore, there has been a fourfold increase in sales of food products containing kiran, a substance that a scientific study has shown reduces cholesterol. This trend is also evident in reduced sales of sulia, a food that few of the healthiest citizens regularly eat.

Write a response in which you examine the stated and/or unstated assumptions of the argument. Be sure to explain how the argument depends on these assumptions and what the implications are for the argument if the assumptions prove unwarranted.

145. The following appeared in a memo to the board of directors of a company that specializes in the delivery of heating oil.

"Most homes in the northeastern United States, where winters are typically cold, have traditionally used oil as their major fuel for heating. Last heating season, that region experienced 90 days with below-normal temperatures, and climate forecasters predict that this weather pattern will continue for several more years. Furthermore, many new homes are being built in the region in response to recent population growth. Because of these trends, we can safely predict that this region will experience an increased demand for heating oil during the next five years."

Write a response in which you discuss what questions would need to be answered in order to decide whether the prediction and the argument on which it is based are reasonable. Be sure to explain how the answers to these questions would help to evaluate the prediction.

146. The following appeared in a memo to the board of directors of a company that specializes in the delivery of heating oil.

"Most homes in the northeastern United States, where winters are typically cold, have traditionally used oil as their major fuel for heating. Last heating season, that region experienced 90 days with below-normal temperatures, and climate forecasters predict that this weather pattern will continue for several more years. Furthermore, many new homes are being built in the region in response to recent population growth.

Because of these trends, we can safely predict that this region will experience an increased demand for heating oil during the next five years."

Write a response in which you discuss what specific evidence is needed to evaluate the argument and explain how the evidence would weaken or strengthen the argument.

147. The following recommendation was made by the president and administrative staff of Grove College, a private institution, to the college's governing committee.

"We recommend that Grove College preserve its century-old tradition of all-female education rather than admit men into its programs. It is true that a majority of faculty members voted in favor of coeducation, arguing that it would encourage more students to apply to Grove. But 80 percent of the students responding to a survey conducted by the student government wanted the school to remain all female, and over half of the alumnae who answered a separate survey also opposed coeducation. Keeping the college all female will improve morale among students and convince alumnae to keep supporting the college financially."

Write a response in which you discuss what specific evidence is needed to evaluate the argument and explain how the evidence would weaken or strengthen the argument.

148. The following recommendation was made by the president and administrative staff of Grove College, a private institution, to the college's governing committee.

"We recommend that Grove College preserve its century-old tradition of all-female education rather than admit men into its programs. It is true that a majority of faculty members voted in favor of coeducation, arguing that it would encourage more students to apply to Grove. But 80 percent of the students responding to a survey conducted by the student government wanted the school to remain all female, and over half of the alumnae who answered a separate survey also opposed coeducation. Keeping the college all female will improve morale among students and convince alumnae to keep supporting the college financially."

Write a response in which you examine the stated and/or unstated assumptions of the argument. Be sure to explain how the argument depends on these assumptions and what the implications are for the argument if the assumptions prove unwarranted.

149. The following recommendation was made by the president and administrative staff of Grove College, a private institution, to the college's governing committee.

"We recommend that Grove College preserve its century-old tradition of all-female education rather than admit men into its programs. It is true that a majority of faculty members voted in favor of coeducation, arguing that it would encourage more students to apply to Grove. But 80 percent of the students responding to a survey conducted by the student government wanted the school to remain all female, and over half of the alumnae who answered a separate survey also opposed coeducation. Keeping the college all female will improve morale among students and convince alumnae to keep supporting the college financially."

Write a response in which you discuss what questions would need to be answered in order to decide whether the recommendation is likely to have the predicted result. Be sure to explain how the answers to these questions would help to evaluate the recommendation.

150. The following appeared in a letter from a firm providing investment advice to a client.

"Homes in the northeastern United States, where winters are typically cold, have traditionally used oil as their major fuel for heating. Last year that region experienced 90 days with below-average temperatures, and climate forecasters at Waymarsh University predict that this weather pattern will continue for several more years. Furthermore, many new homes have been built in this region during the past year. Because these developments will certainly result in an increased demand for heating oil, we recommend investment in Consolidated Industries, one of whose major business operations is the retail sale of home heating oil."

Write a response in which you discuss what questions would need to be answered in order to decide whether the recommendation and the argument on which it is based are reasonable. Be sure to explain how the answers to these questions would help to evaluate the recommendation.

151. Benton City residents have adopted healthier lifestyles. A recent survey of city residents shows that the eating habits of city residents conform more closely to government nutritional recommendations than they did ten years ago. During those ten years, local sales of food products containing kiran, a substance that a scientific study has shown reduces cholesterol, have increased fourfold, while sales of sulia, a food rarely eaten by the healthiest residents, have declined dramatically. Because of these positive changes in the eating habits of Benton City residents, we predict that the obesity rate in the city will soon be well below the national average.

Write a response in which you discuss what questions would need to be answered in order to decide whether the prediction and the argument on which it is based are reasonable. Be sure to explain how the answers to these questions would help to evaluate the prediction.

152. The following appeared in a memo to the board of directors of Bargain Brand Cereals.

"One year ago we introduced our first product, Bargain Brand breakfast cereal. Our very low prices quickly drew many customers away from the top-selling cereal companies. Although the companies producing the top brands have since tried to compete with us by lowering their prices and although several plan to introduce their own budget brands, not once have we needed to raise our prices to continue making a profit. Given our success in selling cereal, we recommend that Bargain Brand now expand its business and begin marketing other low-priced food products as quickly as possible."

Write a response in which you discuss what questions would need to be answered in order to decide whether the recommendation and the argument on which it is based are reasonable. Be sure to explain how the answers to these questions would help to evaluate the recommendation.

153. The following appeared in a memo to the board of directors of Bargain Brand Cereals.

"One year ago we introduced our first product, Bargain Brand breakfast cereal. Our very low prices quickly drew many customers away from the top-selling cereal companies. Although the companies producing the top brands have since tried to compete with us by lowering their prices and although several plan to introduce their own budget brands, not once have we needed to raise our prices to continue making a profit. Given our success in selling cereal, we recommend that Bargain Brand now expand its business and begin marketing other low-priced food products as quickly as possible."

Write a response in which you examine the stated and/or unstated assumptions of the argument. Be sure to explain how the argument depends on these assumptions and what the implications are for the argument if the assumptions prove unwarranted.

154. The following appeared in a letter from a firm providing investment advice to a client.

"Homes in the northeastern United States, where winters are typically cold, have traditionally used oil as their major fuel for heating. Last year that region experienced twenty days with below-average temperatures, and local weather forecasters throughout the region predict that this weather pattern will continue for several more years. Furthermore, many new homes have been built in this region during the past year. Based on these developments, we predict a large increase in the demand for heating oil. Therefore, we recommend investment in Consolidated Industries, one of whose major business operations is the retail sale of home heating oil."

Write a response in which you discuss what questions would need to be answered in order to decide whether the recommendation and the argument on which it is based are reasonable. Be sure to explain how the answers to these questions would help to evaluate the recommendation.

155. The following appeared in a letter from a firm providing investment advice to a client.

"Homes in the northeastern United States, where winters are typically cold, have traditionally used oil as their major fuel for heating. Last year that region experienced twenty days with below-average temperatures, and local weather forecasters throughout the region predict that this weather pattern will continue for several more years. Furthermore, many new homes have been built in this region during the past year. Because of these developments, we predict an increased demand for heating oil and recommend investment in Consolidated Industries, one of whose major business operations is the retail sale of home heating oil."

Write a response in which you discuss what specific evidence is needed to evaluate the argument and explain how the evidence would weaken or strengthen the argument.

156. The following recommendation was made by the president and administrative staff of Grove College, a private institution, to the college's governing committee.

"Recently, there have been discussions about ending Grove College's century-old tradition of all-female education by admitting male students into our programs. At a recent faculty meeting, a majority of faculty members voted in favor of coeducation, arguing that it would encourage more students to apply to Grove. However, Grove students, both past and present, are against the idea of coeducation. Eighty percent of the students responding to a survey conducted by the student government wanted the school to remain all female, and over half of the alumnae who answered a separate survey also opposed coeducation. Therefore, we recommend maintaining Grove College's tradition of all-female education. We predict that keeping the college all-female will improve morale among students and convince alumnae to keep supporting the college financially."

Write a response in which you discuss what questions would need to be answered in order to decide whether the recommendation is likely to have the predicted result. Be sure to explain how the answers to these questions would help to evaluate the recommendation.

157. The following appeared in a memo from the marketing director of Top Dog Pet Stores.

"Five years ago Fish Emporium started advertising in the magazine *Exotic Pets Monthly*. Their stores saw sales increase by 15 percent after their ads began appearing in the magazine. The three Fish Emporium stores in Gulf City saw an even greater increase than that. Because Top Dog Pet Stores is based in Gulf City, it seems clear that we should start placing our own ads in *Exotic Pets Monthly*. If we do so, we will be sure to reverse the recent trend of declining sales and start making a profit again."

Write a response in which you examine the stated and/or unstated assumptions of the argument. Be sure to explain how the argument depends on these assumptions and what the implications are for the argument if the assumptions prove unwarranted.

158. The following appeared in a memo from the marketing director of Top Dog Pet Stores.

"Five years ago, Fish Emporium started advertising in the magazine *Exotic Pets Monthly*. Their stores saw sales increase by 15 percent. The three Fish Emporium stores in Gulf City saw an even greater increase than that. Because Top Dog has some of its largest stores in Gulf City, it seems clear that we should start placing our own ads in *Exotic Pets Monthly*. If we do so, we will be sure to reverse the recent trend of declining sales and start making a profit again."

Write a response in which you discuss what specific evidence is needed to evaluate the argument and explain how the evidence would weaken or strengthen the argument.

159. The following appeared in a letter to the editor of the *Balmer Island Gazette*.

"The population on Balmer Island increases to 100,000 during the summer months. To reduce the number of accidents involving mopeds and pedestrians, the town council of Balmer Island plans to limit the number of mopeds rented by each of the island's six moped rental companies from 50 per day to 30 per day during the summer season. Last year, the neighboring island of Torseau enforced similar limits on moped rentals and saw a 50 percent reduction in moped accidents. We predict that putting these limits into effect on Balmer Island will result in the same reduction in moped accidents."

Write a response in which you discuss what questions would need to be answered in order to decide whether the prediction and the argument on which it is based are reasonable. Be sure to explain how the answers to these questions would help to evaluate the prediction.

160. The following appeared in a recommendation from the President of the Amburg Chamber of Commerce.

"Last October, the city of Belleville installed high-intensity lighting in its central business district, and vandalism there declined almost immediately. The city of Amburg, on the other hand, recently instituted police patrols on bicycles in its business district. However, the rate of vandalism here remains constant. Since high-intensity lighting is clearly the most effective way to combat crime, we recommend using the money that is currently being spent on bicycle patrols to install such lighting throughout Amburg. If we install this high-intensity lighting, we will significantly reduce crime rates in Amburg."

Write a response in which you discuss what questions would need to be answered in order to decide whether the recommendation is likely to have the predicted result. Be sure to explain how the answers to these questions would help to evaluate the recommendation.

161. The following is a recommendation from the personnel director to the president of Acme Publishing Company.

"Many other companies have recently stated that having their employees take the Easy Read Speed-Reading Course has greatly improved productivity. One graduate of the course was able to read a 500-page report in only two hours; another graduate rose from an assistant manager to vice president of the company in under a year. Obviously, the faster you can read, the more information you can absorb in a single workday. Moreover, Easy Read would cost Acme only $500 per employee—a small price to pay when you consider the benefits. Included in this fee is a three-week seminar in Spruce City and a lifelong subscription to the Easy Read newsletter. Clearly, Acme would benefit greatly by requiring all of our employees to take the Easy Read course."

Write a response in which you examine the stated and/or unstated assumptions of the argument. Be sure to explain how the argument depends on these assumptions and what the implications are for the argument if the assumptions prove unwarranted.

162. The following appeared in a memo from a budget planner for the city of Grandview.

"It is time for the city of Grandview to stop funding the Grandview Symphony Orchestra. It is true that the symphony struggled financially for many years, but last year private contributions to the symphony increased by 200 percent and attendance at the symphony's concerts-in-the-park series doubled. In addition, the symphony has just announced an increase in ticket prices for next year. For these reasons, we recommend that the city eliminate funding for the Grandview Symphony Orchestra from next year's budget. We predict that the symphony will flourish in the years to come even without funding from the city."

Write a response in which you discuss what questions would need to be answered in order to decide whether the recommendation is likely to have the predicted result. Be sure to explain how the answers to these questions would help to evaluate the recommendation.

163. The following memo appeared in the newsletter of the West Meria Public Health Council.

"An innovative treatment has come to our attention that promises to significantly reduce absenteeism in our schools and workplaces. A study reports that in nearby East Meria, where consumption of the plant beneficia is very high, people visit the doctor only once or twice per year for the treatment of colds. Clearly, eating a substantial amount of beneficia can prevent colds. Since colds are the reason most frequently given for absences from school and work, we recommend the daily use of nutritional supplements derived from beneficia. We predict this will dramatically reduce absenteeism in our schools and workplaces."

Write a response in which you discuss what questions would need to be answered in order to decide whether the recommendation is likely to have the predicted result. Be sure to explain how the answers to these questions would help to evaluate the recommendation.

164. The following was written by a group of developers in the city of Monroe.

"A jazz music club in Monroe would be a tremendously profitable enterprise. At present, the nearest jazz club is over 60 miles away from Monroe; thus, our proposed club, the C Note, would have the local market all to itself. In addition, there is ample evidence of the popularity of jazz in Monroe: over 100,000 people attended Monroe's jazz festival last summer, several well-known jazz musicians live in Monroe, and the highest-rated radio program in Monroe is 'Jazz Nightly.' Finally, a nationwide study indicates that the typical jazz fan spends close to $1,000 per year on jazz entertainment. We therefore predict that the C Note cannot help but make money."

Write a response in which you discuss what questions would need to be answered in order to decide whether the prediction and the argument on which it is based are reasonable. Be sure to explain how the answers to these questions would help to evaluate the prediction.

165. Humans arrived in the Kaliko Islands about 7,000 years ago, and within 3,000 years most of the large mammal species that had lived in the forests of the Kaliko Islands were extinct. Previous archaeological findings have suggested that early humans generally relied on both fishing and hunting for food; since archaeologists have discovered numerous sites in the Kaliko Islands where the bones of fish were discarded, it is likely that the humans also hunted the mammals. Furthermore, researchers have uncovered simple tools, such as stone knives, that could be used for hunting. The only clear explanation is that humans caused the extinction of the various mammal species through excessive hunting.

Write a response in which you discuss one or more alternative explanations that could rival the proposed explanation and explain how your explanation(s) can plausibly account for the facts presented in the argument.

166. The following memo appeared in the newsletter of the West Meria Public Health Council.

"An innovative treatment has come to our attention that promises to significantly reduce absenteeism in our schools and workplaces. A study reports that in nearby East Meria, where fish consumption is very high, people visit the doctor only once or twice per year for the treatment of colds. This shows that eating a substantial amount of fish can clearly prevent colds. Furthermore, since colds are the reason most frequently given for absences from school and work, attendance levels will improve. Therefore, we recommend the daily use of a nutritional supplement derived from fish oil as a good way to prevent colds and lower absenteeism."

Write a response in which you discuss what questions would need to be answered in order to decide whether the recommendation and the argument on which it is based are reasonable. Be sure to explain how the answers to these questions would help to evaluate the recommendation.

167. The following appeared in a memo from a vice president of Alta Manufacturing.

"During the past year, Alta Manufacturing had thirty percent more on-the-job accidents than nearby Panoply Industries, where the work shifts are one hour shorter than ours. Experts believe that a significant contributing factor in many accidents is fatigue caused by sleep deprivation among workers. Therefore, to reduce the number of on-the-job accidents at Alta, we recommend shortening each of our three work shifts by one hour. If we do this, our employees will get adequate amounts of sleep."

Write a response in which you discuss what questions would need to be answered in order to decide whether the recommendation and the argument on which it is based are reasonable. Be sure to explain how the answers to these questions would help to evaluate the recommendation.

168. The following is a letter that recently appeared in the *Oak City Gazette*, a local newspaper.

"The primary function of the Committee for a Better Oak City is to advise the city government on how to make the best use of the city's limited budget. However, at some of our recent meetings we failed to make important decisions because of the foolish objections raised by committee members who are not even residents of Oak City. People who work in Oak City but who live elsewhere cannot fully understand the business and politics of the city. After all, only Oak City residents pay city taxes, and therefore only residents understand how that money could best be used to improve the city. We recommend, then, that the Committee for a Better Oak City vote to restrict its membership to city residents only. We predict that, without the interference of non-residents, the committee will be able to make Oak City a better place in which to live and work."

Write a response in which you discuss what questions would need to be answered in order to decide whether the recommendation is likely to have the predicted result. Be sure to explain how the answers to these questions would help to evaluate the recommendation.

169. The following appeared in a memo from the mayor of Brindleburg to the city council.

"Two years ago, the town of Seaside Vista opened a new municipal golf course and resort hotel. Since then, the Seaside Vista Tourism Board has reported a 20% increase in visitors. In addition, local banks reported a steep rise in the number of new business loan applications they received this year. The amount of tax money collected by Seaside Vista has also increased, allowing the town to announce plans to improve Seaside Vista's roads and bridges. We recommend building a similar golf course and resort hotel in Brindleburg. We predict that this project will generate additional tax revenue that the city can use to fund much-needed public improvements."

Write a response in which you discuss what questions would need to be answered in order to decide whether the recommendation is likely to have the predicted result. Be sure to explain how the answers to these questions would help to evaluate the recommendation.

170. The following appeared in a memo from the vice president of a company that builds shopping malls around the country.

"The surface of a section of Route 101, paved just two years ago by Good Intentions Roadways, is now badly cracked with a number of dangerous potholes. In another part of the state, a section of Route 40, paved by Appian Roadways more than four years ago, is still in good condition. In a demonstration of their continuing commitment to quality, Appian Roadways recently purchased state-of-the-art paving machinery and hired a new quality-control manager. Therefore, I recommend hiring Appian Roadways to construct the access roads for all our new shopping malls. I predict that our Appian access roads will not have to be repaired for at least four years."

Write a response in which you discuss what questions would need to be answered in order to decide whether the recommendation is likely to have the predicted result. Be sure to explain how the answers to these questions would help to evaluate the recommendation.

171. The following appeared as a letter to the editor from the owner of a skate shop in Central Plaza.

"Two years ago the city voted to prohibit skateboarding in Central Plaza. They claimed that skateboard users were responsible for the litter and vandalism that were keeping other visitors from coming to the plaza. In the past two years, however, there has only been a small increase in the number of visitors to Central Plaza, and litter and vandalism are still problematic. Skateboarding is permitted in Monroe Park, however, and there is no problem with litter or vandalism there. In order to restore Central Plaza to its former glory, then, we recommend that the city lift its prohibition on skateboarding in the plaza."

Write a response in which you discuss what questions would need to be answered in order to decide whether the recommendation and the argument on which it is based are reasonable. Be sure to explain how the answers to these questions would help to evaluate the recommendation.

172. The following appeared in a recommendation from the president of Amburg's Chamber of Commerce.

"Last October the city of Belleville installed high-intensity lighting in its central business district, and vandalism there declined within a month. The city of Amburg has recently begun police patrols on bicycles in its business district, but the rate of vandalism there remains constant. We should install high-intensity lighting throughout Amburg, then, because doing so is a more effective way to combat crime. By reducing crime in this way, we can revitalize the declining neighborhoods in our city."

Write a response in which you discuss what specific evidence is needed to evaluate the argument and explain how the evidence would weaken or strengthen the argument.

173. The following appeared in a letter to the editor of the *Balmer Island Gazette*.

"The population on Balmer Island doubles during the summer months. During the summer, then, the town council of Balmer Island should decrease the maximum number of moped rentals allowed at each of the island's six moped and bicycle rental companies from 50 per day to 30 per day. This will significantly reduce the number of summertime accidents involving mopeds and pedestrians. The neighboring island of Torseau actually saw a 50 percent reduction in moped accidents last year when Torseau's town council enforced similar limits on moped rentals. To help reduce moped accidents, therefore, we should also enforce these limitations during the summer months."

Write a response in which you examine the stated and/or unstated assumptions of the argument. Be sure to explain how the argument depends on these assumptions and what the implications are for the argument if the assumptions prove unwarranted.

174. A recent sales study indicates that consumption of seafood dishes in Bay City restaurants has increased by 30 percent during the past five years. Yet there are no currently operating city restaurants whose specialty is seafood. Moreover, the majority of families in Bay City are two-income families, and a nationwide study has shown that such families eat significantly fewer home-cooked meals than they did a decade ago but at the same time express more concern about healthful eating. Therefore, the new Captain Seafood restaurant that specializes in seafood should be quite popular and profitable.

Write a response in which you discuss what questions would need to be addressed in order to decide whether the conclusion and the argument on which it is based are reasonable. Be sure to explain how the answers to the questions would help to evaluate the conclusion.